Shakespeare as Children's Literature

Shakespeare as Children's Literature

Edwardian Retellings in Words and Pictures

VELMA BOURGEOIS RICHMOND

McFarland & Company, Inc., Publishers
Jefferson, North Carolina, and London

ALSO BY VELMA BOURGEOIS RICHMOND

Chaucer as Children's Literature: Retellings from the Victorian and Edwardian Eras (McFarland, 2004)

Frontispiece: *A Midsummer Night's Dream,* the play most associated with children, often provided the frontispiece to engage children's interest in fairy tales, animal transformation, and diminutive size. Arthur Rackham's delightful and distinctive image for *Tales from Shakespeare by Charles and Mary Lamb* (1899) has many imaginative details.

LIBRARY OF CONGRESS CATALOGUING-IN-PUBLICATION DATA

Richmond, Velma Bourgeois.
   Shakespeare as children's literature : Edwardian retellings in words and pictures / Velma Bourgeois Richmond.
     p.   cm.
   Includes bibliographical references and index.

   ISBN 978-0-7864-3781-8
   softcover : 50# alkaline paper

   1. Lamb, Charles, 1775–1834. Tales from Shakespeare.
2. Lamb, Mary, 1764–1847 — Criticism and interpretation.
3. Shakespeare, William, 1564–1616 — Adaptations. 4. Shakespeare, William, 1564–1616 — Stories, plots, etc. 5. Children's literature, English — History and criticism. 6. Children — Books and reading — Great Britain — History — 19th century. I. Title.
   PR2877.L33R53   2008
   823'.7 — dc22   2008008597

British Library cataloguing data are available

©2008 Velma Bourgeois Richmond. All rights reserved

No part of this book may be reproduced or transmitted in any form or by any means, electronic or mechanical, including photocopying or recording, or by any information storage and retrieval system, without permission in writing from the publisher.

On the cover: J.R. Skelton's depiction of Shakespeare — used in H.E. Marshall's *English Literature for Boys and Girls* (1909) and Henry Gilbert's *Stories of Great Writers* (1914).

Manufactured in the United States of America

McFarland & Company, Inc., Publishers
  Box 611, Jefferson, North Carolina 28640
  www.mcfarlandpub.com

For Hugh, on our fiftieth anniversary

Table of Contents

Preface   1

1 • Contexts for Charles and Mary Lamb's
    Tales from Shakespeare   7

2 • The Tradition of Charles and Mary Lamb's
    Tales from Shakespeare   25

3 • Lamb's *Tales* Continued: Completion, Addition,
    and Selection   71

4 • Victorian Alternatives   110

5 • Edwardian Elegance and Exuberance:
    Retellings Large and Small   155

6 • Shakespeare in Schoolbooks   230

7 • Home Libraries, Literary Histories,
    and Pedagogical Advice   273

Epilogue   321
Tables   325
Chapter Notes   333
Selected Bibliography   345
Index   351

Preface

William Shakespeare is widely recognized as one of the greatest writers in the world, but he is not generally discussed in relation to children's literature. This book parallels my book *Chaucer as Children's Literature: Retellings from the Victorian and Edwardian Eras* (McFarland, 2004), which is part of an endeavor to establish the crucial role of traditional literature retold as children's literature and its significance for English studies. The resources for the first two major authors are substantially different for many reasons. Chaucer wrote narrative poems, which are readily rendered as stories for children, while Shakespeare's plays require a change in genre before they can become stories for children. Moreover, Shakespeare's plays are accompanied by both a massive performance history (and visual representation in paintings) and a negative view of the theatre, especially within the American Puritan tradition. A natural affinity between medieval writers and children is assumed by late Victorians and Edwardians: stories from the "childhood of the race" (epics, romances, legends) are apt choices for child readers. Although inadequately recognized, Shakespeare's obvious affinity with Chaucer is that he used *The Knight's Tale* for both the early comedy *A Midsummer Night's Dream* and the late play *Two Noble Kinsmen*, as well as *Troilus and Criseyde* for *Troilus and Cressida*. In *Shakespeare, Catholicism, and Romance* (2000) I argued the centrality of medieval romance and belief to his habit of mind and plays. Here I try to show how crucial romance is in the development of Shakespeare as children's literature. The favored play, *A Midsummer Night's Dream*, suits children because it is about fairies and deeply rooted in traditions of romance, as are *The Tempest* and *The Winter's Tale*, also popular choices.

Nevertheless, Shakespeare was regarded as very difficult for young children, though there was a concurrent wish that they early become acquainted with the plays to establish some knowledge upon which to build as more adult readers. Yet as the publication of *Family Shakespeare* (1807)—"acknowledged" as the work of Dr. Thomas Bowdler (with no reference to his sister Harriet who probably did most of the work) in the second edition of 1809—makes very obvious, in the nineteenth century much of Shakespeare was also considered unsuitable for adults. Thus the essential question of "adjustments" for children is vastly amplified for Shakespeare's plays; every reteller reiterates care taken to achieve high sentiment and claims only a modest introduction. A belief that literature strengthens moral character is an accepted tenet, typically rated above pleasure, the other desired end.

The Puritan animosity toward plays that led to the closing of the theatres from 1642 to 1660 is significant in the reception of Shakespeare, and elements of anti-theatrical prejudice long persisted. Puritans also objected to fiction both as a distraction from proper and profitable work and because it was not true, an early manifestation of anxiety and subsequent suppression of fairy tales and other fantasy. In the United States Peter Parley (Samuel Goodrich [1793–1860]), author and publisher, was enormously successful in the 1820s-1830s with books of instruction that satisfied Puritan expectations of serious knowledge; his books were widely pirated and imitated in England. A concurrent "anti–Peter Parleyism" was led by "Felix Summerley" (Sir Henry Cole [1808–1882]), a distinguished Victorian public servant — the first director of the South Kensington Museum (Victoria and Albert) — who retold fairy tales in *The Home Treasury* (1843–1844). One is "Robin Goodfellow," a lively account of fairyland and pranks, accompanied by a beautiful color illustration that resembles many subsequently made for *A Midsummer Night's Dream*.[1]

In this context belongs the judgment of the Rev. Heman Humphrey, a Congregational minister, president of Amherst University (1825–1845), who could find few books of fiction to praise for children (*Robinson Crusoe* is one, no doubt because of its nonconformist theology as well as much factual and practical information) and was anxious lest fiction become an addiction. In *Domestic Education* (1840) Rev. Humphrey utters astonishing opposition to Shakespeare:

> I am sorry that most of his plays were ever written. I believe it will appear in the Great Day, that they have done more harm than good.... It is scarcely possible they should pass through the youthful mind and imagination, without leaving a stain behind.[2]

Some years later a young Horace Scudder (1837–1902), who became a distinguished author and editor of children's literature, made the counterargument. As an editor of *Riverside Magazine for Young People*, published by Houghton Mifflin, he included in the second issue (1867) a list of "Books for Young People" that highly recommended Shakespeare because he has "what no other writer has in like measure, the power of furnishing material to the imagination."[3] Scudder acted upon this advocacy of imaginative writing when he secured ten stories from Hans Christian Andersen for the magazine. Although it did not continue long, "Riverside" became a name associated with publication for children, especially schoolbooks.

While there was less immediate dedication to Shakespeare in the United States, schoolbooks and home libraries increasingly made him a central figure, so that in the early twentieth century his prominence paralleled advocacy of Shakespeare for children in England, where Henry Newbolt's Report, *The Teaching of English in England,* published in 1921, recorded that *Tales and Stories from Shakespeare* was number one in the list of books "in great and steady demand" for use in London Elementary Schools.[4] A salient point made by Newbolt, and the distinguished scholars on the committee, many of whom are noted Shakespeareans (F. S. Boas, Sir Arthur Quiller-Couch, Caroline F. E. Spurgeon, J. Dover Wilson), is that stories of the plays are crucial for children, who generally will not be pleased or ready to read the plays successfully until they are older. The prevalence of similar attitudes in the United States explains the extraordinary richness of a tradition of Shakespeare stories for children in the early twentieth century.

The singular component of Shakespeare as children's literature is Mary and Charles Lamb's *Tales from Shakespeare* (1807). Almost immediately recognized as a classic of children's literature, it was constantly reprinted and became a standard — not least because of the literary reputation of Charles Lamb and the poignancy of his filial devotion to his sister through intermittent spells of madness. Some Edwardian collections of Shakespeare even include biographies of both Lamb and Shakespeare. No other retelling of a major writer has achieved and sustained this status. A partial explanation is that Lamb's *Tales* were enhanced by the pictures that accompanied them in myriad editions.

The Golden Age of Children's Literature is also the Golden Age of Children's Book Illustration, a time when publishers relied upon the quality of the illustration even more than the text. A monumental tradition of historical painting extends from eighteenth-century pictures of the Boydell Gallery; through major works by Sir John Everett Millais, Daniel Maclise, Sir Joseph Noel Paton, William Dyce, John H. Bacon, and many more; to all the great book illustrators — Gordon Browne, Walter Crane, Arthur Rackham, Edmund Dulac, W. H. Robinson, Charles Folkard, Gertrude Demain Hammond, and many less well remembered — whose visual images told the stories of Shakespeare's plays. While I argue that pictures retell the plays as memorably as words, the books I discuss are not picture books; each is a happy combination of verbal and visual texts. A remarkable characteristic of Edwardian books is their physical beauty, certain to attract and sustain child readers. Yet even cheap paper pamphlets, W. T. Stead's Books for the Bairns, contain engaging pictures.

Lamb's *Tales* comes at the moment when eighteenth-century and Romantic writers had put more emphasis on childhood and the child, with a corollary increase in works specifically intended for children that reached its height in the Golden Age of Edwardian children's literature. Chapter 1 situates Lamb's *Tales* within contexts of earlier traditional literature for children, notably chapbooks and ballads, and raises issues about adapting classics for children, especially "adjustments" made to create "suitable" stories. Then the place of illustration and distinguished artists who interpreted Shakespeare are indicated, followed by an examination of Shakespeare's place in education, specifically the Newbolt Report on *The Teaching of English in England* (1921) that codifies and evaluates Shakespeare at all levels from elementary through university and adult education. Chapter 2, "The Tradition of Charles and Mary Lamb's *Tales from Shakespeare,*" describes and compares a few of the finest complete editions with special attention to their variety of illustrations. Chapter 3 examines books that continue the Lamb tradition. Some add stories, either to complete the Shakespeare canon or to increase diversity, especially the history plays. Selections record which plays and combinations were deemed most likely to please child readers—and the adults who usually chose children's books.

"Victorian Alternatives," Chapter 4, begins the examination of Shakespeare stories not written by the Lambs. Two very different anthologies, by David Murray Smith and Abby Sage Richardson, combine Shakespeare with other English writers. Mary Seymour's *Shakespeare's Stories Simply Told* (1880) began as a large selection and then expanded as two companion volumes that included all of the plays. In contrast, Robert R. Raymond presented only three plays, very elaborately detailed and with more quotation. Shakespeare is even featured in a geography book.

Chapter 5, "Edwardian Elegance and Exuberance: Retellings Large and Small," shows how alternatives to the Lambs flowered. Books of Shakespeare's stories range from nursery books, like two by Jeanie Lang in the "Told to the Children" series, to sophisticated collections by Mary Macleod, R. Hudson, Thomas Carter, A.T. Quiller-Couch, Alice S. Hoffman, and Constance and Mary Maud. E. Nesbit's *The Children's Shakespeare,* a journeyman work, simplifies Lamb's *Tales* and was perhaps its nearest rival. Interlaced within stories are contemporary attitudes and judgments that show the accuracy of F. J. Harvey Darton's seminal definition of children's books as records of "social life," an early example of "cultural studies." Again illustrations contribute substantially to the distinction of books that are consistently beautiful and thoughtful, typical examples of Edwardian extravagance in printing.

Reproductions of great paintings, and some original work, made schoolbooks similarly attractive and available to those who could not afford Edwardian Reward / Prize books. Educational efforts to increase children's knowledge of Shakespeare are the subject of Chapter 6. Here Lamb's influence is great, since the versions most often printed are from the *Tales,* usually with some pedagogical materials. Graded readers, six or seven books for primary or elementary school, that survey different authors give Shakespeare an honored place. One of the best series, Nelson's *Highroads of Literature,* has a different story from year to year to build a cumulative foundation for later study of Shakespeare, while providing good stories and pictures—and exercises that increased cognitive skills. The relation between literature and history is a major point in Edwardian pedagogy. Schoolbooks of history typically employ Shakespeare's plays to present the English Middle Ages; indeed many believed they most effectively captured these centuries and were a source of racial identity and patriotism. These schoolbooks were disseminated throughout the English-speaking world.

As a balance to English schoolbooks, Chapter 7 concentrates on home libraries in the United States, many-volume collections — *The Children's Hour* (1907), *Journeys through Bookland* (1909), *The Junior Classics* (1912), *My Book House* (1920/21). Literary histories for children, by both British and American authors — H.E. Marshall, Henry Gilbert, Amy Cruse, Eva March Tappan, William J. Long — evaluate Shakespeare's role, give synopses of plays, and stress biography and social history as did William Rolfe's *Shakespeare the Boy* (1896). Finally, three Americans, one educator and two librarians, record Shakespeare's place in children's reading and report reactions to him.

An epilogue acknowledges outstanding examples of present-day books of Shakespeare for children, and tables provide a quick reference for plays retold in different books and for illustrations.

Collectors of Victorian and Edwardian children's books — and I am a passionate one — know that they are listed as "Antiquarian," "Collectible," "Nostalgia." In the current era of online multiplicity, with countless ways to introduce Shakespeare to children, it is easy to dismiss the Edwardians with a smile as irrelevant or quaint.[5] The excitement and challenges of the digital world are likely only to increase and much can be said in favor of technological development. However, concurrent with this is a general loss of quiet, thoughtful reading and a valuing of the humanities, especially a strong sense of the moral tradition of English literature, which reached its ascendant as a discipline in the twentieth century.[6] My hope is that an awareness of Edwardian Shakespeare as children's literature — its significance in the development of capacities to discern and honor humanity, an education that is not mere information and that stimulates reading — will be a contribution to current efforts to defend English studies. J.B. Priestly, who concludes his study *The Edwardians* (1970) with a recognition of fact and illusion about his own era, yet finds a salient trait in those who survived the Great War: "a kind of optimism, not large and wide and one huge smile, almost tiny but very compact and somehow indestructible. It encourages us to engage in all manner of doubtful ventures — as, for instance, trying to huddle Edwardian England between the covers of a book."[7] As a child of Edwardian parents and teachers, I have inherited something of that spirit, which explains why I have been optimistic enough to write this book at a time when optimism is rarely found in the academy.

There are, nevertheless, many who have encouraged and helped me. I want especially to thank the staffs of libraries where I often work: the British Library, the National Library of Scotland, Edinburgh University Library, the Hunterian Library in Glasgow, the Harry Ransome Center at Austin, Texas, the Huntington Library, and Doe Library at the University of California, Berkeley. Antiquarian booksellers in the United Kingdom and the United States — and sometimes online — have made it possible for me to acquire most of the books discussed here, so that I have had a tangible contact with the world that they embody. I am also grateful for invitations to present papers about Shakespeare for children at the University of Bristol in March 2006 and at the Conference of the International Shakespeare Association at Brisbane, Australia, in July 2006. As always, my deepest gratitude is to my husband, who for fifty years has been the person with whom I most often talk about Shakespeare and who always both challenges and encourages me. Moreover, we have attended conferences and countless productions, not least those of his students, including a performance of *Much Ado About Nothing* at the rebuilt Globe in London, where we also early offered a course for teachers; these experiences provided a broader and deeper context for my devotion to books and storytelling and Shakespeare.

1

Contexts for Charles and Mary Lamb's *Tales from Shakespeare*

Works written for children in the Middle Ages and early picture books like John Amos Comenius's *Orbis Pictus* (1659) are identified as children's literature.[1] However, the general assumption is that children's literature had a significant beginning in the eighteenth century, fueled by the thoughts of philosopher and educationalist John Locke (1632–1704), whose *Some Thoughts Concerning Education* (1693) was continuously reprinted in the eighteenth century.[2] Debates about the discovery/recognition of childhood, fueled in part by Philippe Ariés's *Centuries of Childhood: A Social History of Family Life* (1960), abound. Ariés recognizes medieval creation of images of the child (especially of Jesus) in art, but finds the seventeenth century pivotal as the time when portraits of children and families became commonplace.[3] Major painters yield evidence of the celebration of children: Diego Velázquez (1599–1660), Peter Paul Rubens (1577–1640), Franz Hals (c. 1580–1666), Philippe de Champaigne (1602–1674), and Sir Anthony Van Dyke (1599–1641), whose work in England is especially cogent. In the eighteenth century Sir Joshua Reynolds (1723–1792) and Thomas Gainsborough (1727–1788) provide many examples, well demonstrated in the 1995 exhibition *The New Child: British Art and the Origin of Modern Childhood, 1730–1830*, which argues that Georgian Britain led the way for the Continent in privileging the child.[4] Similarly, early American artists often painted children and families. An analogous increased interest in children's reading occurred at the same time.

Chapbooks

Printed literature specifically written for children developed from chapbooks, penny paper pamphlets provided for the emerging literate poor — albeit one of the most important surviving collections is "The Penny Merriements" assembled by Samuel Pepys (1633–1703). Adventures, retellings of medieval romances and murders, songs and ballads were popular with both adults and children who read the same chapbooks, well established in England. Shakespeare's audiences would have been familiar with chapmen, itinerant sellers, whom he immortalized in the character Autolycus in *The Winter's Tale*. That Autolycus sells his printed materials to country people at the sheep-shearing festival indicates a degree of literacy. In the same play a small child, Mamilius, loves to hear and tell tales, "sad or merry," so that Hermione, his mother, challenges him "do your best / To fright me with your sprites. You're powerful at it" (II.i.27–28). Such excitement was typical in later child readers. The essayist Richard Steele (1672–1729), Isaac Bickerstaff in *The Tatler* #95, November 17, 1709, testified that the eight-year-old son of his friends has spent a twelvemonth with lives and adventures of chapbook heroes, while "the little girl ... a better scholar ... deals chiefly in Fairies and Sprights; and sometimes in a Winter Night will terrify the Maids with her Accounts." Laurence Sterne (1713–1768) attested the continuance of such enthusiasm when Uncle Toby in *Tristram Shandy* (1759–1767) recalls his schoolboy practice of sharing such chapbooks, "purchased with my own pocket money." James Boswell (1740–1795), like Pepys, left an important collection, eighty-three chapbooks that he purchased in 1763 and had bound as *Curious Productions*. On the flyleaf is a note that explains: "Having when a boy, been much entertained with Jack the Giant-Killer, and such little Story Books, I have always retained a kind of affection for them, as they recall my early days." To this lifelong admiration he added an ambition to write in the style of these little chapbooks and voiced an often repeated judgment about the value of children's literature: "I shall be happy to succeed for He who pleases the children will be remembered with pleasure by the men."[5] One man who recognized and acted on this fact has not been forgotten.

John Newbery (1713–1767), starting with *A Little Pretty Pocket-Book* (1744), a chapbook for children sold with a ball for "Little Master Tommy" and a pincushion for "Pretty Miss Polly"—an early gendering as market strategy—is recognized as the first publisher to develop a large and permanent market, although most of his books were for adults—of 2,400 titles, only 400 were for children.[6] Oliver Goldsmith (1730–1774), who worked for him and is the likely author of *Goody-Two Shoes*, memorialized Newbery in *The Vicar of Wakefield* (1766), itself a children's classic, as "the philanthropic bookseller in St. Paul's Churchyard, who has written so many little books for children; he called himself their friend." In the United States the Newbery Medal, given for "the most distinguished contribution to American literature for children" and first awarded in 1922, is an annual reminder of his role.

Imitations, pirated versions, of Newbery's books by Isaiah Thomas (1750–1831) of Worcester, Massachusetts, a major publisher and founder of the American Antiquarian Society in 1812, signaled affinity between English and American books. Thomas's first American edition of *A Little Pretty Pocket-book* was printed in 1787.[7] More notable is *Mother Goose's Melody; or Sonnets from the Cradle,* probably published by one of Newbery's successors. Its ninety-six pages started with ten pages of introductory material for adults, while the central largest section contained fifty-one nursery rhymes with brief maxims. Significantly, albeit not illustrated, the last twenty pages were thirteen "Songs and Lullabies by Shakespeare." The earliest surviving English edition is 1791. Only Thomas's second American edition of 1794, issued at Gloucester, has survived intact; it contains the songs of "that sweet Songster and Nurse of Wit and Humour, Master William Shakespear."[8] This is remarkable, since the first play of Shakespeare published in Boston was not until the same year. Newbery's precedent is the oldest book of nursery rhymes, Mary Cooper's *Tommy Thumb's Pretty Song Book* (1744); only its second volume, which lacks a Shakespeare section, has survived. Newbery's *Mother Goose's Melody* and Thomas's American edition thus anticipate Edwardian practice of introducing children to Shakespeare through his songs.[9]

But there were Shakespeare stories in eighteenth-century chapbooks, two published in 1794, *The History of Shylock the Jew, and Antonio The Merchant, with that of Portia and the Three Caskets ... Adapted to the Minds of Young Children* and *The History of King Lear and his Three Daughters.*[10] Both had precedents in sixteenth- and seventeenth-century ballads, appreciated by all levels of society; many were preserved in a manuscript that Bishop Thomas Percy (1729–1811) published as *Reliques of Ancient English Poetry* (1765), three volumes frequently reprinted in the nineteenth century.[11]

Among Percy's ballads Thomas Warton (1728–90) believed that Shakespeare knew *Gernutus the Jew of Venice* (106–111), although the fourteenth-century Italian *Il Pecorone* is his ultimate source for *The Merchant of Venice,* while *King Leir and His Three Daughters* (115–119), whether written before or after the play, has a remarkable resemblance to *King Lear.* Ballads could both introduce stories of plays to children and place Shakespeare in the English literary tradition. In one Edwardian schoolbook series, Nelson's *Highroads of Literature,* children read the ballad *The Jew of Venice* in Third Book to prepare them for Lamb's *The Merchant of Venice* in Fifth Book. An alternative series, Arnold's *The Sesame Readers,* Book IV features the ballad *King Leir and His Three Daughters* that American Hamilton Wright Mabie made one of thirteen items in *A Book of Old English Ballads* (1896).[12]

Today's pedagogy often favors performance — reading aloud, presenting speeches and/or scenes — and this was also Victorian and Edwardian practice. Several early nineteenth-century precedents indicate an analogous wish to encourage recreational approaches to Shakespeare. Georgiana Ziegler identifies *Young Albert, The Roscius* (1811), a picturesque storybook with paper dolls, and play sheets, published by William West and his successor Hodgson & Company, who added texts to accompany model stages for toy theatres. Thus play and learning were combined in a rich tradition described by George Speaight.[13] William West, with a total output of 144 play sheets issued from 1811 to 1831, included nine Shakespeare titles, five before 1819. Hodgson & Company, from a total of sixty-eight between 1822 and 1830, added six more Shakespeare plays. Thus Shakespeare became more available within the decade after the publication of Lamb's *Tales* (1807); the interests are analogous, although tragedies and histories were preferred for play sheets and toy theatres. Speaight's cumulative list of Shakespeare items has thirteen titles, of which *The Merry Wives of Windsor* and *A Midsummer Night's Dream* are comedies, while *The Tempest* and *The Winter's Tale* are romances; nine publishers issued *Richard III*, as compared with the usual two or three.[14] Selection may be tied to performances, but it is tempting to see Lamb as a partial inspiration before the trade began to decline about 1850.

A link between chapbooks and Lamb's *Tales* reiterates that publishers perceived these inexpensive booklets as a vehicle for children's literature; chapbook editions of individual tales were issued before the complete *Tales*.[15] The original intention to publish all twenty tales separately as sixpenny booklets was abandoned by 1809; very few copies survived. Based on surviving copies and advertisements, Foxon's list indicates which plays were thought most likely to appeal: *The Winter's Tale, Othello, A Midsummer Night's Dream,* and *Cymbeline* as separate items and a two-tales edition of *Romeo and Juliet* and *Timon of Athens*, 1807; a double issue, *King Lear* and *The Merchant of Venice*, each with two editions, 1808; a double issue *The Winter's Tale* and *Othello*, 1809; and a double issue *Midsummer Night's Dream* and *Cymbeline*, 1811.

The full collection *Tales from Shakespear (sic)*, published in two volumes in 1807, became the standard and most famous retelling of the stories of Shakespeare's plays for children. Although only the name of Charles Lamb (1775–1834) appears on the title page, most (fourteen) of the twenty stories were the work of Mary Lamb (1764–1847), since her brother contributed only the six tragedies. Lamb's *Specimens of English Dramatic Poets who lived about the time of Shakespeare* (1808), which included critical notes, initiated his reputation as a critic. Subsequently he published *On the Tragedies of Shakespeare, considered with reference to their fitness for Stage Representation* (1811), a substantial essay, in Leigh Hunt's quarterly *The Reflector*; *On the Artificial Comedy of the Last Century* appeared in *Elia* (1823). These, like the *Tales*, express a wish to be free of the stagy characteristics of current productions, to make available to children and simple folk something of the Elizabethan spirit.[16] Brother and sister collaborated on other children's literature; Charles claimed about one third of *Poetry for Children* (1809) and also of *Mrs. Leicester's School* (1809), issued anonymously, but the idea and most stories were Mary's.

The publisher of *Tales from Shakespear* was "Thomas Hodgkins," a pseudonym for William Godwin (1756–1836), and his second wife, Mary Jane Clermont, whose M.J. Godwin and Company lasted only from 1805–1822. They commissioned the work and paid sixty guineas. Charles Lamb, who was trying to establish himself as an essayist, expected the *Tales* to be popular and regarded them as a way to earn much needed money; his letters express a view that writings for children are pot-boilers—an often shared sentiment. American Sidney Lanier (1842–1881), for example, contracted for children's books to gain income that his poetry and music did not provide. While this implies a lack of sympathy, Lamb, who later wrote "Dream Children," brought a characteristic humility, warmth, and personal engagement to *Tales from Shakespear* and his other juvenile works—*Adventures of Ulysses* (1808), and *Prince Dorus, or Flattery Put Out of Countenance* (1811). The context is eighteenth-century fascination with childhood—manifested in paintings of children and much didactic literature written for them—and elevation of childhood by the Romantics, especially William Wordsworth (1770–1850), albeit few wrote for children but rather about the child and childhood.[17]

Moral Tales

In the early-nineteenth century alternatives were sought to the moral tale, the dominant type of children's literature, written by Sarah Trimmer (1741–1810) and Anna Laetitia Barbauld (1743–1825). Lamb famously wrote in a letter to Coleridge:

> *Goody Two Shoes* is almost out of print. Mrs. Barbauld's stuff has banished all the old classics of the nursery.... Science has succeeded Poetry no less in the little walks of children than with men—: Is there no possibility of averting this sore evil? Think what you would have been now, if instead of being fed with Tales and old wives fables in childhood, you had been crammed with Geography and Natural History![18]

With characteristic Romantic sensibility Lamb dismissed information, factual knowledge, given in children's books as "insignificant and vapid" and an occasion for giving the young reader an inflated sense, "conceit of his own powers" rather than "that beautiful interest in wild tales, which made the child a man, while all the time he suspected himself to be no bigger than a child."[19] However, granted her objection to anything fanciful—the view of her time—Mrs. Barbauld was a writer of distinction and influence.[20] Lamb's popularity, as well as modern secular and liberal attitudes, have led to a more negative view of such earlier children's literature than its quality justifies.

Paradoxically, in many ways Lamb's *Tales* was of a piece with children's books that he faulted; however, he and Mary had Shakespeare as their resource, a mine of magical and imaginative storytelling and gruesome cruelty—and a national icon. Nowhere is this more apparent than in the fact that Charles Lamb, although an esteemed essayist, had greatest influence as co-author of *Tales from Shakespeare*. But, paradoxically, histories of children's literature (indeed literary histories) devote very little space or comment—a few lines, a paragraph—to *Tales from Shakespeare,* a fate shared by other retellings of traditional literature/classics not originally written for children. However, Henry Newbolt's report of 1921, *The Teaching of English in England,* records that such titles were very much a part of the lives of late Victorian and Edwardian children, for whom Charles Dickens, Sir Walter Scott, and Shakespeare were favorite authors.

Debates about the brute element — and Shakespeare contains much violence — always dominate considerations of "suitable for children." Lamb's letter, March 11, 1808, to Godwin, both friend and publisher, addresses the issue of adaptation of adult classics to children. In response to requests to soften his *Adventures of Ulysses,* he carefully agrees to eliminate a superfluous "nauseous" passage about vomit but refuses to alter "shocking" details and "the terrible" that are a part of great art. Montrose J. Moses, an American librarian and editor of plays for children, quotes this letter and identifies Lamb as a landmark in the development of children's literature, since he initiated "an almost new critical attitude toward Shakespeare":

> in days when psychology as a study was unknown, when people witnessed the different phases of emotional life and judged them before formulae were invented by which to test them scientifically, he saw, with rare discrimination, the part that the spiritual value of literature was to play in the development of culture. He here weighs in the balance a fine terror with a nauseous scene; such a difference presupposes a clear insight into the story and a power to arrive at the full meaning at once; it infers an instinctive knowledge of the whole gamut of possible effects. Lamb's plea to Godwin is the plea of the man who would rather keep a child in the green fields than have him spend his time on wishy-washy matter.[21]

Writing at the beginning of the twentieth century, Moses was appalled and distressed by educational theory, like Felix Adler's *The Moral Instruction of Children* (1892), that eliminated whatever could distress or offend anyone — stepmothers in fairy tales, anything not "of ornamental or ethical value." Any adjustments pose the problem of who decides (138). While the offending books and authors change — *Uncle Tom's Cabin, Huckleberry Finn, The Wizard of Oz,* C.S. Lewis, *Harry Potter,* Philip Pullman — the attitude of control does not. Moses acknowledged the vigor of objectors when he quoted Frederick Harrison's *The Choice of Books* (1886): "Poor Lamb has not a little to answer for, in the revived relish for garbage unearthed from old theatrical dung-heaps.... Why do we still suffer the traditional hypocrisy about the dignity of literature, — literature I mean, in the gross, which includes about equal parts of what is useful and what is useless?" (133). The argument has not been settled; witness current decisions about educational requirements that eschew Edwardian emphasis upon Shakespeare in schools and influential theorists like Stephen Greenblatt, who states, "there's no reason to think reading Shakespeare necessarily makes you a more reflective or deeper person" and offers the Nazis as his evidence.[22] The British (including the Empire) and Americans are surely a cogent alternative. Ian Watt, for example, who had a copy of Shakespeare with him when the Japanese captured him at Singapore in World War II, read it on the rare occasion when his diet was better.

Edwardian critics and educators were subtly aware of the issue. "Possible Dangers in Reading," a section of *The Teaching of English in England* (1921), is part of a comprehensive advocacy of English studies made at the foundation of the discipline and sustained in its curriculum through the middle of the twentieth century when English literature was esteemed as the basis of liberal education.

> The desire of young people to discover all that can be discovered about sensations cannot be effectively repressed, it can only be prevented from becoming an obsession by leaving open the way of exploration, and by taking care at the same time that the discoveries shall be made under the guidance of right reason and right feeling.... Brute physical facts in a newspaper are far more unwholesome than the same facts in the pages of Shakespeare or of Cervantes. In such books they are conveyed by the sanest of voices and set by the greatest of observers in their due place in human life; they are treated naturally, fearlessly and without self-consciousness, whereas in the police news the reader's mind is concentrated upon the criminal aspect and unhelped by any influence which could make for judgment or a sense of proportion.[23]

While the Lambs recognized a need for a brother to protect his sister from unsuitable details, the case for teaching English expresses no such concern. The Newbolt Report notes that girls were always taught English more than boys, whether in school or at university, where English has been continuously favored by more women than men.

Classics of Literature for Children

Lamb's significant role in establishing the idea of making adult literature accessible to children, an alternative to stories created specifically for them, is a correlative to popular chapbooks that were simplified versions, especially old romances like *Guy of Warwick, Valentine and Orson, The Seven Champions of Christendom,* and the classic *Pilgrim's Progress, Robinson Crusoe,* and *Gulliver's Travels.*[24] Moreover, *Tales from Shakespeare* inspired Lamb's friend Charles Cowden Clarke (1787–1877) to write *Tales from Chaucer in Prose: Designed Chiefly for the Use of Young Persons* (1833). Between them they established a tradition of retelling England's two greatest writers for children.[25] Clarke is best known as a Shakespeare scholar who lectured widely and wrote *The Shakespeare Key* (1879). His wife, Mary Cowden Clarke (1809–1898), produced *The Complete Concordance to Shakespeare* (1845). Together they edited *Cassell's Illustrated Shakespeare* (1886), which included their editions, biography, chronology, and glossary. Mary Cowden Clarke's contribution to children's Shakespeare is substantial. Her *The Girlhood of Shakespeare's Heroines* (1850–1852), in three volumes, is a sensitive and insightful analysis of character as well as a collection of engaging and readable stories that also encourage more penetrating thought about the plays. Her dedications of each imaginative story, often to a writer or artist, record the current establishment and mark sympathetic response children's literature.

Alternatives are similarly original but in different ways. The historical novel, the most numerous fictional genre in the nineteenth century, is an extended narrative and a means of introducing Shakespeare and his contemporaries as characters. The best is by John Bennett (1865–1956), an American, whose *Master Skylark* (1896) effectively evokes London theatres; it became a children's classic, even being adapted for performance. In contrast, Sara Hawkins Sterling's *Shake-speares Sweetheart* (1905) is a first-person romance. Such fictional expansions are ancillary to stories of the plays.

The extraordinary success of Lamb's *Tales* is obvious in several ways. Editions, with a wide range of illustrations, proliferated, and not until the 1880s were there significant alternatives. Even E. Nesbit's *The Children's Shakespeare* (1897) retold the same plays but more simply. Thus, histories of children's literature note "this book of the Lambs is the only one of all this period which has really survived, to be a part of the literature that is used and enjoyed today."[26] Moreover, a book intended for children became a resource for adults—as with chapbooks, a reversal of audience.

English literature had become an examination subject when it was introduced as part of the examination for the Indian Civil Service in 1855. Lamb's *Tales from Shakespeare* was a textbook in India for Entrance Examination at Calcutta University.[27] Shakespeare was a favorite at self-educated men's clubs and Working Men's Colleges in Britain, and self-study courses in the United States also used *Tales from Shakespeare*. Cassell's Penny Shakespeare, each play with its colored cover, was popular with working men, especially in the newly industrialized north of England. In the United States Jerome B. Howard rendered Lamb "in the amanuensis style of phonography" (115); some plays— *Hamlet* (1916)—were published in Gregg shorthand to teach stenographers.

Responses oscillate between detractors of children's versions of traditional classics (usually Shakespearean scholars/purists) who fault omissions and adjustments and admirers (those committed to children's literature and education). Mary F. Thwaite is more poetical in expression than many but, to judge by sales, not unduly enthusiastic about Lamb's *Tales from Shakespeare*:

> it has the charm of a wild and woodland garden. The theme was new, the source brimful of poetry and romance, and the reshaping for "little people" was done with taste and skill, so that the result is neither paraphrase nor abridgement, but stories with an artistic quality of their own. Through their love of the great original, the Lambs captured something of the greatness of the plays, cleverly taking up Shakespeare's own phrases at times when they might be woven into the story. Problems for adult understanding are avoided, and there is little writing down or moralizing [88–89].

These characteristics, a model for bringing great adult literature to children, were devotedly emulated and developed further.

The secure place of Lamb's *Tales* as a classic belies the complexity and intensity of dispute about retelling literary masterpieces for children. In some ways, arguments parallel the gradual recognition of children's literature as a proper academic study. In the United States it belonged to departments/faculties of education and library science until the last quarter of the twentieth century, when English studies accepted children's literature as part of sweeping changes. (When I offered my first class in 1979, colleagues expressed disbelief.) Two explanations are salient. First, the cogent argument stated in the title of F.J. Harvey Darton's *Children's Books in England: Five Centuries of Social Life* (1932), matched the vogue for "cultural studies" and including the "disadvantaged." For the Lambs, as observed in the preface, these were girls— who lacked the resources of school or library given to their brothers; for Edwardians, they were also the poor — those who did not attend public school and university and learned in Working Men's Colleges. In the United States public education was limited; many children left school at very young ages, never attending high school. A second reason for the acceptance of English courses in children's literature was their popular appeal, which meant high enrollments at a time when period courses and even major authors (except Shakespeare!) failed to attract students. The typical syllabus, usually written by a Victorian specialist, consisted of fairy tales and novels, an easy elision with modern fiction. However, as a medievalist and Shakespearean, I always included retellings of medieval romance (Guy of Warwick and Chaucer) and of Shakespeare to introduce an alternative, more universal, dimension. Purists object to loss of the poet's words and to presenting canonical authors as storytellers; the counterargument is that these writers are excellent storytellers whose texts are more rewarding and challenging than most children's books written to order. Furthermore, early reading of narrative and visual texts is but the start of an ongoing, increasingly sophisticated experience, both universal and patriotic, a foundation for a sense of history and continuity that might even culminate in academic critical analyses.

Perhaps the strongest objection to "great literature retold for children" is "adjustments," especially those that undercut twenty-first-century obsession with sexuality; thus I offer an apologia. The year 1807 saw the publication not only of Lamb's *Tales from Shakespeare* but also of Thomas Bowdler's *Family Shakespeare,* a book perhaps unmatched as a catalyst for contempt; earlier expurgations (profanity/political/religious [Oldcastle to Falstaff]) lack its fame, signaled by coining the word "bowdlerize" to mean disapproval in 1836. Nevertheless, these socially acceptable renderings were very successful, not least with evangelicals, and Bowdler was favored for family reading aloud.[28]

The first edition of *Family Shakespeare* appeared anonymously; the second in 1809 carried the name of Dr. Thomas Bowdler (1754–1825) as editor, although his sister, Harriet, seems to have done most of the work, as had Mary Lamb. Social phenomenon gave prominence to views of and about women, notably favoring of comedies and romances and focus on characterization. The essential point is that nineteenth-century retellings for children share adult values; and, arguably, they are also more honest. One salient quality is an acknowledgment that stories are changed to make them suitable; editions often silently omit and correct. Many Edwardians preserved Victorian attitudes. Robert Bridges's preface to the 1907 Stratford edition, edited by A.H. Bullen, expresses concern and distress:

> Shakespeare should not be put into the hands of the young without the warning that the foolish things in his plays were written to please the foolish, the filthy for the filthy, and the brutal for the brutal; and that if, out of veneration for his genius we are led to admire or even tolerate such things, we may be thereby not conforming ourselves to him, but only degrading ourselves to the level of his audience, and learning contamination from those wretched beings who can never be forgiven their share in preventing the greatest poet and dramatist of the world from being the best artist.[29]

A key issue, as with all adult classics retold for children, is the language of the original. Both dramatic form (less understandable on the page) and remote qualities of Shakespeare's language (frequently poetry but also sophisticated prose) make this an obvious concern. Lamb's preface sets out the difficulties and explains the solution made in this first attempt to retell Shakespeare for children.

> In those tales which have been taken from the Tragedies, the young readers will perceive, when they come to see the source from which these stories are derived, that Shakespeare's own words, with little alteration, recur very frequently in the narrative as well as in the dialogue; but in those made from the Comedies the writers found themselves scarcely ever able to turn his words into the narrative form: therefore, it is feared that, in them, dialogue has been made use of too frequently for young people not accustomed to the dramatic form of writing. But this fault, if it be a fault, has been caused by an earnest wish to give as much of Shakespeare's own words as possible: and if the "*He said*" and "*She said*," the question and the reply, should sometimes seem tedious to their young ears, they must pardon it, because it is the only way in which could be given to them a few hints and little foretastes of the great pleasure which awaits them in their elder years, when they come to the rich treasures from which these small and valueless coins are extracted; pretending to no other merit than as faint and imperfect stamps of Shakespeare's matchless image. Faint and imperfect images they must be called, because the beauty of his language is too frequently destroyed by the necessity of changing many of his excellent words into words far less expressive of his true sense, to make it read something like prose; and even in some places, where his blank verse is given unaltered, as hoping from its simple plainness to cheat the young readers into the belief that they are reading prose, yet his language being transplanted from its own natural soil and wild poetic garden, it must want much of its native beauty.

There is no ambiguity about the difference between tales retold for children and original texts: they are not the same, as is particularly conspicuous with language. A twofold objective is to introduce young readers to Shakespeare and to inspire subsequent reading as children mature and become knowledgeable. Every prefatory comment in subsequent editions and in other retellings of Shakespeare's plays reiterates the same points. But in varied ways Shakespeare's language is made a part of the retelling. Some retain Shakespeare's language within their narrative, some interlace more and longer passages, others include extensive quotations in appendices.

Illustrations

While Shakespeare's plays and language are the original inspiration, illustrations frequently tell the story as vividly as the verbal texts and are lovingly remembered; they are a salient part of Shakespeare as children's literature. Charles Lamb disliked the pictures in the first edition because they related to the plays rather than the tales. These copper plates were probably the work of the painter William Mulready (1786–1863), an Irish Catholic, who also provided illustrations for some of the "Felix Summerly" *Home Treasury* series and for John Harris's 1807 edition of William Roscoe's popular *The Butterfly's Ball.* William Blake (1757–1827) is believed to have been the engraver. Thomas Hodgkins issued *Tales from Shakespear* (1807) in two volumes, each with ten tales accompanied by a frontispiece illustration; the plain paper covers with green silk spines are austere.[30] Mulready's style is rather plain, but subsequent editions often repeat his choice of subjects. "Prospero and Miranda" stand on the shore, *The Tempest* (I, frontispiece); four fairies circle above a huge Bottom with ass's head, *A Midsummer Night's Dream* (I, 23); "Imogen in the Cave of Bellarius," eating, as three woodsmen peer in, *Cymbeline* (I, 116); "Lear and Fool," in harlequin dress, suffer the storm (I, 188); "Witches Cauldron"—three with backs to the viewer—and bats, a cat, and a hedgehog attract a child's interest, *Macbeth* (I, 215); at "Capulets Masquerade," pilgrim Romeo wears a very visible cross and kneels to his love, his hat and a rosary are in the foreground (II, 145); a Jane Austen dress, not a nun's habit, is her attire when "Isabel pleads for the Life of her Brother," *Measure for Measure* (II, 70); and "Othello preparing to kill his Wife," a scene of sharply contrasted black and white (II, 206). A few subjects are unusual: "Gratiano and Nerissa desire to get married," *The Merchant of Venice* (I, 140); "Pericles is informed that his Armour is saved" (II, 231); "Orlando saves the life of his brother"—the snake and lion echo woodcuts from chapbook and Bible—*As You Like It* (I, 86); "Petruchio, Catherine and the Woman's Taylor," *The Taming of the Shrew* (II, 24). Others have memorable details: "Countess of Rousillon and her Daughter in Law" recall images of the Visitation of Mary and Elizabeth, *All's Well That Ends Well* (II, frontispiece); "Sebastian escapes on a Mast," as the ship sinks in the background, *Twelfth Night* (II, 24); "Hamlet, Horatio and the Grave digger" shows the latter standing knee deep in Ophelia's grave (II, 177). These first pictures for Lamb's *Tales* are a very modest beginning for a book that inspired some of the finest illustrations ever made for children.

In the 1860s British publishers "began to sell books for children principally for their illustrative content."[31] Some Victorian editions of Lamb's *Tales* relied upon the Boydell Gallery, but the "Golden Age of Children's Literature" is also the "Golden Age of Children's Book Illustration." Many of the finest artists produced their best work for children.[32] Some publishers' accounts indicate that writer and illustrator typically were paid equally; advertisements frequently feature the illustrator, who was often the occasion for a book, especially collections of fairy tales. In part, an enthusiasm for illustration was a result of technology; color printing achieved new standards of excellence through a four-color process that was particularly effective in reproducing watercolor; it required the use of glossy paper, sometimes protected by tissue. Compared to lithography, the new process was subtle and sharply defined. And the books are beautiful, often collector's items that are becoming increasingly expensive.

Arthur Rackham, generally recognized as the greatest children's book illustrator of the Golden Age (1890–1914), forcefully and eloquently put the case for art for children:

> I can only say that I firmly believe in the greatest stimulating and educative power of imaginative, fantastic and playful pictures and writings for children in their most impressionable years—a view that most unfortunately, I consider, has its opponents in these matter-of-fact days. Children will make no mistakes in the way of confusing the imaginative and symbolic with the actual. Nor are they at all blind to decorative or arbitrarily designed treatment in art, any more than they are to poetic or rhythmic form in literature. And it must be insisted on that nothing less than the best that can be had, cost what it may (and it can hardly be cheap), is good enough for those early impressionable years when standards are formed for life. Any accepting, or even choosing, art or literature of a lower standard as good enough for children is a disastrous and costly mistake.[33]

Like Lamb, Rackham urged no mitigation of subject or quality. Victorians and Edwardians saw a very close relationship between art and literature, perhaps because painting was not recognized as a profession until the census of 1861. A commonplace British attitude has been that their national strength lies in literature, not in music or the visual arts; to use subjects from literature was a way of being allied with the best of British. Significantly, the connection of art and literature is part of educational standards and schoolbooks, unusually well illustrated and with many exercises based on the pictures.

There were two resources for illustrations of Shakespeare. First is the rich tradition of historical and salon painting in which Shakespeare is a favorite subject. The Boydell Gallery, with widely distributed engravings, was a major resource (William Hogarth, George Romney, William Blake, Henry Fuseli, Johann Zoffany). For some, especially Fuseli, Shakespeare was a principal inspiration.[34] Almost every notable painter working in Britain in the nineteenth century (John Gilbert, Daniel Maclise, John Martin, J. M. W. Turner, John Everett Millais, Richard Dadd, Joseph Noel Paton, William Holman Hunt, William Dyce, Frederick, Lord Leighton, George Cruikshank, and many other lesser names) interpreted Shakespeare's plays—as did French (Eugène Delacroix and Gustave Moreau) and American artists (John Singer Sargent, Arthur Mathews)—or painted famous actors in their roles. *A Midsummer Night's Dream* and *The Tempest*, both children's favorites and popular with a general audience, were essential sources for paintings of fairies by a variety of artists.[35]

Because of great respect for design—especially by William Morris, Edward Burne-Jones, and Walter Crane, and the corollary beliefs and practices of the Arts and Crafts Movements throughout Europe and the United States—book illustration was not regarded as inferior to painting. Thus the second resource for children's books is the exceptional number of splendid book illustrators—Gordon Browne, Arthur Rackham, Edmund Dulac, W. Heath Robinson, Hugh Thomson, to name only the most obvious—who sustained and expanded the tradition of painting to tell stories and characterize people. This was at a time before abstract art—which prevailed only after World War II in large part because of the position of the United States—dominated expectations and favor. The work of late Victorian and Edwardian painters and illustrators is also a far cry from the picture book staple of many of today's children's books, where the text is often not much longer than captions in earlier books. Edwardian illustrators enjoyed considerable freedom to choose both subject and style. A final point is a distinction in gender: more women retold the stories, and more men made the pictures, which partially explains the independence of illustrators.

Education

A key element in Victorian reforms was elementary education for all. It has been estimated that when the Education Act of 1870 was passed, from the English and Welsh working class, only forty per cent of children aged six to ten and only thirty-three per cent of those aged ten to twelve attended school.[36] Alec Ellis's statistics for the years 1870 to 1895 show the advances made: registration in day schools went from 1,802,419 to 5,231,469, while average attendance rose from 68.32 per cent to 81.61 per cent. The number of years spent in school almost trebled: 2.55 years in 1870, 5.19 years in 1880, 6.13 years in 1890, 7.5 years in 1897 (86). Schoolbooks reflected these advances. The Code of 1871 had six standards for reading, from "I. Read a short paragraph from a book not confined to words of one syllable" to "V. and VI. Improved Reading" (89). Literature was made an examination subject in 1871, the year that Matthew Arnold

(1822–1888) in his role as inspector of schools identified literature as "the greatest power available in education" (91). This was in keeping with the educational theory of William Laurie, Professor of Education at Edinburgh University who argued for "a system which would develop in children the nobler feelings of human nature: love, tenderness, sympathy, a desire for approval, and a spirit of sacrifice" (91). Because children were staying in school longer, Standard VII was added in 1882. Shakespeare is named in the requirements: "VI. Read a passage from one of Shakespeare's historical plays or from some other standard author, or from a history of England. VII. Read a passage from Shakespeare or Milton, or from some other standard author, or from a history of England" (90).

Publishers filled the need with a variety of readers, among which inspectors deemed especially praiseworthy Bell's *Readers* and Nelson's *Royal School Readers*, which were "more extensively used than any others." With both schoolbooks and rewards/prizes, expensive and extravagant volumes, Nelson was especially significant. Blackie and Arnold were other major publishers for children. Having managed to keep going during the Great War, many were devastated by enemy action in World War II, when twenty million books were lost. English publishing from the beginning has been centered in London; and a single German bombing destroyed Paternoster Row and hit publishing houses of Bagster, Longman, Nelson, Sheed & War, and Simpkin-Marshall — many noted for their children's books (170).

The Newbolt Report

The Teaching of English in England, a Report by Henry Newbolt (1862–1938), completed in 1921—signed appropriately on April 23rd, the day of Shakespeare's birth and death, codified and confirmed standards at the start of the twentieth century; it provided comprehensive and rich contexts for understanding Shakespeare as children's literature. Newbolt, who first gained his reputation with stirring patriotic poems—*Admirals All* (1897), *Drake's Drum and Other Sea Songs* (1914), *St. George's Day and Other Poems* (1918)—expressed his high sentiments about chivalry and pubic school education (he was an old boy of Clifton College, Bristol) in *The Book of the Happy Warrior* (1918). During World War I Newbolt was controller of wireless and cables and was knighted in 1915; he wrote a naval *History of the Great War* (1920). The Newbolt Report was the work of an impressive committee. Some were scholar/critics especially concerned with Tudor drama: Caroline F. E. Spurgeon (1869–1941), author of *Shakespeare's Imagery and What It Tells Us* (1935); Frederick S. Boas (1862–1957), editor of *The Year's Work in English Studies* and author of *Shakespeare and His Predecessors* (1896), *Shakespeare and the Universities* (1923), *An Introduction to the Reading of Shakespeare* (1927); Sir Arthur Quiller-Couch (1863–1944), prolific editor, both of *New Cambridge Shakespeare* and The King's

Treasuries of Literature Series (251 volumes between 1920 and 1938, in an attractive small format to enhance the appeal of English literature), author of children's books and of *Shakespeare's Workmanship* (1918); and John Dover Wilson (1881–1969), editor of the *New Cambridge Shakespeare* and *Life in Shakespeare's England* (1911) and author of *The Essential Shakespeare* (1932), *What Happens in Hamlet* (1935), *The Fortunes of Falstaff* (1943), and many others.[37]

The Report's basic principle is that education is "guidance in the acquiring of experience"; and "it has been long accepted ... that the three main motives which actuate the human spirit are the love of goodness, the love of truth, and the love of beauty.... [H]eads corresponding to these [divide education] into the training of the will (morals), the training of the intellect (science) and the training of the emotions (expression or creative art)." Literature is "the most direct and lasting communication of experience by man to men" (8–9). Thus the teaching of English is "the channel for formative culture for all English people, and the medium of the creative art by which all English writers of distinction, whether poets, historians, philosophers or men of science, have secured for us the power of realizing some part of their own experience of life" (12). Every other subject will be affected because of "the teaching of English as the instrument of thought and the means of communication" (23). English and English literature are "so inextricably connected as to form the only basis possible for a national education" (14). Newbolt and his colleagues wrote at a time when a strong case had to be made for the study of English, since Latin and Greek classics were favored, in part for historical reasons—the Church's establishment of education in the Middle Ages and advocacy of classical authors by Renaissance humanists. They argue that English literature is a comparable way to connect with the best minds. A paper on English literature in addition to English grammar was not introduced until 1917.

The Report's judgments are informed by devotion to nation/race, the excellence of English literature—"the great national heritage of prose and poetry" to which children will return if they have enjoyed it—and its accessibility across classes. Another pragmatic consideration is even more cogent today. English was already well established as a world language, not least because of the British Empire; a vote of a Northern Peace Conference in 1919 in Stockholm signaled recognition. Of fifty-four replies to the question which is the language best suited for universal use, one was for German, eight for French, one for Latin or Spanish, five for Ido or Esperanto, and twenty-nine for English (67–68). At the start of the twentieth century the English tradition is the tradition of English-speaking peoples.

Like other significant Shakespeare scholars, Sir Israel Gollancz (1863–1930), Professor of English language and literature at King's College, London, and the first secretary of the British Academy, was interested in Shakespeare for children. Although he published books about Anglo-Saxon poetry and was general editor of the Temple Classics, his chief commitment was to Shakespeare.

He edited the forty volumes of *The Temple Shakespeare* (1894–1896), Charles Lamb's *Specimens of Elizabethan Dramatists* (1893), *Ambales-Saga/Hamlet in Iceland* (1898), and *The Book of Homage to Shakespeare* (1916). In 1916 he founded the Shakespeare Association, which publishes monographs, books, and facsimiles. In addition to scholarly work Gollanz was a popular advocate who urged that schoolwork should be joyful. He worked to establish an annual "Shakespeare Day" to be celebrated on April 23 as a way of uniting children in the United Kingdom, the Dominions, and the United States of America. Schools in France also recognized it (319).

A solid foundation for this patriotic and literary recognition was the teaching of English. In preparatory (elementary) schools "some acquaintance with English literature should precede the introduction of foreign and classical literatures"; in secondary schools, the Report suggests, "in Junior Departments, up to the age of twelve, at least one period a day should be devoted to English"; and "throughout the Public Schools English Literature should be regarded as entitled to a place in the regular school course, and not be relegated to spare time" (349–350). At the elementary stage, literature lessons were to seek not only "increased command of the language" and "the acquisition of knowledge" but also "appreciation and enjoyment of literature." Care is to be taken to guard against "the mere desultory reading of books"; the intellects of young adults in secondary schools should be worthily exercised through "a close and intensive study of specially selected works in verse and prose, chosen on account of their intrinsic value" (116). Finally, frequent references to "the other creative arts, music, architecture, painting, etc." were "to illustrate broad principles of criticism" (118). This pedagogy—supported by marketing of children's books—explains the crucial role of illustration. *The Teaching of English* also makes recommendations for universities, evening and continuation schools, ongoing adult education, and the place of English in commercial and industrial life. English literature is to be read long after the child has left school.

Pedagogical comments about specific authors recognize the necessity for tales and stories to introduce Shakespeare to children at the elementary stage.

> "The oldest boys have been interested in Shakespeare when a play was taken through by an appreciative teacher who dramatises certain scenes; but I question whether Shakespeare is not too difficult for an elementary school."
> Another witness remarks that, "as the elementary school is a finishing school, teachers feel that children ought not to grow up ignorant of Shakespeare and Scott [86].

The Report advises teachers who have no other reason to include these authors to omit them and cites a student response to Scott's pages of description as "very uninteresting, but it is intensely good literature" (86). An alternative witness evaluates Shakespeare:

> "There is no doubt that the most popular author with the pupils is Shakespeare. A different play (or plays), one for each Form, is prescribed each term."

> We feel no call to dispute with those who tell us that Shakespeare is over the heads of the children. He is over the heads of us all. It is sufficient to say that in the schools Shakespeare proves an immense success [86].

Textbooks, editions of Lamb's *Tales,* and alternative retellings are the surest argument of a belief in Shakespeare as children's literature. Later, the Report reiterates: "We have to accept as inevitable the fact that many passages of Shakespeare cannot be understood by children" and advises discussions of language and style only for senior pupils (314).

The Report's fullest discussion of Shakespeare comes under "The Drama in Education" in elementary and in secondary school. Only in the higher forms of secondary schools is drama not considered as reading, and Shakespeare is the usual author (312). That German enthusiasm for Shakespeare surpasses English is a result of language, the one written in a current language all understand, while

> English-Shakespeare is written in a language that every Englishman does not understand ... not only difficult, but archaic as well; and thus he seems doubly unsuitable for young readers. Fortunately he is saved for the schools by his wonderful power of re-telling a story in dramatic form, and his equally wonderful power of characterization, and we may add, his incomparable mastery of word-music. Indeed, it is Shakespeare the poet as much as Shakespeare the dramatist to whom we must introduce our pupils [312].

Several pragmatic suggestions for teachers follow, both for performing the plays and for attending public performances; they mark extraordinary changes in pedagogical attitudes and expectations in the twenty-first century. Since Shakespeare cannot be read at sight, "it seems inadvisable that the first reading of a play should be undertaken by the young pupils themselves." The first stage is to be an eloquent, uninterrupted reading from "a skilled and understanding reader" (313). Earlier in describing the training of teachers, the Report observes that "the voice of the teacher is his main instrument, the only model which pupils have to follow" (178). This is, of course, quite a different attitude from present-day uneasiness with recognizing excellence in an effort to exalt equality. A brief explanation of the Elizabethan theatre, ideally accompanied by a model, is useful. A quick reading and informal discussion, followed by a dramatic reading and assigning of parts, are the next steps advised. Production — scenery and properties — can be very modest, as a successful performance of *Richard II* at a Boys' School in South London demonstrated. Today many have a great advantage, most notably visits to the rebuilt Globe Theatre in London, or similar imitations in Rome or Tokyo. Moreover, outdoor theatres throughout the United States offer analogs to Elizabethan performance.

While attendance at public performances is "an officially recognized form of educational activity," and can be a great advantage, there are dangers (317). Ellen Terry's Portia and Forbes-Robertson's Hamlet are estimable, but often professional performances are what children should not see. The favorite plays named indicate recognized problems:

> Boys and girls should never be allowed to see the wood-magic of *A Midsummer Night's Dream* destroyed by the protracted clowning of Bottom, or to find the flower-sweet loveliness of *Twelfth Night* sullied by extravagant orgies of would-be comic drunkenness. Better, far, the feebleness of and inadequacy of school performance than efficiency of this kind.... [T]eachers must therefore recognise their imperative duty of ensuring that a child's first impressions of Shakespeare shall not be misshapen. That does not mean that we must approach Shakespeare in an attitude of artificial solemnity. Shakespeare must not be made either unnaturally dull or unnaturally grotesque. He wrote his plays to give immediate pleasure to a miscellaneous audience, and he resented liberties with his text. Anything in our treatment that makes Shakespeare dull or distorted is a crime against his spirit — it is "from purpose of playing" [318–319].

What the authors of *The Teaching of English in England* would make of most productions of Shakespeare today is not hard to predict, although verbal facility would be stretched to express reactions. Behind concern with quality and the respect of a performance lies anxiety about children's first impression of Shakespeare. For Edwardians this comes from reading stories and tales.

The Report records Shakespeare's place in a "Memorandum by Mr. A. E. Palfery on the Scheme for the Circulation of Books in London Elementary Schools" that classifies books widely used — approximately 2,000,000 volumes in overall circulation, including 1,650 titles. Group A, those in great and steady demand, lists fifty titles in order of popularity; number one is *Tales and Stories from Shakespeare* (374–375). (Chaucer is number twenty-nine and Spenser's *Stories from the Faerie Queen* is forty-six; Milton did not make the list.) "Tales and Stories," a hybrid title, is significant because it suggests variety of texts. Shakespeare's role as the most significant English writer meant whole books devoted to retellings of his plays. Collections are often very beautiful and luxurious examples of Edwardian extravagance in publishing. But at the same time there are numerous modest offerings, some very attractive, and remarkable schoolbooks that reached the widest audience of children. Because Lamb's *Tales from Shakespeare* was the version most frequently and creatively printed, it makes a proper beginning.

2

The Tradition of Charles and Mary Lamb's *Tales from Shakespeare*

Charles and Mary Lamb's *Tales from Shakespeare* (1807), the first book published specifically as "easy reading for very young children," was written in a clear, vigorous style. Although she contributed more than her brother—the preface (except the last paragraph and a half) and fourteen to his six tales—Mary Lamb's name did not appear on the title page until the sixth edition of 1838. Her preface explicitly recognizes the need for writing for "very young children" and the nature of the task:

> It was no easy matter to give the histories of men and women in terms familiar to the apprehension of the young mind. For young ladies, too, it has been the intention chiefly to write; because boys being generally permitted the use of their fathers' libraries at a much earlier age than girls are, they frequently have the best scenes of Shakespeare by heart, before their sisters are permitted to look into this manly book; and, therefore, instead of recommending these Tales to the perusal of young gentlemen who can read them much better in the originals, their kind assistance is rather requested in explaining to their sisters such parts as are hardest for them to understand; and when they have helped them to get over the difficulties, then perhaps they will read to them (carefully selecting what is proper for a young sister's ear) some passage which has pleased them in one of these stories, in the very words of the scene from which it is taken; and it is hoped they will find that the beautiful extracts, the select passages, will be much better relished and understood from their having some notion of the general story from one of these imperfect abridgments.

Gender expectations are explicit, but also appreciation of her brother, who devoted himself to Mary's care after she killed their mother.[1] Of the First Folio plays, twelve of the fourteen comedies (all but *Love's Labour's Lost* and *Merry Wives of Windsor*) are told, plus *Pericles,* added in the Fourth Folio of 1685. This means that all "romances" are retold, an early signal of fostering chivalric stories as children's literature. In contrast, there are only six of eleven tragedies. Four Roman plays are missing (*Coriolanus, Titus Andronicus, Julius Caesar,*

Antony and Cleopatra) and the English history plays. Thus comedies are deemed most suitable for children, especially girls, but not without adjustments.

In the archetypal favorite for children *A Midsummer Night's Dream*, Bottom is a "Clown," the only mechanical; and there is no performance of "Pyramus and Thisbe." Although parent-child relationships are central, and confused young lovers suffer "sad chance indeed," Lamb gives pride of place to the fairies. This is predictable in the context of fairy tales, which were steadily being appropriated for children, while adult delight was strong. *Victorian Fairy Paintings,* the Royal Academy exhibition of 1997–1998, brilliantly showed this, as did *Shakespeare in Art,* the Dulwich Exhibition of 2003. Thus to begin with *The Tempest* suggests both the First Folio and easy engagement of children. Similarly, the witches survive intact in *Macbeth,* while the Porter is absent. *Measure for Measure* seems an unlikely play for children, but here Lucio and other lowlife characters are absent. Lamb keeps the substitution of Mariana, crucial for the plot, and reassures with a didactic ending:

> when she became duchess of Vienna Isabel worked such a complete reformation among the young ladies of that city, that from that time none ever fell into the transgressions of Juliet, the repentant wife of the reformed Claudio. And the mercy-loving duke reigned with his beloved Isabel, the happiest of husbands and of princes.

Because the number and variety of editions of Lamb's *Tales from Shakespeare* published in Britain and the United States in the nineteenth and early twentieth centuries make discussion of them all ungainly, I consider a small selection, based on the quality of illustrations. The text remains the same, but illustrations record both changing emphasis and interpretation, and chronicle key figures in children's book illustration. Also cogent is added material about Shakespeare's life, the theatre, and biographies of Charles and Mary Lamb. Two other categories are: (1) books that add some or all tales not told by the Lambs, or tell only plays not retold by them to complete stories of Shakespeare's plays; and (2) selections from Lamb's *Tales,* either for especially extravagant Edwardian publication or as small books particularly pleasing to introduce the world of Shakespeare. These are discussed in Chapter 3, and the use of Lamb's *Tales* in schoolbooks in Chapter 7. Here I begin with two Victorian editions that combine Lamb's *Tales* with established illustrations for adults.

A Victorian Edition with Illustrations from the Boydell Gallery (1876)

A Victorian edition, published by Bickers in 1876, marks a general audience; it has no explanatory materials and combines *Tales* for children with twelve resoundingly adult engravings from the Boydell Gallery.[2] The frontispiece

A Victorian Lamb's *Tales from Shakespeare* (1876) contains illustrations from the Boydell Gallery, complex adult images (often of performances), but the cover is decorated with enchanting fairies to promise *A Midsummer Night's Dream* and *The Tempest,* popular stories for children.

is "Shylock, Jessica, and Launcelot" from *The Merchant of Venice,* II.v, painted by Robert Smirke (1752–1845), engraved by Jean Pierre Simon (1750–1810), and published December 1, 1795.[3] Its prominent position —*Merchant* is the seventh tale — reflects both an interest in parent-child relations and this play's popularity, which persisted as a school favorite until World War II, when its use became problematic. With thirty-two paintings Smirke was one of the most prolific contributors to the Boydell Gallery. The moment chosen is the last of father and daughter together; a wary Shylock takes his leave and warns Jessica to keep his house safe. Father and daughter are also the subject of *Prospero's Cell, The Tempest,* IV.i (7) by Joseph Wright of Derby (1734–1797), a skilled eighteenth-century painter, especially in his treatment of light. Robert Thew (1758–1802) did the engraving, published June 1, 1800. An entranced Miranda stands beside Ferdinand, while her father stands before them with his staff raised high toward the top of the picture, a well lighted space with figures of the masque that he has conjured to celebrate their engagement. But below and behind him, in another ragged circle of light, are Caliban and Trinculo and Stephano, who holds a stick (a parody of Prospero's wand) and bottle. The pictures show both authority and its undermining, a cogent theme for children's intellectual development.[4] The next illustration captures a moment when a lost child regains a mother, *The Winter's Tale,* V.iii (47), after the revelation of the statue, just before Hermione descends; her gaze is on Leontes, who looks up in wonder. But prominent in the right foreground is the kneeling Perdita, who also looks to the statue, while her new husband Florizel gazes at her face. The painter is William Hamilton (1751–1801), a Scotsman who did history painting and had the support of Robert Adam while he studied in Rome. The engraver was again Thew, published June 4, 1793.

Only after the interest of child-parent relations has been well introduced by the first three images are other themes selected. Smirke's painting for *Much Ado About Nothing,* IV. ii, is challenging (65); *The Examination of Conrade and Borachio* takes place before Dogberry and other members of the comic watch — whom Mary Lamb eliminated from her tale! Always lacking keenness for comedy, she reduced Shakespeare's brilliant scenes of discovery and trial, with their dazzling play of language and advocacy of the determination of the common man amidst aristocratic scheming, to a few lines of exposition to serve the plot:

> While the prince and Claudio were yet talking of the challenge of Benedick, a magistrate brought Borachio as a prisoner before the prince. Borachio had been overheard talking with one of his companions of the mischief he had been employed by Don John to do [65].

Youth's foibles and follies are the sole illustration for *Two Gentlemen of Verona,* V.iii (106). The woodland scene in which the young lovers meet represents stage action, four figures posed against typical eighteenth-century landscape scenery. Valentine intervenes against his false friend Proteus, caught just as he grasps an unwilling Sylvia. Most appealing is loyal Julia, dressed as a page, who stands sadly apart. The disguise needed by women to enter a man's world is especially cogent, since the artist was a woman. Angelika Kauffmann (1741–1807) was born in Switzerland, worked for a time in Rome, and then lived in London, where she was a friend of Joshua Reynolds and was a foundation member of the Royal Academy. Luigi Schiavonetti (1765–1841) did the engraving, published August 1, 1792. A girl disguised as a boy, which Shakespeare favored because boy actors played the female roles in the Elizabethan theatre, is also the subject of Richard Westall's *The Forest and Cave — Imogen in Boy's Clothes,* for *Cymbeline,* III.vi, engraved by Thomas Gaugain (1748–1812), published December 1, 1803 (136). Westall (1765–1836), a history and genre painter, who gave art lessons to the future Queen Victoria, depicted a lone figure, with short doublet and bare legs; she holds a sword (lowered) as she peers into Belarius's cave. While adults might note the pretty girl, children could empathize with a daughter assailed by a wicked stepmother, the familiar menace of fairy tale.

The dead Cordelia in James Barry's painting of the last scene of *King Lear,* V.iii, follows Shakespeare's text and Lamb's story rather than Nahum Tate's happy ending. Barry (1741–1806), an Anglo-Irish painter from Dublin, was helped by Edmund Burke and Joshua Reynolds to go to London, where for a time he taught painting at the Royal Academy. *King Lear Weeping Over the Dead Body of Cordelia,* now in the Tate Gallery, is an impressive creation of the past of ancient Britons, including in the upper right corner, Stonehenge, conveniently moved, since the play's scene is at Edgar's camp at Dover. Barry also redeploys the great Renaissance art of Michaelangelo: he based Lear on the statue of *Moses* and the composition on Michaelangelo's *Palestrina Pieta.* Just as the Virgin Mary holds the body of the crucified Jesus, so Lear holds the dead Cordelia, draped limply. Warriors stand at the center to balance these figures with the bodies of the wicked sisters, Goneril and Regan, dead by suicide and poison, who lie on the ground between the two. This illustration affirms Lamb's estimate of Cordelia, "an illustrious example of filial duty" (167), and reaffirms didactic points made in earlier images; loyalty in a daughter is sanctified, betrayal is punished by death and destruction.

Female behavior is also the subject of the next two images. First, *Macbeth's Castle — Lady Macbeth,* I.v, by Westall, engraved by James Parker (1750–1805), a fellow apprentice and later partner with William Blake, was published June 4, 1800 (170). Lady Macbeth is a very formidable woman at the moment after she has read her husband's letter and renounces her womanly qualities. Westall's statuesque figure clutches the letter in her left hand, at the level of the breast whose milk she has prayed to turn to gall, while her right arm, with clenched fist, is thrust outward. Several editions included this engraving amidst illustrations made specifically for children's reading. Even more disconcerting is Francis Wheatley's *Taming of the Shrew,* II.ii, engraved by Jean Pierre Simon and published January 4, 1795, which reflects contemporary stage performances (207). Petruchio has a whip, a detail totally at variance with Shakespeare's text in which the only blow struck is by Katherine. Petruchio holds her firmly by the wrist, as her father and others watch with astonishment. *Baptista's House*, obviously a stage set, features elegantly dressed principals, elaborate hats with feathers, detailed gowns, fashionable men's attire. Wheatley (1747–1801), portrait and landscape painter, was one of the most successful artists for the Boydell Gallery.

Although included by Lamb, *Measure for Measure* seems an unlikely play for children. Thomas Kirk (1765–1797) rendered the last dramatic scene, V.i, as a powerful moment of moral vindication (254). The Duke stands on the left, a figure in light, his face revealed when the hood of his Franciscan friar's habit has been pulled back. Beside him the aggressive Lucio, with a feather in his hat, shrinks away and bites his nail, while the wretched Angelo, seated on a throne of authority three steps higher than the other figures, covers his face and cringes in shame; other principal characters are bystanders. Lucio and Angelo, both liars, are humiliated. Jean Pierre Simon did this engraving, published September 1, 1796, and also *Romeo and Juliet*, V.ii, by James Northcote (1746–1831), who contributed nine paintings, somewhat indebted in style to his master Reynolds, to the Boydell Gallery. Northcote was a history and portrait painter but also an engraver and writer — biographies of Reynolds and Titian, fables, articles about art. The scene in the tomb is very much an example of storytelling (317). In the background is an effigy of a knight in armor, while the center is brightly illuminated by Friar Lawrence's torch, the tip of which is outside the frame; more light comes from the lantern on the steps down which the friar descends toward a radiant Juliet, who has just awakened and lifts her arm to greet him. Her fair hair, a white dress, and white shroud make her the glowing center of the painting. Below are the bodies of the two youths who loved her. A kneeling Romeo, the bottle of poison still grasped in his hand, has fallen to rest on her bier, while Paris lies on the floor. Their abandoned swords sign their fatal combat; and a winged hourglass, a fine embroidery on the funeral cloths, signals mutability. The tale ends with reconciliation of the fathers of the warring families and a didactic summation:

> So did these poor old lords, when it was too late, strive to outgo each other in mutual courtesies; while so deadly had been their rage and enmity in past times, that nothing but the fearful overthrow of their children (poor sacrifices to their quarrels and dissensions) could remove the rooted hates and jealousies of the noble families [320].

The appeal of romantic love, specially attributed to young girls, is well served by both verbal and visual texts, albeit there is no warning against juvenile excess and impetuosity.

Complexity of parent-child relationships informs the final illustration for *Othello*, II.i (349). Desdemona, like Juliet a daughter who weds without her father's permission and knowledge, is in glowing white at the center of the painting by Thomas Stothard (1755–1834), a prolific artist, painter and book illustrator and engraver. *A Platform* imagines the scene on the ship just arrived in Cypress, where the Venetian general has been successful. Gathered are all the principals — Othello, Desdemona, Iago, Cassio, Roderigo, Emilia — whose gazes are directed to the married couple, he in full plate armor and she in a lovely, elaborate gown. Both Stothard's devotion to historical accuracy in costume and his indebtedness to the formal design of Rubens's court scenes are in evidence. This episode and the facial expressions and body language — rapt devotion from Othello's wife and companions but a sinister apartness in Iago on the far right — communicate the uneasiness of the situation of the newly married and reunited couple from disparate backgrounds. Charles Lamb, who favored reading Shakespeare's tragedies over seeing performances, found seeing a blackamoor on stage painful; his retelling observes, "neither Othello's colour nor his fortune were such, that it could be hoped Brabantio would accept him for a son-in-law," albeit he "had left his daughter free" (346). The "difficulty" of her father's reluctant acceptance of the marriage being "got over," Desdemona begins as a dutiful wife. When Othello is called to Cyprus to fight the Turks, she, "preferring the honour of her lord (though with danger) before the indulgence of those idle delights in which new-married people usually waste their time, cheerfully consented to his going" (348). The next paragraph — which begins, "No sooner were Othello and his lady landed in Cyprus" — avoids the passionate reunion pictured by Stothard. There is no denying that Charles Lamb expresses a racial prejudice. Romanticism prefers boundless "imagination" to specific delineation, but Lamb does not want to see "a blackamoor in a fit of jealousy kill his innocent white wife" and even exonerates lack of knowledge in Shakespeare's time when Moors were thought to be "coal-black," though "the Moors are now well enough known to be by many shades less unworthy of a white woman's fancy."[5]

There is some irony in the use of Boydell engravings in Lamb's *Tales from Shakespeare,* for Charles's anti-theatrical prejudice extended to these visual representations. For him, the verbal was absolutely superior to the visual, reading over seeing. Several other Romantics reviewed the Boydell Gallery; impressions of images echo in lectures by Samuel Taylor Coleridge and William Hazlitt. The popularity and influence of these engravings is part of the early reception of Lamb's *Tales.* Alternative illustrations, not directly tied to the theatre, were commissioned to enhance "reading" the *Tales,* a safer way of "seeing" that Lamb might have found less objectionable than Mulready's pictures in the first edition. Publishers understood the market and exploited the ample resources of Sir John Gilbert.

Sir John Gilbert (c. 1882)

Book illustrations by Sir John Gilbert (1817–1897) are so numerous and memorable that his name is better remembered than journalist and Shakespeare scholar Howard Staunton (1810–1874), who edited the three-volume *The Works of Shakespeare* (1858–1860) and a photolithographic facsimile of the First Folio (1866). Gilbert, a historical painter and a renowned illustrator who became wealthy, early expressed his interest in Shakespeare. *The Arrest of Lord Hastings* (1836) was one of his first exhibition drawings; *The Merchant of Venice* and *Touchstone and the Shepherd* (1867) are later ambitious paintings. Edwardian collections of Shakespeare for children often include Gilbert's *The Morning of Agincourt*, and also reproduced *Richard II, Resigning His Crown* and *Wolsey Going to Westminster*. Gilbert, who taught himself to draw on block, engrave, etch, and model, was one of the first major figures in the revival of wood engraving. He frequently illustrated Christmas books, and from 1843 on provided news illustrations for *The London Illustrated News*. Gilbert, a member of the Royal Academy, was knighted in 1872. His *Poems by Henry Wadsworth Longfellow* (1856) is a fine example of the brilliant engraving of the brothers George and Edward Dalziel published by Routledge. However, most regard *The Gilbert Shakespeare,* as it became known, as his magnum opus; many images were redeployed in an edition of Lamb.

Tales from Shakespeare (c. 1882) has twenty, not thirty-seven, plays, but 184 Gilbert illustrations for 370 pages of text.[6] Sixteen are full pages placed as frontispieces, while 168 smaller illustrations, three-quarter- and half-pages, are printed in combination with the text. Some plays have only seven, but nine or ten illustrations are more typical. The result is concurrent verbal and visual narrative. Like the Bickers edition, Gilbert's *Tales* has a dark green cloth cover stamped in gold; the designs are female figures, muses; a caption scroll, "There's rosemary; that's for remembrance. There's pansies; that's for thoughts," across the bottom promises an experience of classic literature. A modern art critic registers changing values: "The acclaim with which Gilbert's work was met seems almost incredible, the Victorians considering his rather dull historical set-pieces as equal to the work of Doré."[7] Several examples that emphasize the unusual indicate something of Gilbert's choice of subjects and style. The images bear no captions, but a long list of illustrations identifies subjects, although this would require extra effort from child readers.

A Midsummer Night's Dream is not the first play, but provides the frontispiece. At the center is a large Bottom beside a sleeping Titania, while Oberon observes from above and many fairies enchant. Rather less optimistic are illustrations for the first tale, *Romeo and Juliet,* including the "Death of Mercutio," who is still standing (9), "Romeo's Interview with the Apothecary," a sinister moment (17), and "Friar Lawrence at the Tomb of All the Capulets" where three corpses are prominent (19). Of ten illustrations for *Othello*, one is "Cassio in his Cups" (48); the last two are "Iago and his Victims" (57) and a disturbing "Moor in Death" as a footer (58). The final illustration for *Hamlet*, "Funeral of Ophelia," a procession of small figures (146), further expresses Victorian preoccupation with death.

2 — The Tradition of Charles and Mary Lamb's *Tales from Shakespeare*   33

Very original is *The Merchant of Venice* frontispiece, "Shylock Tells Tubal of His Losses" (94); Jews, very Semitic in appearance, are the focus of attention. Subsequent small designs and pictures stress Cupid, notably "Knocking at the Gates" (110) and "Nerissa's Ring," an unusual picture of an iconic Cupid encircled by a ring (108). An effective still life of Prospero's books and wand concludes *The Tempest* (164), a change from a conventional episode like "Ariel Borne on the Back of a Bat" (150). Very different is Gilbert's half-page "Lear abjures his ungrateful Daughter's Roof" (33); the figure of the old man is cropped, and only his daughter's extended hand indicates his rejection. Sharp contrast is not unusual; *The Comedy of Errors* has a frontispiece of a torture scene (111), but also a lightly drawn but very amusing "The Quadruple Twins" (113).

Perhaps the most compelling effects come with openings where facing illustrations are cogently cross-referenced. The supernatural is clearly a primary interest of *Macbeth*. The frontispiece "The Weird Sisters on the Blasted Heath" has three figures neatly differentiated by shading — black, white, and gray — as light comes from a flash of lightning at the center. Two facing three-quarter-page illustrations set "The Ghost of Banquo at the Banquet" opposite "The Witches Cave," complete with crawling serpent (86–87). Another telling juxtaposition is "Gonzago murdered Sleeping in his Orchard" with "The King disturbed at the Play" in *Hamlet* (138–139). Such combinations are as effective for comedies as for tragedies. In *Much Ado About Nothing* facing scenes depict "Entrapped Benedick" and "Hero and Ursula's deception of Beatrice" (189–191). For *As You Like It* Gilbert provides quintessential images of England, a telling contrast between pastoral and urban. In "The Forest of Arden" magnificent deer move across the page, while opposite, Celia and Rosalind are set against a background cityscape (166–167). Later, a three-quarter-page shows an idyllic "A Glade in the Forest," where giant trees dwarf three small figures (171), while "A Sheepcote in the Forest" is a delightful landscape, very different from the usual concentration upon characters (173). Some of Gilbert's illustrations are thought-provoking rather than escapist. Very rare are "The Mock Marriage" (179), a challenging episode to explain to children, and "The Solitary in the Cave," the last half-page (185) that encourages discussion of levels of complexity in *As You Like It,* for all its renown as an analog to Robin Hood. Gilbert's illustrations have the straightforward pictorial quality and storytelling inherent in historical paintings — which like historical novels appealed to Victorians but lost favor as too simple for the sophistication of the twentieth century — that make a good accompaniment to tales for children.

Like John Newbery who valued woodcuts in his chapbooks and Victorians who delighted in the profusion and variety of Gilbert's drawings, Edwardian publishers offered engaging illustrations in a variety of editions and in selections of Lamb's *Tales*. Six especially richly illustrated *Tales*, with pictures reused in several editions, demonstrate possibilities.

Arthur Rackham (1899/1906)

Arthur Rackham (1867–1939) made eleven black and white line drawings and a delicately tinted frontispiece for *Tales from Shakespeare by Charles and Mary Lamb* (1899), published by J. M. Dent and enhanced by leather binding. In 1906 Dent made it one of the first volumes of For Young People in Everyman's Library, edited by Ernest Rhys.[8] Rackham, called the "beloved Enchanter" — his very name conjures worlds of fairies and other woodland creatures, knights and dragons, beautiful princesses, wonder and menace — was probably the greatest Edwardian illustrator for children. Certainly he is one of the finest and most prolific. His first success came with *The Ingoldsby Legends* (1898), which Dent immediately followed with *Tales from Shakespeare*. Among Rackham's early illustrations for children's literature, including several annual gift books, are *Gulliver's Travels* and *Grimm's Fairy Tales*, both in 1900; *Peter Pan in Kensington Gardens* (1906); *Alice in Wonderland* (1907) — which some preferred to the original illustrations by John Tenniel; *Aesop's Fables* (1912); and Malory's *The Romance of King Arthur* (1917). Exhibitions in Paris, Vienna, and the United States enhanced Rackham's international stature. His illustrations for *The Rhinegold and the Valkyrie* (1910) and *Siegfried and the Twilight of the Gods* (1913) were part of enthusiasm for Richard Wagner's operas. With Washington Irving's *Rip Van Winkle* (1905), Rackham had begun to work in color; its scenes of river and forest, children and fairies, assured his career. William Heinemann published most of his first work, including *A Midsummer Night's Dream* (1908), dazzlingly beautiful and complex. During World War I Rackham dug ditches for the Hampstead Volunteers and produced *The Allies Fairy Book* (1916) and *English Fairy Tales Retold* (1918). Several of his earlier books were enlarged and colored, but his black and white line drawings, and silhouettes, still charm.

Rackham's color frontispiece for Lamb's *Tales*, not included in the Everyman edition, announces difference, for it has an Art Nouveau frame of leaves with flowers to enhance the figures of sweet golden-haired children, including two small nudes discreetly reading a book. The subject matter is fairy tale, with a compelling monstrous and nude Caliban (his knee modestly conceals his genitals), who has a long green tail like a lizard's, large feet and hands with claw-like nails. Ariel flies above with gossamer wings and pulls the creature's ear. In the background is one of Rackham's typical great bare, gnarled trees, the top of which frames Ariel. In this original edition the illustrations were signed and dated, but lacked captions except in the list, perhaps to encourage imaginative speculation. However, the Everyman edition, and a *Daily Sketch* reprint, added these captions (quoted from Lamb's text) to each page illustration. The color frontispiece, "When Caliban was lazy and neglected his work, Ariel would come slily and pinch him," contains a warning against lack of responsibility, albeit less compelling than Rackham's strange imaginative creatures. Even in a reassuring archetypal scene, "Where is Pease-Blossom?" (28),

Rackham adds interest to charming Victorian fairies; three in the foreground share the viewer's perspective and are prettily decorative. Their wings are in contrasting positions, they hold hands, and the farthest on the right has raised a hand to his forehead in puzzlement. A fourth, rather masculine fairy (Puck) stands on a mushroom to adjust a garland around the ass's head, as a more mature and feminine Titania sits beside Bottom with her arm encircling his. Rackham followed this amusing vignette with classical restraint and beauty for the brilliant moment in *The Winter's Tale*, "When Paulina drew back the curtain which concealed this famous statue" (42). Hermione, standing on a pedestal before she "awakens," is one of two lovely female figures in classical drapery (hers bordered), their heads covered by cloaks.

Other illustrations are almost equally divided between representations of youth in the comedies and disturbing moments in the tragedies. In *As You Like It*'s "Ganymede assumed the forward manners often seen in youths when they are between boy and man," Rosalind as boy looks like a forester in the tradition of Robin Hood, while Orlando is nicely attired — more a courtier than a refugee (72). Both seem charming, gazing quizzically at each other, beside a characteristically large tree, a dominant image in Rackham's world. In "She began to think of confessing that she was a woman," Viola as Cesario looks less plausible and less confident (230). Sir Toby Belch and Sir Andrew Aguecheek, many children's favorite characters in *Twelfth Night*, dominate the foreground at the moment before the duel, when Viola's courtier second obviously does not reassure her. As Mary Lamb asked her readers, "What should poor Viola do, who, though she carried a manlike outside, had a true woman's heart, and feared to look on her own sword?" (229). Rackham has wittily commented on the quandary with an amusing statue of Pan, a nature figure who presides over the situation, from a column in the highest position of the background.

Cross-dressing is a delight in Shakespeare's plays, a rich catalyst for questions of gender. However, in "Imogen's two brothers then carried her to a shady covert," from *Cymbeline*, Rackham barely suggests male disguise — her long hair is free (120). Fair hair signs British race and sibling relationship at the moment when Bellarius and Polydore believed Imogen dead, "sang repose to her departed spirit," and conducted "funeral obsequies" (119). Sturdy male hunters, part of the Anglo-Saxon heritage so celebrated by Edwardians, are the real subject. Maleness dominates grotesquely in "Petruchio, pretending to find fault with every dish, threw the meat about the floor," from *The Taming of the Shrew* (176). Here Rackham makes great use of black for Petruchio's hair and part of his clothing. His gesture is broad, left arm raised and right foot just completing a kick that has sent platter and joint sprawling. The comic flair resembles that typical of Gordon Browne's illustrations. Katherine and servants are lightly drawn figures in the background behind the table. Several subsequent illustrators selected this moment, a likely way to indulge the child's temptation to throw food about.

Although *The Merchant of Venice* is a comedy, Rackham's style is very different, dark and menacing, an alternate way to excite children who like the "scary." He chose as subject "Shylock was sharpening a long knife" (102) and uses heavy black lines, rather like those in Dürer woodcuts. Shylock is the "other," a stereotypical Jew that in no way resembles the Venetians, with his sinister face, curling hair and beard, and severe long robe and hat. This illustration prepares for the shift to the tragedies, whose episodes inspire emotional anxiety. Rackham again varies moods. *Romeo and Juliet*'s "At the cell of Friar Lawrence" (260) has some resonance of Pre-Raphaelite Dante Gabriel Rossetti. From the left background the friar, who wears a black cope and hood over a white robe, holds a book and looks toward the larger figures of the lovers, drawn in simple line but for bold use of black for hair and Juliet's bodice.

Rackham selected the most theatrical moment, "There upon a heath, exposed to the fury of the storm in a dark night, did King Lear wander out" (138), and drew boldly, streaks of heavy rain and effects of wind. The old king is still royally dressed; but his long white beard and open, raised hands convey the distress that explains the Fool's anxiety, expressed by his fists up to his chin, at odds with his comic dress. Wind and rain in a wild landscape are repeated for *Macbeth,* where Rackham, who excelled with images of magic, features otherworldly creatures, "They were stopped by the strange appearance of three figures" (144). The witches, drawn in profile with some thick blacking, dominate a bleak scene defined by bare trees and winds; they also draw attention to the small figures of Macbeth and Banquo who face them. The entwining quality of nature is most powerful in Rackham's "To this brook Ophelia came one day when she was unwatched" (288). Hamlet's love, enmeshed in nature, sits on a tree trunk, which stretches above the water, and reaches up to place a flower on a nearby bare branch, the movement before she falls into the river. Drowned Ophelia was a popular subject for Victorian painters; Sir John Everett Millais's *Ophelia* (1851–1852) is the most famous Pre-Raphaelite treatment of Shakespeare, rivaled by Eugene Delacroix's *Death of Ophelia* (1853). Rackham's finished illustration has much of the delicate subtlety of his later color illustrations.

Rackham's *Tales from Shakespeare, Gulliver's Travels,* and *Grimm's Fairy Tales,* all published from 1899 to 1900, were republished in 1909 in deluxe editions with colored illustrations sometimes redrawn. His muted palette relies heavily on browns and grays, rose, and soft blues that do not obscure the sharpness of his line.[9] Some images are significantly enriched: Juliet's dress has a luxurious texture and some Art Nouveau pattern in the material. A full-length portrait of Cordelia, whose costume has even more elaborate designs of flowers, is added. She stands before an elaborately carved wooden panel and rests her hand on the back of a similarly decorated bench; both evoke Anglo-Saxon / Scandinavian designs imitated by Arts and Crafts furniture. "Where is Peaseblossom?" retains all details of the original drawing but was enhanced by a

Arthur Rackham was famous as "the Dean of Fairyland," but this Düreresque illustration for *The Merchant of Venice* is an incisive portrait of Shylock as a sinister figure who sharpens the knife he plans to use to get his "pound of flesh." *Tales from Shakespeare by Charles and Mary Lamb* (1899) was reprinted as one of the first books in the For Young People Series in Everyman's Library (1906).

Arthur Rackham's extraordinary gnarled tree envelops the mad Ophelia — a favorite subject for Victorian artists — at the moment before she falls into the water. Several subsequent children's illustrators imitated this image from *Tales from Shakespeare by Charles and Mary Lamb* (1899).

subtle use of blues and grays; moreover, its broad brown frame, decorated with stars and elegant sprays of flowers, is a typical Art Nouveau effect. These early illustrations were only a beginning.

A Midsummer Night's Dream: *With Illustrations by Arthur Rackham, R.W.S.* (1908) is not Lamb's tale but Shakespeare's play printed in very large type, published by Heinemann; it would certainly have fascinated children, whatever their skill in reading the text.[10] The title indicates Rackham's illustrations are a primary attraction; their sheer quantity is remarkable: forty full pages in color, four full pages in black and white, and twenty-five additional black and white design illustrations, including headers and footers. Improved technology in printing at the start of the twentieth century produced images with extraordinary clarity and subtlety. Rackham's palette favors earth tones—browns, greens, grays, cream rather than white, some black—with an occasional soft red, blue, or orange. He stays close to the text and concentrates on exotic creatures— leviathan, "a mermaid on a dolphin's back," goblins, "russet-pated choughs" (black birds), insects, rodents, reptiles—especially exquisitely characterized and varied fairies.

Victorian enthusiasm and fascination with fairies spawned many great paintings, among which Daniel Maclise's *The Disenchantment of Bottom* (1812) and Noel Paton's *The Reconciliation of Titania and Oberon* (1847) and *The Quarrel of Oberon and Titania* (c. 1850) are cogent for their depiction of distinctive fairies, as is Richard Doyle (1824–1883), who followed Cruikshank and made his name as an illustrator of fairies with *The Fairy Ring* (1846), a new translation of Grimm, and *Fairy Tales from All Nations* (1849). In short, Rackham was working in a very rich and respected tradition so that much of his achievement is an intriguing freshness in delineation of kinds of fairies and their activities, both beautiful and endearing and grotesque and frightening. His illustrations for *A Midsummer Night's Dream* compel close reading as surely as the play's poetry; each reinforces the other to expand appreciation and understanding. This book is a singular achievement, brilliant storytelling through images that can stand without reading the verbal text, and thus readily available even to a young child, or read as an exciting visual embodiment of Shakespeare's imaginative creation. The most obvious later influence came when Rackham's unmistakable style was the inspiration for frightening woods in Walt Disney's *Snow White,* and Tolkien's trees show an affinity. Other illustrators, of lesser and varying skill, enhance countless editions of Lamb's *Tales,* several of which are notable.

Norman M. Price (1905)

The value of illustration for Edwardian publishers is clear from the fact that they paid artists as much as writers, and advertisements identify both.

Records for T.C. and E.C. Jack, for example, show that Andrew Lang and Henry H.J. Ford received about the same sums for their many fairy and romance books. For new editions of Lamb, only the illustrator was a cost, and Jack made ample use of the work of Norman M. Price (1877–1951). His sixteen original color illustrations enlivened *Tales from Shakespeare by Charles and Mary Lamb* (1905), an edition of larger format with 324 pages that includes Lamb's original preface but no new materials.[11] Jack's early announcements are for a volume "Beautifully Bound, with Gold Design and Designed End Papers," priced at 7s.6d. But less expensive versions that relied on cloth covers, stamped with one color, and a pasted color picture, were long valued; my copy was a prize for elocution to a student in Form IIIB, "Oberwyl," in 1921. Jack reprinted some of Price's pictures in two nursery books, *Stories from Shakespeare* (1905) and *More Stories from Shakespeare* (1910), both by Jeanie Lang, in the Told to the Children Series, discussed in Chapter 5.

Price, who exhibited at the Royal Academy in 1905, was known as a figure artist. While many illustrations feature characters, he often depicts a scene, even with a suggestion of performance. A List of Illustrations has a short title with the play's name in parentheses below; these are printed at the bottom of each page illustration with added references to act and scene, an incentive for the child to read some of the play itself. The frontispiece, "Titania Sleeps," *A Midsummer Night's Dream*, II.ii, is the favorite way to entice readers. The fairy queen lies in her flowery bower, watched over by two mature, lovely, winged lady musicians, with lute and harp, who are reminiscent of angels by Edward Burne-Jones (1833–1898), as is some of Price's treatment of flowers. Like Titania they have large wings, deep blue in color, a bold contrast to the softer tones of gold and rose gray in their gossamer dresses. Two very young and chubby fairies provide a child presence and perspective, as they hover above with outstretched arms that suggest beginning prowess.

The second illustration fascinates in quite a different way. "The feast vanished away," *The Tempest*, III.iii, is set in a rocky cavern dominated by Prospero, who wears a dark maroon robe and waves his long wand with spectacular effect: a cascade of plates, jugs, and goblets (10). Between these objects and the table's white cloth hovers Ariel, who has flowing golden hair and whose large open wings, richly colored in green, blue, and gray, conceal the body beneath bare shoulders. In the foreground six men show varied expressions of amazement—shrinking, clutching chest or head, fists clenched. While several other illustrators made a comic scene of Petruchio's tossing of food in *The Taming of the Shrew*, Price makes the casting of objects off a table a demonstration of magic.

The only other episode with comparable excitement is the play scene of *Hamlet*, III.ii (270). The performance takes place in an alcove three steps above the main room: Gonzago pours poison into the ear of the sleeping king, whose golden crown glows with the light of a bright torch standard. Two sets of figures frame this scene. On the left, Hamlet, in black, stands beside a seated Ophelia; two guards with spears are behind them. On the right, several soldiers in armor stand back as torch bearers precede the king and queen, while Polonius remonstrates the players. Like Ophelia, Gertrude wears a white gown and has beautiful golden hair; she looks anxiously at Claudius, who has raised his right hand to his head, a mark of consternation like the empty thrones in the right foreground. Claudius's red cloak and crown match those of the player king. Price's handling of spots of light in massive darkness is more exciting and dramatic than either Daniel Maclise's staid Victorian conception of *The Play Scene in Hamlet* (1863) or Lamb's narrative of Claudius's reaction to the play:

> the strong resemblance which it bore to his own wicked act upon the late king, his brother, whom he had poisoned in his garden, so struck upon the conscience of the usurper, that he was unable to sit out the rest of the play, but on a sudden calling for lights to his chamber, and affecting or partly feeling a sudden sickness, he abruptly left the theatre [280–81].

The title/caption, "KING, Give me some light! away!" well matches Price's action in an illustration that indicates performance, lighting, blocking, and an inner stage.

In comparison, an interior scene (I.iii) before the senators of Venice, "OTHELLO, 'She loved me for the dangers I had passed'" (290), is largely a study in costume and textures—red judicial robes, shining breastplates and helmets, and most distinctively Othello's golden cloak embroidered in red, spread wide as he extends his arms. Further details of exotic Orientalism — the typical point of illustrations of Othello— are his turban and collar armor, all of which contrast to his bare brown feet, a racial detail that seems closer to Lamb's prejudice, which a painting like the *Othello and Desdemona* (1834) of Giuseppe Sabatelli (1813–1843) — the lady in white, a suppliant wife, kneels before a proud (and blacker) tyrant of a husband — might explain, if not justify.

Perhaps the most vigorous action is "The Gentle Katherine," from *The Taming of the Shrew,* II.i (170). The caption is an obvious lesson in irony, for the lady has just crashed a lute over the head of the music-master, whose wide-eyed look and mincing stance show him no match for his pupil. Mary Lamb explained Katherine's act as a response to his "presuming to find fault with her performance" (171). A fiercely determined and angry Katherine stands ready for another blow with a small rod in her left hand. The scene is reported to Baptista while Petruchio is asking for permission to court his daughter, having "resolved upon marrying this famous termagant, and taming her into a meek and manageable wife" (170). Lamb quoted much of Shakespeare's text, including in full the sun and moon scene when Katherine finally understands and decides to cooperate with Petruchio. This follows a statement that they go to Padua for her sister's wedding only after her husband "had brought her proud spirit to such a perfect subjection, that she dared not remember there was such a word as contradiction" (178). Although Mary Lamb quoted almost all of the short dialogue of the wager, she merely epitomized Katherine's magnificent speech when she holds center stage and command:

> And to the wonder of all present, the reformed shrewish lady spoke as eloquently in praise of the wifelike duty of obedience, as she had practised it implicitly in a ready submission to will. And Katherine once more became famous in Padua, not as heretofore, as Katherine the Shrew, but as Katherine the most obedient and duteous wife in Padua [182].

Another of Shakespeare's young women becomes a model of the dutiful daughter. Price's illustration, *LEAR, Cordelia, Cordelia,* III.iii, is his most heavily Victorian image, similar to Pre-Raphaelite paintings. It echoes two by Ford Madox Brown (1821–1893), *Cordelia's Portion,* I.i and *Lear and Cordelia* (1849–1854): the first, for costumes and close filling of the frame, as well as the appearance of the figures; the latter — although it pictures Cordelia watching a resting Lear — is a camp setting where warriors have familiar signs of Northern identity, a horned helmet and weapons (124). Price poses father and daughter to echo the Christian pièta; at the center Lear has raised Cordelia to a sitting position with her head on his right knee; he holds her limp left hand, while he raises his own right hand to his balding head with its gold circle crown. His somewhat ruddy complexion contrasts with her death pallor, as does his rich red garment with her pink dress. Her long golden hair is plaited with a blue ribbon running through it, a decorative detail, as is gold embroidery on their garments. Behind Lear, warriors completely fill the space; one kneels to put his arm on the king's to offer comfort, while two others stand behind with sad expressions. At the center a small white tent topped by a streaming banner completes the pyramidal structure, with thick foliage and cloudy sky on either side. Lamb, whose famous critical judgment was that the emotion of *King Lear* was better read than observed on the stage, in his retelling stresses both filial piety and the power that takes all lives. Goneril and Regan, the "wicked daughters" receive the justice of Heaven. However,

> While the eyes of all men were upon this event, admiring the justice displayed in their deserved deaths, the same eyes were suddenly taken off from this sight to admire at the mysterious ways of the same power in the melancholy fate of the young and virtuous daughter, the lady Cordelia, whose good deeds did seem to deserve a more fortunate conclusion: but it is an awful truth, that innocence and piety are not always successful in this world. The forces which Goneril and Regan had sent out under the command of the bad earl of Gloucester were victorious, and Cordelia, by the practices of this wicked earl, who did not like that any should stand between him and the throne, ended her life in prison. Thus, Heaven took this innocent lady to itself in her young years, after showing her to the world an illustrious example of filial duty. Lear did not long survive this kind child [140].

Given the rates of nineteenth-century child mortality, this episode had deep personal meaning. Lamb's last paragraph makes very clear that this is the story's

Norman M. Price relied on techniques of Victorian historical painting — authentic costume and realistic portraits — for King Lear's grieving over dead Cordelia in *Tales from Shakespeare by Charles and Mary Lamb* (1905).

message. He begins a summary list of many events: "How the judgment of Heaven overtook the bad earl of Gloucester, whose treasons were discovered, and himself slain in single combat with his brother, the lawful earl, ... is needless to narrate; Lear and his Three Daughters being dead, whose adventures alone concern our story" (141). Price depicts the most poignant moment.

Somewhat similar is the tomb scene, "Romeo and Juliet," V.iii (250). Gray garments heighten Romeo's pallor of death, also evident in a recumbent Paris in the foreground; both contrast vividly with Juliet's shining white funeral clothes and golden hair. As she sits on the tomb slab to hold her dead husband's head on her lap, her left hand grips a raised dagger and rests on the edge. The lovers are bathed in light from the left, while only a small lamp hangs on the right, faint before a black entrance to another chamber to extend this stark image.

Several illustrations show characters and their costumes without evoking a particular moment. "Beatrice and Benedick," lovers in *Much Ado About Nothing,* IV.i, stand close to each other (42). Cross-legged, he leans languidly (in a pose reminiscent of a Nicholas Hilliard miniature) against a high wall with yellow roses across the top and a few pansies below. Benedict's open arms suggest an embrace of Beatrice, who stands just in front of him; the fact that each is smiling and holds a yellow rose fosters this impression. Price's treatment of satin textures and colors (black and white for him, pink and white with blue trim for her) echo Van Dyke's paintings. A sharp contrast in mood is *Two Gentlemen of Verona,* V.iv, when Thurio's advances to Sylvia are rejected: "VALENTINE, 'I dare thee but to breathe upon my love'" (76). In a dark wood Valentine, dressed in dark brown and green, stands with clenched fist and sword unsheathed. Sylvia, wearing gray satin with white bodice and cuffs, is behind him; two servants sit anxiously behind them. A classical cityscape is the setting for "DROMIO OF EPHESUS, 'Let my master in!'" This moment of vigorous action is part of multiple confusions of identity in *The Comedy of Errors,* III.i (182), which Mary Lamb concludes to be "pleasant and diverting" (199). Price's only classical scene — the facade of a townhouse with glimpses, beyond steps on the street, of a temple — is sharply drawn with muted colors of gray, tan, and blue. An angry twin servant, in short garment and hat, shouts when he strikes the door with a stave, while one angry woman (arms crossed) watches and Balthasar smirks, as another woman weeps in the background. This picture precedes the tale and aptly faces the conclusion of *The Taming of the Shrew.*

Women are the center of attention in four other illustrations where physical appearance is the point. Very beautiful is "Imogen's Bed Chamber," a luxurious interior scene (hanging lantern, fireplace, casement, jewel box, silver canopy over the bed) that displays the heroine of *Cymbeline* before disaster strikes (108). In "KING, 'Why, then young Bertram take her; she's thy wife,'" an opulently costumed Helena covers her face when she is awarded to the reluctant man she loves, *All's Well that Ends Well,* II.iii (154). "Isabel's Pleading" with

Angelo in *Measure for Measure*, II.ii, provides comparable richness in Vienna (200). The severe novice, in religious habit, kneels with hands clasped before the strict and rigid deputy to plead for her brother's life with the increased vigor urged by sly and salacious Lucio. Finally, two women meet to consider female beauty in "OLIVIA, 'But we will draw the curtain and show you the picture,'" *Twelfth Night*, I.v (218). The whiteness of the lady's veil and bodice (above a deep maroon dress), and more subtly fair flesh of Caesario—Viola, attired as a page but with hair exposed for a feminine look—stand out from another dark interior with a heavy drapery background. Special details are Olivia's fan of peacock feathers and hints of Art Nouveau in the decoration of the youth's costume.

Two final woodland scenes vividly contrast comedy and tragedy. "Rosalind and Celia in the Forest of Arden," *As You Like It*, II.iv., is engaging. The center of attention is Touchstone in his bright red jester's attire, with contrasting brown, replete with cap and bells and jester's wand (56). Indeed the cover bears this figure of Touchstone, cropped, while the cover of Jeanie Lang's *Stories from Shakespeare* in the Told to the Children Series uses the whole picture. Arden is a place of escape, friendly and virtuous, the domain of old Robin Hood. Price situates his three figures in a well lighted space among massive tree trunks; the court jester leads the way with a smile and a jaunty step, while the two cousins, one dark and one fair, follow in their country guise as Ganymede and Aliena. Rosalind as page, for all that she holds a spear, looks as feminine as Celia.

Their prettiness could hardly be more different from the ugly and threatening "The Weird Sisters," unquestionably the favorite subject for *Macbeth*, most notably by Henry Fuseli, who made several paintings of it. Price depicted the witches' dwelling for the late meeting (IV.i) as very dark indeed; the only light comes from the orange and yellow flames of a fire in the lower center. Above it, suspended from the roof, is a large black cauldron, from which smoke rises and a bit of heinous brew bubbles over. One witch, who leans on a crooked staff, peers intently at these contents, while another standing behind her looks across to the third sister, who has raised her arm to make a point. Each is barefoot and bearded and has her head covered (one turban and two hoods of cloaks). Also watching the cauldron is a familiar, a black cat that sits and looks with glowing green eyes. The scary quality and mystery that provoke intense emotional involvement make this illustration one to examine acutely. Price extended Charles Lamb's rendering of the witches' brew in their cave:

> [E]ngaged in preparing their dreadful charms, by which they conjured up infernal spirits to reveal to them futurity. Their horrid ingredients were toads, bats, and serpents, the eye of a newt, and the tongue of a dog, the leg of a lizard, and the wing of the night-owl, the scale of a dragon, the tooth of a wolf, the maw of a ravenous salt-sea shark, the mummy of a witch, the root of a poisonous hemlock (this to have effect must be digged in the dark), the fall of a goat, and the liver of a Jew, with slips of the yew tree that roots itself in graves, and the finger of a dead child: All these were set to boil in a great kettle, or

cauldron, which as fast as it grew too hot, was cooled with a baboon's blood: to these they poured in the blood of a sow that had eaten her young, and they threw into the flame the grease that had sweaten from a murderer's gibbet. By these charms they bound the infernal spirits to answer their questions [149–150].

Although Lamb's prose lacks the chanting cadence of Shakespeare's catalog of ingredients for witches' brew, he retains most of the lurid contents. Unfortunately he does not quote the memorable incantation, "Double, double, toil and trouble; / Fire burn, and cauldron bubble" (IV.i.35–36). This may reflect discretion in not wanting children to have a complete process to try to imitate, or an unawareness of the thrill of such a model. Shakespeare's play, children's stories, and fearsome illustrations are, of course, forerunners of the worldwide success of the Harry Potter books, tales of witches, written by a Scotswoman, J.K. Rowling.

A(lbert) E(dward) Jackson (1918)

A more startlingly varied edition of Lamb's *Tales* was published by Ward, Locke — 472 pages, with 44 color plates, the work of A(lbert) E(dward) Jackson (1873–1952), who has greater scope to include more subject matter. Jackson, who was born in London and studied at the Camden School of Art, painted in watercolor and oil. He exhibited at both the Royal Academy and in the provinces, but is best known for his book illustrations. He worked for Amalgamated Press for more than fifty years (1893–1947) and provided illustrations for several children's books published by Ward, Lock, including *Tales from Shakespeare by Charles and Mary Lamb* (1918).[12] Their advertisement lists "uniform" volumes of stories from classics, all with forty-eight illustrations, an unusually large number; but *Tales* has only forty-four. Jackson also illustrated *Tales from the Arabian Nights* and *Robinson Crusoe*; Margaret W. Tarrant (1888–1959) and Harry G. Theaker (1873–1954), each with several books, are the other artists. Since Lamb's *Tales* does not include the original preface or supporting materials, its competitive distinction is visual. Jackson's illustrations have been described as "generally not distinguished, or distinguishable from other illustration of the period," but this is somewhat untrue as well as unkind.[13] Their sheer number probably explains such a reaction; some are inevitably not inspiring. However, others — a few of which have recently been reproduced as notecards — are quite striking. Moreover, a schematic ordering of images engages interest and enhances the narrative value of the *Tales*.

The cover picture is an amusing scene in Arden, "They were strangely surprised to find the name of Rosalind carved on the trees," III.ii, repeated inside with the tale of *As You Like It* (135). Captions, taken from Lamb's text, are printed with act and scene references on each color page. "They" are Rosalind

(Ganymede) and Celia (Aliena), dressed in simple country clothing; their straw hats and shorter hair, and Ganymede's shepherd's crook, suggest pastoral activity. Jackson draws these figures—and all but the very old (Lear)—as adolescents, a youthfulness more likely to entice empathetic response than Frances Brundage's baby characters in E. Nesbit's *The Children's Shakespeare*. One nice touch is Ganymede's pointing to the name "ROSALIND," plainly visible on a large tree trunk. Inside are engaging end papers, a single picture, front and back, with Shakespeare characters who inhabit a brown landscape. Two are immediately identifiable. On the far right Shylock looks fiercely at Portia in her lawyer's red robes and hat; red is repeated for the hood and jester's wand and squares in the jerkin of Lear's Fool, who sits in the left foreground. Directly behind him are two lovers, whose attire does not match any illustration inside. Similarly generic are several groups across the background, all in muted whites and tans. One, with two female figures and a stylish man, suggests Duke Frederick with Rosalind and Celia. Like the cover, it is an excellent contrast to "Frederick, with looks full of anger, ordered Rosalind to leave the palace," I.iii, a slightly shortened caption from Lamb's text (126). Since a portion of column is Jackson's sole indication of the court, the illustration resembles a production sketch for costume. Duke Frederick, with elegant beard and mustache, wears a jaunty hat above white garments decorated with fur. A commanding and mature man, he has a gold chain of office and a sword; the cousins, in blue and white dresses with blue decoration, are differentiated—one blonde and one auburn hair.

Jackson's frontispiece is the perennial "Bottom and the Fairy Queen," IV.i; again *A Midsummer Night's Dream* makes the salient appeal. Titania's long golden hair and voluminous white garment contrast to her very large decorative wings, dark blue on the upper side and rosy fawn on the under, both boldly marked by eyes. She holds the ass's soft gray head close to her. Bottom, in a short red Grecian garment, has closed eyes, while Titania's are alert. As they recline on a grassy knoll, behind them fly a bevy of infant fairies bringing red and orange flowers. Jackson followed this archetypal frontispiece with a more compelling and unexpected image.

In the first and most editions of Lamb's *Tales* the order is the same; *The Tempest* is first. Here *Hamlet* is first, introduced by the ghost on the ramparts, "Bursting from them, Hamlet followed whithersoever the spirit led," I.iv (12). This mysterious illustration is a Whistler-like study of grays and blues—castle, cliff, cloudy skies, armor—relieved only by an orange glow from the interior and the fine clothes of the two young friends—Horatio's dark blue and Hamlet's purple. The opaque ghost of Hamlet's father glides toward the left, but his helmet, armor plate, and sword are sharp above the increasingly fainter lower part of his body. Two other illustrations, Hamlet with his mother (28) and mad Ophelia alone (35), are costume sketches—figures against a white background, with simple gesture to suggest context, and chairs the only furniture.

Jackson's style is similar in the next two illustrations for *The Tempest*, the second tale in this edition. However, since they celebrate the magical, specifically Ariel, they are entrancing. A handsome youth in long purple surcoat, sword at his side, walks through the landscape, "Ferdinand followed in amazement the sound of Ariel's voice," I.ii (46). Ariel, playing a lyre and singing, is a gossamer figure with flowing drapery, whose hair stands up to indicate flight. The entire vision is pale green — an echo of Millais's painting. "Ariel's Song," V.i, repeats the pale green, this time as a swath of drapery across the torso (shoulders, arm, and legs bare); but here Ariel, who now flies on the back of a black bat, has golden hair and a delicate flesh tone (55). Below are seven lines, "Where the bee sucks, there suck I," one of two songs quoted by Mary Lamb and a reminder that school readers and anthologies often introduce Shakespeare's songs before or without the stories.

The charm of fairies finds expression in another accomplished watercolor, "Oberon left the clown to finish his sleep with his own fool's head upon his shoulders," *A Midsummer Night's Dream*, IV.i (71). This counterpart to the frontispiece shows Bottom restored to his own workman's shape. He lies on a green knoll with woods behind him, while small and amusing fairy creatures race down a curving path that fills the lower half of the illustration. A laughing Puck, larger but still with a childish body, has prominent pointed ears and green wings. Added delight comes from creatures that rush along in this fairy procession — a butterfly, a bee, a white hamster, and many white blobs with single orange eye that prompt speculation about what they are. The picture of Helena and Lysander, just awakened, is, in contrast, undistinguished (66).

For *Macbeth*, a favored tragedy for children, Jackson's two illustrations tell a story and evoke the supernatural. By a suffusion of red tones, Jackson signals Lady Macbeth's ruthlessness and blood-letting, "His listening wife began to think he had failed of his purpose," II.ii (244). Outside the chamber she holds open a rose-colored curtain; and, as light falls fully upon her, she casts a large shadow that enhances the dagger in her hand. Red, blood on the dagger's point and hilt, is echoed in red jewels on her breast cups (like nipples) and at the end of the circlet that holds her white headdress in place. Reddish hair and pale blue eyes mark racial identity. In the second illustration, a shaft of bright white light separates Macbeth from three scary witches, who compel attention; their fingers point into the light that rises from a black cauldron set above a fire that glows orange and red. "The witches called the spirits, which were three. The first arose in the likeness of an armed head," IV.i (250). Macbeth, who wears a round steel helmet, wrist and arm bands, a heavy belt and scabbard, kneels on one knee before the witches and their remarkable brew and lifts his sword high. His garment is short, and across his shoulder is a plaid (Scots) blanket. The somber spirit's head, level with Macbeth's sword, is bolder than Hamlet's ghost; its helmet's large wings depict a strong Northern warrior. Jackson typically included small details to catch a child's attention: a white owl hovers just beside

Macbeth's meeting with the witches exploited fascination with the mysterious (and Scotland as a primitive land). A.E. Jackson's dramatic illustration enhances, with a hovering owl and staring cat's eyes, the spooky quality of an apparition — the head of a warrior in a winged helmet — above the bubbling cauldron. It is one of several lively images in *Tales from Shakespeare by Charles and Mary Lamb* (1918).

the cauldron but looks at the viewer rather than the contents, while two green eyes stare from a black creature (cat) that sits apart. The play of light that marks both scenes invites discussion of darkness instead of the frequent stress on character.

Victorian painters, especially Pre-Raphaelites, indulged fascination with beautiful females. A number of Jackson's illustrations are little more than pretty figures, albeit usually with some gesture to suggest the quoted caption. Julia, in white, pieces together the love letter she has torn in *Two Gentlemen of Verona,* I.ii (146), while Portia, in red lawyer's attire for the trial in *The Merchant of Venice,* IV.i, practices declamation (170). Since much of the appeal of *Cymbeline* is its noble heroine, Jackson shows Imogen in both guises: a golden lass asleep in her sumptuous bed (227) and in male attire and presumed dead, so that her two youthful brothers carry her (233). Viola is a lovelier page in *Twelfth Night,* as she walks and talks with Duke Orsino, I.iv (351), or shrinks from her sword in a posture that is unmistakably feminine and comic, III.iv (362). Heroines of the problem plays are less obviously attractive. A single illustration for *All's Well That Ends Well* is "Helena on her knees before the Countess now owned her love for Bertram," I.iii (271). Both women have severe facial expressions that the rich red of Helena's gown does little to offset. The Countess, in black with a large cross about her neck, looks like a superior for nuns. Religious garments are precise for *Measure for Measure,* IV.iii, "The seeming friar bade her take comfort" (346). Isabella, a novice, wears a white habit and cross, while the Duke's brown Franciscan robe is topped by a darker hood and cape. Their concern differs vastly from Angelo's; his costume is bright and elaborate, but he frowns and covers his mouth with his hand as he contemplates his sin and unjust condemnation of Claudio, II.iv (327). Another single male, Proteus, *Two Gentlemen of Verona,* IV.iv (151), is a parallel figure to his love Julia (146).

More often men are shown in pairs or groups: a perplexed Antipholus of Syracuse in *The Comedy of Errors,* II.ii, to whom Adriana kneels (310); a surprised Pericles with his daughter, "Marina presented to the amazed Pericles the features of his dead queen," V.i (447); the master in *Timon of Athens,* II.ii, who comforts his old steward (383). All wear classical costumes. Romeo and Juliet dress in Renaissance style, very much the "golden couple" at the ball, "Romeo, under favour of his masking habit, presumed in the gentlest manner to take her hand and kiss it," I.v (400). Juliet's hair is fair, and Romeo's black, a signal of difference; nevertheless, the illustration is primarily a study in prettiness and wealth. He wears a golden robe and she a white dress—with decorated hem and patterned wide scarf as girdle about her waist; her golden fan (with peacock eyes) links the two. Juliet looks much the same in a second illustration, but for a cap to sign her as a married lady, "Romeo took his leave of his dear wife with a heavy heart," III.v (406). In this balcony scene, not the usual one, Romeo descends a rope ladder but yet the lovers hold hands. His jerkin is another indulgence in decorative pattern, red with ivory, a bright effect above shiny gray tights. In the final image, "Juliet awoke out of her trance," V.iii (409), her white dress is now a shroud — but still stylishly cut — and her golden hair plaited with black ribbons. Behind her solitary figure a tomb lamp's small red flame glows, but light comes from the position of the viewer who sees her worried expression and her huge black ominous shadow cast against the bare white background.

The most unusual, and endearing, treatments of male characters are three scenes with babies, not paralleled by women with babies. One subject is archetypal: "The poor deserted baby was found by a shepherd," *The Winter's Tale*, III.ii (90), a scene made memorable in a landscape painting by Joseph Wright of Derby. Again Jackson has a plain white background with one large boulder; an older man (white hair) stands before it as he looks down in amazement at the charming infant (a year old) resting against a blue cushion next to a black treasure chest. Perdita is enchanting, fast asleep, with her little hands held close. Her extraordinary dress—white cap, a blue bodice over a long, flowing, white skirt richly embroidered with orange and gold — is Art Nouveau. Most unusual and dramatic is action at sea, "I tied my youngest son to the end of a small mast," *The Comedy of Errors*, I.i, (304). A mature Aegeon, with brown hair and beard, dressed in white classical costume, sits astride a heavy mast, athwart which is a broken timber. A little boy, in white with blue circles, stands beside his father's thigh as he tightens the rope. Aegeon's cloak, lifted by the wind, flies out behind him. Finally, "Pericles took the new-born infant in his arms," III.i, depicts a very handsome youth — golden hair, splendid, princely, classical attire (white tunic, purple cloak)—who looks lovingly at a sleeping baby, Marina, wrapped in a very large white blanket that reaches almost to the ship's deck, details of which form the background (424). Taken in sequence, these three illustrations record the devotion of males—old, mature, and young — to the innocent and vulnerable.

The archetypal mother, ever true and loving, a symbol of grace, is Hermione in *The Winter's Tale*. One of Jackson's richest images is the resurrection scene, "To the amazement of the beholders, the statue came down from off the pedestal," V.iii (95). The drawn curtain has a dark blue inner lining, while the outer cloth is an exquisite rose-red, decorated by golden shields with wings and the image of a bird, a phoenix symbol. The lower ivory border has brown patterning. A glowing Hermione, swathed in white and with a jeweled crown on her head scarf, smiles gently as she steps down. On a pedestal on the left are roses, symbol of the Virgin Mary, a resonance that Shakespeare evokes and that Jackson signals by his chosen colors. Hermione, like Mary, is an example of forgiveness and reassuring love.[14]

Three plays have sequenced illustrations to present a self-contained story. *The Taming of the Shrew*, II.i, begins with the single figure of the heroine, "She was a lady of such ungovernable spirit and fiery temper that she was known by no other name than Katherine the Shrew" (282). The moment follows her row with teachers: arm akimbo, she holds a broken lute in her right hand and clinches her left fist; at her feet are an upturned stool, cushion, and book tossed aside. Children here see a rebellious pupil whose outburst succeeds, albeit with consequences of lost favor. This young woman is very far from the one at the end, "Katherine, the most obedient and duteous wife in Padua," V.i (293). A sumptuous white dress with golden decoration replaces the fiery red of the first picture; and she holds her cap, as her sister Bianca, a blonde in blue, stares at her in amazement. The only other detail is an urn with a red rose tree, symbol of love. Between these two representations is one of Jackson's most vigorous and comic illustrations, "Petruchio, pretending to find fault with every dish, threw the meat about the floor," IV.i (287). With a melodramatic expression of anger he stands at table and holds aloft a sizable platter above which hurtle a large joint of meat and potatoes. At the table, lighted by two candles and with a stain of red wine on its white cloth, sits a dismayed Kate. A tapestry on the wall behind, fine furniture, and large columns indicate richness; a servant peers in discreetly. Petruchio's sword, which is still attached to his waist but rests partially on the table, directs the viewer's eye to this observer. One wonders a bit at children's reactions to throwing food but, as for the first angry Kate, expects a delighted response to outrageousness and some envy at adult freedom.

With more somber stories, *King Lear* and *Othello*, Jackson's choices are telling. Like many historical painters, he makes the opening scene of *King Lear* an occasion for medievalism in one of his most detailed and finished illustrations, an interior of the great hall (rug skin, decorated low stool, harp, rich hangings). Lear, white hair and beard, sits on his canopied throne and thrusts out his left arm, while his right hand holds a lowered scepter. Behind him stand the two elder sisters. Cordelia is the main interest, "The King of France took the young maid by the hand, and said that she should be queen of him and of fair France" (193). Her brilliant red hair (favored by Pre-Raphaelites like Rossetti) is in two heavy plaits that lend interest to her plain white dress. The youthful crowned king, in vivid red and blue, has walked up the steps to the throne and looks toward Lear; but Cordelia, who stands lower, stares at the viewer as though asking for understanding. Attendants are in the right background. A second picture shows the consequence of Lear's action, "The old King was now left with no other companion than the poor fool," III.ii (204). Buffeted by the storm on the heath, Lear is bareheaded and bent as he clutches the arm of the Fool, who stands with head held high to sing; he also holds a balloon in his hand, a comic detail like the red and white checks of his clothes and bells attached to his hood. Lear has wrapped a gray blanket (with Art Nouveau pattern) over his white clothes from the first scene. His loving daughter also still wears white in "Cordelia ended her life in prison," V.iii (210). Chained to a column, she sits hunched on a pile of straw; her red hair still glows, but her eyes are closed and her face pressed against her arm. A plate with a piece of bread and

2— *The Tradition of Charles and Mary Lamb's* Tales from Shakespeare   53

A handsome young Pericles, in noble Grecian costume, holds his infant Marina as the ship lurches. A.E. Jackson's illustration, in ***Tales from Shakespeare by Charles and Mary Lamb*** (1918), is an unusual and touching image of a devoted young father, a contrast to the more frequently depicted old shepherd who finds the "lost" baby in ***The Winter's Tale.***

A.E. Jackson uses contrasts of light and dark and fabrics elaborately decorated with Art Nouveau patterns to depict Othello, Shakespeare's notable exemplar of Orientalism. Several images from this profusely illustrated *Tales from Shakespeare by Charles and Mary Lamb* (1918) have recently been used for notecards.

a broken jug indicate her plight — and form a little still life in the foreground. This edition's changed order puts *King Lear* before *Cymbeline* to separate it from the tragedy of *Macbeth*.

Because *Othello,* not *Pericles,* is the last play, the concluding note is tragedy, which favors tales written by Charles Lamb. In a relaxed scene of courtship, "Desdemona and Cassio would talk and laugh together," III.iii (458). Cassio sits on a stool in the foreground, a lute on the floor beside him, as a pretty blonde Desdemona, in white gown with slashed sleeves, smiles at him; beside her Othello looks favorably on the proceedings. The second picture is conventional, "When he saw her asleep, Othello thought he would not shed her blood, nor scar that white skin of hers, more white than alabaster," V.ii (463). Huge white draperies signal enclosure. Desdemona, her golden hair loose, lies propped on pillows in a bed with richly embroidered coverlet and skirting. Having drawn the curtain, Othello looks at her with an expression not unlike that of the first scene; however, his unsheathed sword enhances his warrior image, almost lost beneath his exotic costume, the same surcoat worn in the first scene — golden with bold red patterns. Like the coverings, it marks Orientalism, introduces design — and perhaps ideas of colonial service, and evokes favorite stories in *Tales from the Arabian Nights,* which Jackson illustrated. Those who read Lamb's *Tales* and Jackson's illustrations had many details to identify and ponder.

Louis John Rhead (1918)

An American edition, *Tales from Shakespeare by Charles and Mary Lamb* (1918), illustrated by Louis John Rhead (1857–1926) and published by Blue Ribbon Books in New York, provides a remarkable comparison with the English Edwardian editions illustrated by Norman M. Price and A. E. Jackson. It too has all twenty plays, but also includes Lamb's preface and a distinctive "Artist's Preface." Moreover, the artist identifies the Louis Rhead Series, seventeen volumes of traditional classics, listed opposite the title page. Along with *Tales from Shakespeare* are *Swiss Family Robinson* (1909), *Gulliver's Travels* (1913), *Andersen's Fairy Tales and Wonder Stories* (1914), *Grimm's Fairy Tales* (1917), *Robin Hood and His Outlaw Band* (1923), *Arabian Nights' Entertainment* (1923), and *Treasure Island* (1925). Rhead, a versatile artist — painter, etcher, and ceramic designer as well as a book illustrator — was English but emigrated to the United States and worked mostly in New York. He early collaborated with his elder brother George Woolliscroft Rhead for editions of *The Pilgrim's Progress* and Tennyson's *Idylls of the King* in 1898.

Publishing values in Rhead's *Tales* begin with the cover's "Rainbow Binding": "a unique development in modern book making" that "represents an entirely new process in book-binding by which the illustration is reproduced with the full beauty of the original directly on the cloth ... then specially treated to make it dust proof and water proof and can be cleaned with a damp cloth in a few moments."[15] This is very different from pasted paper illustrations that decorate Edwardian covers. A rainbow arcs across the back cover and a tip of the red cloth front cover that has a stunningly fierce illustration in several colors. Macbeth, a stolid warrior in shining coat of mail, holds a mace in his right hand and a large shield (red with gold center and surround); his parted legs frame two skulls and bones. Macbeth stares at the phantom "likeness of an armed head" rising from a golden light that sweeps across the bottom and left side. The illustration, repeated as frontispiece, is by Frank E. Schoonover (1877–1972), famous for painting Native Americans; his name is on the spine — with its small image of a jester in cap and bells with wand in hand — but not on the title page. Three other full-page color illustrations, signed by Rhead, are very different in style and tone. Each is a rather bland romantic scene, largely in pastel colors; Rhead's vigorous and bold black and white illustrations are the distinction of this volume. They explain why his drawing has been compared to that of Henry J. Ford and Helen Stratton, both esteemed for their treatment of fairy tales, but also of chivalric romance and heroic epic. In *Tales from Shakespeare* Rhead shows qualities of the latter subjects and remarkable originality.

The cover does not belie the book's inner contents. Each opening has a running half-inch title in capitals, "Tales from Shakespeare," across the two pages; captions below page illustrations are also in large capitals, attention-getting and easy to read. Every tale begins with a large decorative capital, an effective but rare device; Gordon Browne's capitals in Mary Macleod's *The Shakespeare Story Book* (1902), discussed in Chapter 5, is the notable exception. Rhead's twenty-seven black and white full pages are vivid and unusual in choice of subject and detail. Sixty-eight smaller pictures of varying size — 16 one-third-page, 19 half-page, and 23 one-fourth-page — enliven 367 pages in a manner reminiscent of chapbooks because they break the text. These illustrations are in different positions — usually on outer edges of either page, but occasionally two face across pages. In one effective opening for *King Lear* an angry father / king points across to his quiet, modest daughter (142–143). Most compelling is the bold contrast between the murderous Macbeths. The great male warrior, clad in battle gear with sword at his side, stands pensively, his body bent as he leans on a huge battle axe and faces away from Lady Macbeth, a strident figure who clasps a dagger in one hand and lifts the other as a clenched fist (162–163). Variety of size and spacing strengthens interest in characters and scenes.

Rhead's preface helpfully glosses attitudes and expectations at the end of the Edwardian era and World War I. He acknowledged that Lamb's *Tales* has imitators, but judged their efforts "only to invariably produce a result inferior in every way, and so quickly vanish from the reading world while these tales have grown in favor and esteem by thoughtful American parents" (xi). Rhead's audience is, then, American, both child and adult readers. He attributed Lamb's excellence to "diligent study" of Shakespeare, being "well fitted to write good English," and to taking pains "to amuse and instruct the youthful mind." Rhead accepted most of Lamb's adjustments and praised his wise refraining "from giving extracts of the well-known orations and speeches, such as spoken by Wolsey and Antony." Here Rhead erred since Lamb retold neither *Julius Caesar* nor *Henry VIII*! The practice of leaving out "well-known characters who do not assist in developing the story" is less acceptable to artist Rhead, who argued for exceptions "like Touchstone, Jaques, etc., in 'As You Like It,' so revered generation after generation, that the illustrator has ventured to picture them although they were not described in the text" (xi). This point, a harbinger of how he often eschewed the conventional when choosing an episode, expresses Rhead's recognition of a need to interest both child and adult. Specifically, he included a significant number of situations that were much harsher than those typically represented for children, and he included tougher, or more violent, details.

Rhead's audience is the "average reader," adult and child, who will find *Tales* helpful:

> Lamb's greatest accomplishment in this volume is to give the average reader of any age a plain, simple description of the story and plot which, after reading the plays, even the adult often does not get or rightly understand. We are carried away by the splendor of words and thought. That is the reason why, it seems to me, these tales can be read with great advantage by those adults or parents who take for granted this volume is especially for younger readers. The plays are far more edifying after these tales have been read, because the magnificence of Shakespeare can be enjoyed to the fullest extent [xi-xii].

Shakespeare's greatness is not questioned, but understanding him requires something more than reading — or, to cite Elizabethan usage, "hearing" his play. The analog is programs for performances of Shakespeare's plays that contain a synopsis of the story and photos of actors / characters and sets.

Capitals that begin each tale are large (nine lines), printed in bold, or boldly outlined, and decorated, usually the head of a character but often with telling detail. The "T" that begins *The Tempest* is superimposed on a half-figure of Ariel whose face peers into a lily, while above is a bee (1), a tidy signal of the song, "Where the bee sucks, there suck I" (16). Bottom with ass's head is on the left and a small fairy in foliage on the right; here the "T" is in bold, but smaller, only about a fourth of the decorated area that introduces *A Midsummer Night's Dream*. More distinctive is the large "W" that begins *Macbeth*, superimposed on Birnam woods, while two helmeted warriors with spears advance to the right (160). Two other capitals are especially memorable. At the start of *Measure for Measure* a distraught Claudio fills most of the space, while a large bold "I" separates him from the text (226). And the bold initial "G" of *Hamlet* frames the head of the drowned Ophelia (304). *Merchant of Venice* and *Othello* introduce scenes of architecture, respectively, a large bold "S" superimposed on the villa at Belmont (105) and an outlined "B" over a cityscape of Venice (326). These substantiate Rhead's point that Shakespeare set most of his plays "outside his native land, mostly in Italy and Greece" (xii); Lamb has no English history plays, but Rhead underestimates Britain as place in *King Lear, Macbeth,* and *Cymbeline.* The most unusual, and charming, capital is the "L" for *The Winter's Tale*, a large black letter that frames a nude baby who sits before a box of treasure, playing with a jeweled necklace (35). Later, the infant is depicted on the seashore, covered but with arms free, next to the open treasure chest; above her stands a shepherd with his crook and dog, authentic details attractive for children (41).

Rhead's distinctive approach is clear in several ways. He started with three full-page illustrations for *The Tempest*, all featuring the strange creatures of the island. "Prospero, Miranda, and Caliban" meet outside the monster's cave; humans are tall and elegant, their control signed by Prospero's wand (3). In contrast to their full robes and hooded cloaks, a short Caliban wears a loincloth made from skin and a cloak. His body, partially covered in scales, is topped by an ugly head with an angry face, and his raised left arm ends in three fat claws. Ariel, introduced in the capital, is progressively delineated. Loosely draped and with hair blown by the wind, Ariel sits on a rock by the seashore to play a lyre to sing, "Full fathom five thy father lies," to a sad Ferdinand (7). Finally, "On the bat's back I do fly" (17) is a dramatic night scene; a bright full moon at the center is background for Ariel's abundant blown hair, wings, and drapery. The huge bat is blacker than the sky, and three owls sit on a branch above on the right.

While others stressed gossamer fairies, Rhead had no picture of Titania; instead he devoted a full page to Puck, the figure with whom children most readily empathize, especially when drawn as a gleeful little boy, who sits on a mushroom and holds a croaking frog in one hand and a wand in the other (21). Moreover, behind him the full moon lights large ferns and grasses of the woodland. Later, a tiny Puck applies the flower charm to one sleeping lover, separated from another by a large tree trunk (32). Rhead's only other picture for *A Midsummer Night's Dream* is comic; in the woods a desperate Greek maid pursues a fleeing Greek youth (25). Here his humorous approach to romantic confusions balances traditional scenes of pretty ladies, like the overhearing in the garden in *Much Ado About Nothing* (55), or elegant pastoral, "Imogen: 'Good masters, do not harm me,'" replete with richly costumed page and hunters—and a well trained dog (131).

The supernatural and military combine in *Macbeth*. Although Rhead interpreted the same moment as Schoonover's cover, his style is very different in "Macbeth, beware of Macduff, the thane of Fife!" (169). From his standing position on the right Macbeth looks toward the upper left to a "likeness of an armed head," with staring eyes; it surmounts a plume of vapor and smoke rising

Louis Rhead demonstrates the sustained power of black and white after the use of color was favored for illustration. In *Tales from Shakespeare by Charles and Mary Lamb* (1918) his scene on the ramparts when Hamlet meets his father's ghost uses subtle shading and architectural detail as well as vigorous action, martial dress, and sighting of the ghost.

in a widening cone from a cauldron on a stand; below a glowing fire makes the foreground white. Three bearded witches with large noses watch intently from the shadowy background. Rhead characterized each: beside the seated one is a cat familiar — a domestic or supernatural animal — and another stands high and holds a broomstick, while the third, nearest the cauldron and Macbeth, leans on a stick.

Among the most exact illustrations is yet another dark scene: "Still am I called, unhand me, gentleman! By Heaven, I'll make a ghost of him that lets me!" from *Hamlet* (307). The style is Victorian, effective, heavy thatched lines with various degrees of shading. Ramparts and castle are well detailed; Hamlet's father, a pale ghost fully armed, stands near the edge and beckons. Hamlet, with both arms lifted high, faces away from the viewer toward this apparition; his billowing cloak indicates movement, as does the restraining arm on his shoulder, the effort of one of the two guards who stand below a portcullis.

Rhead favored martial action in this ghostly warrior and in other armed figures: several in the wood in *Two Gentlemen of Verona* (101); single figures in costumes of old Britain draw a sword (145), or stand with sword drawn and watch alertly in *King Lear* (155); a Greek captain in *Timon of Athens* (275). Scenes of violent action and its consequences are two youths dueling above the body of Mercutio (291), and the slain Paris before the tomb where Juliet cradles the dead Romeo in her arms (301); a fully armed Macbeth with upraised dagger going toward the sleeping Duncan (165), and a triumphant Macduff holding the severed head of Macbeth and looking back to his torso (only the legs are shown, 17). Images of the dead occur frequently in this children's book, published in the context of World War I. The play scene in *Hamlet* is a half-page close-up, where the murderer pours poison into the ear of the sleeping king (311); and Hamlet, dagger in hand, pulls back the curtain to reveal the body of Polonius (317). "Whose skull is this?" is a richly detailed graveyard scene (319). Amidst the tombstones handsome Hamlet and Horatio stand on the right, while in the lower left are two gravediggers. One empties his shovel just above a skull on the ground that is aligned with the skull that Hamlet cradles in his hand.

This toughness, or realism, also finds expression in emotionally painful moments seldom illustrated and probably thought indecorous for children. In a church interior before a priest, Claudio spurns Hero when they come to wed in *Much Ado About Nothing* (61). Iachimo is shown removing the bracelet from the arm of Imogen, as she sleeps in her exotic bedchamber, for which Rhead employed decorative Art Nouveau patterns (125). Advocates of the temperance movement in the United States had something to protest in a small drawing for *Othello*; a drunken Cassio, glass and bottle in hand, sits slumped in his chair (332). Rhead treats Orientalism in two complete pages, both of which are dominated by the Moor, here shown not as a blackamoor but an intriguing figure from the Middle East. Rhead's most precise interior is a palace chamber with a view to the city, "Desdemona loved to hear him tell the story of his adventures" (327). Othello, with pointed goatee and mustache, wears a turban, short pantaloons, a rich short cloak; he stands and gestures broadly for emphasis. In rapt attention Desdemona sits on a stool beside her wealthy father who looks up from his chair. The second interior is the bedchamber, a study in opulence with heavy patterned curtains. What is most compelling and unusual is the moment pictured. Emilia kneels with both arms raised high and an anguished face as she cries, "She loved thee, cruel Moor" (341). Again Othello stands, not in a nightshirt but fully attired with turban and a similarly beautiful costume that sign his heritage and his otherness. Behind Emilia Desdemona lies face down on the bed. Pretty images do not mitigate human destructiveness, which is as terrifying as violent nature.

Mediterranean storms are a commonplace, recorded from classical times. In *The Comedy of Errors* (209) the ship crashes against the rocks, and a mother reaches for but cannot grasp her child who is strapped to the mast. *Twelfth Night* offers a more optimistic prediction of the happy ending of comedy. "Perchance he is not drown'd: what think you, captain?" (247) asks an apprehensive Viola, who is anxious for her brother Sebastian. She stands amidst wreckage on the shore while a rough sea churns about the sinking ship. Rhead's full-page for *Pericles* is another ship in a storm (351). This cropped image features a well drawn prow, on which stand several robed Greeks, two weeping but the others stoical. Below decks are oarsmen, who pull vigorously so that the ship's prow rises in the turbulent waves. A man stands ready to release a coffin, "So they cast the queen overboard."

The above examples indicate Rhead's emphasis upon the serious and somber, but he was not without comic flair, ably shown in *The Taming of the Shrew*. The featured full-page is "Petruchio entertains his wife at dinner" (197). Again a joint of meat flies through the air because he has pulled the trencher; a subdued Katherine sits with hands folded, as servants flee through the door. Preceding this are two small scenes of violent action: Katherine breaks a lute over the music master's head (193), amusing enough; but less reassuringly Petruchio with sword in hand drags a frightened wife along on her knees (195). Nevertheless, a final small illustration signals good intention: Katherine sits exhausted in her chair, while Petruchio sits up in bed and vigorously waves a pillow in the air (199), an action easily read as playful pillow fight, a relatively harmless activity in the nursery.

In the artist's preface, Rhead declared that he drew for an audience of both adults and children, and he succeeds in providing challenges for both. No one looking at his illustrations could fail to be amused, to question and ponder. He gave parents and children ample opportunities to discuss characters and events, a dialogue advocated by pedagogy.

Although the appeal of a ship in a storm is typical for *The Tempest*, Louis Rhead brilliantly depicts a similar moment in *The Comedy of Errors*: the ship crashed against the rocks with struggling survivors, including children, in the foreground, in *Tales from Shakespeare by Charles and Mary Lamb* (1918).

Frank Godwin (1924)

Rhead's edition is an American version of Edwardian extravagance in book production with illustrations by an English artist. A poorer, albeit often reprinted, Lamb's *Tales From Shakespeare* (1924) was published by the John C. Winston Company in black or green cloth covers with a pasted picture on the front. In The Children's Classics Series, fostered by the Encyclopedia Americana, it received wider distribution.[16] The standard text has the preface and twenty plays, in slightly different order. Captioned illustrations are all full pages, on glossy paper, four in color and six black and white, equally divided between tragedies and comedies; a list gives subject and play's title. Both the number and quality suggest thrift, and make this edition less interesting than others. The artist is Frank Godwin (1889–1959), American painter, cartoonist, muralist, and illustrator.

Colors border on the garish. "Oberon, the King, and Titania, the Queen of Fairies ... in This Wood Held Their Midnight Revels" (24) features a light midsummer night, without the mystery of nature created by Rackham. Godwin's woodland combines masses of green foliage and a bit of blue sky (enlivened by golden stars) with a rocky foreground. Bottom, with his peasant's body and light tan ass's head, is the dominant creature beside whom Titania stands. As at a picnic, three pale fairies, clothed in white gossamer, sit on the ground and another atop a mushroom. For *The Taming of the Shrew* Godwin has a bright interior— "Petruchio, Pretending to Find Fault with Every Dish, Threw the Meat About the Floor" (184). A gray-blue drapery and blue door form the background, while a red rug cuts across the center of a multi-colored stone floor. Katherine, with long golden braids and very long white dress, stands beside the brown table whose white cloth she grasped too late to avoid all the food and plates falling at her feet. Petruchio, with his straight black hair in a square bob and thin, up-sweeping mustache, wears clothes of riotous color—one blue and one red leg, a blue doublet and golden blouse. Moreover, this fashionable gallant is gracefully posed, left arm on the table and body leaning as he watches his wife's response.

While Godwin was similarly conventional in selecting the play scene for *Hamlet,* "At the Representation of This Play, the King ... Was Present, with His Queen and the Whole Court" (217), his predilection for vivid colors renders Claudius's "sudden calling for light" meaningless. Elsinore Castle's opulent grand hall—blue column against long red drapery and a swirl of massive blue curtain with gold decoration to fill the upper right corner—has a beamed ceiling and mottled gray walls. Many nobles and guards with spears stand apart from the principals. At the center Hamlet in blue and Ophelia in white face the king and queen (and the viewer), who sit enthroned on a raised dais, before which reclines the court jester in red and green motley—the most prominent figure in the illustration.

Godwin's best color illustration, "Olivia ... Forgetting Her Determination to Go Veiled for Seven Long Years Drew Aside Her Veil," from *Twelfth Night*

(57), is again a popular moment. The lady sits near a table, just inside a balcony with a glimpse of tall green poplars through very large red curtains, patterned with gold circles. Both her costume and the cloth are pale pink. Viola/Caesario is a pretty, auburn-haired page, in blue and yellow. This illustration contrasts with a facing black and white one, also an Italian court scene. "He Swore to Beatrice that He Took her but for Pity" comes at the end of *Much Ado About Nothing* (56). Renaissance costumes, updated with Art Nouveau fabric design, are more attractive than Godwin's cruder splashes of color. The interior is severe, without hangings but a two-tiered frieze, a fresco, at the back, above the stair. Similar attention to decorative designs, especially on Cordelia's dress and a drapery, give interest to "A Tender Sight It Was to See the Meeting Between This Father and Daughter" in *King Lear* (120). But most compelling is a splendid rug, a white bear skin, open eyes and open mouth to reveal teeth!

Like the forest scene in *A Midsummer Night's Dream,* the black and white illustration for *Two Gentlemen of Verona* lacks sharp definition, although the subject is noble, "He Was All at Once Seized with Penitence and Remorse" (89). Looking confused and distressed, the four young lovers stand in a clearing in the trees. Murky grayness is a bit more effective for Lady Macbeth's sleepwalking; dressed in a long white gown, she holds a lighted candle in one hand and touches the wall as she descends the stairs, watched by her physician and maid (153). The caption wrongly declares, "So, with her Own hands Armed with a Dagger, She Approached the King's Bed." A murder is accurately indicated for *Othello*, "He had Her Prepare for Death, and to Say Her Prayers, for he Would Not Kill Her Soul" (281). A wide cummerbund and racial features of hair, beard, and darker skin signal Orientalism. Desdemona, bathed in light, sits up in bed to look at her husband who holds the curtain open. This adds depth that is enhanced by a tapestry behind the innocent wife. Godwin reserved dramatic contrast of black and white for "Here Romeo Took His Last Leave of His Lady's Lips" (248). In a white dress Juliet lies upon a white bordered funeral drape, garlanded with flowers; lighted candles make her tomb brilliant. Romeo, with black hair and doublet, kneels and grasps her. The crypt features a rounded arch and frescoes in the background, including a crucified Christ and those lamenting at the Cross. While this evocation of youth's suffering is poignant, Godwin's illustrations generally lack the compelling interest of analogous storytelling. Not surprisingly, publishers found ways to repeat some of the best Edwardian artists instead of commissioning new work.

Rackham, W. Heath Robinson, Dulac, Thomson, et al. (1914)

In his early career Arthur Rackham worked for Hodder and Stoughton, but in 1907 he moved to Heinemann; and Edmund Dulac (1882–1953), whose style closely resembles Rackham's, immediately filled his place. The same year, W. Heath Robinson (1872–1944), the youngest of the "Three Musketeer" illustrator brothers, also joined Hodder and Stoughton. Dulac showed his exoticism, the influence of Persian and Indian manuscripts and of Art Nouveau, in *Stories from the Arabian Nights* (1907); he created additional fantasy of the East in *The Rubáiyat of Omar Khayyám* (1909). Dulac's imaginative illustrations greatly enriched the world of Edwardian children's literature: Sir Arthur Quiller-Couch's retellings of *The Sleeping Beauty and Other Fairy Tales* (1910), *Stories from Hans Andersen* (1911), *Badoura* (1913) and *Sinbad the Sailor* (1914) from *Arabian Nights*. Like Rackham Dulac made significant contributions to World War I. *Edmund Dulac's Picture-Book for the French Red Cross* earned £1,000, and he contributed profits from his 1915 work to war charities. Most remarkable is *Edmund Dulac's Fairy Book — Fairy Tales of the Allied Nations* (1916), where he created a style appropriate to each nation (Japan, Serbia, France, Italy, Belgium, England). In the 1940s Dulac designed bank notes for General de Gaulle's "French Libre"; after World War II he designed bank notes for Spain, Italy, and Turkey, and postage stamps and bank notes in Britain. His book illustration at this time was in the United States, several classics for the Limited Editions Club of New York.

Like Rackham and Dulac, Robinson was temperamentally suited to fantasy. He provided both color plates and line drawings for *The Arabian Nights Entertainments* (1899), *The Poems of Edgar Allan Poe* (1900), and *Hans Andersen's Fairy Tales* (1913). Robinson was an especially skilled draughtsman; his black and white drawing was as strong as that of Aubrey Beardsley (1872–1898). For color Robinson used a technique, very like Rackham's, of laying a gray wash over line drawing, then softer hues, and finally color on top, to create a subtle atmosphere. Robinson's small color illustrations for Janet Kelman's *Stories from Chaucer* (1906) in Jack's Told to the Children Series, for which he also illustrated H. E. Marshall's *Stories of Robin Hood* (1906), are subtle and pleasing. He provided a variety of patriotic images for Rudyard Kipling's *A Song of the English* (1909). Illustrations for his original fantasies, *The Adventures of Uncle Lubin* (1902) and *Bill the Minder* (1912), early showed the humor that dominated Robinson's later work as an admired eccentric comic artist, whimsical and satirical creator of marvelous mechanical contrivances that ridiculed the triumph of machinery. In a way, this was a defense of the imaginative and fanciful Edwardian vision for children that had lost favor.

The sharpest difference among the three illustrators is that Dulac favored the richness of watercolor. Rackham and Robinson preferred to tint pen and ink drawings with a minimum of color that resulted in a haunting quality and intriguing world of fantasy. Moreover, their sharper draughtsmanship made them less dependent on color, which is crucial in Dulac. Both Rackham's *A Midsummer Night's Dream* and Dulac's *The Tempest* were published in 1908, as was *Twelfth Night* with illustrations by W. H. Robinson. Hodder and Stoughton reused illustrations by these three esteemed artists of the Edwardian Golden Age — although they are not identified in *Tales from Shakespeare* (1914), a handsome volume with unusual visual variety.[17]

Its brown cloth cover promises entertainment. The title and author are stamped in large gold letters against a black circle, decorated with foliage and ribbons at the top. Most compelling are two jesters—fools in motley with cap and bells and wands with jesters' heads—who sit back to back, like bookends; they decorate the lower half of the cover and promise good reading. Richly colored end papers depict a generic Renaissance scene, a broad piazza, two columns on the left and trees on the right; at the top of a broad stairway a youth plays a lute, while below on the paved square a lover gestures invitingly to his lady. Their costumes add tones of orange-red to muted tan, cream, and green. The title page carries red masks of tragedy and comedy that enliven the black lettering and border. There is neither preface nor supporting materials for this collection of eighteen of Lamb's original twenty tales; missing are *All's Well that Ends Well* and *Measure for Measure,* both "problem plays" for adults, let alone children. The sixteen color illustrations are matted, each protected by an onion skin page that bears the caption, title of the play, and page reference to the text. Since only a few bear clear signatures, artist identifications must be based on other books.[18]

The frontispiece, "The King of France ... bade Cordelia take farewell of her sisters and of her father," exemplifies late Victorian history painting and chivalry. The young couple both have golden hair; France, in full armor, looks like a Viking warrior, while Cordelia's white dress, with color borders, echoes Lear, whose robe, hair, and beard are white. They stand on rough animal skins, which, like the smaller figures behind Lear, signal early Britain.

Dulac's Ferdinand and Miranda, "I am your wife if you will marry me" (8), is stunningly beautiful; it was the frontispiece for his *The Tempest,* which has forty color illustrations handsomely mounted. Rocky island cliffs, pale blue sky with white clouds, and deep blue-green sea with touches of white caps establish a wondrous location. The lovers' costumes display Art Nouveau designs in colors that link them. Her white dress is embroidered with gold, as is his short black tunic over which is a golden coat. The scene combines realistic and romantic, a marked contrast to the magical "Where the bee sucks, there suck I" (17), a quintessential Art Nouveau image. Sweeping up from the lower right is a beautiful floral branch, white flowers and golden leaves on green stem. The body of an exquisite nude Ariel, with golden hair and wings, suspended in flight, connects this branch to a green-leafed bough in the upper right. Dulac matched the text by including two bees; one flies just below Ariel, and the other sucks from one of the flowers below. This is one of several illustrations that feature the supernatural in Dulac's *The Tempest*: two mermaids peer at an old man under water in "Full fathom five thy father lies" (34); Nymphs, called Naiads, frolic in the river and its bank (78) and also dance with reapers (82);

Edmund Dulac's Miranda and Ferdinand stand in a spectacular island landscape and embody the beauty of his Art Nouveau style. The illustration, made for an edition of *The Tempest* (1908), was repeated by Hodder and Stoughton in *Tales from Shakespeare* (1914), a gift book that combined illustrations by major Edwardian artists.

Ariel reports to Prospero (94) and flies on bat's wings (122). "Ye elves of hills, brooks, standing lakes and groves" (98) displays fairy qualities but hints of the symbolic found in George Watts, as does "We are such stuff / As dreams are made on" (86), all turquoise and indigo, heavens and sea, small figures. "Deeper than did ever plummet sound / I'll drown my book" is a kind of underwater still life, dominated by a large jelly fish.[19] Always, Dulac's color makes the dominant impression, whether indigo, turquoise, green, or vibrantly decorative Art Nouveau patterns on costumes. For children the more obvious images were chosen.

Similar is "Some of you must kill cankers in the musk-rose buds, and some wage war with the bats," the sole illustration for *A Midsummer Night's Dream* (32). Against a background of pale clouds Titania reclines on a flowery bed to order her fairies, each distinctive, assembled below her. Botanical details are beautiful and accurate — anemones, daisies, forget-me-nots, foxgloves, sprays of wild roses — while two bats in the upper left corner are softly gray rather than menacing black. Titania's body, partially concealed by gray gossamer, curves languidly, as she rests her chin on her right hand and gestures with her left. The changeling boy (with darker complexion and Oriental pantaloons) faces the viewer.

Juliet alone in the balcony scene — "O Romeo, Romeo!" said she, "wherefore art thou Romeo?" (288) — is a softened image of beauty. Her dress is also gossamer, with a yoke and sleeve of rich Art Nouveau design, but all in pale blue-green that allies her to the garden's vegetation — climbing white roses on the balustrade and leafy trees to which the eye is led by the glow of golden panes in a narrow window. White moonlight bathes the corner column and distant city on the right. At an earlier moment Juliet's dress is the same, but her hair darker (304). The interior setting is the Capulet ball, where Romeo, in brown pilgrim garb, grasps her hand. Both are oblivious of guests who fill a brightly-lit background. This scene is more exciting than the parting of husband and wife, indicated by the caption!

The most opulent illustration is a three-quarter-length formal portrait of Portia, a study in rich texture and color, for *The Merchant of Venice* (120). The lady of Belmont sits upon a bench, her left hand resting on a white cushion that flows into the background frame. At its center is a splendid deep-blue-green tapestry with bold golden design and a standing cushion of similar fabric. Portia has auburn hair, surmounted by a strand of pearls, whose whiteness matches the large collar that surmounts her dress. Every detail denotes luxury: the bodice and large skirts are a deep crimson, trimmed with plain gold bars, while her short cloak is brown fur; both colors reflect tints in her hair. A large panel in the skirt and the sleeves are greenish gray, heavily embossed with a pattern that anticipates the tapestry. Portia holds a bright, open fan, whose blue, red, and gold pattern break the mass of fabric. A similar sharpness of costume defines "Shylock leaving the Ducal Palace" (136); his black robe has red bands and long sleeves, rather like an academic gown. Gray hair and beard, a cane, and a hand on the balustrade mark his age and infirmity as he descends a broad staircase. The steps are horizontal and the balustrade a sharp vertical that cuts across the illustration, while an open doorway (through which is seen the lower part of a man) on the right and an opening through an arch on the left break the mass of white marble.

Concern with period detail is a quality often ascribed to Hugh Thomson (1860–1920), most popular for his black and white drawings, exemplified by his liveliness and ingenuity for another children's classic, FJ. Harvey Darton's *Tales of the Canterbury Pilgrims* (1904). Thomson's two illustrations for *As You Like It* are pretty, delicate pastel studies of conventional situations in the Forest of Arden. "Wondering how this could be," Touchstone, Rosalind, and Celia rest against a massive tree trunk, above which light green foliage disappears into the frame (80). Their costumes of peasant maiden, jester, and page have accurate period details, a characteristic Thomson developed during the 1890s when he was influenced by the style of Randolph Caldecott (1846–1886), whose works Macmillan revived in a series of twenty-four classic books, eleven of which had work by Thomson. Thomson's second scene reiterates the displacement of the banished: "They no longer found the convenient inns and good accommodation they had met with on the road" (96). Ganymede stands, while Aliena sits on a fallen tree, in a more open landscape. Again colors are all soft browns, greens, cream; the two comely and modest cousins are differentiated by blond and dark hair as well as male and female costumes.

W. Heath Robinson's two illustrations for *Twelfth Night* are softly colored because of his use of a gray wash. Indeed the woodland scene "Orsino sought the love of fair Olivia" (240) is a study in gray with a bare hint of blue in the Duke's doublet. His large partial figure in the foreground stands and faces away from the viewer to the lady at the center, while Maria and Feste recline on the grass. A stream of light breaks through shadowy gray trees to foreground Olivia and give depth so that the eye looks into the space beyond her. Viola as Caesario is a foregrounded and cropped figure in "The poor lady might as well love a dream" (256), a rueful comment as Viola looks at the ring in her hand. Her page's costume, gray but with a dark red hat and sleeveless jerkin, stands out well against a large, bare, cream wall. But gray prevails on the right; the remainder of the building shaded, before a glimpse of pale green tree on the far right. Thus Robinson creates an effect of landscape not unlike those found in Renaissance paintings, a neat match to the period costumes.

Such distinction is a far cry from a disappointing watercolor of the most painted scene in *Hamlet,* "To this brook, Ophelia came one day when she was unwatched" (320) by W(illiam) G(eorge) Simmonds (1876–1928). His colors are brighter and cruder than in any other illustration: Ophelia, who stands by the river bank, has a very pink face and arms, while the tree trunk behind her has a reddish hue, albeit the bright green grass and leaves seem English. Two additional pages are more realistic than the work of the major artists so far considered. After their wedding in *The Taming of the Shrew,* "They journeyed on through rough and miry ways" (208), a scene with dynamic action and animals of the real world. Kate and Petruchio, both with broad hats decorated by feathers and matching blue-green riding clothes and brown cloaks, ride vigorously away from Padua, indicated by a church tower in the background. His brown horse is much more lively than her white one that looks dogged: behind follows a servant, all in brown like his horse. Katherine's sharp expression is echoed in the frowning face of another challenged wife, Desdemona in *Othello,* "He accused her more plainly of being unfaithful" (334). Against a tapestry-covered wall, she stands in a fashionably cut but plain gray dress that is as much a contrast to Othello's Oriental costume — brilliant red (decorated with black swirls) and long white cloak, the hood of which sharpens his darker face and black beard — as their different skin tones. Moreover, Desdemona's arms are extended slightly from her sides, while his crossed arms on his chest and the dagger at his waist portend violence.

The individual attractiveness of reused illustrations is only part of the interest of Hodder and Stoughton's *Tales from Shakespeare*; it exemplifies ways to profit from earlier work, a variant on the use of reproductions of great paintings in many children's books of literature and history. A salient point of this chapter has been to establish the variety and quality of editions that sustain privileging of the first retelling of Shakespeare's plays for children and to demonstrate that illustrations determined the appeal of a text so readily available. Choice of play becomes crucial with selected editions of Lamb's *Tales,* typically more elaborately produced with supplementary textual material as well as visual illustration.

3

Lamb's *Tales* Continued: Completion, Addition, and Selection

Complete editions of Lamb's *Tales from Shakespeare* still dominate; online bookseller abe.books, for example, typically has a couple of thousand entries. But two alternatives for Shakespeare's stories give different information about expectations and choices: (1) adding tales and/or elaborating on those already told and (2) selecting from the original twenty tales to provide a less daunting introduction to Shakespeare's plays. Edwardian editors typically express admiration and respect for Lamb's achievements before justifying revisions (usually of details omitted) and supplementary materials, especially quotations. A Shakespeare biography—with special attention to his boyhood and schooling—is a frequent enrichment, sometimes accompanied by a biography of the Lambs and quotations from Charles Lamb's letters. Information about Shakespeare's theatre and contemporaries, dates of plays, and sources are not unusual. Many add more sophisticated critical and scholarly insights about how to read Shakespeare as a whole, to go beyond stories to understand his mind and place in defining the English race / nation. Such materials become especially crucial in additions to schoolbooks, discussed in Chapter 6.

The most basic way to continue Lamb's work was simply to retell plays not included, as did Harrison S. Morris's *Tales from Shakespeare* (1893), an imitative completion. Two other fine examples are F.J. Furnivall's *Tales from Shakespeare* (1901), the most elaborate edition ever published, and Winston Stokes's *All Shakespeare's Plays* (1911) that combines Lamb's *Tales* with his own retellings and great paintings as illustrations.

Much more numerous are selections, usually six to eight tales. The finest example is Mrs. Andrew Lang's *The Gateway to Shakespeare* (1908), a handsome reward or prize book, published by Thomas Nelson in their elegant Gateway Series that introduces major English writers—Chaucer, Spenser, Tennyson—with Edwardian extravagance. The opposite end of the market is W.T. Stead's

Tales from Shakespeare (1903), separate plays in the Books for the Bairns Series, slim paper pamphlets that sold for pennies.

Between these two extremes are several small selections, each issued in a series of traditional literature retold. Clearly many felt that further simplification, especially of language, was needed. Like Stead, who made a few adjustments to increase easy reading, Edith Robarts retold Lamb's *Tales from Shakespeare* (1910), published by Ward Lock. Harrap's All-Time Tales Series includes Lamb's *Tales from Shakespeare,* Book I and Book II (1910), respectively comedies and tragedies, in which simplification is less obtrusive. These two modest books had a double purpose; they became school texts. They are considered in Chapter 6, as is Blackie's single volume *Lamb's Tales from Shakespeare* (1917), a combination of comedies and tragedies, in their Stories Old and New Series. But another selection, edited by F. C. Tilney in 1926, was a late addition to Dent's Tales from Many Lands Series. It repeats some of Charles Folkard's illustrations originally published in Alice S. Hoffman's *The Children's Shakespeare* (1911). Small, attractively illustrated, and cloth-bound, but relatively inexpensive, this series volume competed with similar alternative versions of Shakespeare for children, the subject of Chapter 5.

Harrison S. Morris, Tales from Shakespeare *(1893)*

Harrison S. Morris's *Tales from Shakespeare* (1893), published by William Heinemann in London and J.B. Lippincott in Philadelphia, was written to complete Lamb's *Tales,* of which more than fifty editions had already appeared. Thus Morris (1856–1948) retold sixteen plays: ten English histories, three Roman plays (*Coriolanus, Julius Caesar, Antony and Cleopatra*; there is still no *Titus Andronicus*), and two comedies (*Love's Labour's Lost* and *The Merry Wives of Windsor*). Moreover, illustrations, thirteen color plates, are all paintings: a combination of three contemporary portraits—Henry VI (138) and Shakespeare (both a copy of a 1609 original, 6, and the bust in Stratford-on-Avon parish church, 40)—eight mostly Victorian historical paintings, and two theatrical portraits—*Edmund Kean as Richard III* (frontispiece) and *John Kemble as Coriolanus* (232). Morris claimed his added prose retellings were the first, but he modestly hoped not to be compared with Charles and Mary Lamb's excellences but merely to complete their purpose:

> [A] wish to provide the means for readers, old and young, to gain a knowledge of Shakespeare while from lack of time and training they are not able to find their way through the "wild poetic garden" for themselves. Coupled with this was the desire to supplement the uncompleted work, not with tales the equal of the originals in grace, wisdom, or critical penetration, but with such as at least might be accepted as a help to that part of Shakespeare, and no unimportant part it is, left untouched by the earlier authors.[1]

Morris both recognized Lamb's influence and extended the audience, "old and young." His task was in some ways greater, since the Lambs "chose those [plays] in all respects adapted to their purpose, and omitted just such examples as were most difficult to turn into intelligible prose versions." Morris enumerates difficulties: "To bring Falstaff, the chartered libertine of Elizabethan slang, into juvenile phrase, to weave the broken dramatic scenes of the Wars of the Roses into even-pacing narrative; and to conquer the heroic periods of the unconquerable Romans" (vi–vii). An "adventurer in this untried field," he ends with a modesty topos to invoke the mercies of Elia and Bridget Elia and of Shakespeare. Morris succeeds remarkably well; his full readable narratives are competent summaries, with fewer omissions and more close paraphrases of Shakespeare's lines than interlaced quotations. Of greatest interest are his occasional evaluative glosses on character and action that clearly lead reader response.

Morris introduces the sophisticated comedy *Love's Labour's Lost* by explaining that the vow of the King of Navarre and his friends is a "pleasant whim" (1), while the princess and her ladies are "all light of heart and nimble of wit" (3), a match for gentlemen who are "gallants." He narrates the complexities of misdelivered letters, circumventions of vows and discoveries, but only refers to the "mummery" of the rustics, a tiny gesture beyond Mary Lamb's elimination of *Pyramus and Thisbe* in *A Midsummer Night's Dream*. Like others who offer classics to children, Morris quotes lyric verses: Dumain's "ode" [sonnet], "On a day (alack the day!)" (IV.iii.97–116)—although many do not judge it "one of the sweetest and archest of love-songs" (8)—one of Winter's two stanzas from the concluding songs (17).

Because few include Shakespeare's history plays, the moral difficulties of Falstaff are finessed. Thus Morris's handling is especially notable. He introduces Falstaff in *The Merry Wives of Windsor*, which expands Falstaff's story from the history plays, as

> a freebooter of the town, who lived upon his wits and was followed by a band of cut-purses and knaves who throve on his remnant of respectability. He was fat and unwieldy of gait, and his face was crimsoned by the potations of sack he was forever draining in mine Host's taproom of the Garter Inn, in which public-house he dwelt [18].

Set against this negative description is the glee of Mrs. Page and Mrs. Ford, "good wives ... hearty dames of old England," who enact "a merry revenge" (20). Their employment of children, "dressed like urchins, ouphes, and fairies in green and white, ... carry lighted tapers on their heads and rattles in their hands ... encircle him about and pinch him, fairy-like" (29), is an affinity with child readers in a reassuringly familiar world of fairy lore.

Shakespeare's Falstaff of *Merry Wives* is not the great comic character of the history plays, whose role Morris somewhat reduces as he stresses royal figures. The coming to maturity of Prince Hal, a model of good behavior, is a unifying and uplifting theme, apt for children. Thus Hal's participation in Falstaff's robberies is rationalized and warned against:

> [F]rom a love of adventure because, as is the habit with young people who like to indulge their inclinations, he thought that some day he would amend his ways and make all right.... But this is a dangerous argument, for few can resist temptation at will, and evil doing is not so easily cast aside as the prince believed [86].

The Prince, "who loved such mad pranks beyond even reputation," agrees to accompany Poins (88). Although Morris fully relates the robbery, with its comedy of multiplying men in buckram, he diminishes subversive flaunting of authority. Where Shakespeare's Falstaff plays the Prince, who plays the King, and both exhibit virtuosity in insults, Morris mildly observes their "playing in mockery the scene ... while the others hugely enjoyed the sport" (92). A painting, *Falstaff Playing the Prince*, by H(enry) W(illiam) Bunbury (1750–1811) is similarly innocuous, with bright light, and gentle rose and pink costumes, albeit facial expressions are wry instead of laughing (84). Bunbury's *Falstaff Mustering Recruits* is a darker study in grotesques (102).

Filial piety triumphs in Prince Henry's remorse when he meets King Henry IV:

> The prince knew within himself how deep were his offences, and how well-merited were the upbraidings of his father; but he had resolved to throw off his evil ways and to assert the noble traits which had always slumbered within him, so that he bore the king's censure with a manly humility, promising to be more himself thereafter [93].

The young prince is exemplary, superior to court and tavern. In *Henry IV, Part II* when the Chief Justice's fortunes seem at risk, Morris glossed, "The new king loved an honest directness of speech, and was out of humour with the roundabout affectations of the court" (117). Falstaff's rejection is further anticipated by how he gets recruits: "Thus did this jolly vagabond make a disreputable living by selling what was left to his honour and degrading the king's forces with beggarly recruits" (110). The chief justice and officers bear Falstaff "away to banishment until his conversation should appear more wise and modest in the world" (121). In *Henry V* Mistress Quickly reports Falstaff's death, "in her cockney speech," a line in a paragraph describing how all took arms for France (125).

Morris's openings define circumstances of history. Thus *Henry V* recapitulates:

> When the wild Prince Hal, companion of rogues and cut-purses, ascended the throne as King Henry the Fifth of England, wisdom, like an angel, came and whipped the offending Adam out of him. Never was such a sudden scholar made; never was reformation so complete. The whole nation was blessed in the change, for the young king was found to be master of the state craft; he could reason in divinity with his prelates, he was wise in policy, and he had at command the whole art of war [122].

Hal also followed his father's advice to undertake foreign wars to deflect attention from domestic difficulties. The poised new king dominates Henry Fuseli's *The Arrest of Cambridge, Scroop and Grey* (122), engraved for the Boydell Gallery in 1798. The white plumes of his hat are the highest central point. Set opposite the conspirators are men in armor, who introduce a martial theme realized in a Victorian painting that celebrates Henry V; it is often used in history schoolbooks. Sir John Gilbert's *The Morning of Agincourt* (1884) captures the weariness and determination of the small English force, amongst whom old Sir Thomas Erpingham is prominent (132). On the left many priests and soldiers kneel in prayer. In the upper background is a burning camp; above, dark clouds and a flight of birds evoke the terrible costs of battle. Morris's narrative resembles a juvenile historical novel of chivalry. He paraphrases Shakespeare's scenes of the night before the battle, when a worried but brave king brings comfort to waiting men and communes with himself upon "the vanity of kingship," yet plans a practical joke by changing gages with Williams. Interlaced are contrasting French arrogance and overwhelming numbers. The battle itself takes but a line, followed quickly by the confrontation between Williams and Fluellen and the King's clarification. Then King Harry is "impetuous in his love-making as in all else"; Morris paraphrases his exchange with Katherine, but eliminates the French/English lesson (134).

Purposeful and thorough treatment is most obvious in three separate chapters for *Henry VI, Parts I, II, III*. Morris's summary and paraphrase make this complex English history accessible, but also preserve Shakespeare's emphases. Talbot is the hero of *Part I*; his story of chivalry shows the race's quality: "the hearts of English soldiers ever grow stouter with the approach of danger" (150). At the fight at Orleans,

> the valiant Talbot enacted wonders with his sword and lance. He slew hundreds, and none durst stand out against him; he was here, there, and everywhere, till the French exclaimed that Satan was in arms, and the whole army stood at gaze upon him. His soldiers, spying his undaunted spirit, cried out amain and rushed into the midst of the battle [137–138].

This warrior is also a model of chivalry to the French Countess of Auvergne:

> with courtly gallantry, this knight, whom she had called a silly dwarf, assured her that what she had done had not offended him, nor did he crave other satisfaction than a taste of wine and such delicacies as she might be able to provide, for soldiers' stomachs always served them well [144–145].

While this French lady is honored to feast so great a warrior, La Pucelle, Joan of Arc loses sympathy not because she fights the English and is captured but from lack of courtesy and filial respect when she rejects the old shepherd, her father: "the pity which her virgin adventures and her present misfortunes might have awakened in the gallant English hearts was turned to aversion" (152) — a warning to children. Yet the Duke of York, who orders her burnt, "in deference to her maidenhead, told his officers to spare no faggots or pitch, that her torture might be shortened" (153). Such mixed response differs from but is part of nineteenth-century fascination and celebration of Joan of Arc, well reflected in children's literature — history books, saints' legends, juvenile novels— and public art and sculpture in France, especially paintings in the Pantheon in Paris, often reproduced.

Complications of the Wars of the Roses stem from a "weak king" and make *Henry VI, Parts II and III* difficult; the struggle elicits little empathy: "for the fact was that there was little to choose between the claims of the two houses" (175). Nevertheless, Morris evaluated major figures. Margaret is the "dissembling queen" of "too-confiding Henry" (166); her anger and ferocity climax in *Part III*. She mocks the prisoner Duke of York as she taunts him with the blood of his son, slain by Clifford, who now stabs him: "the queen, vengeful beyond her sex, stepped close to the fallen lord and also thrust her dagger in his side" to "right our gentle-hearted king" (179). Gilbert's *Queen Margaret Taken Prisoner* (1875), a chivalric picture of mounted knights riding across an English landscape with Tewkesbury Cathedral on the horizon (174), offers respite before Richard of Gloucester murders Henry VI in the Tower and the Yorkists triumph over the Lancastrians.

One sign of the audience is Morris's careful retention of scenes with boys; Brutus and Lucius in *Julius Caesar* crucially gain empathy. Two paintings show dangers to princes and exemplify how Victorians viewed the beauty and vulnerability of children. *Hubert and Arthur* by W. F. Yeames (1835–1918) is a poignant scene from *King John* (50), albeit not so popular as Yeames's notoriously Romantic depiction of the Civil War, *And When Did You Last See Your Father?* (1878), still a people's favorite in Britain. A prince younger than Arthur is at the center of *Elizabeth Woodville and the Duke of York* by John Opie (1761–1807), which illustrates *Richard III* (194). The boys are fair-haired and blue-eyed, clothed in the white of innocence, and placed at the center.

The frontispiece, J.J. Halls's *Edmund Kean as Richard III* (1814), privileges a tradition of bravura performance of the role.[2] Morris emphasizes villainy. Richard is "wicked ... dark and unscrupulous mind, ... malformed in shape and hideous in face" (195), the "bloody duke" (206); he allies himself with Buckingham, a "crafty confederate" (204), with "dissembling" Catesby, who spreads rumors of the illness of Richard's wife, and with "discontented" Tyrrel, who arranges the murder of the princes in the Tower. Morris lacks Shakespeare's irony and wit, but builds inexorably to the contrasting dreams of the leaders before Bosworth, where Richard shows feeling and the psychological cost of his evil deeds:

> [C]old fearful drops stood on his trembling flesh, and his heart accused him with a thousand several tongues, every tongue bringing in a several tale, and every tale condemning him for a villain. Despair seized upon him in that awful moment. There was, he said, no creature who loved him, and if he died, no soul would pity him [211].

W.F. Yeames's *Arthur and Hubert* was often used to illustrate *King John*, as in Harrison S. Morris's *Tales from Shakespeare* (1893). This Victorian historical painting typifies the poignancy of innocent childhood, a boy threatened by adult violence and his plea to a presumed friend rejected.

Yet when Richmond and Stanley advance, "aroused in Richard [are] all the prowess of his warlike family.... [He] ordered his standards to advance and the onset to begin.... King Richard that day enacted more wonders than a man ... fought on foot when his horse was slain and sought for Richmond in the throat of death" (212). Despite courage Richard loses to the "devout Richmond" to whom Stanley gives the crown, "these long-usurped royalties ... plucked off the dead temples of this bloody wretch" (213).

Morris usually wrote scenes with women cursorily. In *Richard III* he minimized confrontations between Richard and his mother and the interaction of the queens, and Richard does not woo Anne. In *Richard II* neither Hotspur's Kate not Richard's queen, who both elicit sympathy for their husbands, is significant; and there is no garden scene. A reduction of woman's role is similar in *Henry VIII*, which here lacks the spectacular scene of the dying Katherine's vision and much of her defense in Act II, scene iv. However, an opulent illustration, *The Trial* (1817), painted by G(eorge) H(enry) Harlow (1789–1819), offsets this. It recalls memorable performances by the Kemble family at Covent Garden. Katherine, played by Sarah Siddons in splendid robes and crown, stands and points to her seated enemy Cardinal Wolsey. Behind her extended finger sits her husband Henry VIII. She is clearly the dominant figure before whom men, seated or standing in the background, look insignificant. Two pages are a point of empathy for children; one, with his back to the viewer, bends to adjust a cushion (222). A second illustration is Gilbert's *Wolsey Going to Westminster*. This magnificent processional scene, in which many kneel with petitions in their hands, combines symbols of authority from both state and church. Priests bearing crucifixes lead the procession, followed by those who carry maces of office for the Lord Chancellor. Over his brilliant red cardinal's robes, Wolsey wears a rich stole of brown fur and the chain of secular office. The background interior wall, splendidly carved and a glimpse of tapestry above, signs the opulence of Wolsey's palace at Hampton Court, which was grander than the king's, so that the churchman relinquished it to him.

While Morris's texts indicate uneasiness with powerful women in English histories, this is less evident in Roman plays. Both Portia and Calpurnia in *Julius Caesar* and Volumnia and Virgilia in *Coriolanus* receive fuller treatment; and the Egyptian queen remains crucial in *Antony and Cleopatra*, albeit Morris judged her explicitly and severely. Cleopatra is a "voluptuous" and "captious queen" with "clinging caresses and insidious wiles," who distracts Antony "for a little time, but the world is not so wide but a man's sin may sooner or later find him out" (271). Thus on the first page moral judgment is explicit. Though Cleopatra is "impetuous" (276), able to turn Antony's rage with "womanly spells and magic caresses" (282), Morris did not recognize her "infinite variety." And he retained Shakespeare's language from Philo's opening speech (I.i.1–13) to define Antony's failure:

So infatuated was he, indeed, that his officers called his passion a dotage, for, they said, his goodly eyes that once glowed like plated Mars over the files and musters of the war, now bent and turned their devotion upon this tawny face, and his captain's heart, which in the scuffles of great fights had burst the buckles on his breast, had become the bellows to cool a gipsy's lust [271].

But Morris could not ignore Cleopatra's magnificence in the last act (V.i.280–313):

> "I am fire and air, ... my other elements I give to baser life;" then tenderly kissing her women and with a long farewell, she applied the asp to her breast, bidding it with its sharp teeth untie the intricate knot of life. She passed softly into a state like waking-sleep, and, placing another asp upon her arm, fell across her bed in a dying swoon [291].

Death inspires eulogy when Octavius orders that the famous lovers be buried together: "Such high events as these strike those that make them, ... and their story is no less in pity than his glory which brought them to be lamented" (292). In contrast, the Romans "valued Coriolanus truly for his exalted worth and unsullied honour" (251).

There are only two illustrations for Roman plays, and one is a theatrical portrait: G.H. Harlow's *John Kemble as Coriolanus* (232). The other, a very atmospheric classical scene, captures the experience of Rome. *The Ides of March* is the work of Edward Poynter (1836–1919), who was early stimulated by excavations at Pompeii and often painted subjects set in ancient Rome and from classical mythology. In Poynter's night scene huge marble columns dwarf three figures barely visible in light from a lamp on a standard that illuminates a head of Caesar, while a white streak of lightning across the black, cloud-filled sky centers the picture and casts faint light onto a column on the right side of the temple. Conspiracy and chaos seem inevitable in this "tempestuous night with evil dreams and wakefulness" (255).

While Victorian painters devoted their effort to subjects from both classical antiquity (Greece and Rome) and the Middle Ages, illustrations selected for Morris's *Tales from Shakespeare* favor history of the nation, especially medievalism. Already noted are Gilbert's two paintings of chivalric scenes with many small figures—*The Morning of Agincourt* and *Queen Margaret Taken Prisoner*—and his late medieval/Tudor, *Wolsey Going to Westminster*. His final contribution is *Richard II Resigning the Crown to Bolingbroke* (68), a study in medieval costume and furniture—stained glass, tapestry, orb—like Ford Madox Brown's *Chaucer Reading ... to Edward III and His Court*. But the painting is also theatrical; Richard wears black and boldly gestures with his right hand while he still holds in his left hand the crown that Henry IV has grasped. Facial expressions indicate a variety of responses to the deposition. Gilbert's illustrations for *Shakespeare's Works* (1856–1858), noted in Chapter 2, were a substantial resource to tell the stories of the English histories. Historical paintings greatly enriched Morris's *Tales from Shakespeare*, as they enhanced

Richard II Resigning the Crown to Bolingbroke is a dramatic historical painting by Sir John Gilbert, a prolific and renowned Victorian artist and major illustrator of Shakespeare. This painting is one of several reproduced in Harrison S. Morris's *Tales from Shakespeare* (1893). Gilbert's treatment of costume, stained glass, and heraldic tapestry evoke the Middle Ages. His images were popular choices for schoolbooks to enliven less immediately accessible stories and to foster national identity.

Rewards / prizes; in schoolbooks they also often formed the basis of pedagogical exercises, fulfilling educational guidelines to introduce art into the study of English literature.

F. J. Furnivall, Tales from Shakespeare *(1901)*

Substantial size and sophistication indicate high expectations for children's skill and attention. A sumptuous *Tales,* two volumes, each more than 300 pages, edited by F(rederick) J(ames) Furnivall (1815–1910) for Raphael Tuck in 1901, claimed to be "the grandest and most costly one ever issued."[3] Furnivall, a major figure in the development of English studies in Britain and education for the working man, reduced the limited comprehensiveness of Lamb's initial retelling. His edition, illustrated by Harold Copping (1863–1932), had 22 full-page Photogravure plates and 132 other illustrations. Their subjects are more often character than narrative action. All are for tales told by the Lambs, not for six "Sketches" contributed by Furnivall—*Love's Labour's Lost, Merry Wives of Windsor, Julius Caesar, Troilus and Cressida, Antony and Cleopatra,* and *Coriolanus* (II, 267–308). A cloth edition with gilt top sold for 30 shillings, while the Edition de Luxe, in white buckram, with gilt top cost £5.5s. For £6.6s., the deluxe edition was available in handsome white leather, with gilt solid edges, each copy numbered and signed. A simple book of stories for children, written to amuse Mary Lamb and produce some income, has become a sumptuous collector's item with scholarly enhancement. Furnivall's introduction cites Charles Lamb's letters that explain Mary's work for Godwin's bookseller and his expectation that "it will be popular among the little people, besides money. It's to bring in sixty guineas" (I, ix). "Thomas Hodgkins"—a pseudonym—published the two volumes in 12 mo in 1807, with copper plates, illustrations attributed to painter William Mulready and engraved by William Blake (1757–1827). Lamb judged them "very rough and poor ones." M. J. Godwin did a second edition in 1809, duplicated in 1810 with a new title page, and third and fourth editions in 1816 and 1822 (I, xi). There were many English editions, including ones in America and India, and translations in German, French, Danish, and Polish.

Furnivall, indefatigable as an organizer and editor, especially of early English texts, was founder and director of the Early English Text Society and promoted the Oxford *New English Dictionary,* for which he served as principal editor during the preliminary collection of material. He established societies to promote Chaucer, the Ballad, Wyclif, Browning, and Shelley, as well as the New Shakespeare Society, devoted to the study of "the growth, the oneness of Shakespere." All express his passion for literature and delight in company. Furnivall co-edited with John W. Hales *Bishop Percy's Folio Manuscript* (1867–68), a singular achievement. His greatest efforts were devoted to Chaucer; he produced a *Six-Text Print of Chaucer's Canterbury Tales* for the Chaucer Society (1868–1877) and wrote an introduction for F. J. Harvey Darton's children's book, *Tales of the Canterbury Pilgrims Retold from Chaucer and Others* (1904). Similarly Furnivall supervised production of forty-three volumes of facsimiles of Shakespeare Quartos, and the "grandest" edition of Lamb's *Tales* parallels his scholarly work. He included results of verse tests by the Shakespeare Society to establish the order of plays that is the basis of a division into four periods. Furnivall's physical energy found expression in rowing, for he was an enthusiastic oarsman. He is noted for the introduction of a new narrow sculling boat and of races on the Thames for sculling fours and eights, and children's literature owes a debt to him as inspiration for one of its greatest classics. Kenneth Grahame partially based his character of Rat in *The Wind in the Willows* (1908) on Furnivall, who was fond of male company and "messing about in boats."[4]

The most significant and impressive quality of Furnivall's edition of Lamb's *Tales* is a combined respect for its status of classic with what he proffers as modest improvements and ambitions to expand knowledge and admiration for Shakespeare. As a co-founder, with Walter W. Skeat (1835–1912), of the London Working Men's College, Furnivall was passionately involved in extended adult education, a vast audience in need of accessible versions of traditional literature. About the Lambs, he finds the most "odd thing" is how "two such humourful folk ... who enjoyed Shakespeare's fun, made up their minds to keep all that (or almost all) out of his plays when they told the stories to boys and girls who so like fun too." While he quoted Charles's fear that a reduction would lose the humor, Furnivall ruefully concluded, "I can't help thinking that most boys would like the fun put into the Tales, and the stories cut shorter; but they can easily get it all in the plays themselves, so there's no harm done" (I, xi).

Gender expectations after a century both changed and remained the same. Mary Lamb particularly wrote for girls, who needed retellings to gain access to Shakespeare; Furnivall assumed that boys would read the *Tales*, although the original plays were available. Mary Lamb found Shakespeare's frequent use of cross-dressing a bit of a problem. In a letter to Wordsworth, June 26, 1805, Charles wrote that Mary was stuck with *All's Well that Ends Well*: "She complains of having to set forth so many female characters in boys' clothes. She begins to think Shakespeare must have wanted imagination!" (I, x). In contrast, Furnivall was much taken with the practice of boy actors in Shakespeare's theatre—not least as a point of empathy with his child readers. He observed that the different heights of Helena and Hermia in *A Midsummer Night's Dream* give insight into casting that recurs in other plays (I, 32).

In practice, for all his courteous praise, Furnivall was acutely conscious of limitations in Lamb's *Tales* and remedied them through introductory remarks to each play. He recounted the induction of *The Taming of the Shrew* and opined that "Shakespeare didn't approve of old fogies wanting to marry pretty young girls" (I, 113–115); he restored the "fun" of *Twelfth Night* got from "the formal, conceited steward Malvolio, by the sharp-witted lady's maid Maria and her mates; out of his dupe Sir Andrew Aguecheek, by Sir Toby Belch; and out of Viola by her duel with Sir Andrew, both of them being terribly afraid of each other" (I, 201). To *All's Well* he added details about Parolles (I, 231f); for *The Tempest* he described "the fun of the drunken sailors, of Caliban, and their conspiracy to kill Prospero, as well as the plot of Antonio and Sebastian to kill Alonso and make Sebastian King of Naples" (I, 289f). Furnivall was shocked to discover that Mary Lamb did not mention Autolycus, "the gayest and lightest-hearted rascal in Shakespeare," but deemed her justified since he was not part of its story but "comic relief" (I, 319). Thus, while "Mary Lamb told the story of Lear and his three daughters admirably, putting her own feeling into her work," he summarized the missing underplot of *King Lear* that she thought "needless to narrate" (II, 136–139). Furnivall also praised fullness, as in the tale of *Cymbeline*: "The tale of the plot and underplot is so well told by Mary Lamb — the two being so interwoven that they can hardly be treated separately — that I have nothing to add to her work" (II, 236). Similarly, he acknowledged that romance does not follow a straight narrative line but is instead a complex interweaving of materials; he claimed affinity with the treatment of *Pericles* by Charles Lamb, who "has well told the Tale of the play, leaving out notice of scenes not reproducible by him or by me here" (II, 201). (It is, of course, generally accepted that Charles Lamb wrote all the stories of the tragedies and Mary all the comedies.) When needed, Furnivall added full summaries to supplement the original tales, along with cogent quotations.

Although deeply respectful of Charles Lamb's work, Furnivall found omissions in the tragedies harder to countenance: "space fails me to deal with Polonius and Hamlet's caustic humour" (II, 45). Crucially, Lamb "was obliged to leave out almost all notice" of Hamlet's soliloquies, which embody his character, the chief interest of the play:

> Hamlet tells us his thoughts about life and death, about his unfitness for the task set him, his cowardice in shirking it, and the sorry figure he cuts when compared with the man of action, Fortinbras, and even the Player who was moved to emotion and tears by imaginary woes [II, 41].

Absent also are "the most pathetic scene in the play, Claudius's confession of his guilt and his inability to atone for it" and "the talk of Polonius." Furnivall added long quotations, analyzed Hamlet's irresolution and conflict, and ended compassionately, "How many of us are there who are not like him, putters-off and shirkers of unpleasant duties and hasty pledges?" (II, 44). Similarly, Lamb "hardly noticed the most striking scene" in *Macbeth*, especially effective in the theatre, Lady Macbeth's sleepwalking; Furnivall quotes portions (II, 108–109). He also regrets the absence of "the porter's knocking at the gate, the one touch of comedy in the play," that serves "to relieve the strain of the hearer and reader of the play after the dread scene of Duncan's murder" (II, 109). Further, in a useful pointing of relationship between plays, he compares its effect with Emilia's knocking after the murder in *Othello*.

In addition to full details of the stories and critical analyses of characters, scholarly information encouraged further reading and understanding. Furnivall's most significant point concerns the mixed-up order of Lamb's *Tales* that prevents the reader from perceiving "the growth of Shakespeare's mind," defined as a continuum through the plays, for which he provided a dating sequence divided into comedies and tragedies that he follows to arrange the two volumes (I, xi–xii). Furnivall wanted the young reader to gain a critical conception to unite the disparate plays and to deepen understanding that goes beyond stories. He sustained this objective in each introduction when he located the action geographically and emotionally or intellectually in the development of Shakespeare's mind. Thus *A Midsummer Night's Dream*, like *The Comedy of Errors*, remains in the Mediterranean, but is "a triumph of genius, the most brilliant production of Shakespeare's early time," because Shakespeare, who "first brought the fairy world into literature," unites "delicate and charming fairy creatures with the rough humours of the village orators" (I, 31–32). A key point about Elizabethan performance explains the physiques of Helena and Hermia: "Shakespeare evidently had a sharp little boy in his company, as well as a bigger one, and dressed them up as girls." Furnivall anticipated their appearance in *As You Like It*, where Shakespeare "turns the big boy-girl into a boy again for most of the play" (I, 32); the same short and tall boys enact the heroines in *Much Ado* (I, 141). Finally, *Cymbeline* is a reminder that Imogen, like Portia in *The Merchant of Venice*, dresses as a man: "(Shakespeare must get his boy-girls into their own boy's dress whenever he can.)" (II, 233).

In *As You Like It*, "the gem of Shakespeare's comedies," a life of Robin Hood, improbabilities are irrelevant:

> That a wedding dress comes for Rosalind out of a tree, or somewhere else in the forest, and that the heathen goddess Hymen descends from heaven to preside at her wedding, seem just as natural to you as blowing your nose does. You are under the spell of Shakespeare's genius, and you would not be surprised if your spirit flew out of your body and took a trip to the stars [I, 167].

Like most Victorians Furnivall relished Shakespeare's youthful heroines, whether Juliet, his "first grand figure of girlhood" (II, 3), or the "charm of Miranda" (I, 291), or the "fair girl figure of Perdita" (I, 319); perhaps this romantic sympathy lay behind his gentle acceptance of Mary Lamb's omissions.

A corollary of Furnivall's view of the development of Shakespeare's mind is special awareness of the late romances, where biography is a useful (or at least wishful) aid that fosters his admiration for young women in the plays—and indulges Romanticism. He identifies Marina in *Pericles* as the "first sweet maiden of the Fourth Period," along with Miranda in *The Tempest* and Perdita in *The Winter's Tale*:

> All begin in peril as babes by sea, and later on land, they blossom into womanhood, shedding gracious influence around them, and they live to charm the world for ever. I like to think of them as pictures, glorified by Shakespeare's genius, of the sweet English girls he saw about him on his leaving London for his native Stratford (probably about 1608–09), and to fancy that the reunion of father, mother, and daughter, in "Pericles," of father and daughter in "Winter's Tale," of husband and wife in "Cymbeline," has something to do with his own renewed home life by Avon-side (II, 200).

E.K. Chambers was customarily circumspect but convinced enough by the quality of the late romances to speculate that Shakespeare underwent a major psychological and spiritual change. Furnivall intuited a change emerging from altered parent-child relation, an especially appropriate criticism in a children's book. His reordering of the *Tales,* and separation into comedies and tragedies (printed as a list, I, xii), put *The Winter's Tale* last in volume one. This makes a felicitous conclusion: "And so, amidst the scent of flowers and the smiles of happy girls, we take our leave of the comedies of William Shakespeare" (I, 323).

The second volume's introduction discusses printing and publishing of plays, the theatre in which they were performed, some biographical details, and a boy's life in Shakespeare's days. Portions were reprinted in 1912 in Tuck's later edition of E. Nesbit's *The Children's Shakespeare,* considered in Chapter 5. Introductory comments for each play include such matter as Shakespeare's sources or the occasion for composition, but also interpretations by others: Tennyson's case that Shakespeare did not write all of *Pericles* (II, 199), a relation between Imogen in bed and *The Rape of Lucrece* (II, 233), Gollanz's argument in the Temple edition that a source for Imogen was Grimm's fairy tale of Snow White (II, 237). Furnivall viewed *Julius Caesar* as Shakespeare's reaction to the defeat of Essex's rebellion (II, 281) and judged Antony's funeral oration "perhaps the greatest speech that Shakespeare ever wrote," but also quoted his paean to Brutus (II, 283–284). However, all changes in *Antony and Cleopatra,* when the "lover and avenger of a murdered friend" is seen to "lose his honour, his manliness, and his realm, on account of his lawless passion for the voluptuous and beautiful Cleopatra, Queen of Egypt" (II, 295). In *Troilus and Cressida* Shakespeare "purposely rubbed the romance and glory off the popular legend of the Trojan war" (II, 291). Here Furnivall attempted a sense of history, albeit Roman. To do more would have gone beyond his intention modestly to expand Lamb's *Tales.* Moreover, patriotism deserves closer contact; for English historical plays, Furnivall sent readers to Shakespeare (I, xiii). Others—Stokes who retold all the plays, Quiller-Couch and Carter who devoted books to the histories, and editors who added one or two—made histories part of the canon of stories.

A final distinction of Furnivall's elaborate edition is the use of illustration. Lamb disliked and disapproved—an analog to his preference for reading over seeing plays—of Mulready's copper plates, "very rough and poor ones" (I, xi); Harold Copping's work was part of the grand quality of Furnivall's edition.

Copping, who studied at the Royal Academy and won the Landseer scholarship for Paris, traveled widely in Egypt, Palestine, and Canada, before becoming more permanently resident in Sevenoaks in 1902. He concentrated on designing children's books and also illustrated scriptural stories, and made contributions to *The Girls Own Paper* (1890–1900). Furnivall's edition has no color illustrations, but a great many pictures. Full pages are both special plates (thirteen in volume one and nine in volume two) and black and white pages (fifteen in each volume), for a total of forty-two. Smaller images are even more numerous: 13 three-fourth-page, 24 half-page, 29 one-fourth-page in volume one; numbers in volume two are somewhat fewer: 11 three-fourth-page, 13 half-page, and 15 one-fourth-page. There are no illustrations for Furnivall's "sketches" or added accounts of plays not in Lamb's *Tales*.

With such a large number, inevitably many are simple images of characters; but almost half of the full pages involve storytelling, as do some of the smaller images. Notably they either include different circumstances, or are strongly iconic. A few examples indicate Copping's imaginative range and skill in selecting cogent details. The Friar raises his arm over a frightened Claudio in *Measure for Measure* (I, 270), and Romeo blubbers in the presence of another Friar (II, 25). For *The Tempest* Copping has Ferdinand struggle to carry logs (I, 288), but also Caliban fallen with a burden of logs—and the added feature of a monkey on a branch above him (I, 297). A rather lovely female nude Ariel is twice depicted: holding her lyre, she flies aloft so that Ferdinand "followed in amazement the sound of Ariel's voice" (I, 304); and she lies more discreetly on the body of a black bat, held by wings (I, 315). Valentine with robbers in the woods features forester attire to make an iconic Robin Hood band (I, 56). Petruchio's antics of rage are rendered gently; he holds a seated Katherine's cap (I, 112).

For tragedies Copping's images are somewhat more lurid. Macbeth holds a glowing dagger that drips blood (II, 118), and an unusual glow bathes the witches (II, 122). The two most impressive pages are "Upon a heath, exposed to the fury of the storm in a dark night, did Lear wander and defy the winds and the thunder" (II, 134). The Fool clutches Lear, whose cloak swirls across the center—a typical representation, but enlivened by the use of lightning to highlight faces. Even better is the scene on the ramparts in *Hamlet*: "At the sight of his father's spirit Hamlet was struck with a sudden surprise and fear" (II, 52). Copping shows the moon almost hidden by a cloud, but light shines on Hamlet's face. The ghostly spirit of his father is a gray figure, well delineated as a Saxon warrior.

The claims of editor and publisher that Furnivall's *Tales from Shakespeare* is "the grandest and most costly one of them ever issued" seem well justified. However, many alternatives sought to sustain and develop enthusiasm. Not unusually critics respond and evaluate the work of Charles and Mary Lamb in different ways. A measured judgment by Humphrey Carpenter and Mari Prichard may serve as summation:

THE TEMPEST 23

" Come unto these yellow sands,
And then take hands :
Court'sied when you have, and kiss'd
(The wild waves whist),
Foot it featly here and there ;
And, sweet sprites, the burthen bear ! "

And Ferdinand followed the magic singing, as the song changed to a solemn air, and the words brought grief to his heart, and tears to his eyes, for thus they ran—

" Full fathom five thy
father lies ;
Of his bones are coral
made.
Those are pearls that were
his eyes ;
Nothing of him that
doth fade,
But doth suffer a sea-
change
Into something rich and
strange.
Sea-nymphs hourly ring
his knell :
Hark ! now I hear them,
—ding-dong, bell ! "

And so, singing, Ariel led the spell-bound prince into the presence of Prospero and Miranda. Then, behold ! all happened as Prospero desired. For Miranda, who had never, since she could

Harold Copping's small drawings, from F.J. Furnivall's sumptuous two-volume Lamb's *Tales from Shakespeare* (1901), were repeated by publisher Raphael Tuck in E. Nesbit's *Children's Stories from Shakespeare* (1912), a Reward book. An animal and the monster's simian qualities suggest the unusual island of *The Tempest*, while the comedy of Caliban's incompetence as a log-bearer is obvious in the monkey's reaction.

> [T]he first version of SHAKESPEARE to be published specifically for children. They are written in a clear, vigorous style, not often encumbered by the attempt to make the language resemble that of the original. A lot is left out: ... Sometimes, too, there is obvious "writing down" for children. But the literary quality of the *Tales* makes them outshine almost every other English children's book of this period, and they proved an immediate and lasting success.[5]

Nevertheless, these many attempts afford a deep understanding of Edwardian attitudes toward children's books and publishing practices.

Winston Stokes, All Shakespeare's Plays *(1911)*

Like Furnivall, Winston Stokes modestly demurred from any attempt or claim to equal the achievement of Lamb's *Tales from Shakespeare*. His title *All Shakespeare's Plays* (1911) and preface indicate completeness. He put the case and described challenging difficulties.

> It is hoped that the supplementary Tales may not be read in any spirit of comparison with Lamb's wonderfully blended classics; for even were they written with Lamb's skill, their nature and the subjects with which they deal must in themselves preclude so varied and beautiful a result. Here are the earlier and lesser known of Shakespeare's plays, the products of his unripe craftsmanship and the historical pageants best adapted to a stage far different from our own — all less widely read and talked about than the plays that Lamb has treated in so masterful and fairy-like manner. The writing has presented untold difficulties; to portray in foreign form the shifting battle-scenes of "Henry the Sixth," and guide the thread of an unbroken narrative among the horrors of "Titus Andronicus" must forbid an equal literary merit with Lamb's Tales, even if this had been attempted.
> But the purpose of this book is far removed from so presuming an effort, although the writer has, with Lamb, the definite desire to bring Shakespeare nearer to the affections of the young reader. If these Tales awaken interest in the less widely known of Shakespeare's plays, if they serve only as simple guides to render the plays more clear to future readers, they will accomplish their purpose.
> Moreover, there are a few notable omissions from Lamb's Tales, such as "Julius Caesar" and "The Merry Wives of Windsor," which have been fulfilled to the best of the present writer's abilities.
> While any repetition of Lamb's Tales has been strictly avoided — as it is superfluous to attempt what has been performed inimitably — it is believed that there is a need for a book containing *all* Shakespeare's Tales, and in this volume all are gathered — those by Lamb marvelously told, and the others at least with the effort to preserve, so far as possible the spirit of the plays themselves.[6]

Stokes, an American who also adapted *The Story of Hiawatha* (1910), has less knowledge of and enthusiasm for English history plays than Thomas Carter and A.T. Quiller-Couch, who retold with fervor and precision and without seeking the level of "very young children."

Stokes's preface makes clear his high regard for *Julius Caesar,* favored in the United States for its republicanism; and he preferred *Merry Wives,* with its ahistorical treatment of the comic character of Falstaff. These are Stokes's only retellings with illustrations. But his seventeen workmanlike tales, almost as many as the original twenty, are remarkably comprehensive. Lamb's tales fill the first 278 pages, while Stokes's continue to page 453. Unlike many who combined history plays, Stokes has one each for the two parts of *Henry IV* and three parts of *Henry VI,* or ten tales for Shakespeare's ten English history plays. The next largest number is five with classical subjects (*Troilus and Cressida, Coriolanus, Julius Caesar, Antony and Cleopatra, Titus Andronicus*). Stokes had to add only *The Merry Wives of Windsor* and *Love's Labour's Lost* to complete the comedies; all of the tragedies were in the original Lamb's *Tales.* In some ways, then, the new tales make a somber enlargement, albeit pretty illustrations enliven the text.

Typically both cover and frontispiece are fairy pictures for *A Midsummer Night's Dream,* with delicate fabrics, pinks and other pastels, characteristic of the artist. M(aria) L(ouise) Kirk (b. 1860), an American artist, also created pretty pictures used in several versions of Chaucer's *Canterbury Tales.* Here twelve full-page color illustrations usually focus more on character and costume than action. The cover, "On the bat's back do I fly after summer merrily," promises adventure and vacation time; it features a fairy, with golden hair and gossamer wings, carried by a black bat. The subject is conventional, but the picture is sharply organized. Kirk combines figures on the left with a half-setting sun in a pale blue sky above darker blue water and connects the two areas with an angled tree trunk. The frontispiece, "I will give you fairies to attend you," also has flying fairies, here above Bottom (brown ass's head that blends with his arms and legs, in contrast to his green short garment) and Titania (all golden — hair and dress, and gossamer wings). Kirk's best detail is a small naked Puck at the lower right; his short black hair, big ears, and antennae evoke the darkness of the woods and hint at something other than Kirk's usual sweetness and light.

Although many illustrations are conventional, both in choice of episode and treatment, small details pique interest. For *The Winter's Tale,* "This poor deserted baby was found by a shepherd" (30) has charm; abandoned Perdita is pretty, blonde, and bright-eyed as she looks to the viewer — baby's gaze engaging child. She is wrapped in a multi-colored striped blanket, the center of the picture, another effect to draw the child's attention. The shepherd, who kneels to face the pretty bairn, wears a green cloak and red cap above his purple jerkin; he also has leggings above his sandals, gear that suggests times past. These reassuring figures on the shore are in contrast to gray sea and sky. In Kirk's Forest of Arden for *As You Like It,* fair Ganymede's costume is Robin Hood's green, and Touchstone's sack has polka dots (56). The fashionable Renaissance dress of Romeo and Juliet, all golden and white, as they part from a rich palace setting, seems more cogent than the circumstance of separation (218). Italian settings inspire Kirk to echo Renaissance paintings that combine figures and architecture, a movement from balcony to landscape to a distant wall. Another display of rich Renaissance costume is Portia's ermine-trimmed red robe and perky black cap set against Shylock's luxuriant green and beige garments, in *The Merchant of Venice* (218). The Jew is given strongly Semitic features — pointed nose, black hair and goatee — that mark him as other and alien. Othello, while also racially defined (brown skin and black hair), is even more an image of Orientalism (248). The caption, "He beguiled her of many a tear, when he spoke of what his youth had suffered," encourages admiration and sympathy. Othello's beautiful long garment, dark green and trimmed in gold, as are his boots, enhances his white shirt, a contrast to his blackness. Desdemona's pale blue dress and pale green chiffon scarf, like her symbolic string of pearls, are very different. While her long auburn hair, free but held by a circlet, echoes Pre-Raphaelite beauties, her arms are bare, and she clasps her hands on her knees. The setting is again a Renaissance balcony, here with a view over the sea, a glimpse of distant islands.

The witches of *Macbeth* are perhaps Kirk's most unusual depiction. Although they have very long gray hair, they wear colored garments (red, orange, green) that swirl in Art Nouveau curves as they circle round a black cauldron placed above an orange-white fire (128). Suspended in the air, a naked elf stirs the pot. The cave is not simply a dark hole but a place with stalagmites. Macbeth's reddish hair marks his race as Scots, while his fur-lined knee boots and heavy cloak indicate northern climate. Kirk's illustrations are thus competent rather than exciting, but distinctively detailed.

Stokes's tales often deploy more vigorous style. The forest scene of *The Merry Wives of Windsor* is energetic and good-humored:

> [A]nd Falstaff roared in fear and fell upon his face for he believed these apparitions to be no other than uncanny sprites and goblins who had come to torment him. The supposed fairies worked their will on him, pinching him and burning his fingers with tapers, until Page, Ford, their wives and neighbors came forward with gales of laughter to mock Falstaff, who sat up and stared about him with so dazed and bewildered an expression that merriment was doubled at the sight of him [287].

A final judgment is that all forgive Falstaff, in part because he bears his misfortunes with good humor. The great comic figure fares less well in the two parts of *Henry IV*, where Stokes relates how Hal's "monstrous friend and follower, Sir John Falstaff — the dishonest knight who ruled in taverns, ... best of all delighted to go a thieving ... a fat rascal ... coward ... lies" (378). He omits play-acting prince and king, but retains the reforming talk of father and son. Kirk's Falstaff, somewhat a caricature — gray fringe about his bald head, red face and nose — sits in the basket as the wives order more linen to conceal him. This domestic interior is not Italian but English — lattice window, wood panels, stone floor (284).

Roman plays are typically difficult to turn into tales deemed acceptable for children. The horrors of *Titus Andronicus* cannot be specified; Lavinia "was subjected ... to cruel tortures that deprived her, as they believed, of any power to injure them when she should be set at liberty; however, she contrived to disclose to her father both the manner of her cruel fate and ... the authors of these crimes" (354). Stokes's language is evasive, and there is no banquet scene: Titus simply slays Demetrius and Chiron for revenge. Brutus, more appealing than the nominal hero of *Julius Caesar*, elicits challenging analysis:

> [I]n many ways not inferior to his mighty friend, — rather did he surpass Caesar in the pure and self-sacrificing flame of his patriotism, being prepared to render up his life and what was far dearer to him, his personal honour, in any cause that he considered for his country's good. This disinterested patriotism on the part of Brutus was even stronger than his friendship for Julius Caesar [324].

One paragraph covers the assassination, Antony's funeral oration is paraphrased, and Brutus's defeat is briefly told, before a mitigated judgment that the tragedy began "largely through the mistaken patriotism of Marcus Brutus" and his honoring after death (334). Moreover, the illustration implies that Caesar was foolhardy, "An old man — a soothsayer — bade him to beware the Ides of March" (326). Here Kirk depicts a Roman street scene with temples in the background, a large crowd, and the principals (Antony, Calpurnia). She displays sartorial splendor in togas (purple for Caesar and white with purple border for Antony), Calpurnia's yellow dress, and the soothsayer's green cloak over an orange garment. All suggest the greatness that was Rome, shown to decline in *Antony and Cleopatra*, a tale of Antony's "complete ruin" brought about by "Cleopatra's magic" that led to a "mad purpose of fighting Caesar by sea" and a flight that "undid the fame that he had won in many battles ... Antony's blind love which was akin to madness" (341). Antony, "as womanly as the queen he loved" (336), is the antithesis of ideals of manliness urged upon Edwardian boys of the English-speaking race.

An analogous uneasiness with strong women in history informs Stokes's *Henry V*. After Agincourt, Henry "had a sorry time of it with his new bride, for wooing her in her own speech, he said, was harder than the conquering of her kingdom." This truncated summary of a witty and complex scene is further glossed by a negative conclusion: "But the conquest of France was doubtful after all, for the new queen of England was able to rule there with the complete possession that a true wife should ever have over her husband — even though that husband be as great a conqueror and warrior as Henry the Fifth of England" (399). Edwardian attitudes toward gender, as we have seen, often alter Shakespeare's heroines; several others are cogent in *All Shakespeare's Tales*.

Richard II is a sympathetic husband, whose farewell to his queen Stokes included. He also paraphrased much of the deposition and modified an opening statement that Richard lacked great qualities—"lived with idle and profuse extravagance, requiring great sums of money for his royal pleasures" (366) — to judge the murdered Richard an "unfortunate king whose fate, although brought on by himself, seemed far more terrible than he deserved, lost both his country and his life" (376). The extraordinary wooing of Lady Anne in *Richard III* is absent, neither its irony nor sinister evil suitable for young readers.

Finally, Katherine of Aragon, one of Shakespeare's most revered heroines of history, much admired by Victorians and Edwardians, especially in performance and in paintings, is "a noble minded and generous lady who perceived too plainly the malicious purpose of Wolsey in seeking the Duke of Buckingham's death" (446). In contrast to others, Stokes gave full scope to her death:

> [T]he poor divorced queen, Katherine, also pined away in sorrow at the change that had befallen her. Katherine had a vision in her sleep that gave her to know the end was near at hand, for in a dream she beheld spirits robed in white and clad in garlands who crowned her as one of themselves. Katherine believed this vision prophesied her death which she felt was swiftly approaching her, and she sent to Henry, her former lord, a message of farewell commending to his care her daughter Mary, and telling him that even though unkindly treated, she still loved him. She bade her women to use her with all respect and strew upon her when she died white, maiden flowers, that the world might know that she had been a chaste wife to the hour of her death; and thus the life of this unhappy queen came to an end [453].

He accepted the play, which is in the First Folio, and favored one of Shakespeare's most remarkable women. Mary Lamb's preface, here included, stated her concern to provide girls some knowledge of Shakespeare's "manly book." Stokes's completeness emulated this and the Lambs' modesty. Other editions were more selective, assertive, and self-aggrandizing.

Mrs. Lang, The Gateway to Shakespeare *(1908)*

In children's books that include only a selection, chosen plays and added materials are intriguing. Mrs. Andrew Lang (Leonora Blanche, 1851–1933) is the wife of the man who created the rainbow of fairy tale books for Longmans and two collections of romances for children — most of which she wrote (Mr. Lang thought romance inferior to fairy tale!), though her name does not appear on the title page. Presumably religious issues allowed publication of *The Book of Saints and Heroes* (1912) as her work, edited by him. With its distinctively combined riches Mrs. Lang's *The Gateway to Shakespeare* (1908), part of Thomas Nelson's reward series, is her finest achievement.

As the cover promises, this book is fine Edwardian publishing; white cloth carries a bordered image of Titania, Bottom with ass's head, and an assembly of fairies who rest upon a lovely, curving, Art Nouveau frame. Touches of pink and blue and Titania's yellow dress and wings provide color within black line drawing; the title is in large gilt capitals. On the spine is Touchstone, another favorite comic. End papers, printed in a pale golden tint on white, display a procession of characters with identifying name plates above: Benvolio—Mercutio; Rosalind, Celia—Orlando; Macbeth—Lady Macbeth; Portia, Shylock—Antonio; King Lear, and so on. The frontispiece, a color portrait with a "William Shakespeare" signature below, further signals that *The Gateway* is more than stories retold. Its 336 pages include 16 color and 8 black and white full-page illustrations, compelling marginalia, and 203 small black and white drawings. With a debt to medieval manuscripts, these figures are salient, a source of constant amusement and further information in the Gateway Series. They also often proved too tempting; children colored them with varying skill and success! Several artists contributed to the book's compendium of styles—some still Victorian, but also Art Nouveau, including exquisite framing of images.

The introduction has biographies of Shakespeare and of Charles and Mary Lamb that combine facts with Romantic improvisation. Mrs. Lang wrote in a familiar style of "the baby boy" born 23 April 1564: "Of course his father and mother thought him wonderful, but that was just because they *were* his mother and father."[7] Having accepted "how very, very few things we really know about the man of whom we are all so proud," she improvised Shakespeare's boyhood, school days—and curiosity and imagination on market days:

> If there was not much business being done, he might sometimes get a story of past days from an old man, whose father had perhaps fought in the Wars of the Roses, or had seen the two little princes taken to the Tower. He never lost a chance of using his eyes or his ears, and on his lonely rambles he would think of what he had seen or heard, and make up stories of his own; and a few years later he wrote them down, and now we can read them in his wonderful plays [10].

This boy was father of the man in London, where Shakespeare added to his already acquired

> learning from books, from men, from the events that went on around him. The trivial actions and careless words of the people he met gave him the key to their thoughts, and it was out of this sure knowledge that he built up the characters in his plays. As for his stories, he took them where he would—from history, from legends, from romances, from old masques, from his own fancy; but whatever the source from which the tale came, he turned it out stamped with his own genius [15–16].

Details describe theatres, including "the wooden O of the Globe," boy companies, and Shakespeare's parts for boys. Mrs. Lang's speculation about Shakespeare's marriage tells more about Edwardian than Elizabethan views of gender:

> [I]t is rather surprising to find him at eighteen a married man, with a wife of twenty-six, whose maiden name was Anne Hathaway.... [He left after three years.] He did not trouble himself much about his wife or her three children, although, no doubt, he sent them money from time to time....

> [Shakespeare returned to Stratford.] As to his wife, it is probable that she still occupied whatever house she had been living in, and that she and her husband were on friendly terms, but we know nothing for certain. She survived him seven years, and during her widowhood her daughter Susanna took care of her. But she does not seem to have counted for more in Shakespeare's life at the beginning than at the end, although at her own request she was buried in his grave in the church at Stratford.
>
> The poet passed five contented years in New Place, amusing himself with his garden, with the affairs of the town.... When he got a little tired of the dullness of Stratford, he went up to London to have a gossip with his old companions, or to see Burbage acting Hamlet [11, 18–19].

One wonders about the response of child readers to this anti-romantic, if not acerbic, evaluation, but adults were perhaps amused.

The Gateway to Shakespeare has only seven plays, all very popular—four comedies (*The Tempest, A Midsummer Night's Dream, As You Like It,* and *The Merchant of Venice*) and three tragedies (*King Lear, Macbeth,* and *Romeo and Juliet*). An unusual feature is the combination of Lamb's retellings with substantial quotations after each tale. Mrs. Lang's selection of scenes records one Edwardian's judgment about what episodes might interest children and also indicates something about expectations of comprehension. A title precedes each passage.[8] Very often the color illustration, usually with storytelling qualities, is of quoted scenes. In *The Tempest,* "Ferdinand Meets Miranda" (54–62; I.ii.378–506) is part of a very long scene. "The Log Bearers" (63–69; III.i) is a complete short scene with P. Dudd's rather Victorian illustration, "Miranda: 'If you'll sit down, I'll bear your logs the while'" (64), a woodland setting where the two young lovers look anxiously at each other. A storm scene offsets such sentimentality. In a marginal drawing Prospero holds his child Miranda as they sail into exile; the boat is cropped. Opposite is W. Edward Wigfull's dramatic color illustration of another ship, this one sinking in storm-tossed waves that Prospero has called up, an action scene designed to appeal to boys; in the center swims Ferdinand, his head and red cap cresting the waves (37). Not all openings juxtapose the two modes of illustration; this one is unusually apt.

Predictably, Mrs. Lang enhances fairy lore; in *A Midsummer Night's Dream* three quotations are: "A Fairy Scene in a Wood" (94–105; II.i.1–85, 247–258), where the Athenian lovers are judiciously cut; "Another Fairy Scene" (106–108; II.ii.1–32), where Titania calls for a song to sleep; and "The Fairy's Song" (108; V.i.366–385), Puck's description of the end of the day. To create engaging illustrations of fairies is a challenge. In *The Gateway to Shakespeare* they are relegated to a few marginal drawings for *The Tempest,* but triumph in *A Midsummer Night's Dream.* Few illustrators of children's books became more than journeymen. In *The Gateway to Shakespeare* the exceptional artist is Norman Ault (1880–1950), here at the start of a memorable career. His "Titania met Oberon attended by his train of fairy courtiers" combines elegance, the gossamer wings favored by Victorians, and a cropped figure of an earthy, mischievous Puck

TITANIA

Fairies in *A Midsummer Night's Dream* are unquestionably the favorite subject, and Norman Ault's *Titania* in Mrs. Lang's *The Gateway to Shakespeare* (1908) is the most fanciful. The fairy queen's chariot is a snail's shell drawn by dragonflies — an insect modeled for the most famous piece of Art Nouveau jewelry. Ault's commitment to the new style is further evidenced by the curving frame where vines with fruit, leaves, and flowers also represent nature.

(74). In many ways, this is a rather conventional Victorian image, albeit details are fresh. These include pretty costumes, a starry sky glimpsed through dark trees that frame the brightly lit meeting, and a delightful curving row of white mushrooms, like lanterns, that lead from the bottom of the picture to the queen. Ault's extraordinary achievement is "Titania" (106), a beautiful, delicious study of size and of insect life — familiar to children through observation and popular information books. The queen is dwarfed by her chariot and the dragonflies that draw it. Most attractive is the Art Nouveau framing of grapes, vines, and delicate flowers. In these contrasted illustrations one artist explores alternatives. W. Matthews's black and white page, "Helena: 'Good sir, if you are alive awake'" (81) shows Greek dress enlivened by an extra swirling drapery above her back. But there is more: twenty-six small drawings, with a range of size and subjects, both fairy and human, decorate the margins.

Reliance upon traditional materials governs the image for *As You Like It,*

"Under the Greenwood Tree," a phrase often used to describe Robin Hood and as a title for children's books. Familiarity and attractive nature in the Forest of Arden may explain the length of selections: the forest life of Duke Senior and his fellow exiles, Orlando's care of old Adam, songs, the famous "All the world's a stage, / And all the men and women merely players" (142–160; II.i and II.v. and II.vi and II.vii). Jaques's speech sums up a man's life, and the scenes offer variety and a high ideal of manliness. Nevertheless, Dugdale's color illustrations of court scenes favor Rosalind, who presents a necklace to Orlando (116) and kneels to receive her father's blessing when they are reunited (138). Rosalind also dominates a black and white illustration when she and Celia look at Orlando's sonnets as he approaches from the distance (128).

From *The Merchant of Venice* Mrs. Lang gives an even longer quotation, "The Trial Scene" (188–212; IV.i.1–405) that includes "The quality of mercy" speech, which children often memorized. A young woman, Portia, proves herself brilliant in the law court, a defender against revenge and violence. This play encourages discussion to form ideals of service and justice. Two full-page illustrations that stress the idea of justice are very different in style, a suggestion of universality. A.K. Browling's "Mercy arresting the hand of Justice" depicts two classical figures in somber black and white (198), while complex, sometimes vibrant color and small details characterize a court scene by Henry Marriott Paget (1857–1936). Here is much to consider: Portia's red robe and challenging hand, the stereotypical facial modeling of the Jew Shylock, Antonio's splendid aristocratic dress and emotional gesture as he covers his eyes, the Christian image of the Virgin and child at the apex of the picture, the patterned floor of Italian marble that anchors it (206). But the Art Nouveau framing, a combination of plants and serene flight of birds across the top, is the stunning and memorable feature that sets it, and Ault's "Titania," apart. It is a far cry from E.H. Shephard's somewhat muddied picture of Portia bestowing herself on Bassanio, albeit the extraordinary decorative pattern of her billowing gown and his bright orange tights stand out from the impressionistic blendings of rose and brown tones (168).

Consideration of justice continues in the long quotation from *King Lear,* "The Three Sisters" (243–259; I.i.33–286), one of Shakespeare's most provocative and complex explorations of relationships—parent-child, friendship, lovers—with conflicting claims of duty and individual integrity. The theme from an old traditional story, in ballads and histories, fosters elaborate analysis, enriched by an illustration "Cordelia" (246). Lear, all white (hair, beard, and robe), sits on his throne flanked on either side by a kneeling Goneril and Regan. In a lighter foreground (beige and gray with faint patterning) stands tall and slender Cordelia. Her white clothing links her to her father, but her larger size emphasizes her distance from the court, many of whom crowd the background. Design is integral for this full-page story picture; it is elaborately framed by a narrow white border, and then in a large Art Nouveau frame of autumnal leaves against a pale blue background. Other full pages depict an angry Lear. He scowls with his left fist clenched and holds a scepter as if to strike in "Caius tripped up his heels, and laid the unmannerly slave in the kennel" (224), the work of E.F. Skinner (fl. 1888–1935). P. Dudd contributed a bold heath scene, "There did King Lear defy the winds and the thunder" (232). Dudd combines vibrant color (Lear's red cloak, lightning in the sky reflected on his white hair and beard, on the ground and against contrasting black clouds) with aggressive lines to convey threat, part of the darkness and suffering that dominate tragedies.

The quoted scene from *Macbeth*, "The Foul Deed" (282–189; II.i.32–78), is a fascinating study of gender differences and an exciting and bloody murder. On an elementary level, it forms a basis for discussion of good and evil; more intellectually advanced readers can explore psychological consequences. Dudd's disturbing illustration perfectly matches the quoted scene, "Lady Macbeth: 'My hands are of your colour; but I shame to wear a heart so white'" (288). In full stride she lifts her arms to gesticulate, while her husband strokes his beard pensively and supports himself with his left hand on a table. Her brilliant red dress, an aggressive color, is similarly contrasted to his dark green; both costumes are medieval in design. The castle interior is in bare Romanesque style, but bright golden light illuminates the glowing stone, darkened by the shadows of the fierce couple. A further emphasis upon Lady Macbeth, and a remnant of earlier tradition, is the Boydell Lady Macbeth (284), already discussed. Skinner, a prolific illustrator for children, contributed a startling ghostly image of Banquo (272), whose pale whiteness and serene expression contrast sharply to the disturbed Macbeth and solicitous Lady Macbeth. Finally, an archetypal battle scene, a mainstay of chivalric and epic stories, is "Macduff opposed his turning, and a fierce contest ensued" (280). Fighting is fierce, a body in the foreground and another falling from the left, while flights of arrows cross the sky behind. At the center are the antagonists, both in chain mail; Macduff holds his shield and lifts his sword, while a crowned Macbeth, with axe and shield, looks back.

Fascination with fighting, but before bloodshed and with an emphasis on youth, is the inspiration for T.C. Dugdale's "Tybalt draws his weapon" (304). A group of handsome, richly attired young men — Tybalt, as usual, in red — face each other in a street scene that anticipates Zefferelli's brilliant treatment of male adolescence in his film version of 1968. Sharply contrasted is a heavily drawn, black and white scene in the tomb, "Romeo took his leave of his lady" (318). He kneels and clasps the hand of the (believed) dead Juliet as he holds up his phial of poison. A bright candle illuminates her face and marks Tybalt's corpse in the background. These illustrations are at variance with Mrs. Lang's chosen quotation, "The Lovers in the Orchard" (325–336; II.ii.), the balcony scene with its soaring and seductive lyricism, the play's most famous moment. However, another color page, "Juliet: 'I come anon'" (334), glosses. She stands

Mrs. Lang's *The Gateway to Shakespeare* (1908), a Nelson Reward, had fewer plays but long quotations and memorable illustrations, including Macbeth's vision of Banquo's ghost, boldly represented by E.F. Skinner. Details of costumes, the fallen goblet, and serious facial expressions intensify the supernatural, often depicted for children.

on the balcony of a Renaissance palace, while Romeo kneels outside its railing and kisses her hand. A crescent moon and stars bring touches of light to an indigo sky. Romeo, like Tybalt, wears red, emblematic of intemperance, in a play that explores adolescent passion and impetuosity in conflict with filial duty and family loyalty. Juliet is a Pre-Raphaelite beauty; her long auburn hair hangs free, while her gown displays remarkable Art Nouveau style; its golden cloth is covered with circle designs in blue gray, echoed in the inner lining of full slashed half-sleeves that signal opulent fashion.

Mrs. Lang's combination of comedies and tragedies, the addition of well chosen selections from the plays, and the vivid color illustrations of key moments give longer life to *The Gateway to Shakespeare* by appealing to different ages. The Newbolt Report indicated that attention to art enriched the understanding of literature; this book is a rich source for such learning, a worthy Reward / Prize, an expensive volume at five shillings. Other selections were much cheaper; moreover, seeking greater simplicity, some retellers even made minor adjustments to Lamb's texts. Illustrations, even modest efforts, remain an essential part of Shakespeare as children's literature. An Edwardian child could choose among several distinctive series, each a collection of retellings of classic literature to initiate a comprehensive knowledge of the great stories of western literature.

W.T. Stead, Tales from Shakespeare *(1903)*

Books for the Bairns Series, published by W.T. Stead (1849–1912), were intended for the broadest possible audience. Classic texts in simple pink paper pamphlets sold originally for one penny. The series was marketed as a "charming series of well-illustrated and cheap Books for Boys and Girls. Used as an introduction to English Literature, these little volumes are invaluable."[9] The purpose is both pedagogical and social, since Stead's primary aim was to make traditional literature available even to the very poor.[10] He began Books for the Bairns in 1896 and wrote many texts himself. The first series, which ended in 1920, contained 288 titles. Many are perennials favored for children, nursery stories and fairy tales—both European and Eastern. Others are Greek and Roman stories, medieval, Shakespeare, recognized children's classics (*Robinson Crusoe* and *Gulliver's Travels*), retellings of nineteenth-century literature; there are also Christmas stories, plays, activity books, some biographies, and a substantial number of histories.

Stead, "the foremost publisher of paperbacks in the Victorian age," died in the sinking of the *Titanic*; his remarkable and highly influential effort lived on. His daughter Estelle succeeded him as editor and worked until 1920. Influence went beyond Britain; a French edition of some popular titles—but not Shakespeare — was Collection Stead, Edition française, a First Series of thirteen, in 1907, and a Second Series, 1910–1918, with nearly two hundred titles, including many accounts of World War I. Both French and English schools used these little books to teach language. Even after Books for the Bairns ceased, it had a crucial impact. Allen Lane enthusiastically read Books for the Bairns as a child; they gave him the idea for the Puffin Series, the first paperback books published for children by Penguin Books in 1940. Both Puffins and Stead's slim booklets were a modern version of chapbooks; Stead's earliest numbers even carried comparable advertisements — Cadbury Cocoa, Pears' soap, Dr. Scott's Billious and Liver Pills.

Tales from Shakespeare, Books for the Bairns #92 (October 1903), *As You Like It* and *The Tempest*, with thirty-seven pictures at a price of one penny, contains sixty pages, plus advertising.[11] Stead's introduction explains that he based his story on Charles and Mary Lamb, who, "nearly a hundred years ago wrote stories of the Plays in simple ways in order to give you some idea of them. To make the stories still easier for you to understand, I have altered the words here and there, but not very much" (preface). This method partially explains how Stead produced titles quickly. Comparison of texts reveals "not very much" revision except to make smaller paragraphs. Stead, who retold most classics of English and American literature, and stories from British history, including reports of the coronation of Edward VII, provided a rich alternative to didactic offerings of the Religious Tract Society and the Sunday School Union — though some of their little books are engaging.

A corollary of available retellings of English literature and stories from history for children was increased national / racial awareness. Stead's preface to *Nursery Rhymes,* Books for the Bairns #3 (May 1896) was an early answer to those who sneered: "Laugh at them if you please, these nursery rhymes play no small part in creating the ideal world in which we all live at first, and out of which we come to build Empires and to found homes." This guiding principle explains how traditional literature for children is tied to national / racial identity. Ambitions differ by gender, but mothers and fathers both contribute to form English consciousness and greatness. Stead eloquently puts the case for the lasting effects of children's literature and the crucial role of literature in life.

This early Book for the Bairns has an advertisement for The Penny Poets Series, forty-eight titles, of which three are Shakespeare plays: #6, *Romeo and Juliet*; #22, *Julius Caesar*; #42, *As You Like It*. Only Sir Walter Scott has an equal number. While Stead assumes and articulates a Victorian sense of Empire, he does not lack concern for others. Thus, although he refers to "little darkies" and "Curly-headed woolly pated blackies" in the opening remarks in *The Wonderful Adventures of Old Brer Rabbit*, #6 (August 1896), in *More Nursery Rhymes,* #19 (September 1897) Stead revised a detail in Jack and the Beanstalk, to replace "a rascally Jew" with "Screw, to avoid hurting the people who have been most cruelly used for nearly two thousand years." He hoped that his child readers of *Fairy Tales from China*, #52 (July 1900) "may never grow up to despise other people because they are not like yourself: they are often better than you."

Stead, a pacifist, published *War Against War! A Chronicle of the International Crusade of Peace* in the opening months of 1899. He participated in peace conferences—in Russia, the Hague, New York—and opposed the popular Boer War. It was to speak on world peace at Carnegie Hall that he sailed on *The Titanic*. His death was marked by the reprinting of his article, written twenty-six years earlier, about a modern liner (imaginary), where a lack of adequate lifeboats resulted in disaster.

Underlying Stead's work was his idealism as social reformer—he had stayed in Russia with Leo Tolstoy—that extended to literature. Heartily opposed to those who objected to fairy tales as superstitious, he aimed to popularize "these delightful romances of childhood." His preface to *Cinderella and Other Fairy Tales*, #7 (September 1896), is a manifesto: "there have been many collections of fairy tales; they have been the Perquisite of the Rich but with Books for the Bairns, I will make them the Privilege of the Poor." This is a reminder of the limitations of his own early life; Stead attributed his entry into journalism to the *Penny Shakespeare* and being able to use a cheap subscription library.

Edith Ewen's illustrations for *Tales from Shakespeare* repeat the pattern in chapbooks, one at almost every opening. Her simple sketches, which the cheap paper does not enhance, are usually imaginative and encourage the child's participation. *The Tempest* and *As You Like It* demonstrate how Ewen's visual story heightened Lamb's tales. Her imagination and understanding are somewhat stronger in *As You Like It,* with ten full pages and eleven half- to one-third-page illustrations, rather more than *The Tempest,* with nine full and seven half- to one-third pages. The tale begins with a charming little page who sits in the forest looking toward a group of deer in the trees opposite (3). The first full-page illustrations appeal respectively to girls and boys. "The two friends, Rosalind and Celia" (5), one dark and one fair, wear lovely, long dresses with Art Nouveau patterning. Celia rests her hand on the shoulder of her pensive cousin, who sits on a stool. Their isolation contrasts with a crowd scene, "The Wrestling Match" (9). Both Orlando and Charles are young, still standing as one tries to toss the other with a waist grip, but is thwarted by a push against his chin. Next is Ewen's most original and feminine moment, "Rosalind cuts off her long hair" (12). Celia, with long blond plaits, accented by her black dress, watches as a taller Rosalind, already attired as page, brings the scissors to the remaining side; at her feet are many long tresses already cut to create an attractive short bob. Male companions "Orlando and Old Adam," well dressed master and servant, are outside the servant's cottage (17). Next "Orlando finds the Duke at dinner" (20), a picnic in a sylvan setting where men are still courtiers, since peasants are not Ewen's view. Orlando, a line figure, stands in the foreground; opposite, as a three-quarter figure, he faces the viewer (half-page 21).

Although the second forest scene is traditional, "What Ganymede found on the trees" (23), Ewen's treatment is original. Ganymede reads and points to the letter posted on the tree under the carved ROSALIND. At the lower left is a rectangle with the text, "From the east to the western ind...," in large print. A child could amuse himself by comparing this with the small letters on the posted notice. Depth comes from the background, where Celia reads another posted love poem. In "Ganymede meets the Duke in the Forest" two elegant figures stand rather stiffly side by side; trees frame the picture with a cottage in the background (27). Much more distinctive — more figures, elaborate costumes, a sense of motion — is "Rosalind appears before her father and Orlando" (32). Rosalind kneels as the two men she loves extend their arms toward her. Ewen concludes her efforts to provide quotations with two final pages. "A Double Wedding" (34) shows four young people standing forward against a forest background; Rosalind and Orlando frame the group, while Celia and Oliver are half-figures because of the large inset song, "It was a lover and his lass." The lower portion of the final page has a decoration of holly that frames, "Blow, blow, thou wintry wind..." (36). Ewen quotes songs, often included in anthologies and school readers.

Illustration of *The Tempest* begins solemnly; an elderly Prospero (white beard and fringe on a bald head) sits reading in his cell with a view of the sea and sun behind him (37). Then Ewen engages readers in an opening with two half-pages that depict strange creatures of the island; on the left, four sprites emerge from large tree trunks, while on the right is "Caliban and his hedgehog" (38–39), a delightful and amusing animal. Next, three full pages chronicle father and daughter, present and past. "Miranda's distress about the storm" (40) is one of the best drawings, much swirling of waves, sky, and dress, as two figures stand on the shore. Her concern is set against Prospero's calm. His remarkable robe, decorated with flying bats, is here fully articulated, and he wears a black cap. Ewen glosses "How Prospero and Miranda came to the desert island"; toddler Miranda sits on serene Prospero's knee, as they sail in their little boat, while the ship that brought them recedes on the horizon (42). Although their expressions are serious, books and a basket of provisions reassure that all will be well. More amusing is "Prospero touched his daughter with his magic wand" (44); he leans toward Miranda, who lies asleep on the floor of the cave/study. Ewen repeats details of clothing, the same white embroidered dress for her and his flying-bat robe. The illustration that probably attracted greatest attention is of mermaids and fish that swirl gracefully in the water (47). In a box at the bottom is the song "Full fathom five thy father lies," memorable lines that are part of Lamb's text on the facing page. Similarly amusing is "O father, surely that is a spirit!" (48). As Propero and Miranda sit under a tree, Ferdinand, a small figure, walks up a path toward them. Others are conventional: the log-carrying (51), lovers watched by Prospero (53), playing chess (57). Compared to many illustrators, Ewen does not emphasize the fairy element, albeit the cover illustration, repeated as the final image (60), is Ariel flying on a bat's

Edith Ewen's pictures for *Tales from Shakespeare* (1903) in W.T. Stead's Books for the Bairns Series include an underwater scene that features mermaids, fish, and coral, but also a bell that links figures to the words of Shakespeare's song in *The Tempest*. Sold for a penny, the paper booklets, like chapbooks, made the stories available to the widest audience and appealed with illustrations on almost every page.

wings. In another half-page Ariel plays a flute as she flies above those shipwrecked (56). Most grotesque is "The Harpy," a sinister creature with long, straggling black hair, black wings, and claws that grasp the nearest of four men brought to the island (full page 54). But reconciliation comes when "Antonio is comforted by Prospero," an unusual and didactic moment chosen for the last full page (59).

Comparison of #92A with the original #92 indicates that plates were not reset. Although page numbers begin with 35 instead of 37, illustrations and text correspond exactly. The last pages contain two quotations, Act I, scene 2, and Act III, scene 1, broken into sections for easy assimilation. Edwardians expected reading to continue as the child matured enough to understand Shakespeare's plays. The publishers' redeployment of Stead's original Book for the Bairns indicates confidence that the books remained viable.

Ernest Benn attempted to rekindle enthusiasm for Books for the Bairns by reissuing twenty-five titles in 1926–1927 at sixpence each, a substantial increase. The price of one penny had lasted until the effects of World War I led to small increases. In February 1916, with #237, the listed price was two pence and, in September 1918, with #268, another increase to three pence. *Books for the Bairns*—#92A *The Tempest. With Selections from the Play* sold for three pence. The back of the cover lists Stead's Masterpiece Library, "A charming series of well-illustrated and cheap Books for Boys and Girls. Used as an introduction to English Literature, these little volumes are invaluable." In addition to *Stories from Shakespeare, As You Like It* and *The Tempest*, this list includes books of fairy tales, *Wonders of the Round Table, Saint George of Merrie England, Robin Hood and His Merry Men, Stories from Chaucer*, Scott's *The Talisman* and *Ivanhoe*, Longfellow's *The Story of Hiawatha*, and recent children's classics (Thomas Day's *Stories from "Sandford and Merton,"* Ruskin's *The King of the Golden River,* Susan Coolidge's *What Katy Did*).

Stead's Poets Series, devoted mostly to Sir Walter Scott and Shakespeare, had two collections of four: #63A, *Lamb's Tales— The Tempest, The Merchant of Venice, King Lear, Twelfth Night* and #63B, *Lamb's Tales— As You Like It, Hamlet, A Midsummer Night's Dream, Cymbeline*; and seven separate items: #64, *The Merchant of Venice*; #67, *The Tempest*; #68, *Twelfth Night*; #69, *King Henry VIII*; #70, *Hamlet*; #72, *Macbeth*; #73, *A Midsummer Night's Dream*. Several points are notable: Shakespeare is obviously a poet/writer of masterpieces likely to sell; preference is for comedies, but there is a history play, *King Henry VIII*, the Tudor ruler who initiated the Protestant religion in England and a Victorian favorite. Benn also lists *Richard II*, frequently cited for its powerful poetry and patriotic speeches. Both enlarge Stead's books of British history for the bairns.

Benn offered the series in two forms: with paper covers at four pence, or with cloth covers, seven pence, though some were available only in paper. Four Books of Poems for the Schoolroom and the Scholar supplemented Stead's Poets Series.

Book I, *Simple Poems for Reading and Recitation in Junior Classes*, and Book II, *For Recitation and as First Studies in Literature*, were introductory, while Book III, *Scenes from Shakespeare and Milton*, and Book IV, *On the Teaching of Literature in Schools, with more Scenes from Shakespeare*, relied heavily on Shakespeare. Prices were the same as those in Stead's Poets Series, with an extra penny if sent by post. Benn's editions are easily distinguishable; green paper covers replace Stead's original pink. The introduction of cloth covers made Books for the Bairns competitive with other publications for children, including schoolbooks.

Nevertheless, Benn's Books for the Bairns were not particularly successful; their time had passed — though, like earlier chapbooks, they are now eagerly sought by collectors — but they were an important vanguard of small books for children. Many Edwardian publishers, recognizing that children enjoy collecting, had series of retold great literature, typically in hard back with colored illustrations, yet still modestly priced.

Edith Robarts, Tales from Shakespeare *(1910)*

The Victorian publisher Ward, Lock started in 1854, employed the Dalziels — artists and engravers — after 1863, and opened a New York branch in 1882. They appealed to a middle audience; their reward books for children, a specialty, continued successfully in the twentieth century, even after the publishing house lost everything in the Blitz bombing of London, 29–30 December 1940. Edith Robarts "retold" *Tales from Shakespeare by C. and M. Lamb* (1910) in Stories for the Children Series.[12] This small book, approximately four by six inches and ninety-six pages, has a rich appearance. Its dark blue cloth cover is heavily stamped in gold — title, series name, and a frame for the pasted color illustration. End papers are gilt with decorative device — a white circle with red foliage surrounding a gold pilgrim's shell. Robarts's other books are *True Stories from History: Retold for Little Folk* (1909) and *Tales and Talks from History: Historical Stories for Children* (1911), illustrated by T.H. Robinson, published by Blackie and Sons, and *Don Quixote* (1910).

Like Stead, Robarts simplified Lamb's language; moreover, she added glosses to explain circumstances. Stead's changes are comparatively few, but Robarts's are substantial, including reorganization of paragraphs. A comparison of texts shows how the original was greatly reduced. Revisions that impoverish go a long way to explain why Lamb's *Tales* has maintained its popularity for two centuries.

Changes in the opening paragraph of *A Midsummer Night's Dream* indicate what was considered to be in need of revision. Mary Lamb wrote:

> There was a law in the city of Athens which gave to its citizens the power of compelling their daughters to marry whomsoever they pleased; for upon a daughter's refusing to marry the man her father had chosen for her husband,

the father was empowered by this law to cause her to be put to death; but as fathers do not often desire the death of their own daughters, even though they do happen to prove a little refractory, this law was seldom or never put in execution, though perhaps the young ladies of that city were not unfrequently threatened by their parents with the terrors of it.

Edith Robarts retold this as:

> There was once a law in the city of Athens which gave to parents the power to make their daughters marry whomsoever they pleased; for upon a daughter refusing to marry the man her father had chosen to be her husband the father was empowered by this law to cause her to be put to death. But as fathers do not often desire the death of their daughters, even though they do happen to be disobedient, this law was seldom or ever made use of [5].

The first difference is modification of vocabulary to eliminate unusual words and to heighten local domesticity: "citizens" became "parents," "compelling" became "to make" (also a change from gerund to infinitive), "a little refractory" became "disobedient," "put into execution" became "made use of." These changes, like the addition of "once" in the opening, seek direct reader response. Lamb's opening paragraph is one long sentence, ably punctuated for ease of understanding; Robarts broke it into two sentences. But instead of starting a new paragraph to describe Egeus, she continued and incorporated the next two paragraphs into one large opening paragraph, more to assimilate without a bold pause.

In one of her most attractive and self-revealing passages, Lamb deftly elaborated on the analogy between Robin Hood and exiled Duke Senior in *As You Like It,* when he goes

> with his loving friends, who had put themselves into a voluntary exile for his sake, while their land and revenues enriched the false usurper; and custom soon made the life of careless ease they led here more sweet to them than the pomp and uneasy splendour of a courtier's life. Here they lived like the old Robin Hood of England, and to this forest many noble youths daily resorted from the court, and did fleet the time carelessly, as they did who lived in the golden age. In the summer they lay along under the fine shade of the large forest trees, marking the playful sports of the wild deer; and so fond were they of those poor dappled fools, who seemed to be the native inhabitants of the forest, that it grieved them to be forced to kill them to supply themselves with venison for their food. When the cold winds of winter made the duke feel the change of his adverse fortune, he would endure it patiently, and say, "These chilling winds which blow upon my body are true counsellors; they do not flatter, but represent truly to me my condition; and though they bite sharply, their tooth is nothing like so keen as that of unkindness and ingratitude. I find that howsoever men speak against adversity, yet some sweet uses are to be extracted from it; like the jewel, precious for medicine, which is taken from the head of the venomous and despised toad." In this manner did the patient duke draw a useful moral from everything that he saw; and by the help of this moralising turn, in that life of his, remote from public haunts, he could find tongues in trees, books in running brooks, sermons in stones, and good in everything.

This juxtaposes lines from Shakespeare's opening scene, when Charles describes the Duke's situation to Orlando—"They say he is already in the Forest of Arden, and many a merry men with him; and there they live like the old Robin Hood of England. They say many young gentlemen flock to him every day and fleet the time carelessly as they did in the golden world" (I.i.110–114)—with Duke Senior's first speech (II.i.1–17, 23–25) that explains his life in the forest. Lamb followed Shakespeare's language closely, often simply copying it—though sometimes her change loses pungency and memorable diction ("Sweet are the uses of adversity"). Shakespeare wrote within the classical tradition of pastoral, but with resonances of religious controversy in Elizabeth's England. Lamb's rendering glossed her own situation of mental illness and corollary withdrawal from society. Robarts reduced their nuances to a single sentence: "The Duke who was driven from his country, retired, with a few faithful followers, to the Forest of Arden, where they lived a life of careless ease, like old Robin Hood of England" (20). The change from "friends" to "faithful followers" initiates her mitigation of salient values of life in Arden.

Repeatedly Robarts eliminated subtleties, opportunities to consider alternative ways of evaluating human behavior, and suggestions about character. In *The Merchant of Venice* Lamb retained Shakespeare's heroine (III.ii.149–171)— "the accomplished Portia [who] prettily dispraised herself, and said she was an unloosened girl, unschooled, unpractised, yet not so old but that she could learn, and that she would commit her gentle spirit to be directed and governed by him in all things." Robarts's Portia quickly delivers herself and her wealth to Bassanio without considering what is implied in her commitment (41). Adherence to attitudes of the New Woman may underlie the cut, as much as a wish to simplify. In *Hamlet* Lamb makes the people of Denmark note Queen Gertrude's hasty remarriage as "a strange act of indiscretion, or unfeelingness, or worse"; in Robarts's version, they judge her act "very unfeeling, and disrespectful to the late King" (80).

Robarts's six tales—*As You Like It, Hamlet, Macbeth, Merchant of Venice, A Midsummer Night's Dream, Romeo and Juliet*—are equally divided between tragedies and comedies. The cover picture, repeated inside (80), is "Ophelia in her madness," a subject favored by many great Victorian painters, but unusual for children. Ophelia's dress is white and her long golden hair hangs loosely. She looks more pensive than mad, as she gently holds up one flower taken from a large bouquet cradled in her left arm. On the right, Gertrude (green dress) and Claudius (red robe) watch apprehensively. The background is dark, but Ophelia stands in a white foreground. A somber "Hamlet at the grave-side" (88) is also against a white background, a three-quarter figure in black, sword at his side, who looks thoughtfully at Yorick's skull in his hands. On the left is a deep grave; the pale gravedigger's shoulders are at ground level, as he works with his spade. The sharp contrast between these figures makes this a distinctive watercolor.

Women dominate other illustrations. Juliet both meets Romeo at the dance (72) and kneels, "entreating her father not to marry her to Count Paris" (65). She wears a pretty purple gown in the first scene, where Romeo is a figure in gold who holds his black mask as he bends his face towards hers. As suppliant Juliet wears virginal white. Although Lamb's description was simple, "the terrified Juliet was in a sad perplexity at her father's offer," Robarts made it simpler by changing "perplexity" to "state of mind" (73). She also changed "Juliet" to "girl." Portia is illustrated not as the brilliant lawyer who defeats the Jew in the trial in *The Merchant of Venice*, but as a happily engaged young woman. "Portia rejoicing that Bassanio is her successful suitor" (48) wears a stylish golden dress with an Edwardian look that reinforces a clear visual definition of gender. Two scenes for *As You Like It* are conventional, "Rosalind reading one of Orlando's love-sonnets," observed by Touchstone, in red and gold jester's garb (frontispiece); and "Rosalind and Celia in the forest, finding Rosalind's name carved on a tree by Orlando" (20). However, the illustration for *A Midsummer Night's Dream* is unusual. "Oberon dropping the love-potion upon Titania's eyes" (8) features fairies, but not mischievous Puck or undignified dalliance with Bottom in ass's head. The royal fairies are pretty and youthful, he with fair hair and she with dark; their vaguely Grecian attire is tinted in cream and pink, like their wings. Against a plain white background, they have an obviously Victorian look, like a design for a biscuit tin.

Robarts "retold" Lamb's *Tales* with consistent and substantial changes. Some simplification is typical of small volumes, whether nursery fare or school readers printed in larger typeface. But, as one example after World War I indicates, such simplified versions did not supplant the original text of Lamb's *Tales from Shakespeare*.

F.C. Tilney, ed., Tales from Shakespeare by Charles and Mary Lamb *(1926)*

J.M. Dent in London and E.P. Dutton in New York published over several years a distinctive and sophisticated Tales for Children from Many Lands Series, which contains many fairy tales. The editor was Frederick Colin Tilney (1870–1951), who sometimes both translated and illustrated — *The Original Fables of La Fontaine* (1913), *Aesop's Fables* (1913), *Tales from the Arabian Nights* (1914). Several volumes featured famous illustrators: Charles Robinson for *Perrault's Fairy Tales* (1913) and J. Munoz Escamez's *Fairy Stories from Spain* (1913), Herbert Cole for Christopher Hare's *Bayard* (1911/1913) and Ernest Rhys's *English Fairy Tales* (1913). *Tales from Shakespeare by Charles and Mary Lamb* (1926) combines the frequently reprinted original text with illustrations by Charles Folkard (1878–1963) made for Alice Hoffman's *The Children's*

Shakespeare: Being Stories from the Plays with Illustrative Passages (1911), a collection of twenty plays (fifteen titles retold by the Lambs), published by Dent and Dutton.[13]

Since books in the series are 5 by 7 inches and 126 or 128 pages in length, there are only 8 plays: *The Tempest, A Midsummer Night's Dream, The Winter's Tale, As You Like It, The Merchant of Venice, Macbeth, Romeo and Juliet, Hamlet, Prince of Denmark*. One Folkard illustration is included for each. Both on the cover and as frontispiece, "That shrewd and knavish sprite called Robin Goodfellow," from *A Midsummer Night's Dream*, exploits the play's appeal. Puck's picture is certainly the most charming, and like four others will be described in the discussion of Hoffman's book in Chapter 5: "Ariel and Caliban" for *The Tempest* (14); "O Noble judge! O excellent young man!" the portrait of Shylock for *The Merchant of Venice* (65); "Three forms, wild and unearthly," the witches in *Macbeth* (80); "The Ghost solemnly beckoned him on" in *Hamlet* (112). The remaining three are interesting but less distinctive. "Two shepherds found her," a popular moment in *The Winter's Tale*; here the old shepherd stands holding the baby, while his son kneels on the grass; a flock of sheep move behind them toward the horizon (35). "'I care not for my spirits if my legs were not weary,' said Touchstone" (46) features the jester (cap and bells, wand, checkered tunic), who stands with open mouth as he speaks to an exhausted Celia and anxious Rosalind, who rest beneath a tree that owes much to Rackham and represents the forest pastoral of *As You Like It*. Very different is "Romeo whispered that he must be gone" (97). The lovers, beautifully clothed in Renaissance high fashion, stand just inside a chamber framed by a large curtain that Romeo has pulled open to reveal a balustrade, over which red roses cascade, with a distant prospect of trees beyond (97). Juliet, a study in gold (long wavy hair and dress, cinched with blue bands), has her arms about Romeo's neck and looks adoringly at him as he holds her with his left arm. His brown hair, blue doublet, and rose cloak add warmth.

Volumes from the Tales for Children from Many Lands Series were reprinted after World War II, albeit with simple cloth covers and minimal gold stamping. First editions include the same device of a thin, tall bird with open wings and a crown on its head; this fanciful creature stands in the midst of elaborate foliage opposite the pasted illustration and below a box with the name of the illustrator. Titles are framed at the top and the publisher's name and location at the bottom. Books like these perpetuate Lamb's *Tales* and sustain Edwardian extravagance, which was quite a development from Victorian sobriety.

4

Victorian Alternatives

Although the success of Charles and Mary Lamb's *Tales from Shakespeare* was extraordinary and unmatched, distinctive alternative retellings developed, in anthologies and single-author collections. They indicate Victorian attitudes before educational acts greatly strengthened the study of Shakespeare with corollary increased publication of collections and schoolbooks. Two anthologies combine stories from Shakespeare's plays with retellings of other canonical authors. David Murray Smith's *Tales of Chivalry and Romance* (1869) is an English example, while Abby Sage Richardson's *Stories from Old English Poetry* (1871) is American. Different emphases — number and choice of plays, other canonical authors included, and interpretation — reflect differences in nationality and gender. Children could also read about Shakespeare's life and one story in Eleanor Bulley's *Great Britain for Little Britons* (1887/1904), an analog to adult books of topography. Bulley liberally interlaces descriptions of the country with stories. Two collections devoted exclusively to Shakespeare form another useful comparison. Mary Seamer [Seymour]'s *Shakespeare's Stories Simply Told* (1880) is a comprehensive book with twenty-six stories, published in England by a woman, and subsequently issued in two volumes that include all the plays, while American Robert R. Raymond's *Typical Tales of Fancy, History, and Romance from Shakespeare's Plays* (1881) has only three plays but much elaborate and pedagogical material. Alternatively, Adelaide C. Gordon Sim's *Phoebe's Shakespeare* (1894) is personal, with eight imaginative stories, somewhat anticipating Edwardian diversity.

David Murray Smith, Tales of Chivalry and Romance *(1869)*

David Murray Smith's nine *Tales of Chivalry and Romance,* published by Virtue and Company in 1869, combines Chaucer, Froissart, Malory, and Shakespeare. The first three are obvious choices. Chaucer and Froissart lived in the fourteenth century, the high point of chivalry for England during the Middle Ages, when indeed both were at the court of Edward III, while Malory's fifteenth-century *Le Morte D'Arthur* is a synthesis and culmination of chivalric narrative favored in Froissart's *Chronicles* and Chaucer's romances. These authors, in verse and prose, embody and urge the high sentiment of chivalry that inspired nineteenth-century medievalism, which strove to recreate its idealism, not least in the forming of the English gentleman, a process that began with the schoolboy.[1] Shakespeare, a sixteenth-century playwright, is a less obvious but cogent choice. *The Enchanted Isle* (*The Tempest*) and *Shylock's Revenge* (*The Merchant of Venice*), popular choices for children, share themes of mercy and justice and romantic young love.

Smith justifies his decision to include Shakespeare when he recognizes the role of Charles and Mary Lamb, whose idea it was to "reproduce, in a form appreciable by the young people of the present time, a number of the very best stories with which their elders are familiar." However, since their versions "give only the most meager outline of the prominent incidents," his attempt is "to reproduce the whole plot, and all the most prominent characters."[2] The scale of Smith's stories supports his primary objective: forty-six pages for *The Enchanted Island* and fifty-three for *Shylock's Revenge*. The length comes from episodes and characters omitted by Lamb, and from rich descriptive passages and quoted songs.

The most substantial difference from Lamb's *The Tempest* is Shakespeare's subplot of Trinculo and Stephano, whose drunken antics combine with Caliban's wish to murder Prospero in a comic action that parallels Alonso and Sebastian's conspiracy against Antonio. Smith early names and characterizes Caliban—"half-man, half-monster ... so misshapen in body, and so brutish in mind, that he could hardly be counted human" (72). But, identified as "the butler," Caliban reappears only after all the shipwrecked nobles have been sorted. This "wild, ungrateful, and malicious creature, forgetful of all ... taught him, and remembering only the just punishment which had been inflicted upon him for his laziness and brutish habits, had plotted the destruction of his benefactors" (103). Drunkenness and greed for glittering garments delay their reaching Prospero's cell, so that Ariel and Prospero, attended by spirits shaped as dogs and hounds, disperse them. At the end, a sober and obedient Caliban vows to "be wise and seek Prospero's favour" (114)—a secular rendering of "I'll be wise hereafter / And seek for grace" (V.i.298–299). A visual image reiterates the need to choose good/duty over evil/self-indulgence: Caliban lies on the ground with an anguished look, as a head behind him peers from under the blanket; in the foreground are logs that Caliban should be carrying (115).

Ariel is vastly different, here clearly male: "he" in the text and as a nude winged figure plucking flowers in joy (169). His long didactic speech to the usurpers uses religious imagery: "'You are three men of sin,' said Ariel. 'Destiny hath made the ever-hungry sea vomit you forth'" (98). Like much of Smith's text, this is close to the original (III.iii.53–82). Smith cuts Prospero's praise of Ariel as harpy to make Alonzo's remorse and despair more immediate. "Alas, too! and it was for this crime that my son has had to make his bed in the ooze of the sea-bottom. I will seek him deeper than ever plummet sounded, and there lie with him!" (99). Repentance is the essential message: "Thus Prospero had accomplished his main object. By means of the magic visions which the nimble Ariel had so cleverly produced, he had brought home their guilt to the three conspirators" (100). This is kinder than Prospero's original objective—"Now will I justly punish their perfidy; and, if fortune befriend me, I will regain my heritage, and go prosperously back to Milan" (78). An added gloss assures that young readers distinguish between illusion and reality; the Duke/magician clarifies: "but, though your senses have been disturbed by witnessing mysteries and marvels in this enchanted isle, know that what you now see is real. For certain I am that Prospero..." (111).

In addition to "Full fathom five" (82) and "Where the bee sucks there suck I" (109), Smith quotes the sea-nymph's song, "Come unto these yellow sands" (81), inspiration for the most engaging illustration: a ring of winged fairies dance exuberantly along the beach; in the background shines a full moon, reflected on the water, while a row of seashells across the foreground is almost as large as the fairies (full-page 83). Three three-quarter-page illustrations feature the lovers: as they stroll in the forest (95), as they watch the masque (101)—with more acrobatic, dancing, sylvan figures and three quotations of verse (songs of Ariel, Juno and Ceres [100, 102]), and as they play chess in a great cavern (112). They give prominence to the romance of love, but another full-page illustration emphasizes father and daughter. In a three-line caption Prospero explains how they were hurried out to sea in "a rotten craft ... left to the mercy of winds and waves"; as the ship departs, he lifts his arms to the heavens, while Miranda stares anxiously (76). The seascape is Turneresque, wild nature, not the first reassuring picture of several small boats on gentle waves before a cityscape (half-page 69).

In the theatre, sets, sound, and light effects create an illusion of tempest; in a story, description serves the imagination:

> The storm that had separated Alonzo from his fleet, and had swept his vessel far away into boiling seas, grew stronger and stronger, until it became a perfect tempest; thick darkness, relieved only by the lightnings that played around the mastheads or flashed over the deck, shrouded the doomed ship; and the screaming of the wind in the rigging, and the noise of the waves as they rushed past in high white ridges or crashed in over the bulwarks, were varied only by the loud cries of the seamen and by the peals of thunder that cracked and rolled above and around. Every moment destruction seemed more near; and the last hope was dispelled when land was seen on the lee, and the voyagers knew that they must be dashed against an unknown and harbourless shore. But a more dreadful enemy than the rocky shore upon which they were driving now threatened the king and his court. The lightnings had fired the ship, and lights, as of flame, were dancing and flickering on all sides. The terrible moment at last came; and with loud cries and prayer and wild farewells, Alonzo and his kinsmen leapt into the raging sea [70–71].

Victorian enthusiasm explains this exuberant fairy dance beneath a full moon on the seashore of "The Enchanted Isle" in David Murray Smith's *Tales of Chivalry and Romance* (1869), which included *The Tempest* but not *A Midsummer Night's Dream*, where Shakespeare defined fairies, not least their small size, indicated by the shells in the foreground.

This is less Shakespeare or Lamb than sea adventure as lived and written by Captain Frederick Marryat (1792–1848), popular novelist of exciting adventures, or the prolific W.H.G. Kingston (1814–1880), whose best known novels were also of the sea and foreign lands explored by the British. *The Enchanted Isle* is a place of magic where betrayal is set right, all that was taken away restored, and young love blossomed.

Shylock's Revenge signals a different response to wrongful taking; Smith's retelling shifts the balance of interest and responsibility on both Antonio and Shylock, the merchant and the Jew. The trial scene remains central, but Smith restores main episodes/characters from *The Merchant of Venice* that Mary Lamb eliminated. First are attempts by suitors from Morocco and Aragon to win Portia before Bassanio succeeds in choosing the right casket, an elaboration of the subplot derived from the *Gesta Romanorum*, a collection of the kinds of legends retold for Edwardian children, notably *Guy of Warwick*, *The Seven Sages of Rome*, and *Robert of Sicily*, related in Longfellow's *Tales of a Wayside Inn* (1863). The increased romance element makes a case for "miracle-making love" (140) that somewhat offsets the intensity of Shylock's story. But as his title "Shylock's Revenge" signals, Smith concentrates on Shakespeare's complex view of the Jew, whose character depends in part upon Jessica, his daughter. Her betrayal of her father and the Jewish sense of family initiates Shylock's unmitigated rage and heightens his desire for revenge. Moreover, Smith's long account of Tubal, whom Shylock sent to find his daughter, relates her profligate disregard of the Jew's money and values. At the end of their meeting Shylock sends Tubal to get a gaoler to watch Antonio and exclaims, "I'll have the heart of him! at our synagogue, Tubal" (131). Smith explicitly contrasts Shakespeare's two plots in his transition to Belmont:

> We will leave the Jew to triumph in the fallen fortunes of Antonio, to watch over the unfortunate merchant day and night more vigilantly than he ever guarded his money bags, and to sharpen his knife stealthily for the cutting out of his victim's heart, and we will turn now to Belmont, where fair Portia dwells, and learn the fortunes of her many suitors [131–132].

After the casket episode, Jessica and Lorenzo, who increase the romance element, arrive in Belmont just before Antonio's letter requires Bassanio's return to Venice to try to save his friend and benefactor.

Part of the trial's fascination is Shylock's singular obsession. Smith builds horror by describing his preparations as the Duke examines Bellario's letter with Portia's credentials:

> While the duke was reading these, the court were startled by a harsh clashing sound. It was Shylock's scales, that had fallen to the floor; and the Jew himself was now preparing for his deadly work by sharpening his long knife upon his shoe [153].

When Bassanio and Gratiano ask why, "the merciless Jew" insists upon his claim in law. Smith retains Shakespeare's pun in Gratiano's reply and adds a further unresolved opposition in religion: "You are sharpening your knife not on your sole but on your soul, ... Will no prayers move you?" Shylock's reply is "None that you have wit enough to make" (154). Portia's simplified "quality of mercy" speech, is easily understood: "It is by mercy we are saved; and, praying to heaven for mercy, teaches us to render mercy on earth!" (157). The opening description of Antonio faults his liberality that, although

> in itself the evidence of a good disposition, was productive of results the opposite of good. It encouraged his young friends in habits of extravagance, and kindled against him the wrath of the Jews in Venice, who lived chiefly by lending money at usury, and whose business was marred by the generous Christian who freely lent without rate or usance [117].

When Portia asks, "What mercy can you render him?" Antonio's generosity of spirit — valuing human relationships over money — leads him to accept none for himself; he returns half to Shylock for use during his lifetime and holds the other half until Shylock's death, when all will go to Jessica's husband, Lorenzo. Restoration of Shylock's fortune marks a respect for family and exemplifies Venetian mercy, albeit problematic with the salient condition that Shylock become a Christian. Antonio's final intervention further promotes mercy; he pleads for Bassanio, whom "mischievous" (166) Portia playfully holds at fault for not keeping her ring, before the "night of happiness without alloy" (169).

Like *The Enchanted Isle*, *Shylock's Revenge* is a story of thwarted violence. Prospero's island, inspired by the new world but reached by exiles from Italy, and Belmont, outside Venice, are both remote from the friction and greed of opulent Italian Renaissance cities. The illustrations, which show location, not characters or action, encourage discussion of Italy, a place in direct continuity with the setting of Chaucer's *Clerk's Tale*. Five half-pages depict picturesque Venice: a small cityscape behind a foreground of many sailing ships (116), San Marco Piazza (121), gondolas below a bridge (127), a busy piazza with a gushing fountain (148), the Rialto Bridge with gondolas on the canal beside which people stand or walk (169). Shakespeare's fascination with northern Italy introduces children to the Renaissance. Moreover, the stories raise the question why both Chaucer and Shakespeare, major authors in *Tales of Chivalry and Romance*, retold stories set in Italy. Later, Smith pursued more characteristic Victorian fascination with Northernness; his novel *The Silver Star: A Romance of the North Land* (1880) includes a brief account of the mythology of the Northmen.

Abbey Sage Richardson, Stories from Old English Poetry *(1871)*

An American woman, Abbey Sage Richardson (1837–1900), wrote at about the same time as David Murray Smith; her primary objective in *Stories from*

Old English Poetry (1871/1891) was to introduce children to the riches of English literature, especially two major authors. Of sixteen stories, five are from Chaucer and eight from Shakespeare — *A Midsummer Night's Dream; The Story of Perdita; King Lear and His Three Daughters; The Witty Portia, or The Three Caskets; Rosalind, or As You Like It; Macbeth, King of Scotland; The Wonderful Adventures of Pericles, Prince of Tyre; The Tempest.* The remaining stories are also from sixteenth-century literature — two from Spenser's *Faerie Queene,* and three Renaissance plays (by Lyly and Greene), very unusual choices that give a context for Shakespeare, who is unquestionably the major author.[3] Richardson's preface, which leaves no doubt about her attitude toward Shakespeare, begins with an anecdote from her own childhood that vividly provides a context for children's literature in much of the nineteenth century.

She identified herself by age — "just about eight years old" — by race — "tangled masses of curly yellow hair" — and by intellect — "big eyes always hungry for 'something to read'" (iii). The last point is cogent because, unlike children some twenty years later, she had only three books of her own: the Bible, *Pilgrim's Progress,* and *Arabian Nights' Entertainments.* The first two were owned by most nineteenth-century households, and the third by many. They early formed Richardson's appetite for romance; she liked to read only stories from the Old Testament, "investing it meanwhile with the oriental landscape and atmosphere which she borrowed from the Arabian Nights, till she knew all its stories by heart" (iv). She also formed a habit of mind to read texts as adventures of romance. Then, one momentous rainy morning, she made a discovery while rummaging through the garret:

> two little purple-covered books. They were so small — only about four inches long, three inches wide, and an inch thick — that from their size she instantly concluded they must be real "children's books." She opened one of the tiny treasures, which was in print almost small enough to be legible only by aid of the microscope, and read on the title-page: "The Works of William Shakespeare, in 6 vols. — Vol.IV." [v].

As Beatrix Potter later affirmed, small books instantly attract small hands. Poignantly Richardson confessed that "the child did not consult anybody about the propriety of reading these books"; her father had recently taken from her "a delightful novel" as "not a fit story for a small girl to read," and she did not want to risk further confiscations (v). Names and adventures of this novel were long forgotten, but not Shakespeare. The little girl hid the small books, and "I cannot tell you how eagerly this little girl devoured these books ... better than Aladdin's lamp or his ring" (vi). Richardson remembered titles of plays that interested her — *Macbeth, The Winter's Tale,* and *The Merchant of Venice* in one volume, and *Romeo and Juliet* and *King Lear* in the second — and that there were others, now forgotten. Yet devotion to Shakespeare continued. "The dear little books have been lost long ago, the girl is now a grown woman, but years after" she told her son, "an eager little listener, of 'Lear and his Daughters' and

'Hermione and the Statue,' and many others which were locked up in the book and volume of her memory" (vii).

Stories from Old English Poetry is, then, a result of the relationship between an adult and a specific child—the circumstance that inspired many great late Victorian and Edwardian children's classics—*Alice in Wonderland, Treasure Island, The Wind in the Willows, Peter Rabbit, Peter Pan, Winnie the Pooh*. In parallel retold stories from major writers, Mrs. (Mary Eliza Joy) Haweis in *Chaucer for Children: A Golden Key* (1876) recorded her similar inspiration, a mother reading with her son.[4] Most startling is the capacity of young children to read such texts; their verbal skill and comprehension are a far cry from later expectations; indeed enthusiasm for retelling classic literature partially acknowledges both skills. Stories whose action and characters are understandable and exciting can offset lack of sophisticated reading skills. Richardson hoped that children will "love the tales, and the poets who made them, half as well as she does,—through the imperfect medium in which she gives them to you" (vii). This modest disclaimer is also a reminder that stories are not plays.

Richardson introduced the eight stories with a "Sketch of William Shakespeare," identified in the opening sentence as "one of the most wonderful men who has ever lived" (138). Modest origins in Stratford and something of his education, especially keen reading of "everything which came within his eager grasp" (139), define Shakespeare's boyhood. These details correspond to the American success story of the individual who makes good without privileged birth. Richardson even made his too early marriage and departure from Stratford an archetypal adventure, a variant of male Cinderella. Shakespeare "set out for the great city of London, like a boy in a fairy tale, to seek his fortune. And a wonderful fortune it was—greater than Dick Whittington's, or that of any other unfriended youth who ever came, solitary and unknown, to a great busy city" (140). Theatre attracted young William, who progressed from holding horses outside to acting within—after he joined a company to which a fellow-townsman belonged—to writing plays for the company.

> These plays of Shakespeare are the most wonderful of anything in the English language. They were so great that the people of that age hardly understood their value, and it was only after a century had passed that they began to be appreciated. Out of some of the old tales and legends which he had heard, the lowly bred country youth wove the most exquisite tissues of poetry and romance that the world has ever read. The forgotten creatures of some Italian story became like living, real people by the magic of his pen [141–142].

Richardson's paean exalts poetic language and romance as popular tradition: Shakespeare found inspiration in chapbooks—"generally translations from French and Italian tales, or legends, chronicles extracted from old English history, and sometimes translations from Greek or Latin poetry" (139)—and in oral tradition, the "old tales and legends he had heard" (142). Only two stories are tragedies (*King Lear* and *Macbeth*), each a subject from British history. Of the other six, three (*The Winter's Tale, Pericles, The Tempest*) are "romances" in today's genre designations, and the three comedies have strong affinities to romance. *A Midsummer Night's Dream* derives, in part, from Chaucer's *Knight's Tale,* the romance that Shakespeare returned to later for *Two Noble Kinsmen* (Richardson used this title for Chaucer's story). *As You Like It* relies upon the medieval romance *Gamelyn* and Lodge's *Rosalynde: A Pastoral Romance,* and resonates legends of Robin Hood. Choosing among the caskets in *The Merchant of Venice* comes from an old widespread legend / romance found in Boccaccio's *Decameron,* Gower's *Confessio Amantis,* and *Gesta Romanorum.*

Most retellers of Shakespeare's plays keep his sequence of action, but Richardson had her own narrative development. She created longer segments, with comparatively little dialogue, and changed emphases in theme and character, as her titles sometimes signal. Language and sentence structure are quite advanced. Long descriptions, especially of nature, and interlaced judgments add vitality and guide interpretation to high moral values. Parent-child and sibling relationships are major themes in Shakespeare, and Richardson's selected plays feature them. To engage young readers she emphasized already familiar materials before modulating into Shakespeare's stories, where she stressed traditional legends. Thus she frames her collection with plays that depend upon fairy tale, *A Midsummer Night's Dream* and *The Tempest*; between them *Macbeth* has witchcraft. Opening lines, formulaic "Once upon a time" or "A long time ago," promise the mysterious or exotic.

The beginning of *A Midsummer Night's Dream* combines magic of the other world with pragmatic, ordinary response (including popular language), the pathetic fallacy, and brisk judgments. Richardson begins not with the Athenians but with the fairy world.

> The king and queen of the fairies had quarreled, and all fairy-land was in the dumps. Queen Titania sat pouting all day in her most retired bower, and would hardly stir abroad for fear of meeting King Oberon; while he, attended by the mischief-loving Puck, spent his time in devising plots to tease his dainty consort.
>
> Thus it was that the dew forgot to fall; the fairy circles, no longer used for moonlight revels, had overgrown with rank weeds; the thick air breathed pestilent vapors; the moon shone with watery light; and all the months, missing their guardian fairies, were out of humor, so that stately August wept like changeful April, and merry May was as rude and boisterous as March.
>
> The cause of the quarrel was trifling enough [142–43].

Richardson's seasonal reference recalls Chaucer, and she displayed her rich knowledge of Shakespeare. The passage adapts Titania's account of the disruption in fairyland caused by Oberon's jealousy (II.i.81–117). Later Richardson combined a description of a fairy chariot (147) — abbreviated from Mercutio's Queen Mab speech in *Romeo and Juliet* (I.Iv.59ff), a play not retold in this collection — with Titania's bed and "this fairy lullaby" ([II.ii.9–19], 148).

Being called "knights" (151, 153) does not assure that behavior is chivalric.

Richardson's judgments of character — often intense views of gender — are precise: "Oberon, who was both jealous and exacting, — as much so as an earth-born lord, — " (143); "scheming Oberon" (146) approaches "with stealthy step" to drop "some of the baleful juice" (148); "Demetrius, a fickle gallant" (144), "the silly Helena" (147), "the recreant Lysander" (152). Hermia is more sympathetic; she shows pluck in resisting the strictures on marriage "in these happy days of fairies and Amazons" when fathers had absolute control (145). But follies of adolescent behavior, fickleness and friendship forsworn when competing for loves, are not mitigated. Similarly, Richardson pointed up the grotesque relation between Titania and Bottom: "the tiny queen led the huge monster to her bower" (151).

While there is no account of *Pyramus and Thisbe,* the "mechanics, some of the hard-handed men of Athens" (150), "the clumsy but well-meaning artisans" (155), are each named and identified by trade. The common man affords relief from royalty, both human and fairy. Bottom's theatrical ambitions receive special attention:

> stout old Bottom, the weaver, — Bully Bottom, as his comrades called him. He was, in his own conceit, the best actor of them all; the best for tragedy, comedy, or tragical comical, "Seneca was not too heavy, nor Plautus too light," for old Bottom, and he would have taken all parts in the play at once, with great cheerfulness [150].

Again Richardson introduced a line from a different play. She cleverly linked Bottom's pretensions to those of Polonius, who sums up his list of types of plays with this reference to the two Roman playwrights Shakespeare favored (*Hamlet,* II.ii.400) — an invitation to explanation.

Although Richardson's title is *The Story of Perdita,* her story of *The Winter's Tale* stresses adult characters and marriage. Her evaluations are incisive, beginning with Leontes: "a man of hasty temper and strong passions, quick in his judgments and prone to make mistakes, for which he was bitterly accused by his conscience" (158); "miserable Leontes!" (159), "unreasonable in his passions" (161), "all inflamed with rage" (162), "only grew more angry" (163). Leontes is an exemplar of anger, an emotion common in children, the lesson taught by Marmee in Louisa May Alcott's *Little Women* (1868). But a change from "madness" is possible. Initially disturbing, Leontes's emotions gradually evolve into virtuous behavior: "His remorse was as violent as his unjust jealousy, and he tore his robes and his hair in a frenzy of passionate sorrow" (165). But after sixteen years "Leontes, chastened by grief, has become a grave and somewhat melancholy man a little past middle age, a just ruler, and much more loved by his people than in the days of his youthful reign" (167). Hermione's restoration and the nuptials of Florizel and Perdita end the story, but the last phrase is "all the trials of Leontes ended in wondrous happiness" (175).

Women's strength explains this man's change of heart and fortune. When Paulina brings the smiling baby to Leontes, he looks "wonder-struck at her audacity" and tells her husband Antigonous to take her away. "But Antigonous, though a brave man and a soldier, dared not oppose his wife when she was doing what she thought right.... [T]he lords around listened to Paulina, secretly glad of the way in which she talked to the king" (163). Only Paulina can "console" Leontes after the news of his son Mamilius's death brings him to his senses. Her behavior models nineteenth-century response and management of death:

> [A]s she was a woman of tender heart as well as of strong mind, she was a genuine comforter. With her own hands, too, she prepared the body of Hermione for the grave; watched with it while it lay in state before the funeral, and superintended all the obsequies of her dear queen and mistress [165].

The apparent death and burial of Hermione occasion a suspense kept to the end. Paulina, perceiving that Leontes's "face often wore a shadow, and that many a sigh escaped him which only her quick ear heard ... could no longer keep secret a surprise she had been reserving for him ... a life-sized statue of Hermione" (172–173). The loyal and forthright female attendant has a male counterpart, Camillo, who chooses honor above immediate material advantage:

> Camillo felt a momentary struggle between his loyalty to the king his master and his sense of honor and humanity. On the one side was his personal safety, his ambition, all the motives that selfishness could urge; on the other hand, if he yielded to humanity, and spared Polixenes he knew not but the anger of Leontes might fall on him to such an extent as to strip him of his possessions, his title, or even his life. But the hesitation of Camillo was brief [160–161].

However, sixteen years of exile is a high cost; Camillo's subsequent decision to help Florizel follows after he "debated in his own mind how he might best serve the king, the prince, and his own wishes all at once." Richardson judges this male-centered reasoning, "it must be confessed that Camillo did not care much about Perdita in the affair" (170).

Richardson recapitulated analysis of young lovers in *A Midsummer Night's Dream*; love-sick Florizel is "a romantic youth of twenty" (167), full of sighs but honest with Perdita, who cannot "withhold her heart from this royal wooer, who was so superior to all the rustic swains, who only dared worship her at a distance" (168). Her "bright lips and shifting blushes" (169) are slight commonplaces compared to her mother's extraordinary character. Richardson's preface explains that she told her son "Hermione and the Statue," and the mature woman is exemplary. Accused by her mad and jealous husband, "the poor lady could hardly speak with a word of defiance, she was so overcome with sorrow and astonishment, but what she did say was full of dignity and promise" (162); she rightly has the court's sympathy. Brought as a prisoner to hear the oracle, "weak and pale from recent illness," Hermione "never showed to better advantage than in her patient endurance of her wrongs, and the hearts of all the spectators went out to her" (164). Hermione's qualities, like those of Griselda in Chaucer's *Clerk's Tale*, explain why these stories were favorites for children, who could find reassurance in the triumph of maternal love. "When Hermione heard this [Mamilius's death], the woman overpowered the queen. Her fortitude gave way, and uttering one cry, she fell prostrate in the midst of her guards" (165). The last scene's dramatic power, careful building of suspense, reaches a climax when the curtain is withdrawn. Richardson subverts Shakespeare's "wrinkled" and "agéd" (V.iii.28–29) to define an older woman's virtue:

> The face and figure was not that of the girlish queen who had sunk under the unjust anger of Leontes. It was that of a noble, dignified woman, adding to the loveliness of youth the serene and chastened beauty of ripened womanhood [173].

Because Leontes wishes the statue to live, Paulina bids the musicians sing and invokes

> Hermione to come down from the pedestal. Then the white bosom of the statue heaved; the clasped hands stretched eagerly forward; in another moment the image became a woman, and Hermione was weeping on the bosom of her husband and in the arms of her daughter [174].

Next Paulina explains the mystery: Hermione was not dead, but in a trance.

A contrast to this story of male folly and redemption, *The Adventures of Pericles* tells of a peerless chivalric prince, "learned and thoughtful, and possessed of the virtues of mature manhood" (246), "of very subtle and clear intellect, and also possessed of undaunted courage" (247). These personal qualities, not birth, are the point; for most of the story Pericles is an "unknown" who must repeatedly establish himself. Although Richardson did not specify the questing medieval knight in John Gower's adaptation of the Greek romance that is Shakespeare's source, she heightened these details. Pericles puts country before self-interest, accepts exile to forestall invasion, uses this opportunity to bring corn (largesse) to Tharsus, and leaves when tyrant Antiochus pursues him. After the shipwreck Pericles is almost naked when he reaches shore, but quickly acquires needed armor and tunic, through the generosity of poor fishermen, so that he can enter the tournament of King Simonides. Humble folk respect him for who he is. Richardson pointed the relation between appearance and character: "Notwithstanding the meanness of his attire, the princeliness of Pericles shone through his clothing, so that to the clear eyes of the princess he seemed the noblest and bravest of them all" (251). Description of Pericles's jousts in the tourney resembles many in juvenile historical novels. A page illustration marks his triumph; the princess puts "the silver wreath of victory" on Pericles's head as he kneels (252). In his eyes, Thaisa is "the most beautiful woman he had ever gazed upon. Her face was modest, yet full of wit and sprightliness, and she was wonderfully graceful in person" (251). A true knight, Pericles "proved himself as accomplished in the graces of the dance as in feats of arms ... skill in music, he took the lyre and improvised some words and music in praise of the princess" (252–253). Warrior and lover are mutually reinforcing in the chivalric ideal.

Although he dearly loves the princess, Pericles, who "felt it would be ungenerous in him to ask her to share in his fallen fortunes" (253), keeps his rank a secret. Fortunately, Simonides is comparably noble, "one of the rarest of men, for he saw that true nobility was altogether in the man and not in his surroundings" (253). He treats a man "with such distinction as his merits deserved"; and Thaisa, who "inherited her father's spirit," loves "the young hero who had shown himself brave in arms, skilled in the elegant arts, and whose conversation she found sparkling with wit and knowledge" (254). After Pericles explains that he is Prince of Tyre, "she did not love him more, since that was impossible, but she rejoices at his good fortune," encourages him to return home to claim his heritage, and insists that she accompany her love (256).

Subsequent exciting adventures include another storm at sea, the birth of a daughter and assumed death of Thaisa, whose body is cast away in a chest on the waters, her revival by the physician Cerimon at Ephesus, where Thaisa, believing Pericles to be dead, enters the temple of Diana. Chivalric knights like Lancelot, Yvain, and Guy of Warwick go through periods of withdrawal, a kind of madness during which they abandon their places in the community. Thus Pericles's extreme grief leads him to leave Marina, their child in Mitylene, where she is "instructed in all feminine arts"—to embroider, sing and play the harp, and be "an apt scholar in languages" (261). The narrative then focuses on the daughter who matches her father in talents and character—and penchant for misfortune and overcoming it. Marina's supposed protectors betray her. Dionyza is distressed and envious because Marina's beauty and sweetness eclipse her own princess daughter Philoten, "who is deformed and ugly" (261). Dionyza hires a murderer, and husband Cleon concurs after the death is reported; they give an empty coffin "pompous burial" and erect a monument with an inscription of praise. Evil, hypocrisy and deceit are as constant as virtue. In fact, the clever fourteen-year-old, who asked time for prayer, is taken by pirates; thus another set of adventures begin. Since their trade in Mitylene is of a nature to be edited from a children's version, readers get only reference to pirates, and then see Marina, "surrounded by a group of young girls," as she puts her education to good use when she teaches music and embroidery—with the implication that her knowledge of languages has facilitated her new employment. Technical skills are only part of Marina's character; she is also courageous and compassionate. At the request of Governor Lysimachus—"a young and gallant gentleman" (265) and "handsome" (267)—she comforts an ill and despairing stranger. He is Pericles, who revives when, to argue against his grief, Marina tells her own story as an example of overcoming self-pity and despair. Father recovers daughter. Pericles's vision of Diana leads them to Ephesus, where all are at last reunited after priestess Thaisa overhears Pericles's recitation of his adventures; kingdoms are extended and "long years in wondrous happiness and peace" are lived (269).

Because romance fosters high sentiment and affirms a happy ending, it is especially suitable for children. *The Adventures of Pericles* is quite long, twenty-five pages as compared to nineteen for *The Story of Perdita* and only eleven for *The Tempest*. Miranda, who has "grace and beauty" (273), is "the loveliest maiden" Ferdinand ever saw, while "the handsome young prince seemed to her something almost supernatural, and like a hero of romance" (277). Shakespeare's Miranda calls him a "spirit" or "a thing divine" (I.ii.414, 422). Richardson's attitude toward Prospero is ambivalent; now "a wonderful, wise magician," a good prince who had loved his people, but "was too fond of the study of magic, and all sorts of occult arts and sciences." The result is unexpectedly dubious: "one would have imagined that Prospero's inquiries into all the mysteries of magic might have taught him how to read the designs of men, but it seems they did not" (271). Nevertheless, at the end, within his situation on the enchanted island, "all Prospero's plans were working famously" (279). Always identified as the "magician," he gives no indication of abandoning magic, albeit it is less in evidence.

While the fairies in *A Midsummer Night's Dream* are mostly charming and ultimately helpful creatures who live in a parallel world, here they interact directly with humans. Prospero, who needs servants, has Ariel, from whom he forces a vow of loyalty "because he knew that, as fairies had no souls, he could not depend on his gratitude" (273). Ariel, whose principal role is to lead the shipwrecked, sings, "Come unto these yellow sands," to Ferdinand (276); he is given his liberty when Prospero leaves for Milan. To Caliban, "a vicious monster" (272) "whom no kindness could tame," Prospero assigns "all rude offices, the hewing of wood and drawing of water" (273). Caliban drinks from the bottle of "two common fellows," and "the fumes of the liquor" rise straight to his brain so that he becomes "partly intoxicated"; then he is "the stupid monster" (279). Richardson characterizes humans to make didactic points: "Alonzo was overcome with grief and remorse"; but Antonio, "one of those bad men who are not satisfied with their own wickedness and the fruits of it, but wish to tempt others to bad deeds" (278), yields of necessity and "pretended to be penitent" (280).

The opening and closing paragraphs that describe the island are more inviting than the actions that occur there. The place's magic is greater than that of intruders.

> Once upon a time there lived upon an island, far off in the Southern seas, a wonderful wise magician, with one only daughter. The island was far away from all inhabited lands, and no human being had ever set foot on its shores, till the magician came there. But it had been the abode of genii and fairies, and all kinds of elfin creatures, ever since it first rose from the bosom of the green sea. It was an isle of more than earthly beauty. All sorts of plants and flowers

grew there from spring to winter and from winter to spring again. Groves of palms and orange-trees, of willows and of oaks, grew side by side, and the island blossomed with color and beauty such as eye never beheld in any other spot [270].... [A]nd the enchanted island has never since known human inhabitant, but remains lonely and beautiful in the midst of the sea [281].

The resonances are less of Shakespeare than of William Morris, whose *The Earthly Paradise* (1868–1870) was retold for children by Madalen Edgar in 1906.

Much more cultivated than Prospero's cell and enchanted island is "a magnificent palace, built on a strongly fortified island" (189), a few days' sail from Venice. There dwells "the Witty Portia," a famous and wealthy heiress, who interests Richardson more than the Jew or titular character in *The Merchant of Venice*. She praises the heroine's intellect but as a resource to attain and keep her love, signaled by the subtitle "or, The Three Caskets" and by Langridge's illustration of a thoughtful Bassanio at the moment when he reaches out to touch his choice, a dull leaden casket between bright silver and gold (200). In this finely lined engraving Bassanio is a handsome. dark-haired man dressed as a courtier with sword at his side. Inscriptions (191) and the three verses read by the suitors (199–200) define the moment.

Richardson's details reinforce Shakespeare's creation of an intellectually brilliant heiress and define racial characteristics for nineteenth-century Anglo-Saxonism as well as sixteenth-century Italian. The opening description is complex and full:

> very beautiful, and one of the most intellectual women of the age. She was not only skilled in the working of tapestry and all sorts of exquisite embroidery, with which women ordinarily filled up their time, but she was a rare musician, an accomplished scholar, learned in the arts and sciences, and well read in Venetian laws and history.
>
> Portia was of that rare type of Venetian beauty which Titian has made famous in his pictures. Fair as the fairest Northern woman, her fleecy golden hair fell in wavy masses about her lovely neck and shoulders. Tall and elegant in figure, she bore herself like a princess who owed her birth to a race of kings. Her origin was indeed almost royal, for her father was the last of a long line of Venetian merchants, who ruled the commerce of the world, and whose countless ships furled their sails in every civilized port upon the globe [189–190].

Richardson's reference to Titian is another gloss to encourage knowledge of Renaissance Italy.[5] But Portia is also a reflection of Victorian enthusiasm for the Anglo-Saxon heritage that set England apart from classical / Italian / Mediterranean / Catholic traditions. Her father is a merchant, in trade, and very wealthy, as were the newly prosperous upper-middle classes of provincial northern cities in Britain (Birmingham, Liverpool, Glasgow) or industrialists in the United States. Most distinctive are Portia's intelligence and education, which include female and male achievements. Richardson early explained her easy assumption of the role of lawyer—children might well ask how she knew so much so quickly to argue Antonio's case—but more compelling is her insistence upon women's wit — the "witty" of the title implies sharp intelligence and poise. The conditions of Portia's father's will, and her respectful honoring of it, partially explain the unwed state of such a paragon, but another cause is reaction against her intellect and verbal facility. Some suitors

> when they saw her did not desire to marry a woman so superior to themselves in intellect, for she sent keen arrows of her shrewd wit right and left.... [W]eak-minded cavalierts ... retired quickly from the presence of a woman who saw their defects with eyes so quick. Portia used her wit often in self-protection, and with want of womanly delicacy, for in her heart she wished to defeat every wooer who had approached her [192].

Portia's "self-protection" does not exclude feelings for Bassanio; each remembers a love unspoken but felt through glances. The "gentleman ... most courteous in his manners, and in acquirements a very pattern of the time" (192) needs her fortune, but will hazard the choosing of a casket only if he has some token that she would like him as a husband. As a lover he is careful; as a son and friend he is oblivious. Richardson specified filial kinship and described a parent-child relationship to qualify character. Bassanio does not notice that Antonio's lavish generosity has put him at risk; he "accepted all his friend's favors with the graceful carelessness of a son, who finds the same joy in receiving that the indulgent parent finds in giving" (193).

Racial identity intensifies when difference means incompatibility; "the prince of Morocco, a Moor, whose dark complexion formed a strong contrast to the dazzling fairness of Portia" (198), is not a viable suitor. However, race is not defined solely by color; it is salient for Shylock's religion.

> The Jews were then, as ever since in Europe, a most despised and oppressed race. In all countries they were strangers and foreigners. All Christian nations united in persecuting them, and more cruel laws were passed against them everywhere. Their only protection against such social injustice was in making themselves as powerful as possible to resist it; and their means had been in all countries to heap up vast wealth, so that in their homes and synagogues they could feel themselves partly secure from their oppressors, or sometimes even purchase by the power of their money those rights which society otherwise denied them [196].

While recognition of violated social justice suggests sympathy, the Jew's response and behavior make him unsympathetic. Shylock, with a "clear, subtle intellect," feels "his own power and superiority over the Christians" who treat him with contempt. "Those qualities, which in him would have been great and noble if it had not been for his unfortunate birth, were turned to craft to outwit Christians, and to form schemes of revenge upon his enemies," especially Antonio, a rival in business (196). Shylock is resentful, a cunning dissembler, who seeks revenge before Antonio requests a loan and signs the bond. Richardson expressed no compassion for Jessica, Shylock's "frivolous and unfeeling" daughter (201), whose breaking of "her filial trust ... terribly embittered the Jew"

(202). At the trial Shylock assumes command: "his cloak of civility and blandness thrown boldly aside, his eager eyes thirsting for the sight of his victim's blood, and in his hand the sharp, glittering knife with which to exact the penalty" (205). Religion entails difference, and this Shakespeare story is a vehicle to instruct. Shylock and Portia, Jew and Christian, are as starkly differentiated as medieval sculptures of Synagogue and Church, carved on cathedrals in Paris and Strasbourg, one blindfolded and one seeing clearly:

> in a voice of tenderest compassion she urged on him the Christian law of mercy. But the Jew was deaf to her appeal. His religion had taught him that to exact eye for eye and tooth for tooth was the proper rule of dealing with his fellow-man, and he would have no better teaching than that of his own synagogues [205].

In the end Shylock agrees to forced terms, Jessica's inheritance of his money and a "promise to receive baptism and become a Christian ... but it was easy to see as he tottered from the council-hall that the broken-spirited old man would never outlive his baptism" (207). Thus Richardson anticipated a child's likely question, "What became of the Jew Shylock?"

A return to the happy ending of romance comes when Portia and Nerissa, "roguish" ladies, tease their husbands about surrendering their rings and are reunited. Bassanio and Portia "lived to the end of their days in such complete peace and happiness, as proved the wisdom of the old Merchant of Venice in trusting to the inspiration of true love to find out its idol, even though hidden closely in a *leaden casket*" (210). Thus the narrative comes full circle; Portia's father, not Antonio or Shylock, is the "Merchant of Venice." And Richardson made a final point about the parent-child relationship and love that is essential in romance.

Another of Richardson's retellings, *The Story of Rosalind*, shifts emphasis. Nevertheless, Richardson paid tribute to romance and a familiar hero when she began, "A long time ago," the Duke and his followers lived "as free and as happy as Robin Hood and his merry men." These "outlaws" in the Forest of Arden "never attacked and plundered any one, however, not even the rich and powerful, as Robin Hood sometimes did" (211). The "glorious" forest is a comfortable place where courtiers

> talked of art, of science, and of all things about which the outside world was busy, ... a delightful dwelling-place, better than any royal abode, for they lived there a happy and natural life, free from care; while in the palace, "uneasy lies the head that wears a crown" [211–212].

The well-known quotation from *Henry Fourth, Part II* (III.i.31) is a link to English history and a reminder that Shakespeare is part of the English language. Amiens's quoted song "Under the Greenwood Tree" is even more familiar because it is tied to Robin Hood (213–214)

Richardson centered contrasted pastoral simplicity and court intrigue on

Jaques; he is the same age as the Duke but "vented his bitterness against the world, and the Duke restrained him with his serene and happy temper." A world traveler, Jaques "had been so selfish, very likely, in the pursuit of his own pleasure, that he had done no good to anyone; so now, in growing old, he saw no good in other people" (213). The didactic message is that selfishness leads to unhappiness and unpleasant behavior, but a closing line offers rueful and compassionate judgment: "As for old Jacques [sic], the grumbler, he vowed he would go with Duke Frederick and be converted too; and let us hope that really happened to him" (226).

Celia and Rosalind, in contrast to Hermia and Helena in *A Midsummer Night's Dream* or Marina and Philoten in *Pericles,* are loyal friends. "Rosalind was the lovelier and more gifted of the two girls, but Celia felt no jealousy on that account" and delights in praise of her cousin (214). Their plot to go into the forest is "a clever one ... prompted by Rosalind's wit" (219), but she is also vulnerable. Orlando is "a youth of fire and spirit ... some learning and manly accomplishments. He talked well, rode well, was a little of a poet, and a tolerable musician" (216). Rosalind gives him her chain after the wrestling match, "half blushing at her boldness, — with the graciousness of the princess, blended with the coyness of the maiden, —" and then leaves quickly (217). While Shakespeare made Rosalind cleverer and more accomplished than Orlando, Richardson's nineteenth-century views of gender find an even match, explored in the wooing lesson (IV.i). As Ganymede, "a pretty beardless boy" who plays "the saucy stripling to perfection," Rosalind uses all her womanly resources. However, she is "not a whit more sensible than Orlando, except that being a woman, she could dissemble better, but loved the handsome youth after the same fashion that he loved her." Although both pretend at curing love, Orlando is "in spite of himself drawn to her by an interest which was, very likely, a subtle instinct of recognition." What develops is "a friendship ... in which Orlando sighed the more for his true Rosalind, and the masquerading maiden grew more and more deep in love" (221). After "the seeming boy fainted like a weak girl" upon receiving the bloody handkerchief, "events began so to entangle themselves, that Rosalind was fain to disclose her sex" (224).

Affirmation and escapism dominate *Stories from Old English Poetry*, but *King Lear* and *Macbeth*, part of early British history, have dual relevance. In *The Story of King Lear and His Three Daughters,* the parallel Gloucester plot receives sparse reference. The "good old Gloucester had been most cruelly treated for being kind to Lear" and the wicked sisters practice "horrible tortures on the old man." "A crafty Lord Edmund ... this base Edmund, who was a low-born fellow," serves as object of Regan and Goneril's passion and gives the order for Cordelia's death (186–187), but Gloucester is not named as his father. Edgar / poor Tom does not appear at all; in a minimal heath scene Shakespeare's redemptive ending is lost.

Instead Richardson judged the father — "a kind and generous heart," but "so passionate that [sometimes] fits of rage possessed him"—and his daughters. In a Cinderella contrast of temperament signaled by racial characteristics, the older daughters are

> proud and haughty beauties. They trod the halls of their father's palace as if they were already queens. When any story of suffering or complaint of wrong arose from the people, they always took the part of the oppressor. Their radiant black eyes glistened with hatred or sparkled with anger, but they never softened with pity or tenderness.
>
> But Cordelia, blue-eyed, golden-haired little Cordelia, had a heart full of tenderness and goodness. Her sisters disliked her because she was so meek and gentle, just as ugly spirits always dislike that which is pure and beautiful.
>
> [Reacting to her sisters' noisy protestations, she] had grown very reserved and modest in her speech. Sometimes, when she tried to tell the emotions which lay warm and deep in her heart, an impulse, half of shame, would check her,—a feeling as if these things were too sacred to be talked about [176–177].

Goneril, who has "a wicked temper" (181), gazes "unmoved on her aged father's wounded feelings" when she takes away his retainers; Richardson urged, "Imagine how Lear felt at being talked to thus." After more insults Lear "cursed her with a curse so terrible, that one can hardly imagine how she could have heard it and not fallen on her knees and called on God for Mercy" (182). Regan, following her sister's advice, treats Lear with "pointed coldness" and becomes "even more harsh and unyielding than Goneril" (184).

Richardson explained Cordelia's "Nothing" as thoughtful and discreet behavior; and she accepts the "handsome and earnest" King of France, who values her virtues more than gold, without a word: "Even if she had not thought of him before, his noble offer was enough to make her love him as much as a prince of so rare qualities deserved to be loved" (181). Any reference to a prince of rare qualities suggests Albert, Victoria's much loved husband, who died in 1861 and was intensely mourned. Kent's message to France brings Cordelia back to save Lear from her murderous sisters; father and loving daughter are touchingly reunited on the battlefield, and Lear rejoices to have one daughter who loves him and "grieved that he had not understand her sooner!" (186). Perhaps the most telling gloss concerns Cordelia's active role. When the King of France goes back "to his own country on some sudden business," she "was left in charge of the army" (186). She "did the best so young a bride could do without her husband, and marched her army out to meet them. But she was too much taken at disadvantage" (187). Although it was not uncommon throughout the Empire and among American pioneers, a wife's pluck, aggressive action undertaken through necessity, was not wished for.

Regan and Goneril's lack of filial piety and egotism are a mild preparation for Lady Macbeth's initial aggressive opportunism. In an extended and gender-determined analysis, the woman is always defined by her relationship to her husband, even though Richardson stressed her redemptive conscience.

> Lady Macbeth was reputed a worthy match for her noble husband in all the qualities which could become her station. Her beauty was unquestioned, her manners elegant and polished to a remarkable degree in that age of warfare; and though her mind was wonderfully bold and original, she concealed such masculine attributes under a mask of the most womanly softness and delicacy. Not inferior to Macbeth in any of the qualities which won him scores of friends, she far excelled him in strength of intellect and will, and in unshaken purpose. And her ambition was as riotous as his [233–234].

After his crimes overtake "unhappy Macbeth" and his "guilty imagination" conjures Banquo's ghost and dreadful nightmares, "Remorse could not bring him penitence" (238). "The unhappy woman," his subtler wife, is more wretched and reacts differently:

> In the first enthusiasm of her ambition she was not appalled by any crime. She could scorn her weaker spouse because he had feared to look upon the blood his hands had shed. But in her soul the revulsion of feeling had been greater and more terrible. More reticent and heroic than Macbeth, feeding on her remorse in silence lest she should add to the bitter thoughts that poisoned his life, she constrained herself to smile, and flatter, and play the part of royalty, while in her heart she carried an eternal wound, the slow agony of conscience. Nature avenged itself on the mask she wore, and in the dead of night, when she strove to forget her tortures in sleep, remorse became her conqueror [239].

This kind of analysis is very like that of Mrs. Anna Jameson (1794–1860) in *Characteristics of Women, Moral, Poetical, and Historical* (1832), subsequently entitled *Shakespeare's Heroines* and frequently reprinted. Edwardians praised Mrs. Jameson's analyses as "remarkable for delicacy of critical insight and fineness of literary touch. They are the work of a penetrating but essentially feminine mind, applied to the study of individuals of her own sex, detecting characteristics and defining differences not perceived by the ordinary critic and entirely overlooked by the general reader."[6] An advantage of Shakespeare's stories for children is that women, whose interpretations differ from those of male critics, wrote most of them and thus made an impact.

Additionally, the influence of the Gothic novel shows in a compelling first paragraph:

> Upon a naked, blasted heath, where neither tree nor bush could live, so barren was it in its bleakness, three witches, gray, crooked, and misshapen, hovered round a boiling, bubbling caldron. The fire crackled under the huge vessel, from whose blazing depths came forth a vile and sickening odor. The edge was lurid with sulphurous flames, which gleamed upon the horrid faces of the unclean hags who tended it; lighting up their ghastly faces, fringed with grizzled, scattering hairs, which looked like beards, and showing more plainly than the light of day their eyes,— staring and blood-colored, yet expressionless as the faces of the dead [227].

This description continues for another page of thunder, rain, wind, and an explanation that these witches' "only purpose was to foster crime, to hint black deeds to minds still innocent, to poison with venomous suggestion the most wholesome creature" (227). Macbeth's later visit to their cave is more Gothic, a sustained scary narrative — dripping walls that feel like slimy human gore, monstrous bats, gliding reptiles— to fascinate children (241–242).

Witches constitute a substantial threat; Richardson tempered praise of Macbeth the warrior: "His brave spirit, fearless before all real and tangible dangers, was a slave to superstition" (229). When the witches disappear before he can question their prophecies, his mind has "a thousand half-formed thoughts of villainy"; after an initial startled recoil he needs little persuasion to follow Lady Macbeth's design, identified as "*murder* " (234). Richardson also ascribed to Macbeth a manner so "tremulous and eager" that she wondered Duncan has no suspicions: "The shallowest observer could have read his agitation in his uncertain voice, in the tremor of his hand, his restless eye." In part, the decorum of Lady Macbeth, who "wore a mask impenetrable to all scrutiny," forestalls discovery (235).

Richardson again introduced a non–Shakespearean reference, intriguing enough to lead a child to read another classic. The only "consolation" of "the wicked pair" is their love, which she compared to Dante's "story of two guilty lovers, dying in their crimes, whose souls, even in the deepest torment, could never be separated, and who still found consolation in bewailing together their lost happiness" (240). Dante's stories retold for children include Paolo and Francesca, who fascinate, even attract, although they are consigned to hell.[7]

Eleanor Bulley, Great Britain for Little Britons *(1887/1904)*

Eleanor Bulley's *Great Britain for Little Britons,* published in 1887 and reprinted for Edwardian children in 1904, is a topographical survey of England, Wales, Scotland, and Ireland that provides information about cities, towns, the countryside, great buildings, flora and fauna, industries and products, biographical material about famous kings and queens, writers, and inventors. A question-and-answer format allows continuous breaks in the flood of information, involves the child reader, works to effect cumulative understanding, and gives a conversational tone to the telling of stories. *Great Britain for Little Britons* is not a literary collection, but its many and varied references demonstrate how much Shakespeare is part of national identity. That role extends beyond the British isles; Bulley's dedication is to three named children and "all English-speaking children."[8] Her purpose is to provide "many a thrilling story and many a pleasant tale," and also to inform and inspire:

> Besides the stories, there is a description of your own dear country, the land of which we are all so proud. You wish to know something about the kingdom that all the world holds in honour, — do you not? ...

> Remember, little Britons, you will be some day the rulers of this great country; so is it not right that you should know something of the laws, and the soil, and the manufactures of your future kingdom? ...
> I trust you will gain a stronger love of the old country, which, by the aid of her young citizens will, it is hoped, add many a noble deed to the proud roll of her glorious history [viii].

In this context of Empire, an early story is an archetype for rising in the world. In 1750 Warren Hastings, an orphaned schoolboy, could not go to Oxford after Westminster, but "had to go out to India to earn his bread as a clerk in the East India Company's service" (90). His career trajectory was from "a despised clerk," to private soldier, to company agent, and finally Governor-General of India. "It was all his own doing; he owed his prosperity to nothing but his own firm will" (92). Westminster is just one level below the most famous public school Eton, which Bulley describes in detail as the archetype — lessons learned in the schoolroom and on the playing fields — for creating loyal and devoted public servants (126–129). The book's first audience is obviously privileged, but still must work hard to achieve. Descriptions of Cambridge (110–112) and Oxford (120–125) encourage advanced study and sophisticated life — including at women's colleges ("Perhaps you, Winifred, if you work hard at school, may go there and take your degree the same as the men do," 125) — and the names of famous poets (Wordsworth, Tennyson) who attended.

Shakespeare is not among them, but cited as an authority in the account of Christ Church, the Oxford college built by Cardinal Wolsey: "You can read about him in Shakespeare's play, 'Henry VIII'" (123).[9] Monmouthshire, which begins with King Arthur and the Round Table, including an illustration of "Knights Tilting," concludes with the castle:

> [S]pecially famous, as it was here that the brave King Henry V. was born. Monmouth was then a Welsh county, and Henry V. always called himself a Welshman; and Shakespeare in one of his plays, makes a Welshman tell the king: "All the water in the Wye cannot wash your majesty's Welsh plood out of your pody, I can tell you that."
> The Welsh speak English in this way even now; they always put a *p* where a *b* should be. There is a great deal more in Shakespeare about "Madcap Harry," afterwards the wise King Henry V., that I think you would like to read for yourself [68].

Here Bulley linked renowned heroes of chivalry to Welsh contribution to Great Britain; at the same time, the quotation demonstrates Shakespeare's skill in using dialect in *Henry V* (IV.vii.106) and signals the unity of British races against a common enemy, France. Less serious is the fact that Shakespeare is at least partially responsible for an unusual piece of furniture: "Perhaps you have heard of the Great Bed of Ware. Shakespeare mentions it in one of his plays" (134).

Bulley referred to Shakespeare more than to any other writer. A reminder that he wrote plays, and a bit of theatre history, comes in the biographical note about David Garrick:

> We must always honour him, for he was the first man who ever acted the plays of Shakespeare in the way they ought to be acted. Other actors who had been before him never acted the plays naturally, so that the people who spoke in them would seem to be real living people. When Garrick, however, acted a king you felt you were listening to a real king, and if he had to act a clown (for there *are* clowns in Shakespeare's plays), why, then, he changed his face and voice, and was so merry and funny that no one could help laughing [61].

Garrick was born at Hereford but attended school in Lichfield — Dr. Samuel Johnson was a schoolmaster — near Shakespeare's birthplace, Stratford-on-Avon.

> That little town is well known all over the world; and I have heard that a man who came from America, crossed the great Atlantic Ocean to see Stratford-on-Avon, and then went home again without visiting any other place in England [96].

This may be a wry observation about the provincialism and eccentricity of Americans, but it is also a statement that for some, Shakespeare is England. The traveler wanted to see "a little white-washed cottage, quite a common-looking place: there are fifty better in many villages." Today not all would describe the birthplace as "a humble cottage"—another indication that the audience are of considerable means!—but Bulley's characterization stands easily: "He was a wonderful man, and he seems to have written about almost everything you can think of. You will like to read his books when you are a little older; perhaps even now you might like to read such a play as the 'Merchant of Venice'" (96).

Bulley told of the Jew's bond, Shylock's dissembling and hatred of Christians, the trial, and Portia — "a beautiful young lady ... [who] could not bear to think of such cruelty being done to this Antonio" (97). Bassanio, the caskets, betrothals, weddings, Jessica — none is mentioned. The story, longer than most, progresses through the child's questions and comments, which are italicized: "*What is it about? / What a horrid man! did he get the pound of flesh? I hope he didn't. / I am so glad! But how vexed Shylock must have been!*" (96–98).

The final critical response is, "*I did not know Shakespeare's plays were stories like this; I thought it was all one piece of poetry.*" Bulley explained that Shakespeare wrote plays to be acted and indeed acted himself. "*Which?* ... he acted the Ghost — a very humble part — in his play of *Hamlet*" (98). At the bottom of this page is an illustration of Anne Hathaway's cottage opposite another small picture — a roundel portrait in the center, Shakespeare's house on the left and Stratford church on the right (99). Child readers who visited Shakespeare's home would know what to look for.

Mary Seamer Seymour, Shakespeare's Stories Simply Told *(1880)*

The most impressive Victorian collection devoted entirely to Shakespeare is Mary Seamer's *Shakespeare's Stories Simply Told* (1880) in a small Classic Stories Simply Told Series, to which she later contributed *Chaucer's Stories Simply Told* (1884). Other volumes were Charles Henry Hanson's *Stories of the Days of King Arthur, The Siege of Troy, and the Wanderings of Ulysses* and *The Wanderings of Æneas and the Founding of Rome*. Publisher Thomas Nelson, a Scottish Evangelical, issued many books with religious content, but built financial success upon children's books, including extravagant Edwardian volumes like *The Gateway to Shakespeare*, considered in Chapter 3. Seymour's goal is broad:

> These stories have been put together in the hope that they may familiarize children with our great national dramatist. Care has been taken to omit any expression which might be deemed unsuited to young readers, and to introduce all the familiar passages aptly termed the "Beauties of Shakespeare."[10]

Here are both Victorian patriotism and high moral standards, a continuing tradition begun in fiction published by the Religious Tract Society (RTS) and the Society for the Propagation of Christian Knowledge (SPCK).[11] In addition, beautiful language marks Shakespeare's quality and popularity. Seymour's inclusiveness is impressive: 26 plays retold and 123 of 483 outline engravings from *The Spirit of the Plays of Shakespeare* (1833) by Frank Howard (1843?–1901) — narrative scenes with captions from Seymour's text. In 312 pages *Shakespeare: Stories Simply Told* is comprehensive, accessible, and constantly diverting. Changing running titles on each page and captioned pictures make the action easy to follow. Sturdy binding and quality reproduction of pictures attain Reward quality.

Some of Seymour's omissions indicate a Victorian modesty not found in Lamb's *Tales*: *All's Well*, *Measure for Measure*, *Much Ado*, and *Two Gentlemen*, which all have somewhat tricky sexual matter. But she included *Troilus and Cressida*, albeit mostly about the Trojan War and without cynical and manipulative Tiresias. With Seymour's addition of *Coriolanus* and *Julius Caesar*, *Shakespeare's Stories Simply Told* has a rich component of classical stories. Later editions include both *Titus Andronicus* and *Antony and Cleopatra*, initially deemed unsuitable but necessary for completeness. Seymour's greatest innovation is her emphasis on English history plays, which support the racial pride sounded in "our great national dramatist." But this is more than simple patriotism; many thought that Shakespeare presented history with greater understanding than any account in a history book. Indeed Shakespeare stories are in schoolbooks of both history and literature, discussed in Chapter 6.

The original collection was reprinted as "two companion volumes," each priced at 3s.6d. The combined *Shakespeare's Stories* has 312 pages; *Shakespeare's*

Stories Simply Told: Comedies (1883) and *Shakespeare's Stories Simply Told: Tragedies and Historical Plays* (1899) are, respectively, 234 and 235 pages, for a total increase of 157 pages to accommodate all of the plays.[12] The *Comedies* number sixteen, an increase that comes with the four original omissions from Lamb, plus *Love's Labour's Lost* and *The Merry Wives of Windsor*. Most startling is *Titus Andronicus,* perhaps placed here because *Tragedies and Historical Plays* was crowded. *Cymbeline* is with historical plays, an early recognition of Shakespeare's comprehensive treatment of English history and also an adherence to divisions of the First Folio. Seymour would have been unlikely to employ Edward Dowden's argument, in *Shakespeare* (1877), that the four late plays are neither comedies nor tragedies but a special category of romances—now the usual division in Shakespeare's *Works*. *Antony and Cleopatra,* the previously absent Roman history / tragedy, brought Seymour's total number of stories to thirty-four. Since she told *Henry IV* and *Henry VI* as each one story rather than two and three separate items, she retold all thirty-seven plays. Thus before the end of the nineteenth century one woman had written a complete children's stories of Shakespeare's plays. Identical prefaces to the companion volumes indicate "the favourable reception" of the first book. Seymour's second paragraph modestly claims that her stories are but outlines: "The appreciation of the Plays themselves, and of their detailed beauties, belongs to more mature years; but that will not be the less keen because the appetite has been whetted and the curiosity aroused in early youth" (v).

The number of illustrations also increased; *Comedies* has 83 and *Tragedies and Historical Plays* 98, a total of 181, an added 58. The number of drawings for added plays tends to be higher than in the original edition, perhaps to offset challenging material. *Hamlet* and *Othello* are highest with seven, also the number for *Much Ado About Nothing* and *The Merry Wives of Windsor*. More notable are eight for *Measure for Measure* and nine for *Antony and Cleopatra*. Seymour interlaced Victorian ideas and substantial use of Shakespeare's words. Captions from her text for Howard's illustrations emphasize the link between verbal and visual, while the list of illustrations gives descriptive statements.

Cymbeline begins, "In the old times, when our country was called Britain, a king reigned whose name was..." (45 and 80). Happy workings of chance inform Imogen's flight:

> [S]trangely enough the lady unconsciously took her way to the dwelling where her own brothers had lived since their disappearance when they were infants! ... [Belarius had] reared them with all tenderness. Though they lived in a forest cave, they were not uneducated, and grew up into fine youths, fond of hunting and other sports, and desirous above all else of going to the wars [49 and 84].

Two illustrations depict the siblings: "They stopped at the entrance of the cave" (50 and 85), the initial meeting; and "Then carrying her to a shady spot, the youths laid their unknown sister upon the grass" (51 and 86). They wear rough skins, a contrast with Imogen's boy's apparel. Most telling is the felicitous conclusion, when all are together after the battle:

> Every one was happy — too happy to think of punishing even the wicked Iachimo....
> "Kneel not to me," said Posthumus. "The power that I have on you is to spare you, the malice towards you to forgive you. Live, and deal with others better."
> The bad queen was taken ill, and died more from despair than from any other cause, having failed in her wicked plans; and her son Cloten was slain in some miserable quarrel. But those who deserved happiness won it; and a peace was concluded between the Romans and the Britons which remained uninterrupted for many years; and these were the words in which Cymbeline proclaimed it: "Publish we this peace to all our subjects. Set we forward: Let a Roman and a British ensign wave friendly together" [54 and 89].

Even though he won the battle Cymbeline submits to the greater authority of Imperial Rome, a model for colonial relations within the British Empire in the nineteenth century.

Cymbeline, the fourth item in *Shakespeare's Stories Simply Told* — after three set in Italy (*The Tempest, The Merchant of Venice, The Taming of the Shrew*) — introduces early British history. *Macbeth* is thirteen, while *King John* through *King Henry VIII* are eighteen through twenty-four, followed only by *Troilus and Cressida* and *Coriolanus,* glosses from classical history. In the companion volume *Cymbeline* is fifth, after *Coriolanus, Julius Caesar, Antony and Cleopatra, Troilus and Cressida.* Tragedies are VI through XI, and English histories XII through XVIII.

Seymour managed the complexity of Shakespeare's history plays by simplification and focused emphasis through well selected episodes. *King Richard II* begins with the quarrel, quotes the strongest case for divine right, and stresses the deposition. In five illustrations, young readers saw Richard intervene to stop the chivalric contest (218 and 173); Bolingbroke and his adherents (220 and 175); Richard surrender his crown (224 and 179); the Queen meet Richard as prisoner (225 and 180); and Exton kill Richard (226 and 181). When Seymour combined two plays in *King Henry IV,* she showed little delight in Falstaff, who is not part of the conclusion when the new king appoints the Lord Chief Justice. Stress on the madcap prince's thoughtfulness and his father's guilt makes the father-son relationship the main interest, with Henry IV's death the principal episode. Four illustrations enhance this narrative: Falstaff and Hal enact an imaginary scene (231 and 186), Harry at his father's deathbed (234 and 189), and a prince not eager to be king (236 and 191), but the new king appoints Gascoigne as adviser, a signal that he supports a firm order (237). *King Henry V*'s simpler narrative line is matched by three illustrations: war, climaxed at Agincourt, "God for Harry, England, and St. George!" (240 and 195); wooing the French princess, with chaperon in attendance (244 and 199); and the wedding that assures peace (245 and 200). Very different from these triumphs of chivalry is scheming *King Richard III,* with murder victims illustrated: Clarence to the tower (260 and 215) and smothering the young princes (265 and 220). Two long quotations, Queen Margaret's curses (13 lines) and conscience (15 lines), typify Shakespeare's rhetorical language, open analysis of Richard's character, and recognize a powerful female character.

King Henry VIII was popular in the nineteenth century in spectacular productions and in historical paintings; both strove for accurate period details.[13] George Henry Harlow (1787–1819) painted *The Trial of Queen Katherine* (1817) as played by the Kemble family, with sister Sarah Siddons as Katherine gesturing at her accuser Cardinal Wolsey, played by John Philip Kemble. Henry Andrews (d. 1868) painted the same scene (II.iv) from Charles Kemble's Covent Garden production of 1831, when Fanny Kemble played the queen. Frank Howard's first two illustrations are of this scene. First, Katherine kneels to her husband Henry VIII (270 and 225). Seymour quotes the opening five lines of the queen's great speech, "In what have I offended" (270 and 225). In the second picture Katherine defies Wolsey (272 and 227), whose demise is marked by quotations from his farewell (275 and 229–230) and warning speech to Cromwell (276–277 and 231–232), followed by an illustration of his sudden illness (278 and 233). The final image, as in the play, is more encouraging, the christening of Elizabeth (279 and 234).

Katherine of Aragon is the historical precedent for Hermione, the falsely accused queen in *The Winter's Tale,* a play that Seymour treated with unusual interest and compassion. The story begins with a happy marriage: "Leontes of Sicily, and Hermione his lovely queen, lived together in the greatest harmony, — a harmony and happiness so perfect that the king said he had no wish left to gratify, excepting the desire to see his old companion Polixenes, and present him to the friendship of his wife" (72 and 179). Even after his cruel and false accusation and its dire consequences, Seymour retained sympathy for Leontes. When he learns that Perdita is his daughter, "Joyful as such tidings were, his sorrow at the thought of Hermione, who had not lived to behold her child thus grown into a fair maiden, almost exceeded his happiness, so that he kept exclaiming, 'Oh, thy mother! thy mother!'"; Howard illustrated, "When the curtain was drawn back his sorrow was stirred afresh" (80 and 187). Unlike Lamb's version, Seymour's features the sheep-shearing feast with a delightful illustration, "Young lads and ladies chaffering with a pedlar for his goods" (77 and 184). A bearded Autolycus, dressed in motley with slashes in his pants, stands amidst a crowd of country folk. His pack (which promises treats), a boy, and two dogs invite the gaze of young readers, who thus had lighter amusement amidst serious issues of adult behavior pictured on the opposite page when Polixenes reproaches his son (78 and 185).

Seymour frequently evaluated gender roles. In the domestic comedy *The Taming of the Shrew* Katherine acquires the admirable patient obedience of Griselda. But illustrations are outrageously funny, where captions describe the melodramatic action precisely. "This gentle maiden had struck him upon the head with her lute" (35 and 134) shows the teacher's head caught in a lute still held by Katherine, while a music stand falls to the floor; Petruchio and others observe from the doorway. Amidst the debris, Petruchio holds Katherine's hand and clucks her chin as she faces away: "He would marry her whether she willed or no" (37 and 136). Seymour explained: "All the while they were being married he behaved so strangely and roughly that the high-spirited Katherine trembled with fear: nor did she understand that he was assuming this wildness only that he might succeed in his plan for curing her shrewish temper" (38 and 137). Taming continues in "Away they went, mounted upon lean, miserable horses" (38 and 137); her very anxious look is not surprising, since Petruchio holds a whip as he bids farewell. Apprehension has turned to horror when Petruchio's training of his wife progresses to tearing her new clothes, "He made just the same complaint of its cut and fashion" (41 and 140). Anticipating Germaine Greer, albeit with a muted ending,[14] Seymour highly praised Katherine's teacher:

> No one, perhaps was so well suited to the task as Petruchio; for though high-spirited, he was both wise and merry; nay, he could even feign to be very angry when he was perfectly calm within, so that the airs he gave himself when he was Katherine's husband were only assumed as the best means of controlling her passionate temper [34–35 and 133–134]....
>
> [A]t his bidding Katherine addresses the wilful ladies upon the duty of obedience. You may easily imagine that from this time she became as celebrated as the most dutiful and submissive wife in Padua. Her name of "Kate the Shrew" was forgotten, and everyone praised Petruchio's wisdom in choosing such a method for transforming a violent, imperious woman, into one so gentle and kind [43–44 and 143].

The English domestic comedy *The Merry Wives of Windsor* specifies Falstaff's reprehensible conduct ("so bad and so bold, he transgressed every law and troubled the general peace so sorely," 144) and lack of compunction ("in no wise abashed," 145). But it also shows the clever playfulness of Mistress Ford and Mistress Page and enumerates strenuous female tasks, performed by Mistress Quickly in the house of Doctor Caius ("I wash, wring, brew, bake, scour, dress meat and drink, make the beds, and do all myself," 147). The appeal of a rotund Falstaff and Mistress Quickly are recognized in the frontispiece. More amusing are action pictures that record Falstaff's humiliation: "Emptying the contents of their basket into the wet ditch," where he tumbles out, followed by a heap of laundry (154); "Cudgelling the disguised Falstaff soundly," when his cross-dressing made him the fat woman of Brentford (156)—a motif that Kenneth Grahame (1859–1932) redeploys with Toad in *The Wind in the Willows* (1908)—and assaulted by children disguised as elves and fairies—"Pinch him, and burn him, and turn him about!"—the most familiar appeal to young readers (161). The cumulative effect is laughter from frequent heightening of Shakespeare's infusion of seriousness into comedies.

Several adjustments enhance even the most chaste heroines. Prospero is always present when Miranda and Ferdinand meet in *The Tempest*; there is no competition to choose the casket in *The Merchant of Venice*; Rosalind is not allowed to teach Orlando how to woo in *As You Like It*. However, when Seymour added *Much Ado About Nothing* in the companion volume of *Comedies*, she retained some of the opening biting insults (105–107), much of Beatrice and Benedick's exchange at the church when she challenges him, "Kill Claudio" (119–120), and final teases as they wed (123). Most complete is the overhearing through which the two discover and admit their love, well depicted in an opening with facing pictures of concealment (111–115). Like Lamb, Seymour reduced farcical Dogberry to "a man" who leads in Borachio, who was overheard. Similarly, she echoed Lamb's finesses in *Measure for Measure*. Details of Angelo's exposure are vague — nothing that could identify the bed trick — and Isabella's decision to accept the Duke is rationalized: "she had not joined herself to the sisters of the convent" and is grateful for "his exceeding kindness in his character of friar." Moreover, consequences are exemplary: "her influence over the people was sufficient to exterminate the vices to which they

Mary Seamer Seymour's *Shakespeare's Stories Simply Told* (1880), in two expanded volumes, retold all of the plays, including *Much Ado About Nothing*. Many openings have line drawings on facing pages. Here Benedict and Beatrice overhear that each is loved by the other and readers see how friends have set up their eavesdropping — note Beatrice concealed in the bushes. Captions and running titles direct attention and facilitate reading.

had so long been prone, and the state became once more prosperous and glorious" (178).

An ideal of Victorian maidenhood is spared threats of prostitution in *Pericles,* where Seymour altered "unsuitable" material:

> Meanwhile the pirate who had seized upon Marina had sold her as a slave; and her master grew rich with the money she earned by teaching the music and dancing and embroidery she was so skilful in. It was not long before the city of Mitylene knew the beauty and also the virtue of Marina; and Lysimoclus the governor, who went to visit her, was so surprised by her purity of mind and grace of manner, that he said, — "Thou art a piece of virtue" [121–122 and 229–230].

Nevertheless, Frank Howard depicted a very exciting moment: "He was just about to take the life of the poor maiden" (120 and 228). The would-be murderer is poised, knife in hand and ready to stab, as pirates come round the rocks.

Cross-dressing presented additional hazards with regard to Victorian propriety. A bold young woman who crosses gender expectations has self-doubts: Viola "began to think she had been wicked in thus disguising herself, if it were to bring unhappiness to others" (131 and 98). *Twelfth Night* ends with a pragmatic view of marriage, Victorian negotiation: "When Orsino found that his admiration for Olivia was useless, he began to feel much attracted to Viola; and remembering how, when believed to be a page, she had avowed her love for him, he thought he could not do better than ask her hand in marriage" (136–137 and 103–104). Alternatively, in *The Comedy of Errors,* "the abbess was a wise and prudent woman" who "had entered the convent, and lived a happy life there in the practice of piety and charity" (62 and 56). Sexual morality was air-brushed by Victorian views of adult behavior and propriety in children's literature, but remained a prominent theme.

Sex and violence in *Titus Andronicus,* although popular among Elizabethans and in the late twentieth century, are a major challenge to nineteenth-century sensibility. Lavinia is "cruelly injured" (215), and Titus's slaying his daughter is a "horrible sight" even to Saturninus. Seymour, in six lines, recorded Titus's killing of Chiron and Demetrius and the banquet (but not that they were the food!) before, "maddened by all his miseries and full of revenge, he plunged his sword into the wicked empress Tamora, "and was himself slain by Saturninus in what was "indeed a scene of bloodshed and horror" (218). Of six illustrations the most telling shows Lavinia inscribing the names of Chiron and Demetrius in the sand by using her stumps to guide the stick held in her mouth (223).

Seymour's interpretive glosses in tragedies are less revealing, but Howard's visual images often expand exciting adventure. Hamlet vows to forget learning and pleasure and keep only the memory of the ghost (162 and 105); Seymour quoted his summary response, "Why, what should be the fear?"

(I.iv.64–67). Nevertheless, Hamlet's "unpremeditated slaying of Polonius gave Claudio [sic] a pretext for banishing him from the kingdom" (168 and 110). Three action-filled illustrations display armor and brandished weapons: "The ghost appeared and beckoned to the young prince" (162 and 104); "Claudio [sic] called for lights, and, pretending to sudden illness, left the theatre" (167 and 109); "Hamlet ... turned on the false king and thrust him through" (172 and 114). Quotations from two soliloquies are the first eight lines of "To be or not to be" (III.i.57ff), and nine lines from "O what a noble mind" (153–161), both on the same page (165 and 107).

Stories from Shakespeare Simply Told has both cautious and spectacular treatment of the supernatural. In *The Tempest*, first in Lamb and the combined volume, Seymour mused: "Strange as it may seem, this old man of the island could get the spirits to rouse the winds and waves at his pleasure" (10 and 190). Although she sustained interest in gender with Helena's query about friendship, "O, is all forgot?" (III.ii.201–206), passages from *A Midsummer Night's Dream* present fairy lore: Puck's "I'll put a girdle round about the earth / In forty minutes (II.i.175–176), Oberon's "I know a bank where..." (II.i.249–258), the fairies' charming song (II.ii.9–30). Two archetypal illustrations face each other: Bottom with ass's head in a forest scene with both fairies and sleeping lovers (102 and 92) and a bevy of dancing fairies, "They held high festival" (103 and 93). The disturbing image is from *The Tempest*, Ariel as harpy, "a monster, who carried the untasted food away" (19 and 199). *Macbeth* illustrations are most frightening; witches are in three of the seven. The opening "These three witches had agreed to meet Macbeth thus" (139 and 116) is conventional—concealed by hooded cloaks, one facing the viewer, one turned away and one in profile — as is "Eight shadowy kings passed by" (145 and 121) when Macbeth goes to their cave. However, their presence is entirely unexpected, yet very apt, at the last battle, where "A desperate encounter followed" between Macbeth and Macduff; three witches hover over the fighting warriors (147 and 124).

Seymour's *Shakespeare's Simply Told* is comprehensive and attractive. A German edition in 1890 marked its significance.[15] Heinrich Saure retained twenty of Seymour's twenty-six stories; gone are *The Comedy of Errors, The Taming of the Shrew, Timon of Athens, Troilus and Cressida, Pericles, The Winter's Tale*. His selection indicates less enthusiasm for comedy, problem, and romance; an absence of illustrations reinforces this. Fairly extensive notes facilitate use of Shakespeare's stories to teach English to German students and to introduce the great author so admired and influential in Germany, as elsewhere in the world. English-speaking children typically read books written in England. However, Americans had alternatives to inspire and satisfy different values, both patriotic and pedagogical.

Robert R. Raymond, Typical Tales of Fancy, Romance, and History from Shakespeare's Plays *(1881)*

Robert R(aikes) Raymond's (1817–1888) *Typical Tales of Fancy, Romance, and History from Shakespeare's Plays* (1881) is quite different from simple English retellings; it is an American pedagogical effort, as explained by the subtitle — *In Narrative Form, Largely in Shakespeare's Words, with Dialogue Passages in the Original Dramatic Text*. The title page identifies Raymond (1817–1888) as editor and "Late Principal of the Boston School of Oratory and Former Professor of the English language and literature in the Brooklyn Polytechnic Institute."[16] The intended reader is "the youthful mind" that is eager but, when it finds a difficulty, exercises — in keeping with the Bill of Rights —

> the inalienable right of "skipping." What the young mind can assimilate, it appropriates; the rest is passed over. It is the loss necessarily incurred in this process that the present version — of story and play together — proposes to supply. In other words, it assumes to "skip" *for* the youth, judiciously; bridging the dreary void of omitted passages, with a lively representation of the original, in which the language of the author is to be reproduced only so far as is consistent with the interest of the young reader, — in this case, the prime consideration. Similar service has been attempted also with reference to single obscure expressions, occurring in connections otherwise attractive; the aim being to put the reader in possession of the entire work, so far as he is capable of receiving it [v–vi].

Thus, for obscure words, Raymond substituted the nearest synonym in brackets, or at the bottom of the page when the substitution would distort the rhythm. He also added occasional explanatory footnotes, some very sophisticated; for example, to identify Robin Goodfellow, he quoted Burton's *Anatomy of Melancholy* and Harsenet's *Declaration of Popish Impostures* (28c). A few small changes — distinctions between *should* and *could* instead of Shakespeare's interchangeable usage, *its* for *his* — adjust linguistic development. Yet although "such archaisms as might tend to repel the young reader" were brushed out, "care has been taken to preserve the 'marrys' and 'pr'ythees,' and similar minute colloquialisms, which, as having a certain 'smack of the time,' [the young reader] has generally appeared to appreciate and relish" (vii). This effect, as in Howard Pyle's successful retellings of Robin Hood and King Arthur, gives the lie to later critics who fault such "gadzookery!" Raymond's brief "Memoir" combines a few dates (birth, return to Stratford, death) with familiar stories. Most amusing is Shakespeare's supposed poaching, the act of "a rather frolicsome boy ... very fond of hunting," who, if he lacked permission, is "not for a moment to be defended; but we ought to remember that the English law was far more strict on such matters than ours and although the youngster made himself liable to punishment, his fault was not much greater than that of stealing apples from an orchard would be in our day" (8). One half-page heading contains a portrait (dubious), a roundel with a frieze of cupids, above Shakespeare's signature and name in capital letters (7); a second is an idyllic "Trinity Church at Stratford on Avon" (8), while the memorial bust fills the last quarter-page (10).

In the nineteenth century, American literature was still largely English literature, with some modern American writers in tandem with English—Longfellow and Tennyson are the most popular poets, often retold for children. Nevertheless, there is an American point of view. Raymond's "typical tales" are *A Midsummer Night's Dream, As You Like It*, and *Julius Caesar*. The first is a constant favorite and the second likely, but the Roman play is a quintessentially American choice—*Julius Caesar* was the first Shakespeare I read in school, and its popularity continues.[17] Raymond explained why.

> It deals with characters and events belonging to a period in Roman history better known and more interesting to us as American republicans than any other epoch in the life of the world; because it shows us how a true and pure republican, so many centuries ago, was wrought upon to commit a great crime to save the liberties of his country, and teaches us, by the disastrous result of his effort, the vanity of expecting to do good by evil means [139].

His opening identifies the Roman populace as "of very different material from what we are accustomed to see on similar occasions.... [T]hey were very ignorant. There were then no printed books, no newspapers or periodicals, no reading-rooms, where the common people might learn about public affairs." While "all great crowds are excitable and fickle," these ignorant Romans were especially so, easily swayed by orators (151). Later Raymond's professional expertise noted Brutus's fatal error when he chose to speak first and gave Antony the advantage of speaking last: "Any American boy in a school debating-society could have taught him better than that" (194).

Illustrations amplify Brutus's importance. The headpiece, a third of a page, is an elaborately set great eagle's head, an emblem that serves both Rome and the United States of America (147). Republican issues continue in the first episode; tribunes Flavius and Marullus confront a crowd of workmen and chide them for not wearing signs of their professions (half-page 152). Next Antony kneels to offer a crown to Caesar, who sits on a stepped dais (half-page 162); Caesar has stretched out his arm to refuse, but bystanders look uneasy. The quotation is Casca's account of this moment to answer Brutus's questions (I.ii.215–290). Two very small pictures represent unrest in the state and in nature. Casca and Cicero speak of tempests and winds (164), and a wide-eyed Brutus reads a letter planted by Cassius (167). The first major illustration is "Brutus in His Garden": he stands pensively, arms crossed with a letter in one hand, half-lighted by a flash of lightning on the right (two-thirds-page 169). Behind, a classical building tops a dark background of trees and water below. A brighter "Brutus and the Conspirators" shows him at the top of stairs with one attendant, while five stand below. Light comes from inside and a full moon partially behind trees (full-page 172). In a small picture within text Brutus turns away from Portia, whose lantern illuminates her expression of worry and anger (175). Raymond paraphrased all but the most telling lines about the marriage (II.i.299–310). The next two quarter-page illustrations depict Caesar: he stands proudly, arm akimbo, flanked by Antony and soldiers, as citizens hold petitions toward him (183); and he lies dead, a dagger stuck in his chest (187). Much of the most famous scene, Antony's funeral oration, is quoted (III.ii.75ff) with interlaced explanation of the effects he achieves (195–201). Antony shows Caesar's wounds to the crowd — some weep, others hold weapons high, or simply raise their arms, others stand silently (half-page 198). After Antony plans with Lepidus and Octavius (quarter-page 203), the focus returns to Brutus: his quarrel with Cassius over treasure, quoted with some interlaced summary and comments (204–210); and Brutus bids the boy Lucius fill the cup (quarter-page 209). Most dazzling is the appearance of Caesar's ghost, who stands regally, grasping his staff in his right hand and pointing with his left. Brutus, reclining on a couch, lifts his arm to shield his eyes from light emanating from the figure, while sleeping Lucius leans on his lyre (212). Brutus and Cassius's parting speeches (V.ii.100–129) are broken by a cropped picture of noble Brutus ready to engage in the battle. There is no great fight scene but "Pindarus Reporting to Cassius" (full-page 218); a youth stands on a rock to see distant horses, while below him the leader listens. The final image echoes Caesar's assassination; Brutus lies dead with his sword in his chest, and Antony in full armor kneels beside the corpse. The final quotation is paeans by Antony and Octavius (V.iv.68–81).

While Raymond's sympathy was with Brutus—"O, if Brutus had only permitted Cassius to make short work of this shrewd and brilliant politician"— his moral judgment won out: "But it is better so: a revolution failed which ought never to have succeeded, especially by such means, and Brutus remains— a noble picture—the just, magnanimous, but unskillful patriot that history and Shakespeare have presented to us" (194). Brutus is married to "a glorious woman, [yet] still a woman, and her heart was not strong enough for the burden it is called to bear" (180). Moreover, Brutus is a "scholar and book-lover," who reads by "the dim taper in his tent" before Phillipi (211). Raymond began by insisting that "the life and character of Caesar are the pivot on which the whole action of the drama turns, and that the spirit of Caesar, strong and terrible, is present, as a controlling and an avenging power, to the very end" (144), but his emotional hero was the noble republican.

Raymond's method was to interlace Shakespeare's text with explanations and occasional summary; intact are all the orations and pivotal scenes: the initial exchange among conspirators, the murder of Caesar, the quarrel between Cassius and Brutus over treasure, Brutus with his boy Lucius—a point of view for the young reader. Visual reinforcement is substantial: six full-page, ten three-quarter-page, eleven half-page, thirty-three quarter-page, and seven small images are directly tied to the play / tale. There are also thirty-four quarter-page designs (often bars), another fifteen small devices, and thirteen decorated capitals. To facilitate study *Julius Caesar* is divided into ten large parts (with Roman numerals); each begins with a reference to Act and Scene, so that passages could be found in a complete text. Raymond treated all three plays in the same way.

In *A Midsummer Night's Dream* the story and quotations, divided into eight parts, were more systematically chosen: Shakespeare for scenes with fairies and rustic mechanicals — both in rehearsal and performance; Raymond's summaries for others, especially bits with the young lovers that children would "skip." Illustrations of humans are small and mostly static: Theseus and Hippolyta pose together (18); Hermia and Helena, two very young girls, examine the design on a scroll (19); Hermia turns from Demetrius, while Helena sleeps on the ground behind (47); Philostrate bows to the brides before the mechanicals begin their play (59); the audience in the background watch the actors (three-quarter-page 62). Although Raymond introduced the play as "a curious composition, full of exquisite poetry and jolliest fun," he was uneasy about the complexity of "dream" and "variety of personages." His great anxiety was the "strange and unnatural conduct" of some humans:

> their jealousies, their petty passions, and their little meanness are such as might well have been born in a haunted grove, — the children of magic and the moonlight. We might be amused with their fantastic doings as the shifting shadows of a dream, but would never think of trying them by the waking judgments of the cold, gray morning [13–14].

After Raymond's warning to keep reality in mind, Puck's epilogue invites participation in the dream, "fancy" from the poet with the greatest understanding of "the ways of Fairy-land" (15).

Adults are always divided about the efficacy of fairy tales for children; Raymond's cautions reflect apprehension, but Shakespeare gives legitimacy to imaginative fancy. Several illustrations depict fairy creatures, always with beautiful decorative wings: a gossamer fairy roundel and song around a crescent moon (full-page 33); "the fairies errands" include some with shields and swords who attack two black bats, while several bow to praise an owl (three-quarter-page 34); Cobweb, Peas-blossom, Squash, and Mustard-seed bow courteously to Bottom with his ass's head (three-quarter-page 44). "And so this funny procession — poor donkey-headed Nick, lumbering along, escorted by these droll little children of the air — makes its way toward the leafy chamber of the Fairy Queen" (45). In a thick woodland setting, Oberon applies love juice to a sleeping Titania (three-quarter-page 36); later she embraces Bottom in the same leafy setting (three-quarter-page 54). Oberon also stands elegantly as he waits for Puck (46). Indeed Puck is most frequently depicted: he talks to a female fairy (27), brings confusion and destruction to gossips (29), playfully leaps over a mushroom (42), stands high on a tree branch above a young Greek (50), and bows after his "If we shadows have offended" epilogue (V.i.418–433).

Paintings of fairies inspired by *A Midsummer Night's Dream* are numerous and excellent, the work of many distinguished artists. Those from the Boydell Gallery include the popular work of Henry Fuseli (1741–1825), but also Sir Joshua Reynolds's *Puck* (1789), copied by William B. Essex (1784–1869) in 1847. Major Victorian paintings are *The Disenchantment of Bottom* (1832) by Daniel Maclise (1806–1870); watercolors of a *Fairy Scene* (1831) and of *Oberon and Titania* (1837) by Francis Danby (1793–1861); *Titania and Bottom* (1848–1851) by Sir Edwin Landseer (1802–1873), his only illustration of Shakespeare; and the extraordinarily complex and dazzling *The Quarrel of Oberon and Titania* (1849) and *The Reconciliation of Oberon and Titania* (1847) by Joseph Noël Paton (1821–1902).[18] Shakespeare's fairies did much to inspire Victorian fascination that persisted among Edwardians, including so rational a man as Arthur Conan Doyle (1859–1930), who in 1920 wrote an article for the *Strand* to accompany the "Cottingley Photographs" that appeared to prove the existence of fairies. Iconic fairies of *A Midsummer Night's Dream* are the most reliable way to entice young readers.

Raymond began with the classic formula, "Once upon a time there lived a mighty hero, Theseus," and added a brief account of his legends (17), an easy articulation of mythology. But at strategic moments Raymond reiterated that *A Midsummer Night's Dream* was not to be thought real, and he made moral judgments. Helena's act of following Demetrius in the wood is "— a queer thing for a nice and well-behaved young lady to do! But you are not to forget that all this took place in a dream, and in dreams people never act as they do in the wide-awake world" (37–38). Moreover, as Raymond later wryly observed, "in this enchanted wood every one seems to have easily fallen asleep" (47). He was most at ease with the mechanicals; obvious pretend / performance reassures as does the common man. They inspire the most original illustrations. The heading to Part II shows a room in the cottage of Quince the carpenter that is reassuringly ordinary—a beamed ceiling, three-legged stool, large table with tools, stacks of wood, a ladder leading to a loft, great pots (22). Most delightful is a rehearsal scene with a vigorously gesturing Bottom at the center, "A part to tear a cat in, to make all split" (three-quarter-page 24). Quince reads the script, a long scroll, while others watch with varying degrees of amusement. Opposite is a small cropped picture of five very anxious actors, "*All.* That would hang us, every mother's son"; the footer is an actor's mask (25). At the performance three actors wear masks and stand in a playing area before an audience seated four steps above them (62). A lion's mask device separates Snug's speech to reassure the ladies (V.i.217–224) from responses of Athenian nobility. Most energetic is the Bergomask: six figures, all masked, kick high as they move rapidly in a circular dance (67). Their costumes and masks signal Greek theatre.

But Raymond extended English commentary with a poem attributed to

The importance of the common man is a major theme in American Robert R. Raymond's *Typical Tales of Fancy, Romance and History* (1881). Thus the play rehearsal of Bottom and his fellow mechanicals — not included in *A Midsummer Night's Dream* in Lamb's *Tales* — shows their simplicity and energy. Here the workmen are in Greek costume, albeit their manner remains English.

Ben Jonson, "The Pranks of Robin Goodfellow." Five additional illustrations expand fascination with Puck, the mischievous native fairy most closely allied with humans. First, he dances, holding his side with mirth, as a smiling Oberon leans on a grass and watches (71). In the middle of the second page Robin Goodfellow leads human "wanderers" astray; the next heading, a dancing Robin and a horse under a crescent moon, suggests shape-shifting (73). Finally, Puck springs down through the air with a childlike crescent moon and star behind him (74), while a laughing Robin from the first border marks the end (75).

Although both *A Midsummer Night's Dream* and *Julius Caesar* are highly appealing, for Raymond, *As You Like It* was most pleasing and reassuring. He introduced the play as a "lovely picture of life in the woods"— an illustration features deer in the Forest of Arden with the Duke's company dining in the open air (full-page 98)—written by Shakespeare at mid-career, perhaps as a "recreation" after writing plays with "mighty themes,—of kings, and courts, and camps,—and we may well believe that he was strained and weary" (79). The first illustration establishes Orlando's youth; he is shown with Old Adam and a dog (half-page 81), and a note identifies Adam: "beautiful character is rendered doubly interesting by a curious tradition that Shakespeare himself played it on the stage" (82). More compelling is "Orlando's Victory over Charles, the Duke's Wrestler" (83), a full-page with a strong message: youth triumphs over a bully. Orlando, fair-haired and simply dressed, stands astride an opponent twice his size, as bystanders gossip or gaze in amazement. Because there are different illustrators, characters are not consistent. The young Orlando who bows to receive Rosalind's chain has dark hair (91); he is transformed into a mature and elegant courtier, with hat and small beard, when he draws his sword to demand food from the Duke, whose well laid table is set in the forest (three-quarter-page 109). Raymond quoted the episode that demonstrates the hero's care and concern for his old servant and the Duke's generosity and poise (II.vii.85–134). The long wooing lesson (IV.i.36–188) merits only a small illustration; Orlando and Rosalind take hands before Celia (as witness she makes the marriage a binding contract by sixteenth-century custom). Rosalind's page attire matches the style of mature Orlando; only Celia dresses as peasant (127). Orlando's courtier brother Oliver and peasants Phebe and Silvius join them in a final image (three-quarter-page 136).

Because the play is prose, Raymond's summary explanations and connections blend neatly with quoted Shakespeare. Thus the woodland encounter continues with Jaques's "Seven ages of man" speech (II.vii.135–165). Stories often reduce Touchstone's role and infrequently cite passages that show his wit. But Raymond, who clearly relished the lively spirit and playful qualities of *As You Like It*, treated the clown fully and quoted extensively (I.ii.53–88; III.ii.04–113; V.i.10–57). Moreover, the most compelling illustration is "Corin and Touchstone," a full-page with many details to interest a child: Touchstone, in motley, sits on a bank and talks to the old shepherd seated across from him; his sheep are just behind them, and in the foreground the shepherd's dog sits patiently and looks toward viewers as if to ask what they make of this (115). While many Edwardian editions feature Touchstone with Rosalind and Celia as they make their way in the woods or rest beside a tree, this unusual depiction of the common man suits Raymond's American audience, many of whom lived in rural communities. Opposite is another long quotation about the shepherd's life (III.ii.1–75, 84–85), from which Raymond omitted only the comment about "the copulation of cattle" and an "old cuckoldy ram." He glossed ironically: "in spite of his motley dress and fool's cap and bells, Touchstone liked to seem wise, and to give good advice on every occasion. And Corin was quite ready to minister to this self-importance, for he had the deepest respect for the superior knowledge of the gentleman from the Court" (114). Touchstone

The pastoral quality of *As You Like It* is marked by this meeting of Corin and Touchstone, shepherd and court clown, in a woodland setting made especially appealing to children because of the dog in the foreground and sheep in the background. It is another example of how illustrations in Robert R. Raymond's *Typical Tales of Fancy, Romance and History* (1881) were unusual in their glorification of the ordinary.

demonstrates wit, but Corin's answers define his unpretentious and pragmatic philosophy as a humble worker: "I am a true laborer; I earn what I eat, get that I wear; owe no man hate, envy no man's happiness; am glad of other men's good, content with my own harm; and my greatest pride is to see my ewes graze and my lambs suck" (116). Like the republicanism of *Julius Caesar,* this suits American nationalism that stresses independence, work, and happiness.

Perhaps nationalism also explains why Raymond demurred and did not exploit Shakespeare's use of traditional legend for Duke Senior's life "in the Forest of Arden, and many merry men with him; and there they live like the old Robin Hood of England" (I.i.110–112). Outlaws were, seemingly, not appropriate models, in spite of the Duke's didactic explanation of reconciliation to straightened circumstances: "Sweet are the uses of adversity" (II.i.12–17). Raymond quoted two parts of Amiens's song "Under the greenwood tree" (II.v.i.8, 35–42) — but not the acerbic third stanza composed by Jaques (106–107). "Blow, blow, thou winter wind" (II.vii.173–194) celebrates friendship and healthy and honest outdoor life, and all join in the chorus: "This song, you see, was quite appropriate to the situation of many of the persons of our story, who were preferring the rough merry forest-life to the deceit and cruelty found in cities" (112).

Raymond, who was very confident about the play's appeal and at ease with its subject matter, concluded rhapsodically and optimistically:

> And now, in looking back over our finished story, and seeing how bright and fresh and out-of-doors it has been; how the pleasant people who have suffered, have not suffered so very much, while out of their suffering happiness has come; how all the good have been rewarded, and all the bad have become good, and then been rewarded too; how everybody who ought to get married has got married, and to just the right person; and how the queer folk who could not well be fitted in to the new order of things have been snugly provided for in forest-caves and such out-of-the-way corners, — are you not ready to say that the whole is rightly named, and everything exactly AS YOU LIKE IT? [140].

Typical Tales combines quotations and narrative, but interlaces them seamlessly and is markedly more sophisticated than the introduction of brief passages as in Lamb's *Tales.*

Robert R. Raymond is significant; his treatment of Shakespeare was thorough and skillful, but he also formulated attitudes toward Shakespeare in the United States, including a strong sense of American patriotism. He published *The Patriotic Speaker* (1864), a collection of "modern specimens of eloquence, together with poetical extracts adapted for recitation and dramatic pieces for exhibition," and his own oration, *The True Scholar,* delivered at Madison University, Hamilton, New York, on July 4, 1848. Nevertheless, retelling Shakespeare for children was very much the work of British writers, eagerly accepted in the United States at a time when the heritage of the English language and literature was viewed as an essential way of defining race / nation. Not all Shakespeare stories were inspired by didactic and pedagogical interests; one Victorian woman's retellings are fanciful and emotional.

Adelaide C. Gordon Sim, Phoebe's Shakespeare *(1894)*

As its title indicates, *Phoebe's Shakespeare* was written for a special child, a niece of Adelaide C. Gordon Sim, who gave it as a Christmas present with a wish that "you learn to know them, and love them, while you are still a little girl."[19] "Auntie Addie" explained that "Mr. Shakespeare wrote some stories that even children can understand" [iv]. Eight plays—seven comedies (*The Tempest, Midsummer Night's Dream, Twelfth Night, Two Gentlemen of Verona, Taming of the Shrew, Merchant of Venice, As You Like It*) and one tragedy (*Romeo and Juliet*)—retold in 146 pages of large print, are not difficult. Sim's narratives are relatively complete, with discreet omissions, but other details, like drunkenness, are not often included. In *The Tempest* Stephano, the king's butler, sings "a vulgar song" and cheers himself up with a bottle of wine, and Caliban "became so tipsy and eager for more" (9). "Sir Toby Belch, and a friend of his, Sir Andrew Ague Cheek, were always drinking and sitting up half the night with the clown: making a most terrible noise and disturbance" (42). But "they behaved themselves much better, and left off getting drunk and riotous" when Sebastian became master of the house, so that *Twelfth Night* concludes with their improvement (49). In *Two Gentlemen of Verona* no comic scene is told, although Proteus's servant has "a poor, ugly, starved, dirty old dog, called Crab, that Launce *would* take with him" (52). In *As You Like It* Sim identified "a sport called wrestling, in which men catch hold of each other and struggle until the strongest throws the other down; and as the men in those days were rough, and didn't mind hurting each other, even in play, people often had their bones broken and sometimes were killed" (103). Orlando "was a good wrestler and rather proud of his strength" (103); however, Sim did not share Castiglione's view of wrestling as a skill suitable to *The Courtier* (1528), admired by Elizabethans in Sir Thomas Hoby's translation of 1561. Her fascination with Italy and reliance on fairy tales parallels Shakespeare's, while her firm judgments of gender and unusually bold negative assessment of Jews differ.

Sim explicitly enhanced fairy elements in *The Tempest*: "Prospero knew directly that he was in an enchanted country, and, as he understood all about fairies and their ways, he was very glad to go on shore and make a home there for himself and his child" (3). To induce Alonso and Antonio to repent, Prospero draws a magic circle around them with his wand; accompanied by sweet music, "a troop of fairies, dancing and tripping in," carry in dishes for the banquet (10). Sim emulated Shakespeare's deployment of *Sea Venture* of the Bermudas; given his liberty, Ariel returns to Fairy-land:

> but they have never found it to this day, and I don't think they ever will, for, after Prospero and Miranda left, I believe the fairies gave it to the mermaids, who took it down to the bottom of the sea and used it for a palace, and Caliban went down with it. He'll never be able to do any more mischief [13].

This neatly disposes of Caliban. Echoes of Darwin supplement Trinculo's noting of Caliban's resemblance to a fish: "a dreadful looking creature, something like a large monkey, and as hairy as a great bear; he had a hump back, and long nails like claws" (8).

Sim directly confronted attitudes toward the role of fairy tales with an opening paragraph to *Midsummer Night's Dream*:

> All the children, who I hope will read these stories and learn to love them, have, I am sure, heard of fairies, and have seen the green rings on the grass where they dance on moonlight nights; but I have never known a child who had seen a fairy or heard it speak. But Mr. William Shakespeare was a poet, and a poet is a person who can see fairies, and one lovely summer night, when he was lying under the trees on the soft moss in the woods, he heard and saw some wonderful things, and wrote them down and made this story [15].

Sim cast the story as the great quarrel between Titania and Oberon, which prompts dire warnings against bad behavior, anger, the emotion that children readily recognize:

> Fairies have tempers, like other people, and if good beautiful fairies get cross and passionate, and give way to bad feelings, they grow by degrees into wicked fairies, and lose their looks and get hump-backed, and wrinkled and ugly; and then they leave off doing kind things, and amuse themselves by spoiling christening parties, and giving children horrid presents, and changing handsome young princes into beasts and princesses into cats, and altogether making themselves very troublesome to everyone [15].

A rich description of Titania's happy court—dresses of flower petals, butterfly wings, dewdrop jewels, elves who ride on bats' wings and carry glowworm lamps—and quoted songs point what can be lost. Sim summarized the lovers' confusion and Oberon's "unkind trick." Bottom—whom Puck transforms with a wave of his wand (22)—and the fairies are central, with funny details of his longing for hay (21–27) and the conclusion that he had a dream. Her main point was the end of the quarrel, when Titania and Oberon "determined never to be ill-natured and quarrelsome any more; and, as Mr. Shakespeare has made no more stories about their not agreeing, I think they must have kept friends ever after" (32).

A quarrel causes tragedy in *Romeo and Juliet*, a play written at the same time as *A Midsummer Night's Dream* and a serious inversion of the mechanicals' play of *Pyramus and Thisbe* that Sim did not describe. She stressed "these foolish passionate people," two families in Verona who have constant battles.

Part of Romeo's suit to Juliet is that he will try to end the strife (127). The Capulets seem worthy; Sim noted, "I think she [Juliet] would have been quite fond of Paris, if it had not been that something happened that same evening which put a stop to all her parents' plans" (123); upon their daughter's death they are deeply grieved and repentant. Sim interjected odd moments of comedy. The long balcony scene is undisturbed because the old nurse is "rather deaf, so she didn't hear them talking, and as she had rheumatism, she didn't venture out on to the balcony to see what her young lady was doing" (127–128). Juliet's impatience to have her nurse's news from Romeo is a main scene. After dueling and deaths, entombment and poison, Sim rejected tragic sympathy to voice her disapproval of adolescent—and Italian—excess with the rhetorical question

> Was it not dreadful?
> If only Romeo had been a little more patient and less selfish, and had remembered that he had no right to kill himself just because he was unhappy; or if poor Juliet had waked up a little sooner; or if the Friar had come before Romeo took the poison, everything might have been right; but Shakespeare himself says:
> "Never was a story of more woe
> Than this of Juliet and her Romeo" [145–146].

Nevertheless, there are delights for a little girl: Capulet's ball is Juliet's first, and much is made of her dress (white, "trimmed all over with silver thread, and little seed pearls: and round her waist, instead of a sash, she had a girdle of great big pearls, and another long string of them that went round and round her neck four or five times") and her person ("all her fair hair fell curling down her back, far below her waist, and in it she had a wreath of white roses," 124–125). A remarkably similar dress and beauty enhance *Two Gentleman of Verona*: "Sylvia herself wore a cream-coloured satin gown, all embroidered with gold, her long fair hair fell in curls all down her back, she had great strings of pearls round her neck" (53). Fashion in Padua resembles that in Verona. In *The Taming of the Shrew* Katharina, "very handsome, tall and fair, with beautiful golden-red hair" (64), has "a lovely white satin wedding dress, all embroidered with silver thread and little pearls, and ... some beautiful jewels on her neck, and a wreath in her hair, and a white veil over her face" (68). Images painted by Titian or Veronese provide the Italian ideal, and fair hair is salient for Northern beauties. Predictably, heroines wear male costume reluctantly. Viola, who can find no alternative work, "made up her mind to put on boy's clothes and go into his [Orsino's] service" (38). Julia puts on boy's clothes from fear of robbers (55), as does Rosalind. But she and Celia "packed up their jewels, and their dresses, and their money in bundles, and started off on foot to walk all the long miles to the Forest of Arden" (110).

Sim framed *As You Like It* as a fairy tale: "Once upon a time" (99) ... "they all went back to their own homes and lived happy ever after" (120). Homely details are Rosalind and Celia's skill at housekeeping at the farm although they are ladies (115), whose occupations—embroidery, reading, playing viols, keeping dogs and birds (108)—have an affinity with Edwardian upper-middle-class pastimes.

Quoted passages heighten the stories: there are four songs ("Come unto these yellow sands," 6; "You spotted snakes with double tongue," 18; "Who is Silvia?" 56–57; "Tell me where is fancy bred," 88). The longest quoted passages are Katharina's delineation of wife and husband (V.ii.139–178) in *Taming of the Shrew* (78–79) and Duke Senior's idea of the universal theatre and Jaques's "All the world's a stage" (114–115) in *As You Like It* (II.vii.135–165). Rather surprisingly Portia's "quality of mercy" speech reduces to "a beautiful speech about mercy" (94); then Sim quoted her citing of the bond and triumphant case (94–95).

This suits strong anti–Semitic sentiments in *Merchant of Venice*, which begins with a declaration that Venice is "the most wonderful and beautiful town in Europe, and perhaps in all the world," and describes its palaces and canals, boats, and gondolas—and the absence of "horrid fogs" (80–82)—a very English perspective! Antonio, the greatest merchant, is most hated by Shylock, not because of anything he said but "partly because he was good and charitable, and partly because he was so rich" (85). Shylock's character and circumstances are absolutely different:

> There was an old Jew in Venice, called Shylock, who was richer than any of the merchants, because he never spent more of his money than he could help, but hoarded it up, and saved it; and sometimes when other people were hard up, he would lend them a little; but on condition that when they paid him back they should always give him more than he had lent them; and as they wanted the money in a hurry they used to agree to this, and for every fifty pounds Shylock lent his neighbors he got back eighty, or even a hundred, and so he grew very rich. But, as he was mean and hard, the people in Venice hated him, and he knew it, and hated them even more; and was always glad when he could screw more money out of a poor Christian, who wanted a little help; for you know there was always a quarrel between the Jews and the Christians, because it was the Jews who crucified our Saviour, whom the Christians know was the Son of God; and for many years they could not forgive the Jews, and would not treat them like fellow countrymen, but rather like slaves [84–85].

This passage, the most protracted and overt articulation of religious difference in Shakespeare stories for children, is also unusually aggressive in raising economic issues. Portia's first response to the letter about Antonio's plight is to offer money: "she thought that Shylock was like all Jews, and loved money so much that he would be delighted to have the gold instead of a pound of flesh, which could be no good to him" (90). Sim's Shylock has telling stereotypical physical characteristics: "long matted hair that hung on his shoulders"; he grows white with rage and dances with fury at the defeat of "his wicked, cruel plan." Sims's final judgment came when "he crawled out of the Court like the cowardly sneak that he was" (95). In contrast, Antonio, "who was ready to forgive even his worst enemy" refuses to take half of Shylock's money but returns it "on condition that he made friends again with Jessica and her husband Lorenzo" (96). Sim added a final disposition of fortunes; when Antonio dies, he leaves his own money to Portia's children (98). Economic emphasis, like elaborate descriptions of opulent dresses and jewels, says something about Edwardian extravagance and religious prejudice. The pressure to earn money among the middle classes, and limited opportunities for women, underlies the work of many who wrote for children. Among them is the remarkable Edith Nesbit, an Edwardian toiler who became a classic writer.

5

Edwardian Elegance and Exuberance: Retellings Large and Small

The nearest rival to Lamb's *Tales from Shakespeare* is *The Children's Shakespeare* (1897), published while Victoria was still queen and popular through Edwardian editions. E(dith) Nesbit (1858–1924) adhered closely to Lamb's *Tales,* including the same plays but simplifying their texts, in a journeyman work that preceded her Bastable stories, highly imaginative novels that rank as "classics" of children's literature and define Nesbit's talent as a writer. Various editions of *The Children's Shakespeare,* even single stories, in both Britain and the United States, are distinguished by illustrations and qualities of book production. An alternative *The Children's Shakespeare* (1902), by Ada Baynes Stidolph, had only three plays and is little known. But its origin in South Africa exemplifies that Shakespeare stories for children were part of the tradition of the British Empire.

Several Edwardians wrote sophisticated retellings that eschewed dependency upon Lamb, with different choices of plays, fullness of treatment, and critical glosses. Supplementary introductions by scholars add distinction and signal serious intentions. Typically these original collections contain fewer plays. Mary Macleod's *The Shakespeare Story-Book* (1902) is a serious effort. The publisher was Wells Gardner, Darton, the house directed by F. J. Harvey Darton, himself author of several children's retold literary classics and of the seminal *Children's Books in England* (1932), in Cambridge University Press's literary history, which put children's literature into the canon.

A cogent reminder of Edwardian devotion to introducing great writers at an early age is a nursery series called Stories Told to the Children, published by E.C. and T.C. Jack. Although adjusted to attract very young children — small books, emulation of fairy tale, and overt storytelling techniques — Jeanie Lang's *Stories from Shakespeare* (1905) and *More Stories from Shakespeare* (1910) are models for initial reading of classics. A reiterated objective is to delight and encourage increasingly sophisticated exposure until children can read the plays for themselves, fortified by knowledge of the action and characters that facilitate greater understanding. Alternatively, Fay Adams Britton's unmitigatedly imaginative *Shakespearian Fairy Tales* (1907) builds upon early reading. Her charming tales transform plays into palimpsests, magical and reassuring stories of fairies who serve Shakespeare's famous characters. She judiciously selected situations and characters to infuse with traditional elements of fairy tale and retains some original language or paraphrase.

R. Hudson's *Tales from Shakespeare* (1906) from Collins Clear-Type Press is a small book, but totally unlike in intention: Hudson included different plays, notably histories, and significant quotations, while his narratives stress character. Edwardian commitment to the English history plays is a major difference from Lamb's *Tales*, most expansions, and Nesbit's *The Children's Shakespeare*. The change contrasts sharply with Lamb's feminization for girl readers, the original audience. A.T. Quiller-Couch's *Historical Tales from Shakespeare* (1910), which includes two Roman plays as well as the English histories, is a prime example. With patriotic exuberance and historical contexts, Quiller-Couch sought to revive or instill enthusiasm for history among the young, especially boys. Thomas Carter's *Shakespeare's Stories of the English Kings* (1912) has a similar intention. It and Carter's earlier volume, *Stories from Shakespeare* (1910), are both in Harrap's Told Through the Ages Series, a remarkably comprehensive, well written and illustrated collection of titles, largely western literature and history, designed for the older child and for adult readers not up to the complete original texts.

Two further collections, both beautiful examples of Edwardian extravagance in publishing, are praiseworthy. Alice Hoffman's *The Children's Shakespeare: Being Stories from the Plays with Illustrative Passages* (1911) furthers the concept of interlacing quotations and narrative to enhance familiarity with Shakespeare. The publishers, Dent and Dutton, also issued some of Hoffman's stories as separate small books. *The Tempest*, with pictures by Walter Crane, is exquisite. Finally, Constance and Mary Maud's *Shakespeare's Stories* (1912) is idiosyncratic: interlaced, forthright interpretations and Boydell Gallery engravings.

E. Nesbit, The Children's Shakespeare *(1897)*

In *The Children's Shakespeare* (1897) Nesbit included only twelve of twenty plays chosen by Charles and Mary Lamb: *The Winter's Tale, Romeo and Juliet, The Tempest, A Midsummer Night's Dream, King Lear, Cymbeline, The Taming of the Shrew, Hamlet, Twelfth Night, As You Like It, Pericles, The Merchant of Venice*.[1] Moreover, Nesbit undertook further simplification; she explains conversationally in her introduction that Lamb's retellings were hard to understand. The original illustrations signal a child audience even more aggressively;

notoriously, all characters are small children. Several artists contributed: Frances Brundage, "a rather sugary artist not improved by chromo-lithography,"[2] did twelve full, color pages, of which two are signed, "W & F Brundage." M. Bowling's title page and five other full pages were all black and white, while J. Wilis Grey and André Sleigh each contributed three black and white pages. Edric Vredenburg edited this first edition, published by Raphael Tuck and Sons.

An alternative to the original child figures, copied by Max Bihn in America, was undertaken by Tuck. Several artists illustrated a sumptuous E. Nesbit's *Children's Stories from Shakespeare* (1912) for the Raphael House Library of Gift Books for Boys and Girls, a series with more than twenty volumes— Scott, Tennyson, Longfellow, fairy tales, legends, poets, and history. Each crown quarto book has 144 pages; seven by nine and a half inches, a large dimension especially effective for illustration.

Tuck reused some of F.J. Furnivall's biography, "When Shakespeare Was a Boy," from his lavish *Tales from Shakespeare by Mary and Charles Lamb* (1901), discussed in Chapter 3. This introduction is only one of Furnivall's contributions to children's literature, a corollary to other educational efforts as enthusiastic proponent of English literature. His role as co-founder, with W.W. Skeat, of the London Working Men's College, was part of Victorian advance of study in Mechanics Institutes and Working Men's Colleges, where English was a kind of poor man's classics. Furnivall's essay has essential biographical facts and patriotic claims for the "King of Literature, the greatest genius the world has yet seen, the pride of England, the bond between her and all the nations who speak and understand her tongue."[3] But most of his essay describes boyhood in Shakespeare's time. He cited a contemporary source, Francis Seager's *Schoole of Vertue and booke of good Nourture for chyldren* (1557), recommended by John Brinsley in his *Grammar Schoole* (1612), an assurance of scholarly aptness. In great detail a boy's day is described, with special attention to food (and the shortage of forks), courtesy to parents, and cleanliness. Severe flogging is a school practice that remains, one Furnivall shared with Shakespeare. A long list of play activities and "fun" at events like harvest-homes, sheep-shearing, and holidays somewhat offsets it. Furnivall improvised an archetypal physical description—"chestnut hair, blue eyes, and rosy cheeks"— and assumed that Shakespeare would have been "in the thick of whatever fun and mischief were going." His exuberant peroration is a direct appeal:

> Only think what good company he must have been, and what jolly stories he told the boys he was with! Don't you wish you'd been one of them, even if you did have to put your meat in your mouth with your fingers instead of a fork? I do [13].

Furnivall met a criticism that Shakespeare put few children into his plays by pointing out limitations of the earlier era, a typical Whig view of progress in history:

> Englishmen in the sixteenth century were not, on most points, so enlightened as they are now. They hadn't then learnt the real value of boys and girls, and didn't properly appreciate the blessing and the virtues of them.
>
> Besides, most plays wanted villains or sinners in them; and of course no boy or girl was a villain or a sinner. If Shakespeare could but come to life again now, he'd assuredly put plenty of boys and girls into his new plays. We mustn't expect too much of a man who lived so very long ago. He did his best, and an uncommonly good best it was; so let's forgive him for only using his boys as girls [13].

There is playfulness, a knowing empathy, cogent flattery, acknowledged limited awareness of girls ("we know very little of their school life — if they had girls' schools, other than convents— in Shakespeare's youth," 13). Four precise line drawings give a visual impression of Shakespeare's world — the birthplace, grammar school, Anne Hathaway's cottage in Stratford, and De Witt's 1596 sketch of a London theatre. Nineteenth-century confidence in progress, the quality of Empire that brought English and thus Shakespeare to the world, is almost unmitigated.

Twelve plays are as in Nesbit's first edition, except that *The Winter's Tale* is last, a small gesture to Furnivall's concern to show the development of Shakespeare's mind, but there is no convincing chronology. Types of plays are mingled, three tragedies with nine comedies; if romance is a separate category, all four are present, but not grouped together. The intention was to have a happy book, and illustrations contribute significantly: ten full-page color plates on glossy paper, eleven black and white full-page illustrations, and ninety-two additional black and white images ranging from three-quarter pages to small devices. This reward book is more vibrant and inviting than the first edition.

The principal artists of *Children's Stories from Shakespeare* are J(ohn) H(enry) Bacon (1865–1914), portrait painter and illustrator; Harold Copping (1863–1932), illustrator of children's books and scriptural stories; A(rthur) A. Dixon (fl. 1893–1920), genre and historical painter and illustrator, and Howard Davie (fl. 1914–1935), who illustrated several books in the Raphael House Series. Bacon's opulent colors and adolescent young people make his interpretations a far cry from Brundage / Bihn's small children, and his paintings were often reproduced. He contributed glowing representations of young lovers. In the balcony scene, Juliet, in a white dress and with long flowing golden hair, leans to touch the hands of a raptly adoring Romeo, who stands just below her (30). His dark red doublet, cloak, and cap with feather are intense against the muted white and gray stone balustrade and clouds. Even more Pre-Raphaelite in style are *Ophelia and Hamlet,* shown in happy wooing days (52). She, fair and golden-haired with a wreath of white flowers round her head, wears a gold dress and white satin overdress. Hamlet, with jet black hair and small mustache, is dressed in deep purple; his cloak's gold lining links the lovers, as do their gently clasped hands, while the garden suggests fecundity and promise. Observed by the king and queen, Posthumus and Imogen, husband and wife, embrace more closely,

Paintings by John H. Bacon, usually reproduced in vivid color, greatly enriched E. Nesbit's *Children's Stories from Shakespeare* (1912), a Raphael Tuck Reward book. Young lovers, beautiful and handsome, exquisitely dressed, holding hands but separated by the balcony, foster Romantic interpretations of *Romeo and Juliet*.

for she hangs upon his neck (88). Her auburn hair and striking profile are reminiscent of Pre-Raphaelite beauties; again the man has dark hair. Costumes, suitable for *Cymbeline,* a play that juxtaposes eras, are vaguely medieval; the courtyard setting provides a glimpse of sea and the sail of a boat to take Posthumus away. Another couple, Katherine, a blonde Titian-like beauty in shining satin, and Petruchio, with fair hair and small mustache, sit elegantly at table (110). The taming husband smiles; he has deftly flicked a joint of meat off the platter he still holds, and a servant's open hands suggest he may catch it. This episode's indulgent horseplay is often used to amuse children. Here beauty, not temper or messiness, prevails in a scene made bright by glittering candles. The only incongruous lovers are Titania and the Clown, a lovely fairy queen whose arms encircle a country man with an ass's head. In Bacon's sylvan scene, many flowers are white and pink, while attendant fairies are bright red. Titania, whose beautiful, long red hair is held in place by a garland of white flowers, wears what is probably the longest swirling garment, so that she seems larger, albeit a solid Bottom the weaver, his ass's ears entwined by a garland of pink roses, dominates the center of this archetype for *A Midsummer Night's Dream.*

Resemblances between Bacon's illustrations and those of other artists indicate unity of design—and a frequent delight in red. Dixon's *Touchstone and Audrey,* the frontispiece from *As You Like It,* look more courtly than rustic, although in conventional costumes of shepherdess and fool. Touchstone is also featured in Howard Davie's popular forest scene; he sits to rest with Celia and Rosalind, as Aliena and Ganymede (80). Dixon made Touchstone's motley costume mostly red, while Davie made it green. Both depicted characters more childlike than Bacon's and thus much closer to Brundage's original figures.

Anti-Romantic illustrations characterize *Twelfth Night.* Dixon's splendid *Malvolio* proudly stands in a formal garden with precisely trimmed hedges, including a witty iconic cockerel, and rose bushes (120). The moment is Malvolio's reading of Olivia's supposed love letter, which he holds, arm extended, in his left hand, while his right hand lifts his staff from the ground. His exaggerated figure—legs wide apart, swelling chest, head tipped back to point his small goatee and large mustache—fills the center, made vivid by his doublet's alternating red stripes and wider, gold-decorated blue stripes. Malvolio is oblivious of Maria behind the hedge; she watches him preen. In a second image of vanity, *Viola and Olivia,* Ceasario fascinates the vain lady who lifts her veil to show her face (128). Her bright red dress, here a bold change from mourning, would be startling on anyone. One wonders whether red is relied upon to catch children's attention, or an artist's joke. With Gordon Browne (1858–1932), a prolific illustrator perhaps best known for images in adventure stories, joking is likely; the faces show a mild form of his satirical style, earlier deployed in Mary Macleod's *The Shakespeare Story-Book* (1902), considered later in this chapter. While the ten color pages dominate this Reward *Children's Stories from Shakespeare,* much of the book's appeal lies in black and white images, fine line

Katharina and Petruchio are beautiful figures in brightly lighted and elegant surroundings in Bacon's painting for *The Taming of the Shrew,* E. Nesbit's *Children's Stories from Shakespeare* (1912). However, the scene is comic, since the hero has flipped the platter to hurl the joint of meat (like a football) into the servant's waiting hands. Several illustrators depicted this moment of tossing food, a kind of child's play as well as indulgence of interest in food.

A.A. Dixon created a fancifully dressed and laughable figure in vain Malvolio of *Twelfth Night*, for E. Nesbit's *Children's Stories from Shakespeare* (1912). A lush formal garden provides the setting for his arrogant stance as he reads the fake letter, watched from behind a hedge by Maria, who has planned the trick. Most delightfully, at the top of the shaped bush a cock provides an analog to the proud, deluded steward.

drawings by Harold Copping and A.A. Dixon that frequently convey intense feelings: eleven full pages, twenty-five half- or three-quarter pages, fifty-five quarter pages, and twelve small devices. With these numbers a child always had a picture to look at. Eight full pages, outlined in black and signed, are Dixon's work. Captions, lines from Nesbit's text, identify episodes and signal differences in pictorial conception; color pages simply give names of characters. Smaller figures, signed only occasionally, are by Copping, taken from Furnivall's Lamb's *Tales*, published by Tuck in 1901. This is a notable example of reusing illustrations. As in other volumes in Raphael House Library, partial page illustrations, in a variety of positions, break the lines of text; some facing images in a single opening provide a little narrative.

Dixon's pages vary in interest, some rather conventional, but others as excellent as vivid color illustrations. All are sharply drawn with a sure sense of design equal to qualities of storytelling in well chosen moments. For *The Tempest*, "Prospero and his little one landed in safety" (20), from a boat partially glimpsed behind huge white cliffs that dominate the background. A thoughtful father — holding in his arms Miranda, a bundle of clothes, and a stack of books — wades through water. The dark lines of his royal costume separate the white cliff and child's white dress; she gazes in wonder at a site that looks promising — fruit on the tree before a cave, flowers, shells on the shore. *The Winter's Tale* offers another scene of wonder at the seashore: "The poor, deserted little baby was found by a shepherd," who lifts an arm in amazement (44). Perdita, whose name is written on the note beside her, smiles contentedly as she looks up. On her blanket, decorated with a heraldic device, is a jewel box; a flock of sheep on the left and a small ship on the right horizon are additional details. But the force of the illustration comes from its position; it faces Copping's drawing of a bear that stands atop the unfortunate man it has "torn to pieces" (44). Another central white background highlights "Romeo made his way to the fair lady" (33). They stand on a pavement of black and white squares; on the left is a glimpse of garden with a crescent moon, while guests dance on the right. Romeo's doublet and mask are black, but his cloak and Juliet's dress are white.

A brilliant opening from *Hamlet* supplements Furnivall's introduction about the theatre. On the left, as the court watch the players, "The wicked Claudius suddenly rose" (54). Dixon depicted a tense tyrant who grasps the throne; his eyes stare and his mouth is agape, while behind his shoulder Gertrude is wide-eyed. Hamlet, in black, sits on the dais and looks toward the king and the viewer. On the right, on a raised platform the player murderer pours poison into the sleeping king's ear. Two figures watch the play. A jester sits on a cushion beside the king and dominates the foreground, while Ophelia sits on the right, her back to the viewer. Opposite, Copping's drawing is a close-up: an anguished Claudius grips his cloak and chair, while Gertrude looks ahead, intent on the play.

In an opening for *The Tempest*, a pensive Miranda stares at the viewer;

Along with many color pages in E. Nesbit's *Children's Stories from Shakespeare* (1912) are fine black and white drawings, like A.A. Dixon's play within the play in *Hamlet*. Its carefully delineated interior frames varying reactions of the principals to the moment when the player pours poison into the ear of the sleeping king. Hamlet is at the center as he watches Claudius, who is rising from his ill-gotten throne. A jester, a prominent comic figure, and Ophelia are unaware, but Gertrude looks anxious.

opposite, a nude Ariel rests on a large bat, his body an arched horizontal against the bat's vertical wings (28–29). Of Copping's many portraits, several are memorable: Lear's Fool (75) and mad Lear (77), a winsome Rosalind as Ganymede (88), a plaintive Imogen as boy (97), a rueful Viola as Caesario with Orsino (126), and mad Ophelia (130). Some small, dynamic scenes are extraordinary: Caliban, wearing only a hide around his waist, has fallen and dropped the logs he was carrying, while on a branch above a monkey grins at the monster and the viewer (23); Lear's loyal servant Kent sits in the stocks (79); Iachimo emerges from the chest in Imogen's bedroom in *Cymbeline* (94); Katherine and Petruchio meet Vicentio on the road in *The Taming of the Shrew* (106); two fishermen find a chest on the seashore in *Pericles* (112), and Cerimon and his three attendants peer at the casket's contents (115); Horatio kneels beside the dead Hamlet (61).

Ever enterprising, Raphael Tuck included Shakespeare in The Children's Gem Library, a series of eighteen small books—Beatrix Potter size—divided into three parts. The first, "Children's Stories by Popular Authors," are by contemporary writers associated with Tuck: E. Nesbit's *The Rainbow Queen*, L. T. Meade's *Tic-tac-too*, and others (Edric Vredenburg, Nora Chesson, M. A. Hoyer) scarcely remembered today. The second and third parts are "Children's Stories from Dickens" and "Children's Stories from Shakespeare," the latter all by E. Nesbit: *The Winter's Tale, Romeo and Juliet, A Midsummer Night's Dream, Cymbeline, The Taming of the Shrew, The Merchant of Venice*. Presumably, these stories were deemed most likely to interest young readers. The listed prices were, in Britain, "6d. each or Six Books complete in fancy case, 3s.6d.," and, in the United States, "25c. each, or Six Books complete in fancy case, 1.50."

Not listed is a sixty-four-page book (the size given at the top of the advertisement) with three stories—*The Winter's Tale, Macbeth, Othello*—"By E. Nesbit and Hugh Chesson. Illustrated by Frances Brundage, M. Bowley, Etc., etc." Pictures are unsigned, but most are from other editions. The color frontispiece is a charming "Prince Florizel and Perdita." Fair-haired and simply dressed in brown, she stands to hold a lamb wrapped in a blue blanket, while two sheep lie beside her; Florizel, with long brown hair and a red costume (hose, doublet, cap with feather), embraces her, as he sits beside a tree trunk and looks up lovingly. Black and white illustrations are numerous: four full-page, six three-quarter-page, and eleven half-page. Two are unusual, an architectural picture of Venice, with the domes of St. Mark's in the background and a procession of people (57), and a final simple drawing of a little girl, with a partial drape, who carries a large branch (64). Eight pages advertise books, "Father Tuck's patent Paintbox Post Card and Painting Books," and a variety of "Indestructible" items—nursery mats, curtains, bedspreads.

The most complex edition of Nesbit's stories is an expanded American one, *Twenty Beautiful Stories from Shakespeare: A Home Study Course* (1907), printed by John A. Hertel in Boston and Chicago in 1907.[4] The editor E.T. Roe began with a panegyric:

Shakespeare instructed by delighting. His plays alone (leaving mere science out of the question), contain more actual wisdom than the whole body of English learning. He is the teacher of all good — pity, generosity, true courage, love. His bright wit is cut out "into little stars." His solid masses of knowledge are meted out in morsels and proverbs, and thus distributed, there is scarcely a corner of the English-speaking world to-day which he does not illuminate, or a cottage which he does not enrich. His bounty is like the sea, which, though often unacknowledged, is everywhere felt. As his friend Ben Jonson, wrote of him, "He was not of an age but for all time." He ever kept the highroad of human life whereon all travel. He did not pick out by-paths of feeling and sentiment. In his creations we have no moral highwaymen, sentimental thieves, interesting villains, and amiable, elegant adventuresses — no delicate entanglements of situation, in which the grossest images are presented to the mind disguised under the superficial attraction of style and sentiment. He flattered no bad passion, disguised no vice in the garb of virtue, trifled with no just and generous principle. While causing us to laugh at folly, and shudder at crime, he still preserves our love for our fellow-beings, and our reverence for ourselves [3-4].

Although Roe expressed didactic high sentiments more flamboyantly, they were not unusual. His emphasis upon moral values leads easily to an observation that Shakespeare and the Bible "are the most highly esteemed of all the classics of English literature." Moreover, Shakespeare's characters have been so drawn upon by "artists, poets, and writers of fiction ... that to be ignorant of the plot of these dramas is often a cause of embarrassment" (5). But there is a problem for children: "Shakespeare wrote for grown-up people, for men and women, and in words that little folks cannot understand"; thus Nesbit wrote "to reproduce the entertaining stories contained in the plays of Shakespeare, in a form so simple that children can understand and enjoy them" (5). These sentences indicate children are the audience, and Roe concluded reassuringly. To prevent "the youngest readers" from stumbling in pronouncing the names, he has included a "Pronouncing Vocabulary of Difficult Names." However, the unique feature is "Shakespeare Quotations," not set speeches from each play, but an alphabetical compendium of passages, usually two or three lines but sometimes as many as six, that define and encourage moral virtue. They treat a range of subjects — braggarts, calumny, doubts and fears, drunkenness, equivocation, fear, feasts, filial ingratitude, honesty, and so on. This overtly didactic argument for Shakespeare should have inspired and sobered children's thoughts.

The colorful cloth cover features Romeo and Juliet, here framed by a theatrical curtain topped by a mask that blends tragedy and comedy. Max Bihn, who copied the original edition's child pictures by Brundage, Bowley, and others, is given sole credit for the seventy-six black and white illustrations. Pages have borders — decorated with a knight and lady, shields, and written scrolls — that give *Twenty Beautiful Stories* a distinctive appearance, part of the American Arts and Crafts movement, parallel to William Morris. Facing images can tell a story, as in *A Midsummer Night's Dream*, when Titania is placed under a spell and awakes to see Bottom (30–31). Puck is a toddler, while the fairy queen is a bit older. Portraits are most numerous, usually three-quarter-length, including several distinctive choices: Æmilia as abbess in *The Comedy of Errors* (181), Benedick as a saucy courtier (94) and a tonsured Friar Francis in *Much Ado About Nothing* (101). Hermione as statue inside the alcove wears simple Greek dress, but the curtain is heavily embroidered (65). Several portraits are racially distinctive. Othello's shaded face indicates his difference, a fact reinforced by chains that he wears (a disturbing echo of slavery), albeit his elegant dress includes a fez, bolero, pantaloons (213). He wears a long striped robe, when he tells a strikingly fair-haired Desdemona his adventures (211). The black Prince of Morocco's attire includes a turban with feather and matching wide sash, bolero, robe and cloak, earrings and a necklace (187). Jessica, a Jew in *The Merchant of Venice,* is a female example of Orientalism — beaded headdress that matches the wide sleeves of her dress, a large necklace, a shawl tied just below her hips to make an overskirt — as she leaves home carrying a bag of gold and a jewelry box (191). These contrast with figures like "King and Queen Macbeth," fair Europeans in medieval dress (159), or a sturdy outlaw in *Two Gentleman of Verona,* whose circumstance is signed by an animal cloak over his hunter's dress; he looks very western, a boy dressed up for play (267). Children costumed as adults have a winsome air. The most saccharin image is in *Macbeth*; "The Three Witches" are pretty sylphs (153).

Unusual episodes can be amusing: "Ganymede Faints" into the arms of Aliena and Oliver in *As You Like It* (51), or a "Poet reading to Timon" from a scroll, both richly dressed in the style of Athens (194). Images of physical combat keep a sense of adventure: in an urban setting (a rare background) "Romeo and Tybalt Fight" as Benvolio tries to intercede (105); "Pericles wins in the tournament," a Greek warrior fights with sword and shield against another Greek (122); "Macbeth and Macduff fight" on foot in vaguely Roman short armor with sword and shield (166).

Twenty Beautiful Stories features eight four-color plates, all in rather muted tones. Petruchio points with his left finger and holds a whip in his right hand as he dominates Katherine, one of Brundage / Bihn's plump child-ladies (228). In contrast, a gracious Bassanio looks down while Portia apprehensively watches him "Choosing the Casket" and Nerissa bites her nail (183). Imogen is a golden-haired gamin with bare legs, as she cools her feet in a stream (141). "Titania and the Clown" sit formally as though for a studio portrait; he with ass's head and a red blanket, the golden-haired fairy in a pink dress. Two color pages are totally different with distractingly adult figures: Romeo and Juliet embrace on the balcony (104), and Prospero watches Ferdinand and Miranda at log-carrying (33). Both, although typically Victorian, seem to have strayed into the wrong book. However, the frontispiece of William Shakespeare, "From Mr. Ozias Humphrey's Drawing of the Chandos Portrait made for the late Mr. Malone in the Year 1783," is an attractive pastel study.

The most notorious illustrations of Shakespeare stories for children were those made by Frances Brundage and others for E. Nesbit's retellings; characters are depicted as very young, rather plump children. Petruchio's manly command, pointing arm and whip at the ready, are one approach to *The Taming of the Shrew.* Max Bihn copied the images for an American edition, *Twenty Beautiful Stories from Shakespeare* (1907).

Two versions of selected Nesbit's *The Children's Shakespeare* indicate not all editions in the United States were so splendid. Henry Altemus's 1900 edition, published in Philadelphia, is rather fine, printed on glossy paper with eleven full-page black and white illustrations for thirteen plays: *Romeo and Juliet, The Tempest, A Midsummer Night's Dream, King Lear, Cymbeline, The Taming of the Shrew, Hamlet, Twelfth Night, As You Like It, Pericles, The Merchant of Venice, The Winter's Tale.*[5] The cloth cover's color design is pretty — the balcony scene of *Romeo and Juliet*, now framed in a profusion of flowers. Delicate colors and ribbons about the title resemble Victorian postcards. Seventy-six pages include Nesbit's introduction. The birthplace is a header, and Shakespeare's portrait and signature the frontispiece. Very different indeed is a cheap edition on paper of such poor quality that the smudgy illustrations, again from Brundage / Bihn, are almost unreadable. Its fifty-two pages contain five plays: *The Winter's Tale, Romeo and Juliet, The Tempest, A Midsummer Night's Dream, King Lear.*[6] The cloth cover's color illustration, pasted into a design below the title, is a feeble imitation of Millais's *The Princes in the Tower* (1878) — inappropriate since Nesbit did not include history plays, but a way to interest boys. The color frontispiece is unique: Santa Claus, with his white beard, in his red suit and mittens, drives his sled, filled with toys, across the rooftops under a crescent moon! It is perhaps a stretch to interpret this icon as a promise of presents (stories from Shakespeare's plays) to be opened eagerly. But there is no doubt that writers, scholars, and publishers had great confidence that books of Shakespeare stories were desirable, and indeed were an opportunity for singular new interpretations by Edwardians who followed the Lambs and Nesbit.

Ada Baynes Stidolph, The Children's Shakespeare *(1902)*

Major Edwardian publishers had offices in major cities throughout the Empire to distribute children's books written in England. Ada Baynes Stidolph's *The Children's Shakespeare* (1902) was published in London but written in Wynberg, South Africa.[7] With only three plays and 116 pages, it is slighter than Nesbit's with the same title; however, it exemplifies the unity of English-speakers and gives insight to colonial service. Stidolph dedicated her book to Natalie, daughter of Sir Walter Hely-Hutchinson, K.C.M.G., governor of Cape Colony. The child's portrait, seated in formal Victorian dress (including a hat), is the frontispiece. Unusually, it is a photograph, as are three others of actors in famous roles: Sir Henry Irving as Shylock (1), Ellen Terry as Portia (37), Julia Neilson as Oberon (57). These photographs from current theatre are an updating of Boydell and Victorian paintings. Presumably there was no memorable actor from *As You Like It*, the least effective retelling; John Faed's painting *Shakespeare in His Study* is its frontispiece (91).

A preface, by Very Rev. Charles W. Barnett-Clarke, Dean of Cape Town, identifies a need; "so far as I am aware, of late years no one has attempted a 'Children's Shakespeare'" (viii). The thrust of his recommendation is patriotic and religious. Barnett-Clarke "dotes" on Shakespeare, "perchance [because] 'Gentle Will' was born and died on April 23, the festival of St. George, the martyr and patron saint of dear old England, and also of the cathedral of which I am Dean" (vii). He cited Lamb's view of Shakespeare as a way to teach virtues, and then developed his own extraordinary argument:

> I deem it right that all that tends to foster loyalty to the Throne and Crown and sceptre should be heartily supported, as Shakespeare says, "No man's too good to serve his Prince."
>
> For these three chequered centuries, fraught with so much of weal and want, woe and war, progress in peace, and stress in storm, William Shakespeare "being dead, yet speaketh"; and he has been wondrously influential in moulding the minds of many men, women, and children for ten generations, to the good and Godward excelsior zenith of all that maketh for national advancement and honour. True, the keenness of realm-wide interest hath ebbed and flowed ever and anon. Princes, prelates and priests, lords and ladies, lads and lassies, have evinced periodically a loving regard for "dear sweet Will," for, as Ben Jonson said so truly, "He was not of an age but for all time." And so, we venture to bespeak for this, "The Children's Shakespeare," a right royal reception by boys and girls—yea, and grateful parents of the many millions of right loyal subjects of our mighty monarch Edward VII., not solely in Great Britain, but in "the dominions over the sea." And "so mote it be," pray I. Cordially, therefore, do I wish "God-speed" to this earnest endeavour to place in the hands of the hope of the whole realm and vast Empire—"Our Beloved Young Folk"—a wholesome, edifying publication, well calculated, I feel confident, if studied together with the Holy Scriptures—that "Book of Books"—to prove a powerful helpmeet in the attainment of that sublime safeguard for King and peoples, "the righteousness that exalteth a nation," and the practice and fulfilling of the four divine precepts—"Honour all men, Love the Brotherhood, Fear God, Honour the King"—all of which are so strenuously taught and set forth in the dramas and sonnets of William Shakespeare [ix–x].

This panegyric, resonating both high sentiment and Elizabethan language, interlaces Shakespeare, religion, and nation; admitted vagaries quickly fade in a plethora of eulogy. For understanding Shakespeare as children's literature, these comments are more significant than the stories that they introduce.

Nevertheless, Stidolph's point of view and style, "her winsome way of telling in attractive language the plot and story" (viii), are noteworthy. The manner is easy, conversational, pointed to children with dramatic explanation, description, questioning. *The Merchant of Venice*, which requires serious moral judgments, has the most variety. Stidolph early warned about Bassanio, tall, distinguished-looking, expensively dressed:

5 — Edwardian Elegance and Exuberance

> And now I am sorry to say that I must tell you a little tale about him, because all the trouble that follows is chiefly caused by one great fault of Bassanio's. Although he was such a fine, good-natured, handsome fellow, he had got into a very bad habit of wasting his money, and many times he had run into debt, and had to borrow money from his friends [30].

She alerted her readers/listeners to a frightening antagonist:

> Who is this old man, speaking in a deep, low voice, with eager-looking eyes, a long beard, and hooked nose, and wearing a loose gown, bound round with a coloured girdle, who leans forward upon his stick...?
> This is Shylock, the Jew, the money-lender....
> Watch Shylock now. See what an evil look he gives him, as he mutters to himself that he hates Antonio, and will never forgive him [9–10].

Later she made Shylock's servant Launcelot occasion for a didactic lesson, when he tries to decide whether it is right or wrong to run away:

> Now you all know what your conscience is, do you not?
> Have you not often heard a little still voice inside you which tells you if you are doing a wrong thing? [13].

Jessica, introduced as "a lovely young girl, with black hair and dark eyes. One can see at once that she is a Jewess," recognizes her filial ingratitude as she plans to become a Christian wife: "Poor Jessica! Do you not feel sorry for her, little boys and girls, who have good kind fathers who do all they can to make you happy" [18]?

Suspense is crucial to Stidolph's storytelling: "Are you not anxious to know what Portia's wonderful plan can be?" (32). She sustained excitement with an alternative appeal to imagination; evocative description introduces the trial.

> I do not suppose any of you, my dear little children, have ever been inside a court-room, have you?
> Well, I am going to take you to a court to day for the first time in your life.
> How beautiful! how wonderful! You almost hold your breath in amazement... [34].

Finally, Stidolph complemented details of crimson walls and carpet, gilt carvings, painted ceiling, golden throne with an exciting entry — and sound effects:

> Have you ever seen any place like this in your life before? I think not. Listen! There is a sound of trumpets, and you can hear the steady tramp, tramp of soldiers' feet [34].

Even judgment of Shylock, moving from initial harshness to compassion, involves suspense:

> What a change has come over Shylock! Utterly broken down and dazed ... with slow and tottering steps he turns to go. Will he reach the door without falling?
> We cannot help feeling sorry for him now, for he has lost everything, and even has to turn Christian, which is a terrible thing to him [41].

After a challenging *The Merchant of Venice*, the second story, *A Midsummer Night's Dream*, familiar and escapist, occasions comfort:

> Hold up your hands, children, those of you who would like to hear a fairy story.
> Ah! I see everyone's hand going up in a minute and bright eyes smile back into mine at the thought of such a pleasure in store as a real fairy tale.
> Come along, then, children; bring your footstools and sit beside me on the rug. Settle yourselves quite comfortably, and then we will turn the lights down low and imagine ourselves, not in the nursery which we know so well, but in a new and wonderful world called *fairyland* [48].

This depiction of "the children's hour" is charming, an evocation of Edwardian dedication to children's literature, happy meeting of nursery and family. The vagaries of the fairy world are acknowledged, but not threatening. Attention focuses on a boy-like Puck; his "work is to amuse Oberon and make him laugh, and be merry with all my funny..." (58):

> What dreadful mischief that naughty little Puck has been doing, has he not?
> Don't you hope that he will be able to alter his mistake when he finds out what he has done? ...
> "Oh, naughty Puck! ... Oh, Puck, what a terrible muddle you have got them into! What are we to do with them all?" cries Oberon....
> I wonder if all their troubles will be over when they wake again?
> [65, 73–74].

Stidolph's language — "mischief," "naughty," "muddle" — reassures and triggers amused delight rather than serious contemplation of fiscal responsibility or conscience. The child audience is placed within the nursery; amusement — leavened with some moral teaching — and simplified plot are the objectives. Older children had more sophisticated books.

Mary Macleod, The Shakespeare Story-Book *(1902)*

Dissatisfaction with Lamb's *Tales* informs Sidney Lee's introduction to *The Shakespeare Story-Book* (1902) by Mary Macleod, who had earlier written *Stories from the Faerie Queene* (1897) and later wrote *Book of Ballad Stories* (1906) and *The Story of King Arthur* (1908), often reprinted. Publisher Wells Gardner, Darton here relied on a scholar to introduce retellings of classic literature. Sidney Lee (1859–1926), author of the highly praised *A Life of William Shakespeare* (1898), began with the critical debate about whether plot or character gives excellence to drama. Like many Victorians, Lee identified interest in characters as "the final effect of supreme dramatic genius."[8] However, he recognized that, for the young, plot is first:

> When the youthful mind has grasped the manner and matter of the plots, it will in adult age be in a far better position than it could be otherwise to comprehend

all the excellences, all the subtleties of the characters. Only when plot and character have received equally full attention will Shakespeare stand revealed to the mature student in his manifold glory [viii–ix].

This is the premise of Lamb's *Tales*; but their execution was inadequate, since Mary Lamb "had little of her brother's literary power ... none of his wealth of fancy, his pliancy of style, his humorous insight, or his learning" (ix). Some prejudice about gender seems implicit, albeit Lee was introducing stories by another woman. He found Lamb's tales of the comedies "often trace the course of the stories too faintly and imperfectly to recall Shakespeare's own image ... frequently pertinent intricacies of plot are blurred by a silent omission of details, knowledge of which is essential to a complete understanding of the Shakespearean theme" (ix–x). After citing examples, Lee judged that Lamb offered young readers "a very fragmentary knowledge of the scope of Shakespeare's plays" (x). Thus he welcomed a new volume that endeavored to be more complete.

Sidney Lee, who specialized in sixteenth-century writers, was probably the best informed authority to introduce children's stories from Shakespeare. Concurrent with *The Shakespeare Story-Book* was the Oxford facsimile of the First Folio, which Lee edited (1902). His edition of the complete *Works* and *Shakespeare and the Modern Stage* were both published in 1906, as was *Great Englishmen of the Sixteenth Century*, a culmination of his more than 800 articles, most about Elizabethans. He also worked to create the *Dictionary of National Biography,* of which he ultimately became chief editor. That Lee, like Furnivall, was committed to fostering great English writers as children's literature says much about Edwardian practice of literary criticism that was strenuous but not elitist.

No contradiction exists between making Shakespeare's plays into readable stories for children and providing academic details and a cogent defense of the study of great literature. Lee allowed himself a brief note on sources. Asserting that "Romantic fiction was born for modern Europe on Italian soil" (xi), he cited Boccaccio, Bandello, Cinthio, and Belleforest's French translation. However, Shakespeare's debt to them is greater in appearance than in reality; he "freely altered and adapted the borrowed stories in accordance with his sense of dramatic and artistic fitness" (xi). Having introduced some idea of the complexity of artistic creation, Lee quickly asserted that knowing the stories was most important, a first step to future love and knowledge of Shakespeare's plays, the study of which

> may, in a far higher degree than the study of other literature, enrich their fancy, strengthen them in virtue, withdraw them from selfish and mercenary thoughts. Life will bring them no better instructor in the doing of sweet and honourable action, no better teacher of courtesy, benignity, generosity, humanity; for of both stories and characters profferring the counsel to seek what is good and true and to shun what is bad and false Shakespeare's pages are full [xii–xiii].

The justification for the study of literature is to cultivate moral virtue, and few passages state this objective more confidently and clearly.

The Shakespeare Story-Book has only sixteen of Lamb's twenty tales; the four omissions—*All's Well, Measure for Measure, Pericles, Timon of Athens*—are an initial comment about the suitability of subject matter that is less inspiring and / or poses difficult moral judgment. Macleod's ordering also suggests this awareness; she began with *The Tempest*, then seven other comedies (*Two Gentlemen, Much Ado, A Midsummer Night's Dream, The Merchant of Venice, As You Like It, Taming of the Shrew, Twelfth Night*), followed by five tragedies (*Romeo and Juliet, Macbeth, Hamlet, King Lear, Othello*) two romances (*Cymbeline* and *The Winter's Tale*), and finally *The Comedy of Errors*, which is farcical but also a recovery narrative as in romance. The absence of history plays suggests they lacked interest, were almost a separate canon, as to a lesser extent were the Roman plays. Macleod's rich details usually met Lee's criteria for fullness, while her discreet glosses of character and customs of earlier ages foster an appropriately moral understanding. Her writing is clear, often quite close paraphrase and usually without verbal simplification. Some of Shakespeare's best songs are in the original verse (22, 96, 144, 146–147, 386), as are a few short speeches from *Hamlet* and *Macbeth*.

While most stories begin with an expository paragraph of fact, several openings evoke fairy tale, whether the play is romance, tragedy, or comedy:

> There was once a lonely island far away in the midst of the sea [*The Tempest*, 2].
>
> There lived once in Verona two friends... [*Two Gentlemen*, 27].
>
> Long ago in Britain there lived a certain King... [*King Lear*, 335].
>
> There was once a merchant of Syracuse called Ægeon... [*The Comedy of Errors*, 445].

Another encouragement for young readers is the division of each story into several parts, usually four or five, often with enticing subtitles (The Magician's Isle, A Plain-dealing Villain, The Three Caskets, A Vision at Midnight, The Guest at the Banquet, The Oracle Speaks, and so on). Shorter sections aid both the pacing of reading and comprehension in a book of 460 pages. Moreover, running titles (play on the left and subtitle on the right) both entice and allow the young reader to find his place.

The physical appearance of Macleod's *The Shakespeare Story-Book* marks it as an example of Edwardian extravagance in publishing. The cover is blue cloth, with some gradation in shades of blue; figures are outlined in black, titles and a few details are gold. The spine has a small device: two faces / masks rest on two books, marked "COMEDIES" and "TRAGEDIES." "Illustrated by Gordon Browne" is on the cover and spine, but "Mary Macleod" only on the spine. This highlights the artist's fame and popularity, and the importance attached to illustration. The cover image promises the favorite play, *A Midsummer Night's*

Dream. At the center sits a splendidly drawn Bottom with his ass's head; he brays through his open mouth, flings his right arm into the air, touches the head with his left hand, and looks to the right. Thus his profiled head partially covers the gold moon above. Behind the grassy knoll a line of bushes defines the background. Four small fairies, in simple shifts that do not impede their open wings, hold hands as they dance. Bottom also supports the title page: he sits at the bottom and faces the viewer directly; on either side flits a small fairy and at the very top a large fairy (all more faintly drawn than human figures). Jester Touchstone and a youth who holds a book make a first tier just above Bottom; Rosalind and Celia, a page with a spear and a lady with a fan, stand higher. Surrounding decorative scrolls are red.

Gordon Browne (1858–1932) is one of the greatest illustrators of his era, both skilled and prolific. Here his black and white illustrations number twenty full-pages, nine three-quarter-pages, fifteen half-pages, sixteen third- or quarter-pages, and seventeen headings, sixteen with decorated initials. Browne, who made more than five hundred illustrations for *The Henry Irving Shakespeare* (1895), was a sophisticated and original artist, often more wryly humorous than the writer he illustrated. He was the son of "Phiz," who illustrated Dick-

One of Gordon Browne's most compelling illustrations for Mary Macleod's **The Shakespeare Story-Book** (1902) features Titania and Bottom, attended by the Queen's fairy subjects. However, tiny small fairies are the most diverting figures as they engage in a multitude of activities: a round of tiny figures fly in the upper left and gentle female fairies play in the lower right, while many tiny figures stand guard, engage in martial arts, or ride a snail.

ens; many consider the son a superior draughtsman, albeit less famous because he worked with so many different writers. Browne's drawing is dynamic, yet painstaking, with details for the child to discover. The first page of *A Midsummer Night's Dream* is typical (82). The heading features not pretty, gossamer fairies but a mischievous sprite who has pulled the three-legged stool of one old woman — the sort who believe in fairies. Bottom is a sleeping figure in the "T" that begins the Duke's name. The full-page, "Oh, how I love thee! how I dote on thee!" is complex (97). Again Bottom, here distinctive as the only figure drawn with very close black lines, sits among myriad fairies. Titania sits back on her knees, clasps her hands, and looks doting. Much more fascinating are lesser fairies engaged in different lively activities: very small figures dance a fairy round in the left corner, while below, other female fairies stand amidst flowers, and one larger male fairy stands on one leg to thrust his lance at three huddled dwarves. On the opposite side, two seated fairies point similarly at another small dwarf who defends with a sword, as another rides away on a snail, while a third creeps behind him. Seated nearer the queen a larger female fairy holds one of these small creatures and peers at it as if it were a doll. Above, more male fairies indulge their martial arts. One, with back to the viewer, points with raised lance at the aerial combat between a charging fairy, with lance and a leaf for shield, as he attacks a bee. A picture like this fascinates for quite a long time.

Browne's first pages for each play, which contain a heading and a large decorated initial, are consistently amusing, thoughtful, often witty, sometimes disturbing, always tantalizing. *The Tempest* begins with a composite of imaginative creatures: a pretty winged Ariel hovers on the left to point at a monstrous Caliban, who squats apelike on the ground and holds a log on one shoulder. Both his feet and hands are webbed, and he has a simian nose and wide mouth. The decorated initial for "There" is superimposed on a sinking vessel (1). *As You Like It* begins with a precisely drawn conventional scene — Touchstone leads Ganymede and Aliena through the forest — but the decorated "D" of "Deep," quaintly placed over a forest scene, has become an entrance through which Rosalind / Ganymede steps (133). For tragedy, images are somber: a pensive friar listens to an anxious Juliet, while the capital in "There" shows her white funeral bier against a black background (210). Later, the friar gestures desperately over a prostrate young lover, "Romeo, arise; thou wilt be taken!" (229); he must cope when Romeo "past all reason ... flung himself down on the ground in a perfect frenzy of grief" (228). In "Oh, I am slain!" Romeo is a dark figure as he slays the hapless Paris, who falls into a black space (241). The book's frontispiece, Juliet entombed with suicidal Romeo, anticipates both illustrations. Browne had no ecstatic balcony scene; many illustrations give the lie to romantic indulgence. Two for *Cymbeline* form a miniature narrative. In the heading Iachimo is climbing into the trunk, while the initial "D" (Daughter) frames him as a man in black pulling the lid of the trunk (391). Macleod described how Iachimo took Imogen's bracelet and observed details of her appearance and the book she was reading. "Then, satisfied with his ignoble work, he went back into the trunk. The lid shut with a spring, and once more there was apparently nothing in the room to disturb the innocent serenity of the sleeping Princess" (399).

Macleod found it necessary to explain attitudes of earlier times, especially a father's right to determine a child's marriage, whether a daughter's by "custom" in *Two Gentleman of Verona* (35), or "the law of Athens" (83) in *A Midsummer Night's Dream,* or to preserve the son's heritage in *The Winter's Tale* (435–436). In contrast, the old shepherd is firm but solicitous when he encourages a shy Perdita to take her place as queen of the sheep-shearing. For King Lear Macleod showed little sympathy:

> [Always rash and headstrong, even in his best days, old age and infirmities had rendered him still more unruly and wayward, and his fits of unreasoning anger were often beyond control.... [T]he most violent language ... flagrant injustice.... Lear, always fiery-tempered and impetuous, was certainly not one to submit tamely to such insulting treatment, and almost out of his mind... [337, 338, 342].

The King of France, who believes in Cordelia, comforts her with "manly and chivalrous words" (340). Macleod praised Kent and the Fool, while acknowledging that their "unswerving fidelity" cannot stop the forces unleashed by Lear (344). In Browne's main illustration Lear faces filial ingratitude (346), proud and scornful daughters who humiliate him. Nevertheless, Macleod praised Lear's humility when he is reunited with Cordelia, if only briefly: "It would be pleasant if the story could end here, and if we could leave the tempest-tossed old King in the cherished keeping of the gentle Cordelia" (355). Instead, they die: "And so, with all his faults and follies, which had assuredly wrought out their own bitter retribution, the fiery-hearted King passed into the realm of eternal rest" (359). Gloucester and his sons are a very minor theme, referred to as absolutely needed: "Edmund in the meanwhile, wounded to death by his own brave half-brother Edgar, who had appeared as champion to punish Edmund for his many horrible acts of treachery and wickedness, now confessed..." (357).

The Shakespeare Story-Book, Sidney Lee's remarks indicated, was written for an audience not so sophisticated as to understand character. Thus Macleod interlaced her plots with pungent evaluations that removed any ambiguity. Juliet's nurse has a "shallow, selfish nature" (225); she is a "selfish, base-minded old woman" (233). Don John in *Much Ado* is "a man of sullen, envious, and malicious temper" (59). Iago is "a man of utterly unscrupulous character" (361), who with "diabolical cunning" (367), "in a serpent-like manner, began to insinuate suspicions" (376), to "poison ... the guileless Othello" (366), who is a man of "frank, valiant nature" (360).

Several of Browne's portraits are visual equivalents of Macleod's glossing. Dressed in motley, a relaxed Touchstone sits quietly, smiles slightly, and looks at his dial before saying, "It is ten o'clock." This illustration breaks text that describes Jaques's reaction to a fool in motley who moralizes on time; Jaques would follow in the same suit: "Dress me in motley, and give me leave to speak my mind, and I will guarantee to cure the world of much evil" (145). For *Twelfth Night* Browne's fat and jovial Sir Toby Belch sprawls in a chair to cry out, "Farewell, dear heart, since I must needs be gone!" (187), a response "in mock melancholy" to Malvolio's "stern rebuke." An incisive portrait of Malvolio is sufficiently distinctive to serve as frontispiece to the table of contents (xiv). Browne's Malvolio is a fop (tiny goatee, elevated tufts of hair on either side of a bald head, high ruff, excessive long sleeves, and decorated shoes), who vainly preens with a small mirror as he observes, "Some have greatness thrust upon them." More lighthearted is the mirror image of the two Dromios, servant twins, in *The Comedy of Errors*; they lean back slightly with heads slanted to observe with ironic playfulness, "I see by you I am a sweet-faced youth" (459).

The most detailed story is *Hamlet*; and Ophelia, "a beautiful young maiden ... long yellow locks ... sweet blue eyes" (323), is understandably absorbed in a paragon:

> [P]eerless in grace and beauty, gallant in bearing as noble in nature, the young Prince shone forth far beyond any of his companions. As soldier, courtier, scholar, he was alike distinguished — ready in wit, skilled in many exercises, highly accomplished, deeply thoughtful, studious in learning, a prince of courtesy, and an affectionate comrade [294].

Macleod, who favored Hamlet, mitigated his killing of Polonius: "Thus the officious old man's prying ways met their punishment"; nevertheless, Hamlet's "lack of resolution" in carrying out "what he believed to be his duty" led him to trust "the blind impulse of the moment" and thus sacrifice "a comparatively innocent life" (316). However, at the end, "his customary sweetness of disposition" makes him apologize to Laertes (332). Browne's page illustration again features a parent-child relationship, the moment when Hamlet sees his father's ghost while he is confronting his mother after the play (319). It has perhaps the finest precision, subtle contrasts of an ethereal figure, a young man in black, and a young woman in white whose looks suggest why Claudius wed her. The detailed interior, especially the furniture and a glowing fire, reinforce the Elizabethan costume that Browne favored. But he followed principles of Victorian historical painting: ancient Briton garb for *Cymbeline* and *King Lear*, classical costume for *The Comedy of Errors*, and an exotic mixture for *The Winter's Tale*. "O, thus she stood ... when first I wooed her!" is Browne's rendering of the statue scene. Hermione has a simply cut, but well decorated Grecian drapery, while Leontes is signed an exotic Sicilian by his headgear and beard that contrast to Camillo's plainer style. Their long robes, with patterned borders, are vaguely medieval, as is Paulina's headdress and full gown, seen only from the back (441).

Evaluations of characters in the texts remove complications and tell something of social mores. Very compelling are two glosses on disturbing issues of

The variety and number of Gordon Browne's illustrations for Mary Macleod's *The Shakespeare Story-Book* (1902) combine with her sophisticated retellings to make one of the most compelling collections. Of special interest for children is the appearance of the ghost when Hamlet is in his mother's chamber; it stresses both the supernatural and the family relationship that is at the heart of the play.

belief and race that persist today. A corollary to the anxiety expressed by many (especially fundamentalist Christians in the United States) about subject matter in J.K. Rowling's Harry Potter books, the opening of *Macbeth* begins:

> Witchcraft is now a thing of the past, as far as England is concerned, unless there still lingers in some very remote corners a belief in the power of evil of some poor old body, whose only claim for such distinction is, perhaps, her loneliness and ugliness. But in ancient days, and even into the last century, such a belief was a very usual thing. "Wise women," as they were often called, who pretended they had the power of foretelling the future, were by no means uncommon, and even learned people and those in high positions were not ashamed to consult them with regard to coming events. In Scotland this belief lingered much longer than in England, and even to this day, in remote parts of the Highlands, there are some who claim they have the gift of "second sight"— that is, that they can see in advance events that will happen several years hence [245–246].

A date of 1039 puts the action as pre–Conquest and before the union of Scotland and England, an oblique explanation of difference. Browne's heading has dramatic lighting and movement as three witches circle a cauldron, while through the capital "W" move soldiers from Birnam wood (245). An illustration of Macbeth's later visit, "What is this that rises like the issue of a King?" conveys a sense of marvel (271): a ghostly crowned child rises through the fumes above the cauldron; it contrasts sharply with the ugliness of hags, three bent figures with faces as sharply individual as those in Fuseli's painting *The Weird Sisters* (1783). Macbeth is a tall and handsome warrior, whose short garment and winged helmet connote Northernness (Viking), while his checked cloak shows Victorian enthusiasm for tartan. Although Macleod is somewhat sympathetic to Lady Macbeth, especially when she has to recover social propriety after Macbeth sees Banquo's ghost, Browne depicted the "contemptuous" wife, "Infirm of purpose! Give me the daggers" (259/257); her long black plaited hair is severe, while his tousled fair hair indicates vulnerability. Boys might have been more amused by a smaller image, "Lay on, Macduff!" that captures the exciting moment of fierce single combat — and could be readily imitated in play (281).

Uneasiness after World War II altered the great popularity enjoyed by *The Merchant of Venice*, but anti–Semitism was not unknown among Victorians and Edwardians, as previously described in Adelaide Sim's *Phoebe's Shakespeare*. Browne's heading signals the stereotype not only of Venice with a gondola but also of a Jew through physiognomy, the difference between an upright Christian in white and a bowed Jew in black. The figure in the capital S for "shunned" is Shylock, a felicitous match, albeit his large nose intensified in profile, is not reassuring (104). The resemblance suggests Dickens's Fagin rather than Victoria's exceptional Prime Minister Benjamin Disraeli. Macleod's opening gives a context:

> Shunned, hated, despised, insulted, the Jews in the Middle Ages led a cruel and embittered existence among their Christian brethren. But beaten down and oppressed as they were in most of the countries of Europe, they still prospered as far as money matters were concerned, and, in spite of the demands continually levied on them, they contrived to amass large hoards of wealth. When the great nobles or merchant princes of those days got into difficulties, it was to the Jews they turned for help, and the enormous sums charged as interest for the loan enabled the Jews to fill their coffers rapidly [104].

Sympathy is not salient; Macleod quickly described Shylock as one who "lived in a wretched, penurious style, with only a clownish lad to act as a servant" (104). This man obviously lacks an Edwardian sense of the proper display of affluence; but his "pretty, flighty daughter ... gay, extravagant, without much heart, and with no respect or affection for her own race and kindred" is not a winning alternative (105). After stealing away, Jessica "in her heedless extravagance, squandered money right and left" with a "reckless prodigality [that] cut Shylock to the heart." Shylock turns with "reckless glee" toward Antonio's misfortunes and speaks to him "with a snarl like a tiger" (116–117). The Jew's end is relentlessly chronicled: "Baffled of his revenge, stripped of his wealth, forced to disown his faith, his very life forfeited — a hated, despised, miserable old man — he stood alone amidst the hostile throng. Not one face looked at him kindly, not one voice was raised in his behalf" (128). The trial, which anticipates this total judgment, is Browne's fullest drawing of the Jew — and a crowd of Christians who look on smugly and triumphantly as Portia wins the case (125). Disguised by her lawyer's robes, she is a woman in a courtroom where only men are present; Browne repeated the figure with Bassanio (129). Just as Macleod explained that young women needed male attire if they were to move about, so Browne delighted in drawing pretty pages: Julia in *Two Gentlemen* (49), three times each for Rosalind in *As You Like It* (133, 141, 153), Viola in *Twelfth Night* (176, 181, 199) and Imogen in *Cymbeline* (406, 409, 414). He favored sylvan scenes, and costumes of the ancient Britons were an additional opportunity for Victorian medievalism.

Both Mary Macleod's narratives and Gordon Browne's illustrations make *The Shakespeare Story-Book* an inviting and amusing volume for children who could find its size and sophistication attractive. The *Standard Catalog for High School Libraries* (1929), which begins with a statement that there are so many editions of Shakespeare that it is not practicable to list them, recommends having an attractively illustrated, cheaper edition of Lamb's *Tales*. The only other recommended children's version is Mary Macleod's *Shakespeare Story-Book*, published in the United States by A.S. Barnes at a price of $3. The American Library Association's review is quoted: "Charming stories of 16 plays with dialogue in words of original."[9] Clearly a retelling that retained much of Shakespeare's language had cogency beyond a child's initial reading. Nevertheless, publishers reckoned that younger children might be better served by simpler and smaller books of Shakespeare stories, those suitable for the nursery.

Jeanie Lang, Stories from Shakespeare *(1905)*, More Stories from Shakespeare *(1910)*

Edwardian publishers needed several versions of Shakespeare to reach children of different ages; but the same illustrations, a substantial part of the cost and recognized primary element, could serve several levels. In 1905 T.C. and E. C. Jack issued Lamb's *Tales from Shakespeare*, with sixteen color illustrations by American painter and draftsman Norman M. Price, discussed in Chapter 2. Five were also in Jeanie Lang's *Stories from Shakespeare,* published the same year as #12 in Jack's Told to the Children Series of nursery books, edited by Louey Chisholm, author of *In Fairyland* (1904) and *The Enchanted Land* (1906). The little books in this series retold major works of literature, classical and European, through the nineteenth century. With eight illustrations and 114 to 145 pages, they are more up-market than Stead's Books for the Bairns, as the cloth cover of the most elegant edition, which sold for one shilling and sixpence, indicates. Stamped in gold with a design derived from Charles Rennie Mackintosh

(1868–1928) and an illustration pasted on the front, each "dainty volume" was four and a quarter by five and three quarter inches. The one-shilling edition had ornamental boards, black lettering and a simpler picture or device.

Touchstone, in bright red costume, cap and bells, dominates the cover of *Stories from Shakespeare*; he promises adventure, leading readers as well as Celia and Rosalind into the Forest of Arden. Sondheim's musical proclaims the nature of fairy tale is "Into the Woods," and with Lang this is a magical and happy place. All seven stories are comedies—*As You Like It, The Merchant of Venice, The Taming of the Shrew, A Midsummer Night's Dream* and *A Comedy of Errors*—and romances—*The Tempest* and *The Winter's Tale*. Lang is acutely aware of the child's point of view. Her comments "About This Book" address limitations of books of "grown people," which "look very dull": "Most of them have no pictures; and if there are any, either they are not interesting, or else you have to read through pages and pages of what is hard to understand, before you come to anything about a picture that looks exciting."[10] Even with pictures of fairies or a funny man in cap and bells, soon children put the adult text aside when confronted by long words and difficult things. Only older children can read Shakespeare and understand why "people call him the greatest writer that ever lived." Lang's stories are "like a faint pencil outline" of a great picture that will be seen later, helped by early encounter (viii).

Like Mary Macleod, Jeanie Lang evokes fairy tales in opening sentences:

> Once on a time there lived in Milan, a city of Italy, a Duke... [*The Tempest*, 1].
>
> In France, long years ago, there lived two girls... [*As You Like It*, 15].
>
> Far away in a land where the sky is nearly always blue, and the sun... [*The Merchant of Venice*, 32].
>
> In one of the beautiful cities of Italy there once lived a rich gentleman... [*The Taming of the Shrew*, 53].
>
> Long, long ago, in the days when fairies danced in the twilight and held their fairy balls in the woods, there lived in Greece... [*A Midsummer Night's Dream*, 77].
>
> Far away in the sunny sea that lies south of Italy is an island called Sicily.... Once, long ago, there was a king of Sicily... [*The Winter's Tale*, 99].
>
> Once on a time the states of Ephesus in Asia, and of Syracuse in Sicily, were at war [*The Comedy of Errors*, 120].

But Lang did more than establish a far away time and place; her narratives have the simplicity of fairy tale. Five are set in Italy, a warm place of beautiful sun and sea that Lang equated with fairy tale; she also expected that her readers would visit Venice.

> And one day, when you go there and see the white marble palaces close to the water, and the little boats with sails of red and yellow and orange, and the gondolas all black, and the great white-sailed ships from other lands, you will think you are in Fairyland [32].

Ariel is "a gentle, pretty little fairy" (3), whose carrying out of Prospero's commands becomes a main theme. He is "a beautiful sea-fairy," unseen by all but Prospero, although "others could hear his little voice singing, and ringing like a clear, sweet bell" (7). Ariel also becomes "a horrible bird that flapped its wings over the table and made everything vanish away," illustrated by Price at the moment after it has sent plates and goblets flying in the air (11–12). When Prospero, a "magician," extends his wand, his enemies cower. Caliban scarcely appears, the drunken Stephano and Trinculo never. Thus Lang spared children unsavory subject matter and fostered the role of the good fairy.

Making *A Midsummer Night's Dream* primarily a fairy tale simplifies and involves child readers more completely. The young lovers are minor characters, unable to perceive fairies because they lack "ears that are quick enough" and their heads are too "full of their own affairs" (81). They wander through the wood "hearing no fairy music, and seeing no fairy forms, full only of their own unhappiness" (92). Lang explained what they are missing, and how her readers might attain it.

> Perhaps if a little girl or boy had been there — a little girl or boy who had done nothing mean or selfish or cruel or greedy all that day — they might have heard soft rustling in the long green grass, and merry, tinkling laughter, as if the bluebells were nodding their heads and singing. They might have heard tiny voices, as sweet as the sweetest birds,' and they might even have seen a flash and a shimmer of shining wings, as if some beautiful butterflies were still astir, or as if some big fire-flies were playing hide-and-seek amongst the bushes [80–81].

The frontispiece, archetypal gossamer and beauty, features shining wings, musical instruments, flitting lights, and flowers. This is the icon faked in a notorious photograph of fairies that played upon longings for such lovely creatures; even Arthur Conan Doyle credited it. Quoted songs enhance Lang's description. In this magical world Bottom — although he is the subject of a second illustration (90) — appears only briefly, before Oberon has compassion for Titania's infatuation. Hippolyta is absent, as are the rustics and their play. Puck, or Robin Goodfellow, is a "merry, mischievous little elf" who plays tricks, but also "a good little fellow indeed to those who treated him kindly"; he does their household chores (84–85). When Puck precipitates confusions, this is just a "mistake" that Oberon quickly corrects without reprimand (92–93).

Endless mistakings in *The Comedy of Errors* prompt Dromio's fright: "This is fairy land," where "We talk with goblins, owls, and elvish spirits" that injure those who do not obey (130). However, the day ends "in peace and joyousness and contentment" (144). Little Prince Mamilius, "laughing to think how he would frighten them," tells "a tale of sprites and goblins" in *The Winter's Tale* (101). Lang also retained the shepherd's identification of the treasure found with abandoned baby Perdita as "fairy gold" (109), and Price illustrated (108). Perdita is the princess of fairy tale, by birth and by Florizel's selection, yet there is a contemporary note; she "was looking lovelier than ever in a pretty frock" (111).

Through such Edwardian references Lang pointed difference between Shakespeare's time and her own. Celia and Rosalind attend the wrestling match in *As You Like It*, "for in those long ago days it was the custom for gentle ladies to look on at things that now seem to us very rough and very cruel" (18–19). In the forest Orlando "does not know them in the dress they wore and with their stained brown faces, and took them for the shepherd boy and his sister that they pretended to be. He made great friends with them" (28). Expectations of class and gender are properly handled. When Rosalind faints at the sight of the handkerchief stained with Orlando's blood, those who "thought she was a boy laughed at her for being so womanish" (31).

Admiration for Portia partially explains the popularity of *The Merchant of Venice*, although the play's subject poses difficulties that require rationalization. Whether to avoid sophisticated ambivalence or to excuse racial prejudice, Lang—like Sim and Macleod—made Shylock a villain, "the worst of all the Jews in Venice," who "in those long ago days were not good" because they lent money too dearly to make themselves rich and others poor (34). Shylock only "pretends to be very good and kind" when Bassanio asks for the loan; actually he is delighted to have his hated enemy Antonio in his hands. Jessica eloped because "Shylock was not kind to her, and she knew he would never let her marry any man who was not a Jew" (39). At the trial "Shylock would not hear of mercy" (46). At the end "the Jew, whose money was more dear to him than anything else, was broken-hearted," after the Duke gave his wealth to Antonio, who, in contrast, refuses the half of Shylock's money due him on condition that the Jew will all his riches to his daughter. Because here Shylock is not forced to convert, Jews are simplistically greedy and materialistic. Set against this is the selection of the "box" to win Portia; Lang quoted the maxims of gold, silver, and lead to confirm the theme. The illustration, styled like a Renaissance painting, depicts Bassanio, watched by an anxious Portia, as he touches the smaller lead box (38).

The list of books in Jack's Told to the Children Series grew steadily in the opening years of the twentieth century; five years after *Stories from Shakespeare*, Jeanie Lang contributed *More Stories from Shakespeare* (1910), illustrated by eight more pictures by N.M. Price. Again there are seven stories—*Hamlet, Prince of Denmark, The Life and Death of King John, Macbeth, The Tragedy of King Richard III, King Lear, Pericles, Prince of Tyre, Julius Caesar*—but very different from those in the first book. Lang's "About This Book" opening has much to say about the suitability of Shakespeare for children. She explained her initial selections: "because I thought they would best like stories that ended happily, I left the sad ones out."[11] Lang's second book responds to people who said she had not told any of the histories or tragedies—"which is the name by which unhappy tales are known"—that children should also know.

5 — *Edwardian Elegance and Exuberance* 185

Jeanie Lang's *Stories from Shakespeare* (1905) was followed by *More Stories from Shakespeare* (1910), both volumes in the nursery Jack's Told to the Children Series that introduced great literature. Norman Price's lively illustration of Touchstone, Celia, and Rosalind, who move lightly into the Forest of Arden, signals the comedies of the first book, while his sinister figure of Richard III before the Tower of London is portentous of more stories from Shakespeare's tragedies and histories. The gold decoration, with Mackintosh influence, of the cloth edition marks a more expensive book than the simple paper cover, but the illustrations are the same.

Nevertheless, Lang cited a little girl's response to hearing these stories before they were printed:

> Some stories begin happy and end miserable, and some begin miserable and end happy. I like best the ones about the adventures, where they are happy all the time; but it seems to me that in these stories, the people begin miserable and go on being miserabler. The only happy story is the story of Pericles [v].

Pericles is, of course, a romance. Lang ended with an explanation that Shakespeare, who wrote for grown-up people, was deeply concerned with moral values:

> one of the greatest teachers. And in each of these plays that are so sad, there is a big lesson to be learned. We see how selfishness and cruel wickedness and envy can bring misery upon innocent people; how the longing to be great, the greed of power, can lead men and women into every sort of evil; how unselfish love and goodness must always bring true happiness in the end [vi].

Children will derive these lessons from the stories; as adult readers of Shakespeare's plays they will recognize the greatness of one who saw Life with "true eyes."

To render the "miserable stories" more accessible, Lang used simple language and typically started with a gloss that makes a contemporary reference and evokes fairy tale or legend. Thus *Hamlet* begins:

> In a little country by the North Sea, the home of our own Queen Alexandra, long, long ago there lived a King who was very brave and very good.
> He had one son called Hamlet, and a wife whom he loved.
> He was a clever and handsome Prince, with a careless, happy heart that did not like to be troubled by serious things.
> Now Hamlet's mother was a bad woman. She was far more fond of the King's wicked brother than she was of her noble husband, and together she and this wicked man planned how they might kill the King [1].

Almost nothing of the play's ambiguity survives; any child reader would have no cause to consider alternate judgments. After meeting the ghost, "All the gaiety and happiness seemed from that night to go out of Hamlet's heart. His father's death had made him very sad, but now he was sadder still" (4). Since revenge is the only possible course of action, the prince chides himself for delay: "I must be a coward, ... a miserable weak villain, a John-a-Dreams who has no courage to avenge an evil deed" (6). The illustration is the player's scene, when the King calls for light (8). Like a hero from Northern sagas, Hamlet beheads those who would kill him on the way to England. The drowning Ophelia, favored by Victorian painters, is appealing in Lang's description, "as she floated, she sang, like a lovely mermaid, snatches of old tunes" (14). Lang quoted, "Good-night, sweet Prince," when four captains bear his body, but added a final didactic summation: "So, like a soldier, ended Hamlet, who might have been a great and happy king had not the wickedness of others made him one of the most unhappy princes that ever lived" (17).

Lang's judgment of *Macbeth* is similar: "So, fighting to the last, died one who had been a brave soldier until that evil day when, by their wicked magic, the witches poisoned what had been a true and gallant heart" (48). The other influence, Lady Macbeth, "was a proud, bad-hearted woman, [who] plotted and planned how she could gain the crown for him" (35). In short, Lang's tragic heroes are more victims of circumstances than molders of their own destinies. Openings that create a remote past partially explain and exonerate:

> In the long, long ago days, when history and fairy tale seem to have got mixed up together, so that it is not easy to tell which is which, the King of Scotland was a good old man, named Duncan.
> Scotland was a wild country when Duncan reigned. Where there are now houses and towns there were then thick forests in which wolves sheltered, and lonely moors where the red deer and wild cattle grazed. From Norway there came ships full of warriors who fought with the Scottish King and tried to take the kingdom for their own, and in those battles King Duncan owned no better general than his friend and kinsmen, Macbeth [31].

Lang exploited children's enthusiasm for Viking tales, while her contrast between modern and medieval acknowledges difference that becomes more specific when Macbeth and Banquo ride on a stormy evening on a lonely moor: "Had they known who they would meet there, they would certainly have stuck sprigs of rowan in their helmets because in those days people fancied that the rowan could keep away all evil spirits, and witches and warlocks" (32).[12] Price's illustration is again dark, an interior dominated by a huge cauldron over a fire that gives the only light, enough to reveal three thin figures, with beards and pointed noses, who wear cloaks, one with a turban. A black cat watches them chant, "Double, double toil and trouble" (42). It is a familiar for children to watch.

The two English histories are somewhat obvious choices. *The Life and Death of King John* is here primarily a story of Prince Arthur's pleading with Hubert not to blind him, a memorable episode of pathos as in Yeames's famous painting, and subject of Price's illustration, "Oh, save me, Hubert! save me!" (26). In a beautiful interior with medieval details a boy pleads; his fair hair, accented by his golden tunic and green cape, contrasts to the russet and maroon worn by the adult.

The Tragedy of King Richard III is more intriguing; Lang's introduction explains:

> Were it possible for us to call up a long procession of kings and queens, such as we sometimes have in pantomimes, we should see in the line of English Kings, about midway between William the Conqueror and our own King George, a little, slight figure, more like that of a boy than of a man. His face would be thin, clever, and very sad. Perhaps you might like him until you realized from one of his shoulders being higher than the other that he was Richard III, whom we have been taught to think of as a hunchback, and have learned to hate as one of the wickedest kings of history [49].

Like Hamlet and Macbeth, Richard dies fighting, "ever a brave soldier" but with a "heavy heart" (61). Lang repeated the evaluation of character that has been taught, but she also implied an alternative. Richard is a man of his time, but cleverer than others:

> There were many savage battles in those days, many dark plots and secrets, when kinsman warred against kinsman, brother plotted against brother. And chief of all the plotters was Richard, Duke of Gloucester. He was very clever, very sly, and he thought to wear the crown of England. So cunning was he in his wickedness that he was able to get others to carry out his plans, and to have all the blame and punishment fall upon them, while he himself won greater honours by the evil he had made them do [50–51].

The juxtaposition of cleverness and wickedness in Richard makes him a less easily didactic character; quotations ("I seem a saint, when most I play the devil" and the dreams before Bosworth) enrich possibilities. In Price's illustration, Richard, who looks at the viewer with sad, lidded eyes, walks along the Thames across from a white Tower of London, scene of his infamous murders—signaled by the bag of coins that he holds and his arms behind him — and a contrast to his rich, dark clothing, deep red cap and doublet and brown fur cape (cover, 50).

King Lear is more fairy tale, "Once upon a time there was an old King of Britain whose name was Lear" (67). Like Lamb's tale, Lang's story lacks the complexity of the Gloucester plot and historical interest of Edgar. But she situated *Julius Caesar* in a Christian context: "One hundred years before the shepherds of Bethlehem heard the angels' song of peace and good-will, there was born in Rome a baby boy who afterwards became a very great ruler" (97). A dominant message is "there has never been a great man who had not enemies" (98). Substantial quotations from the funeral orations, often used in schools to train in elocution, display the power of rhetoric.

More Stories from Shakespeare is a weak example of history plays in a small book, and the combination with tragedies heightens the miseries that the little girl found so obvious. Only *Pericles* has the affirming adventure of romance/comedy—"many a gallant knight came to the tournament" (84) and a pretty, efficient, cheerful heroine who lives. A singular way to gain the advantage of cheerful retelling and appeal to girl readers was to expand Lamb's feminization and turn Shakespeare stories into fairy tales.

Fay Adams Britton, Shakespearian Fairy Tales *(1907)*

Fay Adams Britton told something of plots and characters in eight of Shakespeare's plays by using fairy lore to create a palimpsest. She relied upon the "fancy" of children who respond to fairy tales even before they can read. Her style was that of the oral storyteller, for she constantly addressed her audience, simple statements about behavior and questions—not infrequently as a way of defusing possible concerns and of securing agreement with the judgment she was making. The book is "fondly" dedicated to her own sons, while her author's note is primarily an argument for children's Shakespeare. She perceived that "the minds of children dwell in the realms of fancy. With magical eyes they see the things which are read or told to them, and retain the pictures in memory ever after."[13] Because older people remember the stories of childhood more than things read later, early introduction to classic literature is advantageous: "familiarize the childish mind with the work of the great English poet," and "the youthful reader" will already have "the desire for Shakespeare's plays and ... find them full of interest and easier understanding" (1–2).

Britton's eight fairy tales derive from *A Midsummer Night's Dream, The Merchant of Venice, King Lear, The Winter's Tale, The Taming of the Shrew, Macbeth, The Tempest,* and *Cymbeline.* Clara Powers Wilson contributed twenty-four full-page illustrations—three for each story, one color and two black and white. Like Britton's simple vocabulary and sentence structure, Wilson's depictions of children signal a young audience. Unlike the infantile figures of Frances

Brundage, and his adapter Max Bihn, for Nesbit's *The Children's Shakespeare*, Wilson's are elegant; they are not plump, and their costumes are influenced by Art Nouveau. Moreover, fairies who serve / help / direct characters appear in most pictures. The book's 143 pages of large print are thus very much enlivened; each tale is a good length to read aloud. The cover is paper boards, with a cloth spine and an engaging color illustration (red and black on a cream background). Two fairies stand on either side of a clock where the time is a minute before midnight. One is dressed as a jester (cap and bells, checked tunic, striped stockings); the other, who has a bare chest and legs, wears a long, beautifully bordered cloth about his waist but trailing from his arm to his sandals. Each has two small horns on his head to signal fairy identity. Both hold large smiling masks that promise comedies only. Britton's distinctive characteristic is to infuse elements from fairy tales, familiar motifs, to amplify Shakespeare's plots—and be a cogent reminder that Shakespeare depended upon traditional motifs; the kernel of many plays is a fairy tale.

The demands of transformations vary greatly, as does the extent of Britton's alterations. Easiest is *A Midsummer Night's Dream*, Shakespeare's richest treatment of fairies and the foundation for subsequent depictions, most notably their diminutive size, as in *Nymphidia* (1627), a poem by his friend Michael Drayton. Mortals are only incidental; Britton centers on the quarrel between Oberon and Titania, but immediately involves her audience with a commonplace experience: "Now, we find that fairies sometimes quarrel and do naughty things, just as do little girls and boys—and even grown-ups at times" (9). In Wilson's black and white line drawing Titania stands with the changeling boy atop a huge flower, while Puck sits on another and holds his head in confusion (11). When Oberon seeks revenge on Titania, Britton again observes human similarity: "Fairies, my dears, did not like to be made fun of any more than people do, as you will learn when you hear how King Oberon wished to tease and humble Queen Titania" (12). Oberon's attempt to sort out the confused young lovers is an incidental act of kindness. Britton's view of Bottom is not dissimilar to Lamb's: "a clown, my dears, as you may know, is a very foolish man who does silly things" (15). Her closest adherence to Shakespeare's text is for the fairies that attend Bottom. They dominate the color illustration, where Titania's long swirl of dress and wings and several fairies crowded behind the donkey's head almost equal his size (frontispiece). Later Oberon removes the donkey's head—Britton does not use the word "ass"— "which so pleased the fellow that he just cracked his heels together and scampered out of the wood; and he has never been back again" (18). King and queen are happily and lovingly reconciled, while "dear, laughing little Puck ... continued his merry pranks secure in the friendship of everybody" (19), reiterated by a visual image of Puck as he rides on a bat's wings (16). Britton's final question clarified the difference between fantasy and reality, and led her to identify the author:

Now, my dears, what do you think of this story?
It is just a fairy tale — a funny little dream — A Midsummer Night's Dream of a great man who lived long, long years ago, and whose name was—
WILLIAM SHAKESPEARE [19].

Britton reiterated the theme of quarrel in *The Merchant of Venice*. Antonio and Shylock had "quarreled many times, and therefore were not good friends. Antonio had called Shylock some very ugly names, and the man hated Antonio and was anxious to be even with him for past injuries" (23). She quickly recounted Bassanio's success in choosing the right casket, anticipated in Wilson's illustration: three small pages hold the caskets up to him, as Portia watches anxiously in the background (20). Britton's innovation is that Portia's courage and intelligence alone do not resolve the trial: "Portia was surprised by a strange creature who announced herself as Portia's Fairy Godmother" (26) and asks whether Portia wishes to help her husband. The fairy godmother provides a letter of introduction to the Court of Venice, dresses Portia by fairy magic as a Doctor of Laws, and keeps her promise to "whisper in your ear wise and proper words for you to say" (26). "The quality of mercy" is the long quotation, nineteen lines, followed by ten lines from the clinching argument (29). Again in muted tones of brown, orange, and rose, the color illustration is a study in exquisite costume. Portia, ever feminine, wears not a lawyer's dour robes, but a low-necked gown and a beautiful cloak with Art Nouveau designs. In the foreground half-figures of five young courtiers observe — and display beautifully patterned doublets. Finally, the fairy godmother's "warning voice" tells Portia to hurry home before Bassanio (30). Britton's moral lesson concerns Shylock — never identified as Jew or father. She counseled compassion:

> Now, my dears, of course you feel unkindly towards Shylock, but you must remember he had suffered much, and that the poor man had been called a "dog," and many other ugly names. So I think he was to be pitied some, too. Antonio was set free, and Shylock lost all his money because he sought a human life. Poor old Shylock! We must feel sorry for him as he leaves the Court, a broken-hearted old man [29–30].

Britton was, however, unsympathetic to King Lear, who had "many queer notions" and "didn't really know the wicked hearts of his two eldest daughters" (32). The opening scene, with demands for filial piety, fills most of the tale (32–36) and is the subject of the color illustration. Cordelia's very long patterned cloak (echoes of Gustav Klimt) dominates as she stands before her enthroned old father and obscures her two sisters on the left. Others at court are child musicians; a boy stands with a harp on the right side and several others on his left. When Cordelia and the Earl of Kent are banished, he takes the hands of the weeping child and says, "May all the inhabitants of Fairyland attend and shelter thee, sweet maid, that justly think'st and has't most rightly said" (37). Fairies are actively involved with Kent. As he sits to rest, he hears the "wee voice" of Ariel, Queen of the Fairies, who consoles him, "Have good cheer. The Fairies will defend you and the fair Cordelia" (40). She gives him a magic ring for protection, disguises him as a peasant by waving her wand over him, and sends him to serve old King Lear. "The Fairy Guides Lear and Kent" depicts a very strong youth who takes the feeble old man by the hand and supports him with an arm about his shoulder. Ariel hovers as a tiny figure in the foreground, wings widespread (41). Taking on an extra servant occasions Lear's quarrel — Britton returned to consequences of anger — with Goneril and subsequently Regan, whose response to Kent's intercession for Lear is to place him in the stocks, a practice that Britton explained:

> Stocks, my dears, are happily not used nowadays. They were heavy wooden frames, with holes into which a person's legs and arms were fastened, so that no movement was possible. It was customary to put law-breakers in the stocks for hours at a time [43].

Although an illustration depicts Kent's punishment, the fairy hovers above reassuringly (44). Britton explains that Kent saw Ariel smiling; but "of course, no one else saw the Fairy, for the Fairies make themselves visible only to a chosen few." Her "wee voice" reminds him of the ring; after he glances down, "immediately the stocks fell apart and he was free" (43). Thus Kent is able to help mad Lear, while the fairy goes to Cordelia, happily married in France, to bring her back to nurse her father. When a quarrel between Albany and Cornwall precipitates a battle, France wins an easy victory and is able to restore the kingdom to Lear:

> The past seemed a fearful dream to the aged King Lear. Yet he was destined to see many happy days, and to entertain the future King of Britain many times when he came with his fond father, the King of France, and his mother, the dearly beloved Cordelia [48].

Shakespeare's tragedy is now a fairy tale in which all live happily ever after.

The fairy's role in *The Winter's Tale* is somewhat more exacting. There is a surprise for Hermione, who has been shut in a room by her angry husband: "the fairy had something in her arms, and what do you suppose it was? A wee baby girl! Think of that!" (53) — a fairy tale explanation of where babies come from. The message is "Cheer up," for the fairy expects the baby to make the king happy. However, when Hermione gives the infant to Leontes, saying, "My King, a Fairy left this to make us happy," he continues to act "as many spoiled little boys and girls do over imaginary wrongs" (52) and is "cross and ugly" (53). Forced to be ferocious, the fairy scolds his "wicked ways," promises "severe" punishment, and oracle-like announces that his son is dead. Immediate confirmation leads to instant remorse; Britton again engaged her audience with a question: "When we feel we have been naughty we always want to be forgiven, don't we?" (55). Upon finding Hermione gone, Leontes remembers the fairy's prophecy that only when he recovers the baby will he see his queen again. The fairy also sets up the reunion; she gives Camillo a box of the queen's jewels and gold to leave with baby Perdita at the shepherd's door in Bohemia. Although pastoral Act IV is condensed to Florizel's recognition that they must flee, an illustration shows the lovers as shepherdess and pipe-playing suitor (56). Following the reunion of father and daughter, which comes quickly and easily, the fairy counsels Leontes to prepare a wedding feast for two couples, since he too will be a groom. In the art gallery the fairy, "with one wave of her sparkling wand over the statue," says, "Be stone no more," and Hermione comes to life (61; color illustration, 60). Britton concluded with one of her severest didactic lessons:

> Was not the fairy very kind to bring her back to life?
> This little story proves to us that we must be kind and gentle to those we love, doesn't it? Else some fairy may visit our dear ones and take them away. I know my little readers would be sorry indeed to have that happen [62].

Not all fairies are gossamer and winged. In *The Taming of the Shrew* Britton deployed an elf, the tinker Sly, so named "because he always managed to accomplish what he set out to do, either by fair means of foul" (64). To a distraught Baptista he appears

> in his regular uniform which he wore in Fairyland. This consisted of green knee-breeches and a red satin waistcoat, trimmed in brass buttons and bells, a pointed cap of yellow satin with bells, green hose, and red slippers with very pointed toes, at the end of which were bells. He had the funniest of funny faces — a wee mouth that drew up at the corners, a pug nose, sparkling blue eyes that told of his merry interest in all he undertook, and the reddest of curly hair [66].

This precise description follows Wilson's black and white illustration, "Sly Bowed Low to Baptista" (65), where the elf's clothes are modestly detailed in comparison with the human's splendidly decorated costume. Elf Sly also differs in being larger, the size of a small child rather than tiny. But his task, to transform Katherine, is as great as those undertaken in other Shakespearean fairy tales. Sly gives Baptista a magic ring with which he can be summoned at any time for "consultation and advice." This becomes increasingly necessary since Master Sly's first suggestion — to interest the angry shrew in things outside herself, notably art, languages, and music — meets with no success; she beats the tutors. Katherine fully voices her resentment; Britton paraphrased Shakespeare — the elder daughter objects to her father's favoring of Bianca (69) — and then attributed her fury over Bianca's suitors to a discriminating femininity: "And while Katherine was really not interested in the least in the gentlemen themselves, she had enough feminine nature to wish to be admired" (70). Moreover, in her first encounter with Petruchio, closely paraphrased, Katherine is both "enraged" and "half amused" (74–78). Sly takes charge of wedding arrangements; when Baptista turns the magic ring three times Sly and the groom — disreputably dressed — appear. This brings relief after the moment depicted in the color illustration, "And Still no Bridegroom Came," which foregrounds a cropped carriage drawn by prancing horses held steady by pages; at the bottom of a long stairway Baptista waits pensively, at the top the two sisters cover their faces in distress, while a row of pages observe (82). When Petruchio insists that they leave immediately, Britton evaluated, "Katherine had met her match this time" (85). Sly continues her instruction, here briefly told, by placing the groom's house "in great disorder and confusion" (85). Britton tempered the play's toughness in striking ways. Petruchio explains that he is sole heir of all his father's lands and goods, "which I have bettered rather than decreased" (72), and he promises that Kate "will prove a second Grissell" (79). There is no wager at Bianca's wedding feast, but a stunning reversal: "Petruchio tore off his mask, and on bended knees before his wife, vowed his eternal love and devotion to the gentlest and most patient of wives. And Katherine's face was radiant with joy, peace, and happiness" (86–87). As for Sly, he returned to Fairyland, "where he received new laurels for his task" (87).

Britton transformed *King Lear* into a fairy story with a happy ending, but used *Macbeth* to explain that at the same time that fairies lived, there was "another sort of queer little people" (89). She first asked her readers to guess, then proceeded with a helpful — and frightening — physical description (bent figures, long uncombed gray hair, sharp and angular features, rolling eyes, pointed hats) and explanation that "witches" lived in dark caves or the tops of big trees and spent their time plotting wrongs (89). In one illustration five fly on broomsticks across a craggy landscape dominated by a great tree (88). Tempting great men to evil deeds, witches chose their victim: "these witches knew who would listen to them, just as Fairies knew things" (91). The color illustration is at first glance one of chivalry, two mounted knights in armor; but on the lower right are small witches, whose presence explains why horses are rearing (92). Witches are always around, "whispering wicked things" to Lady Macbeth as well as her husband. Britton explained what Macbeth saw at the banquet: "A ghost — and it looked like Banquo! It really was not a ghost, my dears. Macbeth's heart was so guilty and full of sin, that it pictured a ghost" (95). To make a fairy tale of *Macbeth* is a bit beyond even Britton's ingenuity; she catalogued murders and deaths quickly before reassuring her dear readers that Malcolm is placed on the throne and "there was great rejoicing in Scotland" (98). Witches afford a daunting comparison to fairies.

The final two plays offer richer territory for adaptation as fairy tale. Like *A Midsummer Night's Dream*, *The Tempest* already has a fairy, the lovely Ariel. Britton began with the rule of Sycorax, "an old witch" who lived in "a deep, dark cave, hewn out of solid rock, under the earth" (99). On the island live "very queer little people ... very much like the funny little Imps Rip Van Winkle found upon a mountain in his day" (99). Britton thus simultaneously gave a familiar American reference and greatly increased the population of "Fairy Isle" (102); she further explained that the unfortunate fairies had been locked up by Sycorax for refusing to obey her wicked commands. When Sycorax died, there was no one to release them until Prospero arrives. His exploration of the island leads him to the cavern where he finds a book that explains Sycorax's secrets and gives the location of "a glittering wand ... studded with sparkling gems all over its polished surface, causing it to dazzle the eye" (101). When Prospero chances to touch a wall, Ariel, here female, emerges. She explains to Prospero that, filled with rage and grief over such mistreatment, she touched Sycorax with her wand and willed her death; however, unfortunately the witch had time to imprison all the fairies in "walls, trees, and stumps" (102). Himself a victim of persecution, "Prospero Releases the Fairies" (illustration 104). With his great unfurled cloak, decorated with large, black, interlacing shapes, his majestic figure takes up almost as much room as the countless small fairies, also wrapped in cloaks, that he releases with one wave of Ariel's wand. Ariel suggests the fairies make Prospero their king and over the years enlarge his wealth with bags of gold. Miranda is depicted as a child of nature, all rosy and innocent, albeit her dress exposes one shoulder (100). She kneels on the sandy beach to listen to the sea in one of the many white shells she has gathered.

Unfortunately Caliban was among those freed. Britton set up the opposition of the two principal inhabitants as good and bad supernatural creatures on Fairy Isle:

> Caliban, you must know, my little readers, was a son of the wicked Sycorax and had inherited his mother's evil heart and power. He was a dwarf, short and misshapen, but exceedingly strong and powerful. He could not speak, and when addressed would answer only by signs, although when angry he would roar loudly. Ariel well knew that Caliban would never rest until he had revenge upon the Fairies, and herself particularly, for the death of his mother. Henceforth Caliban and Ariel would be at war [106].

Here Britton also referenced the tradition of dwarfs as evil. Caliban's "perverted nature" limits what Prospero can teach him; "a very sulky and lazy Sprite," he neglects his assigned manual labor (106, 107). Ariel, not Prospero, identifies the vessel coming from Naples and suggests that they raise a tempest so that Prospero can deal with his enemies as he likes. Again a fairy, not a human, determines events. In "Prospero Calms the Storm," waves and clouds are turbulent and the ship thrown on its side; father and daughter embrace quietly on the shore (109). Prospero finally tells Miranda his story to explain the tempest, and she falls asleep. Thus Ariel has time to bring Ferdinand, Prospero's choice for her husband, and many fairies:

> Oh what a beautiful sight! Fairies dressed in pink, Fairies in in blue, Fairies in all the rainbow hues. There was low, sweet music, too.
> Prospero waved his wand, and there stood Ferdinand. Poor Ferdinand! He did not know what to make of this strange cave [113].

Britton quickly recounted their love and Prospero's reconciliation with his brother: "Was not Prospero kind and good to forgive Antonio? I think he was" (115). Because his time on Fairy Island has been happy and the fairies faithful and good subjects, Prospero provides a farewell party that also celebrates the impending marriage (115). As an expression of gratitude, "all the funny little folk of the island" build a beautiful ship for Princess Miranda. Prospero returns the island to the fairies whose future is happy, since "the ugly Caliban died." The humans sail away "in their beautiful vessel of pearl and gold on a calm, smooth sea, with all the blessing of Fairyland attending them" (116).

Perhaps her own sons inspired Britton to make Cymbeline's two sons the starting point of a crucial history of the early days of Great Britain, an era of fairies;

> In the woods and dells of Britain there dwelt a band of Fairies, who not only danced and frolicked in the moonlight, but had their little serious life as well, each having his individual cares and duties. These little Fairies were the guardians of Britain's people [118].

The queen of the fairies foresees the death of Cymbeline's good queen and that the household will fall to "a mighty and powerful Witch" when he weds another (119). In "The Fairies Kidnap the Princes," two pretty small boys look a bit apprehensive as a bevy of little fairies dance about them in another color illustration with muted tones of pink, rose, brown and white (120). Myriel, favorite of the fairy queen, is appointed to watch over little Imogen, but difficulties emerge when she is older. As in Shakespeare's play, newly married Imogen is alone after Leonatus is banished; he goes to Rome but is innocent of silly boasting or wager. Iachimo devises his plot with the trunk only after he has been charmed by the witch. Because Myriel does not thwart theft of the bracelet, Iachimo is able to deceive Leonatus, who sends a message for Imogen to meet him at Milford Haven, where he has ordered his servant Pisanio to murder her. However, in the forest fairy Myriel appears to explain all and redirect the action: Pisanio, who is to return to Leonatus with a false report of Imogen's death, gives her the little vial of poison the queen gave him, thinking that it will help her sleep.

The finest moment follows: "The Fairy Changes Imogen into a Boy" (illustration 135). With a touch of her wand Imogen becomes Fidele, "and from now on we must remember that Fidele is Imogen, and Imogen Fidele" (134). Wilson's pretty page kneels as Myriel presents a gleaming sword, albeit symbolic lilies portend difficulties to come. The complexities of Shakespeare's several plots are quickly untangled (or ignored): "You remember we left Imogen (or Fidele, I mean) before the great cave" (138), whose inhabitants Britton described as "hunters, strong, sturdy, and brave, well skilled in military tactics and thoroughly educated. Men with a love for truth; brave men who would fight valiantly for a good cause" (138). In short, they are the worthy princes of Britain, Guiderius and Arviragus, "kidnapped by the fairies," and the banished Belarius, "a wise and learned man and just the man to have charge of these princely boys" (139). War with Rome; Guiderius's swift death blow to the wrong-headed suitor, cowardly Cloten; the fearful and screaming death of his mother, the

Imaginative explanations in Fay Adams Britton's *Shakespearian Fairy Tales* (1907) transform the plays by relying on conventions of fairy tales. Thus when in *Cymbeline* Imogen assumes male attire — a frequent device used by Shakespeare — the agent of her transformation is a fairy. Clara Powers Wilson exploits characteristics of Art Nouveau in the patterns of her doublet and fairy wings and decorative lilies.

witch; Cymbeline's temporary sadness until "the spell of witchcraft passed over Britain" and Myriel restored his sons— all transpire quickly. Finally, "The Fairy Reunites Imogen and Leonatus" (141), so that a happy family can live in the castle for many years. Britton, who deployed formulas of fairy tales and attributed main actions to fairies in a charming and appealing way, included elements to please boys, but books of Shakespeare stories devised for boys were written by three men.

R(obert) Hudson, Tales from Shakespeare (1906)

Published at the same time, R. Hudson's *Tales from Shakespeare* (1906) is another small book. However, Hudson wrote more varied and challenging tales and paraphrased original texts with fewer simplifications and interpretations. Jack published separate series, Told to the Children, Stories from History, and The Children's Heroes; Collins' Clear-Type Press combined literature and history in their Tales for the Children Series that included Hudson's *Tales*. The end papers depict pretty children reading—four girls but only one boy—and juxtapose a fairy and mermaid with blond warrior heroes in the upper border. The cover, Bottom with ass's head and Titania, again relies on *A Midsummer Night's Dream*. Hudson's title "Oberon and Titania" signals stress on fairies, but he also retained complexity—Hippolyta, the rustics and their play, and emotions of the young lovers. Some harshness amidst the laughter and merriment of "the mischievous fairies," including a Puck "chuckling with delight," make this version more than an engaging fairy tale.[14]

Hudson's choice of plays is sophisticated, and he emphasized major characters of some complexity. Of ten tales only one is a tragedy, *Romeo and Juliet*; two are history plays, *Henry IV, Parts I and II*; two popular romances, *The Winter's Tale* and *The Tempest*. Of five comedies, three (*As You Like It, The Merchant of Venice, A Midsummer Night's Dream*) are often retold for children, two (*Much Ado about Nothing* and *Two Gentleman of Verona*) infrequently. What distinguishes Hudson's collection is a combination of simplified story with much of Shakespeare's language. Tales are named for main characters, with titles in parentheses. Lovers are favored, as in "Ferdinand and Miranda," although Hudson included other parts of the story. Quotation in "Romeo and Juliet" is particularly crucial—the lovers' meeting at the Capulets' ball, the balcony scene, and Mercutio's wit in the fight with Tybalt. Lyrical verse reads easily as romantic speech. The exception is "A False Friend," a guide to interpretation of a four-page summary of *Two Gentlemen*. Others elicit complex responses.

"Prince Hal and the Fat Knight" and "Falstaff and the King" introduce Shakespeare's most challenging comic character and two crucial history plays. The frontispiece is a fine historical painting by Ed. Grutzner. The plate armor and jupon worn by Douglas contrast effectively with Falstaff's muted beige, while the background of a faintly visible battle sets the foregrounded moment apart, a telling comment on war and honor, "Falstaff was far from being dead." The facing title page is very different — pretty children's sensitive faces in roundels, among the interlacing rose and foliage that acknowledge Art Nouveau. Falstaff's figure also frames "Contents" and "Illustrations" (1 and 3), a further mark of his dominance in *Tales from Shakespeare.* "Madcap Hal" is "a well-grown, manly lad, ... with spirit showing in every glance of his clear blue eyes; and yet at times a look of reckless wildness crossed his handsome face" (6). Although the prince early recognizes the "folly of his life" (8), the Gadshill robbery is a major scene, including much of the dialogue (8–12). Hudson ends with Falstaff's words about living "as cleanly, as a nobleman should do" (17). But "Falstaff and the King," Shakespeare's darker *Henry IV, Part II* is an inexorable movement from Prince Hal's self-blame, "so idly to profane the precious time" (88), to the rejection scene and Falstaff's subsequent reflection "upon the unexpected change of fortune, which, while promising prosperity and security to England, had ruined his own hopes, and cost him his liberty" (94). Hudson's historical gloss guides the child's evaluation of Falstaff and the triumph of England — and makes his daring emphasis upon Falstaff acceptable.

"Beatrice and Benedick" relies heavily on exact quotations, prose dialogue that is easily kept, and an early encounter with witty and memorable exchanges— the initial meeting, the dance, the overhearing, and the final talk before "Benedick, the sworn bachelor, married the girl in whom he had always met his match" (68). Hudson briefly described the Hero and Claudio plot, thus avoiding painful dialogue of Claudio's malicious condemnation. But Claudio, dressed in white and half-shielding his face with his right hand, is at the center of John H. Bacon's illustration, "This looks not like a wedding," a lavish spectacle inside a huge church (64). Hudson substituted his own explanation for the dazzling repartee of Beatrice and Benedick in the church: "But when she bade him kill Claudio for his cruelty to Hero, Benedick hung back; for Claudio was his dearest friend. But at last, pressed by the weeping girl, who taunted him with his unmanliness, he rushed forth to challenge Claudio to mortal combat" (65).

Since Hudson's retellings praise conventional behavior, Shakespeare's Beatrice is too much a New Woman to be easily assimilated. So too is Rosalind; Orlando thinks her cure of lovesickness by pretend-wooing "a rather foolish plan," and Rosalind herself does not "find it such pleasant sport as she had fancied it would be" (26). Touchstone, whose wit and pungent self-knowledge are absent, merely falls "a prey to Cupid's weapons, the rustic charms of Audrey," whom he "does not consider very good-looking," for he "ungallantly" introduces her as "an ill-favoured thing" (27). Hudson comfortably favored the pretty young woman; he followed eighteenth-century productions and reduced *The Winter's Tale* to "The Story of Perdita," the sheep-shearing of Act IV, illustrated by John H. Bacon's "She is the queen of curds and cream" (48), also used in Nesbit's *The Children's Shakespeare,* a Raphael Tuck reward book. Leontes's mad jealousy is scarcely mentioned, only his belated deploring of it, before Hermione comes quickly to forgive his "injustice and cruelty" (54–55). Mamilius has no part of this tale of "general rejoicing" (55).

"The Merchant of Venice" signals Hudson's emphasis upon Antonio, "of so noble and generous a nature that he was loved and respected by all who knew him — all, that is to say, save one, a miserly, money-lending Jew named Shylock" (69). Antonio frames the story, while Bassanio's choosing the casket is the favored scene. Fred. Barth.'s painting, "Let music sound while he doth make his choice" is a highly unusual double opening (72–73). Venetian Renaissance opulence — costumes of sumptuous fabric, Oriental carpet and table covering, the three caskets, an African boy — is, as in Lang's *Stories*, inspiration for a nineteenth-century artist. Indeed Hudson seemed to have this painting before him to write his description of Portia, a paragon of femininity:

> Standing there, a lovely figure in her beautiful robe, her sunny hair, bound only by a simple ribbon, descending to her waist in ripples of golden light, she watched him as he read the inscriptions and made his choice, her heart throbbing quickly and the colour coming and going in the fairness of her face [76].

The image lingers through a long scene; Hudson quoted Shakespeare's lines for Morocco, the Spaniard, and Bassanio — without the asides — to focus on the test itself. An ideal woman, Portia speaks "softly" in the trial scene, where Hudson quoted much of her "quality of mercy" speech (80). She later exhibits this quality when, after "teasing him for some time," she returns Bassanio's ring (83). Hudson judged Shylock less severely than other retellers, modulating his initial description; the bond is "a merry, fantastical trick," albeit Bassanio does not trust the Jew (73). Most decisively Hudson noted the event that makes "stronger and more venomous the Jew's hatred" — his loved daughter's elopement; "her heartless desertion of him in his old age hurt him very deeply" (78). When Shylock is ordered to become a Christian, Hudson sympathetically quoted his "I — am — not well" (82).

Hudson's *Tales from Shakespeare* is, then, much more sophisticated than Lang's two volumes and Britton's fairy tales with its higher expectations of understanding, greater balance among kinds of plays, and consistently richer language. Plain type and small size suggest a nursery audience, but other qualities put Hudson with large collections that offer comprehensive, challenging introductions to Shakespeare's stories.

A.T. Quiller-Couch, Historical Tales from Shakespeare *(1910)*

In contrast to all who acknowledged indebtedness to Lamb's *Tales from Shakespeare,* Sir A(rthur) T. Quiller-Couch (1863–1944) explicitly set *Historical*

Tales from Shakespeare (1910) apart from the Lambs, who had "found that a certain class of play lay outside their purpose."[15] Like most retellers, Quiller-Couch acknowledged their apt judgment of plays that would appeal to the young, "pleasant and profitable stories"; however, he chose "the historical ones ... with a different purpose." While he recognized difficulties posed by "dramatic form and sophisticated language," Quiller-Couch judged that "nowhere in spite of many inaccuracies can historical pictures be found so vivid or in the main so just as in these historical plays of Shakespeare." Moreover, he hoped to offset young readers' inherent lack of interest in history and to assure they do not "miss so much which might quicken their interest in history and their early patriotism" (iii). To read Shakespeare's historical plays is a very different and serious experience:

> to follow him into his dealings with history, where things cannot be forced to happen so neatly as in a made-up tale, and to persuade my young audience that history (in spite of their natural distrust) is by no means a dull business when handled by one who marvelously understood the human heart and was able so to put life into the figures of men and women long passed away that they become real to us as we follow their thoughts and motions and watch them making war plotting, succeeding, or accepting reverses, playing once more the big drama which they played on earth [iv].

The way was through storytelling; but Quiller-Couch knew that he had to go beyond what was in schoolbooks.

The career of Quiller-Couch, popularly referred to as "Q" and one of the most influential figures in the advancement of English literature in the early twentieth century, is varied and distinguished. Educated at Clifton and Trinity, Oxford, he was early in his career a journalist associated with the Liberal weekly *Speaker*. He also wrote novels, often historical; the first, *Dead Man's Rock* (1887), shows his admiration for Robert Louis Stevenson. He followed *The Sleeping Beauty and Other Fairy Tales* (1910) with his own fairy tales, *In Powder and Crinoline* (1913), illustrated by Kay Nielsen. However, Quiller-Couch is better remembered for his role as editor, especially of *The Oxford Book of English Verse, 1250–1900* (1900), which shaped taste for half a century, and as joint editor with J. Dover Wilson of Cambridge University's "New Shakespeare" (1921–1969). Moreover, Quiller-Couch's appointment, by Liberal Prime Minister Asquith, as King Edward VII Professor of English Literature in Cambridge University in 1912, had far-reaching consequences. By 1917 Quiller-Couch had secured the establishment of an independent honors school of English literature at Cambridge, which included study of "the English Moralists," a sustaining of Liberal principles that were dying out and that he believed "were inextricable from the tradition of an English way of Life."[16] Twelve lectures from 1916 to 1918, *On the Art of Reading* (1920) sought public acceptance. The dates are a reminder of how crucial Edwardians were in the formation of English studies as a discipline.[17]

The title *Adventures in Criticism* (1900), a collection of articles, shows Quiller-Couch's enthusiastic and romantic attitudes. As general editor of The Kings Treasuries of Literature Series, published by J. M. Dent and E. P. Dutton, he significantly influenced directions for reading, especially children's. Many titles, both reprints and original, were versions of traditional literature in convenient and inexpensive little books. They went beyond Everyman's Library volumes "For Young People," edited by Ernest Rhys, that included Shakespeare titles (Lamb's *Tales* and Mary Cowden Clarke's *The Girlhood of Shakespeare's Heroines*). Available and affordable, these conveniently sized books were an Every Child's Library (title of an American series), and some were used as schoolbooks.

Quiller-Couch sought to foster the history plays and Victorian emphasis on personality:

> to lay more stress on the characters in these plays, and on the many springs of action, often small and subtle ones, by uncovering which Shakespeare made history visible; to keep to the story indeed, but to make it a story of men's motives and feelings, as well as of the actual events they gave rise to or were derived from [iv].

The truth, then, does not require absolute accuracy of facts; *Historical Tales from Shakespeare* does not correct inaccuracies of detail or chronology. Quiller-Couch followed Shakespeare "so long as he tells his story with fairness and justice" (v). An obvious example, "the single exception," is Shakespeare's vilifying portrait of Joan of Arc, which "our schoolboys would reject with scornful disgust." Edwardian histories and novels give it the lie, and more tellingly, so do the sentiments: "to-day, if ever, it is necessary to insist that no patriotism can be true which gives to a boy no knightliness or to a girl no gentleness of heart" (v). Edwardian collections of saints' legends for children expressed regret and shame over English mistreatment of St. Joan, a violation of chivalry. If Lamb's *Tales* is a "feminization," Quiller-Couch's *Historical Tales* are a "masculinization" of Shakespeare.

Essentially, the plays are full "of true and fervent patriotism." What is more,

> the real hero of Shakespeare's historical plays is England; and no one can read them and be deaf to the ringing vibrating note of pride, of almost fierce joy to be an Englishman, to have inherited the liberties of so great a country and to be a partaker in her glory. And this love of England is the sincerer for the courage with which he owns and grieves that she has been sometimes humiliated, sometimes untrue to herself.... [T]hese plays might almost serve as a handbook to patriotism, did that sacred passion need one. For nowhere surely in literature is it so confidently nourished and at the same time so wisely and anxiously directed [v–vi].

Similarities between this apology and Victorian responses to the Boer War immediately come to mind. Quiller-Couch's concluding apology is twofold; he could not follow the Lambs' style but used his own voice, and inevitably those who know the original texts (adults, not the intended audience) will find the loss that comes with "ordinary prose ... hard to tolerate" (vi).

The scope of *Historical Tales* embraces two Roman plays, *Coriolanus* and *Julius Caesar,* as well as six English histories: *King John, King Richard the Second, King Henry the Fourth, King Henry the Fifth, King Henry the Sixth,* and *King Richard the Third.* Quiller-Couch's decision to combine plays of Shakespeare's tetralogies, with a play for each medieval king, emphasizes history, rather than individual plays. Appendices support this with the genealogy of the Houses of York and Lancaster (299) and a quotation from *Henry VI, Part II* (II.ii) that sets out the Yorkist claim (300–301); a table explains Henry V's claim to the French crown (185). Quiller-Couch's summaries of action are unusually full, while much dialogue, often using Shakespeare's language, brings immediacy and a sense of drama. Nine illustrations from the Boydell collection add interest and a somber note. These images range from J. Northcote's *Arthur Pleading with Hubert* (82) and *Richard and the Young Princes* (277), both of sinister threats to children, to Francis Rigaud's *Prince Harry and Hotspur at the Battle of Shrewsbury* (147), of chivalric knights.

Ideals of chivalry, enthusiastically redeployed in Victorian medievalism, resonate through many plays, beginning with *King John*:

> His death put a new face on the fortunes of England. As a young king, supported by the barons and the better hopes of his subjects, the troop of a foreigner could not hold their ground for long on this island. And the lesson of this "troublesome raigne" is summed up for us in the wise, brave, and patriotic words of Faulconbridge — the lines which every English boy should get by heart:
>
>> This England never did, nor never shall
>> Lie at the proud foot of a conqueror
>> But when it first did help to wound itself.
>> Now these her princes are come home again,
>> Come the three corners of the world in arms
>> And we shall shock them. Naught shall make us rue,
>> If England to itself so rest but true [91].

The Bastard's summation (V.vii.112–118) explains Shakespeare's acclaim as a national poet, one who captures and perpetuates an English ideal of race. Moreover, an effective way to experience and sustain these sentiments is memorization.

Richard II affords a strong beginning and the most intense expression of Quiller-Couch's patriotism. He did not shrink from pointing out Richard's weaknesses, but focused on the speech of the dying Gaunt, whose "lips began to mutter, over and over, words of love for England and pride in her." His note is "This incomparable lament may only be rendered in Shakespeare's own words, which no English boy, who is old enough to love his country, is too young to get by heart, forgetting the sorrow in it. Tears such as Gaunt's are drawn from a well of joy or pride in England and a fierce love of her goodness.—" The quoted lines (99–100) are from "This royal throne of kings, this scepter'd isle" through "How happy then were my ensuing death" (II.i.40–68). Even disappointing Richard was praised for his manliness at the end:

> He never lacked bodily courage; it has never been the way of English kings to lack it. In his youth he had faced a crowd of armed rebels under Wat Tyler, and cowed them with his rare fearlessness; and the same spirit was alive in him yet. He snatched an axe from the first servant, and clove him down with it. "Go thou, and fill another room in hell!" he shouted, turning on a second and smiting him dead. But this was his last blow. Before he could recover, Exton beat him to the ground with a fatal stroke [115].

This narrative matches juvenile historical novels; Richard's weapon is an axe, a link to Northern heroes, favored ancestors of the English race.

A sense of history combines with characterization to explain Falstaff, very much an individual and a product of his times. Prince Hal's "pet crony" is

> an old disreputable, and immensely fat knight called Sir John Falstaff. There was much good in this old fellow, or rather, much that was amiable in spite of his rascally and loose living. He was, in fact, a gentleman; a poor gentleman shaken loose from the lower degrees of feudalism when that edifice began to rock and totter. Shaken off, he had gone utterly astray, wasting his days in drinking and rioting among unworthy company, which in the end became a necessity to him. His round face and grotesque, fat belly were familiar in every low London tavern, and the butt of men far below him in birth and still further below him in honesty. Yet with all that incurable frailty he kept so large a heart and so sweet a temper that at the sound of his infectious laugh—never so ready as at his own expense—men felt themselves drawn to him even in the act of despising him. The Prince found him the rarest of companions, for you could laugh at him, or laugh with him, or even both together [123–124].

The narrative confirms this judiciously balanced analysis of character, which avoids oversimplified enthusiasm and moral indignation; the plan and execution of the robbery are full, including much exact wording in dialogue (124–134).

Furthermore, the triumph of *Henry V* demonstrates that the young prince did not suffer from his association with Falstaff. Quiller-Couch defined the king as

> sober-minded, of strong will, yet just; masterful, while willing to listen to advice; at once a king with high thoughts for his country's welfare and honour, and a man with a mind of his own ... a born commander, and not least by the ardour of devotion his mere presence kindled ... merciful by nature, but he had hardened his temper to war as every great general must [194–194].

Another set-piece, a description of the battle of Agincourt, shows imaginative skills of Quiller-Couch the novelist in a passage comparable to many in Henty's popular novels:

> The English archers bared their breasts and arms for free play and charged forward with a shout.... [The French came] floundering forward into the open over the sodden ground; which they trod into a quagmire. As they came, Henry called a halt. Each of his archers carried a sharpened stake; and now at a word planting a rough and ready stockade, from behind it they poured their arrows into the throng where no arrow could miss a mark. The slaughter was terrible; yet the French blundered on and by sheer weight drove the archers right and left into the woods, only to find the deadly rain now pouring on either flank from behind the trees, among which they could not pursue. While they swayed mire-bound and exposed to this cross-fire, Henry flung his heavier troops straight on their front, himself charging like a hero and setting an example to all. Once he went down under the blow of a French mace; again, while stooping to lift the Duke of York, felled by a blow of Alençon's, he took a stroke from the same hand which shore away a piece of the crown on his helmet... [205].

Two further passages signal the patriotic fervor of Shakespeare's historical tales. *Henry V* ends with a summary of his learning and achievement, his moral development, from

> a wild scape-grace youngster, little better than a boy. We have seen him confirmed, step by step, in strength and a better judgment; become a wise king, a God-fearing man, a triumphant warrior. Here at the height of his achievement we leave him; happily married, worshipped by his subjects, seated on a throne securely establish'd, and looking forward to a still more splendid inheritance [210].

No hint of Shakespeare's Chorus about the "small time" of Henry V's inheritance mars this account of the ideal exemplar, a reassuringly human boy who makes mistakes but reforms to transcend through dedication and hard work. In addition, Quiller-Couch quoted an Elizabethan gloss, Michael Drayton's "The Ballad of Agincourt" (210–213), another set-piece of patriotic fervor, favored in Edwardian schoolbooks and collections of poetry.

Nevertheless, the tale of heroic chivalry ends; as Quiller-Couch explained:

> Our tale has brought us to a time when the darkness of the Middle Ages was breaking up. Already Caxton had set up his printing press at Westminster, and soon, as the Turks took Constantinople, and its Greek scholars fled for refuge to Italy, a flood of old Greek learning was to come pouring over the west of Europe. In that queer twilight while the old faith was dissolving and before a new one had fairly dawned, there was born — it is one of the wonders of history — numbers of men with utterly pagan souls. They disbelieved in God and scoffed at Him; they were wicked, knew themselves to be wicked, rejoiced in it, and took a pride in their wickedness as if it had been a sort of fine art. Nowadays a wicked man usually tries to persuade himself that he is not so bad after all, that the world has used him ill, that he is "more sinned against than sinning"; but these men were wicked from choice and strove to be devilish. In the history of Italy about this time you may find many such. In England for several reasons this deliberate villainy has never been common; but if there lived in England a deliberate villain, by all accounts Richard was he [257–258].

The footnote modifies "by all accounts" to admit the Tudors set out to "blacken" Richard's memory, not least their historian Polydore Vergil, who destroyed documents. Shakespeare, writing under Elizabeth, a Tudor queen, for "a prejudiced audience," must thus be taken "with more than a grain of salt" (260n). But after minimal acknowledgment of Richard's physical handicaps, Quiller-Couch marveled at Shakespeare's growing knowledge that he could fascinate. The wooing of Lady Anne, omitted by others, is the first example. His broader interpretation of history glosses Edwardian attitudes: praise of Renaissance learning, especially Greek, and facing the reality that men can deliberately deny God and decide to be evil. However, there is patriotic mitigation: few Englishmen were of such evil nature; most were Italian—a nationalist sentiment and denigration that parallel that of France in *Henry V.*

Readers of *Historical Tales from Shakespeare* also read historical tales from Quiller-Couch, whose patriotic fervor and confidence beam radiantly. Study of the classics, especially Latin, and considerations of tyranny and order, explain how *Coriolanus* and *Julius Caesar* are background to European civilizations. But England is the subject, specifically the England of the Middle Ages when chivalry was in flower. Quiller-Couch's omission of *Henry VIII* is not explained, but his consideration of *Richard III* expressed concerns about undue Tudor influence on Shakespeare. Moreover, Henry VIII, while he sustained the pageantry of the Middle Ages at the Field of the Cloth of Gold, was a far cry from the ideals and beliefs of the centuries his dynasty replaced. As general editor of The King's Treasuries of Literature Series and as a member of Henry Newbolt's committee that wrote *The Teaching of English in England* (1921), the influential Quiller-Couch often stimulated the same high sentiments.

Thomas Carter, Stories from Shakespeare *(1910) and* Shakespeare's Stories of the English Kings *(1912)*

Like Quiller-Couch, Thomas Carter, Doctor of Theology, was a scholar who retold Shakespeare for children. His academic books, *Shakespeare Puritan and Recusant* (1897) and *Shakespeare and Holy Scripture* (1905), anticipated much of today's return of interest in Shakespeare's religion, while his two collections for children, *Stories from Shakespeare* (1910) and *Shakespeare's Stories of the English Kings* (1912), are significant contributions. Carter combined the roles of storyteller and scholarly authority. George G. Harrap published both volumes in its Told Through the Ages Series, the best for older children, printed with different quality and prices, often given as rewards. My personal copies illustrate how widespread this practice was, and how encompassing was devotion to Shakespeare. *Shakespeare's Stories of English Kings* was a prize book for St. Hilda's School, Edinburgh—for the Junior Tennis Tournament—while

Stories from Shakespeare was presented by "The Independent Order of Rechabites" as a second prize for introducing new members. Carter's books have beautiful color pictures by Gertrude Demain Hammond (1862–1934), painter and illustrator, an accomplished draughtsman, noted for her female figures, who worked in oil and watercolor. She also illustrated Thackeray, Dickens, George Eliot, and was frequently employed by Harrap, especially for Told Through the Ages Series.

Stories from Shakespeare retells eleven plays in 286 pages, an indication that Carter is thorough.[18] Comedies and two romances alternate with tragedies—*The Merchant of Venice, King Lear, The Winter's Tale, Hamlet, As You Like It, Macbeth, A Midsummer Night's Dream, Julius Caesar, The Comedy of Errors, Romeo and Juliet, The Tempest*—in a selection where a Roman play is the only unusual item. Each story begins with an exposition of circumstances and setting, usually with added details from history to expand the context. Carter did not always follow Shakespeare's sequence of events, but rather focused on one theme / character and then moved to another with similar grouping of episodes. He added elaborate descriptions of nature, especially of storms or forests. He paraphrased many lines and quoted extensively: soliloquies (Hamlet's "To be or not to be," 92–93; Macbeth's "To-morrow and to-morrow," 154; and Bottom's "I have had a most rare vision," 174); public speeches (Antony's funeral oration, 198; Portia's "quality of mercy" defense, 20; Mercutio's "Queen Mab" speech, 236–237; and Jaques's "All the world's a stage," 124–125); and songs. The range of passages to ponder and learn by heart is wide. Most distinctively, Carter's substantial analyses of character and event guide understanding and judgment.

His treatment of *The Merchant of Venice* matches an unusual decision to make it the first story; he began with Portia, a paragon, the beautiful and virtuous woman:

> a mind and heart of richest worth, and an outward form which seemed to centre in itself all the graces of Italy. She was fair, and her sunny locks hung on her temples like a golden fleece, but she was even fairer in the beauty of her mind, which was of wondrous virtue. She had been taught by the best of masters, and loved to have around her beautiful pictures, costly marbles, and precious things. Her palace was in the midst of magnificent gardens, ... [S]he had grown to womanhood under every influence calculated to bring out all that was best in a noble, sunny nature. She was brave and ready, quick-witted and clever, able to devise a plan and capable of carrying it to success, and withal she was gentle and modest. She said to the one who won her love, that she wished she could be trebled twenty times in excellence for his sake, ... happiest of all that her gentle spirit could commit itself to the directing care of a great love. There is no flaw in the beauty of her character, and although it was a man's hand that drew her picture for us, yet she is in all things a true and perfect woman, an ideal of womanly grace and dignity [3].

Carter explained that Portia, who is first to declare her love, gives hints to help Bassanio choose; moreover, he heartily approved:

> Portia was bound by an oath, but when was oath or bond too strait for woman's wit when woman's love was in the question? It is possible to keep a promise in the letter and break it in the spirit. Some bonds are best treated thus, for broken hearts are more sad than a broken bond [13].

Hammond's illustration creates a court scene — a great hall with columns, several elegant ladies and courtiers in the background — for their declaration of love. Portia's elegant Renaissance gown is white and gold, with a saucy hat; with lowered arms and open hands she modestly faces the viewer — and Bassanio, who stands before her in purples and gold (14). Carter's interpretation of Portia as womanly ideal exemplifies one dimension of the play's popularity.

Shylock is "as far from her as though he dwelt in another planet" (4), while his daughter Jessica is "too careless and selfish to strive to learn the secret of a proud man's heart" (5). Thus she is responsible for their cold and bickering household; she adds to Shylock's bitterness and intractable nature when she proves "treacherous and unworthy" (11). Hammond's graceful frontispiece, which shows them in luxurious, exotic costumes, somewhat belies Carter's preliminary judgments. Shylock, who wears a long golden cloak over his beige robe, is a fashionable figure, in a costume highlighted with broad colorful waistband and black hat with trailing scarf. He points to Jessica, who looks more other than he; her dress is Oriental, a splendid contrast to Portia. Both wear white, but Jessica's white dress is straight rather than full, and the sleeves have a wide decorated border with colors that match her bolero; most strikingly, a long red scarf covers her black hair. Although drawn in profile, neither Jew has stereotypical features. Like Carter, Hammond avoided anti–Semitic judgment.

Portia fully displays her intellect and goodness when she demonstrates her love by devising a plan, pleads Antonio's case with "perfect self-possession" (19), explains with Christian gentleness that "the quality of mercy is not strained" in a declaration that "has since re-echoed round the world" (20), warns Shylock twice, and tries to dissuade him from his cruelty. Action is inexorable, but Carter evaluated mercifully a "judgment, stern and sweeping ... well deserved ... yet we feel a throb of pity for the poor old alien who, beggared and doubly outcast, stood overwhelmed before the angry, jeering faces of the court" (23). Even more tellingly Carter put Shylock's moving speech "Hath not a Jew eyes?" at the end (27). This obvious alteration of Shakespeare's ordering of events and sentiments well suited the concerns of a doctor of theology.

Carter was similarly charitable and optimistic about Caliban; "this strange, evil monster, half man and half demon, was not altogether bad, for if in dreams we see and love the higher things there is hope that one day we shall rise to nobler aims" (268). Polonius is facile in shifting his allegiance, "worldly wise and shrewd," and "often his sounding words would tire his hearers," yet he was capable of "exalted sentiments" in his advice to Laertes that "shows him to have been vastly more than a mere windbag" (89). Carter, who quoted the Friar's discourse on nature and virtue (242), deemed his plan to salvage Romeo and

Juliet's "rash, unadvised, sudden love" (241) to be "a plausible but a dangerous scheme" (252). In Hammond's illustration, in brown Franciscan robe, he is as important as the lovers; iconic white lilies provide the foreground (242). Although Ophelia's death causes great sadness, "her end was like a strain of sad sweet music which comes floating to us on the wings of night and silence, and which we rather feel than hear, and so her gentle spirit fled upward to the Unseen" (100). But Hammond's image is disturbing; Ophelia stands in a rocky landscape and clutches flowers; the garland round her head is askew and her eyes mad. A black blanket slipping from her shoulders covers her simple white dress of innocence.

Glowing innocence is the attribute of Cordelia in "Nothing, my lord," Hammond's only illustration for *King Lear*, the initial parent-child interaction (30). Here Hammond's work resembles Pre-Raphaelite painting. Cordelia's gown is brilliantly white, while Goneril and Regan are dark, shadowy figures who separate their sister from a patriarchal father, an enthroned, ancient king of Britain in dark blue with red decoration and a white ermine-lined golden cloak, which with his white hair and beard, links him to Cordelia. She answers Lear's "childish, foolish question" (31); but through Edmund, "a subtle and cynical villain ... the story becomes a tragedy of blood and sorrow" (29). Carter set the tone and circumstances when he identified Lear as "a man of Keltic [sic] blood and race, with all the self-will and passionate intensity of the Kelt" (28), thus iterating Victorian attitudes about racial identity. Lear's traits are manifest at the end:

> [I]n a passionate agony of yearning for the peace and light and love which dwelt for him in the pure and holy heart of Cordelia, we feel that the great writer in the words "Look there, look there!" lifts up the dark curtain for an instant that the light of the Eternal may shine through and speak of hope Beyond [51].

Thus Carter, a devout Christian minister who always sought goodness, explicitly affirmed life after death, even when Shakespeare had not.

Admiration of Portia, a characteristic Victorian response, was only Carter's first pronouncement on the character of Shakespeare's women. Widowed Gertrude, "overleaping the barriers of relationship and unmindful of the claims of rightful mourning," hastily remarried (76–77). Indeed, Hamlet is more distressed by his mother's remarriage than his father's death: "when a son feels that his confidence in his mother is shattered a sadness deep as night falls on his heart" (84). Lady Macbeth elicits a mixed response:

> a faithful and good wife to a loyal and chivalrous soldier ... dignified, courteous, and friendly ... womanly and delicate in her disgust of unlovely things, she sometimes exaggerated the vigour of her language, when under the stress of great excitement, but she was delicate and refined in her shrinking from sights of coarseness and blood.... She little thought as she viewed the awful act of disloyal treachery from a distance ... as she pondered over her husband's letter she meditated with a woman's ingenuity [139].

Woman's love and devoted service to her husband mitigate severe judgment. So too can maidenly innocence. Miranda asks Ferdinand, "'Do you love me?' It was a question which is not usually addressed by a woman to the man she loves, but Ferdinand did not misunderstand the pure nature that expressed itself in glowing words. There was no self-consciousness in the unsullied soul which felt for the first time the mastery of love" (276). However, Carter has little time for extravagant behavior; Helena bewails her situation in *A Midsummer Night's Dream,* "although one would have thought that the running away of Hermia would rather help her to win Demetrius" (159). Yet he finds her outrageous "I am your spaniel" speech a "touching and humble avowal" (159–160).

In contrast, feisty and independent Shakespearean heroines are unsettling; Carter eliminated the wooing scene in which Rosalind teaches Orlando good sense and indulges her own needs. He referred to it as a "strange compact, and later ... a farcical marriage service, with Celia as the priest" (129). Moreover, when Rosalind returns in court attire, "Orlando knew, and he must have been a simpleton not to have guessed it before, that the handsome forester with the swashing, martial air, was none other than the idol of his heart" (131–132). Carter, then, underrated Rosalind, who lacks Portia's womanly subservience. Hammond's "Touchstone laughed at the verses" pictures this Ganymede, in green and brown, as she looks unhappily from the paper to Touchstone, a merry jester in red and white satin, with cap and bells and wand, whose back is to the viewer (126). Touchstone is "of all the fools ... the most joyous, the most philosophical, and the cleverest" (116) — traits that signal nobility and virtue, especially when ridiculing courts and love. Of his relation to Audrey, Carter discreetly observed: "It was a most curious instance of love at first sight, and showed that mating often goes by contrary" (128).

Victorians translated the idea of chivalry into their own medievalism and advocacy of the English gentleman, and Edwardians published an extraordinary number of chivalric stories for children. Carter discreetly used the term in his descriptions. In *King Lear* Edgar is "a young man of great nobility of character, loving, unsuspicious, and chivalrous" (29), while the King of France reveals "the unselfishness of his nature and the chivalrous devotion of his heart" (34), when he declares love for the disinherited Cordelia. In this ethos Lear has concern for his "knights," symbol of his responsibility and dignity.

Carter found greater scope for chivalry and nationalism in *Shakespeare's Stories of the English Kings* (1912). His reading of Shakespeare's history plays urges their comprehensiveness and the influence of the plays on understanding English history.

> Beginning with the period before the Roman invader came to our shores, and passing through the times of the Plantagenet and Tudor to the opening days of Elizabeth, Shakespeare has presented in his wonderful series an almost complete view of the great figures of English history, indicating with a sure touch the movements, crises, and turning-points of our national development. The

canvas is a crowded one, but there is no superfluous figure, and from the king to the peasant he holds a mirror of genius up to nature and reflects life.[19]

He quoted Walter Pater's judgment that Shakespeare emphasized irony in his treatment of kings, pointing up inherent "lights and shadows" but also "keeping very close to the original authorities" (vi). Carter's nine chapters begin with *Cymbeline*; *King Lear* "properly belongs to the group" but had already appeared in his *Stories from Shakespeare*. The three parts of *Henry VI*, combined into a single chapter without illustration, are exacting.

However, each part of *King Henry the Fourth*, here designated "(Before and After Shrewsbury)," gets a separate chapter; and Falstaff is the subject of the frontispiece. Hammond's "Come, thou must not be in this humour with me" signals Falstaff's playful quality with Dame Quickly. Non-courtly medieval costumes in a town scene make a charming study. Hammond's figures are usually attractive; her Falstaff, dressed in red, is not "grotesque," albeit the text so describes his appearance (128). Carter quoted Falstaff's speech on honor approvingly in comparison with the declaration of excessively chivalric Hotspur (120) and tried to recognize his greatness, not least when he cited sympathetic critics Coleridge and Dowden (130–131). Nevertheless, severer moral judgment prevails. Carter stressed the wrong choices made by Falstaff, who "quoted more texts and misused them [the words of Holy Scripture] more cleverly than any other character in the writings of Shakespeare," and "when he gave himself time to think he knew that he was playing an unworthy part" (128–129). Ever the doctor of theology, Carter improvised Falstaff's remorse after King Henry rejects him:

> the reflection that the subtle and brilliant cleverness of one of the ablest of men could be contemptuously thrown aside and committed to the dust of a prison-yard; that the ready wit and joviality of a prince of good companions could be easily and profitably dispensed with, because that in life there are greater things than a splendid unworthiness, and roads upon which the feet of true and honourable men alone may tread [173].

Hammond's frontispiece separates the figure of temptation from the heir, and Carter sought the same distance for her young readers. Her illustration is the reconciliation between father and son, "This in the name of God, I promise here" (140). The regal father — all red, ermine, and gold — sits forward on his throne, while the handsome prince — a gold jerkin, huge flowing purple sleeves, hose with one red leg and one blue — stands with his left hand on his sword and his right arm lifted in gesture. Carter praised Henry IV, "the grave, dark, politic Hereford ... a striking contrast" to the more intellectual and poetic Richard (87–88). Hammond depicted him with the youthful future king, two poised figures that express confidence in the succession. The artist's colorfully detailed costumes, the Gothic chair, and hangings in the background embody the Middle Ages. These figures recapitulate Hammond's illustration for *Richard II*, the parting of Bolingbroke from his father Gaunt (96), whose set-piece panegyric, "this sceptr'd isle," Carter quoted (98–99). Bolingbroke looks like Galahad in his plate armor—iconic in so many children's books of chivalric stories—while his old father's clothes proclaim his great wealth, and shadowy figures in the background evoke the tournament just canceled. Hammond's skill in depicting chivalry is best deployed for Henry V's charge at Agincourt (190), the apogee of knighthood. This unusual action scene differs from her formal settings with a few figures. The King is at the center before a mass of knights in shining armor and the royal standard unfurled. But the bolder figures in the foreground focus sharply on the common man, armed with metal-tipped staves. Carter's narrative explained the crucial role of English bowmen:

> Each man had his long iron-pointed staff in his hand. His good yew bow was slung over his shoulders, and every quiver was full of the grey goose-feathered shafts.... Always maintaining the wedge-like formation, each man was told to drive his staff firmly into the ground, leaving space for a man to slip through, and to advance far enough in front of the staves so as to give every archer plenty of room. When the horsemen charged, the fatal arrows were to be sent speeding in a thick cloud into them, and the attack was to be kept up until the knights were driven back. But if the horsemen came on again in force which threatened to overwhelm the bowmen, each man was to slip through the iron-pointed staves, and allow the knights to hurl themselves upon the rampart, while the re-formed archers galled them from a position of vantage. The King had no reason to doubt the courage and skill of his bowmen, and each man knew that the battle would have to be decided by the grey goose shaft [196].

Ancillary facts greatly enrich the child reader's knowledge and intensify a sense of exciting adventure. Enhanced celebration of patriotic achievement is in keeping with Edwardian sentiments that Lawrence Olivier's film of *Henry V* (1944), timed to coincide with the Allied invasion of Normandy in World War II, brilliantly redeployed. Even Kenneth Branagh's later film (1989), a more skeptical representation, could not forego the glorious flight of arrows.

Readers of *Shakespeare's Stories of the English Kings* were helped by Carter's clear exposition of historical events and persons at the start of each chapter. These summaries, usually a couple of pages of information not in the plays, set the context, while character portraits often predispose evaluations. The most distinctive example is the introduction to *Richard III*, more than six pages about the historical last Plantagenet, an inheritor of "four centuries of warrior ancestors," who was shaped by feudalism, which "produced nobles and followers whose first and chiefest thought was strife and bloodshed" (239). Carter dispelled Romantic medievalism but also rejected Shakespeare's participation in Tudor propaganda that distorted character for "the sinister figure":

> As a King of England it is unfortunate for Richard that the portrait which will live for ever in the eyes of men is that one which was drawn by the hand of the dramatist rather than that which lies buried in the dusty histories of the records of England, but it can be said with fairness that the public records of his reign exhibit the historical King Richard in a very different light [241].

As he enumerated Richard's virtues and benevolence in conducting England's affairs, Carter sounded like a charter member of the Richard III Society. Nevertheless, he retold the play through paraphrase and long quotations that bring Shakespeare's Richard vividly alive, most notably his soliloquy, "Now is the winter of our discontent," two lines of which provide the caption, "I am determined to prove a villain, / And hate the idle pleasures of these days" for Hammond's illustration (247–248). Here her background is again a street scene. Richard strokes his chin as he systematically plans how to achieve his ambition; his costume includes exaggeratedly pointed shoes, full sleeves, and costly fabrics. Not the wooing itself but the conclusion of Richard's response to winning Lady Anne is quoted (249). Similarly, Carter, who lessened Queen Margaret's role across the tetralogy, eliminated the mother's curses of her villainous son, but introduced some of Queen Elizabeth's anxiety for her sons before judging the murder of the princes "indeed the most arch act of piteous massacre that ever the land of England was guilty of, but it did not seem to trouble the mind of the triumphant Richard III" (257). However, Richard's Tudor successor is not an unsullied hero; exile and dangers

> made him serious, silent, suspicious, and reserved. He was selfish and cold, but loved fine clothes, bright jewels, and glittering pageants.... He was no soldier, and hated the strife of battle. King Richard was his superior in everything, and looked upon him as a cowardly runagate. Yet Richmond, by the grace of God, was destined to hurl the powerful Richard from his throne [257–258].

At the battle of Bosworth, "Richmond fought with the fury of one who realizes that his foeman is skilled with the sword beyond ordinary men, and his associates hurried to his assistance, whereupon Richard was beaten down and slain" (261). Finally, Carter expanded stage directions to make Richmond somewhat less heroic than Tudor panegyric indicated.

Carter's retellings stress, as do Shakespeare's plays, the culmination of the Middle Ages in the Wars of the Roses, with all their violence and lack of honor; but he found much to admire in an earlier period. His introduction to *King John* sets out details of dynasty and possessions and becomes an occasion to celebrate Richard Lion Heart:

> a Knight of wonderful prowess, tall, stalwart, and handsome, with fair hair and bright blue eyes. His reckless bravery impelled him to enter quarrels on the most trivial causes, and he would travel many leagues in search of adventure. He was marvelously expert in the use of weapons, and had been trained from his boyhood in all the knightly exercises of the times. It was said that only one Knight in Christendom, William of Barre, could match him in the lists. He was a great lover of music and poetry, and took delight in the lays of troubadours and minstrels [50].

He also "sailed to the Holy Land, where Knights of Christendom were gathering to wrest the Holy City of Jerusalem from the hands of Saladin the Saracen" (51). Richard's chivalry allowed John to scheme in England, but unlike modern historians Carter did not fault Richard, who is important to the play because of Faulconbridge:

> a stalwart, broad-shouldered giant, with curly, clustering fair hair, and steady blue eyes. He carried himself like a knightly champion, and his bold demeanour and laughing grace and confidence reminded Queen Eleanor of her wayward knightly son who lay buried at his father's feet in the stately old Abbey Church of Font-Evraud [54].

Father and son are archetypal warriors with racial characteristics of Northernness, so often praised by Victorians and Edwardians. At Angiers "Sir Richard had fought with all the joyous and reckless bravery of his valiant father, and had swept across the field of battle with mighty force, beating his adversaries out of his way" (60). Although Carter never called him "Bastard" and reduced his role as choric commentator, he quoted about half of Philip's incisive judgment of Commodity (II.i.562–81), "Mad world! mad kings! mad composition!" (62–63). Hammond's only illustration shows Queen Eleanor in conference with the French claimant, "Philip now learned that he was the son of King Richard," albeit "base-born" (56). The medieval costumes are splendid, and heraldic shields painted on the wall signal heritage. The Queen's green dress and long white veil contrast delicately with the handsome young man's short red gown and long blue surcoat, also bordered in gold. Queen Eleanor, one of three images of women in *Shakespeare's Stories of the English Kings,* is a noble and elegant lady very different from tradeswoman Dame Quickly. The third picture is androgynous. In *Cymbeline* Imogen as a page calls, "Ho! who's here?" (34); this is the only illustration with a single figure. Although the landscape is appealing, the cave's dark entrance signals danger. Perhaps this is the sharpest correlation between visual and verbal text; Carter's retellings minimize the roles Shakespeare gave to women in his histories, even when they are as compelling as those in the comedies. This is striking in his treatment of Katherine of Aragon, a role — and a woman — much admired by Victorians, even though she was Spanish and Roman Catholic.[20]

Carter introduced *King Henry VIII* as "the beginning of a new epoch" in which modern states were formed and new colonial empires begun by France and Spain, while "England had yet to learn that her greatest power and mightiest rule were to lie upon the seas and beyond them" (264). The allusion to the British Empire is salient. Hammond's illustration, "Read o'er this!" shows the familiar, magnificently dressed Henry with Wolsey, the brilliant and ambitious churchman and statesman, who shares emphasis as they plot the divorce and compete for power (279). Carter quoted copiously from the men's speeches (278–282): Wolsey's "Farewell" (III.ii.352–372) and reply to Cromwell (III.ii.429–458), and Griffith's summation of the Cardinal's character (IV.ii.48–68). But, as always, Carter reduced the role of women; neither Anne Boleyn nor Katherine is fully drawn, and the latter's great speeches, which raise domestic and theological issues, are largely unheard. Although Carter quoted

Thomas Carter's *Stories of the English Kings* (1912) afforded Gertrude Demain Hammond an opportunity to display her knowledge and skill at historical painting. This leading illustrator for George G. Harrap's popular Told through the Ages Series for older children emphasizes the beauty and color of the Middle Ages. In *King John* Queen Eleanor speaks to Philip, bastard son of Richard the Lion Heart, chivalric hero of the Crusades. Costumes, chair, and heraldic hanging are evocative, part of Medievalism, developed in the nineteenth century.

the first part of Cranmer's prophesy of Elizabeth's greatness (V.v. 18–39), he stopped before expectations of her heirs and added his own final paragraph to tie Shakespeare's English kings to the present:

> Thus with stately words of prophetic insight were the spacious days of great Elizabeth ushered in, and the curtain falls upon the magnificent series of historical plays which the kingly genius of Shakespeare has presented as a precious heritage to Britain's sons and daughters [283].

Entire volumes devoted to retelling Shakespeare's history plays, by Carter and Quiller-Couch, mark a union of patriotic pride with English history represented by the greatest English playwright and poet. Carter even claimed tragedies—*King Lear* and *Cymbeline*—as the opening phase of Shakespeare's study of British history. But histories were not consistently chosen for collections, as two final Edwardians demonstrate. Alice S. Hoffman, who was devoted to Britain's Northern heritage, made histories a genre within Shakespeare's oeuvre, but Constance and Mary Maud did not.

Alice Spencer Hoffman, The Children's Shakespeare: Being Stories from the Plays with Illustrative Passages *(1911)*

Alice Spencer Hoffman, one of the more skilled Edwardian retellers of traditional literature for children, also wrote *The Book of the Sagas* (1913) and *Heroes and Heroines of English History* (1913), collections that celebrate the Northern heritage of Britain. J.M. Dent and E.P. Dutton published her *The Children's Shakespeare: Being Stories from the Plays with Illustrative Passages* (1911).[21] This impressive volume is notable for its fluid introduction of many quotations, with unobtrusive notes at the bottom of each page to give meanings of unfamiliar words, and for illustrations by Charles Folkard (1878–1963). Hoffman's rich descriptions and frequent dialogue suggest performance, so that stories rise above competence to excellence. Further, she was original in her choice of plays. Like Lamb's *Tales*, *The Children's Shakespeare* contains twenty, fifteen of which are the same as Lamb's. But Hoffman replaced four comedies (*Comedy of Errors, Two Gentlemen, All's Well, Measure for Measure*) and one tragedy (*Timon*) with two Roman plays (*Coriolanus* and *Julius Caesar*) and three English histories (*King John, Richard II, Henry V*). Thus she provided greater comprehensiveness, and history plays furthered her celebration of English heroes.

Hoffman explained actions and responses in glosses that express a clear point of view. "To My Readers" states her expectation:

> When you grow older, you will read all the great plays from which these stories have been written, and they will be to you like old friends who have lived with you all your lives, whose very thoughts you know and whose delights

Alice S. Hoffman's thoughtful and full retellings in *The Children's Shakespeare* (1911) were enhanced by Charles Folkard's illustrations. In *A Midsummer Night's Dream* Puck or Robin Goodfellow is the center of mischief and a character who elicits empathy for boys. Folkard's delightful night picture depicts him springing aloft with a lantern that lights his way and illuminates his winning grin. Dent/Dutton later used the image for the cover of F.C. Tilney's *Tales from Shakespeare by Charles and Mary Lamb* (1926), Tales from Many Lands Series.

and sorrows you have shared. Like old friends, too, they will in their turn, give of their best to you—their words of comfort and of strength: of joy or of peace [vi].

The case for early experience of masterworks—an easy familiarity with plot is essential to later more informed reading—is made agreeably. Equally, Hoffman urged the case for the sustaining quality of literature, its capacity to affirm and inspire.

Only *A Midsummer Night's Dream* has two full-page color illustrations. Folkard's frontispiece combines a large Bottom with ass's head and a tiny, diaphanous Titania and countless gnome-like fairies and curious beetles. Robin Goodfellow, the traditional English fairy, here an elfin sprite with a lamp, is his other subject (30). Blue misty background and leaves at the top make a woodland scene.

Hoffman was judicious in her explanatory comments. Children are told, "Theseus is one of the Greek heroes you know" (26). However, adolescent behavior requires clarification:

> Helena's jealousy made her blind to their tenderness and kindness. She could think only of how to spite them, and so she made up her mind to tell Demetrius of their flight to the wood. She was sure he would follow and try to stop them, and for the joy of being near him she meant to follow too [29].

Hoffman's fullest attention and sympathy went to the rustic mechanicals:

> These poor men knew very little about anything except the work by which they earned their living. They had little learning and they knew nothing at all about acting. But they had a real wish to give their master pleasure on his wedding day [35].

She followed this supportive view of the working class with an unusual, brief summary of the story of their play, the casting, and rehearsal. At the wedding feast its full title is announced, and the action quickly described. Continuing her initial recognition of the limited skills but boundless good will of the players, Hoffman was more concerned with the audience's response:

> How Theseus and his friends laughed over them and their queer acting! But they were too kind-hearted to let the good men see their amusement, for they felt that each one was trying to do his best; and indeed, when Pyramus found the blood-stained mantle, and thought his Thisbe dead, Bottom's simple show of grief quite touched Hippolyta's tender heart.
> "Beshrew me, but I pity the man!" she cried [47].

Thus Hoffman quoted the kindest evaluation rather than the witty comments and competitive attempts at cleverness. She removed Shakespeare's complexity—including Bottom's over-acting, which is far from a "simple show of grief"—to provide a kind and appreciative response to good intentions and conscientious efforts. This models sympathetic response to the limitations of student productions, and to the eager and hard work they entail. Hoffman cut

Puck's epilogue and ended with the attendant fairies: "So we leave Theseus and Hippolyta, Demetrius and Hermia, Lysander and Helena, sure of their happiness while such sweet fairies guard them" (48).

Making Leontes a sympathetic and noble character in *The Winter's Tale* required greater finesse, since his loss of children and sexual jealousy (adult experiences) are crucial, and his behavior is mad and irrational. Thus Hoffman began:

> It may be that these fears were due to a serious flaw in the otherwise noble character of Leontes—to a jealous distrust which had always been there, but which had no opportunity of showing itself till now. But however we may explain it, a sudden change had come over Leontes, so that he almost hated his wife and the friend whom he had so dearly loved, and a fierce mad longing for revenge took hold of him [171].

Hoffman enhanced the poignancy of childhood, as when Mamilius tells his tale:

> The boyish face and voice were so grave, as warning his hearers of the woefulness of his story, that the Ladies could not keep from laughing. The reproach on the child's face at this irreverent interruption brought his mother's arm about him, and the rest of his sad tale was told softly into her sympathetic ear.
>
> That was the picture Leontes saw when he burst into the room, but the sight of even that sacred love had no power to move him from his purpose. The hatred within him closed his eyes to all beauty and his heart to all pity. He roughly seized the boy and ordered him from the chamber, and while Hermione looked from one to the other in wonder, he bade the Lords mark her outward beauty and learn that she was a traitor [174].

Hermione's response (174–175) is quoted (II.i), as is the final scene with the statue (V.iii, where dialogue is interlaced with narrative, 190–191). Hoffman, who preceded the climax with a gloss on the shepherd's story, added a precise picture of Leontes's remorse and suffering when he recognizes Hermione's mantle:

> How often had he seen it in the years that were past! Its colour, its soft folds, the jewel clasping the neck, brought to his mind a lovely face that once had looked into his with tenderest love—gone now for ever. He buried his face in the mantle and sobbed aloud [189].

The color illustration both interests and reassures. Folkard depicted the discovery of the baby by two shepherds in a pastoral scene with precisely drawn lambs on green grass below a blue sky; an absence of stormy effects anticipates the happy ending (176).

Folkard's twenty-one full-color illustrations, as well as black and white title headings, provide great visual interest to *The Children's Shakespeare,* an early success of a skilled illustrator who was productive throughout a long life. His Edwardian achievements have been somewhat obscured by the fame of his cartoon character Teddy Tail, "the Mouse in your House," created ten years before Walt Disney's Mickey Mouse and the first newspaper cartoon animal famous throughout the world, particularly bringing amusement in the dark days of World War I. The year 1911 was extraordinary for Folkard, with the publication of *The Children's Shakespeare,* and classic illustrations for *Pinocchio* and *Grimm's Fairy Tales* — both published by A. and C. Black. Several other books — *Aesop's Fables* (1912), *The Arabian Nights* (1913), *Ottoman Wonder Tales* (1915) — established his brilliance in drawing animals and authentic Orientalism. In some details his style resembles that of Arthur Rackham. In "Ariel and Caliban," for example, Folkard's Rackham-style trees are background for a simian hairy monster with long nails, who wears a greenish gray tunic, while Ariel, made decent by a white drape, has green wings and pointed ears (20). Caliban registers pain from Ariel's pinching his shoulder and drops his burden of firewood. Two frogs at the bottom of the picture provide realism, and another point of discovery for the child viewer.

While many subjects are familiar — jester Touchstone with a weary Rosalind and Celia in the woods for *As You Like It* (122), Petruchio throwing the plates in *The Taming of the Shrew* (138), Lear and his Fool on the stormy heath (294), the Ghost beckoning Hamlet (256), a balcony scene for *Romeo and Juliet* (394), Prince Arthur begging Hubert not to blind him in *King John* (204) — some are quite original, notably for the histories. Folkard chose the garden scene (III.iv) for *Richard II* (228). The Queen is a compelling figure, whose gray dress features an Art Nouveau design. He introduced similar detail in fittings of the chest in *Pericles,* where costumes at Ephesus demonstrate his skill with Oriental design. Most elaborate is the full-length portrait of Shylock for *The Merchant of Venice* (100), a very disturbing image. Shylock is a stereotypical stage Jew with a large nose, black hair and beard. Like his physical characteristics, his Oriental dress (loose robe, a wide striped cummerbund, hat with jeweled tassel) and dagger at his waist set him apart; Folkard also featured the scales that Shylock brings to weigh his pound of flesh. Not chivalric battle at Agincourt but "The chest contained nothing but tennis balls" is his illustration for *Henry V,* an opportunity to depict lavish costumes of bishop, king, and courtiers. Moreover, the episode is a stunning challenge to youth and nation (236). Combat is the subject for *Coriolanus,* where two brave men in Roman dress wield their swords from horseback (454), again an opportunity to draw animals well. Folkard gives interest to the ubiquitous iconic witches in *Macbeth*; three black birds fly about the three wild and unearthly crones, whose green pointed hats and loose dresses echo their gray-green flesh. A gnarled tree stump, in an otherwise barren land, resembles a monster's head (406). Most mysterious is the ghost scene in *Hamlet,* a fine example of misty gray wash — atmospheric sky and large solid castle, and a ghost just perceptible in white outline (256). Three tiny human figures stand out in their strong colors of brown, red, and gold. Dent later reprinted eight of Folkard's illustrations in an edition of Lamb's *Tales,* edited by F.C. Tilney for the Tales from Many Lands Series, discussed in Chapter 3.

Although Hoffman's large volume is compelling, an earlier series of small books of single plays, with different illustrators, is also memorable. These sold for 1s. in cloth and 1s.6d. in leather. The first six titles, published 1904–1905, indicate expectations of readers' interests: *A Midsummer Night's Dream, As You Like It, The Tempest, Richard II, Merchant of Venice, Henry V*. R. Anning Bell illustrated the first and Dora Curtis all the others except *The Tempest*, the gem of the series, illustrated by Walter Crane (1845–1915).[22] Crane is probably better known for his color work, especially in children's books, but here all illustrations are black and white, in a style close to that used by William Morris's Kelmscott Press, where Edward Burne-Jones (1833–1898) was the principal artist. Starting with an Art Nouveau design for the end papers, many pictures enthrall: three half-page drawings of places in Stratford in the introduction (viii, x, xiii), four incisive portraits (Prospero, 4; Ariel, 41; Trinculo, 50; and Stephano, 55) each a third of a page, and eight full-pages with episodes from the story. Part of their brilliance comes from the way that Crane totally filled the space and framed each picture with a border that bears a caption across the bottom. Intricate design and detail make his illustrations finer than many in color, which was becoming standard.

Hoffman's address "To My Child-Readers" offered "these little stories" for children to "love" as "you love all the old stories that have belonged to children for ages past"; she also hoped that at a very young age they would know something of the writings of their "great countryman." As a storyteller, the great writer had affinity with traditional tales. Hoffman combined a child perspective — "the good fairies surely gave him all their gifts" — with patriotism — Shakespeare was appropriately born and died on the "day set apart for St. George, the patron, or guardian, saint of England" (vii). Her didactic biographical sketch assumes a boy wonder:

> [H]e had been taught the Latin language as well as reading, writing, and arithmetic. What happy years [six at the Grammar School] those must have been to the boy, so eager to seize every chance of gaining knowledge! What questions he must have asked! And how worried his parents must have been when they could not answer him! But we may be sure, they were very proud as they listened to him and watched the growth of his glorious mind [ix].

A more inspiring example of a schoolboy would be hard to find.

While many think that Shakespeare's early marriage and unfortunate choice of wife explain why he left Stratford, Hoffman prudently reported that we do not know the facts. But she reassuringly posited a belief that there must have been a good reason, "or surely he never would have given up his home and the happiness of watching over his children and teaching them to love him" (xi). Perhaps to give a context for *The Tempest*, she correlated Shakespeare's life and the types of plays written:

> While he was still young and hopeful the plays that he wrote were full of fun, and love, and joy of life. Then there came a time when youth had gone and he

Folkard's depiction of Shylock is of a sinister stereotype, as Shylock holds the scales he brought to the trial to measure payment of his bond in *The Merchant of Venice*. The Orientalism of the Jew's attire further sets him apart as other.

was passing through troubles and temptations. Then he wrote the great tragedies, telling of all the sins and sorrows of this life of ours. And afterwards, when peace and calm came to him again, he wrote three more plays with something of the old joy of life in them, and all teaching the great lesson of forgiveness [xi–xii].

This more sophisticated argument, pressed by Furnivall in his 1901 edition of Lamb's *Tales* and accepted by so careful a scholar as E.K. Chambers, stresses a moral ideal, Christian forgiveness, rather than fairies and spectacle. In Hoffman's biography the mature Shakespeare is reunited with his family and makes up what was lost while he was in London. She linked *The Tempest* to *A Midsummer Night's Dream*, a return to "the beautiful world of fancy," but now a story "of the pure and perfect love of man and woman, and of pity, and above all, of the forgiveness of man by man" (xiv). Her thoughtful religious interpretation explains why Edwardians favored these plays and supports their expectation that child readers would return to Shakespeare as adults to find an old friend who has always been with them, ready with "words of comfort or of strength: of joy or of peace" (xvi).

Hoffman wanted "the little book and its charming pictures" to please her readers, but she also wanted love and reverence, a place "in your hearts, next to the things that are already beautiful and precious to you — your Father — your Mother — your Home" (xvi). She was not simply domestic, but combined nationalism and didacticism in her peroration:

> [T]he words that he wrote are still with us, and are as full of power and of truth as ever they were, and will last as long as the world lasts. There is nothing in all England's history of which we have more right to be proud than this, that it was in this "dear, dear land," as Shakespeare called it, that he was born, that here he lived and wrote, and here he died. We can show our love and honour of him in no better way than by reading and learning to understand the great plays he has left us. By so doing we shall be the better and nobler men and women, and this England of ours, so proud of her greatness and wealth, will be more truly great and truly rich than ever [xiv–xv].

A theme of valued education, sounded in Hoffman's introductory remarks, developed in her retelling of the relation of father and daughter in *The Tempest*:

> He had in these long quiet years been her schoolmaster, and it had been his great delight to fill her mind with such knowledge as she could not have had if they had lived in the great world, where there would have been many other things to take up their time.
>
> He had given her beautiful thoughts, and so her mind had grown as beautiful as her body. Perhaps you do not know what is meant by a beautiful mind. It is the mind which makes us think and do, and if the mind is beautiful and good, we shall think and do beautiful and good things, while if it is bad, we shall think and do bad things [7].

Miranda pays rapt attention to Prospero's teaching in Crane's "He told her all that old sad story" (15), a picture with marvelous details of plants, repeated in each illustration, to evoke the luxuriant nature of the enchanted island. This, combined with the elegant figures, shows Crane's relation to Edward Burne-Jones, which is even more obvious in "The Dance of the Nymphs and Reapers" (65), although Crane's pretty ladies in swirling draperies lack the Gothic slenderness that signals the most esteemed Victorian painter.

Whenever possible Hoffman heightened high sentiment. Miranda's reaction to Ferdinand is well advised; he has "all the beauty of young and noble manhood made greater by the events of the last hour. Deepest sorrow and tenderest love shone in his face, together with a strange calm" (25). Crane's frontispiece, "The Meeting of Ferdinand and Miranda," is richly detailed in a style whose affinity to that of Burne-Jones explains why Morris asked Crane to illustrate a Kelmscott book—albeit Crane's illustrations were less effective than expected. Ariel is an overarching figure, while on the left Prospero watches thoughtfully. This scene conveys wonder, but monitored, a sense that the picture's framing reinforces. In another outdoor scene Miranda offers to carry the logs borne by a muscular Ferdinand (31). The lovers gaze raptly at each other in a drawing that displays the beauty of physical bodies. The gaze persists in a lighted, well furnished interior where the lovers sit, with knees almost touching, to play chess (78). Visual images reiterate that their marriage is Prospero's primary objective, though a sense of loss tinges his feelings.

Hoffman's moral context is that Prospero "had no thought of revenge as a man not so good would have had; he only wished to forgive" those who harmed him (9); "his purpose in bringing them to the island was not to punish, but to pardon, if only they were sorry for their sin" (73). Prospero uses his magic power for good, and when the "three men of sin" have their new life "there will be no need of magic—love will take its place and reign supreme" (86). Consistent sweetness and beauty pervade Hoffman's story.

Nevertheless, although Prospero taught Caliban to speak well, he "kept all his brutish ways" (5); thus the master becomes stern "because of his unwillingness to work or be useful in any way" (49). Hoffman described Caliban as "half-man, half-animal ... his body crooked, and covered with hair; his ugly face full of spite and cunning; and his hands and feet with long nails like claws" (5). Crane's illustrations depict a monster—with a rather startling resemblance to Tolkein's Gollum—whether he kneels to Stephano and Trinculo while holding their wine bottle, again watched by Ariel (57), or flies in terror before hounds that Prospero and Ariel set on the three conspirators (70). Evil figures fill most of the space, but are clearly being driven away; Ariel and Prospero in the upper right corner extend their arms like divine forces. Children had, then, a powerful picture of sinful creatures to compare with the gentle beauty and plenitude of the lovers and the thoughtful, loving, and forgiving Prospero.

Crane's most dramatic picture is the tempest itself (11). A cropped section of a ship, with deck awash as high waves crash all round, epitomizes the play's opening, which Hoffman puts after an exposition of how Prospero came to the

Walter Crane's many illustrations for Alice S. Hoffman's *The Tempest* (1904), a small volume with only one story, made it astonishing. From the upper left Prospero and Ariel observe Caliban and his evil companions, who flee before spirits in the shape of hounds.

island. Italians in court dress are juxtaposed to the sturdy Boatswain, Viking-like in simple garb and with a knife at his waist; moreover, his knowledge of the sea and fearless disregard for royalty set him apart. The book's illustrations, a mark of the quality of Edwardian achievement in publishing, make clear why Crane, who was master of the Art-Workers Guild, President of the Arts and Crafts Exhibition Society, and Principal of the Royal College of Art, was a leader in the Arts and Crafts Movement. His *Of the Decorative Illustration of Books Old and New* (1896) remains a crucial document of Victorian attitudes and methods.[23]

Constance and Mary Maud, Shakespeare's Stories *(1913)*

While Crane's illustrations subtly questioned Hoffman's consistently high sentiments, the reverse relationship between picture and text characterizes Constance and Mary Maud's *Shakespeare's Stories* (1913), published by Edward Arnold.[24] Glosses are Edwardian witty remarks reflecting current social mores, but they are juxtaposed with elaborate eighteenth-century Boydell Gallery engravings. The Mauds chose nine plays: four comedies (*As You Like It, Twelfth Night, A Midsummer Night's Dream, The Merchant of Venice*), four tragedies (*Romeo and Juliet, Macbeth, King Lear, Hamlet*), and one romance (*The Tempest*). The order is different; *As You Like It* is first, *A Midsummer Night's Dream* and *The Tempest* come past the middle; *Hamlet* is the last play and the subject of the frontispiece. Stories are substantially paraphrased, largely written as dialogue with narrative linking. Each is divided into parts, the usual device to facilitate and encourage reading to the end. Interlaced comments about character and action make fascinating comparisons with Victorian collections by Mary Seymour or Edwardian Mary Macleod. The Mauds seem almost to have set out to undercut Victorian propriety, or at least to propose an alternative sophistication.

The fairies in *A Midsummer Night's Dream*, as we have seen repeatedly, are the most exploited subject for children. The Mauds began, "fairies can see and hear the mortals, and it is of that our story tells us" (241), but then quickly introduced skepticism to undermine favorite conventions through a comparative description of Puck:

> Now Puck was not one of those light, gossamer, rainbow-tinted fairies, more like a soap-bubble than anything else — only a soap-bubble shaped like a tiny mortal, of course — he was a sturdy little fellow, dressed in green and brown, and he wore a kind of hood with two rather large ears attached to it, which gave him a waggish look. He folded his little green wings so close to his back that you could hardly see he had any; but when he wanted to use them —flash! and away he was; no other fairy could fly so fast, and no steamer or aeroplane

will ever be able to go with his swiftness. We mortals can hardly think so fast [242].

Authors and readers here engage; the Mauds forestalled any rejection of tree fairies, evoke outlaws of the greenwood in the description of Puck, and acknowledge modern technology. Thus they are as "waggish" as the sprite himself. Nevertheless, the conclusion features pretty and comforting fairies; when all in the palace are asleep,

> from room to room they tripped, light as birds, and with their soft song, that woke no one, but only gave most pleasant dreams, they blessed the happy couples; and when they flew off to their delightful wood, they left behind them the blessed gift of sweet peace [266].

The illustration for *As You Like It* (II.ii) is by John Dowman: Rosalind (Sarah Siddons) bestows her necklace on Orlando, as the wrestler Charles is carried off in the background and Duke Frederick hurries off to the right. Engraved by William Satchwell Leney and published in 1800, the image is typical of eighteenth-century productions. But the Mauds combined gaiety and practicality in an Edwardian rationale for Rosalind and Celia's decision to make Touchstone their traveling companion:

> Some people may think this a strange choice, and that two young Princesses starting alone on an unknown journey would rather have an able-bodied swordsman; or, bethinking them of the difficulty of obtaining food, that they would have engaged the service of a cook, or perhaps a lady's maid, since never in their lives had they dressed without the assistance of one. But think how wise, after all, were these young maids. Though so little experienced, they realized that such hardships as were likely to befall them would count for little were they only kept thoroughly amused in cheerful company, and this they knew would be with the Fool — who was no fool. Under the cover of his cap and bells and motley coat he had always enjoyed a perfect liberty of speech permitted to no one else in the Palace. From him you got no empty compliments and soft phrases, and the relief of this to ladies brought up in Court circles cannot be imagined, for too much sugar is a far worse evil than none [12–13].

This gloss works on many levels; it is a delicious send-up of the pretensions of Edwardian society, and also a playful but useful delineation of what is most helpful when one is in adversity. Nevertheless, conventional suppositions were allowed: the repentant Oliver "had changed not only within, but also without, and no one to look at him could have thought him capable of unkindness, much less of cruelty" (31). Thus the match with Celia is made, but lest the reader wallow in sentimentality, Orlando, the long-smitten swain, finishes pragmatically:

> People in love can swallow a wondrous large dose if it proves the thing they desire. And so Orlando, his heart beating high with hope, wisely never questioned this tale of sorceress-uncles and magic, but went straight to the point, which was getting his true love by hook or by crook [34].

Since tragedies do not encourage playful glosses, the Mauds sounded quite didactic and Victorian. Thus Richard Westall's *Lady Macbeth* (1800), with its dramatic gesture in the manner of Fuseli, is less at variance. "That Banquo was greater, as a giant is greater than a dwarf, Macbeth knew in his craven, distorted soul" (137). Lady Macbeth, who recognizes that she has sacrificed all that was worth living for, discovers her initial mistake quickly, "Gladly she would have turned Macbeth's energies into sane and useful directions," but she is "powerless to stop him"; thus "remorse and horror" fill her brain and the strain breaks her (153). The play's opening portends disaster: "In the olden days Scotland was the haunt, not only of the good fairies, but of witches and wizards. The latter had no power over those of good and true heart, as this tale will show, but in those whose hearts were as evil soil they planted seeds which grew to terrible deeds of darkness" (125). Like Macleod, the Mauds stressed setting, where supernatural phenomena had greater presence; however, they clearly established personal choice and responsibility. Macbeth responds to the witches' prophecy:

> Black thoughts and murderous wishes sprang from the evil seed in his heart. He feared to face his own thoughts, but he nursed them carefully instead of strangling them. He bade his eye wink at what he wished his hand to do. But his hand trembled at the thought of the deed.
>
> Macbeth's wife was made of more daring stuff. She was a woman who feared nothing and cared for nobody but her husband.... [S]ince only by murder could he obtain the throne, she would fan up his flickering courage. For when once her mind was made up to a deed, she could not abide shilly-shallying [129–131].

The metaphor of the seed is scriptural (Matthew 13.19–23, Mark 4.3–32) and much of the language somber, but "shilly-shallying" has an Edwardian ring of triviality and command. Constance and Mary Maud reinforced currency in the plays — and moral choices.

Relations between parent and child in tragedies, as already noted, require complex explanation. Hamlet regards his mother's remarriage "with horror and amazement" (303), but when Gertrude keeps her promise to stay away from Claudius, "one object was to protect her son" (329). Although Hamlet's "sole object in life was to fulfill the ghost's command and deal vengeance on the evil Claudius ... the Queen, his mother, was the great difficulty, for he desired to spare her all he could" (340–341). More exacting is evaluation of "poor old Lear," who stages "an ill-timed competition" (213) among his daughters. Henry Fuseli's painting (212), engraved by Richard Earlom in 1792, is here captioned: "How, how, Cordelia! Mend your speech a little, / Lest it may mar your fortunes" (I.i.94–95). Fuseli's characteristic vigor has melodramatic gestures but no trace of beauty except that of force. Lear finds that his daughters and his knights draw away when he foregoes power: "They thought to offer their services to one going up hill, not to a poor old man going down so fast! Poor old Lear! both daughters against him!" (323, 325). Applicability to an ambitious society resonates, but with hope as well as bleakness. The story is "sad ... all the foolishness and wickedness of base ingratitude; but, like bright stars between the dark driving clouds of a stormy night, shine out the love of Cordelia, and the faithfulness of Kent" (240).

Capulet, also a dominating father, is torn by conflicting emotions of love and pride after he insists that Juliet wed Paris:

> [T]he wrathful parent turned on his heel, feeling very righteous, very wrathful, and very miserable, for, after all, his little daughter was the person he loved best in all the world; but, of course, parental authority had to be upheld, and if he did not know what was best for his child's good, who did? [68–69].

William Miller's view of the Capulets' ball, engraved by Georg Siegmund and Johann Gottlieb and published 1792, is a beautiful representation of the lovers, brightly lit in the lower left corner and watched by the nurse, Mercutio, and Benvolio. The cross of Romeo's pilgrim's staff points toward a wall torch, as he takes Juliet's hand to declare, "If I profane with my unworthiest hand / This holy Shrine" (I.v.94–95). Opposite, Capulet restrains Tybalt, while before them a charming page looks directly at the viewer, a point of contact for child readers. At the center are dancing graces. Perhaps the most interesting gloss is a distinction based on gender, not simply their identities as "pilgrim" and "fair saint" but also how each responded at first meeting: love enters through Romeo's eyes and through Juliet's ears (49).

In *The Tempest*, on the other hand, there is no denial of Miranda's loving Ferdinand at first sight: "I call him a thing divine. I never saw a mortal look so noble" (176). Fortunately, this is the reaction that Prospero intends. Positive support of a father's authority and choice of husband for a beloved daughter is wittily made in *The Tempest*. After Miranda expresses delight in Ferdinand, who kisses her in the log-carrying episode, the text asks:

> And who do you think was looking on all the time? and looking on with great pleasure and no anger at all — why, Prospero himself. No tyrant he, and no cruel father either; he had all along been planning this very thing [201].

Glosses like these encourage child and adult to talk as part of the moral learning that Edwardians expected children to acquire when they read stories from Shakespeare's plays. The conversational manner and wit of Constance and Mary Maud were risky but also more engaging than sober pronouncements; they inspired adult self-recognition and were likely to amuse children, not least by flattering them.

As the last few chapters have shown, Edwardian children could choose from a splendid variety of books with Shakespeare stories / tales and intriguing illustrations. The strength of the tradition of Lamb's *Tales from Shakespeare*, and artists' ingenuity in selecting and skills to illustrate episodes, had a significant counterpart in many alternatives developed by Edwardian writers, illustrators, and publishers. Thus far the books considered have often been upmarket, reward and prize volumes, albeit some relatively inexpensive. However, another very large and attractive resource was available to all schoolchildren. Edwardian schoolbooks of literature, and of history, are remarkably well presented. The plays chosen — one to three a year — indicate those preferred; exercises are a sign of how interpretations were guided and demonstrate the interrelation between verbal and visual texts.

6

Shakespeare in Schoolbooks

While late Victorian and Edwardian children of prosperous parents could choose from the proliferation of Shakespeare tales / stories in beautiful and elaborate editions, those of lesser means could read—and see images—in schoolbooks. This chapter begins with two small collections, Blackie's Stories Old and New Series and Harrap's All-Time Tales; these books were sold both as part of a child's inexpensive library and as readers. Like many schoolbooks, they reprinted Lamb's *Tales from Shakespeare*. A. Syms-Wood's edition of 1909, the remarkable Oxford and Cambridge text, combines stories from Lamb with quotations and much pedagogical detail. Designed to prepare students for preliminary examinations, it signals qualities of mind expected at eleven-plus years to indicate capacity for university education. Clara L. Thomson, an outstanding Edwardian educator and author, in an alternative *A First Book of English Literature* (1906) gave an overview of Shakespeare in the context of the national tradition.

School readers, six or seven to serve forms / classes in the preparatory education that all received, conformed to current educational standards. They indicated Shakespeare's role in national life and literature; children studied his works over several years, a cumulative effect of increasing complexity. The chosen plays record those deemed suitable. Educational standards meant similarities between series, but there are differences. Edward Arnold published *Literary Reading Books* (1902–1909) and *Steps to Literature* (1905), and a third series, *Sesame Readers* (1908), not exclusively devoted to literature. Thomas Nelson's *Highroads of Literature* (1913–1915) is similar to Arnold's *Literary Reading Books*, but exceptional because of its use of historical paintings and cogent exercises. School editions of plays are not within this study's scope—stories retold. Thus although Macmillan's Pocket Classics series in the United States included volumes of plays and Lamb's *Tales*, only the latter is discussed, along with a picturesque edition from Edwin Ginn.

Learning about Shakespeare was not limited to schoolbooks of literature. Nelson's parallel *Highroads of History* series is sophisticated enough to identify Shakespeare's changed interpretations of history. Harrap's Illustrated Story of

England Series introduced his plays in accounts of earlier periods, as had Charlotte Yonge's *Westminster Historical Reading Books* (1892). Clara Linklater Thomson, a forceful and effective proponent of the interlace of literature and history, relied on Shakespeare's plays to present the Middle Ages in *A First History of England* (1901–1909). Tom Bevan's *Stories from British History (B.C. 454–A.D. 1485)* had a praising but more limited use.

Harrap's All-Time Tales

George G. Harrap published two series of traditional stories for young people. Thomas Carter's two original volumes of Shakespeare stories were in the sophisticated Told Through the Ages Series, discussed in Chapter 5. The simpler All-Time Tales has two books of *Lamb's Tales from Shakespeare* (1910).[1] Each was "bound in limp cloth strengthened with tapes," 128 pages of large print, priced at sixpence. A Prize Edition in cloth boards, with color frontispiece, sold for one shilling. Inscriptions in my copies mark non-class use: Book I is "from Aunt Ethel, Xmas 1912," while Book II is "For best progress in school work during the year 1921." This indicates appeal, as gift and as prize, over the years for books from a "Series of Supplementary Readers on the lines of the Suggestions from the English and Scottish Education Departments." Five tales in Book I are all comedies—*As You Like It, A Midsummer Night's Dream, The Tempest, Twelfth Night, The Winter's Tale*; Book II has four tales: one comedy—*The Merchant of Venice*—and three tragedies—*King Lear, Romeo and Juliet*, and *Hamlet*. Texts are unchanged, but there is no preface or supporting notes. M. Lavars Harry illustrated both; each has a color frontispiece, also pasted on the cover, and seven full-page black and white illustrations.

The color picture of Book I is ever-popular Bottom and Titania, with a remarkable discrepancy between his large size and her fairy daintiness. Bottom has an unusually expressive face, as he responds to the gentle stroking of his nose by Titania, an Art Nouveau lady with short bob and patterned costume and wings, a delicate design that reiterates the contrast between the two figures. Bottom, in simple Greek workman's dress, with bare arms and legs, sprawls beneath a tree. Because Harry's palette was soft grays and tans, the seven black and white illustrations are bolder. One distinctive image is Puck, who "proceeded to pour some of the juice of the little purple flower into his eyes" (59). An elegant Athenian youth sleeps peacefully, while a small Puck hovers above him. The woodland background is well executed with swirling lines that make the trees seem alive and intimidating; roots of one on the left look like feet and a branch reaches out.

Especially engaging is "Prospero was standing by them invisible, to overhear what they said," *The Tempest* (21). Ghosts or invisible creatures add mystery. Prospero is drawn with thin vertical lines and fused to the tree, also a

Orlando's pretend wooing of Ganymede (his Rosalind in boy's guise) in *As You Like It* is a cogent but unusual subject chosen by M. Lavars Harry to illustrate Lamb's *Tales from Shakespeare,* Book I (1910), Harrap's All-Time Tales Series, an attractive small volume that was sometimes a schoolbook. The young people sit before a huge tree whose girth provides background for bench and figures.

vertical study. Between the lovers is a stack of logs, all horizontal lines, but for four in the foreground. Ferdinand and Miranda are in white costumes, lightly bordered in black. In Harry's depiction of this popular moment Ferdinand kneels and Miranda holds a flower. "And Orlando called the shepherd his Rosalind" (93), from *As You Like It,* is one of Shakespeare's wittiest and most brilliant scenes, a rarely illustrated wooing. The picture develops Mary Lamb's brief narrative: "and every day talked over all the fine words and flattering compliments which young men delight to use when they court their mistresses" (92). The pair sit on a bench before a massive tree trunk; he holds her left hand in his right hand, and lowers his left arm expressively. Celebration of physical action is the point of "he performed wonders" (76). Orlando stands before his fallen opponent, the wrestler Charles, while behind them many spectators watch carefully; figures are drawn against a plain white background.

Viola, another heroine in male attire, faces greater challenges in *Twelfth Night.* She must dissemble before Olivia, who entices, "I will draw the curtain and show the picture" (113). This is Harry's only interior, simply indicated by casement windows. The drawing is in lighter, minimal lines, but deftly placed, most tellingly in a splendid Art Nouveau pattern for the lady's cloak. Here Viola, a page with cap in hand, controls the situation; but Harry also depicted her in danger: "She saw her formidable rival advancing towards her with sword drawn" (119). Viola's anxiety is plain to the viewer she faces, while her stalwart opponent fills the foreground. The complexity of a girl pretending to be a boy strengthens the duel's excitement. Cross-dressing, interchange of genders, leads to awareness of sexual identity. The lightly sketched setting is a palace courtyard. A more severely drawn, conventional episode for *The Winter's Tale,* "This poor deserted baby was found by a shepherd" (37), is compelling — triangular composition, a bold but minimal use of black to give depth to costumes and trees that frame a bare landscape. A lamb in the shepherd's arm, like the baby's outstretched arms, adds empathy.

The visual images of Book 2 belie its emphasis upon tragedies. The frontispiece / cover is a romantic moment from the one comedy, *The Merchant of Venice.* Portia signs surrender of herself and all her worldly possessions to Bassanio, "I give them with this ring." Elegantly dressed lovers stand before a plain background, a large curtain but for a portion of stained glass window with heraldic crest. The colors are soft, mostly fawn and gray. Similarly, in *King Lear,* France gently kisses Cordelia's hand as he promises their future, "And be queen of him and of fair France" (17). Lear and two daughters are just visible behind France's large cloak with its minimal decorative border; slender Cordelia's slighter mantle is patterned. A large curtain crosses the entire background, while a modest pattern indicates a floor rug.

The second image is a traditional storm on the heath, "There did King Lear defy the winds and thunder" (29). At the center with billowing cloak and streaming beard and hair, Lear extends his left arm. The Fool crouches before him, nearer the viewer, his body bent forward. A bold diamond pattern on his stockings and linings of his jerkin contrasts sharply with Lear's white cloak and the thin lines of rain that fill the background. Just as this illustration points to the tragic hardship of King Lear, so does the trial for *The Merchant of Venice*, "O wise and upright judge!" (53), an uneasy moment before Shylock's defeat. All figures are staid. Antonio in courtier's dress and Shylock in a long robe face toward Portia, who stands to read the bond before a long table where several hefty volumes indicate that the case will be thoroughly argued. The judge, seated above, is barely visible behind the parchment, while a youthful Bassanio watches anxiously on the far right.

Two illustrations for *Romeo and Juliet* also afford contrast. The first, happy lovers that kiss in the balcony scene, "The day was breaking when they parted" (73), is the finest picture in Book II. Drawn very precisely are effective contrasts of black and white — the squares of the pavement on which Juliet stands, the diamond design of Romeo's doublet and stripes of his hose, the dark trees against very tight black lines with a small white patch to mark the end of night. Harry echoed Renaissance painting with its focus on the principals and a distant landscape in the background, separated by the strong line of the balcony. A fine detail is Romeo's position, his left leg kneels on the balcony and curves to link the intensity of their moment of union with the darker outside world.

Only for *Hamlet* do Harry's illustrations convey unmitigated darkness. First, "A bloody deed, Mother," cried Hamlet, "but not so bad as yours" (114). A courtier in black, he stands dagger in hand above slain Polonius, whose head protrudes under a large curtain. Gertrude's costume is medieval in style, white with a small border, similar to Ophelia's dress in a second illustration. A bold sash about the waist echoes a line in the garland of flowers that Ophelia holds out from her shoulder. With head uncovered and hair in disarray she stares upward. "To this brook she came when she was unwatched" (123), echoes Arthur Rackham's identically captioned illustration — the brook's edge and a massive tree — but Harry's leaning tree forms a balance to Ophelia's standing figure and is less entangling. Harry's pictures comment on Lamb's texts and occasion questions.

Blackie's Stories Old and New

With the same marketing appeal (*A Midsummer Night's Dream* on its cover) and similar scope, *Lamb's Tales from Shakespeare* in the Stories Old and New Series was published by Blackie in 1917.[2] A preface, used in every volume, seductively invites child readers, explains the intention, and urges care in reading and keeping of the volumes:

> A small chosen library is like a walled garden where a child may safely play. In that charmed seclusion the love of books, like the love of flowers, grows of itself. If the reading habit is to be acquired, the child ought from the first to be given real books, which may be handled with pleasure and kept with pride — books containing literature suited to its own age.
>
> This volume belongs to a series of "Stories Old and New" which has been prepared specially for children. The books have been carefully chosen so as to include, along with the most charming stories by the best children's authors of to-day, a due proportion of those older tales which never grow old.
>
> To secure simplicity and right gradation, the text has been prepared to suit the different ages of readers. Care has been given to the illustration, print, and binding of the series, for it is believed that this is the best way to secure from the children that careful handling of the volumes which is the mark of the true book-lover [1].

The flower analogy is Romantic but apt because it is easily accessible to children. Insistence upon retellings of traditional literature, "stories old," along with modern books, "stories new," is the most significant pedagogical point. This both affirms confidence in the lasting appeal of earlier works and a belief that knowledge of them is fundamental. The final paragraph combines a pragmatic reassurance that the books are well made with a plea for their value and an encouragement to collect them.

A list of titles, divided into four overlapping categories (Grade I or II, Grade II or III, Grade III or IV, Grade IV or V), reflects expectations for different age levels and signs the popularity of classic texts. In the 1920s the books were published with uniform covers, tan cloth stamped with an interlaced pattern of foliage and bearing heraldic shields— reminiscent of Edward Burne-Jones. Generally, earlier grades were assigned fairy tales and myths, while middle grades add romance and adventure (King Arthur, Robin Hood, Knights of Charlemagne). Lamb's *Tales* is assigned to the last group, Grade IV or V, with more legends (*The Story of Don Quixote, The Arabian Nights,* and *The Lady of the Fountain* [*Mabinogion*]).³ Shakespeare, then, comes late in primary education that leads up to the eleven-plus examinations; the school edition contains questions.

Blackie's selected six tales combine comedies and tragedies, in order: *As You Like It, Hamlet, Merchant of Venice, A Midsummer Night's Dream, Much Ado about Nothing, The Winter's Tale.* The last two, although favored for children, are more demanding. Like Edith Robarts's version, this Lamb's *Tales* simplifies vocabulary and complex sentences and divides longer paragraphs into short ones. Moreover, each tale is divided into parts, roughly corresponding to acts. While advertisements for the series claimed "beautifully illustrated in colour by the best artists," no one is named; few images are signed, although some contain initials. Six full-page and four half-page illustrations in black and white supplement five (including the cover) full-color pages. A green cloth cover forms an appropriate setting for the pasted picture of Bottom, Titania, and small fairies in the woods. Unusually, Bottom's ass's head is very dark gray, as is his upper garment; a solid mass that makes his exposed human flesh (wrists and hands, knees, feet in sandals) more startling. A fair-haired Titania, in gossamer white and with large open wings, kneels beside him and appears smitten, a further contrast to the amazement suggested by Bottom's supporting his head in his right hand. Although attendant fairies are very small and infantile, they have assumed bold stances, enhanced by jaunty little hats, short garments, and blue wings. This is the only illustration of fairies. A rather somber Hermia and Helena, "The fair ladies became once more true friends" (black and white 79), two decorous figures (one sewing) model forgiveness. More lively, "Bless thee, Bottom" depicts his friends and fellow actors, the mechanicals, in flight across a desolate landscape (73).

Favored *As You Like It* and *The Winter's Tale* have two color pages each. Both for *As You Like It* show "the greenwood," an escapist world. Dorothy King's *Greenwood Tales: Stories of Robin Hood and His Merry Men* (1920) in Blackie's Stories Old and New Series, used the popular phrase as title and printed Amiens's song "Under the Greenwood Tree" as epigraph.[4] The frontispiece "Orlando and the Duke," a male focus, recalls the play's analog, the story of *Gamelyn*, a popular romance for children. The design is one of contrasts, age and youth, large and slight, rich dark blue courtier's clothes decorated with gold and forester's simple brown attire. Contrast also defines the two pretty young people resting during their flight from the court when "A Countryman chanced to pass" in the forest. Celia, in navy and white, rests her head on Rosalind's lap. Rosalind's attire as Ganymede matches Orlando's. Two half-pages are somber. Orlando comforts Adam in "O my dear master, I die for want of food" (18), while Touchstone (jester's suit, cap and bells) holds his wand and peers solemnly at a skull on the ground before him (33).

Illustrations for *The Winter's Tale* combine conventional situation with distinctive treatment. "The deserted baby was found by a shepherd" is frontispiece to the tale (81). Again a dark palette of navy and brown, his clothes and the sea / landscape, gives vividness, as does the striped blanket tightly wrapped about infant Perdita. Very curious is "Would you not think it breathed?" (96), an exotic Hermione as statue, an example of Orientalism built on details from ancient art of the Middle East, a hybrid Egyptian and Assyrian style that children could compare to sculptures in the British Museum. Bold stripes on the curtain pulled aside and on the costumes give definition. Hermione, with long black plaits and a golden headdress, holds her white mantle (with blue borders) as she stands in an alcove a step above Leontes, Camillo, and Paulina. Her faithful attendant watches the response of the jealous and cruel husband, whose character was portrayed in a black and white half-page, "The King commands Camillo to poison his guest" (83), a dark and sinister aggressor with his still, obedient subject.

For *The Merchant of Venice*, "I would be friends with you and have your love" (full-page 105), is fine work by the skilled and prolific illustrator Gordon

Various exotic costumes, an indulgence in Orientalism to signal Sicily, suggest Shakespeare's shifting locations and circumstances in his romance *The Winter's Tale*. A colorful illustration in Lamb's *Tales from Shakespeare* (1917), Blackie's Stories Old and New Series, shows Hermione standing in a raised alcove from which the curtain has been drawn aside. Leontes with Paulina and Camillo view the "statue" that is soon to come alive when the falsely accused queen is restored in a moment of magic and resurrection.

Browne, who averaged six books a year, but whose accurate and vivid drawings are always pleasing. Shylock, a stereotypical Jew, makes a fawning bow to proud Antonio, whose eyes are lowered. Beside him handsome Bassanio, a figure in white, does not deign to look at Shylock; but a boy with a basket of loaves rests against a pillar and looks at viewers as if to ask what they make of this. A second image of defeated Shylock, "I am ill. Let me go home" (121), leaves no doubt that a simple negative response to the Jew, the other, is inadequate. Browne also contributed an untitled but familiar image for *Hamlet*. The dead Ophelia floats on the river; her face is sharply drawn against a dark woody background (152). A smaller black and white picture, not signed by Browne, is clearly his style. *Much Ado About Nothing* ends with a delightful figure, a jester who lies on his back and bounces aloft a ball with his legs (57). This playful summary parallels the title and produces a smile, if not laughter.

The Educational Times evaluated Blackie's Stories Old and New Series: "A very attractive series, sure to fulfill its most useful object. The stories are simply told and effectively. The type is excellent, and the get-up is agreeable." This praise mirrors characteristics of these handy books, four and three-quarters by seven inches, that invited Edwardian (and later) children into the world's great literature and to begin a library.

A. Syms-Wood, ed., Tales from Shakespeare *(1909)*

Austere in appearance, with no visual illustrations, the Oxford and Cambridge *Tales from Shakespeare,* edited by A. Syms-Wood, B.A., London University and Balliol College, Oxford, and Prizeman of the New Shakespeare Society, was "specially prepared to meet the requirements of the Oxford and Cambridge University Examination bodies, the selection of tales being suggested by the University authorities as a subject for Preliminary Candidates at the Local Examinations."⁵ The six plays—*A Midsummer Night's Dream, The Winter's Tale, Much Ado about Nothing, Macbeth, Comedy of Errors,* and *Othello*—were frequently reprinted, but never with such penetrating and comprehensive materials and a confidence that there is "no necessary incompatibility between fostering in children a taste for good literature, and at the same time training them to answer examination papers" (iv). Syms-Wood offered "Lives of Charles and Mary Lamb" (vi–viii), "A Life of Shakespeare" (ix–x), Lamb's *Tales,* substantial quotations, more information than Mrs. Lang or F.J. Furnivall, and deliberately difficult questions to "educe the thinking powers of the young student." Extracts from plays are chosen to compare with Lamb's texts to recognize differences, to "take a lesson in the useful art of précis writing," and to be "suitable for committing to memory" (v). Finally, a key intention is didactic, sustaining Lamb's purpose to teach "*a lesson of all sweet and honourable thoughts and actions*" (iv). Moreover, their lives redolent of "consistent cheerfulness in spite of poverty and their unselfish devotion to each other will make a lasting impression upon the minds of the young" (v). Advocates for teaching English asserted this affirmation of the moral tradition in English literature, rooted in Christianity.

Each play begins with an introduction containing several headings, with only minor differences to suit particular needs. Four pages for *A Midsummer Night's Dream* comprise "Date of the Play," "Text of the Play," "The Title," "Source of the Play," "Nature of the Play and the Tale," "Lessons from the Tale," "Omissions in the Tale — Characters Omitted and Incidents Omitted," "Divergences from the Play in the Tale," and "Additions to the Play in the Tale" (3–6). Another section has "Dramatis Personae,"

> intended to serve as an abstract of each story and to help the student to answer the familiar question, "What do you know of So-and-so?" Character sketches or studies are added in the case of the more important personages. In these all attempt at deep philosophical analysis has been studiedly avoided: nothing will be found in them which the "young reader" could not have culled for himself from the Tales themselves, and they are inserted chiefly for the purpose of teaching him how to use for himself, in the study of character, the materials provided by Charles and Mary Lamb [iv].

After a list of "Characters of the Tale" (7–9) comes the tale itself, followed by extracts from the play, referenced to passages in the tale. Seven from *A Midsummer Night's Dream* explain young loves or fairies. Like Furnivall, Syms-Wood pointed out limitations in Mary Lamb's rendering, principally the absence of "most of the real comedy," although "the underlying motive — caprice" justifies calling the play a comedy (4). He further observed that "Pyramus and Thisbe" and the menials are the part best known and loved by the British public (5). Several changes seem arbitrary. Oberon, not Puck, puts the ass's head on Bottom and takes it off, and Puck does not speak the epilogue. The not-too-obvious lesson is to recognize daily human vexations and worries that explain lovers' inconstancy and that moods must be set aside to renew love. Two sets of ten questions each test close reading of phrases and their contexts, including recognition of Lamb's language as distinct from Shakespeare's, explanations of characters and their motives, and demonstration of skill in quoting (28). Questions are of

> every type set in elementary examinations ... intended to test the written work of the candidate, containing, as they do, a preponderance of questions of the more difficult type and such as are calculated to educe the thinking powers of the student ... well adapted for purposes of revision before examinations, inasmuch as they cover the whole field of research likely to be exploited by the examiner [iv].

Pedagogical apparatus in the introduction for *The Winter's Tale* is the most sophisticated; it has the same general topics plus one addition, "Anachronisms, etc." Most significant is an expansion that follows the "Dramatis Personae" and

"Characters in the Tale"; four additional pages — "Character Study: The Leontes and Hermione of the Tale: Their Counterparts in Othello" (41–44) — develop the complexities of this late comedy's characters and actions and take the young student into a comparative study of a comedy and a tragedy. Syms-Wood early marked how Shakespeare changed his source to let Hermione live (31) and defined her character in the tale: "the patient virtues of the long-suffering Hermione that were rewarded by the happy reunion and reconciliation with her lord" (39). Lamb's additions "form, as usual, a running commentary on the text, revealing traits of character, explaining motives, and pointing morals." A simple example is Antigonus: "A bear came out of the woods and tore him to pieces; *a just punishment on him for obeying the wicked order of Leontes*" (36). The tale's egregious limitation is removal of Autolycus as "the minister of fate in the comedy part," to

> regard it [the play] as a pure and simple love story rather than as a tragi-comedy, and thinking that a comic minister of fate would detract from the moral of the Tale she therefore chose higher instruments, instruments acting from within rather than from without, to unloose the knots. It may be that her story is better suited to teach the young how to overcome the difficulties of life by one's own efforts, but I think that the lesson taught by all Shakespeare's comedies — how Providence moves in a mysterious way its wonders to perform — a deeper and more profound one, more difficult, perhaps to penetrate, but truer to life [33].

Besides obscuring Shakespeare's Christian message, Lamb's Hermione "leaves much to the imagination," without which she is "either an impossibility or a singularly colourless personality," as when "she is apparently silent at her trial" (42). Lack of imagination is offset by quoting Hermione's first response to Leontes's accusation and the editor's portrayal

> of a heroine indeed, calm with the dignity of injured innocence, full of pity for those who have wronged her, patient but not abject, above recrimination and almost silent in rebuke, ready to suffer for those she knows will suffer, ever confidently trusting in a Providence that will right the wrong [43].

Extracts buttress this view; two center on Hermione, her request — a response to Leontes's wish — to Polixenes that he linger (I.ii.1–107) and her defense before her judges (III.iii. 21–114). In short, supplementary materials and Syms-Wood's analysis of character present a sophisticated interpretation and methods that are useful in literary analysis. These go far beyond his simple statement of the tale's lesson: "that life itself is like a tale, that we must all expect ups and downs, and that seeming accidents and trifles are in reality the mysterious workings of providence on our behalf" (32).

Moreover, at the end of the comparison between *The Winter's Tale* and *Othello*, largely devoted to Hermione, Syms-Wood advised students that when they read the plays themselves they would do well to compare Paulina and Emilia, who are both types — and so intended by Shakespeare —

of the clearheadedness and right-mindedness of the ordinary individuals we meet in daily life. Both see that wrong is being done to their mistresses, and both are fearlessly outspoken on their behalf, equally in the presence of the husbands of their unhappy ladies and in that of their own husbands—the ministers of crime. And the verdict of such is the verdict of the world at large [44].

The lesson is salutary, a simple and straightforward affirmation of modest courage in speaking the truth, not least because it is possible for persons not in authority, women — and schoolchildren. The eleven-plus examinations always had opponents because they placed very young children under great pressure; they were essentially abandoned some years ago. Nevertheless, Syms-Wood's edition, sanctioned by Oxford and Cambridge, is a dramatic reminder of how advanced training in reading and comprehending literature, and corollary moral understanding, could be for Edwardian children. Workday schoolbooks of Lamb's *Tales*, often without illustrations or pedagogical apparatus, were very different from his scholarly and critical materials.

Macmillan's The Children's Shakespeare *(1910)*

The Children's Shakespeare, published by Macmillan in 1910 and priced at four pence, was a good value. Alternatives, *The Children's Rossetti* and *The Children's Tennyson*, indicate the ongoing competitive advantages between nineteenth-century and earlier classic literature. The subtitle declared *The Children's Shakespeare* to be *Scenes from the Plays. With Introductory Readings from Charles and Mary Lamb's 'Tales from Shakespeare.' Arranged as a Continuous Reader with Exercises in Composition.*[6] Thus its pedagogical aspiration is analogous to Syms-Wood, but more modest and with some quite different emphases. Six plays combine comedies and tragedies: *As You Like It, King Lear, The Merchant of Venice, The Tempest, A Midsummer Night's Dream,* and *Macbeth*. Four sepia illustrations by J. Macfarlane enliven the text of *As You Like It*, the first and featured play, presented in eight parts. The first two scenes are the meeting between "Oliver and Orlando" in the orchard (I.i) and the "Wrestling Match" (I.ii), longer at five pages, and with an illustration of Rosalind giving Orlando a chain (14). An exercise asks: "What is wrestling? How was it looked upon in the time of the play?" (15). To answer requires a recognition of changing values from one historical period to another. "The Flight of Celia and Rosalind" (I.iii) has two sections, the banishment and plan, and the acquiring of the cottage. Part IV, "In the Forest of Arden" (II.iii), describes the pastoral pleasure of Duke Senior, shown as a kind of Robin Hood figure with four companions in the forest (28), while Part V is "The Flight of Orlando and Adam" (II.iii). Part VI is the encounter of "Orlando and the Duke" (II.vii), when he seeks food and includes the song "Blow, blow." One exercise is "Write out Amiens' song"— memorization; another asks for interpretation —"Explain 'All the world's a stage'" (45). Reinforcing the illustration of foresters is another popular subject — Rosalind, Celia, and Touchstone in country and jester costume (45). The final parts, "Rosalind and Orlando" and "Rosalind and Orlando cont'd" are long, quoted passages, nine pages (III.iii. and IV.i.) that include the wooing scene and an illustration of them as woodsmen. The exercise requires subtlety: "Give an account of Rosalind's attempt to cure Orlando" (63). Pupils read an interlace of Lamb and Shakespeare, albeit rather simplified through a concentration on pivotal scenes. Moreover, they were challenged by discriminating exercises in composition that encouraged character analysis that went beyond surface summary.

Macfarlane's three illustrations for *King Lear* make an appropriate contrast to those for *As You Like It*. All are conventional subjects with details of ancient Briton costumes that feature horned helmets usually associated with Saxons or Vikings. The opening scene shows the three princesses with long gowns and circlet crowns, while the old king sits on his throne to divide the kingdom (11). Lightning dominates the heath scene of a buffeted, bare-headed old man (43), who is most impressive in "Lend me a looking glass" (58). Lear stands holding a stiff, dead Cordelia; Viking figures (horned helmets) watch in the background. Schoolbooks like *The Children's Shakespeare* aimed at the best of both worlds. Lamb's *Tales* gave the stories, but long quotations introduced Shakespeare's language and allowed concentration on key passages.

Macmillan's Pocket Classics (1916)

In the United States an influential series was Macmillan's Pocket American and English Classics, advertised as "A Series of English Texts, edited for use in Elementary and Secondary Schools, with Critical Introductions, Notes, etc." These books are very manageable, four and a quarter by five and a half inches, sturdily and uniformly bound in brown cloth, with title stamped in gold, and priced at twenty-five cents. Many of Shakespeare's plays were single volumes for secondary or high school. For elementary schools there was *Lamb's Tales from Shakespeare* (1916): all twenty plays and the original preface, no illustrations, but the critical introduction of Lamb's editor, the Rev. Alfred Ainger, M.A. (1837–1904), whom the eleventh edition of *The Encyclopedia Britannica* (1910) identified as "English divine and man of letters." Ainger was the major nineteenth-century authority who wrote *Charles Lamb* (1882) in the "English Men of Letters Series," produced early editions of *Essays of Elia* (1883) and *Letters* (1888), and finally *The Life and Works of Charles Lamb*, in twelve volumes (1899–1900). He was educated at King's College, London, and at Trinity College, Cambridge. For a time he was an assistant master at Sheffield Collegiate School. He had a long association with Temple Church, London, served as canon at Bristol Cathedral, and was chaplain-in-ordinary to Queen Victoria and King Edward VII. In short, Ainger belongs to the mighty army of Victorian priests of the Anglican Church who made monumental contributions to the study of English literature. *Lamb's Tales* could have found no more congenial advocate; Ainger was amiable and generous, a sympathetic reader of the *Tales* who believed in its purpose and achievement.

Ainger's 1878 introduction, written seventy years after first publication of the *Tales*, unites biographical and publishing information with discreetly poised critical analysis. He commented that Mary Lamb was not named as co-author— "Perhaps it was the sister's own wish that her name should be suppressed."[7] However, he pointed out that the original preface makes clear that Charles was not the only author; he cited several of Charles's letters—to Manning and Wordsworth—written while the Lambs were sharing the work of retelling, before concluding, "her name therefore appears in the title of the present edition" (vi). The most fascinating part of Ainger's analysis is his comparison of the two authors and insistence upon the praiseworthy merits of each. While some later editors favored the tragedies and lauded Charles, Ainger was quick to recognize and praise Mary's achievement:

> In fact, the share of the work undertaken by Mary Lamb was the more difficult and the less grateful.... The differences of genius in the two narrators appear very evidently in their shares of the joint task. As already pointed out, Mary Lamb's part was the least rewarding, for she had to give to the improbabilities of the Comedies an air of probability, while denied the compensations of glowing poetry and brilliant wit. And it was no brotherly prejudice on the part of Charles that made him praise her workmanship in the letter to Manning. She constantly evinces a rare shrewdness and tact in her incidental criticisms, which show her to have been, in her way, as keen an observer of human nature as her brother [vii–viii, x–xi].

Nevertheless, Ainger found

> in the Tragedies, and in the profounder problems of human life there treated, ... the master-hand of Charles Lamb distinctly declares itself. The subtle intellect and unerring taste that have elsewhere analysed for us the characters of Lear and Malvolio are no less visible even when adapting Shakespeare's stories to the intelligence of the least critical of students [ix].

Ainger referred to *Hamlet* and *Romeo and Juliet* for examples of brilliant insight and skill in communicating complex experience with great clarity. Balanced against these is Mary Lamb's gloss on Beatrice and Benedict's rivalry in *Much Ado About Nothing*—"there is nothing that great wits so much dread as the imputation of buffoonery, because the charge comes sometimes a little too near the truth." Ainger exclaimed:

> How illuminating, in the best sense of the term, is such a commentary as this! The knowledge of human character that it displays is indeed in advance of a child's own power of analysis or experience of the world, but it is at once intelligible when thus presented, and in a most true sense educative [xi].

Here he articulated principles about the essential nature of children's literature, a perilous balance between a child's experience and capacity to understand complexities wisely made available. It is an apologia for the retelling of adult classics for children of which Lamb's *Tales* is the only begetter.

While Ainger succinctly identified two clear objectives set forth in Lamb's preface — "to interest young persons in the story of each drama, to supply them with a clear and definite outline of the main argument, omitting such episodes or incidental sketches of character as were not absolutely necessary to its development," he devoted greater attention to their elusive third objective, "to initiate the young reader into the unfamiliar diction of the dramatist, and by occasional slight changes in it to remove difficulties and remove obscurities" (viii). Again Mary Lamb provided the example — her treatment of Prospero's narrative in the first act of *The Tempest* — by shortening and making intelligible to a child with "a kind of running annotation or commentary ... for the reader — unsuspected by him or her" (ix). Subtlety in transposing Shakespeare into stories for children, a "casual and diffused method," is also the key to the Lambs's success in "enforcing the many moral lessons that lie in Shakespeare's plays" (xi).

Ainger's principles as a Victorian Anglican clergyman, sustained by readers and viewers of Shakespeare's plays until the later twentieth century, are salient for many today, although the diversity of the early twenty-first century makes their reception less commonplace. Ainger simply averred that the moral lessons, "at least in his judgment," constituted the "one special value of this little book in the training of children." Furthermore, the Lambs succeeded because they were not "ordinary compilers" who "would have been tempted to make these little stories sermons in disguise, or to have appended to them in set form the lessons they were calculated to teach. Happily, both as moralist and artist, Charles Lamb knew better how hearts and spirits are touched to 'fine issues'" (xii). Lamb's *Tales,* replete with lessons of "tenderness and wisdom," have a unique position in the annals of English literature.

> And so it happened that these trifles, designed for the nursery and the schoolroom, have never been superseded, nor are they ever likely to be. Written in the first instance solely with a view to being read by children, they are marked here and there by a certain needless concession to the supposed phraseology of the nursery. But the genius of the writers had unconsciously ministered to the wants of children of a larger growth [xii].

While publishers of a second edition presented it with "suitable elegance" for "young ladies advancing to the state of womanhood" (xii), Ainger went much farther: "More and more is a knowledge of Shakespeare coming to be regarded as a necessary part of an Englishman's education; and the Editor knows of no first introduction to that study at once so winning and so helpful as that supplied by these narrative versions" (xiii). He could have enlarged "Englishman" to the English-speaking world.

Edwin Ginn (1915)

American publisher, Ginn and Company, with offices throughout the United States, made a few adjustments that signal national differences. Lamb's *Tales from Shakespeare* (1915) reprinted the original edition of Edwin Ginn (1838–1914), one of the first titles in Classics for Children Series, "which first made available for school use many of the standard works in literature."[8] Its distinctive features are: Ginn's revisions of the prefaces by Ainger and Lamb, the elimination of *Measure for Measure*, the addition of eighteen full-page illustrations, and a "Pronouncing Vocabulary of Names."

Adaptation for use in schools required "a few verbal alterations" and most tellingly the elimination of *Measure for Measure*, a play now identified as a "problem play" and popular because of fascination with sexuality. Ginn did not explain his decision, but avoided the exacting sexual circumstances of venereal disease and the bed trick, however deftly the tale elided the problems. He was explicit about changes to Lamb's preface that sharply divided boys and girls:

> It also seemed wise to omit the portion of Lamb's preface especially applicable to English schools, as the following quotation would indicate: "Instead of recommending these Tales to the perusal of young gentlemen, who can read them so much better in the originals, their kind assistance is rather requested in explaining to their sisters such parts as are hardest to understand."
>
> Such a recommendation would be hardly appreciated in our schools, where the misses have equal advantages with their brothers and do not feel the need of such assistance [vi].

Proud satisfaction in the American ideal of public education informs this passage, which also resonates of difference from English / European attitudes toward freedom rightly accorded to girls. It glosses fictional heroines of Henry James (1843–1916) in *Daisy Miller* (1879) and *The Portrait of a Lady* (1881) and is cogent for today's debates about gender.

Illustrations, which distinguish and differentiate editions of Lamb's *Tales*, in Ginn's schoolbook are old-fashioned, eighteen full-pages made from "the beautiful outline plates in the Valpy Shakespeare, which are based on the famous Boydell pictures" (vii). The explanation may be economic, or a long-lasting appreciation for eighteenth-century images from the Boydell Gallery; identifying plates on the title page indicates they were thought an asset. The effect is quite different from the original engravings that are rich, subtle, and clearly adult. Line drawings gave easier access and a challenge to draw—to imitate or copy—an exercise that enriches the study of literature. A great advantage of the Boydell pictures, previously discussed for a Victorian edition in Chapter 2, is their relation to performance. There is more vigorous action and storytelling than in several Edwardian illustrators who favored character and relied on color. Shakespeare's plays abound in situations of parent-child conflict and resolution, obvious choices, as we have seen, for children's books.

Two illustrations, printed to precede the two plays as frontispieces, immediately engage. George Romney's "Prospero and Miranda Witness the Storm" (2) depicts the violence of the opening scene (I.i) with surging waves and howling winds that toss a small vessel, crammed with frightened sailors, as a staid Prospero and apprehensive Miranda observe the working of his magic. This excitement is reiterated at the center of the book. "Lear, Kent, and the Fool Find Shelter in the Hovel" (161), by the American painter Benjamin West (1738–1820), is a brilliant depiction of the ferocity of nature against vulnerable men. The magic of fairies, both mischievous and grotesque, is embodied in "Puck" (18), who also disturbs nature. Henry Fuseli pictured Puck in flight at the center of a wind that has made a horse shy and plunge its rider toward the water. Relationships of parent and child combine with those of lovers at the shepherd's dwelling in *The Winter's Tale* (43) and "The Marriage of Claudio and Hero" in *Much Ado About Nothing* (67); both reassuringly depict moments before denunciation takes place. In contrast, Angelika Kauffmann's "Valentine, Proteus, Silvia, and Julia" in *Two Gentlemen of Verona* (107) shows exposed disguises and deceits in the forest. William Hamilton's "The Duke Learns of Viola's Marriage to Olivia" (249) is another moment of short-lived anxiety and distress before the happy ending when all are neatly paired and wed. "The Marriage of Rosalind and Orlando in the Forest of Arden" (89) is Hamilton's bright and happy celebration — with three dogs in the right foreground! Parallel is an opulent interior, William Miller's "Romeo at the Feast of the Capulets" (275), with its bevy of dancing maidens in the background. Like "Othello's Departure for Cyprus" (323) by Thomas Stothard, this is an evasion of tragedy and another staging of handsome court figures elaborately costumed.

Nevertheless, several illustrations pose issues of failure and distress. Richard Westall's "Hamlet Again Sees the Ghost of His father" (311) perhaps most obviously signals difficult child-parent relationships. The encounter on the ramparts, with the added attraction of a castle and soldiers, is frequently depicted in children's Shakespeare; however, here the scene is Gertrude's chamber, where mother, son, and father's ghost come together. Old Hamlet is a warrior whose ghostly quality is not obvious; he differs only by being set against a darker background of thin lines, while a seated Gertrude and standing Hamlet are framed against white. As Hamlet reaches toward his father, Gertrude's gaze is fixed on her son who sees ghosts. "Shylock and His Daughter" (121), Robert Smirke's depiction of the father's uneasy departure for dinner in *The Merchant of Venice,* illustrates incipient betrayal. Perhaps the most daunting image is "Petruchio, Katharine, Baptista, Guests, and Servants" (203) from *The Taming of the Shrew*; the aggressive suitor holds his intended bride with one hand and cracks his whip in the other. Francis Wheatley's icon of public humiliation is a sobering expression of earlier attitudes toward gender, much at odds with Ginn's assertions about the achievement of girls in American schools. However, they might have been reassured by "The Countess and Helena" (187), who sit demurely in conversation, an honest exchange of feelings in *All's Well That Ends Well*, albeit a time of quiet domestic decorum rather than excitement.

Three other illustrations tell of isolation: "Timon departs from Athens" (265); "Lady Macbeth" (170) stands resolutely clutching her husband's letter in Westall's dramatic pose, the Boydell image most often repeated for children. Westall's "Imogen before the Cave," from *Cymbeline* (135), in contrast, conveys exciting adventure in the wilderness. Reassurance is the message in what is unquestionably the most exotic illustration, "The Abbess Makes Herself Known" in *The Comedy of Errors* (233). While Othello was marked as other by his dark skin and armor, John Francis Rigaud makes figures at Ephesus intriguing examples of Orientalism — men's turbans and cinched robes for an effect of pantaloons, a wide flat umbrella — that contrast with a Christian nun's habit. The moment is one of justice — half-naked and bound Egeus embodies the threat of execution — and a time when members of a family presumed dead are reunited and reconciled because the mother, after long years of piety and service in a religious community, sets right the errors that stemmed from initial loss. Only the tale of *Pericles* — where reunion and reconciliation come after years of separation and multiple hardships— lacks an illustration; there is none in the Boydell Gallery. Use of outline plates from the Valpy edition gave Ginn's edition rich variety, occasion for amusement, and an alternative way to understand. Its cover was gray cloth, but attractively stamped in red and black, with a decorative frame around the title and a picture from *As You Like It*: Celia and Rosalind in the forest with Touchstone, the delightful jester with cap and bells and wand, who stands before them offering encouragement. School children would not have been disappointed.[9] They could also deepen their knowledge of Shakespeare through a variety of surveys of English literature.

Schoolbooks of English Literature

C. Linklater Thomson

C(lara) Linklater Thomson was a prolific and passionate advocate of English literature and history for Edwardian children. She contributed many retellings— *The Adventures of Beowulf* (1899), *King Arthur of Britain* (1902), selections from *Morte Darthur*, *Tales from Chaucer* (1903), an edited *Pilgrim's Progress* (1913), and an anthology *Carmina Britanniæ* (1901). Her classroom experience resulted in thoughtful analyses of pedagogy, implemented as a major editor of schoolbooks and series published by Horace Marshall and Son. *A First Book of English Literature, Part III From Lyndsay to Bacon* (1906) features Shakespeare, albeit his name is not in the title. In part, this reflects Thomson's dedication to understanding the development of English literature and history. Her preface acknowledges "a commendable and justifiable reaction against teaching the history of English literature in schools."[10] However, the fault lies not in the subject but in pedagogy — "mere lists of names and dates, with a few borrowed lines of criticism":

> [A]s an examiner, and a teacher of English literature, I have felt the want of some book which shall provide a simple chronological framework into which later details may be fitted. I have found that pupils whose work in English has been confined to the study of two or three books are deficient in grasping their significance in the development of our literature, and in relation to the political history of the country. And as a teacher of English history, I have felt the need of some cheap and easily portable book which contains sufficiently long and interesting extracts from contemporary literature to illustrate the thought and social movements of the period studied [I, v].

Thomson aimed to meet "both wants" through a combination of literature and history, the only way to understanding. She treated only "great authors of each age"; for the sixteenth century, Shakespeare is central: forty pages in Chapter IX. Thomson followed Sidney Lee's *Life of Shakespeare* for the biography, included details about the theatre and the De Witt drawing (211), gave sources and a paragraph summary of each play, and accepted a chronology for Shakespeare's works that showed "the growing seriousness with which he closed advancing years, for the deepest problems of life were the subjects of his maturity" (219).

Choice of material and critical evaluations indicate what was deemed appropriate, while an interlace of literature and history explains some emphases. Local allusions led Thomson to stress the Induction in *The Taming of the Shrew* and say nothing about the play itself, while *A Midsummer Night's Dream* is notable for Theseus, the first sketch of kingly ideals afterwards perfected in *Henry V* (229). Thomson recognized Shakespeare's dependence upon Plutarch for *Julius Caesar*, but praised Antony's wonderful speeches in Act III, which were entirely Shakespeare's invention (233). Similarly, *Coriolanus* is close to Plutarch, but Shakespeare developed "the central motive of the play — the struggle between the domineering pride of the aristocrat and the ignorant self-confidence of the multitude" (238). In contrast, the "greatest merit" of *Antony and Cleopatra,* although "full of many magnificent passages," is "wonderful characterization. Thus, Shakespeare's conception of Cleopatra has so impressed men's minds that the historic Queen of Egypt is to most people Shakespeare's Cleopatra, and nothing more or less" (239). Thomson discussed his English history plays in the companion series *A First History of England* (1901–1909), also in seven parts, where she observed that history had become the history found in Shakespeare's plays. Comment about *Macbeth* reflected commitment to the value of plays as social commentary: "with his usual wonderful insight, Shakespeare reproduced the Celtic atmosphere, bringing into prominence that belief in the existence of supernatural things which is so characteristic of Highland temperament" (235–236). But other points interest students.

A leitmotif about gender runs through Thomson's brief epitomes of plays:

> Beatrice is one of the most fascinating of Shakespeare's heroines; strong, high-spirited and independent, she melts into the most womanly tenderness for her cousin's sorrow, and defends her with unflinching courage and loyalty....
>   Rosalind is in some respects like Beatrice; she is at the same time brave and womanly, and willingly puts on the clothing of a boy, acknowledging it to be her duty to comfort the weaker vessel....
>   Isabella is one of the noblest and purest creations....
>   Imogen and Hermione are the very flower of suffering and faithful womanhood, while Perdita and Miranda show that the poet's sympathy and comprehension of youth were as fresh and keen as ever [231–232, 235, 240].

In short, there was no falling off in Shakespeare's creation, one quality of which was to honor noble women.

As repeatedly recognized, retellings of tragedies are less favored for children; however, Thomson neatly urged their merits. *Hamlet,* "which has been the most discussed of all the author's works, depends for its interest on the inward struggle between Hamlet's conviction that he ought to punish his uncle for killing his father and his reluctance to take any decided action" (234). *Othello* is deemed one of the finest tragedies—"so heart-breaking in its pathos, so skilful in its characterization, so rich in mingled poetry and wisdom" (235)—in spite of its villain Iago, who is comparable only to Angelo in *Measure for Measure*. King Lear is viewed as an example of severest distress:

> Shakespeare, in his present gloomy mood, seems to have been intent on showing that the fortunate conclusions which we love in fiction are untrue to the facts of life.... Shakespeare sounded the deepest note of tragedy in this terrible and beautiful play, where human passions struggle and jostle together like the stormy winds about the head of the aged king. But the piece is not all gloom for it is relieved by the strong and gracious character of Cordelia, unequalled even among Shakespeare's women, and by the tender loyalty of Kent to Lear and of Edgar to Gloucester [236–237].

To find idealism even in the midst of bleakness is salient, especially for children. Thomson signaled her late Victorian / Edwardian sensibility in the Romantic imagery of storm and her confidence in ideal woman, attributed to Shakespeare but interpreted in the kindest and most inspiring way. High sentiment characterizes the sixteenth-century writer who has been honored through the centuries and stands as England's greatest. Fittingly, Thomson concluded by quoting Dryden's paean.

Two additional features were aids to students, visual and verbal illustrations. The Chandos portrait accompanies the opening biography (205), while a photo of the church at Stratford-upon-Avon, a tangible reminder, comes at the end (241). Following the discussion are illustrations from the plays, quotations divided into five parts: before 1594, 1594–1599, 1599–1604, 1604–1609, 1610–1611. Passages vary in length, some as long as four pages: *Macbeth,* II.ii, the murder of Duncan; *The Tempest,* I.ii, the meeting of Ferdinand and Miranda.

Included are traditional fairy lore (*Romeo and Juliet,* I.iv, Queen Mab; and *A Midsummer Night's Dream,* II.i, dialogue with Puck); Greenwood (*As You Like It,* II.i, the outlawed Duke in the Forest of Arden); a parent-child scene—*Henry IV, Part I,* II.iv, Hal and Falstaff pretending to be king and prince; three sonnets—(73, 102, 106). The pedagogical apparatus provides sophisticated questions and responses.

Among Thomson's many publications *Our Inheritance* (1910) is her most accomplished statement about Edwardian racial / national sentiments and the interconnection of history and literature.[11] This small pamphlet is in part a mini-literary history, but its emphasis upon education makes it a suitable gloss in a discussion of schoolbooks. Thirty-nine pages in paper covers, published by Cambridge University Press and sold for sixpence, offer a succinct review of English master writers. The frontispiece, Arthur Rackham's *Titania and Bottom,* marks Shakespeare's honored place, the play preferred for children, and a brilliant illustrator. Thomson's survey of English heritage emphasizes the Middle Ages: Chaucer, the English language, and the role of Caxton in printing (*The Canterbury Tales,* Malory, and Aesop). After special attention to Sir Walter Scott and Tennyson among many nineteenth-century writers, *Our Inheritance* ends in 1889, the death of Robert Browning. Most major writers (Milton, Bunyan, Swift, Defoe, Pope, Burns) from the intervening centuries have a place.

At the center of *Our Inheritance* is Shakespeare, consistently the exemplar of the interlace of literature and history; the pamphlet includes a photograph of a room in Shakespeare's house in Stratford (21). Thomson identified *A Midsummer Night's Dream* as his most poetical early play, while among later plays *King Lear,* a story derived from Layamon's *Brut,* is one of the most beautiful and terrible. Many schoolbooks reflect this judgment, but Thomson made another entirely distinctive proposal for selecting plays. Her expectations for Edwardian children included knowledge of both Shakespeare and history:

> assume already read something: In beginning to read him it is best to take first one of the historical plays because we know the plot already, and it is therefore easier to follow. And it is wonderful how much more living and real such people as Richard II and John of Gaunt and Hotspur and Henry V seem when we meet them in Shakespeare's plays than when we read about them in our history text book [23–24].

The premise of national identity and love of "our inheritance" that undergird this recommendation ceased at the end of the twentieth century to be automatically a part of educational policy. However, recent actions in the United Kingdom suggest a growing awareness that this change was misguided. Thousands of reprints of H.E. Marshall's *Our Island Story* (1905)—*An Island Story* (1906) in the United States—were given to schools, and the Price of Wales has joined with Cambridge University to establish the Prince's Cambridge Programme for Teaching to "reinspire" the values defined by C.L. Thomson in *Our*

Inheritance.[12] These efforts can be seen as a positive response to her peroration: "We have tried in a little space to tell you of some of its glories. The inheritance is yours. Will you not enter in and possess it?" (39). Edwardian publishers, through many schoolbooks, made every effort to fulfill educational guidelines and assure Shakespeare's crucial place.

Thomas Nelson Readers

The publisher Thomas Nelson had a strong Evangelical commitment, expressed in the issue of many books with religious content — descriptions of the Holy Land, hymns, a Living Purpose Series with biographies of admirable persons and lessons to be learned from "earnest" and "noble" lives. Nelson's other great commitment was to children's literature that ranged from Reward or Prize books — the already discussed handsome Victorian Classic Stories Simply Told Series and extravagant Edwardian Gateway Series — to schoolbooks, *The Royal Treasury of Story and Song* (1907–1909) and *The Royal School Series Highroads of Literature* (1913–1915). *The Royal Treasury of Story and Song* is an attractive series, not least because of the variety and quality of illustrations; but it does not feature a cumulative knowledge of Shakespeare through several books over years, as does *Highroads of Literature*. That often reissued series is my archetype.

Although the second book of *Highroads of Literature, Bards and Minstrels* contains mostly medieval stories, it introduces Shakespeare. The lesson on Layamon identifies King Lear as part of the *Brut*, but explains that "the great writer Shakespeare made a noble play out of this story, and I shall tell it to you as he wrote it."[13] A full-page color illustration of the first scene, "I love your majesty / According to my bond; nor more or less" (143), by W(illiam) H(enry) Margetson (1861–1940) makes the play's issues clear. Cordelia's truth and Kent's loyalty contrast with the sisters' meanness. Albeit Lear is foolish and angry, the question is, "Do you not pity the poor old man even though he had brought all this unkindness upon himself?" (150). Moreover, this retelling ends with the reunion of Lear and Cordelia: "So here we will leave this poor old king, happy once more in his faithful Cordelia. As for the cruel daughters, they and their husbands came to a sad end, as they deserved to do" (154). This is the medieval historical account, but desire for a happy ending is also cogent. Furthermore, it reiterates family accord, signaled in Rosa C. Petherick's "She asked his blessing" (152), a black and white picture in which Cordelia kneels beside a wild-eyed Lear, who sits on a bed in a dungeon room.[14]

The third book, *The Morning Star*, as its title indicates, is primarily a celebration of Geoffrey Chaucer, with other writers from the Middle Ages and Caxton's role as England's first printer.[15] The sixteenth century, less than half of the volume, features Spenser's *The Faerie Queene*, a logical continuation of medieval romance and King Arthur's story; similarly, Sir Philip Sidney, who embodied the chivalric ideal, is singled out, as is Sir Walter Raleigh. Shakespeare is only anticipated; lessons 38 and 39 are *The Jew of Venice* with a note, "the story told in the following old ballad forms the plot of Shakespeare's play, *The Merchant of Venice*" (140). Four small, marginal, black and white drawings show characters in nicely detailed costumes. Two exercises are to "copy the figure of Gernutus," depicted in two different drawings (141 and 145); the first explains that Shakespeare named this character Shylock (188). The ballad gave pupils early familiarity with the simple story before they encountered Shakespeare's complexity. Another point is that famous writers derive their plots from old stories; recognition of tradition is one objective in the series.

Already well introduced through sources of two plays in the second and third books, Shakespeare becomes the major figure—nineteen of fifty-seven lessons—in fourth book, *Captains and Kings*, as the frontispiece announces.[16] *The First Performance of 'The Merry Wives of Windsor,' 1599*, by Edgar Bundy (1862–1922), is an occasion of bustling activity, a colorful picture of Elizabethans inside their theatre. Lesson 8, "The Theatre in Shakespeare's Day,"

Thomas Nelson, a distinguished publisher of children's books, characteristically combined great paintings with stories from literature. The frontispiece of *Captains and Kings, Book IV* in *Highroads of Literature* (1913–1915), which features Shakespeare, is Edgar Bundy's *The First Performance of "The Merry Wives of Windsor."* The painting vibrantly represents the Elizabethan theatre where members of the audience sat in galleries, stood as groundlings, and a few had a place on the stage. While most of the latter (the large figures in the foreground) watch the actors, one looks toward the viewer—an indication that some came to be seen as much as to see. A careful pupil could identify just behind the pillar the head of Shakespeare, who looks as he does in famous portraits and faces the viewer.

includes a contemporary drawing (34). Bundy's figures are both fashionable rich and poorer groundlings. In the gallery, an alert child could discover Shakespeare, with features like "the Shakespeare Bust," also shown in color (14). Both are a far cry from *Shakespeare at the Age of Twelve*, an "imaginary portrait" (11) by James Sant (1820–1916) to accompany full biographical material, including a lesson on Shakespeare's school. *Shakespeare before Sir Thomas Lucy*, a painting by Thomas Brooks (1818–1891), depicts the young man brought to answer for poaching (23). Details of hunting are fascinating: a slain deer dragged into the hall to the dismay of a small dog, a large hunting dog that sniffs the crossbow of the gamekeeper, who points an accusing finger at the central figure. Lady Lucy and two daughters watch from the doorway. These pictures, and episodes, exemplify the juxtaposition of legend and fact in "Biography," the first lessons.

The first quotations are songs, interspersed in three lessons of biography. All are brief, and the subject is nature ("Winter" from *Love's Labour's Lost* and "Morning Song" from *Cymbeline*, 16–17, followed by "Over hill, over dale," sung by Puck and the fairies in *A Midsummer Night's Dream*, 24–25). Since nursery poems and stories favor nature, all reinforce earlier knowledge. Variety and special amusement come with Sir John Davies's lyric "To the Month of September," an acrostic for ELISABETHA REGINA (39). Finally, Ariel's three songs from *The Tempest* ("Come unto these yellow sands," "Full fathom five thy father lies," "Where the bee sucks, there suck I," 47–48) are preceded by a brief note identifying Prospero as a magician, and perhaps Shakespeare's retirement. Daniel Maclise's *Miss Priscilla Horton as* Ariel is frontispiece to this lesson (46). She is obviously an adult performer in costume, a winged fairy with bare arms and legs in a picturesque sylvan scene. While songs are a gentle introduction, Shakespeare is not always accessible: "Shakespeare did not write for young boys and girls, but for grown men and women. For this reason you cannot understand and appreciate his works. Nevertheless, before we pass on, I think you would like to read two of the stories which are told in his plays" (49).

Hamlet and *As You Like It* each make three lessons. Both begin "Once upon a time"—to signal fairy story—and urge, "Listen" (49) and "you shall now hear" (64)—the promise of storytelling. These formulae reassure but are not the only resource for understanding. Students already know that "a tragedy is a grave and sad play." Chaucer's definition is applied to Shakespeare's "greatest tragedy, ... the story of how Hamlet, Prince of Denmark, fell out of high degree into misery and ended wretchedly" (49). Hamlet, who pretends madness and is unkind to Ophelia, is "a man of weak resolution" (55) and dies at the end of "the miserable story" (62). Two color illustrations are inspiring works by great Victorian artists. Irish painter Daniel Maclise's *The Play Scene in "Hamlet"* dramatically depicts players in an inner stage above a large audience (42). Ophelia's white dress is a central light in a dark scene, as are the bright faces of several women spectators on either side. A dark and pensive Hamlet stands beside Ophelia. Opposite, Gertrude watches the play, but Claudius turns away in distress and holds his forehead. Maclise's historical painting is less well known than Sir John Millais's *Ophelia* (59). Painted 1851–1852, this memorable oil is preeminent among Pre-Raphaelite paintings.[17] It combines beautiful and painstaking botanical observations (many plants with symbolic meanings) and several birds with a poignant, beautiful young woman who raises her hands and sings as she floats on the water; her long and heavy dress foretells her drowning in the river. Since Victorians favored scenes from Shakespeare for their celebration of literature and painting (then considered the lesser art), Nelson had rich resources to draw upon for their trademark "children's books illustrated by great paintings." *John Kemble as Hamlet*, by Sir Thomas Lawrence (1769–1830), reinforces the idea of performance (52).

In spite of such enrichment, this schoolbook recognizes a somber response and reassuringly promises a cheerful alternative:

> You have now read the plot of *Hamlet*, and I am sure that you have found it very sad and gloomy. Let us turn for relief to one of the bright and merry plays which Shakespeare wrote. In all he composed more than a dozen comedies, which still afford playgoers amusement. These comedies are full of jokes, shrewd sayings, sweet songs, laughable muddles, and queer mistakes. One of the most delightful of them is called *As You Like It*. The story of this play you shall now hear [64].

As You Like It begins with banished Duke Frederick, who "withdrew to the Forest of Arden, where he lived in the greenwood like the famous Robin Hood of old English story" (64). Reference to a story already known is always reassuring; the third book, *The Morning Star*, includes the ballad of "Robin Hood and Allen-a-Dale," pictures of Sherwood Forest, and drawings of the outlaw. The story then turns to the Duke's daughter Rosalind, shown standing with Celia as she offers a chain to the kneeling Orlando, "Gentleman, wear this for me" (66). Another reused image, Dugdale's illustration is black and white here, but color in Nelson's *The Gateway to Shakespeare*. In Millais's painting *Aliena and Ganymede*, also in black and white (72), they rest under a tree, with Touchstone—even though this retelling has no clown, and the shepherd who shows them the cottage is the only rustic. Changing fortunes of court figures, reconciliation, and happy marriages are main subjects: "and so this pretty story ends with wedding bells, wrongs righted, misdeeds forgiven, sins atoned for, and truth and loyalty rewarded. I am sure that the end of the story is just *As You Like It* (80–81). Two more songs—"Under the greenwood tree" and "Blow, blow, thou winter wind"—are about nature but more explicitly tied to human attitudes. Many exercises develop vocabulary and writing of sentences, while others ask for character analysis. The last exercise quotes eight lines of Ben Jonson's eulogy to be copied and memorized (254), an assured continuity of praise for England's great poet / playwright.

Shakespeare continues to be the principal writer in the fifth book, *Books of All Time,* a kind of mini-survey of great English writers. An opening lesson explains that the title comes from John Ruskin's distinctions between good and bad books, for the hour and for all time; "books for all time" are ones in which "the author feels that he has a true and useful message to deliver to mankind, and he strives to set it forth with all the clearness, sincerity, and beauty of which he is capable."[18] While earlier books emphasized medieval literature, this one stresses modern writers. Shakespeare is first, and Tennyson—whose Arthurian poems are something of a recapitulation of earlier stories—is last. Extracts, a proper length for lessons, are from works by authors whose life stories were told in the fourth book, *Captains and Kings.* Thirteen sections, from a total of fifty-three, are Shakespeare. The stories of *The Tempest* and *The Merchant of Venice* are by Lamb, but with added quotations interlaced, and four full-page illustrations. A.C. Michael's *Prospero* is compelling (11); a powerful man, with long white beard and hair, dressed in a purple robe, stands on the seashore with arms extended and wand raised amidst gray clouds and swirling seas. Behind him crouches Caliban, a hairy monster with webbed hands, a grotesque head with spiky horns, and coarse features. Above Prospero's arm, in the center is beautiful Ariel, a female figure with long flowing hair and dress. Michael used muted colors for both. The second color page unites history and literature: "A Warship of Shakespeare's Time," the *Ark Royal,* copied from hangings in the House of Lords (14). Symbolic figures of winds and sun, furled sails, flowing flags and pennants, and an heraldic crest are among fine details. The first quotation, "Ferdinand meets Miranda" (25–32), is accompanied by a black and white copy of Millais's *Ferdinand Lured by Ariel* (1849–1850), an image of magic, not least the music that the young man hears. More conventional is P. Dudd's *Miranda and Ferdinand,* used in Mrs. Lang's *Gateway to Shakespeare,* a Nelson Reward. Its woodland setting and lovers (23) are explained in a quotation, "The Log Bearers" (41–45). Exercises are tied to previous books (vocabulary, paraphrase, comprehension, etc.) but here go farther; one, "Compare the story of *The Tempest* with that of *As You Like It*" (299), revises work of the previous year.

Three lessons—two for the last fight of the *Revenge,* one for *The Faerie Queene*—separate Shakespeare lessons. Sir Walter Raleigh and Edmund Spenser, both introduced in Book III, are identified as "bosom-friends" (55). Opening stanzas, "The Red Cross Knight and Una Set Out," amplify Book III's prose retelling of *The Faerie Queene.* Similarly, Book III contained an old ballad, *The Jew of Venice,* a "bald story" that Shakespeare "developed, ... clothed its somewhat lifeless characters with flesh and blood, and made them living, breathing creatures, more real to us than many of our friends" (60).

Four lessons are Lamb's *Tales;* two others quote scenes from *As You Like It,* including choosing the caskets, omitted by Lamb. Probably because of its comic quality—for Edwardians not mitigated by anxiety about racial stereotyping—the effort of the Prince of Morocco is quoted (75–78), while Bassanio's

A.C. Michael's Prospero stands with arms outstretched in the opening moments of *The Tempest.* At his feet cowers the monster Caliban, while Ariel's head is just visible above Prospero's arm that holds his magic wand. The fury of the storm and promise of strange creatures encourage pupils to read Lamb's story in *Books of All Time, Book V* of Nelson's *Highroads of Literature.*

trial makes a splendid color illustration, F. Barth's *Choosing the Caskets* (70), a sumptuous recreation of Renaissance Venetian beauty and color. A dominant blonde Portia, dressed in white, stands closest to the viewer. Behind her are several seated observers, all luxuriously dressed. Portia's hand on her cheek signals her anxiety as handsome Bassanio rests his hand on a white cloth that covers the table where three caskets await his choice. Abel Truchet's *The Doges' Palace*—a landscape painting of the pink and white building, is foregrounded by tall pillars and gondolas on shimmering water that reflects both land and sky; two tall sails make a vertical center, while a white foot bridge on the right leads to further buildings (67)—establishes the reality of Shakespeare's setting. Two illustrations reinforce the trial (94–100), quoted until Antonio declares his readiness to submit. Sir James D. Linton's *The Trial Scene* reinforces the splendor of Venice (80). The Doge, in white and gold, presides from a raised dais; Portia, in black, stands at the center before a desk with elaborate covering. Lawyers and courtiers fill the chamber. On the left Shylock stands with a knife in one hand and a scale in the other; at the far right is a stool with rejected bags of money. Shylock looks down, as Portia gestures with her right arm. Like Barth's work, this is popular Victorian historical painting. A photograph of "Miss Ellen Terry as Portia" records a famous performance (84). In another painting, M. Gottlieb's *Shylock and Jessica, His Daughter,* the Jew gently embraces his child, who looks sadly thoughtful (88). Its final position is a subtle reminder that mercy and compassion are due. One exercise is to "ask teacher to let you discuss the question: 'Was justice done to Shylock?'"; another is "Write out and learn Portia's beautiful speech on Mercy" (304). Thus more discriminating analysis is encouraged, along with practical exercises to build vocabulary, write longer sentences, and increase reading comprehension.

Although Book VI, *Thoughts and Voices,* does not feature Shakespeare, he is still present, with three lessons, spaced at intervals to indicate that his words and characters pervade English literature.[19] Expectations are much more advanced; reading assignments are extracts rather than retellings. No play's story is retold; students, now deemed ready for the original text, are expected to interpret great speeches. Lesson 7, "Gems from Shakespeare," has three sections and emphasizes nation. Short passages from history plays (*Henry V,* I.ii; *Richard II,* II.i; *King John,* V.vii) affirm English patriotism, epitomized in two lines from a chorus of *Henry V*: "O England, model to thy inward greatness, / Like little body with a mighty heart!" (11). A longer speech, "All's the world's a stage" (*As You Like It,* II.vii) is represented in W. Mulready's *The Seven Ages of Man.* Even in black and white, its complex details engage (54); an exercise is to explain how it illustrates the quotation (333). Lesson 30 is an extract from Marc Antony's "Speech over the Body of Caesar," the object of which was "to inflame the populace against Caesar's murderers" (213–219). J.D. Court's painting is a historical representation of orator, corpse, and crowd (214). Much more thrilling in color is *The Ides of March* (216), an example of the classical style of

Sir Edwin Poynter (1836–1919) but with melodramatic effects. This evocative night scene shows portents in the sky, a bust of Caesar lighted eerily from below, and two men in togas walking out from a grand Roman building. Exercises include the usual vocabulary and sentence writing, more advanced identifying of meters—and to describe each picture.

Nelson's *Highroads of Literature* series are schoolbooks, but an imaginative choice of materials, particularly great paintings, photographs, and drawings, make the series appealing and pedagogically strong. The study of art and literature together is mutually reinforcing, although support for classes in art history is less consistent than for language and literature. *Highroads of Literature* books were recognized as attractive objects; inscriptions in the end papers indicate they were rewards and presents. In my copies of the 1915 edition, Book II is inscribed, "Chrystal Hindley from Dad," while the third book was "Presented to Amy Lowe for neatness in work and good conduct during school year 1920–21." Other publishers, vying for adoption, prepared competing series, different executions to fulfill educational standards.

Edward Arnold Readers

Edward Arnold published three distinctive series. *Arnold's Literary Reading Books* (1902–1909) concentrates on English literature, with an added seventh book relating literature and history. *Steps to Literature* (1905), with six books, combines British and world interests. *The Sesame Readers* (1908), six volumes, offer a broad, general invitation to acquire wider knowledge; reading is the "Open Sesame" for all areas.

Because *Arnold's Literary Reading Books* is the nearest equivalent to *Highroads of Literature*, its six volumes (four for Junior Forms and two for Middle Forms) afford a basic comparison.[20] While books in *Highroads of Literature* increase steadily (176 pages for the second book, 192 for the third, 272 for the fourth, 319 for the fifth, and 351 for the sixth), *Arnold's Literary Reading Books* are consistent (224 pages for four books for junior forms and 256 for two books for middle forms). Both series include famous paintings. Arnold's advertisements for single volumes identify artist and title for illustrations but only names of writers. There is heavy but not exclusive reliance upon Lamb's *Tales*; the first book *In Golden Realms* (1902) combines Lamb's *The Tempest* with Sir Walter Scott's *Macbeth*, from his history of Scotland for children, *Tales of a Grandfather* (1827–1830). *The Greenwood Tree: A Book of Nature Myths and Verses* (1903) includes short quotations, each of two or three lines, to form "Trees and Flowers in Shakespeare." *Chips from a Bookshelf* (1908), edited by H.B. Browne, has Lamb's *A Midsummer Night's Dream*, with a fine illustration by Sir Edwin Landseer (1802–1873). Titania and Bottom are very large figures, while in the right corner with his back to the viewer is Puck, a tiny nude dwarfed by two large rabbits. *Rambles in Bookland* (1909), edited by C.E. Byles, includes Lamb's *As*

You Like It. Pupils encounter Shakespeare's language and a history play through a long quotation, the death of Hotspur from *Henry IV, Part I* (V.iv), supported by Frances Rigaud's print "The Death of Hotspur" (91). Increased complexity continues in the first volume for Middle Forms, *In the World of Books* (1902); Lear's story is quoted from Geoffrey of Monmouth's *History of the British Kings* (23–30).[21] Passages from Shakespeare are the death of Duncan from *Macbeth* (70–72) and "Under the Greenwood Tree" from *As You Like It* (64–69). Returning to a play previously introduced is a review and way to gain deeper understanding.

The first four *Arnold's Literary Reading Books* were priced at 1s.3d., and the last two at 1s.6d. Two positive reviews, quoted in an advertisement for *In the World of Books*, evaluate the schoolbook, indicate expectations for the study of literature, and sympathize with some of the problems faced by teachers:

> Infinitely varied in subject and style, containing nothing commonplace or mean, they not only give a very fair conspectus of the field of English literature, but provide plenty of opportunities to the teacher to dwell on those matters of knowledge which the reading lesson ought to suggest [*The Guardian*, n.p.].

> The selections are particularly well chosen, and enough is given to stimulate the child's appetite for more. The passages, too, are sufficiently unhackneyed for the most part not to bore the teacher in advance — a by no means unimportant factor in teaching [*The Saturday Review*, n.p.].

Arnold's seventh volume gives Shakespeare a curiously small part. *The Storied Past: A Book of Selections from English Literature Illustrative of English History* (1911) has 248 pages and an explicit theme of nationalism. King John usually has a place in children's histories because of the Magna Carta and the development of English liberty. Alternatively, he is attractive to Protestants as an English king early opposed to a Catholic Pope. However, Shakespeare's *King John* is closest to children's feelings in the scene between Prince Arthur and Hubert (IV.i). Its extraordinary poignancy comes from threatened innocence and conflicting loyalties felt by a royal subject commanded by John to destroy his nephew, a measure to solidify his claim to the throne. Sympathy and understanding are significantly enhanced by Yeames's favored painting *Hubert and Arthur*. The Prince — an archetypal angelic English boy, fair-haired, sweet-faced, and dressed in white — has put his arms around the retainer he believes to be a friend. A scowling Hubert, who has come to blind Arthur, grips the table behind him and holds his right hand between his knees as he struggles to resist the boy's affection. Hubert is dressed in black, his head covered with a dark hood. The interior, bare but for the table and a bench where they sit, contrasts dark and light with an opening and a heavy stone wall. Ominously, a length of coiled rope fills the lower right of the picture, ready to bind the boy who is to be blinded. Victorians loved this kind of historical painting, not least because of its sentimental view of children.

Given the broad scope of *Steps to Literature* it is perhaps to be expected that Shakespeare play a lesser role.[22] He is not in the first two books, *Tales of the Homeland* and *Tales of Many Lands,* both rather simple and devoted to folk and fairy tales. However, Book III, *Stories from English and Welsh Literature,* includes *Cymbeline,* retold in four lessons (96–110). A combination of Wales and Britain and of different periods of history makes it a logical, if unusual, text; its thematic emphasis upon forgiveness, a virtue urged for children. is useful. An alternative Book IIIA, *Stories from the Literature of the British Isles,* has Shakespeare's *The Winter's Tale,* again a romance that expounds forgiveness and reconciliation (50–68). While much is made of the Festival over which Perdita presides, the longest quotation is the awakening of Hermione, the statue. A more unusual and light-hearted quotation is the pedlar's song (68–70). By definition Book IV, *Literary Readings relating to the Empire,* offers mostly non–British texts, while Book V, *Literary Readings relating to Europe,* has a heavy emphasis upon medieval chivalric stories. So does Book VI, *Glimpses of World Literature,* but it returns to Shakespeare, indeed to his first inclusion in the series. "Imogen in the Cave" (113–121) combines a précis of the story with several quotations (III.vi and IV.ii) somewhat cut. *Steps to Literature* is also "a graduated series," both in cost and size: Book I, 112 pages, price 10d.; II, 144 pages, price 1s.; III, 192 pages, price 1s.3d; Books IIIA, IV, V, 224 pages, and VI, 256 pages, all priced at 1s.6d.

The Sesame Readers, "graduated general reading books, are based on the idea that reading is an 'Open Sesame' to the treasures of literature and knowledge."[23] Shakespeare's role is smaller but cogent. The first four books contain elementary fairy and folk tales, rhymes, and a scheme to teach phonetics. *Characters and Scenes, Book IV* has a didactic purpose of giving examples rather than precepts "to awaken the enthusiasm of hero-worship" through various readings, "both tales of heroism and adventure from real life and passages from fiction and romance" (v). The featured story is *King Lear and His Three Daughters,* told by the old ballad and three illustrations: Cordelia banished (211), Lear's decline when he is with the evil sisters (213), and Lear and his Fool on the heath with Stonehenge in the background (217). All die, and the moral is "Thus have you seen the fall of pride, / And disobedient sin" (219). Juxtaposed to this somber didacticism, "The Poor Players" finishes on a positive note. The rehearsal scene from *A Midsummer Night's Dream* is quoted, and a half-page illustration shows the rustics paying attention as Peter Quince holds a script. While these do not conform to the book's heroic themes, chivalric romances, and nineteenth-century success stories, the mechanicals exemplify the common man and give respite from strenuous and exacting characters.

As the greatest writer in English, Shakespeare provides a transition to the final book, *Britain of To-day,* which aims to inspire young readers to assume their social and political responsibilities as inheritors and preservers of the great British Empire. The preface leaves no doubt about what this means: the British

Empire covers more than one-fifth of the land surface of the globe, approximately 11,437,000 miles, with a population of 400,000,000:

> Does it not fill you with wonder, and a sense of power and security, to think that you belong to such an immense body of people, all living under the same flag, governed by similar laws, speaking to a large extent the same language, and loyally acknowledging one King as their head? [7].

The question "How is it you live a free life?" returns to King John, shown signing the Magna Carta (9), iconic of interdependence and community. Finally, the role of children is directly expounded:

> An empire is not a thing that manages itself. It is not merely so many millions of square miles of land that in itself would not make an empire. It is the people who live in it who make the British Empire, and twenty years hence its continuance will depend on those who are at present boys and girls. The fate of the Empire is in the hands of its children! [11].

Many selections exemplify British accomplishment and character. *Rule, Britannia!* is an obvious choice; but there is also *The Fatherland* by American poet James Russell Lowell (1819–1891), minister to London from 1877 to 1885. Tennyson's *Locksley Hall* is cited as a vision for the future. Shakespeare contributes high moral sentiment in Portia's "quality of mercy" speech from *The Merchant of Venice*, a model of Christian behavior to express the visionary ideals advocated for Edwardian children.

Nationalism in *Britain of To-day* includes information about how boys and girls addressed in the preface should proceed; education is the ladder to success. A survey of "Our Schools and Colleges" explains in detail the structure of education in Britain, citing nineteenth-century acts of Parliament of 1870 and 1872 that required primary schools, and administration by School Boards. The "public schools"— Eton, Harrow, Winchester, Rugby — are exemplars of secondary education, with Henry Newbolt's "play up, play up the game" a commended exposition of how the country's battles are won on their playing fields. Extracts from several Victorian school stories are cited: *Tom Brown's School Days, Vanity Fair, Jane Eyre* and *Villette*. A brief survey of the founding of colleges and universities gives special attention to Oxford and Cambridge, with a description of degrees granted. Most crucial is an assertion that advanced study is "not out of reach of the poorest boy, if he is clever and works hard at school" (237). Samuel Smiles's popular *Self Help* (1859), still reprinted by Edwardians, provides "The True Gentleman" (240–248), the objective sought for sustaining the Empire. Mention of women's colleges, Lady Margaret Hall and Somerville at Oxford, and Girton and Newnham at Cambridge, indicates that clever girls might also continue their studies. Recognition of the place of English studies as preparation for the civil service, for examinations for colonial service, is made at an early age. Shakespeare is at the heart of the tradition; further knowledge of his plays came from history schoolbooks.

Shakespeare in History Books

George G. Harrap's Illustrated Story of England Series serves as a counterpart to their much larger and more diverse Told Through the Ages Series, discussed in Chapter 5; it is nicely printed, includes no exercises, and was not listed with schoolbooks. Estelle Ross wrote three volumes devoted to the Middle Ages, two for periods in Shakespeare's history plays.[24] All have pictures by Evelyn Paul (fl. 1906–1928), a prolific illustrator of some of Harrap's most sumptuous volumes, notably for the Middle Ages.

A key figure in *From Conquest to Charter (1066–1215)*, published in 1911, is King John. Ross described Shakespeare's often cited scene between Prince Arthur and Hubert de Burgh, here illustrated by Paul (271), and recounted the boy's murder. Her judgment was measured; she acknowledged uncertainty about Arthur's death but also recorded that the trial in France found John guilty. In *Barons and Kings (1215–1485)*, published in 1912, Ross's interlace of history and literature includes a quotation for the rebellion of "Glendower and Hotspur (1400–13)," part of the heaviness of the crown, from *King Henry IV, Part II*. She then rendered a highly laudatory account of Henry V, the great chivalric king renowned for piety as much as bravery. Quotation from *Henry VI* glosses the beginning of the War of the Roses, and a passage from *Richard III* dramatically portrays the tyrant's dreams before the battle of Bosworth to mark its end. For many, Shakespeare's history is the history of England.

The extent of that reliance is exemplified in Alice Cockran's *The Dawn of British History* (1912).[25] "Dramas from the Legends" refers to fairies in *A Midsummer Night's Dream*, but explains, "I will not tell you more about Shakespeare's play, because you will read it for yourselves, and it will give you a better idea than I can of how much the fairies entered into the thoughts of our ancestors" (52). This recognizes Shakespeare as a recorder of folk history and histories of kings. Cockran related a story of Rhuhudibras, who was perhaps the father of Lear, then linked *King Lear* to the popular Irish legend of *The Daughters of Lir*, often retold in Edwardian chivalric collections. Finally, *Cymbeline* recounts the most important link in Britain in the time of Augustus Caesar. Cockran concluded, "Thus we find Shakespeare's genius clothing with life and grace old legends that were told in ancient times by mothers to their little ones" (54).

Some did not quote relevant passages but cited Shakespeare's treatment of episodes. A.J. Church's *Stories from English History: From Richard II to Charles I* (1896) both corrects Shakespeare's errors in historical fact and approves his imaginative recreation of certain moments.[26] Thus in "Hotspur and Glendower," he explained that at Shrewsbury

> Hotspur was killed, not as Shakespeare describes, by the young Prince Henry, who was a lad of fifteen, but by a chance arrow, as he was leading his men. The Earl of Douglas was taken prisoner. Prince Henry was in the battle, and was wounded by an arrow in the forehead [17].

However, at "Bosworth Field" Church found "Shakespeare has described how Richard spent the night before the battle, seeming to see in his dreams the ghosts of those whom he had slain, King Henry, the two young Princes, and Buckingham, his last victim, among them" (87). Shakespeare's close reliance upon chronicles meant that sometimes Church's quotations from them sound like Shakespeare.

Sidney Dark's *The Book of England for Young People* (1923) affords an amusing contrast to Church, a Victorian Anglican priest.[27] Two factors are crucial: Dark was writing after World War I, which forever changed perceptions of nationalism, not least because the Old World had to rely on the New; and Dark wrote specifically for Americans. His address "To All the American Children Who Read This Book" begins:

> My Dears,
> There is nothing in the world that matters so much as that the American and English people, who speak the same language, read the same books, and generally think the same kind of thoughts, should understand each other and should be good friends. There are so many evil things in the world that ought to be destroyed and there are so many muddles that ought to be cleared up. And the evils will never be destroyed unless the Americans and the English join hands and work together. When you grow up to be men and women, you will be able to help America and England to be friends or you will be able to make the friendship difficult [v].

English history is both the beginning of American history and its future — even though immigrants come from other nations, this is not difference, since the English are themselves descendants of several different races. Most importantly, these two nations share traditions, of which literature is of greatest import: "The splendid thing is that the great English writers like Shakespeare and Milton and Bunyan and Dickens belong to you just as much as to us" (vi). Dark minimized potential negative reactions against British royalty; thus he

> tried to write much more about simple people. Only a very few kings have mattered much in the history of England and none of them has mattered so much as Shakespeare, the son of a Stratford-on-Avon butcher, and Bunyan, the Bedfordshire tinker [vii].

Writing about "Merrie England" of the Middle Ages, Dark explained that in 1413, "Henry V, generally called Harry of England, a brave, light-hearted soldier, became the English king. You can read about Harry of England in Shakespeare's plays 'Henry IV' and 'Henry V'" (86). Like Church, Dark carefully distinguished historical facts from Shakespeare's history:

> The Battle of Agincourt was fought on St. Crispin's day, and, if you will read Shakespeare's "Henry V," you will find that the English poet has written a splendid speech of the king in which he says that St. Crispin's day will never be forgotten in England. As a matter of fact, very little good came to the English from the Battle of Agincourt [87].

He ended his discussion of the battle of Bosworth Field by noting that Richard III "died fighting very bravely. You can read about this king in Shakespeare's play 'Richard III,' which I hope you will find time to read when you have finished this chapter" (96). Dark's history thus introduced a valuable recognition of difference between accounts of moments in history and encouraged further, more exacting reading. His peroration about Shakespeare came in a chapter about the sixteenth century, "To Shakespeare and Elizabeth," giving them equal billing; but Dark reiterated the superiority of writer to monarch. Many writers of plays, which were performed before both queen and people, enriched this age:

> The greatest of these writers of plays was William Shakespeare, the son of a butcher at Stratford-on-Avon, and the greatest poet who ever wrote in the English language. I have advised you to read two or three of Shakespeare's plays and I can promise you that you will find them thrilling and exciting. Nowadays we remember Elizabeth largely because she was the friend of Shakespeare. A great writer is greater than a great queen, and the Stratford-on-Avon's butcher's son has given immortality to the daughter of Henry VIII [116–117].

Ender's painting *Shakespeare Reading "Macbeth" to Queen Elizabeth* (112) is a quality engraving of the court, ladies and lords beautifully dressed. Shakespeare stands at the center and rests his manuscript on a table. He looks directly at the viewer — the actor facing his audience — while Elizabeth leans forward from her throne, her eyes fixed on the writer. Enders's title does not accord with modern scholars' dating *Macbeth* as the last of the four great tragedies (1606-1607), Shakespeare's choice of a Scottish subject in response to King James's accession in 1603 upon the death of Elizabeth I, who reigned from 1558 to 1603. Nevertheless, the painting exactly represents Dark's view of the relation between author and queen. The cover picture is the Edwardian favorite, Yeames's *Prince Arthur and Hubert*, although it never achieved the affection felt for his *And When Did You Last See Your Father?* (1878) — among Victorians, as a wax tableau at Madame Tussaud's in London, and winner of the vote in a television contest (2006) to be part of the People's Museum in Britain.

Schoolbooks of History

Although Arthur Quiller-Couch and Thomas Carter wrote books exclusively devoted to Shakespeare's history plays, discussed in Chapter 5, retellings are rare in most literary collections and schoolbooks. However, the plays are often mentioned in history schoolbooks. An early example, Charlotte M. Yonge's *Westminster Historical Reading Books* (1892), responded to recent requirements of the New Code of 1891. In *Part III: Twenty Stories and Biographies: From 1066 to 1485*, "Poetical Pieces" are part of the increasingly advanced instruction that makes more of biography than story, the elementary approach of the first two books.[28] Scenes from Shakespeare include the encounter between Arthur and Hubert from *King John* (91–94). Yonge relied on Shakespeare's more precise history to help explain the complex genealogy of the Wars of the Roses; she quoted a passage from *Henry VI, Part II* (II.ii.7–38, 43–55) in which Warwick and York review lineage, and the playwright helped his audience sort rival claims (190–192). Enthusiasm for the exemplary Henry V prompts defense against his misrepresentation as the young prince, best known in Shakespeare's plays, and heightened piety:

> He was never liked by his father, and all sorts of stories were told of the "madcap" prince, as he was called—of his wild amusements, bad companions, and even of his robbing the King's treasure-waggons—but it is most likely that none of these are true, since he was always a good and devout man. He was, however, lively and merry in his ways, and, as he was not allowed to be much at court, these stories grew up about him [169–170].

Two black and white illustrations—an engraving "King Henry V. Addressing His Troops at Agincourt, 1415" (171) and a line drawing "Battle of Agincourt" (173)—and an abridgment of Michael Drayton's celebratory "The Battle of Agincourt" (175–178) mark this defining moment of patriotism and nationalism. Yonge paraphrased the king's response to the victory:

> Henry gave thanks on the field of battle, and had the Psalm "Not us, O Lord, not unto us, but unto Thy name, be the praise," sung beneath his standard [174].

Yonge, a devout Anglican, described Henry's death as a model of piety: "he sent for the priest for his last Communion, and died while the Penitential Psalms were being read to him" (181). Not Shakespeare's tetralogy that recounts the Wars of the Roses, but Robert Southey's "The Royal Plantagenet Graves at Windsor" (216–217)—which opens with praise of the saintly Henry VI—sums up what followed. Thus Yonge, a prolific and successful writer of juvenile historical novels of the Middle Ages, selected from Shakespeare's history plays what she agreed with and refuted biographical details that she deemed false or uninspiring.

Like Yonge, Clara Linklater Thomson wrote both literature and history books and used Shakespeare to teach the Middle Ages. Her *A First History of England* (1901–1909) has seven parts.[29] The second division in *Part II* treats the House of Anjou. Richard I dominates as archetypal legendary crusader, but Thomson cited Shakespeare's *King John* as contrast. Shakespeare's view, which "provides an unrivaled literary documentation of the Middle Ages by a Tudor poet," prevails with the House of Lancaster in *Part III*. Included are scattered lines and long quotations: the king's description of Hereford in *Richard II* (I.iv), Worcester and Hotspur in *Henry IV, Part I* (I.iii), the battle of Agincourt in *Henry V* (IV.iii), the thoughtful Henry VI's soliloquy before the battle at

Towton in *Henry VI, Part III* (II.v), the murder of the princes in *Richard III* (IV.iii).

Thomson relied upon Shakespeare but advocated Henry V as the supreme chivalric hero: "No English king has ever been more beloved than Henry V. He was handsome in face, kindly and gracious in his bearing, a wonderfully skilled general, and intensely religious" (157). Clearly children's literature promotes adult patriotic and religious sentiment. *A First History of England* served a wide audience in a variety of schools, ranging from leading public schools, to grammar schools, to secondary schools—Eton, Harrow, Westminster, Cheltenham College, Burton-on-Trent Grammar School, Manchester High School for Girls, The Park School, Glasgow, Newcastle-upon-Tyne High School, Oxford High School, and Norwich High Schools. The volumes were priced at 1s.6d. for I, II, IV, V; 2s. for III; 2s.6d. for VI and VII. Alternatively two combined volumes—I, II, III, IV and V, VI, VII—sold for 6s. each.

Other writers did not always match Thomson's extraordinary commitment to the mutual enrichment of literature and history. Tom Bevan, also a writer of juvenile historical novels of the Middle Ages, recognized that Shakespeare took great license with history. His *Stories from British History (B.C. 54– A.D. 1485)*, published in 1910, offers greatest opportunity to cite history plays.[30] Moreover, Shakespeare is the occasion for instruction about the relationship between history and storytelling, in both old and present times. Bevan's chapter "Truth and Fable" begins with a lesson to distinguish fact and legend:

> Our great poet, Shakespeare, wrote many plays that deal with the history of England and the lives of her kings. Into these plays he put much good and true history; but he also put many fables and stories that the story-telling folk told to one another in the long winter evenings.
>
> The ballad-singers, too, sang of the old heroes and kings, and their songs often had but a small grain of truth in them. Thus it happens that men who write of the history of our land have great difficulty, at times, in sifting through the true from the false in the old books and papers that they study so carefully.
>
> Now Shakespeare wrote a very long play concerning the life and times of Henry IV; indeed it is so long that it is divided into two parts. You ought to read this play some day, and when you do, you will learn much [153–154].

Nevertheless, Bevan limited himself to Prince Hal / Henry V, paragon of chivalric virtue. He began with several rhetorical questions—"What would you think of a prince if someone told you that he spent much of his time in ale-houses and taverns, with such people as frequent those places?" (154)—as a way of telling something of Henry's youthful exploits, chronicled by "our great poet, Shakespeare," as the "wild life ... of a hot-headed, yet a sensible young fellow." However, Bevan concluded, after "a rather pretty story," that "none of these stories have much truth in them. Let us see what history really can tell us of prince Henry's youth" (157–158). Thus he disputed legendary stories. He related recorded military feats, yet his narrative account of Agincourt reads like one

For many, Shakespeare's history plays are English history, the truest evocation of the Middle Ages. Their stories are told in schoolbooks of history as well as of literature. The exemplary king is always Henry V, a courageous and pious man, the chivalric hero who led his men to the great victory of Agincourt. This iconic moment of charging horse, shining armor, and bold knights is from Tom Bevan's *Stories from British History, B.C. 54–1485 A.D.* (1903).

of his novels. Bevan concluded, "though he reigned but nine years, he won more glory as a soldier than any king of England since his day" (158). Paean, not Shakespearean ambiguity, is the point. *Stories from British History* is unusually well illustrated, and Henry V is nobly served. The color page is iconic chivalry, "Prince Henry Leading His Men to Battle" (155). Gloriously attired in shining armor and royal heraldry, Henry rides a fine charging horse as he lifts his standard to urge on the knights behind him. A black and white page is formal *Henry V* from the National Portrait Gallery (156), while the last half-page reproduces a painting *The English on the Field of Agincourt Before the Battle* (160). Here all traits of Henry V's character combine: fully armed, he sits on his white horse, head bowed, as a priest, who holds a crucifix, stands to lead prayer; behind the warrior and pious king are his mounted knights, while on either side kneel his men at arms, and in the distant background are massed knights with raised lances.

Shakespeare dominates several volumes of Nelson's *Highroads of Literature;* but his role in their parallel *Highroads of History* is limited and questioned. Book VII, *Highroads of British History,* a recapitulation for twelve- and thirteen-year-old students, mentions Shakespeare only incidentally but not infrequently.[31] While Chaucer appears only once, as "the first great English poet," Shakespeare, whose plays range across the whole of British history, becomes a recurrent theme. At the end of "Alfred the Truth-Teller," a last paragraph explains that King Duncan was defeated and slain by his thane Macbeth, and that his son and heir lived at the court of King Edward of England for fifteen years before Macduff persuaded him to return to Scotland with an army against Macbeth, who was defeated and slain. The episode concludes: "This is the 'Macbeth' of Shakespeare's great play, but the story as told by the poet has little real foundation in history" (45). In contrast, "The Wars of the Roses" praises Shakespeare's rendering of the battle at Bosworth Field: "In one of the finest scenes of his historical plays, Shakespeare describes the defeat and death of Richard in this battle and the triumph of his opponent, who was hailed on the field as Henry the Seventh" (116). Black and white illustrations show Shakespeare's significance in memorable Victorian historical paintings: John Pettie's *Plucking the Roses* (112) and T.A. Houston's *The Death of Warwick at the Battle of Barnet* (115).

Unlike other schoolbooks, *Highroads of British History* does not celebrate Henry V as the finest medieval king, although it acknowledges Shakespeare's treatment:

> Many stories have been told of the wild youthful days of this prince; and Shakespeare, in his dramatic account of the battle [Shrewsbury], tells how the fiery young leader meets Hotspur in single combat; how the latter finally falls with a mortal wound; and how Prince Henry in noble words mourns the death of his brave foe [105].

The triumph of youthful chivalry is a strong message. Agincourt — "How he fought and won this fight is a well-known story" (105) — is one in a list of battles. The conclusion, shared by many historians, makes clear why Henry V's victory in France is not celebrated:

> But the forced union of the two countries was not destined to last for any length of time, and the next great event in our history is the severing of the unnatural bond. The English and the French were separate and distinct nations; only in the mind of an ambitious, self-seeking monarch could they ever be united [107].

The monarch could be Edward III or Henry V, but the sentiment resonates with British imperialism of a later century. The death of Joan of Arc and loss of all of France except Calais "ended the unnatural connection between the French and English crowns" (108). Only two small marginal drawings depict Henry V: Prince Henry places a cushion on his head in a madcap play at king (105), while Henry V, in armor, stands alone on the field (107). No mention is made of Shakespeare's Henry VI, who is characterized as "of feeble mind, and a mere puppet in the hands of the great lords" (110), or of his *King Henry VIII*.

However attractive and effective schoolbooks of history were, many pupils did not find the study of history appealing. Clara L. Thomson, whose traditional schoolbooks have already been considered, was acutely aware of the problems of creating and sustaining children's interest in history. She addressed the issue in an innovative book built upon her classroom experience, writing of textbooks, and dedication to the interlace of literature and history. Thus for the study of Shakespeare as children's literature, probably her most compelling and inspiring effort is an anthology, *Carmina Britanniæ: A Selection of Poems and Ballads Illustrative of English History* (1901), also published by Horace Marshall. Thomson's preface, a straightforward and sound analysis that explains her pedagogy, is worth quoting at length:

> It is no new plan, but it is a plan which has not yet been universally adopted by teachers of English history, to illustrate their lessons by the reading or recitation of poems on historical subjects. Such readings give a welcome variety to the lesson, and since men and women are here treated exclusively from the romantic and imaginative point of view, they form a useful antidote to the dry statements of the text-books into which are compressed the splendid annals of our past. For many reasons, histories for school use must necessarily be somewhat dull; to write accurately and soundly the story of two thousand years, in such a manner that the book may be both cheap and portable, is no easy matter, and much picturesque detail must inevitably be omitted. But it is the imperative duty of every teacher to see that these dry bones do not represent to children the glorious body of history; it is his duty to animate and vivify the tale by recalling the motives and passions that thrilled our ancestors, to remember that chronology is not history, and to seize one of the few opportunities afforded by the school curriculum to appeal to the human sympathies and moral judgment of his pupils.
>
> One of the best means of doing this, I submit, is by reading of ballads and poems on historical subjects. It may be argued that such poems are seldom historically accurate; that they give a perverted view of men and facts. This is quite true. But it is for the teacher to guard against these dangers, to point out

discrepancies, and to show where the poetic story is biased by party feeling. If this is done, little harm can ensue, and I venture to affirm that the class will have a much better chance of remembering and realising the causes of, let me say, the deposition of Richard II., if the bare account of the same subject in the text-book be supplemented by the dramatic view of the same subject in Shakespeare's *Richard II.* and *Henry IV.* For after all, the permanence of any fact in the memory depends altogether on the depth of the impression it has made on the mind, and it is better to give a vivid and clear-cut impression in the first instance than to disgust the learner by the continual repetition of unadorned statements.[32]

Thomson, with a sure sense of the need to engage children, argued that literature does this better and more memorably than history schoolbooks. While she acknowledged that imaginative treatments may "pervert" facts, she lauded the truth that comes from fiction, an artistic view, especially cogent for historical novels. Although Scottish novelist Muriel Spark (1918–2006) wrote about contemporary circumstances, her philosophical distinction between truth and fiction is useful: "I don't claim that my novels are truth — I claim that they are fiction, out of which a kind of truth emerges."[33] This recognition mirrors the relationship between history and Shakespeare — who was writing about times past in an attempt to understand what led to Tudor England. Thomson's critical explanation includes matter that today's academics identify as modern historicism and reception theory, distinctions between historical fact and imaginative recreation, while her concern with "human sympathies and moral judgment" signal her Edwardian values. Moreover, her pedagogy includes memorization and recitation, a kind of performance that increases skill in public speaking.

Thomson's example of Shakespeare and Richard II is not accidental but substantive. Shakespeare's work dominates *Carmina Britanniæ,* so that a further lesson is the poet/ playwright's significance as a writer of history. The most egregious omission from Lamb's *Tales* is history plays; their addition to collections and entire books of stories from history indicate Edwardian understanding and patriotism that Thomson's "songs of Britain" celebrate.

Carmina Britanniæ was designed to be "serviceable to both teachers and pupils by reason of its convenient size and moderate price" (vii). The 251 pages have a type face large enough to be read easily. The sweep of history begins with "Boadicea" by William Cowper and ends with Lord Tennyson's "To Queen Victoria." A date for each event is at the start of each poem. Comparative weight by periods is notable. The first 150 pages contain fifty-two poems, while there are fifty-eight in the last 101. A significant number of items are anonymous; twenty-three are identified as contemporary poem, old ballad, or old song. Among named writers, Shakespeare, with eleven, is the largest contributor. Wordsworth is nearest with six, followed by Tennyson with four. The Elizabethan period (extending to "On Sir Walter Raleigh's Death" [1618] and "The Pilgrim Fathers" [1620] by Felicia Hemans) is the most fully represented, with twenty-eight poems, including Shakespeare's.

Quotations from Shakespeare's history plays are comprehensive; Thomson gave each a title and a reference to act and scene — to which I have added line references:

"Prince Arthur and Hubert," *King John*, IV.i.1–132 (38–43).

"John of Gaunt Consoles Bolingbroke for His Exile," *Richard II*, I.iii.247–309 (66–68).

"The Death of Richard II," *Richard II*, V.v.67–118 (76–78).

"Henry IV.'s Advice to Prince Hal," *Henry IV, Part I*, III.ii.29–91 (83–85).

"Henry V.'s Speech Before Agincourt," *Henry V*, IV.iii.16–67 (89–91).

"Soliloquy of Henry VI. at the Battle of Towton," *Henry VI, Part III*, II.v.1–54 (91–93).

"The Murder of the Princes in the Tower," *Richard III*, IV.iii.1–57 (96–99).

"Bosworth Field," *Richard III*, V.iv.1–12 & v.1–40 (99–101).

"The Disgrace of Wolsey," *Henry VIII*, III.ii.351–458 (108–112).

"Katharine of Aragon Hears the News of Wolsey's Death," *Henry VIII*, IV.ii.1–80 (112–115).

"In Praise of Queen Elizabeth," *Henry VIII*, V.iv.15–63 (115–117).

These well chosen passages introduce interesting characters and situations and meaningful themes. Three feature children: the blinding of Prince Arthur and the murders of the princes offer danger and pathos, while Elizabeth's birth is a cause for optimism. Gaunt's words to his son are both a father's advice — as is Henry IV's advice to Prince Hal — and a statement of patriotism. Love of country and courage are favored themes, best exemplified in Henry V's magnificent speech before Agincourt. Its stirring call to arms is in sharp contrast with Henry VI's melancholy reflections before Towton Battle. Nevertheless, the saintly king is there, a kind of heroism, albeit not equal to Richard II's extraordinary valor and strength when he dies fighting his murderers. Similarly, Richard III dies fighting valiantly at Bosworth. In short, Thomson made good use of Shakespeare's view that English kings die with courage, whatever their faults at other times. Two passages about Cardinal Wolsey are a powerful example of ill-placed ambition, fall from fortune, and forgiveness — a Christian message — and a key moment in the formation of the Church of England. The absence of illustrations in *Carmina Britanniæ* is symbolic; Shakespeare's words create pictures.

In one way Shakespeare's history plays are a return to techniques employed in early chronicles, histories of the Middle Ages (Bede, Matthew Paris, William of Malmesbury, and Henry Knighton, to name a few) that give factual information but also tell stories, including imagined scenes, dialogue, and character summations. Shakespeare's principal sources, Raphael Holinshed's *Chronicles* (1587) and Edward Hall's *The Union of the Two Noble and Illustre*

Families of Lancaster and York (1542), are part of this tradition, while poems in *A Mirror for Magistrates* (1559) are a model for the self-revelation of soliloquies as well as "dry bones" (facts). In short, Thomson's pedagogy of teaching history through literature has sound precedents.

At the end of several years of schooling, and repeated exposure to Shakespeare in literature and history schoolbooks, students faced sharper distinctions between the two disciplines and questions of representation — but Shakespeare is always an unmatched strong presence, woven into the fabric and mind of the nation / race. The beginning of the twentieth century was an extraordinary period in the development and expansion of ways to increase reading and knowledge; and Shakespeare is recognized as the greatest author in home and public libraries, as well as at school.

7

Home Libraries, Literary Histories, and Pedagogical Advice

Elegant books of stories for pleasurable reading at home and attractive schoolbooks for enjoyable study dominate Shakespeare as children's literature for Victorian and Edwardian children, but there were appealing alternatives. This chapter considers a type especially popular in the United States, a "home library," often ten volumes, but sometimes more, that brought together stories from great literatures, history, biography, and special topics. Especially recommended for use at home where parent and child read together, home libraries were on the model of the *Harvard Classics,* "Dr. Eliot's Five-foot Shelf of Books," volumes that contained the "wisdom of the world"—information as in an encyclopedia, but through primary texts. Editor-in-chief Charles Eliot Norton, President of Harvard, also contributed an introduction to *The Junior Classics,* "The Young Folks' Shelf of Books"; P.F. Collier published both. American writers were prominent; however, Shakespeare — along with medieval legends and chivalric stories, favorites for young children — had an honored place. Most printed the story of the masterpiece / classic by itself; pedagogical notes, even a fully articulated guide, came in a final or supplementary volume. Usually stories were reprinted, and illustrations were rarely original; thus choices were significant. Lamb's *Tales from Shakespeare* was most popular, but E. Nesbit's *The Children's Shakespeare* was also used. Volumes of poetry contained some Shakespeare songs.

Home libraries flourished in the opening decades of the twentieth century, but new editions continued after World War II. Several with varied design and emphases upon Shakespeare were *The Young Folks' Library* (1901–1902), edited by Thomas Bailey Aldrich; *The Children's Hour* (1907), edited by Eva March Tappan; *Journeys through Bookland* (1909), edited by Charles Sylvester; *Young Folks' Treasury* (1909), edited by Hamilton Wright Mabie, Edward Everett Hale and William Byron Forbush; *The Junior Classics* (1912), edited by William Patten; and *My Book House* (1920/21), edited by Olive Beaupré Miller. The subtitle of Logan Marshall's single volume epitomizes the underlying purpose of home instruction: *Young People's Home Library: A Book to Delight, Entertain, Amuse and Instruct Both Young and Old. Especially Prepared for All Social and Home Occasions* (1910). Shakespeare's stature inspired Percy MacKaye's *Caliban by the Yellow Sands* (1916), American community theatre at its grandest.

Concurrent literary histories for children, which stressed biography and presented a chronological survey but also retold major texts, consistently honored Shakespeare. There is no doubt about his premier place in the canon defined by the English language and heritage. Particularly noteworthy is the recognition that Shakespeare's plays are difficult for young children. Nevertheless, he is the "genius," the most remarkable author and most highly praised. Literary histories for children typically use techniques of storytelling for biography, indicate development over centuries, and establish a sense of patriotic identity from nation / race. Within this larger story are smaller retellings of individual great works. Four such histories are by English authors who worked primarily as writers, not in schools: H(enrietta) E. Marshall's *English Literature for Boys and Girls* (1909), Edward Parrott's *The Pageant of English Literature* (1914), Amy Cruse's *English Literature through the Ages* (1914), and Henry Gilbert's *Stories of Great Writers* (1914). All are Prizes / Rewards, examples of Edwardian extravagance in publishing with compelling illustrations, attractive type, and handsome covers. None includes American writers, not even Longfellow, often regarded on a par with Tennyson. However, they address Britain (encompassing the Empire) and the United States.

Analogous books in the United States are less handsome, but make American writers part of English literary history. Eva March Tappan's *A Brief History of English Literature* (1904/1914/1920/1932) concludes with American writers. Harrap published it in Britain in the same year as Parrott, Gilbert, and Cruse. The date is thus memorable for something other than the start of the Great War, albeit these books unquestionably further nationalism — one inspiration for children's literary history — and are a part of the zeitgeist of Europe. William J. Long's *Outlines of English and American Literature* (1919) — the title states the affinity — was published at the end of World War I. Both are workmanlike — not beautiful gift books — with some qualities of the textbook, which is not surprising given the pedagogical experiences of the authors. Later revision by Tappan resulted in two separate volumes, *A Short History of England's Literature* (1920 and 1933) and *A Short History of America's Literature* (1932), published by Houghton Mifflin. By the 1930s, then, a separation was made; American schoolbooks increasingly favored national writers.

Closely related to children's home libraries and literary histories are pedagogical studies and works by librarians that recommend reading to further children's appreciation of literature. Three notable guides to practices in school and library in the United States came from on-site experience: Mary E. Burt's *Literary Landmarks: A Guide to Good Reading for Young People, and Teachers' Assistant* (1897), Montrose J. Moses's *Children's Books and Reading* (1907), and

Frances Jenkins Olcott's *The Children's Reading* (1912). Each combined a philosophy of reading with extensive lists of recommended texts. Intended as guides for adults, but including children's responses, they glossed educational theory and reception. They included non–English classics, but marked Shakespeare's premier place.

Home Libraries

Thomas Bailey Aldrich, ed., *The Young Folks' Library* (1901–1902)

The editor-in-chief of *The Young Folks' Library*, twenty volumes, was Thomas Bailey Aldrich (1836–1907), who is best known for his autobiographical *The Story of a Bad Boy* (1870). Aldrich also wrote short stories and light verse and followed William Dean Howells as editor of the *Atlantic Monthly*. A subtitle of *The Young Folks' Library* describes the subjects covered: "Selections from the Choicest Literature of all Lands: Folk-lore, Fairy Tales, Fables, Legends, Natural History, Wonders of Earth, Sea and Sky, Animal Stories, Sea Tales, Brave Deeds, Explorations, Stories of School and College Life, Biography, History, Patriotic Eloquence, Poetry."[1] Exact titles of the ten volumes are slightly different: I. *The Story Teller*, II. *The Merry Makers* (edited by Joel Chandler Harris, author of *Uncle Remus* [1880]), III. *Famous Fairy Tales*, IV. *Tales of Fantasy*, V. *Myths and Legends*, VI. *The Animal Story Book*, VII. *School and College Days*, VIII. *Book of Adventure*, IX. *Famous Explorers*, X. *Brave Deeds*, XI. *Wonders of Earth, Sea, and Sky*, XII. *Famous Travels*, XIII. *Sea Stories*, XIV. *A Book of Natural History*, XV. *Historic Scenes in Fiction*, XVI. *Famous Battles by Land and Sea*, XVII. *Men Who Have Risen*, XVIII. *Book of Patriotism*, XIX. *Leaders of Men, or History Told in Biography*, XX. *Famous Poems*. History is as dominant as literature; no single volume is devoted to masterpieces / classics, but many are included. Subjects suggest boys are the likely audience, and emphasis on the United States is strong. Shakespeare, represented only by Lamb's *A Midsummer Night's Dream* in *The Story-Teller*, volume I, is not favored. Subsequent home libraries give him greater recognition.

Eva March Tappan, ed., *The Children's Hour* (1907)

Eva March Tappan (1854–1930) is an early example of a very successful professional woman, an educator who began as a teacher and then devoted herself to writing. Her father was a pastor of the Free Baptist Church, and she graduated from Vassar in 1875. For a time Tappan taught at Wheaton College in Illinois and in private schools in New Jersey and Massachusetts. She then completed a Master's degree in 1895 and a Ph.D. in 1896 from the University of Pennsylvania. Her dedication to the young, particularly from poor and immigrant families, expressed itself in her return to high school teaching. Her influence in Britain was substantial because Harrap published her books in its Told Through the Ages Series. Tappan's specialty was the Middle Ages—*Robin Hood: His Book* (1903), *In the Days of King Alfred* (1905), *The Chaucer Story Book* (1908), *When Knights Were Bold* (1911)—issued by Harrap as *In Feudal Times: Social Life in the Middle Ages* (1913) and *Heroes of the Middle Ages (Alaric to Columbus)* (1911). All express a pedagogy that finds heroic and mythic stories especially suitable for children. Tappan also wrote an influential *A Brief History of English Literature* (1904/1914, rev. ed. 1920/1932), which is discussed later in this chapter. She selected stories from distinguished children's versions of great literature and arranged them in Houghton-Mifflin's *The Children's Hour* (1907), ten volumes, one of the most interestingly organized and nicely illustrated home libraries.

The title, which comes from Henry Wadsworth Longfellow's popular poem, identifies a time when parents and children could meet and read together. The opening lines—"Between the dark and the daylight, when the night is beginning to lower, / There comes a pause in the day's occupations, that is known as the Children's Hour"—signal an ideal intention to foster family relations; they are printed at the bottom of each volume's title page. Red cloth covers bear gold-stamped titles and a drawing that indicates something of the contents. The ten volumes are *I. Folk Stories and Fable, II. Myths from Many Lands, III. Stories from the Classics, IV. Stories of Legendary Heroes, V. Stories from Seven Old Favorites, VI. Old-Fashioned Stories and Poems, VII. Out-of-Door Books, VIII. Adventures and Achievements, IX. Poems and Rhymes,* and *X. Modern Stories.* This library is, then, primarily imaginative literature; stories of adventures and achievements (VIII) are historical.

Shakespeare is in *V. Stories from Seven Old Favorites.* Tappan's "To the Children" explains that all are very different but liked by most boys and girls because they are more "real" than most other stories.[2] Studies of children's literature continue to recognize them as classics: John Bunyan's *The Pilgrim's Progress,* Daniel Defoe's *Robinson Crusoe,* Jonathan Swift's *Gulliver's Travels,* Miguel Cervantes's *Don Quixote, The Arabian Nights,* Rudolf Erich Raspe's *The Travels of Baron Munchausen,* and Lamb's *Tales from Shakespeare.* Each classic was written originally for adults and then appropriated for children, with adjustments, including some early chapbooks. The original texts date from the seventeenth or eighteenth centuries—the much older *Arabian Nights* became known in Europe only in the eighteenth century. They passed the test of time needed to be world classics.

Shakespeare's premier place is signaled by the color frontispiece (Millais's *Ferdinand and Ariel* [1849–1850]), his position as final author, and Tappan's esteem of "a great genius." A play always has a story—what is here offered—but there is much more:

> Now when Shakespeare puts a thought into words, we find that no one else has expressed it so well. Moreover, he sees more clearly than any other writer how a person would feel and behave in various circumstances. We think of them as real people. We talk of what they would have done if circumstances had been different [xiv].

Tappan selected three of Lamb's stories: *The Comedy of Errors, The Merchant of Venice,* and *The Tempest.* All are comedies, the last two special favorites for children. The only illustration within the text is also from *The Tempest,* a moment of great excitement, the opening storm. George Romney's "The Vessel will be dashed to pieces" features William Hayley as Prospero and Emma Hamilton as Miranda (426). Safe within Prospero's cell, against which waves break, these figures stand on the right to balance the bright light in the upper left corner where Ariel is seen on white clouds, while a boat crowded with standing men fills most of the painting. Benjamin Smith did the engraving for the Boydell Gallery, September 29, 1797. Like others, Tappan added cultural depth by using famous paintings.

Her "Introduction to the Mothers and Fathers," which sketches the variety of stories and some responses of children, includes a significant reference to Shakespeare. Pointing to the role of literature in forming the imagination and its relation to science, she recorded that "when Agassiz started for the South to make his study of the structure of the Florida reefs, he carried Shakespeare's 'Tempest' with him that his imagination might be aroused and stimulated to suggest all possible theories of their foundation" (I, xvii). Tappan concluded with her own experience as a reader who became a writer:

> The selection of texts has been made carefully and critically; and yet of greater authority than all the formal canons of literary and pedagogical wisdom, are the memories of what stories and poems were dearest to my own childhood. To recall when and where I entered into the world of marvel and delight that lay between the covers of each, to think of the many children who have felt the same pleasure in these beloved little volumes, and then to lay the books happily side by side, has been a rare enjoyment. The work has been a gladsome little journey back into the happy land of childhood; and when I recall it in days to come, it will not seem work, but will take its name from the collection itself, and be to me "a pause in the day's occupation that is known as The Children's Hour" [I, xx-xxi].

The end-papers, bright red printed with white designs, signal great resources. At the spine the trunk of a tree (of knowledge?) rises into foliage and fruit that spread across the top, while on either side identical rows of small figures advance from each side: Viking ships, bushes, dwarfs, knights on horses, foliage, castles, double rows of foliage. Tappan selected and arranged a great many stories; a supplementary volume advises how they might be read.

Robert Newton Linscott's *A Guide to Good Reading: With Practical Directions for the Use of* The Children's Hour *in the Home,* published by Mifflin in 1912, is a valuable record of attitudes. His introduction explains that the ten volumes, although inspired by a wish that children not have to "shift for themselves," are designed to attract the child, unhampered by obvious instructions for use; freedom to roam through the books is advised, and flexibility for age levels.[3] Tappan's essay "How to Get the Most Good from The Children's Hour," one of two addressed to parents,[4] affirms these principles by identifying five salient features: (1) the stories are interesting (President Eliot of Harvard and Edward Everett Hale both wanted to read the volumes themselves), (2) "these stories are of distinct educational value," (3) and of moral value, (4) "there are no hard and fast divisions," artificial groupings to make points, and (5) each volume generally moves from simplicity to greater difficulty, but no expectations of matching age levels inhibit individual children from choosing what interests them (7–9). Although she offered a few examples of how to choose, Tappan concluded with Charles Lamb's wise judgment about his sister Mary, who "was tumbled early by accident or design into a spacious closet of good old English reading." Tappan's ordering suggested Shakespeare's complexity, and she affirmed that "to read and to think about what one has read is a most excellent groundwork for all education" (12). Linscott identified a key objective: "every story in The Children's Hour has been selected with a view to developing character in one way or another" (ix). There is no ambiguity; literature embodies a moral tradition as crucial as learning to read words and sentences.

Most of Linscott's book is an encyclopedic "Guide to Good Reading" to facilitate use of *The Children's Hour* and to identify related books for further reading. Each volume begins with a quotation that epitomizes its contents and is described in three columns: "The Stories," "Their Source," "Other Related Books." Oliver Goldsmith introduced *Stories from Seven Old Favorites:* "The first time I read an excellent book, it is to me just as if I had gained a new friend; when I read over a book I have perused before, it resembles a meeting with an old one" (31). Stories of Shakespeare's three plays come from Lamb's *Tales*. A recommended edition is the one profusely illustrated by Norman M. Price, described in Chapter 2; Charles Scribner's Sons published it in the United States. Also recommended is an inexpensive Riverside School Library edition, published by Mifflin, whose Cambridge edition, edited by William A. Neilson, is the only listing of "other related books"—a bit of advertising. Comments about progressive reading of Shakespeare are practical:

> Lamb's Tales are chiefly valuable as an introduction to Shakespeare himself. "The Tempest" and "A Midsummer Night's Dream" are the best to begin with. "The Merchant of Venice may be read shortly after, "Julius Caesar" in connection with the selection in Volume III, then "King John," "Richard III," "Twelfth Night," "Macbeth," and the rest of "that noble company" [32].

Two of Tappan's selections comply. Although *The Comedy of Errors* is not an obvious choice, it is a farce, classical, and about a reunited family. Suggestions for tragedies and history plays match titles in Jeanie Lang's *More Stories from*

Shakespeare (1910) — apt reading about republicanism, a vulnerable young prince, an archetypal villain, and witches.

Other sections of *A Guide to Good Reading* are substantial aids for reference. First, "Noteworthy Characters and Events Referred to in 'The Children's Hour'" provides a thorough explanation of persons, places, and events from history, and identifies volume and page. A second large section, brief biographies of "Authors of 'The Children's Hour,'" includes Charles and Mary Lamb (108) and William Shakespeare, "the world's greatest poet and dramatist" (114). Commendation is unusual; most entries are restricted to facts — dates, places, titles. Finally, a very comprehensive index to Linscott's *Guide* indicates whether a writer or story is in any of the ten volumes.

A special English edition of *The Children's Hour* was published in 1909 in nine volumes by the Waverley Book Company. Hall Caine's Foreword to I. *Folk Stories and Fables* is notable, since he defined the universality of selections at a time when Europeans were preoccupied, if not obsessed, with ideas of race / nation:

> [C]hildhood knows nothing of nationality or of race, and therefore the book is best that best takes account of this touching universality. Only as we grow up do we become Englishmen and Americans, Germans and Frenchmen, with separated interests, divided aims, different faiths and ways of thinking. The child fresh from God belongs to the Empire of Childhood — an Empire that has no boundaries except the far-off borderlands of love and belief and awe and wonder.... [In an anthology gathered from every part of the world] turning their pages is like opening the door of a room that rings not only with music but with the merry laughter of an innumerable company of children — children of all countries and all ages, all nations and races, all classes and colours. Beautiful thought, making a book like this a melting-pot for our little racial differences, set up in that sweet chamber of childhood when alone the human family is one![5]

Similarly, *Stories from Seven Old Favorites* are neither exclusively English nor European. Reprints in 1912 and 1913 indicate a good reception, while Caine's remarks resonate with a blend of Edwardian consciousness of Empire and a poignancy for lost innocence and good will that in 1914 became catastrophic.

Mabie, Hale, and Forbush, eds., *Young Folks' Treasury* (1909)

Young Folks' Treasury resembles *The Children's Hour* in subject divisions, but has twelve volumes and three editors, all men with distinctive achievements in the United States. Hamilton Wright Mabie (1879–1917) practiced law for six or seven years but became an educator and prolific writer. He received B.A., M.A., and L.H.D. degrees from Williams College, and was awarded an LL.B by Columbia University. The University Society published both *Young Folks' Treasury* and the Every Child Should Know Series, for which Mabie edited *Myths*

(1905), *Heroes* (1906), *Legends* (1906), *Fairy Tales* (1907), *Heroines* (1908), *Folk Tales* (1910).[6] Edward Everett Hale (1822–1909) was a Boston Unitarian clergyman. With his sister Susan he wrote the *Family Flight* series of travelogue storybooks, a type to which Americans were particularly devoted. However, Hale is best remembered for his patriotic novel *The Man Without a Country* (1865), which inspired many to care about their identity as citizens of the United States. William Byron Forbush, a Congregational minister in Vermont, founded in 1893 an organization for boys, The Knights of King Arthur, an inspiration for Robert Baden-Powell to create the Boy Scouts. Forbush's *The Boy Problem* (1901), in a sixth edition by 1907, explains that these Arthurians—boys who took the names of knights and turned their games and outings into quests and battles and were led by Merlins (adults)—sought to revive "the spirit of chivalry, courtesy, deference to womanhood, recognition of the *noblesse oblige,* and Christian daring."[7] Forbush wrote to improve the moral character of children in *Young Folk's Book of Ideals* (1912), and the introduction to III. *Classic Tales and Everyday Stories* (1919/1921). Tappan put Shakespeare with old favorites; Forbush placed him among classic tales—although with uneasiness.

His introduction explains that the book is really two volumes in one. A particular concern with "the boy problem," which inspired his redeployment of Arthurian stories to inspire chivalry, perhaps explains why "everyday stories" precede "classic tales" in his explanation, although not in the volume. "Stories of Play and Athletics," "Stories of Adventure," "Stories of Heroism," and "Stories of Human Love" are recognized as appropriate for high school, while "Old-fashioned Stories"—selections from Maria Edgeworth's *Simple Susan* (adapted by Louey Chisholm in 1907)—are "quaint and funny," with "charming color prints" and have a "sweet flavor and savor."[8] Stories in this second book are separated from the first by "Funny Stories"—perhaps to allow young readers to recover from the first part—and appeal directly to boys. Differences in gender influence preferred writers: girls frequently read boys' books, but boys seldom like girls' books. A survey of 790 boys, aged eleven to nineteen, made in 1884 by Charles Welsh, favored *Robinson Crusoe* and writers of adventure stories and novels, the most influential Victorian books for boys. A similar survey of 1000 found that girls also liked Shakespeare and Bunyan, and Dickens, Scott, and Yonge.[9] Ellis pointed out that girls had many fewer books and periodicals to choose from. Forbush warned, reassured, and enticed:

> The CLASSIC TALES in the first part of the book may look a bit alarming at first. They are placed here so that the names of Homer, Shakespeare, Chaucer, Cervantes, and Lamb may become as familiar as "Cinderella" and "The Three Bears." Really read them through and you will be spellbound. You will find something more than a silly old man in noble Don Quixote, you will see the sly fun that Swift was poking at us all in Gulliver's adventures, you will lose your way in magical Bagdad during fascinating Arabian Nights. Those daring mariners, Ulysses and Robinson Crusoe, will make you forget your home for a while. Chaucer will take you on a journey that you will never wish to end and

Bunyan on a pilgrimage that closes only with the Celestial City. Charles and Mary Lamb will carry you to Fairyland and Prospero's isle of magic [v].

These brief descriptive advertisements argued that the best way to encourage children to read classic tales was to present them as similar to popular adventure novels. Most titles duplicated Tappan, except Homer (both *The Iliad* and *The Odyssey*) and Chaucer replaced *Travels of Baron Munchhausen* (perhaps reaction to World War I). Forbush's final wish was that childhood reading would introduce great writers that later would become lifelong friends.

The Tempest and *A Midsummer Night's Dream* from Lamb's *Tales* indicate that fairies and magic are most likely to engage young readers; they are supported by three full-page color illustrations. The frontispiece is N. M. Price's "The Fairies Sing Titania to Sleep" that was also frontispiece for *Tales from Shakespeare by Charles and Mary Lamb* (1905) and Jeanie Lang's *Stories from Shakespeare* (1905) in the Told to the Children Series, published by E. C. and T.C. Jack. Although many selections in *The Young Folks' Treasury* come from this series, the editors chose the best known version, Lamb's *Tales*. A second picture, Oberon: "Ill met by moonlight, proud Titania" is a well lit, simply drawn gathering of fairies in the wood (244). In contrast, "Miranda Watching the Storm" is a portrait of a dark-haired beauty in an orange dress of classical style; she rests one hand on a large rock before a seascape with turbulent waves, dark clouds, and a flash of lightning (234). Neither is as exciting as thrilling combats in other classic tales.

The Young Folks' Treasury often is overtly didactic, especially selections from history. Mabie and Hale phrased a collection of predominantly American biographies as an argument for hard work, IX. *Men and Women of Achievement; Self-Help,* while VII. *Heroes and Patriots,* edited by George Cary Eggleston and John H. Clifford, has great dedication to American ideals, signaled by the frontispiece portrait of Theodore Roosevelt. Examples from the United States are more numerous than European; substantial space deals with topics like "Good Citizenship"; "Nation-building, Progress, and Patriotism"; "Party Politics and Public Opinions." In short, this home library does not favor literature as did Tappan and Patten.

After World War II The University Society combined material from *The Young Folks' Treasury, The Boys and Girls Bookshelf* (1912, 1915, 1920), and several later collections to make a "meaty volume" (368 pages with double columns), VI. *Famous Stories and Verse* in *The Bookshelf for Boys and Girls* as "an introduction to the best literature."[10] The editors explained their selections were made for entertainment, but still urged intentions common to Edwardians: "Much of it is inspirational, although not obtrusively so. The stories teach nobility of character, and high endeavor. And further, they give the young reader a taste and desire for the really worthwhile in the world's literature" (iv). *The Arabian Nights,* medieval chivalric stories (including Chaucer), Spenser,

Cervantes, many nineteenth-century novels (both juvenile and adult) are "Some Good Stories Retold," among which is Lamb's *The Tempest*. Katherine Worthington enriched it with quotations: a dozen of Ariel's lines to describe the results of the storm, Prospero's recollection of how he freed Ariel from Sycorax, the first stanza of Ariel's song, "Come unto these yellow sands," and "Full fathom five," lovers' speeches—Ferdinand's first greeting of Miranda and her response to so fair a young man, their exchange over the logs, his identification of himself as a prince. Two quotations come from the feast, the marriage blessing and Prospero's address to the nymphs and farewell, "Our revels now are ended." *The Tempest* survives as the featured play; its combination of supernatural creatures and family relationships well suit the book's purpose. Other selections, mostly nineteenth- and twentieth-century, are arranged thematically—"Fancy," "Magic and Mystery," "Love of Country," "Holidays," "Nature," "The Best Things in Life," "Funny Verses," "Story Poems," "Tales of Joy and Sorrow." *The Bookshelf for Boys and Girls* is thus in the vein of earlier home libraries, still defined in part by a purpose of informing national and family identity.

William Patten, ed., *The Junior Classics* (1912)

Quite similar to *The Children's Hour* and *The Young Folks' Library* is *Junior Classics: The Young Folks' Shelf of Books*, ten volumes edited by William Patten (1868–1936), managing editor of the Harvard Classics, and published by P. F. Collier in 1912. It has the same physical dimensions, approximately five by seven and a half inches. Its cloth cover has different colors rather than uniform; however, the device on the front is always the same, "Sir Galahad," icon of chivalry, from the 1862 painting by George Frederick Watts (1817–1904), a version of which hangs in Eton Chapel. The end papers, the same front and back in every volume, reproduce Watts's "Sir Galahad," faced by Robinson Crusoe, drawn in pale green lines. The volumes are *1. Fairy and Wonder Tales, 2. Folk Tales and Myths, 3. Tales from Greece and Rome, 4. Heroes and Heroines of Chivalry, 5. Stories That Never Grow Old, 6. Old Fashioned Tales, 7. Stories of Courage and Heroism, 8. Animal and Nature Stories, 9. Stories of To-day,* and *10. Poems Old and New, Reading Guides and Indexes.*

Stories That Never Grow Old parallels Tappan's *Stories from Seven Old Favorites* and Forbush's *Classic Tales*. The seven titles are *Arabian Nights, Robinson Crusoe, Gulliver's Travels, The Plays of Shakespeare, Pilgrim's Progress, Ivanhoe* and *Guy Mannering,* and *The Startling Adventures of Baron Munchausen*. Sir Walter Scott's two novels instead of Cervantes's *Don Quixote* and / or Chaucer and Homer add a modern emphasis. Similarly, retellings of Shakespeare are by E. Nesbit, who simplified Lamb's *Tales* and suited Patten's concern about children's responses. A brief introductory note gives a few details about Shakespeare's life, praises his "two rare gifts" (the ability to understand people and to write so that the reader feels and sees as he did), and defines his eminence: "To read Shakespeare's plays is the height of an actor's ambition. To read and enjoy them has been for over three hundred years one of the greatest pleasures known to English-speaking people."[11] A tradition of performance in the United States included the Booth family, touring companies from England, notably Henry Irving's, and Charles Dickens's readings.

Four comedies, "here represented by short stories, in which the plot of each play is briefly told," are popular choices for children: *A Midsummer Night's Dream, The Tempest, As You Like It, The Merchant of Venice.* Notable artists of the Golden Age did the illustrations. The color frontispiece is Arthur Rackham's "And I will wind thee in my arms" from his remarkable *A Midsummer Night's Dream.* The other three stories have black and white full pages. "This was Caliban, the son of the wicked witch," by F. O. C. Darley (322), combines storm effects and rocky shore with contrasting figures of "a hideous, deformed monster, horrible to look on, and vicious and brutal in all his habits" (340) and a startled survivor. Caliban, who cowers above logs he dropped on the beach, has webbed feet and a fierce face but does not quite convey Nesbit's vivid description of him in *The Tempest.* Two others depict pastoral and court. Charles Folkard's "They were very tired when at last they came to the forest of Arden" is a lively rendering of Touchstone, Celia, and Rosalind during their flight in *As You Like It.* Already described, Folkard's illustrations were created for Alice Hoffman's *The Children's Shakespeare* (1911) and repeated in F. C. Tilney's selected Lamb's *Tales from Shakespeare* (1926). Alex Cabanel's *Portia and the Three Caskets* features a stunning beauty in extravagant Renaissance costume and in the background a handsome courtier (354).

The color frontispiece of 10. *Poems Old and New* signals Shakespeare's pre-eminence in a second volume. Folkard's engaging "And for my pranks men call me by the name of Robin Goodfellow" is here referenced to an anonymous lyric.[12] But Patten included three poems from *A Midsummer Night's Dream*: "Over hill, over dale," "I know a bank where the wild thyme blows," and "The Fairies' lullaby." Songs from *The Tempest* are "Where the bee sucks" and "Come unto these yellow sands," while "Jog On" and "The Pedler's Pack"—Autolycus's song, "Lawn as white as driven snow"—are from *The Winter's Tale.* Use of lyrics/songs to introduce Shakespeare to children is commonplace. More unusual, and an indication that *The Junior Classics* is a home library for different ages, are quotations that exemplify salient qualities of character, the cultivation of which is one stated objective of the study of literature. From *Henry VIII,* "Cardinal Wolsey Speech to Cromwell" (III.ii. 429–458) and "Wolsey's Fall" (III.ii. 352–373) make a lesson in the consequences of overweening ambition, while Jaques's "Seven Ages of Man" speech from *As You Like It* (II.vii.138–165) reflects on how men decline with age. Most distinctive is "Hotspur's Description of a Fop" from *King Henry IV, Part I* (I.iii.30–64), both outrageously funny and a warning against unmanliness. Several quotations are best read without awareness of the complexity of speaker and circumstance: a portion of Polonius's advice to his son Laertes in *Hamlet* (I.iii.68–80), Iago's comment on "Reputation" in *Othello* (III.iii.168–174), and "Perfection," Salisbury's remarks in *King John* (IV.ii.11–16). Brutus's observation on "Opportunity" in *Julius Caesar* (IV.iii.217–222) and Portia on "Mercy" in *The Merchant of Venice* (IV.i.182–195) are better known, sometimes memorized. With eighteen "poems," Shakespeare has the second highest number. This is surpassed only by Robert Louis Stevenson's nineteen from *A Child's Garden of Verses* (1885), the finest Victorian poetry written for children; William Allan Neilson suggested it was appropriate for Grade III. The next highest contributors are the most popular nineteenth-century poets, one American and one English: thirteen from Longfellow, and only eight from Tennyson.

An introduction by Charles W. Eliot (1834–1926), President Emeritus of Harvard University and one of America's most distinguished educators, supported Patten's selection and arranging of *The Junior Classics*, while a reading guide was made by William Allan Neilson (1869–1946). Born in Scotland, first educated at the University of Edinburgh, but a Harvard Ph.D., Neilson taught in Canada, at Bryn Mawr, at Columbia, was Professor of English at Harvard (1906–1917), and then was President of Smith College. He was editor-in-chief of the second edition of *Webster's New International Dictionary* (1934). Most relevant is Neilson's work as a sixteenth-century scholar; he edited *The Chief Elizabethan Dramatists excluding Shakespeare* (1911) and *The Complete Dramatic and Poetic Works of William Shakespeare* (1906), with the text from the early quartos and First Folio. *The Tudor Shakespeare* (1911–1913), forty volumes edited with Ashley Horace Thorndike, uses the same text, and includes *The Facts about Shakespeare* (1913). As a major academic who worked assiduously to advance literature for children in the United States, he paralleled F. J. Furnivall, Sidney Lee, and Arthur Quiller-Couch in England.

Neilson's reading guide for *Stories That Never Grow Old* at the end of volume 10 adds a few comments about each selection and a "List of Best Books." The relevant paragraph is: "Of the stories of Shakespeare's plays and Scott's novels there is no need to speak. Their chief function here is to give a taste of these writers as will entice the reader to go direct to the fountain head" (467). In the arrangement according to assumed maturity, E. Nesbit's four stories are assigned to Grade VI (487), while Shakespeare's poems are recommended for Grade VII (491–492), which is fairly late in the normal eight grades then in effect in American public schools. While Neilson insisted that "no hard lines" could be drawn, his assignments reinforced Forbush's uneasiness about responses and the findings of the Newbolt Report in England. England and the United States agreed in rating Shakespeare as the "greatest genius/writer," but Americans were less confident about early teaching. The four home libraries considered thus far are similar in attitude and design; however, another was quite different, with unusual organization and pedagogical apparatus.

Charles H. Sylvester, *Journeys through Bookland* (1909)

Charles H. Sylvester, author of *English and American Literature*, proposed a very different approach in *Journeys through Bookland*, published in 1909 in Chicago by Bellows-Reeve Company. The black (or dark red) cloth covers with titles and a floral design stamped in gold are rather austere and formal. However, end papers are more encouraging: on the left a shepherd plays a flute to his sheep on a hillside, a pastoral scene linked to the opposite side by a sweep of coastline and sea with several ships in the distance. The right side features footmen and knights marching across the bottom, while a medieval castle fills the upper half. Sylvester's *Guide to Journeys through Bookland* is a handbook of literary terms and methods of study (character, literature and its forms, how to read fiction and poetry, close reading, memorizing, reading aloud, recitations and special days in school) — with model analyses for all parts of interpretation. The unique characteristic of this ten-volume home library is that selections are not divided by subjects or types; the subtitle promises "A New and Original Plan for Reading, Applied to the World's Best Literature for Children."[13] The masterpieces are the same, but generally the only ordering is some increase in difficulty within a volume; items at the end of one volume are harder than those at the start of the next. This encourages fluid selection, as the child progresses from nursery rhymes to the difficulties of Shakespeare, Browning, and Goethe (18), but also repeated readings. Moreover, it prohibits saturation in any one type — fairy tales, for example. Nevertheless, Sylvester provides several tools for conventional groupings. A "Graphic Classification of Masterpieces" gives volume numbers across the top and a column with familiar subjects: "Fables," "Fairy Stories and Folk Lore," "Stories Old and New," "Myths and Classic Literature," "Legendary Heroes," "Biography," "Travel and Adventure," "History," "Biblical Moral and Religious," "Patriotism," "Nature," "Humor," "Poetry," "Drama," and "Studies" (14). For high school students Sylvester provided a formal arrangement: lists of items from different volumes for studies in character, plot, description, rhyme, meter and melody, interpretation, biographies, and so on. "Supplementary Book Lists" are classified according to kinds of literature, and a "Handy List of Studies" references texts by volumes. Working one's way through the journeys can be strenuous, but this design fosters thinking and continuous reading — the most important, prime study (387).

A rubric on the title page of *Guide to Journeys through Bookland* epitomizes the intended audience and purposes of home libraries in the United States:

> For parents, teachers, and all who have children under their charge; for adults who wish to renew their acquaintance with the friends of their youth, or to open for the first time the world's great treasure house of literature; for youthful readers who must study the classics.

While the role of the home / family is crucial (2), the variety of readers indicates broad expectations and a need to interest different levels. *Journeys* is not intended to teach reading, but to serve the child who by the third grade should know how to read and by the fourth grade be reading independently (26). Sylvester recognized that children can and should read masterpieces that are beyond their comprehension — skipping words and parts is not a sin — for great literature should be read more than once and with increasing perception (282). High school students should be capable of reading readily, but may well lack knowledge of the classics that are found in *Journeys through Bookland*.

Sylvester reiterated that he had chosen "masterpieces" and placed them in three categories. First is "the literature of culture, those things which you and I and everybody must know if we expect to be considered educated or to be able to read with intelligence current writings of the day." This assumed a common canon and a relation between early literature and the present. The second kind has commanded greatest attention and was expected to have greatest influence: "selections whose power lies in the profound influence they exert upon the unfolding character of the boy or girl. As a child readeth so is he." Last are "masterpieces which lend interest to school work and make it pleasanter, easier and more profitable" (8–9).

For the study of Shakespeare as children's literature Sylvester's treatment is quite revealing; he both separated drama, declared more suitable for older children, from other types and left it until volume IX. Moreover, the only dramatist is Shakespeare, introduced through a single masterpiece, *The Tempest*, both Lamb's *Tale* and the play itself. The *Guide* contains a few additional references to Shakespeare, but most information is here (IX, 283–438). This emphasis offsets preceding works as different as Washington Irving's *The Alhambra* and Robert Burns's poem "The Cotter's Saturday Night," and three essays (Macaulay's "The Impeachment of Warren Hastings," and Charles Lamb's "A Dissertation upon Roast Pig" and "The Praise of Chimney Sweepers").

Sylvester's prefatory note, "reading Shakespeare," makes abundantly clear that in the United States many did not read "the greatest author the world has known" with understanding and / or appreciation:

> Not every reader of Shakespeare loves him, but that is because not every reader appreciates him. He wrote in the English of his times, and used many words and expressions that have since dropped out of the language, changed their meaning, or become unfamiliar in common speech. Then again, his knowledge of life is so profound and his insight into human nature so keen and penetrating, that the casual reader is liable not to follow his thought. In other words, Shakespeare must be studied to be appreciated; but if he is studied and appreciated, he gives a pleasure that cannot be equaled.
>
> Young people are liable to think that study is laborious and uninteresting, a nuisance and a bore. Nothing of the sort is true of the study of Shakespeare, because for every effort there is a present reward, there is no waiting to see results [IX, 283].

Sylvester's essential point was that the young reader would have to work but should give Shakespeare a good try. He faulted poor teaching and urged that properly prepared children could and should read by themselves. From many plays with a wide range of activities and characters, he chose *The Tempest* and made a final emotional appeal to his audience:

> Will you then, our young readers, go hand in hand with us into the reading of Shakespeare? Do as we say this one time, and read as we ask you to, even if it does take some time from your play. If, while you are doing it, you do not enjoy yourselves, or if at the end you do not feel repaid, then take your own course in your reading thereafter. It will be a better course for having studied one great play carefully [IX, 284–285].

The prelude to reading the play is to read the "charming tale" written by Lamb, which gives the story, "though a wealth of incidents is omitted" (IX, 285).

Sylvester expected substantial work—and pleasure. An introductory note calls for two readings of the play, one quick—during which not everything will be understood or recognized—and a second slow—every sentence and the footnotes (some of which point out that no one is absolutely sure of the meaning of a few passages; IX, 402n.23, 407n.39). For example, "It is not known whether *line* refers to a clothesline or to a line tree. Only Shakespeare himself could tell to a certainty" (IX, 393n.50). Three notes guide response to the supernatural and discussion of fairy tales for children. When Ariel reports to Prospero how he managed the storm and passengers, Sylvester observed: "To enjoy *The Tempest*, we must lay aside our reason to the extent of believing in charms and magic, in witchcraft and in Ariel's wonderful powers. Prospero's control of the magic art is part of what he gained from his studies while Antonio was stealing his principality" (IX, 322n.69). A gloss on Prospero's reference to "weak master" explains: "The fairies are weak masters, that is, they can accomplish little if left to themselves, but under the direction of a human mind like Prospero's they could work such wonders as he describes" (IX, 399n.9). Concerning the Man in the Moon, his dog and bush: "All these things the fanciful used to think they could see in the face of the moon" (IX, 361n.27). The combined argument affirms human dominance and dismisses fancy as outdated. Most footnotes simply give meanings of words. A rare commentary is about Prospero's telling his story to Miranda: she is not inattentive to her father; rather Prospero lacks clarity, as his mind wanders and he speaks imperfect sentences (IX, 315n.31). As an interpretation of parent-child interplay this is provocative.

Exacting reading is enlivened by ten black and white illustrations, each a full page but for two or three lines of text printed at the bottom. In the *Guide* Sylvester averred that "pictures are in themselves a language—the oldest as well as the most universal tongue of the world" (48). He devoted a full chapter to illustrations, stressing that they greatly help young readers to understand literature—by encouraging them to read on and find out what the pictures hint, and by giving visual details of character, costume, and place. "All lost! All lost!" is a very dramatic rendering of a listing ship buffeted by extraordinary waves (IX, 308). Terrified sailors and passengers rush to the edge, cling to the mast, prepare to jump — enough action to fascinate any young reader, who upon looking carefully will see the gleaming figure of Ariel against the sail at the top. Ariel is clearly delineated in a line drawing where he hails Prospero as master (IX, 320). Later, Ariel asks, "Do you love me, Master?" (IX, 386), lightly touches Prospero's sleeve, and looks up; Prospero, again in contrasting dark clothes, looks down gently as he holds his wand and book. Ariel wakes Gonzalo in another line drawing that emphasizes lush vegetation and shows two other small figures on the beach (IX, 352). The island's landscape is more prominent in a remarkable drawing of Caliban, who trudges up an incline with a heavy load of wood strapped to his back; Caliban stares directly at the viewer, inviting a response to his extraordinary face and short garment of animal skin (IX, 354).

Several illustrations simply depict character and costume: on the beach, Ferdinand asks Miranda to marry him, as they hold hands (IX, 367); a satisfied Prospero stands between the lovers, as he assures the young man "She will outstrip all praise" (IX, 384). Very distinctive is Prospero's meeting with his enemies, "Behold the wronged duke of Milan" (IX, 403), again a study in costume — Prospero's cloak is marvelously decorated — and expressions of pain on worried faces. In one comic scene, a light line drawing, "Ariel plays the tune" (IX, 374). A small figure, he looks directly at the viewer; but Caliban (with bottle in hand), Stephano, and Trinculo do not see him concealed behind a bush. A similarly amusing half-tone, signed by K. Maxey, is "What things are these?"— three drunken creatures brought before Alonso, Prospero, Ferdinand and Miranda (IX, 412). Both the number and different subjects—all illustrations are original in *Journeys through Bookland*— stimulate the imagination and enable young readers to understand the play without depending entirely upon words. Another half-tone page portrait of Shakespeare introduces "Studies for *The Tempest*" (IX, 416–438).

Studies are many and wide-ranging, a combination of critical explanation and questions to inspire independent thinking. Several topics cover the spectrum of literary analysis. "The Author," a brief biography (that urges the author controversy should be avoided), stresses genius and friends; "The Play" points out the original plot, three unities, blend of supernatural and natural, and high sentiments. "Characters," one of the longer discussions, begins with advice against superficial judgments—albeit Sylvester fully praised Prospero and Miranda before encouraging answers about others: What kind of young man is Ferdinand? Find all the references to Ariel and come to know him. What do you think of Prospero's judgment of Caliban, and why should such a character be in the play? Finally, identify the other characters as good or evil. "Story or Plot" proceeds scene by scene —first a statement of the purpose, and then a series of questions that require detailed knowledge. "Poetry or Prose" asks which characters use each and why, the number of songs and who sings them, and finally whether any character speaks in rhyme. "Conclusion" advises how to read: stop when one loses interest and the work seems drudgery and come back renewed. Sylvester admitted that precise and sustained study may result in loss of a sense of the whole and appreciation of *The Tempest* as a work of art. Thus he advised yet another reading,

> in a leisurely manner, pausing merely to enjoy its beauty, to smile at its playfulness and to feel our hearts expand under the benign influence of the grand old man Prospero. Now Miranda, Ferdinand, and Ariel have passed the line of mere acquaintances, and have become fast friends, who though they may be forever silent, have yet given us a fragment of their lives to cheer us on our way [IX, 437].

The final topic, "Other Plays of Shakespeare," points out that not all are equally good, and some are more difficult for young readers; he recommended the most appropriate:

> *A Midsummer Night's Dream* is a charming fairy story; *The Merchant of Venice* is a good story, contains fine characters and shows some of Shakespeare's most beautiful thoughts, although some people are inclined to believe he has dealt too severely with the Jew. *Much Ado About Nothing* is a jolly comedy to match with *The Comedy of Errors*. *Julius Caesar, Richard III* and *Coriolanus* are interesting historical plays, and *Hamlet, Macbeth* and *Romeo and Juliet* are among the best of his tragedies. If a person would read just the plays mentioned in the thoughtful way we have indicated here, he would gain a benefit whose great value never can be estimated, and thereafter all reading would seem easier and more delightful [IX, 437–438].

Because *Journeys through Bookland* was designed for readers young and old, the list of recommended plays encourages choice and breadth. Those who follow Sylvester's scheme to read Shakespeare gain knowledge of the work of the greatest writer in English and also increase reading skill and appreciation that will enhance whatever they read. Shakespeare requires work, but coming to know his plays is the crowning achievement in reading and also gives pleasure.

Olive Beaupré Miller, ed., *My Book House* (1920/1921)

My Book House (1920/1921) serves as a summation of home libraries. The first edition had six volumes, I–IV published in 1920 and V and VI in 1921. Through sixteen editions the six-volume set changed little; then Edition 17 (1932 and 1933) introduced vast changes in format; sets of six became twelve, with books of about 216–240 pages instead of the original hefty 448 pages. The first Rainbow Edition in 1937 introduced some alterations in contents, and updating continued in subsequent editions. The story of publication, documented by Dorothy Loring Taylor, is both complicated and exciting.[14]

Olive Beaupré Miller (1883–1968) was a native Mid-Westerner, of a distinguished family that encouraged her early intellectual interests; she graduated from Smith College in 1904.[15] An energetic and imaginative writer, she followed *My Book House* with *My Book of History: A Picturesque Tale of Progress,* four volumes (1929–1933), subsequently published in eight volumes as *A Picturesque Tale of Progress* (1935). Concurrent with revising, Miller wrote stories and poems, some for her collections. *Heroes of the Bible* (1940), her last major effort — 82,000 copies — was a more overt expression of her deep religious feeling, with ecumenical qualities; Miller was a member of the Christian Science Church. Writing about *My Book House*, religious leaders and educators judged her stories "one of the greatest things you could provide for a home or church school library"; they shared "a broad Christian concept of social living" (67).

Until their divorce in 1935, Henry Miller, Olive Beaupré Miller's husband, managed the business aspects of the publishing house they founded together; then she added that responsibility to her writing and editing. In addition to the longevity of this home library, two other distinctive points are remarkable. First, the work for *My Book House,* both production and sales, was done almost entirely by women, including marketing by door-to-door sales; and second, the Depression of the 1930s did not lessen the success of the series, although constant ingenuity was used to make the books attractive. The first edition was packaged in a cardboard house, which explains the name *My Book House* and suggests a home library. Books published by The Bookhouse for Children never had jackets; Miller wanted "to arouse in the child a deep love of his book ... and anything that separates the hand of the child from the beloved possession — his book — defeats the purpose" (94).

My Book House is devoted to literature and emphasizes English and American authors, but also includes major non–English writers. Importantly, Miller's work demonstrates that a home library which sustains Edwardian attitudes and literary choices was successful throughout the twentieth century. Letters affirm childhood delight and strong influence. A mother who purchased the set in 1931 recorded its salient qualities — "In addition to supplying beloved stories, it built character. Truth, honesty, generosity, persistence; these are abstractions beyond the concept of small children except in story form with a moral in terms they can understand" (51) — and the academic success of her daughters to attend university. High sentiment, a view of literature as the epitome of moral tradition, has not changed from Edwardian ideals for children's literature.

Volumes in *My Book House* are large (seven by nine and a quarter inches), but big print and bright illustrations make pages friendly and accessible. The original edition was bound in black cloth, but then other colors, especially a whitewashed green "Fabrikoid" were introduced; the gilt lettering and paste-on pictures on the covers, different for each title, did not change. Beginning with the seventeenth edition, blue cloth covers became standard, still with titles stamped in gold and a pasted paper color illustration, an Edwardian style. End papers for earliest volumes depict small children who point toward a magical castle on a cliff, an image later revised to include a large tree on the left and a more fanciful and slender castle on the right with children still moving across the center; still later came mounted knights in armor on the left and a Viking ship on the right, bordered by a city wall above and shoreline below. Here style is unmistakably 1920s/1930s modern, bold lines and bright color, an Art Deco characteristic. Later end papers introduce figures from the texts. While illustrations in early editions are colorful, they are muted in comparison to later bright reprintings, dominated by a palette of orange, deep blue-green, and brown.

At first Miller did not particularly emphasize Shakespeare. Early editions contain six songs—"Jog On" and "When Daffodils Begin to Peer" (*In the Nursery,* I, 32 and 54), "Ariel's Song" (*Up One Pair of Stairs,* II, 269), "Lullaby for Titania" and "The Peddler's Song" (*Through Fairy Halls,* III, 25 and 256), and "Under the Greenwood Tree" (*From the Tower Window,* V, 74)—and a substantial biography that incorporates accounts of medieval drama and the Elizabethan theatre (*The Latch Key,* VI, 49–63).[16] Stories of plays came in the expanded twelve volumes (with old and new titles, so that numbers change). First was the perennial *A Midsummer Night's Dream,* an original retelling made for *Through Fairy Halls* (VI, 36–57); then Lamb's *The Winter's Tale* in *The Magic Garden,* VII; followed by an original *The Tempest* in *Flying Sails,* VIII. *As You Like It* was added in *From the Tower Window,* X, to give "*older*" children another story from Shakespeare. Since these additions came much later, I note them only to mark the increasing prominence of Shakespeare for children in the United States—situated within traditions of fairy tale, magic garden, sea story, national epic—and his biography in "halls of fame."

"Down by the River Avon. William Shakespeare (English, 1564–1616)" follows two biographies of Americans (Phineas T. Barnum and Louisa May Alcott) in *The Latch Key* (VI, 49–63; *Halls of Fame,* XII, in later editions), so that he is first among non–Americans. The cover picture shows a young girl and younger boy reaching to open a great door, clearly an iconic gateway to further reading. For later editions, the scene is a great hall with columns, through which stroll an older boy, who gazes at a painting of a man, and a girl who faces the opposite way. All costumes are Edwardian, but the children became significantly older. Miller's biography identifies Shakespeare's father John and describes the town of Stratford, including the school and delights of free countryside, market days, and neighboring castles. But it is also an account of festivals, particularly May Day, when the school had a holiday and Will could attend. A small illustration shows a boy skipping happily (VI, 52), while opposite participants (St. George and the dragon, with its queen and fool, Morris dancers, Robin Hood, Marion, and Friar Tuck) dance with linked hands to the Maypole, as a man plays a bagpipe (VI, 53). Such information stemmed from early twentieth-century attraction to folklore. A fascinating description of miracle or mystery plays—episodes from the Bible—includes accounts of properties and costs, and vivid pictures of Hell's Mouth and Noah's ark, high on its pageant wagon (VI, 56–57). An early example of cultural history is *Shakespeare the Boy: With Sketches of The Home and School Life, The Games and Sports, The Manners, Customs, and Folk-lore of the Time* (1896), a biography for children, by American educator William James Rolfe (1827–1910). It is a compendium of information, long quoted sources, and appended recommendations for "School Courses in Shakespeare."

Biographical details explain that Will left Anne for London; she waves goodbye in front of the cottage (illustration VI, 60). A description of the theater is supported by a picture of a performance, observed by people in the galleries, lords on the stage, and groundlings standing below (VI, 61). A sign explains, "This is a Court Room in Venice"; Portia, Shylock, Antonio, Bassanio, and the Doge are easily identified. *The Merchant of Venice,* then, is a play connected to children, even though *My Book House* lacks a retelling.

Success in the big city need not and does not corrupt youth:

> [Y]oung Will kept his head marvelously well in spite of his success, and he avoided the wild dissipations that were ruining his fellow-dramatists, though he loved life and mirth as well as any and had no smallest trace of harshness in his blithe and genial nature. He worked hard, studying at French and Italian in his spare time, saving money for his family and making visits every year to his beloved Stratford [VI, 61–62].

Thus William Shakespeare was an exemplary human being for children to emulate. He was part of his exciting age, the time of Queen Elizabeth with its awakening spirit of inquiry and adventure and emerging nationalism, exemplified by explorers like Drake, Hawkins, and Frobisher. Indeed, "the drama of the day became the mirror in which all these active forces were reflected." Shakespeare explored not the Americas but "the world of human nature.... Into that unknown sea sailed the intrepid mariner, Shakespeare, and he charted it in his mighty dramas as none other has ever done, the great Columbus of the newly discovered world of man's heart and mind and spirit." The analogy is an engaging comparison of writer and adventurer, embarked upon discovery to find great rewards for himself and others. The references also point to American affinity with the English writer who "still remains the greatest dramatist of all ages who wrote 'not for an age but for all time'" (VI, 63).

Combined with biographies in *The Latch Key* are several indexes to direct reading and use of *My Book House.* These changed over the years and many editions. The first had a "General Index of Authors, Titles and Leading Characters" (368–389), "Geographical Index" (390–396), "Special Subjects Index" (397–419), and "Ethical Theme Index" (420–445), as well as "A Guide to the Pronunciation of Proper Names in My Book House" (446–448). Later editions dropped the "Geographical Index." The most telling alteration is the replacement of "Ethical Theme Index" with "Character Building Index. A Guide for

Parents," with monumental changes. For example, "Compassion" and "Chivalry" were gone, but "Courage" remained, and there was a very long "Child's Daily Activities." Nevertheless, the unchanged account of Shakespeare could gloss many surviving traits of character.

Percy MacKaye, *Caliban by the Yellow Sands* (1916)

Admiration for Shakespeare marks a consistent and strong affinity between the United States and England, and a fitting concluding gloss to this section is a work by Percy MacKaye (1875–1956), poet and dramatist, teacher and lecturer. *Caliban by the Yellow Sands: A Community Masque of the Art of the Theatre* (1916) was "Devised and Written to Commemorate the Tercentenary of the Death of Shakespeare." MacKaye's preface situates 23 April 1916 in "a self-destroying world," where World War I, which was to mark the end of Edwardian idealism, raged and devastated:

> Over seas, the choral hymns of canon acclaim his death; in battle trenches artists are turned subtly ingenious to inter his art; War, Lust, and Death are risen in power to restore the primeval reign of Setebos.
> Here in America, where the neighboring waters of his "vexed Bermoothes" lie more calm than those about his own native isle, here only is given some practical opportunity for his uninterable spirit to create new splendid symbols for peace through harmonious international expression.[17]

MacKaye drew inspiration from *The Tempest* but created his own characters. Caliban is

> that passionate child-curious part of us all [whether as individuals or as races], grovelling close to his aboriginal origins, yet groping up and staggering — with almost rhythmic falls and back-sliding — toward that serener plane of pity and love, reason and disciplined will, where Miranda and Prospero commune with Ariel and his Spirits [xv].

He called his work a masque to indicate its symbolic qualities, and a photograph of his *Pageant and Masque of Saint Louis* (May 1914) shows the scale of community participation: 150,000 spectators and 7,500 citizens took part. MacKaye's theme — "Caliban seeking to learn the art of Prospero— is, of course, the slow education of mankind through the influence of coöperative art, that is, of the art of the theatre in its full social scope" (xvii) — is a cry for education, high moral sentiment. A swift chronological survey of the theatre — similar to those in biographies — comes through three interludes: classical, medieval, and Elizabethan. Most telling are "inner scenes" interlaced with the main action. Like editors of home libraries, MacKaye provided his audience with selections from Shakespeare, ten Inner Scenes, "conceived as being conjured by Prospero and enacted by the Spirits of Ariel" (xvi). The plays quoted are diverse: *Antony and Cleopatra, Troilus and Cressida, Julius Caesar, Hamlet, King Henry VIII, Romeo and Juliet, The Merchant of Venice, The Winter's Tale,*

As You Like It, The Merry Wives of Windsor, and *King Henry V.* Members of the audience, children and adults, were likely to recognize items familiar from home libraries. Although the United States had not yet entered the Great War, the final quotation leaves little doubt about where sympathies lay: "Once more unto the breach, dear friends, once more, ... Cry, 'God for Harry, England, and Saint George!'" (137–138). A preliminary sketch shows a warrior with shield and sword scaling a great rise, while flights of arrows in the background and staves stuck in the ground behind him depict combat. Patriotism, pride in nation / race is a major inspiration for literary histories for children.

Literary Histories

H(enrietta) E. Marshall, *English Literature for Boys and Girls* (1909)

One of the most enterprising writers of traditional stories for children was H(enrietta) E. Marshall (b. 1876). T.C. and E.C. Jack published many of her books, notably *Our Island Story* (1905), the most popular Edwardian children's history, published as *An Island Story* in the United States. *English Literature for Boys and Girls* (1909) is a companion volume, both in physical appearance and patriotic enthusiasm. Their common intention was storytelling and an unapologetic appeal to enjoyment, an objective that Marshall, echoing Kenneth Grahame, justified in a preface addressed, "To 'the Olympians'— An Explanation":

> [M]y desire has been to produce a book which a boy or girl will read, not as a task, but as a pleasure.... The object with which I write being to amuse and interest rather than to teach, a great deal has been left out which must of necessity have been included in a book meant for school use.[18]

She included not "all the great names" but representative writers, especially those who "widened and deepened our literature." However, she chose some items "chiefly because of appeal to young readers" and selected not necessarily the greatest work "but that which most easily comes within the grasp of young minds," while she "silently passes over others for obvious reasons." Marshall had already written for Jack's Told to the Children Series—*Robin Hood, William Tell, Guy of Warwick, Roland*—all from the Middle Ages. *English Literature for Boys and Girls* gives more space to the early period in the "belief that what was attractive to a youthful nation will be most attractive to the young of that nation" (x). Chapter I, "In the Listening Time," explains that there have always been stories, even when there were no books "in the dim, far-off times when our forefathers were wild, naked savages" (1). Marshall, then, took a Whiggish view of history and linked the development of literature—stories, then history, then poetry—to the growth of a nation. She saw a parallel to the growth of a child's understanding and taste, a gradual increase in knowledge, with ever more keys to "rooms in the fairy palaces of our Literature" that gradually open only to reveal so many others that "you can never hope to open all the doors even to peep inside" (4).

English Literature for Boys and Girls is massive; its 687 pages include a chronology, an index, and lists of "Books to Read" at the end of each chapter. Eighty-five chapters span from "The Cattle Raid at Cooley" through "Tennyson — the Poet of Friendship." Only three writers (Chaucer, Spenser, and Shakespeare) warrant three chapters; illustrations signal Shakespeare's honored place. He is at the center of five writers on the white cloth stamped cover, one of two on the end papers (Sir Walter Scott is the other), and the only writer in a small decoration on the title page. Marshall, in typical Victorian fashion, stressed biography, which the illustrator J(oseph) R(adcliffe) Skelton (fl. 1888–1927) reinforced. Seventeen of twenty color pages are portraits, usually in a situation that tells a story. Shakespeare with children in Stratford is iconic. Three non-portraits depict the transmission of English literature — a monk writes in a scriptorium, a minstrel sings in an Anglo-Saxon hall, a medieval play is performed on a platform in a market square.

"About the First Theatres" chronicles the story from monk and minstrel, the later split between poet and dramatist, including references to *Ralph Roister Doister* and *Gorboduc*. Marshall surveyed theatrical practices and listed thirteen dramatists of the sixteenth century, when acting and shows replaced the storytelling of the Middle Ages. The next two chapters relate the life of the "bright star" that outshines all others, not only in England but for "the whole world ... wherever poetry is read and plays are played, the name of William Shakespeare is known and revered" (278).

Chapter XLV, "Shakespeare — The Boy," describes his family, birth, and life in Stratford until after his marriage and early departure — following his being caught as a poacher, an activity that he enjoyed from boyhood. Marshall's speculation has two main points. Shakespeare seems not to have enjoyed the grammar school as much as he loved the outdoors: she quoted "A whining schoolboy ... creeping like snail unwillingly to school" (280). He perhaps saw performances of strolling players and the pageantry of Queen Elizabeth's visit to the Earl of Leicester at Kenilworth. Artists recreated the latter: Sir Walter Scott in his novel *Kenilworth* (1821) and Frederick Cowie in his painting *Queen Elizabeth at Kenilworth* (1849). The Warwick Pageant of 1906, one of several popular, patriotic celebrations in the decade before World War I, dramatized the meeting of the boy Shakespeare with Queen Elizabeth to reenact the popular myth. The episode tied the poet dramatist to local history and established a point of view for children, as does Skelton's picture. Master Shakespeare stands before the birthplace in Stratford-on-Avon; with him are children — in the foreground a little girl holds her doll, three boys play at marbles on the right, and two others at tag on the left (290). According to the book's iconography,

Shakespeare as children's literature is the point of J.R. Skelton's depiction of him as a familiar and friendly figure in Stratford-upon-Avon, where the young include a little girl he has stopped to greet, while in the background boys run or play at marbles. T.C. and E.C. Jack used the illustration in H.E. Marshall's *English Literature for Boys and Girls* (1909) and in Henry Gilbert's *Stories of Great Writers* (1914), In Days of Old Series.

then, Shakespeare is the friend of playful children; all other writers are pictured alone or with adults, often fellow writers. The only other image of a child is a fair-haired boy in the Anglo-Saxon hall who listens to the minstrel's song of the deeds of heroes.

"Shakespeare — the Man" begins in London, where his earliest work was to hold horses outside the theatre, but soon he was writing plays. Marshall stressed that their stories were not original, but original treatments of old stories; she also said that children would be interested to follow Shakespeare's sources when they were older. The paean of Shakespeare is for his knowledge of human character and feeling that is both Elizabethan and universal; he is not, and never could be, "old-fashioned," for as his contemporary claimed, "He was not of an age but for all times" (288). Marshall deflected charges that Shakespeare was "coarse," acknowledging that "it was the fashion of his day to be more open and plain spoken than we are" (291). She limited factual details to number of works, division of plays into histories, comedies, and tragedies for convenience, and as markers of the stages of his life. Chapter XLVI ends with Shakespeare's happy return to Stratford and untimely death from a "fever, brought on, no doubt, by the evil smells and bad air by which people lived surrounded in those days before they had learned to be clean in house and street" (291). After this assertion of Edwardian superiority, Marshall described the burial and monuments in Stratford Parish Church and quoted the inscriptions.

This final chapter also retells *The Merchant of Venice*. Marshall was mainly interested in the trial, with its lesson of mercy and forgiveness, and to a lesser extent the Jew Shylock. She observed, "In those days Jews were ill-treated and despised, and there was great hatred between them and Christians" (294), but quoted in full Shylock's long apologia (295–296). She omitted other suitors, made Bassanio's choice come quickly, and focused on Portia, "happy, triumphant, humble, no longer the great lady with untold wealth, with lands and palaces and radiant beauty, but merely a woman who has given her love" (297–298). From Portia, the womanly ideal, a long declaration of love is quoted (297–298). Unlike most retellers, Marshall specified the play's structure: "this part of the story has brought us to the fourth act" (299). The trial scene (IV.i.180–261 and 297–341) is quoted with only a few lines paraphrased, the longest quotation in the book (300–303). Thus Marshall enhanced challenge and pleasure, assuming that the scene and language are sufficiently compelling to inspire effort beyond simple storytelling, a first step toward how children would read as they grew older. Similarly, she challenged understanding of humanity, when she applied the principle of mercy in her judgment of Shylock, who is not allowed to go "until he is humiliated, and so heaped with disgrace and insult that we are sorry for him" (303). The giving of rings ends this section, and a very short paragraph summarizes the final act. Marshall's recommendations for further reading come at the end of this third chapter devoted to Shakespeare (304). A complete list of plays is her most specific and extensive bibliography. But she also recommended collections of children's stories of Shakespeare — Mary Macleod, Charles and Mary Lamb, and Jeanie Lang, all discussed in earlier chapters. Marshall's popular survey significantly promoted great works of literature by giving a context and critical observations not characteristic of brief introductions to retellings. It could, despite her disclaimer, be useful in school.

Edward Parrott, *The Pageant of English Literature* (1914)

Not quite so large, and Romantic in a different way, Edward Parrott's *The Pageant of English Literature* (1914) makes Shakespeare most dominant, the only writer given four chapters — Chaucer and Milton each have two.[19] "23. Shakespeare, the Boy" begins with Stratford, in "the heart of England," which is "the literary mecca of the English-speaking world" (178). Parrott, who earlier wrote *The Pageant of British History* (1908), described Queen Elizabeth's visit to Kenilworth, when according to legend the boy Shakespeare met the queen. Parrott's imaginary boy Shakespeare thinks of plays, and London players visit the area. An account of an Elizabethan schoolday, a ten-hour experience, refers to Lilly's *Latin Grammar* and Erasmus's *Colloquies*. Time out of doors was happy, and Parrott quoted the song "When daisies pied" from *Love's Labour's Lost*. "24. The Stage in Shakespeare's Day" interlaces biographical information — his father's fortunes, his own early marriage at age eighteen, the deer-stealing episode — with accounts of companies of players and a description of the Globe Theatre. "25. Shakespeare the Man" summarizes his career in London, Greene's attack and Meres's praise, lists plays, notes Shakespeare's indifference to publication, the First Folio from Heminge and Condell, and retirement to Stratford. Parrott declared Theodore Watts-Dunton's painting *Christmas at the Mermaid* an epitome of "the early rapture of his Elizabethan models" — Ben Jonson, Raleigh, Drayton, Lodge, Dekker, Chapman — who toast Will (198).

"26. The Visions of Shakespeare," justifies such praise; Coleridge called him "the greatest genius that perhaps human nature has yet produced" (200). Parrott's selected plays and succinct judgments are significant. He favored admirable role models: faithful Imogen and Cordelia, paragon daughters, exemplars of filial love, and attractive young lovers Romeo and Juliet. The "happy music" of the comedies begins with *A Midsummer Night's Dream* and *Merchant of Venice*. However, Parrott paid most attention to Sir John Falstaff, "the crown of all Shakespeare's comic invention, and, indeed, the most humorous figure of all English literature" (207). Parrott admitted in this unusual evaluation for children that Falstaff is gross and coarse and has "no moral sense, and no self-respect"; but he admired his skill with the quick lie and that he is first to laugh at himself and ended with sympathy:

> We ought to find Falstaff utterly repulsive, yet, strange to say, everybody has a kindly thought for him, and when, at last, he babbles of green fields and passes away, "an it had been a Christom child," only the sourest of moralists can refuse him the tribute of a smiling regret [208].

This challenging passage is also exceptional because Parrott otherwise "passes unnoticed the heroes and heroines of history and Roman plays" (208).

Generous and thoughtful appreciation of Shakespeare's understanding unfortunately did not extend so far to women. *The Taming of the Shrew* is a "noisy, bustling, almost farcical story"; and Kate at the end embodies "a temper of mind wholly out of consonance with the ideals of the modern woman" (208). These Edwardian perceptions were less insightful and flexible than those sympathizing with male complexity. Parrott deemed *Twelfth Night* a "poetical romance" with "abounding mirth and delicate charm." Beatrice and Benedict provide greatest interest in *Much Ado about Nothing,* while the statue scene is salient in *The Winter's Tale,* an exemplary moment for a noble woman.

Parrott's book of pageants includes five historical paintings, four color pages and one black and white. Edgar Bundy's *The First Performance of "The Merry Wives of Windsor," 1599* shows audience and players (184), while Daniel Maclise's *The Play Scene of "Hamlet"* is a dark interior lightened by the whiteness of Ophelia (192), also the subject of Sir John Millais's famous *Ophelia* (200). Millais's engaging *Rosalind and Celia,* resting in the forest as Touchstone drowses, is not in color (204). "The Shakespeare Bust in The Parish Church, Stratford-on-Avon" supports the biography of England's most glorious poet (208). Again the publisher Nelson combined great art and great literature for children.

Amy Cruse, *English Literature through the Ages* (1914)

The most sophisticated literary history, one from which undergraduates could learn, is Amy Cruse's *English Literature through the Ages,* also published in 1914. Another large volume, 592 pages, it is divided into two books, with the eighteenth century, characterized as "urban," as the point of separation. Cruse (b. 1870) professed to concentrate upon individual masterpieces, to tell the story of English literature "through the stories of individual books" in "considerable detail, aiming at making each appear to her readers as a living reality, not merely a constituent part of a great whole known as English literature."[20] In practice, she presented much biographical material and social context. "Chapter XVIII: The Plays of Shakespeare" begins with a speculative account of his boyhood, somewhat supported by references to information in the plays and what "tradition" says. Cruse posited a change of heart, a maturing. Shakespeare left school early to help after his father John's loss of fortune, according to one biographer working as a butcher and noted "as an idler, seeking abroad some relief from the harshness of his home circumstances" (157). Early marriage to Anne Hathaway at age eighteen came when his father's circumstances were most acute. Cruse cited the birth of a daughter in 1583 and the twins in 1585. Now Shakespeare's story becomes an inspiring model for change by idle and irresolute youth:

> By this time, it would seem, the better mind of William Shakespeare was coming back to him. He had allowed himself to become disheartened by the unfortunate circumstances of his life, had drifted along without any set purpose, and had yielded easily to the temptations that came in his way. Now the resolution that had so much influence on his after career was slowly forming in his mind—the resolution to mend his father's broken fortunes, to make the name of Shakespeare respected once more in Stratford-on-Avon, to give his family a happy prosperous home in his native place. The careless, happy-tempered lad whose good looks and frank manners had gained for him many friends in whose company it was so easy and pleasant to be idle, was soon to develop into the brave-hearted strenuous worker who, from the humblest beginning, rose by his own exertions to fame and fortune [158].

Here Cruse rivaled Samuel Smiles (1812–1904), the enormously popular and influential Victorian author of *Self-Help* (1859), often reprinted by Edwardians, and American Horatio Alger (1834–1899), who wrote exemplary novels of adventure for boys. Cruse, like many biographers (Victorian and recent!), laced her narrative with disclaimers—"says a tradition ... may perhaps infer ... we do not know ... it would seem ... we believe"—as she filled in from known facts.

These included naming plays in sequence of composition with brief comment on Shakespeare's developing mind, as urged by Furnivall. Cruse's fullest effort to tell the story of a masterpiece is *As You Like It*, praised for its evocation of nature, one of his "company of girl-characters which is one of the notable glories of Shakespeare's works," and especially interesting because Shakespeare took the part of Adam (166). In *King Lear* she found

> an agony so stupendous and heart-breaking that to contemplate it calmly is almost an impossibility.... There is no fearful national convulsion, no devastating war, no deeply laid plot... The rending of natural, human ties, the rejection of natural human duties—from these apparently small beginnings the great agony begins [168].

Cruse strove for balance: disregard of filial obligations is uplifted by a reminder that "the simple, loving fulfillment of a daughter's duty suffices to make a heroine," and so with "a stern sense of the compulsion laid upon a man to do the plain duty appointed for him and not to evade it upon pretext"; she concluded, "The cloud was thick and black, but Shakespeare never lost his faith that somewhere behind it there was still a sun in the heavens; and soon the sun shone through the clouds, and made a glorious ending to the poet's splendid, though not unclouded day" (169).

In his last years Shakespeare wrote three dramas, "full of a radiant loveliness which transfigures and etherealizes them without taking away their warm living interest" (169–170). The term "romance" for *The Winter's Tale, Cymbeline*, and *The Tempest* signals these qualities and departs from earlier comedies; their difference is manifest in heroines:

> Perdita, Imogen, and Miranda stand apart. There has been nothing like them in any of the previous plays. They are neither brilliant nor witty, they have nothing of the charming airs and graces that delight us in Shakespeare's earlier creations. They are sweet, lovable, loving girls, of an exquisite purity and rare beauty that, in some wonderful way is shone in their every word and action. It is perhaps not too fanciful to see Judith Shakespeare once more as her father's model. He has learnt now that there is more in his daughter than the high spirits and the grace which first charmed him; he has learnt to reverence girlhood in her person, and to spend all his creative skill in doing it honour [170].

By current theories of gender, this argument is unsettling, but it parallels Cruse's earlier improvisation of Shakespeare as a reformed youth. Biography as interpretation urges high sentiment and unselfish behavior, ideals for young readers. Cruse's last point is predictable: "In Prospero it is inevitable that we should see some shadow of the writer of the play. Shakespeare himself, one cannot help thinking, meant to signify an intention of bringing his work as a dramatist to a close when he wrote the words 'I'll break my staff'" (170).

The experience of the Great War did not destroy Cruse's idealism, which survived in *The Golden Road in English Literature: From Beowulf to Bernard Shaw* (1931):

> It is difficult to say just why Imogen, and Perdita, and Miranda, so charm the heart of all who read them.... They are such pure, bright figures that they seem, like Spenser's Una, to make "a sunshine in the shady place" and give something of their own beauty to the whole play.
> All three plays come very near to being tragedies, and the happy ending is only reached through much suffering.... In all three plays there are older characters who take parts as important as those of the young lovers; the story of Hermione, in *The Winter's Tale,* is as interesting as that of her daughter Perdita; and Prospero, Miranda's father, is the character in *The Tempest* on whom the whole plot depends.[21]

Cruse recounted something of the lovers in Act IV, but also Leontes's rejection of Hermione. Here her longest summary is *A Midsummer Night's Dream,* and she quoted Dogberry from *Much Ado about Nothing*. Moreover, she acknowledged that much of Shakespeare's biography is fanciful, since few facts are known [sic!].

Henry Gilbert, *Stories of Great Writers* (1914)

The third literary history for children in 1914 was Henry Gilbert's *Stories of Great Writers,* published by T.C. and E.C. Jack, in their In Days of Old Series that combined history (*Stories of Rome, Stories of France, Stories of Scotland*) and popular legendary literature (*Robin Hood and His Merry Men* and *The Knights of the Round Table*). Gilbert was selective, major authors rather than a broad survey. Since he supported Victorian and Edwardian views that writers from the childhood of the race best suit children, four are from the Middle Ages ("A Bard of the Britons" [the battle of Cattraeth], "When the Gleemen Sang of *Beowulf,*" "The Poet of Poor Men" [Langland] and "The Father of English Writers" [Chaucer]). But Shakespeare, with the longest chapter, is at the center of *Stories of Great Writers,* followed by three shorter chapters ("The First Journalists" [Clibborn, Defoe, Addison and Steele], "When Poets Lived in Garrets" [Johnson and Goldsmith], "The Wizard of the North" [Sir Walter Scott]). Gilbert was closer to Parrot than Cruse. He stressed history, of which literature is another side; his aim was to tell the stories of lives, which he believed would engage children more readily.[22]

> Literature is really the record of the feelings and thoughts of men and women, which they have written down as the result of their experiences, or of experiences which they imagine others might have. Actual experience, or the vivid imagination which appears to be most like actual experience, forms the basis of the finest and most enduring of our literature [vi].

While this seems to echo moralists who oppose fancy, fairy tales and legends, Gilbert was inspired not by a sense of moral rectitude but an urge to bring alive "great personalities of British literature," to make British children realize that they are connected to earlier literature and should take pride in this relationship. He urged that writers and the people whose stories they tell are as alive as friends. Moreover, they are of the same race:

> They were of the same blood as yourselves, had the same colour of eyes and hair, and the same "family likeness"; they liked to play games and practical jokes, and generally enjoyed the sun and the wind as much as you do. They are as much your "relations" as those of the past generation of your own kindred [vi].

Patriotism is the subtext; each chapter combines specific biography and cultural history, evocations of the world in which writers lived—great hall, court, theatre, city.

"The Story of Shakespeare" opens with a recreated scene in which "The players have come!" echoes though the streets of Stratford on a May afternoon in 1577. Gilbert described how players transformed themselves and the crowd who beheld them. Under the patronage of Her Highness, the Countess of Essex, actors are to perform *The Misfortunes of Arthur* and *Ralph Roister Doister* in the Guildhall. Among those who hear them are boys from the Free School, especially "a square-built little lad of about thirteen years of age, with ruddy cheeks, chestnut curls, and hazel eyes, which are full of life and spirit, ... little Will Shakespeare" (80). Gilbert recounted his prior encounters with actors and an early impulse to set out—"thus we may imagine" (81). He interlaced biographical facts (father John's fortunes) and traditions (a butcher, a teacher) with interpretations of character. At school with the quick and sensitive mind that he possessed, [Will] must have been an apt pupil, and I do not doubt that, like many another studious village boy before and since his time, he ransacked the chests and shelves of all his parents' friends, if they yielded to his frequent inquiries, and read all the books he could discover [82].

Poetry and a love of nature, precisely observed, are early attributes, but the boy also adventures with his fellows. Will Shakespeare, in short, is the ideal schoolboy; any child reading his story would be inspired to work hard and seriously, and to retain a spirit of play.

The turning point in Shakespeare's life was his marriage and need to support a wife and three babies. When in 1587 his father was imprisoned and the Lord Chamberlain's Players came to town, the young man resolved to go to London to improve his fortunes. A rich and bustling account of the city (85–88) contrasts sharply with the pastoral idyll of Warwickshire. Gilbert imagined how hard it was for a country youth to make his way, citing a tradition that Shakespeare began running errands and caring for the horses of theatre patrons. One large section is a general description of Elizabethan theatrical practice interlaced with details from Shakespeare's life. Soon he became a reviser of plays for James Burbage. Shakespeare's success came from close observation, theatrical imagination, and "a strangely fine way of writing poetry" (90). Information about contemporaries includes his rivalry with Robert Greene, "a dissolute but clever man" who reviled him, even after death in *A Groat's Worth of Wit bought with a Million of Repentance;* and, more characteristically, friendship and collaboration with Marlowe, Francis Meres's praise in *Palladis Tamia, Wit's Treasury,* witty exchanges with Ben Jonson and acting in *Every Man in His Humour.* Gilbert, who gave titles of Shakespeare's plays in clusters by dates of composition, again evaluated his personality and process of composition as he learned more and more, especially from meeting people of keen wit. Shakespeare is a man of his age, but "with finer thoughts and feelings, amiable and friendly, very good company, but not self-indulgent in the taverns": "He was a serious and conscientious man, thoughtful beyond his fellows, and with the grip upon himself which the finest natures often possess" (92–93). The greatest English writer is an exemplary model of balance, discipline, and good will. Further inspiration for young people is to be found in Shakespeare's filial piety.

Gilbert explained his return to Stratford — "the runaway son having now returned with a fortune, was determined to force men's regard by making a display which should impress them"— payment of his father's debts and purchase of New Place, to which he retired only in 1609 and wrote the last four romances. His life was then one of serenity, a wise man aware of the evil in human nature but also of forgiveness: "The whole of his later plays teach the great lesson which, two centuries and a half before, Langland taught — let your charity be infinite." Although Shakespeare's "tender" attachment to his daughter Susanna was a joy after the death of his parents and his youngest brother

Edmund, the retirement granted him after "a hard and strenuous life" was brief (104–105). Skelton's repeated color illustration "It was only Master Shakespeare" signals him as the poet / playwright for the young (104). It is one of eight illustrations from Marshall's *English Literature for Boys and Girls*. Jack was a thrifty — and astute — publisher.

Eva March Tappan, *A Brief History of English Literature* (1905/1914)

Eva March Tappan, already discussed as editor of *The Children's Hour*, wrote *A Brief History of English Literature* (1905/1914), published by Houghton Mifflin in the United States and then by George G. Harrap in Britain. It is comparatively modest, fourteen chapters in 320 pages. In contrast to English literary histories, this American one included more facts in a comprehensive survey that details principal events, writers in all genres, and astute critical analyses.[23] Tappan's preface enumerated her convictions:

> *First:* That the prime object of studying literature is to arouse the impulse to read the greatest English masterpieces.
> *Second:* That it is more important to understand the times during which an author wrote, and the reasons for his writing as he did, than to be familiar with a mere catalogue of names, titles, and dates.
> *Third:* That it is better to be well acquainted with a few authors and their works than to know many superficially [i].

Her first four chapters present the Middle Ages; two, the Elizabethans; another two, Puritans and Cavaliers; one to the Age of Anne, and another to literature under the Georges; the last four chapters, writers of the nineteenth century, then finished with two on American literature (Poetry and Prose). A revised edition *A Short History of England's Literature* (1920 and 1933) was reorganized into eight chapters; it eliminated American writers who became part of another book, *A Short History of America's Literature* (1932) that included the twentieth century with chapters added by Rose Adelaide Witham. The revision organized chapters by centuries with subtitles to describe periods ("V–XI, The Early English"; "XII–XIII, The Norman English Period"; "XIV, Chaucer's Century"; "XV, The People's Century"; "XVI, Shakespeare's Century"; "XVII, Puritans and Royalists"; "XVIII, The Century of Prose"; "XIX, The Century of the Novel"). Changes recognized two dominant writers (Chaucer and Shakespeare) and genres (for the later centuries) rather than British monarchs. In the early twentieth century, period courses characterized English studies — along with major authors (Chaucer, Shakespeare, Milton) and genres (drama, novel) — although there were discrepancies. Tappan acknowledged limitations of arbitrary dates in *A Short History of England's Literature* in the life and work of Shakespeare; she discussed earlier works as the climactic conclusion of the sixteenth / his century and began the seventeenth century with his later plays and death in 1616.

Topics are numbered (148 in all) and subtitled in bold type, while insets in bold highlight authors, titles, dates, events. The sixteenth century begins with item thirty-nine; "William Shakespeare, 1564–1616" is item fifty-eight, an indication of thoroughness. Tappan's biographical matter puts Stratford in context — its proximity to Kenilworth, where the eleven-year-old boy Shakespeare was likely to have seen Queen Elizabeth and entertainments in her honor, several visits of London actors to Stratford — as well as John Shakespeare's changing situation and William's early marriage and move to London. Specially noted early plays reflected personal and current preferences for children. *Love's Labour's Lost* is a "Merry little comedy ... full of fun and frolic, and fairly sparkles with witty repartee" (98). While Tappan merely named *A Midsummer Night's Dream* and *The Comedy of Errors,* both "merry, sparkling comedies," she emphasized Shakespeare's skill in the historical plays, a product of "a time when the poet seemed fascinated by the history of his own land" (98). Never a "student-author" who searched old records, he had a "special power as a dramatist of history ... his sympathetic imagination by which he understood the men of bygone days." Later historical research has often proved "his interpretation of some historical character, opposed as it was to the common belief of his time, ... correct" (99).

Nevertheless, Tappan's archetype, richly justified, is *The Merchant of Venice*:

> In the *Merchant of Venice* perhaps quite as much as in any other play, Shakespeare shows his power to make us hold a character in the balance. Shylock is cruel and miserly, but we cannot help seeing with a touch of sympathy that he is oppressed and lonely; Bassanio is a careless young spendthrift, but so boyish and so frank that we forget to be severe; Portia is perfectly conscious of the value of her wealth and her beauty, but at love's command she is ready to drop both lightly into the hands of Bassanio [100].

Rather than a worrying example of anti–Semitism to be avoided, Tappan found Shakespeare's play a fine model to teach the complexity of human behavior; she perceived good and bad qualities in all characters so that absolute, simplistic evaluation was impossible. Portia's famous argument for the quality of mercy stated the ideal. Tappan's summary ended with a judgment that Shakespeare "solved the great dramatic problem, how to make the characters seem like real people" (102).

This prepares for the later plays, written when Shakespeare's "genius broadened and deepened" beyond his skill in writing comedies and histories to "his deeper comedies and a superb group of tragedies, *Hamlet, King Lear,* and others."

> His plays grow more intense, more powerful. Sometimes he uses bitter irony. Stern retribution is visited upon both weak and wicked. There is a touch of gloom. Magnificent as these dramas are, it is good to come away from them to the ripple of the sea, to the breeze of the meadow land, to his last group of

plays, the joyous and beautiful and romantic dramas, such as the *Winter's Tale, Cymbeline,* and, last of all, it may be, *The Tempest,* that marvellous production in which a child may find a fairy tale, a philosopher suggestion of mystery and that "solemn vision" of life that comes in the midst of the wonders of the magic island [103].

Brief but cogent juxtaposition of readers—from child to philosopher—points the argument to read on many levels, at different stages of life. Tappan reaffirmed a positive and uplifting vision, the achievement of the romances that mirror the contentment of Shakespeare's later life. Of his retirement to Stratford, "a quiet village now grown so puritanical that its council had solemnly decreed that the acting of plays within its limits should be regarded as an unlawful deed" (105), away from the excitement and success of London, she noted: "No word of complaint or loneliness has come down to us" (106).

Tappan concluded with a paragraph about the sonnets to introduce their variety and range, illustrated by quoted lines "perfect" and "honest," that rightly lead "every student to have his own interpretation" (104). Two final sections support that "Shakespeare is the world's greatest poet" and signal assumption of the relation between author and work. She defined "Shakespeare's Genius" as threefold:

> first, in reading men and women better than any one else has ever read them, in knowing what a person of certain traits would do under certain circumstances, and how the scenes through which that person passed would affect his character; second, in his ability to express that knowledge with such perfection of form and such brilliancy of imagination as has never been equalled; third, in the fact that his power both to read and to express was sustained [104].

Sustained achievement is crucial, a telling superiority over contemporaries who "often had flashes and gleams of insight and momentary powers of expression that were worthy of him" (104). This makes Shakespeare a man of his age and a genius who transcends it. Yet "Shakespeare as a man" is convincingly pragmatic and ordinary, for he was not a

> supernatural being; he was a very human man. Certainly he never thought of himself as sitting on a pinnacle manufacturing English classics. He threw himself into his poetry, but he never forgot that he was writing plays for people to act and people to see. No really good work flows from the pen without thought. Shakespeare worked very rapidly, but the thinking was done at some time, either when he took up pen or beforehand. He was a straightforward business man, who paid his debts and intended what was due to him should be paid. He loved his early home and planned, perhaps from the time that he left it, to return to Stratford. Money came to him rapidly, especially after 1599, when the Globe Theatre was built, in which he seems to have had a generous share [105].

Tappan ended *A Short History of England's Literature* with a list of recommended books for future reading. Of Shakespeare, she noted, "Good editions are numerous" up to Furness's variorum. "For the beginner, *Julius Caesar, The*

Merchant of Venice, Macbeth, The Tempest, and selections from the sonnets are recommended." Her list of plays matches those in collections and schoolbooks. Tappan also added that *The Winter's Tale* was available in Cassell's edition, along with Greene's *Pandosto* (272). Noting that Mary wrote the comedies and Charles the tragedies, Tappan named *Tales from Shakespeare* (1807) in her later account of Charles Lamb. She quoted Mary's observation that her brother did the work "groaning all the time" as he struggled to make sense of the tragedies (216).

Tappan's *A Short History of America's Literature* (1932) documents devotion to Shakespeare at the close of the nineteenth century, in a section about "American Scholars." She identified Thomas Raynesford Lounsbury (1838–1915) of Yale University as an authority on Chaucer and Shakespeare, while Felix Emanuel Schelling (1858–1945) is greatest for Elizabethan Literature. "In fact, the Shakespeare plays seemed to hold the attention of American scholars." Three are named for their "excellent editions"—Richard Grant White (1821–1885), William Rolfe (1827–1910), and Henry Norman Hudson (1814–1886), while Horace Howard Furness (1833–1912) made the greatest achievement with the *Variorum Edition,* a work continued by his son (131). Moreover, American scholars contributed to study of the history and etymology of language, work in the scientific style of German universities, which most attended, so that "American research began to take its place with European scholarship" (132). Tappan also recognized Shakespeare as a popular author, celebrated on a massive scale through Percy MacKaye's *Caliban* (1916), produced in the stadium of New York University as part of the Shakespeare Tercentenary. With a cast of 2500 this spectacle was designed for a large audience (179). An inheritance from Shakespeare's own tradition of popular theatre with an emphasis on spectacle, civic pageants thrilled audiences and built pride and community in England and the United States.

No other English author is so inextricably entwined with artistic and academic development in the United States, even when the breadth and achievement of American writing is regarded as sufficient to merit a literary history separate from that of England. The Anglo-American special relationship stems from qualities recognized by Edwardians and their counterparts in the United States. Tappan's peroration in *A Short History of England's Literature* exalts traits of faithfulness, historical accuracy, unprejudiced biography, reasoning without fallacy, genuine thought, and truth to life (263). These are the ideals of the Edwardian era, a time of unparalleled possibilities that somehow went terribly wrong with the Great War. Thus there is an extraordinary poignancy in Tappan's final sentence: "Whatever the future of England's literature may be, it has at least the foundation of honest effort and an inexorable demand for sincerity and truth" (264). Political and national events of 1914, the year that saw publication of many fine English literary histories for children, were to change everything, to dismantle the Edwardian apogee of high sentiment and idealism; but Shakespeare's extraordinary position remained secure.

William J. Long, *Outlines of English and American Literature* (1919)

The Chandos portrait, as frontispiece and only color illustration, signals Shakespeare's importance in *Outlines of English and American Literature* (1919). A facing catalogue description quotes the paper note that gives this canvas' provenance and is attached to the back: "property of John Taylor, the player, painted by him or Richard Burbage, who left it to Sir William Davenant, upon whose death Betterton, the actor bought it. The portrait thus far was firmly kept in the world of the theatre, but then changed when Mr. Keck of the Temple purchased it for forty guineas; he willed it to Mr. Nicoll of Michenden House, Southgate, Middlesex. His only daughter married James, Marquess of Caernarvon, afterwards Duke of Chandos, father of Ann Eliza, Duchess of Buckingham." More recently it was "purchased at the Stow Sale, September 1848, by the Earl of Ellesmere, and presented by him to the nation, March, 1856."[24] Since the National Portrait Gallery was founded in London in 1856, Shakespeare is among the first honored.

In "An Essay on Literature (Not a Lesson, but an Invitation)," an introductory chapter, William J. Long (1867–1952), author of textbooks of English literature, specified traditional literature read by children and their basic understanding:

> Since childhood we have been familiar with this noble subject of literature. We have entered into the heritage of the ancient Greeks, who thought that Homer was a good teacher for the nursery; we have made acquaintance with Psalm and Prophecy and Parable, with the knightly tales of Malory, with the fairy stories of Grimm or Andersen, with the poetry of Shakespeare, with the novels of Scott or Dickens—in short with some of the best books that the world has ever produced. We know, therefore, what literature is, and that it is an excellent thing which ministers to the joy of living [1–2].

Seeking to provide a definition of literature, Long began by eliminating books of knowledge (information—science, history, philosophy, and the rest) and focusing on literature of power, "consisting of poems, plays, essays, stories of every kind, to which we go treasure-hunting for happiness or counsel, for noble thoughts, or fine feelings, for rest of body or exercise of spirit—for almost everything, in fine, except information" (3). As Chaucer said, the aim of literature is pleasure. It appeals to the imagination and emotions to "awaken in us a feeling of sympathy or admiration for whatever is beautiful in nature or the soul of man" (3). Long defined greatness as lasting and broad appeal derived from universality and youthfulness:

> Its only subjects are nature and human nature; it deals with common experiences of joy and sorrow, pain or pleasure, that all men understand; it cherishes the unchanging ideals of love, faith, duty, freedom, reverence, courtesy.... Such ideals tend to ennoble a writer, and therefore are great books characterized by lofty thought, by fine feeling, and, as a rule, by a beautiful simplicity of expression [5].

His final Arnoldian definition of literature is "the written record of men's best thought and feeling." Moreover, English literature is not just that written in Britain but "everything written in the English language" (6).

Three quotations — Hallam, Emerson, and Goethe — introduce the chapter devoted to Shakespeare to exalt him as the greatest name in all literature, the horizon beyond which we do not see, the heavenly genius whose works made the greatest impression (87). Shakespeare's name is "a signal for enthusiasm," yet Long wrote a measured evaluation — a sketch of dramatic practice (chronicle play, domestic drama, court comedy, melodrama, tragedy of blood, romantic comedy and romantic tragedy — all of which Shakespeare wrote), meager biography, periods with titles of plays, definitions of comedy and tragedy, but with blended elements. He discussed the juxtaposition of practical affairs of life with poetical dreams in *A Midsummer Night's Dream* and *The Merchant of Venice,* epitomized protagonists in the tragedies, and found the most "wholesome expression of life" in *The Winter's Tale* or *The Tempest.* He recommended reading three different types of plays in succession: *As You Like It, Macbeth, Julius Caesar*; or *The Merchant of Venice, Romeo and Juliet, Henry IV* with *The Tempest* read as a conclusion.

Throughout, Long exalted Shakespeare's genius; his final pages seek to define "The Quality of Shakespeare." First is a recognition of an "imagination both sympathetic and creative," overpowering but for other qualities — especially "an observation almost as keen as that of Chaucer and the saving grace of humor" (97). Nevertheless, Long quoted Ben Jonson's wish that his friend had "blotted a thousand lines" and discerned imperfection:

> Even in his best work Shakespeare has more faults than any other poet in England. He is in turn careless, extravagant, profuse, tedious, sensational; his wit grows stale or coarse; his patriotism turns to bombast; he mars even such pathetic scenes as the burial of Ophelia by buffoonery and brawling; and all to please a public that was given to bull-baiting [98].

Shakespeare was a man of his age as well as a genius, a writer in sympathy with his sources that dealt with problems, a form of evil, and provided a solution that was moral.

While Long found "Shakespeare's women are his finest characters," his concluding "Moral Emphasis" elaborates Lamb's identification of "this manly book." This is yet another example of complex contemporary attitudes toward gender. More crucial is the world's judgment that while Shakespeare introduced evil, his "emphasis is always upon the right man and the right action" (99). Long's peroration affirmed Shakespeare's role as brilliant, moral, popular, and influential:

> This may seem a trite thing to say in praise of a great genius; but when you reflect that Shakespeare is read throughout the civilized world, the simple fact that the splendor of his poetry is balanced by the rightness of his message becomes significant and impressive. It speaks not only for Shakespeare but for

the moral quality of the multitudes who acknowledge his mastery. Wherever his plays are read, on land or sea, in the crowded cities of men or the far silent places of the earth, there the solitary man finds himself face to face with the unchanging ideals of his race, with honor, duty, courtesy, and the moral imperative,

> This above all: to thine own self be true
> And it must follow, as the night the day,
> Thou canst not then be false to any man [99–100].

Shakespeare, paragon of writers, gives pleasure, moral guidance, and inspiration — perfect reading for children. Today's ambiguous and negative views may deem Long's commitment to literature as the conveyor of morality obsolete. But it is well to remember that this judgment was formative, and commonplace, when English literature was admired and its academic study developed.

Pedagogical Advice

Mary E. Burt, *Literary Landmarks* (1892/1897)

While literary histories were written for children, books of pedagogy were for teachers. *Literary Landmarks: A Guide to Good Reading for Young People, and Teachers' Assistant* (1897) by Mary E. Burt (1850–1918), is especially notable; it passionately advocates use of traditional literature, rather than school texts deliberately made for children and typically "written down," and of whole books rather than selections or "Epigrammatic Literature." Moreover, she insisted upon the necessity of a clear sense of order and provided many charts or guides with authors in correct historical sequence. Burt, a teacher at Cook County Normal School and a member of the Chicago Board of Education, also included samples from her twenty years in the classroom, helpful diagrams, and extensive book lists. Comprehensive coverage means non-literary chapters — "Scientific and Geographical Reading, Books of Travel"; "History and Biography"; "Utilitarian Literature, Books of Reference, Miscellaneous." However, her longest chapter is "Works of the Creative Imagination." *Literary Landmarks* places English literature in the larger context of world literature — in part, a reflection of the complexity of cultures in the United States — but still embodies Victorian and Edwardian attitudes. Nineteenth-century multi-culturalism is Eurocentric; Greek and Roman, and even Chaldean, which precede Christianity (indicated by a cross to divide each chart), balance European authors Chaucer and Dante, Shakespeare, Goethe, Present Age. A system of value is similarly British:

> [T]he child can easily see that the work of art which portrays a national life, a religion, is greater than one which shows some pettier feeling. Macaulay tells us that religion is at the foundation of the best art, and that national life is at the foundation of religion.[25]

Thomas Babington Macaulay (1800–1859), historian and member of Parliament, a Whig and strong Protestant, advocated English education, most notably in India, over an Oriental type. Children often knew his poetical *Lays of Ancient Rome* (1842), in Burt's List of Books, Number 45 of the Riverside Literature Series (154).

Burt's first chapter, "Theories of Children's Reading," sets out problems and principles that still resonate. Textbooks are a huge market, much governed by economics and politics. Burt, who stressed quality, deplored "the modern school-reader with its ill-assorted, namby-pamby, scrappy selections" and identified the "goody-goody" books as an even more "pernicious class of reading" (9, 76). She listed "fantasies" about young people's reading of the classics—too difficult, appropriate only for young men in college; scholars, who read in the original, know more than translations; the young who mastered the classics would have nothing left to read when they were older (23)—and observed:

> The truth is that the classics are simpler by far than the great mass of modern writing. They are nearer to children and the childhood of the race. They are the a, b, c of literature and history, and give clue to modern thought.... Many teachers have proved to their own satisfaction that young children prefer great classics to weak reading [24, 29].

Among her poignant stories of classroom experience are reactions against the vapid or simplistic. But her most startling point, a stark reminder of limited earlier education, is that she worked on "the fact that fifty per cent of all children who ever enter school leave before the age of ten" (63). This meant that a child needed an outline in mind on which to base further reading; it also explains Burt's belief that working men could read the classics with profit. Since children started school at age six, and many left from the fifth and six grades, the most interesting literature should be introduced to the young. The key writer to be added was Shakespeare: building upon fourth-grade knowledge, the pupil could separate the golden age of Greek literature into the ages of Homer and Pericles, already introduced, and "insert the age of Shakespeare between the age of Dante and Chaucer and the present age" (67). Pedagogical studies reiterate that, in the early years, the most effective texts are legend and myth, both immediately engaging and with a continuing presence in later eras that teaches continuity.

Burt gave most attention to *A Midsummer Night's Dream*, comparing it to Chaucer's *Knight's Tale*. She quoted two end-of-year essays from a seventh- and an eighth-grade student. The first girl drew a clock and marked periods of history on the face and names of writers in surrounding sections. Chaucer's *Knight's Tale* was a favorite, and *A Midsummer Night's Dream* was similar (48). The eighth-grade girl, who drew a river system to demonstrate her knowledge, added a connection: "We read Midsummer Night's Dream, and were delighted to find that Shakespeare used the same old woods which Chaucer used in The Knight's Tale, and that Shakespeare used the same form which Aeschylus used, but Shakespeare uses more characters than Aeschylus" (56). A long list of works designed to increase connecting links in seventh and eight grades names "the myth of Theseus and the Amazons, followed by Chaucer's Knight's Tale, and Midsummer Night's Dream" (73).

Subsequent references to Shakespeare are not extensive. Examples of the law that a work is greater when its parts are correctly related include "Midsummer Night's Dream and Philoctetes (Plumptre's translation) for seventh and eight grades, Lamb's The Tempest for sixth grade, the Antigone of Sophocles for older people, are all interesting studies and illustrations of this law of structure" (33). An example that literature presents national law is "the drama of Julius Caesar" (38) — perennial favorite in the United States. Burt's guiding principle for teachers in Normal Schools was to lead "primary and grammar pupils ... into a perception of the fact that literature is but the evolution of the thought of humanity." Here she added "Marlowe's Jew of Malta, followed by Shakespeare's Merchant of Venice" (75). Dowden's *The Mind and Art of Shakespeare* is one suggestion for essays in criticism ("Utilitarian Literature") for seventh and eighth grades (107).

The "List of Books" is substantial, nearly fifty pages of small type (109–157). Burt's introductory comment combined the ideal with the practical:

> I used to have great sympathy with cheap editions of books, but I am not sure but I shall change my mind regarding them, since I observe that children treat well-bound volumes with more respect than pamphlets, and perhaps invest the thoughts with more dignity and reverence. And yet I know what it is to place the two-cent pamphlets in the hands of those pupils whose money has been worse than wasted in well-bound copies of "My Nag can Run" literature, the pamphlets serving as stepping stones to better ideas of books— real books. And so I have catalogued in my list many of these cheap pamphlets, much against my taste [109].

This glosses both the pleasure of Edwardian extravagance in printing children's literature and pragmatic reliance upon cheap paper pamphlets, like those of the long established Religious Tract Society or Stead's Books for the Bairns Series. Titles are followed by publisher and price. Many are Riverside Classics, or Cabinet Edition of Favorite Works, illustrated and in uniform volumes, published by Houghton Mifflin, each at a price of $1.00. Number 55 is Shakespeare's *Merchant of Venice*, edited for school use by Samuel Thurber, Master in the Girls' High School, Boston (154). Also in the list, but without detail, are Number 67, Shakespeare's *Julius Caesar*; Number 93, Shakespeare's *As You Like It*; and Number 99, Shakespeare's *Macbeth* (157).

Houghton Mifflin, "assisted by more than one hundred of the best educators of American youth," published The Riverside School Library: "Books of Permanent Value Carefully Chosen, Thoroughly Edited, Clearly Printed, Durably Bound in Half Leather, and Sold At Low Prices with Introductions, Notes, and Illustrations." The publisher's note goes beyond advertising the appeal of dark red half leather to moral objectives:

> It is hoped that the reading of these books will promote a love for good literature, and prevent or correct the taste for trashy and unwholesome stories that constantly tempt the young.
>
> It is believed that the use of this series will give a strong impetus to the movement for supplying schools with thoroughly good libraries, which must be regarded as among the most potent instrumentalities for the promotion of good citizenship, and the development of intelligence, refinement, and high character among the boys and girls so fortunate as to enjoy their influence [inside cover].

Such statements, using terms usually found in chivalric stories, proclaim ideals of education as both nationalistic and honorable. Eleven pages, in large type, identify classics of children's literature: *Pilgrim's Progress, Robinson Crusoe, Gulliver's Travels,* Hans Christian Andersen, Brothers Grimm, *Fables and Folk Tales* (by Horace Scudder); novels like Scott's *Ivanhoe,* Goldsmith's *The Vicar of Wakefield,* Dickens's *A Christmas Carol,* James Fenimore Cooper's *The Last of the Mohicans*; many books of poetry (Longfellow, Whittier, Lowell, and Tennyson); other key American writers (Benjamin Franklin, Washington Irving, Oliver Wendell Holmes, Nathaniel Hawthorne, Harriet Beecher Stowe, Sarah Orne Jewett, Kate Douglas Wiggin).

Shakespeare is the only drama: Lamb's *Tales from Shakespeare,* 324 pages for 60 cents, which included an introductory sketch and portraits of the artists; and Richard Grant White's edition of *Julius Caesar* and *As You Like It,* 224 pages for 50 cents. As discussed in Chapter 4, Robert R. Raymond's *Typical Tales* in 1881 included these as two of his three choices. Most significant is a description of Lamb's *Tales*:

> There is a story behind every great play, and it is only after one has got at the story that one thoroughly understands and enjoys the play. Charles and Mary Lamb were themselves delightful writers, and to read their Tales from Shakespeare is not only to have a capital introduction to the great dramatist's works, but to hear fine stories finely told [7].

Their biography is the "account of the brother and sister, whose life together is one of the most touching tales in English literature." The success of Lamb's *Tales* rests on its being the first retelling and Charles's reputation as a Romantic, but the siblings' perseverance in adversity and family devotion add appeal. Burt listed as an alternative Abby Sage Richardson's *Stories from Old English Poetry* (1871 and 1891), discussed in Chapter 4.

Librarians

The creation and development of libraries in the United Kingdom followed from the Education Act of 1870; by 1900 local authorities in 401 districts had adopted the Public Libraries Act.[26] Andrew Carnegie's generosity greatly furthered free libraries between 1897 and 1913, when 225 were established in England and Wales. But facilities were inadequate or unavailable to many children, and financial resources were insufficient. The Library Association, always concerned with the needs of children, was founded in 1877. Usually children's libraries were in separate rooms, and after a stipulated age children were often allowed to read books in the adult library. The most successful results came through cooperation with children's libraries in schools; approximately forty-five per cent of elementary schools contained libraries in the opening years of the twentieth century. A report of the London County Council in 1907 set out five needs and expectations:

1. a place for reading by children in the evenings, on Saturdays, and during school holidays;
2. books for home reading;
3. skilled advice for children regarding their choice of books;
4. books of reference in connection with school work;
5. specially adapted sets of books for loans to schools [137].

Librarians in many different locations made various efforts—appropriate opening times, story hours, study circles, special lists of books—to encourage children's reading.

Library work with children was more advanced in the United States and provided a model. Caleb Bingham, a bookseller, established the first library exclusively for children in Salisbury, Connecticut, in 1803; others soon followed in New Jersey and Massachusetts. The American Library Association was established in 1876, but did not hold the first public general discussion of library work with children until their 1897 conference. Librarians were trained at the Pratt Institute to work with children as early as 1898, the same year that Frances Jenkins Olcott "organized the children's department of the Carnegie Library of Pittsburgh, developing a pattern for reaching children through the children's rooms of branch libraries, through the schools, and through the homes."[27] A Section for Children's Librarians of the American Library Association was formed in 1905. Children's rooms were inviting because they were designed on a smaller scale to suit their readers. In the opening years of the twentieth century two American librarians offered a different perspective, albeit they were similar to writers and teachers in commitment to children's literature and values.

Montrose J. Moses, *Children's Books and Reading* (1907)

As noted in Chapter 1, Montrose J. Moses (1878–1934) discussed Lamb's *Tales* in "The Old-Fashioned Library" chapter of his history of children's literature, but was more skeptical than impressed by its place as a favored text for children. This is incidental to his overview of a falling off from "then" to "now" and inadequately appealing schoolbooks. Moses worked in the New York Public Library, and in consultation with librarians at Columbia, in Hartford, Pittsburgh, and Cleveland. Much of *Children's Books and Reading* (1907) is an account of how libraries developed and should be used; about a third is lists of children's books—seventy-two of the 272 pages plus another dozen pages of lists at ends of chapters.[28] Unusually, substantial sections were devoted to French (232–237) and German (238–246) books, a likely reflection of the population of New York City. Moses compared resources available to "the second generation of ignorant emigrant in New York or Chicago or Cleveland or Pittsburgh [that] is far more fortunate than the new generation peopling our Blue Ridge Mountains in Virginia" (188). Educational surveys identified discrepancy between urban education (distinct from the inner city that emerged after the mid-twentieth century) and that in the rural South.

Recognizing that modifications in beliefs, knowledge, and aspirations of adults were the same for children except for a difference in intensity, Moses stressed correlation between developments in children's literature and the increasing role of elementary education and social change (143, 146). He argued how

> the educational impulse dominated over all elements of pure imagination; how the retelling craze given a large literary sanction by such a writer as Lamb, and so excellently upheld by Charles Kingsley, lost caste when brought within compass of the text-book. He [the student] will finally see how this educational pest has overrun America to a far greater extent than England, to the detriment of much that is worthy and of much which should by rights be made to constitute a children's reading heritage [146–147].

Schoolbooks that dilute and exploit provoked Moses's negative evaluation of Lamb, the begetter of retellings of classics. His list of "Classics" is very brief, including only eleven: Cervantes's *Don Quixote* (Judge E. A. Parry), Chaucer, Herodotus, Homer's *Iliad*, *The Adventures of Ulysses* (Charles Lamb) and *Adventures of Odysseus* (F. S. Marvin), Plutarch's *Lives,* Swift's *Gulliver's Travels, Spenser for Children* (M. H. Towry), and Shakespeare. He listed four editions of Lamb's *Tales*—Ainger, published by Macmillan; E. V. Lucas, published by Putnam; Scribner's edition, with illustrations by Norman M. Price; an edition published by Nister; Scribner's edition of Quiller-Couch's historical tales (221). Also named is Mary Cowden Clarke's *Girlhood of Shakespeare's Heroines,* a brilliant example of fiction rooted in a classic, illustrated by Sir John Gilbert, published by Scribner, expensive at $3.00, obviously a prize or gift book.

Moses, who recognized that terms of classification in libraries and lists were often baffling, had a substantial list of "Myths, Folk-lore, Legends, Fairy Tales, and Hero Tales" (210–216), where he included titles—many of traditional stories—that others designated "classics." Salient characteristics, found abundantly in classics, were interest and style:

> Literature has been made cold to the child, yet there is nothing warmer than a classic, when properly handled. Each man lives in his own age; we are creatures of timeliness, but we see the clearer for being at times on a mountain peak. The traveller from an antique land is part of our experience quite as much as the man around the corner. What I contend is that the attraction, the appeal of a story depends largely on the telling [171–172].

The heights were as available to a tenement boy as to Keats because the public library eschewed mediocrity to "purchase for those empty shelves the best of a class, the best of an edition, and the most authentic of texts" (172). This procedure assured Moses's democratic ideal: "Children are entitled to their full heritage; education is paramount, culture is the saving grace" (14).

Later, Moses praised English-made books over American schoolbooks (206). Like Burt, and many others—not least publishers and collectors—he observed the importance of a book's physical appearance to attract child readers who are not drawn to schoolbooks. (That negative is borne out only in part by my study, given the beauty of series—with great paintings, often in color, as illustration—published by Nelson, Arnold, and Harrap for the school market, albeit they originate in England.) However, quality in physical books was subordinate to Moses's insistence and plea for excellence. The problem was mediocrity, a corollary of the reading democracy created by public libraries, and patently false (8). Like anyone with a knowledge of children's literature, Moses recognized the flow between adult and child, appropriation of adult texts by children and adult delight in the best children's books. However, an abundance of fiction, especially the "series" class of storybook led to a view "in the popular mind that literature is synonymous with dullness; that only current fiction is worth while" (8). Later he reiterated, "the amount of inane fiction concocted for children is pernicious" (171).

Differences between the past and now explain Moses's anxieties and passionate desire that children read the classics. He offered a telling reminder of changing standards:

> Can we recall any of our great men—literary, scientific, or otherwise—who were brought up on distinctively juvenile literature. A present-day boy who would read what Lamb or Wordsworth, Coleridge or Tennyson, Gladstone or Huxley devoured with gusto in their youth, would set the psychologists in a flutter, would become an object for head-lines in our papers [7].

One hundred years later, the mind boggles to contemplate how to update Moses's recognition of different standards; to modern psychology must be added fluid pedagogy and politics.

Frances Jenkins Olcott, *The Children's Reading* (1912)

A few years after Moses's study another American librarian argued for the relation between reading Shakespeare and success in the world. "A Table of

Classics and Notable Persons Influenced by Them," a bordered, two-page opening, introduces *The Children's Reading* (1912). Frances Jenkins Olcott (1872/3–1963) explained:

> This table cannot show to full extent the number of famous people influenced by the books which are listed. Biographies often state merely that such a man was a voracious reader in his youth, devouring every book that came to hand. Most of the books listed here were read before the readers were sixteen years old, and many before they were twelve.[29]

The table, a kind of nineteenth-century literary canon, names four individuals influenced by each of twelve classics: The Bible, *Arabian Nights, Don Quixote, Faerie Queene,* Fairy Tales, *Gulliver's Travels, Odyssey, Pilgrim's Progress,* Plutarch, *Robinson Crusoe,* Scott's Novels and Poems, Shakespeare. Most are writers, but some are statesmen or scientists. The four influenced by Shakespeare are distinctive because none is a poet or novelist — Daniel Webster, Lincoln, Darwin, Emerson. Although Olcott favored imaginative literature — she is the author of *Fairy Tales* (1898), *Arabian Nights* (1913), and *Story-telling Poems* (1913) — *The Children's Reading* is a comprehensive work by a librarian who recognized and made concrete suggestions for a wide range of interests with indications of some approximate age levels. Her work, both as author and librarian, was seminal. Between 1890 and 1900 public libraries, which had not previously recognized children, established rooms for children, partially inspired by Olcott, who in 1898 set up a children's department and established outreach programs through branch libraries, schools, and homes for the Carnegie Library in Pittsburg.

The Children's Reading particularly stresses the role of mothers at home, often noted for their influence on great men. Criteria for recommending juvenile books are "standards based on Christian ethics, practical psychology, and the literary values of generally accepted good books" (vii). These values assumed a uniform society in the United States, albeit facing lowered standards with the influence of moving-picture shows, dime and nickel novels. Like most who write about children's literature Olcott fully accepted that children love adventure, emotional and sensational experiences. However, she hoped for better choices, books that would have a strong, positive influence rather than merely distract: "the books that may forcibly impress on character ideas of justice, truth, honor, loyalty, and heroism, these must be introduced to the children through tactful and enjoyable methods, which will stimulate the imagination" (25). The ideals are chivalric, and romances are among stories highly praised. Olcott, who charted a reading plan from ballads to epics of *Beowulf, Siegfried,* and *The Faerie Queene,* was a strong advocate for Chaucer and Arthurian and Carolingean romances as children's literature.[30] She boldly addressed the "much-mooted" question of "whether great literature should be rewritten for children, and whether it should be expurgated" (117). Within her scheme of values she showed great flexibility. She accepted both adaptations and excerpts, which could lead to later reading of the full original texts; moreover, she acknowledged that expurgations express adult anxieties more that children's cognizance.

Olcott was similarly realistic about how books attract young readers by their physical appearance. She reiterated Moses's eschewing of classics that look like textbooks (dull cover, small, close-set type) and cited a librarian's experience that such books are

> rarely stolen, and rarely worn out; two proofs of unpopularity. But place on the shelf the same work in a gayly covered edition, illustrated in color, printed in clear, attractive type, and presto! the book disappears legitimately or otherwise. And often a child who reads this attractive volume will tell other children about the story, and behold, the formerly despised, homely volume becomes fashionable [148].

Red was the favorite color for covers, and illustrations should be story-telling pictures.

There could scarcely be a more accurate description of numerous and luxurious editions of Lamb's *Tales from Shakespeare,* a major title in the list at the end of Chapter X. "Some Classics and Standards" divided into "Books," "Novels," "Essays and Miscellanies," and "Drama." The final section, in six parts, begins with "Everyman and Other Miracle Plays," followed by "Plays (Shakespeare)," "Plays (Sheridan)," "She Stoops to Conquer (Goldsmith)," "Stories of Famous Operas (Guerber)" and "Stories of the Wagner Operas (Guerber)." The Shakespeare entry is longer than all others combined; clearly he is a writer for children:

> There is no finer gift for boy or girl than a good one-volume edition of the great dramatist, or, if preferred, a set of "Temple Shakespeare," bound in leather. The advantages of the set are that the individual volumes are inexpensive and one may be bought at a time; also, if wished, a selection of the plays may be made. If a selection is desired, the first plays that should be bought for a child's own bookcase are "Midsummer Night's Dream," "The Tempest," "As You Like It," "Merchant of Venice," "Twelfth Night," "The Winter's Tale," "Comedy of Errors," "Romeo and Juliet, "Taming of the Shrew," "Hamlet," "Julius Caesar," "King John, "Henry IV," "Henry V," "Macbeth," and "King Lear." Good prose renditions of the plays are Lambs' "Tales from Shakespeare," Quiller-Couch's "Historical Tales from Shakespeare," which supplements Lamb; and a charming set of books called "The Temple Shakespeare for Children." The stories in this set are attractively told in prose by Alice Spencer Hoffman. Parts of the original plays are woven into the narratives. Each play is published separately bound in leather, and illustrated. "The Tempest" is illustrated by Walter Crane. For the "Ben Greet Shakespeare," see page 240 [166].

A "Dramatics and Story-Telling" list is at the end of Chapter XIII. "Useful Books" identifies "four attractive volumes for the use of amateur players" — *Midsummer Night's Dream, As You Like It, The Merchant of Venice, The Tempest.* Olcott's note is reassuring: "Objectionable parts are cut out, and the sequence of a few scenes is altered to facilitate presentation. General rules for acting are given and also diagrams showing positions, together with full directions for playing each part" (240). Recognition of what will work in performance is crucial; Shakespeare's text is always adapted—from his own day to the present—to suit the company. Since *The Children's Reading* is essentially an argument of general principles and recommendations for specific books, these notes are the nearest Olcott came to critical evaluation. Her only other naming of Shakespeare was in Chapter III. In "Children's Interests," *King John*, Act IV, is suggested reading under "Infancy and childhood." Parents needed to take care in suiting text to child; Olcott set no rigid timeline, and posited that reading the books is a way of "renewing one's youth" (25).

The time to read Shakespeare accords with recommendations in Newbolt's Report, *The Teaching of English in England*, completed in 1921. Olcott confidently expected earlier childhood reading to concentrate on chivalry and folk-lore (ballads, romances, and epics) to establish a basis for judgment. Carefully chosen, these stories, in which the child would clearly discern the difference between good and evil, strength and weakness, were effective at ages when idea was more important than form. Yet a strong style that supported the ideas was necessary. By the age of fifteen or sixteen the child with "a moral sense" that is both trained and independent was capable of making his or her own judgments, "to perceive for themselves when an author fails to uphold uniformly high standards of virtue, or confuses falsehood with truth" (118–119). Thus "good renditions" serve as literary guides, when the original literature is beyond the child (146–147). Before offering her list of suggestions Olcott admitted it "is not on the whole a popular one," but for fortunate boys and girls "whose parents and teachers have introduced them step by step to fine ennobling literature, and who are ready to take keen pleasure in stories that have character and strength" (153).

The appendix explains in two sections how to procure books: through the public library, with precise accounts given for many states, and by purchase, with booksellers for new and used books; an alphabetical purchase list covers every book mentioned in *The Children's Reading*, with page references, names of publishers and prices. Houghton Mifflin's Cambridge edition of Shakespeare's plays is listed at $3.00; Dutton's Everyman Library, three volumes, leather, are seventy cents each; Temple Shakespeare, leather, is fifty-five cents each; Doubleday's four volumes of Ben Greet's acting versions are sixty cents each. "Purchase List of Children's Books for Children and Young People from One to Sixteen Years of Age"—each chapter's list with many added items—fills thirty-six pages of small print.

Several points emerged from Moses and Olcott, two librarians distressed about ever-growing numbers of cheap books with a corollary wish to provide children with classics. Each paid most attention to earlier, medieval literature that was generally regarded as especially suited to younger children. The alternative retellings of Chaucer, for example, received greater mention than Shakespeare stories, notably Lamb's *Tales*. In contrast, *Standard Catalog for High School Libraries* (1929) was much more extensive and varied. Neither Moses nor Olcott devoted space to an analysis of Shakespeare; his works are simply accepted as essential "classics." The twenty-first century has not lost that designation, but Shakespeare stories are no longer told to children in the same ways.

Epilogue

Today's Shakespeare industry designs verbal and visual texts for children who live in a vastly different world from that inhabited by Victorian and Edwardian children. Most obviously they can see and hear *The Animated Tales* (*Romeo and Juliet, As You Like It, The Taming of the Shrew, Macbeth, A Midsummer Night's Dream, Richard III, Hamlet, The Tempest, Julius Caesar, Twelfth Night, Othello, The Winter's Tale*), produced in association with the BBC and now available on DVD. Shakespeare films (and palimpsests), the twentieth century's contribution to art, also provide enjoyment and instruction. Films are outside this study's scope, but several recent books of Shakespeare stories that combine verbal and visual texts afford apt comparison with Edwardians.

Terry Deary, Britain's popular and prolific author, in *Top Ten Shakespeare Stories* (1998) has employed a wide range of contemporary fashions.[1] His title is a link to pop culture; the introduction declares that Shakespeare is as entertaining as a soap opera, and urges HAVE FUN. *Top Ten Shakespeare Stories* is a compendium of popular genres, each story written in a different aptly chosen familiar form, numbered to progress from Story 10 to Story 1: *A Midsummer Night's Dream, King Lear, Twelfth Night, The Tempest, Merchant of Venice, Romeo and Juliet, Julius Caesar, Taming of the Shrew, Macbeth, Hamlet*. "Top Facts" follow each. An early joke is that the favorite *A Midsummer Night's Dream* is the first told, as "Nightmare in Elm Trees"; however, it is Story 10, bottom of the charts. Top Facts 10 is biography, a life corresponding to the seven ages of man with three updates of fame after death (First Folio, Garrick celebration, films). In subsequent Top Facts, Shakespeare's Theatre is 9, Timeline is 7, Audience is 3. Among devices of storytelling *The Tempest* is Miranda's diary; Brutus explained "The revenge of Caesar's spirit"; "The Ballad of Big Mac" (another pun) is followed by "The Macbeth curse"; *Hamlet*, "The topped ten," uses a police report and has a "Quick quiz." Challengingly revisionist is "Shylock shocker" in the *Venetian Times*, a Jewish newspaper report; "Shakespeare's Blind Date," a cartoon of the caskets for *The Merchant of Venice*, follows. Top Facts 6 is "Villains or victims?"— a chronology for Jews. Deary's ordinary paperback, with black and white drawings by Michael Tickner, recalls the modest appearance of chapbooks, as do his titillating stories. Supplementary information and popular references establish Shakespeare as part of modern culture, without abandoning learning.

Alternative originality is manifest in *Mr. William Shakespeare's Plays* (1998) and *Bravo, Mr. William Shakespeare!* (2000) by Marcia Williams, an English reteller and illustrator of classic literature for children. Late Victorian and Edwardian illustrations favored high sentiment through beautiful and uplifting images of often idealized people in magical, heroic, and romantic situations. Williams's pictures employ the artistry of the comic strip—bright colors, caricature figures, obvious situations—the printed analog to animated films. Her books also feature language: two concurrent texts, a few words from Shakespeare (in smaller typeface) across the top and a straightforward story of the plot across the bottom of each frame. In addition, every page on the sides and bottom has a running commentary of audience response, another set of figures that make funny comments in a low style that deflates serious and formal qualities. The selected plays also indicate some significant alteration in favored titles, proportionately more tragedies and later, sophisticated comedies. The first book contains: *A Midsummer Night's Dream, Romeo and Juliet, The Winter's Tale, Macbeth, Hamlet,* and *Julius Caesar,* while the second has *Much Ado about Nothing, As You Like It, Richard III, Antony and Cleopatra, Twelfth Night, King Lear,* and *The Merchant of Venice.* Although Williams makes a direct challenge to Lamb's *Tales from Shakespeare,* there is some continuity amidst substantial change to express differences in sensibility from the beginning of the nineteenth to the start of the twenty-first century.[2] Williams, who recreates favorite classics—*The Adventures of Robin Hood, Don Quixote, Greek Myths, The Iliad and the Odyssey, King Arthur and the Knights of the Round Table, Sinbad the Sailor*—notably sustains Victorian and Edwardian tradition.[3]

Aliki, who wrote and illustrated *William Shakespeare and the Globe* (2000), uses something of the comic book style of narrative pictures; however, her drawings are usually not caricature.[4] She divides her picture book into five acts, some with several scenes. Acts One through Four describe Shakespeare's life and world of sixteenth-century England, while Act Five recounts the rebuilding of the Globe, inspired by American actor Sam Wanamaker (1919–1993) on the Thames in London. Thus Aliki combines biography and celebration of the most authentic modern recreation of Shakespeare's theatre, which opened formally with a performance of *Henry V* before Queen Elizabeth II—and supporters of the rebuilding—on June 12, 1997. (As a member of that audience, I found it one of the most thrilling moments ever experienced in theatre.) Aliki introduces scholarly detail, but the book's distinction lies in her illustrations based upon buildings in Stratford, Elizabethan paintings and drawings, and pictures of the process of modern reconstruction.

Juan Wijngard's *Shakespeare's Globe: An Interactive Pop-up Theatre* is both a tribute to the rebuilt theatre (the single pop-up) and a redeployment of a nineteenth-century form of book.⁵ Included are two booklets with speeches from twelve plays: *A Midsummer Night's Dream, Twelfth Night, As You Like It, The Merchant of Venice, King Lear, Hamlet, Julius Caesar, The Tempest, Romeo and Juliet, Richard III, Henry V, Macbeth*. The child could read or recite to give a sense of character, but not within a story.

With even this sampling of current attractive and accessible Shakespeare books for children, a stronger enthusiasm and greater familiarity with the plays could be expected, and a corollary enthusiasm for reading great literature. However, this seems not the case. An article in *The Sunday Telegraph*, April 23, 2006, entitled, "Brush up your Shakespeare: for a pass you need to know ... nothing," points out that students "can now score zero on the Shakespeare section and still achieve a pass."⁶ Not unexpectedly, many, including the Prince of Wales, are distressed and seek remedies. He protests that schools are depriving children of their cultural heritage: "For all sorts of well-meaning reasons and for too many pupils, teaching has omitted to pass on to the next generation not only our deep knowledge of literature and history, but also the value of education."⁷

This observation is at least as cogent for schools in the United States. An article, "The Arts May Aid Literacy, Study Says," *The New York Times*, July 27, 2006, suggests a potential argument to restore enthusiasm for Shakespeare as children's literature. Students who participated in the program sponsored by the Guggenheim Museum performed better in literacy and critical thinking.⁸ Surely these qualities are essential even at a time when technology and business dominate; recognition of qualities of "the beautiful mind" is a sound beginning, and minds grow beautiful from reading and understanding Shakespeare.

Tables

The following tables bring together data about collections of Shakespeare's stories retold for children, both the occurrence of titles and kinds of illustrations. Each table is accompanied by a key; details of books are in the bibliography.

Table 1, which does not include complete editions of the twenty stories included in Lamb's *Tales from Shakespeare,* records nine distinctive books of selections and additions, beginning with one Victorian and ending after World War I. They indicate which plays were deemed suitable for shorter introductions to Shakespeare.

Table 2 shows how E. Nesbit's *The Children's Shakespeare,* the only rival in popularity to Lamb's *Tales,* was offered in a similar but more limited variety of Edwardian editions, both in Britain and the United States.

Table 3 records seventeen alternatives to Lamb and Nesbit, collections of Shakespeare's stories for children by many different writers, again British and American, from the Victorian era until World War I.

Table 4 is a record of visual texts that parallel verbal stories. The use of illustration was extensive, as much a part of Shakespeare as children's literature as the retold plays. Indeed pictures are another way to read and understand the plays, for they focus and comment on both characters and actions. The list of illustrators includes many of the most distinguished artists—pictures from the Boydell Gallery, Sir John Gilbert, Harold Copping, Gordon Browne, Arthur Rackham, Charles Folkard, Edmund Dulac, W. Heath Robinson, Hugh Thomson, Gertrude Demain Hammond, and many others. Their interpretations engage the imagination and are a major resource for understanding Shakespeare. The form of illustration is indicated by giving the size of each book, different sizes of images, color and black and white, and total number of images.

Table 1. Distribution of Plays in Edwardian Editions
Charles and Mary Lamb, *Tales from Shakespeare*

	Bickers[1]	Blackie[2]	Furnivall[3]	Harrap[4] I	Harrap[4] II	Hodder & Stoughton[5]	Mrs. Lang[6]	Robarts[7]	Tilney[8]
All'sWell			X						
AsYouLikeIt		X	X	X		X	X	X	X
ComError			X			X			
Cymbeline	X		X			X			
Hamlet		X	X		X	X		X	X
KingLear	X		X		X	X	X		
Macbeth	X		X			X	X	X	X
Measure	X		X						
Merchant	X	X	X		X	X	X	X	X
Midsummer		X	X	X		X	X	X	X
Much Ado	X	X	X			X			
Othello	X		X			X			
Pericles			X			X			
Romeo&J.	X		X		X	X	X	X	X
Taming	X		X			X			
Tempest	X		X	X		X	X		X
Timon			X			X			
TwelfthNight			X	X		X			
TwoGent	X		X			X			
Winter'sTale	X	X	X	X		X			X
Antony&C.			X						
Coriolanus			X						
JuliusCaesar			X						
Troilus&C.			X						
LoveLaborLost			X						
Merry Wives			X						
TOTAL	12	6	26	5	4	18	7	6	8

Table 1 Key

1. *Tales from Shakespeare.* Permanent Photography from the Boydell Gallery.
2. *Tales from Shakespeare: From the Collection by Charles and Mary Lamb.* Stories Old & New Series.
3. *Tales from Shakespeare by Mary and Charles Lamb with Introductions and Additions.* 2 vols. Illustrated by Harold Copping.
4. Lamb's *Tales from Shakespeare*, Book 1 and Book 2. All-Time Tales Series.
5. *Tales from Shakespeare by Mary and Charles Lamb.* Illustrations by Edmund Dulac, Arthur Rackham, Hugh Thomson, W. Heath Robinson, etc.
6. *The Gateway to Shakespeare for Children.* Illustrations by E.F. Skinner, Norman Ault, T.C. Dugdale, A.K. Browling. The Gateway Series.
7. *Tales from Shakespeare by C. and M. Lamb.* Illustrated.
8. *Tales from Shakespeare by Charles and Mary Lamb.* Illustrated by Charles Folkard. Tales for Children from Many Lands Series.

Table 2. E. Nesbit, *The Children's Shakespeare*

	First[1]	Beautiful[2]	Graham[3]	R. Tuck[4]	TuckGem[5]	Altemus[6]
All'sWell		X				
AsYouLikeIt	X	X		X		X
ComError		X				
Cymbeline	X	X		X	X	X
Hamlet	X	X		X		X
KingLear	X	X	X	X		X
Macbeth		X				
Measure		X				
Merchant	X	X		X	X	X
Midsummer	X	X	X	X	X	X
Much Ado		X				
Othello		X				
Pericles	X	X		X		X
Romeo&J.	X	X	X	X	X	X
Taming	X	X		X	X	X
Tempest	X	X	X	X		
Timon		X				
TwelfthNight	X	X		X		X
TwoGent		X				
Winter'sTale	X	X	X	X	X	X
TOTAL	12	20	5	12	6	12

Table 2 Key

1. *The Children's Shakespeare*, ed. Edric Vredenburg. Illustrated by Francis Brundage, M. Bowley, J. Willis Grey, etc.
2. *Twenty Beautiful Stories from Shakespeare: A Home Study Course*. Illustrations by Max Bihn, from Brundage.
3. *The Children's Shakespeare*. Illustrations from Brundage.
4. *Children's Stories from Shakespeare*. Raphael House Library of Gift Books. Illustrations by J.H. Bacon, Harold Copping, A.A. Dixon, Howard Davie, Gordon Browne.
5. E. Nesbit with Hugh Chesson, *The Winter's Tale, and Other Stories*. Illustrated by Frances Brudage, M. Bowley, and others.
6. *The Children's Shakespeare*. Illustrations from Brundage, etc.

Table 3. Alternative Books of Shakespeare's Stories

	S[1]	SA[2]	SB[3]	Raymond[4]	Morris[5]	Sim[6]	Macleod[7]	Stidolph[8]	Hudson[9]	Britton[10]	L1[11]	L2[12]	H1[13]	H2[14]	C1[15]	C2[16]	Maud[17]
All'sWell		X															X
AsYouLikeIt	X	X		X		X					X		X		X		
ComError	X	X									X				X	X	
Cymbeline	X									X							
Hamlet	X		X				X					X	X		X		X
KingLear	X		X				X			X		X	X		X		X
Macbeth	X		X				X			X		X	X		X		X
Measure		X															
Merchant	X	X					X		X	X	X		X		X		X
Midsummer	X	X		X		X	X	X	X	X	X		X		X		X
Much Ado	X	X				X	X	X	X				X				
Othello	X		X				X						X				
Pericles	X											X	X				
Romeo&J.	X		X			X	X			X	X		X		X		X
Taming	X					X	X		X	X	X		X				
Tempest	X					X	X		X	X	X		X	X	X		X
Timon	X		X														
TwelfthNight	X	X				X	X		X				X				
TwoGent	X	X				X	X		X	X							
Winter'sTale	X	X					X		X		X		X		X		
Antony&C.	X		X		X								X				
Coriolanus	X		X		X								X				
JuliusCaesar	X		X	X	X								X				
K.John	X		X		X							X	X				
K.RichII	X		X		X							X	X				
K.HenryIV1					X				X							X	
K.HenryIV2		X			X				X							X	
K.HenryV	X				X											X	
K.HenryVI	X		X		X (x3)										X	X	
K.RichIII	X		X		X							X				X	
K.HenryVIII	X		X		X											X	
Troilus&C.	X		X		X											X	
LoveLaborLost		X			X												
MerryWives		X			X												
TitusAndron	X																
TOTAL	26	16	18	3	16	8	16	3	10	8	7	7	20	1	11	9	8

N.B. The section above the rule lists plays included in Lamb's *Tales from Shakepeare* and E. Nesbit's *The Children's Shakespeare*. The section below the rule lists other plays added. Books in the table are in order of publication.

Table 3 Key

Books in the table are in order of publication.

1. Mary Seamer Seymour, *Shakespeare's Stories Simply Told*. 1880.
2. Mary Seamer Seymour, *Shakespeare's Stories Simply Told. Comedies*. 1883.
3. Mary Seamer Seymour, *Shakespeare's Stories Simply Told. Tragedies and Historical Plays*. 1899.
4. Robert R. Raymond, ed. *Typical Tales of Fancy, Romance, and History from Shakespeare*. 1881.
5. Harrison S. Morris, *Tales from Shakespeare*. 1893.
6. Adelaide C. Gordon Sim, *Phoebe's Shakespeare*. 1894.
7. Mary Macleod, *The Shakespeare Story-Book*. 1902.
8. Ada Baynes Stidolph, *The Children's Shakespeare*. 1902.
9. R. Hudson, *Tales from Shakespeare*. 1906.
10. Fay Adams Britton, *Shakespearian Fairy Tales*. 1907.
11. Jeanie Lang, *Stories from Shakespeare*. 1905.
12. Jeanie Lang, *More Stories from Shakespeare*. 1910.
13. Alice Spencer Hoffman, *The Children's Shakespeare: Being Stories from the Plays with Illustrative Passages*. 1911.
14. Alice Spencer Hoffman, *The Story of the Tempest from the Play of Shakespeare*. 1904.
15. Thomas Carter, *Stories from Shakespeare*. 1910.
16. Thomas Carter, *Shakespeare's Stories of the English Kings*. 1912.
17. Constance and Mary Maud, *Shakespeare's Stories*. Illustrations from Boydell. 1913.

Table 4. Illustrations in Books of Shakespeare for Children

Artist [or publisher]	Total Pages	Full Color	Full B&W	Partial	Small	Total
Blackie[1]	157	5	5	5		15
Boydell Bickers[2]	386		12			12
Boydell, Maud[3]	345		8			8
Boydell, Quiller-C[4]	301		9			9
Browne, Gordon[5]	460		20	40	33	93
Brundage Gem[6]	64	1	4	17		22
Brundage Altemus[7]	76		12			12
Brundage Graham[8]	52		3	17		20
Brundage/Bihn[9]	317	8		76		84
Copping, Harold[10]	655	[22]	30	61	44	157
Engravings[11]	224		6	22	102	130
Ewen, Edith[12]	60		19	18		37
Folkard, Charles-1[13]	425	21				21
Folkard, Charles-2[14]	120	5				5
Gilbert, John[15]	372		16	168		184
Godwin, Frank[16]	311	4	6			10
Hammond, G.D.-1[17]	286	16				16
Hammond, G.D.-2[18]	385	8				8
Harry, M.L.-1[19]	128	1	7			8
Harry, M.L.-2[20]	128	1	7			8
Howard, Frank[21]	312			123		123
Howard, Frank-A[22]	234			83		83
Howard, Frank-B[23]	235			98		98
Jackson, A.E.[24]	472	48				48
Kirk, M.L.[25]	453	12				12
Mulready, William[26]	486	20				20

Artist [or publisher]	Total Pages	Full Color	Full B&W	Partial	Small	Total
Price, N.M.[27]	324	16				16
Price, N.M.-1[28]	144	8				8
Price, N.M.-2[29]	118	8				8
Rackham, Arthur[30]	327	1	11			12
Rhead, Louis[31]	367	4	27	35	23	89
Ward, Lock & Co.[32]	96	8				8
Wilson, Clara P.[33]	143	8	16			24
Nesbit*[34]	130	10	11	55	12	88
Gateway*[35]	336	16	8		203	227
Hodder & Stoughton*[36]	380	16				16
Paintings-1*[37]	292	18				18
Paintings-2*[38]	126	7		2	10	19
Photographs/paint*[39]	116		4			4

*Several artists contributed illustrations.

Table 4 Key

1. *Tales from Shakespeare: From the Collection by Charles and Mary Lamb.* Stories Old & New Series. Illustrated by C.B.
2. *Tales from Shakespeare.* Permanent Photography from the Boydell Gallery.
3. Constance and Mary Maud, *Shakespeare's Stories.*
4. A.T. Quiller-Couch, *Historical Tales from Shakespeare.*
5. Mary Macleod, *The Shakespeare Story-Book.*
6. E. Nesbit with Hugh Chesson, *The Winter's Tale, and Other Stories.* Illustrated by Frances Brudage, M. Bowley, and others.
7. *The Children's Shakespeare.* Brundage Illustrations. Altemus.
8. *The Children's Shakespeare.* Brundage Illustrations. Graham.
9. *Twenty Beautiful Stories from Shakespeare: A Home Study Course.* Illustrations by Max Bihn, from Francis Brundage, M. Bowley, J. Willis Grey, etc.
10. F.J. Furnivall, *Tales from Shakespeare by Mary and Charles Lamb with Introductions and Additions.* 2 vols.
11. Robert R. Raymond, ed. *Typical Tales of Fancy, Romance, and History from Shakespeare.* Engravings.
12. W.T. Stead, *Tales from Shakespeare: "As You Like It" and "The Tempest,"* Books for the Bairns, #92.
13. Alice Spencer Hoffman, *The Children's Shakespeare: Being Stories from the Plays with Illustrative Passages.*
14. Tilney, F.C., *Tales from Shakespeare by Charles and Mary Lamb.*
15. Charles Lamb, *Tales from Shakespeare designed for the Use of Young People.* Engraved by Dalziel.
16. *Tales from Shakespeare by Mary and Charles Lamb.*
17. Thomas Carter, *Stories from Shakespeare.* Told through the Ages Series.
18. Thomas Carter, *Shakespeare's Stories of the English Kings.* Told Through the Ages Series.
19. *Lamb's Tales from Shakespeare,* Book 1. All-Time Tales Series.
20. *Lamb's Tales from Shakespeare,* Book 2. All-Time Tales Series.
21. Mary Seamer Seymour, *Shakespeare's Stories Simply Told.*
22. Mary Seamer Seymour, *Shakespeare's Stories Simply Told. Comedies.*
23. Mary Seamer Seymour, *Shakespeare's Stories Simply Told. Tragedies and Historical Plays.*
24. *Tales from Shakespeare by Charles and Mary Lamb.*
25. Winston Stokes, *All Shakespeare's Tales. Tales from Shakespeare by Charles and Mary Lamb and Tales from Shakespeare by Winston Stokes.*
26. Charles Lamb, *Tales from Shakespear. Designed for the Use of Young Persons.*
27. *Tales from Shakespeare by Charles and Mary Lamb.*
28. Jeanie Lang, *Stories from Shakespeare.* Told to the Children Series.

29. Jeanie Lang, *More Stories from Shakespeare*. Told to the Children Series.
30. *Lamb's Tales from Shakespeare*.
31. *Tales from Shakespeare by Charles and Mary Lamb*.
32. Edith Robarts, *Tales from Shakespeare by C. and M. Lamb*.
33. Fay Adams Britton, *Shakespearian Fairy Tales*.
34. E. Nesbit, *Children's Stories from Shakespeare*. Raphael House Library of Gift Books. Illustrations by J.H. Bacon, Harold Copping, A.A. Dixon, Howard Davie, Gordon Browne.
35. Mrs. Lang, *The Gateway to Shakespeare for Children*. The Gateway Series. Illustrations by E.F. Skinner, Norman Ault, T.C. Dugdale, A.K. Browling.
36. *Tales from Shakespeare by Mary and Charles Lamb*. Illustrations by Edmund Dulac, Arthur Rackham, Hugh Thomson, W. Heath Robinson, etc. Hodder & Stoughton.
37. Harrison S. Morris, *Tales from Shakespeare*. Color Plates.
38. R. Hudson, *Tales from Shakespeare*. Illustrations from Paintings.
39. Ada Baynes Stidolph, *The Children's Shakespeare* (3 actors, 1 painting).

Chapter Notes

Preface

1. *The Home Treasury of Old Story Books* (London: Sampson Low, Son, & Co., 1859), 191–208. "Ambrose Merton" (William Thoms [1803–1885]), librarian at the House of Lords and founder of *Notes and Queries*, added other traditional stories in *Old Story Books of England*. Joseph Cundall's original (1843–1844) expensive books resemble medieval manuscripts; other publishers reprinted different stories more cheaply.
2. Heman Humphrey, *Domestic Education* (Amherst, MA: J. A. & C. Adams, 1840), 94–99 passim, quoted in Gillian Avery, *Behold the Child: American Children and Their Books 1621–1922* (Baltimore: The Johns Hopkins Press, 1994), 26.
3. Avery, *Behold the Child*, 150.
4. Henry Newbolt, *The Teaching of English in England: Being the Report of the Departmental Committee Appointed by the President of the Board of Education to Inquire into the Position of English in the Educational System of England* (London: His Majesty's Stationery Office, 1921).
5. A danger phrased by Meg Pearson's online review of the Folger Library Exhibition. The exhibition was titled, "Golden Lads and Lasses," and was held 21 January–13 May, 2006. Meg Pearson, "From Hornbooks to Comic Books: 'Shakespeare for Children,'" *Borrowers and Lenders: The Journal of Shakespeare and Appropriation*, n.d., <http://lachesis.english.uga.edu/cocoon/borrowers/request?id=423239>
6. Ongoing controversy about canons of literature and history is substantial; e.g., E.D. Hirsch, Jr., *Cultural Literacy: What Every American Needs to Know*, with an updated appendix, "What Literate Americans Know" by Hirsch, Joseph Kett, and James Trefil (New York: Vintage Books, 1988); and C. John Sommerville, *The Decline of the Secular University* (Oxford and New York: Oxford University Press, 2006).
7. J.B. Priestly, *The Edwardians* (New York and Evanston: Harper & Row, 1970), 290.

Chapter 1

1. Humanists emphasized the Middle Ages in early volumes of *Children's Literature:* vol. 1 (1972), pp. 16–20 and 21–29; vol. 2 (1973), pp. 40–49; vol. 4 (1975), pp. 36–63; vol. 6 (1977), pp. 17–33. Daniel T. Kline, ed., *Medieval Literature for Children* (London: Routledge, 2003). Kline selects from nearly twenty texts. In contrast, critics note the absence of convincing characterization in Leslie Fielder, "The Child in Shakespeare," *Children's Literature* 2 (1973): 209–212. John Amos Comenius, *Orbis Pictus: A Facsimile of the First English Edition of 1659*, ed. John E. Sadler (London: Oxford University Press, 1968).
2. Samuel F. Pickering, Jr., *John Locke and Children's Books in Eighteenth-Century England* (Knoxville: University of Tennessee Press, 1981).
3. Philippe Ariés, *Centuries of Childhood: A Social History of Family Life*, trans. Robert Baldick (New York: Vintage Books of Random House, 1962), 46; Joel T. Rosenthal, ed., *Essays on Medieval Childhood: Responses to Recent Debates* (Donington, UK: Shaun Tyas, 2007); and Keith Thomas, "Children in Early Modern England," in *Children and Their Books: A Celebration of the Work of Iona and Peter Opie*, eds. Gillian Avery and Julia Briggs (Oxford: Clarendon Press, 1989), 45–77. Among distinctive studies are: Lloyd de Mause, ed., *The History of Childhood* (New York: Harper & Row, 1975); Lawrence Stone, *The Family, Sex and Marriage in England 1500–1800* (New York: Harper & Row, 1977); Linda Pollack, *Forgotten Children: Parent-Child Relations from 1500 to 1900* (New

York: Cambridge University Press, 1983); Linda Pollack, *A Lasting Relationship: Parents and Children over Three Centuries* (Hanover, NH: The University Press of New England, 1987); Ralph A. Houlbrooke, *The English Family 1450–1700* (New York: Longman, 1984).

4. James Stewart, *The New Child: British Art and the Origin of Modern Childhood, 1730–1830* (Berkeley: University of California Press, 1995), Exhibition Catalogue. See also J. H. Plumb, "The New World of Children in Eighteenth-Century England," *Past and Present* 67 (1975): 64–95.

5. Quoted in William Coolidge Lance, ed., *Catalogue of English and American Chap-Books and Broadside Ballads in Harvard College Library*, Bibliographical Contribution #56 (Cambridge, MA: Library of Harvard University, 1905), Item 57, p. vii.

6. John Newbery, *A Little Pretty Pocket-Book*, ed. Mary F. Thwaite (London, 1760; repr. London: Oxford University Press, 1966, and New York: Harcourt, Brace & World, 1967). Victor E. Neuburg, *The Penny Histories: A Study of Chapbooks for Young Readers over Two Centuries*, The Juvenile Library Series (London: Oxford University Press, 1968). For context, see Victor E. Neuburg, *Popular Literature: A History and Guide from the Beginnings to the Year 1897* (Harmondsworth, UK: Penguin Books, 1977); Leslie Shepard, *The History of Street Literature: The Story of Broadside Ballads, Chapbooks, Proclamations, News-sheets, Election Bills, Tracts, Pamphlets, Cocks, Catchpennies and Other Ephemera* (Newton Abbot, UK: David & Charles, 1973); Margaret Spufford, *Small Books and Pleasant Histories: Popular Fiction and Its Readership in Seventeenth-century England* (Athens: The University of Georgia Press, 1981). Histories of children's literature include additional information: F. J. Harvey Darton, *Children's Books in England: Five Centuries of Social Life*, ed. Brian Alderson (Cambridge: Cambridge University Press, 1932; repr. 1982); Percy Muir, *English Children's Books, 1600–1900* (London: Batsford, 1954); Mary F. Thwaite, *From Primer to Pleasure in Reading* (Boston: The Horn Book, 1963, repr. 1972); Mary V. Jackson, *Engines of Instruction, Mischief, and Magic: Children's Literature in England from Its Beginnings to 1839* (Lincoln: University of Nebraska Press, 1989). Humphrey Carpenter and Mari Prichard, *The Oxford Companion to Children's Literature* (Oxford and New York: Oxford University Press, 1984), 374–376. This work is a succinct overview with a list of winners of the Newbery Medal, the most prestigious American award for children's books.

7. Isaiah Thomas, *A Little Pretty Pocket-book* (Worcester, MA: Isaiah Thomas, 1787); facsimile reprint (West Haven, CT: Antique Educational, n.d.).

8. Gillian Avery, *Behold the Child: American Children and Their Books, 1621–1922* (Baltimore: The Johns Hopkins University Press, 1994), 60–61.

9. Carpenter and Prichard, *The Oxford Companion*, 363–364. E.F. Bleiler, *Mother Goose's Melodies* (Boston: Munroe and Francis, 1833), facsimile reprint (New York: Dover Publications, 1970). Although the Shakespeare section was not retained in the facsimile, "Fie, foh, and fumme, I smell the blood of a British man" (*King Lear* III.iv) is among the nursery rhymes; "Fee, Faw, Foe, Fum, / I smell the blood of an Englishman, / Dead or alive, I will have some" is the last rhyme before the alphabet in Munroe and Francis (Bleiler, *Mother Goose's Melodies*, 92). See Iona and Peter Opie, *The Oxford Dictionary of Nursery Rhymes* (Oxford: Clarendon Press, 1951); and William S. Baring-Gould and Cecil Baring-Gould, *The Annotated Mother Goose* (New York: Clarkson N. Potter, 1962).

10. Georgianna Ziegler, "Introducing Shakespeare: The Earliest Versions for Children," *Shakespeare* 2 (Dec. 2006): 137–139. Notable is a popular presentation, *Young Albert, the Roscius, Exhibited in a Series of Characters* (London: S. & J. Fuller, 1811), with five paper dolls and speeches for Richard III, Hamlet, Othello, Orlando (*As You Like It*), and Falstaff (*Henry IV*).

11. Thomas Percy, *Reliques of Ancient English Poetry: Consisting of Old Heroic Ballads, Songs, and Other Pieces of Our Earlier Poets, Together with some Few of Later Date*, ed. Robert Aris Willmott, Routledge's British Poets Series (London: George Routledge and Co., 1857). References are to this edition and page numbers are given in parentheses. Other Shakespearean items—"Titus Andronicus's Complaint" (111–114) and "Take, oh take those lips away," *Measure for Measure* (115)—are less relevant, since these plays were not popular for children. Percy identified a stanza of a later ballad, "Willow, willow, willow" (98–101), as derived from Shakespeare.

12. Hamilton Wright Mabie, *A Book of Old English Ballads* (New York: The Macmillan Co., 1896), 48–58; Hamilton Wright Mabie, *Short Studies in Literature* (New York: Dodd, Mead & Co., 1891, 1893). *Short Studies* has chapters about "Genius and Personality," "The Race Element," and "Personality and Race" that gloss relations between American and English identity, including many references to Shakespeare.

13. George Speaight, *Juvenile Drama: The History of the English Toy Theatre* (London: Macdonald & Co., 1975). This is the definitive study. Play sheets for nine Shakespearean titles—*Macbeth* (1811), *Julius Caesar* (1812), *The Merry Wives of Windsor*, *Romeo and Juliet*, *A*

Midsummer Night's Dream (1815), *Richard III* (1817), *Hamlet* (1819), *Henry IV* (1824), and *Richard II* (n.d.) — were issued by William West. His successor, Hodgson & Son, published texts of plays to accompany toy theatres; six Shakespeare titles (*Hamlet, Romeo and Juliet, The Tempest, Othello, Macbeth,* and *Richard III*) were among sixty-eight titles, published 1822–1830.

14. Speaight, *Juvenile Drama*, 236.

15. David Foxon, "The Chapbook Editions of the Lamb's *Tales from Shakespeare*," *The Book Collector* 6 (1957): 41–53.

16. Darton, *Children's Books in England*, 191.

17. In addition to those named in note 6, other important histories show how study of children's literature evolved in the late twentieth century: Cornelia Meigs, ed., *A Critical History of Children's Literature* (New York: Macmillan Co., 1953); John Rowe Townsend, *Written for Children: An Outline of English-Language Children's Literature* (Harmondsworth, UK, Middlesex, UK: Penguin Books, 1965, rev. 1974, 1976); Peter Hunt, *An Introduction to Children's Literature* (Oxford & New York: Oxford University Press, 1994); Peter Hunt, ed., *Children's Literature: An Illustrated History* (Oxford & New York: Oxford University Press, 1995). Revised editions of Sheila Egoff, G.T. Stubbs, and L.F. Ashley, eds., *Only Connect: Readings on Children's Literature* (Toronto, New York: Oxford University Press, 1969) reflect changing interests; cf. 3rd ed. of 1996, eds., Sheila Egoff, Gordon Stubbs, Ralph Ashley, and Wendy Sutton. Peter Hunt, *Criticism, Theory, and Children's Literature* (Oxford: Basil Blackwell, 1991). This study situates developing study of children's literature, theory, and cross-disciplinary work exemplified in Peter Hunt, ed., *Understanding Children's Literature* (London and New York: Routledge, 1999).

18. Quoted by Darton, *Children's Books in England*, 129. Chapbooks inspired writers of moral tales who imitated their style but added virtuous argument. Mrs. Trimmer, who is remembered for condemning fairy stories, prolifically wrote tracts for Sunday schools, a periodical called *The Guardian of Education* (1802–1806), and *The History of the Robins*, an animal story much loved by Victorians and illustrated by famous artists. Charles Welsh, *Goody Two-shoes: A Facsimile Reproduction of the Edition of 1766* (London: Griffith & Farran, 1881; repr. Detroit: Singing Tree Press, 1970). Almost the first book written to amuse children, it was long admired and remained of antiquarian and popular interest. Darton, *Children's Books in England*, 126–131, includes examples from the eighteenth century to 1940.

19. Charles Lamb, *The Letters of Charles Lamb*, vol. 1, ed. E.V. Lucas (London: Methuen, 1935), 326. Cited by Thwaite, *From Primer to Pleasure in Reading*, 82.

20. *Lessons for Children* (1778), two to three and three to four years old, a series written for an adopted son, attempted an appropriate level of comprehension; it was popular until the 1860s. *Hymns in Prose for Children* (1781) was translated into French, German, Spanish, Italian, and Hungarian and printed until the early twentieth century. Thwaite, *From Primer to Pleasure in Reading*, 57–59, 189, and Carpenter and Prichard, *The Oxford Companion*, 44–45, 267, 309. Mrs. Barbauld, who urged printing on good paper, in large and clear type, and with large spaces, anticipated publishing standards in children's books. A unique archive of a mother's materials for home education provides evidence of alternatives to published materials. Gillian Avery, *A Very Pretty Story: Facsimile of a Manuscript Held in the Bodleian Library* (Oxford: Bodleian Library, 2001); this is Jane Johnson's imaginative story, dated 1744. Evelyn Arizpe and Morag Styles with Shirley Brice Heath, *Reading Lessons from the Eighteenth Century: Mothers, Children and Texts* (Lichfield: Pied Piper, 2006); these scholars consider the entire archive — lesson cards, reading games, a commonplace book of quotations, and the imaginative story.

21. Montrose J. Moses, *Children's Books and Reading* (New York: Mitchell Kennerley, 1907), 136 and 137. All references are to this edition and page numbers are given in parentheses. Moses's selected "Book Lists for Children" cite several editions: Alfred Ainger's, E.V. Lucas's, Scribner's illustrated by Norman M. Price, and Quiller-Couch's historical tales.

22. Julie Henry and Chris Hastings, "Brush up your Shakespeare: for a pass you need to know ... nothing," *Sunday Telegraph*, April 23, 2006, p. 13; and Maureen Dowd, "Much Ado About Reading," *The New York Times*, Sat., 2 Sept. 2006, p. A23.

23. Henry Newbolt, *The Teaching of English in England: Being the Report of the Departmental Committee Appointed by the President of the Board of Education to Inquire into the Position of English in the Educational System of England* (London: His Majesty's Stationery Office, 1921), 337. All quotations are from this edition and page references are given in parentheses.

24. Neuburg's *The Penny Histories* is an excellent introduction, with both a history and facsimiles of examples. See also Velma Bourgeois Richmond, *The Legend of Guy of Warwick* (New York: Garland Publishing, 1996), 237–241, 313–315, 345–356.

25. Velma Bourgeois Richmond, *Chaucer as Children's Literature: Retellings from the*

Victorian and Edwardian Eras (Jefferson, NC, and London: McFarland & Co., 2004), 24–35.

26. Meigs, ed., *A Critical History of Children's Literature*, 92.

27. David Daiches, "Presenting Shakespeare," in *Essays in the History of Printing*, ed. Asa Briggs (London: Longman, 1974), 61–112. This readable, detailed summary of editions includes a few particulars about Shakespeare for children, notably Lamb's *Tales* and school texts.

28. Quoted by Daiches, "Presenting Shakespeare," 94.

29. *Lamb's Tales from Shakespeare: Being the Textbook in English Appointed by the Senate of the Calcutta University for the Entrance Examination* (Calcutta: Roy Press, 1879).

30. Charles Lamb, *Tales from Shakespeare: Designed for the Use of Young Persons*, 2 vols. (London: Thomas Hodgkins, 1807). Volume and page references are from this edition and given in parentheses.

31. Alec Ellis, *A History of Children's Reading and Literature* (Oxford: Pergamon Press, 1968), 76.

32. Information about many illustrators is difficult to find; histories of children's literature stress verbal texts. The most helpful general reference works on which I have relied are: Simon Houfe, *The Dictionary of 19th Century British Book Illustrators and Caricaturists* (1978, rev. ed. Woodbridge, Suffolk: Antique Collectors' Club, 1996); Alan Horne, *The Dictionary of 20th Century British Book Illustrators* (Woodbridge, Suffolk: Antique Collectors' Club, 1994); Susan E. Meyer, *A Treasury of the Great Children's Book Illustrators* (New York: Harry N. Abrams, 1983); John Barr, *Illustrated Children's Books* (London: The British Library, 1986); Joyce Irene Whalley and Tessa Rose Chester, *A History of Children's Book Illustration* (London: John Murray with the Victoria & Albert Museum, 1988); Richard Dalby, *The Golden Age of Children's Book Illustration* (New York: Gallery Books, 1991).

33. Quoted in Margery Darrell, ed., *Once Upon A Time: The Fairy Tale World of Arthur Rackham* (New York: Viking, 1972), 12.

34. Walter Pape and Frederick Burwick, eds., in collaboration with the German Shakespeare Society, *The Boydell Shakespeare Gallery* (Bottrop: Peter Pomp, 1996). Jane Martineau, et al. *Shakespeare in Art*, Exhibition Catalogue, Dulwich Picture Gallery (London and New York: Merrell Holberton Publishers, 2003); see Velma Bourgeois Richmond, "Exhibition Review—Shakespeare in Art at the Dulwich Picture Gallery London," *Art on the Line* (2004/1): 1–4.

35. Jane Martineau, ed., *Victorian Fairy Painting*, Exhibition Catalogue, Royal Academy of Art (London: Merrell Holberton Publishers, 1997).

36. Ellis, *A History of Children's Reading*, 82.

37. Newbolt was chairman; other members were John Bailey, K.M. Baines, Frederick S. Boas, H.M. Davies, D. Enright, S.H. Firth, J.H. Fowler, L.A. Lowe, Sir Arthur T. Quiller-Couch, George Sampson, Caroline F.E. Spurgeon, G. Perrie Williams, and J. Dover Wilson. Chris Baldick, *The Social Mission of English Criticism, 1848–1932* (Oxford: Oxford University Press, 1983), 93–105. Baldick explains the context of the report and interests and qualifications of its authors.

Chapter 2

1. Jean I. Marsden, "Shakespeare for Girls: Mary Lamb and Tales from Shakespeare," *Children's Literature* 17 (1989): 47–63, argues, "feminization, rewriting to provide an ideal of what young ladies should learn." See Janet Bottoms, "'To read aright': Representations of Shakespeare for Children," *Children's Literature* 32 (2004): 1–14.

2. Charles and Mary Lamb, *Tales from Shakespeare by Charles and Mary Lamb*, with Boydell Gallery illustrations (London: Bickers & Son, 1876).

3. Illustrations are identified by play, act, and scene. Details of artist, date, and engraver are from Walter Pape and Frederick Burwick, eds., *The Boydell Shakespeare Gallery* (Bottrop, Essen: Peter Pomp, 1996), published in collaboration with the German Shakespeare Society to accompany The Boydell Shakespeare Gallery Exhibition at Museum Bochum.

4. Grant F. Scott, "To Play the King: Illustrations from *The Tempest* in the Boydell Shakespeare Gallery," in Pape and Burwick, *The Boydell Shakespeare Gallery*, 120–121. Scott argues that the image is designed to question Prospero's powers and refer to the instability of King George III.

5. Quoted by Frederick Burwick, "The Romantic Reception of the Boydell Shakespeare Gallery: Lamb, Coleridge, and Hazlitt," in Pape and Burwick, *The Boydell Shakespeare Gallery*, 146. I am indebted to this excellent essay, 143–157, for much of this discussion.

6. Charles Lamb, *Tales from Shakespeare Designed for the Use of Young People*, illustrated by Sir John Gilbert, R.A. (London: Routledge, 1882). All references are to this edition and pages are given in parentheses.

7. Simon Houfe, *The Dictionary of 19th Century British Book Illustrators and Caricaturists* (1978, rev. ed. Woodbridge, Suffolk: Antique Collectors' Club, 1996), 151.

8. Charles and Mary Lamb, *Tales from*

Shakespeare by Charles and Mary Lamb, illustrated by Arthur Rackham (London: J.M. Dent & Co., 1899); and Ernest Rhys, ed., *Tales from Shakespeare by Charles and Mary Lamb*, illustrated by Arthur Rackham, Everyman for Young People Series (London: J.M. Dent & Co., 1906; New York: E.P. Dutton & Co., 1906). All quotations are from the latter and page references are given in parentheses. Dent reprinted it four times in the first two years. *Great Stories from Shakespeare by Charles and Mary Lamb*, illustrated in line by Arthur Rackham (London: Daily Sketch Publications, n. d.) has only seven of the original twelve illustrations and eighteen of Lamb's twenty tales; two less obviously unsuitable for children and not illustrated by Rackham—*Pericles* and *Timon of Athens*—have been dropped.

9. Twelve color illustrations are in a facsimile of the 1909 edition: Charles and Mary Lamb, *Tales from Shakespeare* (New York: Weathervane Books, Crown Publishers, 1975).

10. William Shakespeare, *A Midsummer Night's Dream: With Illustrations by Arthur Rackham, R.W.S.* (London: William Heinemann, 1908). A facsimile, *Shakespeare's A Midsummer Night's Dream: Illustrated by Arthur Rackham* (Mineola, NY: Dover Publications, 2003), has some adjustments, notably placing captions with each illustration and adding bracketed references to the repaginated text. My page references are to this edition.

11. Charles and Mary Lamb, *Tales from Shakespeare by Charles and Mary Lamb*, illustrated by Norman M. Price (London & Edinburgh: E.C. and T.C. Jack, 1905). All page references are to this edition. Charles Scribner's Sons was the publisher in the United States.

12. Charles and Mary Lamb, *Tales from Shakespeare by Charles and Mary Lamb*, illustrated by A.E. Jackson (London and Melborne: Ward, Lock and Co., 1918). Quotations and descriptions are based on this edition and page references are given in parentheses.

13. Alan Horne, *The Dictionary of 20th Century British Book Illustrators* (Woodbridge, Suffolk: Antique Collectors' Club, 1994), 259.

14. Velma Bourgeois Richmond, *Shakespeare, Catholicism, and Romance* (New York: Continuum Publishing, 2000), 197–201.

15. Charles and Mary Lamb, *Tales from Shakespeare by Charles and Mary Lamb*, illustrated by Louis John Rhead (New York: Blue Ribbon Books [Harper & Brothers], 1918), 368. Quotations and descriptions are based on this edition and page references are given in parentheses.

16. Charles and Mary Lamb, *Tales From Shakespeare by Charles and Mary Lamb*, illustrated by Frank Godwin (Philadelphia: John C. Winston Co., 1924). Quotations and descriptions are based on this edition and page references are given in parentheses.

17. Charles and Mary Lamb, *Tales from Shakespeare by Charles and Mary Lamb*, illustrated by various artists (London: Hodder & Stoughton, 1914).

18. Maurice Clare [Mary Clarissa Gillington Byron], *A Day with William Shakespeare*, Days with the Poets Series (London: Hodder & Stoughton, 1913), reprints and identifies some illustrations.

19. *Shakespeare's Comedy of The Tempest with Illustrations by Edmund Dulac* (New York and London: Hodder and Stoughton, 1908). Quotations and descriptions are based on this edition, and page references are given in parentheses.

Chapter 3

1. Harrison S. Morris, *Tales from Shakespeare* (Philadelphia: J.B. Lippincott Co. and London: William Heinemann, 1893), vi. All quotations are from this edition and page references are given in parentheses.

2. Hugh M. Richmond, *Shakespeare in Performance: King Richard III* (Manchester and New York: Manchester University Press, 1989).

3. F.J. Furnivall, *Tales from Shakespeare by Mary and Charles Lamb: With Introductions and Additions* (London, Paris, New York: Raphael Tuck & Sons, 1901), xi. All references are to this edition and given in parentheses.

4. Furnivall is a subject of debate among scholars. Useful for understanding him is William Benzie, *Dr. F.J. Furnivall: Victorian Scholar Adventurer* (Norman, OK: Pilgrim Books, 1983). See also Derek Pearsall, "Frederick James Furnivall," in *Medieval Scholarship: Biographical Studies on the Formation of the Discipline*, ed. Helen Damico with Donald Fennema and Karmen Lenz, vol. 2: Literature and Philology, Garland Reference Library of the Humanities Series (New York: Garland Publishing, 1998), 125–138; David Matthews, *The Making of Middle English, 1765–1910*, vol. 18, Medieval Cultures Series (Minneapolis: University of Minnesota Press, 1999), 138–161.

5. Humphrey Carpenter and Mari Prichard, *The Oxford Companion to Children's Literature* (Oxford and New York: Oxford University Press, 1984), 515.

6. Winston Stokes, *All Shakespeare's Tales: Tales from Shakespeare by Charles and Mary Lamb and Tales from Shakespeare by Winston Stokes* (New York: Frederick A. Stokes and

London & Edinburgh: W. & R. Chambers, 1911). All references are to this edition and given in parentheses.

7. Mrs. Andrew Lang, *The Gateway to Shakespeare for Children: Containing a Life of Shakespeare, by Mrs. Andrew Lang, a Selection from the Plays, and from Lamb's Tales* (London, Edinburgh, Dublin, New York: Thomas Nelson & Sons, 1908), 7. All references are to this edition and given in parentheses.

8. After page references I add act, scene, and line references, from David Bevington, ed., *The Complete Works of Shakespeare*, updated 4th ed. (New York: Longman, 1997). All subsequent act, scene, and line references are to this edition.

9. *Tales from Shakespeare*. "The Tempest," Books for the Bairns— 92A repr. (London: Stead's Bairns' Library, 1918); blurb on inside cover.

10. Sally Wood, *W.T. Stead and His "Books for the Bairns"* (Edinburgh: Salvia Books, 1987). Wood surveys his career, lists titles and dates, and includes sample illustrations. Much of my discussion of Stead's life and work comes from her biography, 3–17.

11. *Tales from Shakespeare Books for the Bairns*, #92 "*As You Like It*" and "*The Tempest*" (London: Mowbray House, 1903). All references are to this edition and page numbers are given in parentheses.

12. Edith Robarts, *Tales from Shakespeare by C. and M. Lamb*, Stories for the Children Series (London: Ward, Locke & Sons, 1910).

13. F.C. Tilney, ed., *Tales from Shakespeare by Charles and Mary Lamb*, Tales for Children from Many Lands Series (London: J. M. Dent & Sons and New York: E.P. Dutton & Co., 1926). All page references are to this edition and given in parentheses.

Chapter 4

1. Mark Girouard, *The Return to Camelot: Chivalry and the English Gentleman* (New Haven: Yale University Press, 1981). Girouard makes the case brilliantly and thoroughly. But Debra Mancoff, "Mark Girouard, An Enthusiast for Chivalry: The Return to Camelot: Chivalry and the English Gentleman," in *History and Community: Essays in Victorian Medievalism*, ed. Florence S. Boos (New York: Garland Publishing, 1992), 209–220, points to the book's popular, non–academic quality and concludes him to be "a bit chivalry-mad," although appropriately enthusiastic given his subject. Children's literature heavily supports Girouard's thesis, in collections of chivalric stories and explicit arguments, notably Henry Newbolt, *The Book of the Happy Warrior* (London: Longmans, Green & Co., 1917). Eva March Tappan, *When Knights Were Bold* (Boston and New York: Houghton Mifflin Co., 1911), a children's social history, identifies chivalry as central to understanding the Middle Ages.

2. David Murray Smith, *Tales of Chivalry and Romance* (London: Virtue & Co., 1869), Preface. All quotations are from this edition and page references are given in parentheses.

3. Abby Sage Richardson, *Stories from Old English Poetry, 1871* (Boston: Houghton, Mifflin & Co., 1891). All quotations are from this edition and page references are given in parentheses. Spenser's tales are the conclusion of the *Squire's Tale* and the *Adventures of Fair Florimel*; the plays are John Lyly's *Campaspe and the Painter* and Robert Greene's *Friar Bacon's Brass Head* and *Margaret, the Fair Maid of Fresingfield*.

4. Mrs. H.R. Haweis, *Chaucer for Children: A Golden Key*, new ed. (London: Chatto & Windus, 1900). See Velma Bourgeois Richmond, *Chaucer as Children's Literature: Retellings from the Victorian and Edwardian Eras* (Jefferson, NC, and London: McFarland & Co., 2004), 36–48.

5. Edwardian books of art history for children show that study of painting, especially Italian painters, was popular. Two early examples, one English and one American, are Lawrence Wilson, *Painting Shown to the Children*, Shown to the Children Series, ed. Louey Chisholm (London & Edinburgh: T. C. & E. C. Jack, 1907); and Dolores Bacon, *Pictures Every Child Should Know*, Every Child Should Know Series (New York: Grosset & Dunlop, 1908). Amy Steedman, *Knights of Art: Stories of the Italian Painters* (London & Edinburgh: T.C. & E.C. Jack, 1907), is a reward book.

6. *The Encyclopædia Britannica*, 11th ed. (1910–1911), XV, 147.

7. Susan Cunningham, *Stories from Dante*, Told through the Ages Series (London: George G. Harrap, 1911); and W. E. Sparkes, *Paolo and Francesca*, The World's Romances Series (London: Thomas Nelson & Sons, 1912).

8. Eleanor Bulley, *Great Britain for Little Britons* (1887; repr. London: Wells Gardner, Darton & Co., 1904), v. All quotations are from this edition and page references are given in parentheses.

9. The account of Ipswich, Wolsey's birthplace, later provides a biographical sketch, 169–170.

10. Mary Seamer [Seymour], *Shakespeare's Stories Simply Told* (London, Edinburgh, New York: Thomas Nelson & Sons, 1880), 5. Page references for quotations from this edition are the first number given in parentheses; the second

number refers to pages from the later companion volumes described in note 12.

11. J.S. Bratton, *The Impact of Victorian Fiction* (London: Croom Helm, and Totowa, NJ: Barnes & Noble Books, 1981). Bratton argues that the early work of Sunday schools, the Religious Tract Society (RTS), and the Society for the Propagation of Christian Knowledge (SPCK) were crucial to the development of children's literature; their publication of "Rewards" and adaptations of popular romance models established basic principles. Alec Ellis, *A History of Children's Reading and Literature* (Oxford: Pergamon Press, 1968), describes publishing practices for children within contexts of nineteenth-century development of literacy for the working class and of schools and libraries. John Feather, *A History of British Publishing* (London and New York: Routledge, 1988), is a comprehensive survey with some attention to children's books.

12. Mary [Seamer] Seymour, *Shakespeare's Stories Simply Told: Comedies* (London, Edinburgh, and New York: T. Nelson & Sons, 1883); and Mary [Seamer] Seymour, *Shakespeare's Stories Simply Told: Tragedies and Historical Plays* (London, Edinburgh, and New York: T. Nelson & Sons, 1899). Page references for quotations are the second number given in parentheses; first numbers refer to the first edition.

13. Hugh M. Richmond, *Shakespeare in Performance: King Henry VIII* (New York and Manchester: Manchester University Press, 1994).

14. Germaine Greer, *The Female Eunuch* (1970; repr. New York: Bantam Books, 1971), 220–221.

15. Heinrich Saure, *M. Seamer Shakespeare's Stories für Schulen bearbeitet und mit Anmerkungen Versehen* (Berlin: F.A. Herbig, 1890).

16. Robert R. Raymond, *Typical Tales of Fancy, Romance, and History from Shakespeare's Plays* (New York: Fords, Howard, and Hulbert, 1881). Quotations are from a second printing in 1892 and page references are given in parentheses.

17. Some English children also had strong attitudes. Records of child responses are few, but Emily Shore (1819–1839), after hearing *Julius Caesar* read aloud—a reminder of the nineteenth-century practice—recorded her sharp judgments: "Brutus is my favourite.... I am fond of Portia also, but not Julius Caesar, nor Mark Anthony." *The Journal of Emily Shore* (London: 1891), 22, cited by A.O.J. Cockshut, "Children's Diaries," in *Children and Their Books: A Celebration of the Work of Iona and Peter Opie*, ed. Gillian Avery and Julia Briggs (Oxford: Clarendon Press, 1989), 390. The child's diary, kept from July 1831 to July 1839, shows remarkable perspicacity; she records her enthusiasm for Milton.

18. Jane Martineau, ed., *Victorian Fairy Painting*, Exhibition Catalogue, Royal Academy of Arts (London: Merrell Holberton Publishers, 1997). Several articles are cogent for Shakespeare as children's literature: Pamela White Trimpe, "Victorian Fairy Book Illustration," 54–61; and Russell Jackson, "Shakespeare's Fairies in Victorian Criticism and Performance," 38–45. Illustrations are mostly in color and Shakespeare is the most frequent reference throughout. See also Jane Martineau, et al., *Shakespeare in Art*, Exhibition Catalogue. Dulwich Picture Gallery (London and New York: Merrell Publishers, 2003).

19. Adelaide C. Gordon Sim, *Phoebe's Shakespeare* (London: Bickers & Son, 1894), iv. All quotations are from this edition and page references are given in parentheses.

Chapter 5

1. E. Nesbit, *The Children's Shakespeare*, ed. Edric Vredenburg and illustrated by Frances Brundage, M. Bowley, J. Willis Grey, et al. (London, Paris, New York: Raphael Tuck & Sons, 1897). The best biography is Julia Briggs, *A Woman of Passion: The Life of Edith Nesbit* (London: Hutchinson, 1987).

2. Simon Houfe, *The Dictionary of 19th Century British Book Illustrators and Caricaturists* (1978, rev. ed. Woodbridge, Suffolk: Antique Collectors' Club, 1996), 80.

3. E. Nesbit, *Children's Stories from Shakespeare*, ed. Capt. Edric Vredenburg, The Raphael House Library of Gift Books for Boys and Girls Series (London, Paris, New York: Raphael Tuck & Sons, 1912), 10. All quotations are from this edition and page references are given in parentheses.

4. E. Nesbit, *Twenty Beautiful Stories from Shakespeare: A Home Study Course. Being a Choice Collection from the World's Greatest Classic Writer*, ed. E.T. Roe and illustrated by Max Bihn (Chicago and Boston: The John A. Hertel Co., 1907). All quotations are from this edition and page references are given in parentheses. For text and illustrations—but not the first edition's beauty, decorative borders and positions of illustrations—see http://www.worldwideschool.com/library/books/lit/Shakespeare/BeautifulStoriesfromShakespeare/chap18.html (Seattle, WA, June 1998). A paperback, E. Nesbit, *The Best of Shakespeare*, The Opie Library Series (Oxford and New York: Oxford University Press, 1997), includes ten plays: *Romeo and Juliet, The Merchant of Venice, Twelfth Night, Hamlet, The Tempest, King Lear, Macbeth, As*

You Like It, The Winter's Tale, and *Othello.* Peter Hunt makes the case that Nesbit was learning her craft in this apprentice work in his Afterword, 103–108.

5. E. Nesbit, *The Children's Shakespeare* (Philadelphia: Henry Altemus Co., 1900).

6. E. Nesbit, *The Children's Shakespeare* (New York: Charles E. Graham, 1900).

7. Ada Baynes Stidolph, *The Children's Shakespeare* (London: Allman & Sons, 1902). All quotations are from this edition and page references are given in parentheses.

8. Mary Macleod, *The Shakespeare Story-Book* (London: Wells Gardner, Darton & Co., 1902), viii. All quotations are from the fourth edition of 1910 and page references are given in parentheses.

9. Zaidee Brown, ed., *Standard Catalog for High School Libraries* (New York: The H. W. Wilson Co., 1929), 137.

10. Jeanie Lang, *Stories from Shakespeare,* Told to the Children Series (London: T.C. and E.C. Jack; and New York: E.P. Dutton & Co., 1905), vii. All quotations are from this edition and page references are given in parentheses.

11. Jeanie Lang, *More Stories from Shakespeare,* Told to the Children Series (London: T.C. and E.C. Jack; and New York: E.P. Dutton & Co., 1910), v. All quotations are from this edition and page references are given in parentheses.

12. Andrew Wawn, *The Vikings and the Victorians: Inventing the Old North in Nineteenth-century Britain* (Cambridge: D. S. Brewer, 2000), is the definitive study, although there are few references to children's literature.

13. Fay Adams Britton, *Shakespearian Fairy Tales* (Chicago: The Reilly & Britton Co., 1907). All quotations are from this edition and page references are given in parentheses.

14. R(obert) Hudson, *Tales from Shakespeare* (London and Glasgow: Collins Clear-Type Press, 1906), 120 and 119. All quotations are from this edition and page references are given in parentheses.

15. Sir Arthur T. Quiller-Couch, *Historical Tales from Shakespeare* (London: Edward Arnold, 1910). All quotations are from this edition and page references are given in parentheses.

16. Terence Hawkes, "Entry on Q," in *Shakespeare and Appropriation,* ed. Christy Desmet and Robert Sawyer (London and New York: Routledge, 1999), 37, 42. Hawkes analyzes the New Cambridge edition of *As You Like It* (1926), a joint effort by Quiller-Couch and J. Dover Wilson, to support his argument about Q's Liberalism: set in "the Heart of England," this play's essential Englishness, an articulation of English "free from Teutonic distractions" and beyond criticism, has "feeling that goes deeper into moral concern." Hawkes, "Entry on Q," 39–40.

Both E.M.W. Tillyard and Basil Willey confirm Quiller-Couch's importance in defining the Cambridge tripos.

17. Sir Arthur T. Quiller-Couch, *On the Art of Reading* (Cambridge: Cambridge University Press, 1920).

18. Thomas Carter, *Stories from Shakespeare,* Told through the Ages Series (London: George G. Harrap & Co., 1910). All quotations are from this edition with page references in parentheses.

19. Thomas Carter, *Shakespeare's Stories of the English Kings,* Told through the Ages Series (London, Bombay, Sydney: George G. Harrap & Co., 1912). All quotations are from this edition and page references are given in parentheses.

20. Velma Bourgeois Richmond, *Shakespeare, Catholicism, and Romance* (New York: Continuum, 2000), 201–206. An example of conflicting religious attitudes toward Catherine of Aragon during family stories in the evening is *Peter Parley's Tales about the Kings and Queens: With an Historical Review of Their Characters, and the Great Events of Their Respective Reigns* (London: Thomas Holmes, 1848), 47–65. Recitations from Shakespeare's *Henry VIII* include daughter Eliza's "the best part of Catherine's defense of herself" (II.iv.13–32), while Mamma reminds her "dear children of their favorite lines" (IV.ii.83–84, 87–92), 51 and 56.

21. Alice Spencer Hoffman, *The Children's Shakespeare: Being Stories from the Plays with Illustrative Passages Told and Chosen,* illustrated by Charles Folkard (London: J. M. Dent; and New York: E.P. Dutton, 1911). Page references for quotations from this edition are in parentheses.

22. Alice Spencer Hoffman, *The Story of The Tempest from the Play of Shakespeare,* illustrated by Walter Crane (London: J.M. Dent & Co.; and New York: E.P. Dutton & Co., 1904), vii. Page references for quotations from this edition are given in parentheses.

23. Walter Crane, *Of the Decorative Illustration of Books Old and New* (London: G. Bell & Sons, 1896) was reissued in 1972 and reprinted in 1979 by Bell and Hyman.

24. Constance and Mary Maud, *Shakespeare's Stories* (London: Edward Arnold, 1913). All quotations are from this edition and page references are given in parentheses.

Chapter 6

1. Charles and Mary Lamb, *Tales from Shakespeare,* Book I and Book II, All-Time Tales Series, illustrated by M. Lavars Harry (London:

George G. Harrap, & Co., 1910). All quotations are from these editions and page references are given in parentheses.

2. *Tales from Shakespeare*, Stories Old and New Series (London, Glasgow, Bombay: Blackie, 1917). All quotations are from this edition and page references are given in parentheses. It was reissued in 1955, when patriotic interest in English traditional literature followed victory in World War II.

3. The list is from Albert Meyrac, *The Flower of Gold and Other Legends*, trans. Dorothy King, Stories Old and New Series (London and Glasgow: Blackie & Son, 1927), 1.

4. Dorothy King, *Greenwood Tales: Stories of Robin Hood and his Merry Men*, Stories Old and New Series (London and Glasgow: Blackie & Son, 1920), 3.

5. A. Syms-Wood, ed., *Tales from Shakespeare by Charles and Mary Lamb for Preliminary Students, with Introduction, Notes, Examination Papers, Extracts from the Plays, Etc.* (London: George Gill & Sons, 1909), iv. All quotations are from this edition and page references are given in parentheses.

6. *The Children's Shakespeare: Scenes from the Plays. With Introductory Readings from Charles and Mary Lamb's 'Tales from Shakespeare.' Arranged as a Continuous Reader with Exercises in Composition* (London: Macmillan & Co., 1910).

7. Rev. Alfred Ainger, ed., *Tales from Shakespeare by Charles and Mary Lamb*, Macmillan's Pocket American and English Classics (New York and London: The Macmillan Co., 1916), vi. All quotations are from this edition and page references are given in parentheses.

8. Edwin Ginn, *Tales from Shakespeare by Charles and Mary Lamb, Edited for the Use of Schools, with Illustrations from Plates in the Valpy Edition of Shakespeare's Plays* (Boston, New York, Chicago, London, Atlanta, Dallas, Columbus, and San Francisco: Ginn & Co., 1915). All quotations are from this edition and page references are given in parentheses.

9. In contrast, *Tales from Shakespeare by Charles and Mary Lamb* (Rahway, NJ, and New York: The Mershon Co., n.d. [c.1910]), is austere — no pictures — with rich pedagogical materials. This little volume (actually two books, each with ten tales, combined comedies and tragedies, in no obvious order) is "an ill-favored thing, but mine own," found in my grandmother's attic on a hot summer's day a very long time ago, and was my first reading of Shakespeare's stories.

10. Clara Linklater Thomson, *A First Book of English Literature*, vol. 1 of 7 (London: Horace Marshall & Son, 1903–1909?), v. Each volume repeats the Preface with different book lists. All other quotations are from volume III and page references are given in parentheses.

11. Clara Linklater Thomson, *Our Inheritance* (Cambridge: Cambridge University Press, 1910). All quotations are from this edition and page references are given in parentheses.

12. John Clare, "Free — a proper history book for every school," *The Daily Telegraph*, Weds., 21 Sept. 2005, p. 25; Tony Halpin, "Prince to promote old-school teaching," *The Times*, Thurs., 8 June 2006, p. 5.

13. *Highroads of Literature, Book Second, Bards and Minstrels* (London, Edinburgh, Dublin, and New York: Thomas Nelson & Sons, 1915), 141. All quotations are from this edition and page references are given in parentheses.

14. Lear's story, largely because of Shakespeare's play, was told in several ways. The old verse ballad "King Lear and His Three Daughters" is with tales of Beowulf, Siegfried, King Arthur, Robin Hood, Roland and Oliver, and others in *The Hall of Heroes, Book III, The Royal Treasury of Story and Song* (London, Edinburgh, New York: Thomas Nelson & Sons, 1907), 178–184.

15. *Highroads of Literature, Book Third, The Morning Star* (London, Edinburgh, Dublin, and New York: Thomas Nelson & Sons, 1915). All quotations are from this edition and page references are given in parentheses.

16. *Highroads of Literature, Book Fourth, Captains and Kings* (London, Edinburgh, Dublin, and New York: Thomas Nelson & Sons, 1915), 14. All quotations are from this edition and page references are given in parentheses.

17. It is the back cover of Leslie Parris, ed., *The Pre-Raphaelites* (1994; repr. London: Tate Gallery, 1996). See Millais, *Ophelia*, 96–98. This exhibition and catalog contributed greatly to a return of favor for Pre-Raphaelite painters.

18. *Highroads of Literature, Book Fifth, Books of all Time* (London, Edinburgh, and New York: Thomas Nelson & Sons, 1919), 10. All quotations are from this edition and page references are given in parentheses.

19. *Highroads of Literature, Book Sixth, Thoughts and Voices* (London, Edinburgh, and New York: Thomas Nelson & Sons, 1920), 54. All quotations are from this edition and page references are given in parentheses.

20. *Arnold's Literary Reading Books*, 6 vols. (London: Edward Arnold, 1902–1909), including: *In Golden Realms* (1902), *The Greenwood Tree* (1903), *Chips from a Bookshelf* (1908), *Rambles in Bookland* (1909), and *In the World of Books* (1902). An added seventh volume is *The Storied Past: A Book of Selections from English Literature Illustrative of English History* (1911).

21. "King Leir and His Daughters," retold from Geoffrey of Monmouth's *History of the*

Kings of Britain (1148), is the final and only item of "History" in M(ary) Sturt and E(llen) C. Oakden, *Minstrel Tales*, #159 of The King's Treasuries of Literature Series (London and Toronto: J. M. Dent, 1928), 235–239. Other categories are "Adventure," "Romance," "Tricks and Jests," "Animal Tales," "Saints' Legends," and "Fairy Tales."

22. *Steps to Literature*, 7 vols. (London: Edward Arnold, 1905), including *Book I: Tales of the Homeland*, *Book II: Tales of Many Lands*, *Book III: Stories from English and Welsh Literature*, *Book IIIA: Stories from the Literature of the British Isles*, *Book IV: Literary Readings relating to the Empire*, and *Book VI: Glimpses of World Literature*.

23. *The Sesame Readers*, 6 vols. (London: Edward Arnold, 1908), including *Introductory Book: Open Sesame*, *Book I: Stories and Fables*, *Book II: Fairy Land*, *Book III: Wonder Land*, *Book IV: Characters and Scenes*, and *Book V: Britain of To-day*. Quotations are from this edition and page references are given in parentheses.

24. Estelle Ross, *The Birth of England (449–1066)*, *From Conquest to Charter (1066–1215)*, *Barons and Kings (1215–1485)*, Harrap's Illustrated History of England Series (London: George G. Harrap, 1910, 1912, 1911).

25. Alice Cockran, *The Dawn of British History*, Harrap's Illustrated History of England Series (London: George G. Harrap, 1912).

26. A. J. Church, *Stories from English History: From Richard II to Charles I* (London: Seeley & Co., 1896). Quotations are from this edition and page references are given in parentheses.

27. Sidney Dark, *The Book of England for Young People* (New York: George H. Doran & Co., 1923). Quotations are from this edition and page references are given in parentheses.

28. Charlotte M. Yonge, *Part III: Twenty Stories and Biographies: From 1066 to 1485*, Westminster Historical Reading Books Series (London: National Society's Depository, 1892), 91–94. Quotations are from this edition and page references are given in parentheses.

29. Clara Linklater Thomson, *A First History of England*, 7 vols. (London: Horace Marshall & Son, 1901–1909).

30. Tom Bevan, *Stories from British History (B.C. 54–A.D. 1485)* (Boston: Little, Brown & Co., 1910). Quotations are from this edition and page references are given in parentheses.

31. *Highroads of History, Book Seventh, Highroads of British History* (London, Edinburgh, Dublin, and New York: Thomas Nelson & Sons, 1903).

32. Clara Linklater Thomson, *Carmina Britanniæ: A Selection of Poems and Ballads Illustrative of English History* (London: Horace Marshall & Son, 1901), v–vi. All references are to this edition and given in parentheses.

33. Quoted in an interview by Frank Kermode, "The House of Fiction," *Partisan Review* 30 (Spring 1963): 80.

Chapter 7

1. Thomas Bailey Aldrich, ed., *The Young Folks' Library*, 20 vols. (Boston: Hall & Lock Co., 1901–1902). As late as the 1950s, these books were reprinted, albeit in cheaper editions; e.g., Charles Eliot Norton, *The Story Teller* (Chicago: Auxiliary Educational League, 1953).

2. Eva March Tappan, *The Children's Hour: Stories from Seven Old Favorites*, vol. 5 of 10 (Boston: Houghton Mifflin Co., 1907), ix. All quotations are from this edition and page references are given in parentheses. Five additional volumes (history, science, and so on) were added in 1916 to supplement the original ten volumes of literature.

3. Robert Newton Linscott, *A Guide to Good Reading: With Practical Directions for the Use of The Children's Hour in the Home* (Boston: Houghton Mifflin Co., 1912), vii. All quotations are from this edition and page references are given in parentheses.

4. Elizabeth McCracken, "The Selection of Stories for Little Children," in *The Children's Hour*, 10 vols., ed. Eva March Tappan (Boston: Houghton Mifflin & Co., 1907), 1–12. McCracken tells anecdotes of children's immediate and long-term responses to stories. Linscott's annotated bibliography "Books for Parents" advises practical considerations, including sex and health, as well as values of high sentiment. Also in Eva March Tappan, ed., *The Children's Hour*, 10 vols. (Boston: Houghton Mifflin & Co., 1907).

5. Hall Caine, Foreword, *Folk Stories and Fables*, vol. 1 of *The Children's Hour*, ed. Eva March Tappan (London: The Waverley Book Company, 1909), v–vi.

6. The Parents' Institute and Grosset and Dunlap also published editions of this series.

7. Byron Forbush, *The Boy Problems*, 100–104, cited by Mark Girouard, *The Return to Camelot: Chivalry and the English Gentleman* (New Haven and London: Yale University Press, 1981), 254. See also John Neubauer, *The Fin-de-Siècle Culture of Adolescence* (New Haven: Yale University Press, 1992), 47, 52, 182–203.

8. Hamilton Wright Mabie, Edward Everett Hale, and William Byron Forbush, eds., *Classic Tales and Everyday Stories, Young Folks' Treasury*,

vol. 3 (New York: The University Society, 1909), v. All quotations are from this edition and page references are given in parentheses.

9. Alec Ellis, *A History of Children's Reading and Literature* (Oxford: Pergamon Press, 1968), 72.

10. The Editorial Board of The University Society, *Famous Stories and Verse, The Bookshelf for Boys and Girls*, vol. 6 (New York: The University Society, 1948), iii–iv. Page references are given in parentheses.

11. William Patten, ed., *The Junior Classics: Stories That Never Grow Old*, vol. 5 of 10 (New York: P.F. Collier & Son, 1912), 330. All quotations are from this edition and page references are given in parentheses.

12. William Patten, ed., *The Junior Classics: Poems Old and New*, vol. 10 of 10 (New York: P.F. Collier & Son, 1912), 85. All quotations are from this edition and page references are given in parentheses.

13. Charles H. Sylvester, *Journeys Through Bookland*, 10 vols. (Chicago: Bellows-Reeve Co., 1909). *Guide* is volume 10. All quotations are from this edition and references are given in parentheses.

14. Dorothy Loring Taylor, *Olive Beaupré Miller and The Book House for Children* (Chicago: Chicago Review Press, 1986) includes a well-illustrated bibliographical history, 93–104. My discussion is derived from Taylor; page references are given in parentheses.

15. Her grandfather Lorenzo Dow Brady was in the Illinois legislature, founded the C. B. & Q. Railroad, and was instrumental in establishing the first free school in Aurora, Illinois, public education outside Chicago. Among Brady's friends was Mathias Beaupré, her other grandfather, who was French, from Canada, a business clerk who became Deputy Collector of Internal Revenue. Her father William was a banker, who organized the first public library in Aurora.

16. Olive Beaupré Miller, ed., *My Book House*, 6 vols. (Chicago: The Book House for Children, 1920–1921). This edition was reprinted with only minor changes until 1937, when a revision established the twelve-volume format and contents. Given in parentheses, book and page references for the songs and biography are from the first edition; stories from the 1937 edition.

17. Percy MacKaye, *Caliban by the Yellow Sands* (Garden City, NY: Doubleday, Page & Co., 1916), xiii. All quotations are from this edition and page references are given in parentheses.

18. H.E. Marshall, *English Literature for Boys and Girls* (London: T.C. and E.C. Jack, 1909), ix. All quotations are from this edition and page references are given in parentheses.

19. Edward Parrott, *The Pageant of English Literature* (London, Edinburgh, Dublin, New York: Thomas Nelson & Sons, 1914). All quotations are from this edition and page references are given in parentheses.

20. Amy Cruse, *English Literature through the Ages* (London, Calcutta, Sydney: George G. Harrap & Co., 1914), 5. All quotations are from the reprint of 1925 and page references are given in parentheses.

21. Amy Cruse, *The Golden Road in English Literature: From Beowulf to Bernard Shaw* (London, Bombay, Sydney: George G. Harrap, 1931), 208–209. All quotations are from this edition and page references are given in parentheses.

22. Henry Gilbert, *Stories of Great Writers*, In Days of Old Series (London, Edinburgh, New York: T.C. & E.C. Jack, 1914), v. Quotations are from this edition and page references are in parentheses.

23. Eva March Tappan, *A Brief History of English Literature* (London: George G. Harrap & Co., 1914). Quotations are from the revised American edition, *A Short History of England's Literature* (Boston: Houghton Mifflin Co., 1933); and *A Short History of America's Literature* (Boston: Houghton Mifflin Co., 1932); page references are given in parentheses.

24. William J. Long, *Outlines of English and American Literature* (Boston, New York, Chicago, London, Atlanta, Dallas, Columbus, San Francisco: Ginn & Co., 1919). Quotations are from this edition and page references are given in parentheses.

25. Mary E. Burt, *Literary Landmarks: A Guide to Good Reading for Young People, and Teachers' Assistant with a Carefully Selected List of Seven Hundred Books*, rev. ed. (Boston and New York: Houghton Mifflin & Co.; and Cambridge: The Riverside Press, 1897), 37–38. Quotations are from this edition and page references are given in parentheses.

26. My discussion follows Ellis, *A History of Children's Reading and Literature*, 100–18, 136–46.

27. Elizabeth Nesbit, "Major Steps Forward," in *A Critical History of Children's Literature*, ed. Cornelia Meigs, Elizabeth Nesbit, Anne Eaton, and Ruth Hill Viguers (New York: The Macmillan Co., 1953), 419.

28. Montrose J. Moses, *Children's Books and Reading* (New York: Mitchell Kennerley, 1907). Quotations are from this edition and page references are given in parentheses.

29. Frances Jenkins Olcott, *The Children's Reading* (Boston and New York: Houghton Mifflin Co.; and Cambridge: The Riverside Press, 1912), xii–xiii. Quotations are from this edition and page references are given in parentheses.

30. Velma Bourgeois Richmond, *Chaucer as Children's Literature: Retellings from the Victorian and Edwardian Eras* (Jefferson, NC, and London: McFarland & Co., 2004), 196–198.

Epilogue

1. Terry Deary, *Top Ten Shakespeare Stories* (London: Scholastic Children's Books, 1998). Terry Deary, *The Lord of the Gleaming Globe*, Tudor Chronicles (London: Dolphin, 1998; repr. London: Orion Children's Books, 2006), is an amusing novel.
2. Marcia Williams, "Bravo, Mr. William Shakespeare!" in *Reimagining Shakespeare for Children and Young Adults*, ed. Naomi J. Miller (New York and London: Routledge, 2003), 29–38. Williams traces her own attitudes toward an early, and unpleasant, encounter with Lamb's *Tales*. This volume, which includes writers, artists, and scholars, is an excellent source for current treatments of Shakespeare. It contains few references to Victorian and Edwardian books.
3. Marcia Williams, *Tales from Shakespeare: Seven Plays* (New York: Scholastic, 1998). This is the American edition of the English edition: *Mr. William Shakespeare's Plays* ; *Bravo, Mr. William Shakespeare!* (London: Walker Books, 2000).
4. Aliki, *William Shakespeare and the Globe* (London: Mammoth, Egmont Children's Books, 2000).
5. Juan Wijngard, *Shakespeare's Globe: An Interactive Pop-up Theatre* (Cambridge, MA: Candlewick Press, n.d.).
6. Julie Henry and Chris Hastings, "Brush up your Shakespeare: for a pass you need to know ... nothing," *The Sunday Telegraph*, 23 Apr. 2006, p. 13.
7. Tony Halpin, "Prince to promote old-school teaching," *The Times*, Thurs., 8 June 2006, p. 5.
8. Randy Kennedy, "The Arts May Aid Literacy, Study Says," *The New York Times*, 27 July 2006, p. B1.

Selected Bibliography

Primary Sources

Charles and Mary Lamb

Complete Editions

Furnivall, F.J. *Tales from Shakespeare by Mary and Charles Lamb with Introductions and Additions.* 2 vols. Illustrated by Harold Copping, some photogravure. London, Paris, New York: Raphael Tuck & Sons, 1901.

Lamb, Charles. *Tales from Shakespeare. Designed for the Use of Young Persons.* 2 vols. Illustrated by William Mulready. London: Thomas Hodgkins, 1807.

Lamb, Charles and Mary. *Lamb's Tales from Shakespeare by Charles and Mary Lamb.* Illustrated by Arthur Rackham. London: J.M. Dent, 1899.

Lamb, Charles and Mary. *Lamb's Tales from Shakespeare by Charles and Mary Lamb.* Everyman's Library for Young People Series. Illustrated by Arthur Rackham. London: J.M. Dent, 1906.

Lamb, Charles and Mary. *Tales from Shakespeare by Charles and Mary Lamb.* Illustrations in Permanent Photography from the Boydell Gallery. London: Bickers & Son, 1876.

Lamb, Charles and Mary. *Tales from Shakespeare by Charles and Mary Lamb.* Illustrated by A.E. Jackson. London & Melbourne: Ward, Lock & Co, 1918.

Lamb, Charles and Mary. *Tales from Shakespeare by Charles and Mary Lamb.* Illustrated by Norman M. Price. London & Edinburgh: T. C. and E. C. Jack, 1905.

Lamb, Charles and Mary. *Tales from Shakespeare by Charles and Mary Lamb.* Illustrated by Louis Rhead. Louis Rhead Series. New York: Blue Ribbon Books, 1918.

Lamb, Charles and Mary. *Tales from Shakespeare by Mary and Charles Lamb.* Illustrated by Frank Godwin. New York: The John C. Winston Co., 1924.

Lamb, Charles and Mary. *Tales from Shakespeare designed for the Use of Young People.* Illustrated by Sir John Gilbert, engraved by Dalziel. London: Routledge, ©1882.

Stokes, Winston. *All Shakespeare's Tales: Tales from Shakespeare by Charles and Mary Lamb and Tales from Shakespeare by Winston Stokes.* Illustrated by M.L. Kirk. New York: Frederick A. Stokes and London & Edinburgh: W. & R. Chambers, 1911.

Selections

Lang, Mrs. Andrew. *The Gateway to Shakespeare for Children—Containing a Life of Shakespeare by Mrs. Andrew Lang, A Selection from the Plays, and from Lamb's "Tales."* The Gateway Series. Illustrated by E. F. Skinner, A. K. Bowling, Norman Ault and others. London, Edinburgh, Dublin, New York: Thomas Nelson & Sons, 1908.

Robarts, Edith. *Tales from Shakespeare by C. & M. Lamb*. Illustrated. Stories for the Children Series. London, Melbourne, Toronto: Ward Lock & Co, 1910.

Stead, W.T. *Tales from Shakespeare. As You Like It*, #92 and *The Tempest*, #92A. Illustrated by Edith Ewen. Books for the Bairns Series. London: Stead's Bairns' Library, 1903.

Tales from Shakespeare by Charles and Mary Lamb, Book One and Book Two. All-Time Tales Series. Illustrated by M. Lavars Harry. London: George G. Harrap & Co., 1910.

Tales from Shakespeare by Charles and Mary Lamb, Illustrated by Edmund Dulac, W. Heath Robinson, Hugh Thomson, etc. London: Hodder & Stoughton, 1914.

Tales from Shakespeare: From the Collection by Charles and Mary Lamb. Stories Old & New Series. Illustrated. London: Blackie & Son, 1910.

Tilney, F.C. *Tales from Shakespeare by Charles and Mary Lamb*. Illustrated by Charles Folkard. London: J.M. Dent & Sons and New York: E.P. Dutton & Co., 1926.

E. Nesbit

Children's Stories from Shakespeare. Ed. Capt. Edric Vredenburg. The Raphael House Library of Gift Books for Boys and Girls. Illustrated by J.H. Bacon, Harold Copping & Others (A.A. Dixon, Howard Davie, Gordon Browne). Intro. by Dr. F. J. Furnivall. London, Paris, New York: Raphael Tuck & Sons, 1912.

The Children's Shakespeare. Ed. Edric Vredenburg. Illustrated by Francis Brundage, M. Bowley, J. Willis Grey, etc. London, Paris, New York: Raphael Tuck & Sons, 1898.

The Children's Shakespeare. Illustrated from Brundage, etc. New York: Charles E. Graham & Co., ©1905.

The Children's Shakespeare. Illustrated from Brundage, etc. Philadelphia: Henry Altemus Co., 1900.

Twenty Beautiful Stories from Shakespeare: A Home Study Course. Being a Choice Collection from the World's Greatest Classic Writer. Ed. E.T. Roe. Illustrated by Max Bihn from Brundage, etc. Chicago & Boston: The John A. Hertel Co., 1907.

_____, and Hugh Chesson. *The Winter's Tale, and Other Stories*. [Macbeth, Othello]. Illustrated by Frances Brundage, M. Bowley, etc. London, Paris, Berlin, New York: Raphael Tuck & Sons, ©1912.

Alternative Retellings

Britton, Fay Adams. *Shakespearian Fairy Tales*. Illustrated by Clara Powers Wilson. Chicago: The Reilly & Britton Co., 1907.

Carter, Thomas. *Stories from Shakespeare*. Illustrated by Gertrude Demain Hammond. Told through the Ages Series. London: George G. Harrap, 1910.

_____. *Shakespeare's Stories of the English Kings*. Illustrated by Gertrude Demain Hammond. Told through the Ages Series. London: George G. Harrap, 1912.

Hoffman, Alice Spencer. *The Children's Shakespeare: Being Stories from the Plays with Illustrative Passages*. Illustrated by Charles Folkard. London: J.M. Dent & Sons; and New York: E.P. Dutton & Co., 1911.

_____. *The Story of the Tempest from the Play of Shakespeare*. Illustrated by Walter Crane. London: J.M. Dent & New York: E.P. Dutton, 1904.

Hudson, R(obert). *Tales from Shakespeare*. Illustrations from Paintings. London: Collins' Clear Type Press, 1906.

Lang, Jeanie. *More Stories from Shakespeare*. Illustrated by N.M. Price. Told to the Children Series. London, 1910.

_____. *Stories from Shakespeare*. Illustrated by N.M. Price and others. Told to the Children Series. London: T.C. & E.C. Jack and New York: E.P. Dutton, 1907.

Macleod, Mary. *The Shakespeare Story-Book*. Illustrated by Gordon Browne, intro. by Sidney Lee. London: Wells Gardner, Darton, 1902.

Maud, Constance and Mary. *Shakespeare's Stories*. Illustrations from Boydell Gallery. London: Edward Arnold, 1913.

Morris, Harrison S. *Tales from Shakespeare*. Color Plates from Paintings. Philadelphia: J.B. Lippincott, 1893.

Quiller-Couch, Sir Arthur T. *Historical Tales from Shakespeare*. Illustrations from Boydell Gallery. London: Edward Arnold, 1910.

Raymond, Robert R., ed. *Typical Tales of Fancy, Romance, and History from Shakespeare*. Engravings. New York: Fords, Howard, & Hulbert, 1881 and 1882.

Seymour, Mary [Seamer]. *Shakespeare's Stories Simply Told*. Illustrated by Frank Howard. London, Edinburgh, New York: Thomas Nelson & Sons, 1880.

_____. *Shakespeare's Stories Simply Told: Comedies*. Illustrated by Frank Howard. London, Edinburgh, New York: Thomas Nelson & Sons, 1883.

_____. *Shakespeare's Stories Simply Told: Tragedies and Historical Plays*. Illustrated by Frank Howard. London, Edinburgh, New York: Thomas Nelson & Sons, 1899.

Sim, Adelaide C. Gordon. *Phoebe's Shakespeare*. London: Bickers & Son, 1894.

Stidolph, Ada Baynes. *The Children's Shakespeare*. Photographs. London: Allman & Son, 1902.

Schoolbooks

Literature

Ainger, Alfred Rev., ed. *Tales from Shakespeare by Charles and Mary Lamb*. Macmillan's Pocket Classics. New York and London: The Macmillan Co., 1916.

Ginn, Edwin, ed. *Tales from Shakespeare by Charles and Mary Lamb*. Illustrations from the Valpy Edition. Boston, New York, Chicago, London, Atlanta, Dallas, Columbus, San Francisco: Ginn & Co., 1915.

Highroads of Literature, Book Second, Bards and Minstrels; Book Third, The Morning Star; Book Fourth, Captains and Kings; Book Fifth, Books of All Time; Books Sixth, Thoughts and Voices. London, Edinburgh, Dublin, and New York: Thomas Nelson & Sons, 1915–1920.

In Golden Realms: An English Reading Book for Junior Forms. Arnold's Literary Reading Books. London: Edward Arnold, 1902.

Syms-Wood, A., ed. *Tales from Shakespeare by Charles and Mary Lamb for Preliminary Students, with Introduction, Notes, Examination papers, Extracts from the Plays, etc*. Oxford and Cambridge Edition. London: George Gill & Sons, 1909.

Tales from Shakespeare by Charles and Mary Lamb. Rahway, NJ, and New York: Mershon Co., ©1910.

The Children's Shakespeare: Scenes from the Plays. With Introductory Readings from Charles and Mary Lamb's "Tales from Shakespeare." Arranged as a Continuous Reader with Exercises in Composition. Illustrated by J. Macfarlane. London: Macmillan & Co., 1910.

_____. *A First Book of English Literature, Part III: From Lyndsay to Bacon*. London: Horace Marshall & Co., 1906.

History

Bevan, Tom. *Stories from British History (B.C. 54–A.D. 1485)*. Illustrations from Paintings. Boston: Little Brown & Co., 1910.

Bulley, Eleanor. *Great Britain for Little Britons*. 1887. Illustrated. repr. London: Wells Gardner, Darton & Co., 1904.

Church, A(lfred) J(ohn). *Stories from English History: From Richard II to Charles I*. Illustrated. London: Seeley & Co., 1896.

Corkran, Alice. *The Dawn of British History*. History of England Series. Illustrated by M. Lavars Harry. London: George G. Harrap & Co., 1912.

Dark, Sidney. *The Book of England for Young People.* Illustrations from Paintings. New York: George H. Doran & Co., 1923.

Ross, Estelle, *From Conquest to Charter (1066–1215).* Illustrated by Evelyn Paul. History of England Series. London: George G. Harrap & Co., 1912.

———. *Barons and Kings (1215–1485).* History of England Series. Illustrated by Evelyn Paul. London: George G. Harrap & Co., 1912.

Thomson, C(lara) Linklater. *A First History of England, Parts II, III.* 7 vols. London: Horace Marshall & Son, 1901–07.

———. *Carmina Britanniæ: A Selection of Poems and Ballads Illustrative of English History.* London: Horace Marshall & Son, 1901.

Yonge, Charlotte M. *Twenty Stories and Biographies: From 1066 to 1485.* Westminster Historical Reading Books, Part III. Illustrated. London: National Society's Depository, 1892.

Anthologies, Home Libraries, Literary Histories

Anthologies

Richardson, Abby Sage. *Stories from Old English Poetry.* Illustrated 1871; repr. Boston: Houghton, Mifflin & Co., 1891.

Smith, David Murray. *Tales of Chivalry and Romance.* Illustrated. London: Virtue & Co., 1869.

Home Libraries

Aldrich, Thomas Bailey, ed. *The Young Folks' Library*, 20 vols. Boston: Hall & Lock Co., 1901–1902.

Mabie, Hamilton Wright, Edward Everett Hale, and William Byron Forbush, eds. *Young Folks' Treasury*, 10 vols. New York: The University Society, 1909.

Marshall, Logan, ed. *Young People's Home Library.* n.p. W.E. Scull, 1909.

Miller, Olive Beaupré. *My Book House*, 6 vols. Chicago: The Book House for Children, 1920–1921.

Patten, William, ed. *The Junior Classics*, 10 vols. New York: P.F. Collier & Son, 1912.

Sylvester, Charles H. *Journeys Through Bookland*, 10 vols. Chicago: Bellows-Reeve & Co., 1909.

Tappan, Eva March. *The Children's Hour*, 10 vols. Boston: Houghton Mifflin & Co., 1907.

Literary Histories

Cruse, Amy. *English Literature through the Ages.* Illustrated by Paintings. London, Calcutta, Sydney: George G. Harrap & Co., 1914.

Gilbert, Henry. *Stories of Great Writers.* In Days of Old Series. Illustrated by John R. Skelton. London, Edinburgh, New York: T.C. and E.C. Jack, 1914.

Long, William J. *Outlines of English and American Literature.* Illustrated. Boston, New York, Chicago, London, Atlanta, Dallas, Columbus, San Francisco: Ginn & Co., 1919.

Marshall, Henrietta E. *The Child's English Literature.* Illustrated by John R. Skelton. London: T.C. & E.C. Jack, 1909. Reissued as *English Literature for Boys and Girls.*

Parrott, Edward. *The Pageant of English Literature.* Illustrated by Great Paintings. London, Edinburgh, Dublin, New York: Thomas Nelson & Sons, 1914.

Tappan, Eva March. *A Brief History of English Literature.* London; George G. Harrap, 1914.

Thomson, Clara Linklater. *Our Inheritance.* Cambridge: Cambridge University Press, 1910.

Secondary Sources

Ariés, Philippe. *Centuries of Childhood: A Social History of Family Life.* trans. Robert Baldick. New York: Vintage Books of Random House, 1962.

Baldick, Chris. *The Social Mission of English Criticism, 1848–1932.* Oxford: Oxford University Press, 1983.

Bevington, David, ed. *The Complete Works of Shakespeare,* updated 4th ed. New York: Longman, 1997.

Bottoms, Janet. "'To read aright': Representations of Shakespeare for Children," *Children's Literature* 32 (2004): 1–14.

Brown, Zaidee, ed. *Standard Catalog for High School Libraries.* New York: The H.W. Wilson Co., 1929.

Burt, Mary E. *Literary Landmarks: A Guide to Good Reading for Young People. and Teachers' Assistant with a Carefully Selected List of Seven Hundred Books,* rev. ed. Boston and New York: Houghton Mifflin & Co.; and Cambridge: The Riverside Press, 1897.

Carpenter, Humphrey and Mari Prichard. *The Oxford Companion to Children's Literature.* Oxford and New York: Oxford University Press, 1984.

Daiches, David. "Presenting Shakespeare." In *Essays in the History of Printing,* ed. Asa Briggs, 61–112. London: Longman, 1974.

Dalby, Richard. *The Golden Age of Children's Book Illustration.* New York: Gallery Books, 1991.

Darton, F.J. Harvey. *Children's Books in England: Five Centuries of Social Life.* 1932. rev. ed. Brian Alderson. Cambridge: Cambridge University Press, 1982.

Ellis, Alec. *A History of Children's Reading and Literature.* Oxford: Pergamon Press, 1968.

Feather, John. *A History of British Publishing.* London and New York: Routledge, 1968.

Home, Alan. *The Dictionary of 20th Century British Book Illustrators.* Woodbridge, Suffolk: Antique Collectors' Club, 1994.

Houfe, Simon. *The Dictionary of 19th Century Book Illustrators and Caricaturists.* 1978. rev. ed. Woodbridge, Suffolk: Antique Collectors' Club, 1996.

Houlbrooke, Ralph A. *The English Family 1450–1700.* New York: Longman, 1984.

Klein, Holger and James L. Harner, eds. *Shakespeare and the Visual Arts.* Shakespeare Yearbook, vol. 11. Lewiston, Queenston, Lampeter: The Edwin Meller Press, 2000.

Linscott, Robert Newton. *A Guide to Good Reading: With Practical Directions for the Use of The Children's Hour in the Home.* Boston: Houghton Mifflin Co., 1912.

Marsden, Jean. "Shakespeare for Girls: Mary Lamb and *Tales from Shakespeare,*" *Children's Literature* 17 (1989): 47–63.

Martineau, Jane, et al. *Shakespeare in Art.* Exhibition Catalogue. London: Merrell Holberton Publishers, 2003.

———. *Victorian Fairy Painting.* Exhibition Catalogue, Royal Academy of Arts. London: Merrell Holberton Publishers, 1997.

Meigs, Cornelia, ed. *A Critical History of Children's Literature.* New York: Macmillan Co., 1953.

Meyer, Susan E. *A Treasury of the Great Children's Book Illustrators.* New York: Harry N. Abrams, 1983.

Montrose, Moses J. *Children's Books and Reading.* New York: Mitchell Kennerley, 1907.

Newbolt, Henry. *The Teaching of English in England: Being the Report of the Departmental CommitteeAppointed by the President of the Board of Education to Inquire into the Position of English in the Educational System of England.* London: His Majesty's Stationery Office, 1921.

Olcott, Frances Jenkins. *The Children's Reading.* Boston and New York: Houghton Mifflin Co.; and Cambridge: The Riverside Press, 1912.

Pape, Walter and Frederick Burwick, eds., in collaboration with the German Shakespeare Society. *The Boydell Shakespeare Gallery.* Bottrop: Peter Pomp, 1996.

Parris, Leslie, ed. *The Pre-Raphaelites.* Exhibition Catalogue. 1994; repr. London: The Tate Gallery, 1996.

Priestly, J.B. *The Edwardians.* New York and Evanston: Harper & Row, 1970.

Quiller-Couch, Sir Arthur T. *On the Art of Reading.* Cambridge: Cambridge University Press, 1920.

Richmond, Velma Bourgeois. *Chaucer as Children's Literature: Retellings from the Victorian and Edwardian Eras.* Jefferson, NC and London: McFarland & Co., 2004.

_____. "Exhibition Review — Shakespeare in Art at the Dulwich Picture Gallery London." *Art on the Line* (2004/1): 1–4.

_____. *The Legend of Guy of Warwick.* New York: Garland Publishing, 1996.

_____. *Shakespeare, Catholicism, and Romance.* New York: Continuum, 2000.

Rosenthal, Joel T. Ed. *Essays on Medieval Childhood: Responses to Recent Debates.* Donington, UK: Shaun Tyas, 2007.

Stewart, James. *The New Child: British Art and the Origin of Modern Childhood, 1730–1830.* Exhibition Catalogue. Berkeley: University of California Press, 1995.

Thomas, Keith. "Children in Early Modern England." In *Children and Their Books: A Celebration of the Work of Peter and Iona Opie,* ed. Gillian Avery and Julia Briggs, 45–77. Oxford: Clarendon Press, 1989.

Whalley, Joyce Irene and Tessa Rose Chester. *A History of Children's Book Illustration.* London: John Murray with the Victoria & Albert Museum, 1988.

Index

Adam, Robert 28
Addison & Steele 302
Adler, Felix 12
adjustments for children 2–3, 12–13, 15–17, 24, 16, 60, 81, 82, 88, 100, 105–07, 122, 134, 138–39, 141, 147, 150, 166, 173, 174, 177, 183, 184–85, 189–90, 210, 215, 217, 239, 244, 248, 254, 257, 270, 276, 281, 285–87, 294, 298, 311, 316, 318–19
adventure & travel stories 275, 276, 280, 283, 285
Adventures in Criticism 201
Aeneas 133
Aeschylus 311
Aesop 108, 219, 250
Agassiz, Louis 277
Ainger, Alfred 242–44, 245, 315, 341n7
Alcott, Louisa May 119, 291
Alderson, Brian 334n6
Aldrich, Thomas Bailey 273, 275, 342n1
Alger, Horatio 300
The Alhambra 286
Alice in Wonderland 34, 117
Aliki 322, 344n4
All-Time Tales Series 72, 230, 231
All's Well 17, 44, 50, 66, 82, 83, 133, 174, 215, 246–47
Altemus, Henry 169
American Library Association 314
American perspective 1, 2, 23, 110, 117, 141–43, 147, 149, 193, 245, 263, 270, 273–75, 279, 281, 284, 290, 291, 293, 300, 314, 316, 335n18
Andersen, Hans Christian 2, 55, 65, 308, 313
Andrews, Henry 136
Animated Tales 321
Anjou 265
Antony & Cleopatra 25, 72, 78–79, 81, 85, 89, 91, 133, 134, 248, 293, 322
The Arabian Nights 46, 55, 65, 108, 116, 219, 235, 276, 281, 282, 317, 322
Ariès, Philippe 7, 333n3
Arizpe, Evelyn 335n20

Arnold, Edward 20, 225, 230, 258–61, 316
Arnold, Matthew 19–20, 309
Art Deco 291
Art Nouveau 34, 36, 39, 45, 51, 52, 60, 64, 66–68, 90, 92, 93, 95, 96, 99, 101, 189, 196, 198, 219, 220, 231, 233
Arts & Crafts Movement 19, 36, 166, 225
As You Like It 17, 32, 33, 45, 46–47, 57, 69, 84, 89, 92, 94, 95–96, 100, 101–02, 104, 106–07, 109, 116, 118, 126–27, 138, 146–49, 150, 152–53, 156, 160, 165, 167, 169, 174, 176, 177–78, 181, 182, 184, 197, 206, 209, 219, 220, 225, 226, 231, 232–33, 235, 236, 241–42, 246, 247, 249, 250, 253, 254, 257, 259, 283, 291, 293, 300, 309, 312, 313, 318, 322, 323
Ashley, L. F. 335n17
Asquith, Herbert Henry 200
Atlantic Monthly 275
audience 8, 14, 24, 57, 61, 66, 73, 76, 101, 117, 131, 136, 151, 158, 166, 169, 173, 181, 182, 184, 185, 188, 189, 191, 197, 202, 215, 217, 219, 220, 222, 228, 233, 234–36, 238, 244, 250, 259, 261, 263, 264, 266, 275, 276, 280, 284, 285–89, 293–94, 295, 297, 305, 306, 310, 315–16, 319
Ault, Norman 94–96
Avery, Gillian 333n2, n3, 334n8, 335n20, 339n17

Bacon, Dolores 338n5
Bacon, John H. 3, 158–60, 198
Baden-Powell, Robert 280
ballads 3, 8, 9, 81, 96, 172, 252, 254, 255, 260, 266, 269, 317, 319
Bandello 173
Barbauld, Anne Laetitia 11, 335n20
Baring-Gould, W. S. & C. 334n9
Barnes, A. S. 181
Barnett-Clarke, Charles W. 170
Barnum, P. T. 291
Barons and Kings 262, 342n24
Barr, John 336n32
Barry, James 29

351

INDEX

Barth, Fred 199
Bayard 108
Beardsley, Aubrey 65
Bede 271
Behold the Child 333n2, n3, 334n8
Bell, R. Anning 220
Bell Readers 20
Belleforest 173
Bellows-Reeve Co. 285
Benn, Ernest 104–05
Bennett, John 14
Benzie, William 237n4
Beowulf 247, 301, 302, 317, 339
The Best of Shakespeare 339n4
Betterton, Thomas 308
Bevan, Tom 231, 266–68, 342n30
Bevington, David 338n8
Bible 116, 166, 285, 290, 292, 308, 317
Bickers 26–31, 32
Bihn, Max 157, 166, 189, 339n4
Bingham, Caleb 314
biography 275, 276, 281, 285, 310; *see also* Shakespeare
Black, A & C 219
Blackie 20, 105, 230, 234–41
Blake, William 17, 19, 29, 81
Bleiler, E. F. 334n9
Blue Ribbon Books 55–56
Boas, F. S. 3, 20
Boer War 201
The Book of England for Young People 263–64, 342n27
A Book of Old English Ballads 9
The Book of Sagas 215
The Book of Saints & Heroes 92
book quality 3–4, 18–19, 24, 36, 46, 55–56, 63–68, 71–72, 80–81, 92–93, 99–100, 105, 108, 155, 156, 157, 158, 166, 169, 174–75, 181–82, 189, 201, 218, 225, 229, 230, 231, 235, 242, 251, 258, 270, 274, 276, 277, 285, 289–91, 312, 315–16, 318, 321–22, 339n4
The Bookhouse for Children 290
Books for the Bairns Series 3, 72, 99–100, 181, 312, 338n9, n10, n11
The Bookshelf for Boys and Girls 281, 282, 343n10
Booth family 283
Boswell, James 8
Bottoms, Janet 336n1
Bowdler, Harriet & Thomas 1, 15–16
Bowley, M. 165, 166
Bowling, M. 157
The Boy Problem 280, 342n7
Boy Scouts 280
Boydell Gallery 3, 17, 26–31, 75, 97, 169, 202, 225–29, 245–47, 277, 336n34
The Boys & Girls Bookshelf 281
Branagh, Kenneth 211
Bravo, Mr. William Shakespeare! 322
Brer Rabbit 100

Bridges, Robert 16
A Brief History of English Literature 274, 275, 304–07, 343n23
Briggs, Asa 339n17
Briggs, Julia 333n3
Brinsley, John 157
Britton, Fay Adams 156, 188–97, 199, 340n13
Brooks, Thomas 253
Browling, A.K. 96
Brown, Zaidee 340n9
Browne, Ford Maddox 42, 79
Browne, Gordon 3, 19, 35, 55, 160, 174–81, 237
Browne, H. B. 258
Browning, Robert 81, 250, 285
Brundage, Frances 47, 158, 160, 165, 166–67, 189
Bullen, A. H. 16, 336n29
Bulley, Eleanor 110, 130–32, 338n8
Bunbury, H. W. 74
Bundy, Edgar 252–53
Bunyan, John 250, 263, 276, 280, 281
Burbage, Richard 94, 303, 308
Burke, Edmund 29
Burne-Jones, Sir Edward 19, 40, 223, 235
Burns, Robert 250, 286
Burt, Mary E. 274, 310–13, 343n25
Burton, Robert 141
Burwick, Frederick 336n34, n3, n5
The Butterfly's Ball 17
Byles, C. E. 258

Cabanel, Alex 283
Caine, Hall 279, 342n5
Caldecott, Randolph 69
Caliban by the Yellow Sands 274, 293–94, 307, 343n17
Cambridge 155, 238, 241, 250
capitals 56, 57, 144, 175, 176, 179, 180
Carmina Britanniae 247, 269–72, 342n32
Carnegie, Andrew 314
Carpenter, Humphrey & M. Prichard 86–87, 334n6, n9, 335n20, 337n5
Carter, Thomas 4, 88, 156, 205–15, 231, 264, 340n18, n19
Cassell 13, 14, 307
Castiglione 150
Caxton, William 204, 250, 251
Centuries of Childhood 7, 333n3
Cervantes 276, 280, 281, 282, 315
Chaldean 310
Chambers, E.K. 85, 222
Champaigne, Phillipe de 7
chapbooks 3, 7–11, 13, 33, 56, 100, 101, 105, 117, 276, 322, 334n6, 335n18
Charlemagne 235, 317
Chaucer 1, 13, 15, 24, 65, 71, 79, 81–82, 89, 110–11, 115, 116, 117, 118, 120, 133, 247, 250, 251, 253, 268, 276, 280, 281, 282, 295, 301, 304, 307, 308, 310, 311–12, 315, 317, 319, 335n25, 338n4

Chesson, Hugh 165
Chesson, Nora 165
Chester, Tessa Rose 336n32
childhood 3, 7, 11, 116–17, 277, 278, 279, 281, 290, 302, 308, 311, 317, 319, 341n9
Children and Their Books 333n3
Children's Books and Reading 12, 274, 314–16, 343n28
Children's Books in England 15, 155, 334n6, 335n16, n18
The Children's Classics Series 63
Children's Gem Library 165
The Children's Heroes Series 197
The Children's Hour 5, 275–79, 342n2, n3, n4, n5
Children's Literature: Illustrated History 335n17
The Children's Reading 274, 316–20
The Children's Shakespeare 155, 169–72, 340n7, 341n6; *see also* Nesbit, Hoffman
*A Child's Garden of Verse*s 284
Chisholm, Louey 181, 280, 338n5
chivalry 20, 25, 65, 75–76, 97, 110–11, 118, 121–22, 131, 135, 136, 166, 176, 188, 193, 201, 202, 204, 205, 208, 209, 210, 211, 212–14, 219, 235, 251, 260, 262, 266–29, 273, 277, 280, 281, 282, 285, 290, 293, 308, 317, 319, 338n1
The Choice of Books 12
A Christmas Carol 313
Church, A. J. 262–63, 342n26
Cinderella 128
Cinthio 173
Clare, Maurice 337n18
Clarke, Charles Cowden 13
Clarke, Mary Cowden 13, 291, 315
Classic Stories Simply Told Series 133, 251
classics (Greek & Roman) 21, 22, 79, 89, 96, 99, 117, 121, 124, 133, 135, 142, 145, 181, 204, 205, 217, 220, 248, 276, 280, 282, 301, 308, 310, 311, 315, 322
Classics for Children Series 245
Clermont, Mary Jane 10
Clibborn 302
Clifford, John H. 281
Cockran, Alice 262, 342n25
Cockshut, A. O. J. 339n17
Cole, Henry 2
Cole, Herbert 108
Coleridge, Samuel 11, 31, 210, 298, 316
Collier, P. F. 273, 282
Collins 156, 197
Columbus 292
Comedy of Errors 44, 50, 51, 61, 62, 84, 139, 140, 167, 174, 178, 182, 183, 206, 215, 238, 247, 277, 278, 289, 305, 318
Comenius 7
comic strip 322
Conan Doyle, Sir Arthur 183
Confessio Amantis 118
Cooper, James Fenimore 313

Cooper, Mary 8
Copping, Harold 81, 85–86, 158, 163, 165
Coriolanus 25, 72, 78, 81, 89, 133, 135, 202, 205, 215, 219, 248, 289
167, 169, 174, 176, 178, 181, 188, 195–97, 210, 213, 215, 247, 249, 253, 260, 262, 298, 300, 206
"The Cotter's Saturday Night" 286
Cottingley photos 183
Court, J. D. 258
The Courtier 150
Cowie, Frederick 295
Cowper, William 270
Crane, Walter 3, 19, 156, 220–25, 318, 340n23
Cruikshank, George 19
Cruse, Amy 5, 274, 299–301, 302, 343n20, n21
Cundall, Joseph 333n1
Cunningham, Susan 338n7
Curtis, Dora 220
Cymbeline 10, 17, 29, 35, 44, 50, 58, 60, 83, 84–85, 104, 134–45, 156, 158, 160, 165

Dadd, Richard 19
Daiches, David 336n27, n28
Dalby, Richard 336n32
Dalziel brothers 32
Damico, Helen 337n4
Danby, Francis 145
Dante 130, 310, 311
Dark, Sidney 263–64, 342n27
Darley, F. O. C. 283
Darrell, Margery 336n33
Darton, F. J. Harvey 4, 15, 155, 335n16, n18
Darwin, Charles 151, 317
The Daughters of Lir 262
Davie, Howard 158, 160
Davies, John 253
The Dawn of British History 262
Day, Thomas 194
A Day with William Shakespeare 337n18
Deary, Terry 321, 344n1
death 120, 122, 135; *see also* ghosts; witches
The Decameron 118
Declaration of Popish Imposters 141
Defoe, Daniel 250, 276, 302
Dekker, Thomas 298
Delacroix, Eugene 19
de Mause, Lloyd 333n3
Dent, J. M. 34, 72, 108, 109, 156, 201, 215, 219
DeWitt 158, 248
Dickens, Charles 12, 165, 175, 180, 263, 280, 283, 308, 313
Dictionary of National Biography (*DNB*) 173
The Dictionary of 19th Book Illustrators and Cartoonists 336n32, n7, 339n2
The Dictionary of 20th Book Illustrators 336n32, 337n13
Disney, Walt 39, 219
Disraeli, Benjamin 180

Dixon, A. A. 158, 160, 162, 163
Don Quixote 105, 235, 276, 280, 282, 315, 317, 322
Doré, Gustave 32
Doubleday 319
Dowd, Maureen 335n22
Dowden, Edward 134, 210, 312
Dowman, John 226
Doyle, Richard 39
Drake, Sir Francis 292
drama 9, 16, 23–24, 173, 286, 313, 318; *see also* Shakespeare, William
Drayton, Michael 189, 204, 265, 298
Dryden, John 249
Dudd, P. 94, 97
Dugdale, T. C. 96, 97, 254
Dulac, Edmund 3, 19, 64–65
Dürer, Albrecht 36
Dutton, E. P. 108, 109, 156, 201, 215, 319
dwarves 175, 194, 277
Dyce, William 3, 19

Earlom, Richard 227
The Earthly Paradise 124
Edgar, Madalen 124
Edgeworth, Maria 280
education *see* Newbolt Report; pedagogy; schoolbooks
Education Acts 19
Edwardian attitudes 16, 18, 35, 56, 65, 88, 91, 93–94, 104, 107, 128, 145, 153, 154, 156, 158, 170, 172, 180, 184, 186–87, 189, 192, 201, 205, 209, 211, 215, 222, 225, 226, 228, 239, 249, 250, 255, 261, 270, 277–79, 281, 290, 293, 297, 299, 300, 302, 307, 309, 310, 322; *see also* gender
The Edwardians 5, 333n7
Eggleston, George Cary 281
Egoff, Sheila 335n17
Eliot, Charles W. 278
Eliot, George 206
Elizabethan context 147, 150, 157–58, 170, 173, 184, 252–53, 322
Ellis, Alec 236n31, n36, 339n1, 343n9, n26
Emerson, Ralph Waldo 308, 317
Empire (British) 100, 128, 155, 158, 169, 170, 213, 260–61, 269, 274, 279, 342n22; *see also* national/racial/patriotic identity
Ender 264
Engines of Instruction 334n6
English Children's Books 334n6
English Literature for Boys and Girls 274, 294–98, 304, 343n18
English Literature through the Ages 274, 299–301, 343n20
English studies 1, 5, 14, 21, 81–82, 157, 173–74, 200, 239, 243–44, 261, 304, 307, 310, 340n16
epics 56, 97, 317, 319
Escamez, J. Munoz 108
Essays in the History of Printing 336n27

Essex, William B. 145
Every Child Should Know Series 279
Every Man in His Humour 303
Everyman 318
Everyman's Library 34, 201, 319
Ewen, Edith 101–04

Faed, John 170
The Faerie Queene 24, 116, 172, 251, 255, 317, 338n3
fairies 8, 19, 26, 27, 35, 40, 48, 58, 63, 73, 84, 89, 94–95, 102, 108, 118, 123–24, 137, 140, 144–45, 150–51, 167, 175, 182–83, 197, 217–18, 220, 222, 225–26, 227, 236, 239, 246, 249, 253, 280, 281, 287, 295
fairy tales 12, 26, 34, 39, 55, 65, 92, 101–03, 108, 117, 144, 152, 157, 172, 174, 181, 182–83, 188–97, 200, 253, 260, 275, 276, 282, 285, 289, 302, 308, 315, 317, 335n18, 342n23
Family Flight 280
Family Shakespeare 15–16
Feather, John 339n11
Fieldler, Leslie 333n1
The Fin-de-Siècle Culture of Adolescence 342n7
A First Book of English Literature 230, 247–50, 341n10
First Folio 25, 26, 32, 92, 134, 173, 298
A First History of England 231, 248, 265–66, 342n29
The Flower of Gold 341n3
Folger Library Exhibit 333n5
Folkard, Charles 3, 108–09, 215–19, 220, 283, 338n13
folktales 260, 275, 276, 282, 285, 291, 313, 315, 319, 342n5
Forbes-Robertson, Johnston 23
Forbush, William Byron 273, 280–82, 284, 342n7, n8
Ford, Henry J. 40
Foxon, David 10, 335n15
Franklin, Benjamin 313
Frobisher, Martin 292
Froissart, Jean 110
From Charter to Conquest 262, 342n24
Furness, Howard 306, 207
Furnivall, F. J. 71, 81–88, 157, 163, 173, 222, 238, 239, 284, 300, 337n3
Fuseli, Henry 19, 75, 227, 246

Gainsborough, Thomas 7
Galahad, Sir 211, 282
Gamelyn 236
Garrick, David 131–32, 321
Gaugain, Thomas 29
Gateway Series 71, 93, 251
gender 8, 15, 25, 29–30, 35, 44, 50, 78–79, 82, 84, 91, 93–94, 97, 100, 107, 110, 119–20, 122, 124–25, 127, 128–29, 131, 136–39, 142, 145, 147, 152, 157, 158, 180, 181, 184, 190, 192–93,

195, 197, 198, 201, 206–07, 208–09, 213, 233, 241, 245, 246, 249, 261, 280, 299, 300, 301, 309
Geoffrey of Monmouth 259, 341n21
geography books 4, 110, 130–32, 275, 285, 338n8
German use 23, 140
Gernutus see *Jew of Venice*
Gesta Romanorum 114, 118
ghosts 47, 59–60, 86, 97–98, 109, 129, 132, 139–40, 178, 180, 186, 193, 227, 231, 233, 246, 283
Gilbert, Henry 5, 274, 296, 301–04, 343n22
Gilbert, Sir John 19, 31–33, 75, 76, 78, 79, 315, 336n6
Ginn, Edwin 230, 245–47, 341n8
The Girlhood of Shakespeare's Heroines 13–14, 315
The Girls' Own Paper 86
Girouard, Mark 338n1, 342n7
Gladstone, William 316
Globe Theatre 23, 93, 158, 248, 252, 298, 322, 344n1, n4, n5
Godwin, Frank 63–64, 337n16
Godwin, M. J. 81
Godwin, William 10, 12, 82
Goethe 285, 308, 310
The Golden Road in English Literature 30, 343n21
Goldsmith, Oliver 8, 278, 302, 313, 318
Gollanz, Israel 21–22
Goody-Two Shoes 8, 11, 335n18
Gorboduc 295
Gothic novel 129–30
Gottlieb, Johann 228
Gottlieb, M. 257
Gower, John 118, 121
Grahame, Kenneth 82, 137, 294
Grammar Schoole 157
Great Britain for Little Britons 110, 130–32, 338n8
Great War see World War I
Greece 58
Greenblatt, Stephen 12
Greene, Robert 116, 298, 303, 338n3
Greer, Germaine 137, 339n14
Greet, Ben 318
Gregg shorthand 14
Grey, J. Willis 157
Grimm brothers 34, 36, 39, 85, 219, 308, 312
A Groat's Worth of Wit 303
Grosset & Dunlap 342n6
Grutzner, Ed. 197
Guerber, H. E. 318
A Guide to Good Reading 277–79, 342n3
Gulliver's Travels 13, 34, 36, 55, 276, 280, 282, 313, 315, 317
Guy Mannering 282
Guy of Warwick 13, 15, 114, 122, 294, 335n24

Hale, Edward Everett 273, 280, 342n8
Hales, John W. 81
Hall, Edward 271
The Hall of Heroes 341n14
Hallam, Arthur 309
Halls, J. J. 76
Halpin, Tony 341n12, 344n7
Halz, Franz 7
Hamilton, Emma 277
Hamilton, William 28, 246
Hamlet 17, 32, 36, 38, 40–41, 47, 57, 59, 60, 63, 69, 83, 86, 104, 107, 109, 119, 132, 134, 139–40, 156, 158, 163, 164, 165, 169, 174, 178, 179, 184, 186, 206, 207, 219, 225, 227, 231, 234, 235, 238, 243, 246, 249, 253–54, 284, 289, 293, 305, 309, 310, 321, 322, 323
Hammond, Gertrude Demain 3, 206–14
Hanson, Charles Henry 133
Hare, Christopher 108
Harlow, George H. 79, 136
Harrap, George G. 156, 205, 230–34, 262, 274, 276, 304, 316
Harris, Joel Chandler 275
Harris, John 17
Harrison, Frederick 12
Harry, M. Lavars 231–34
Harsenet, Samuel 141
The Harvard Classics 273, 282
Hastings, Chris 335n22, 344n6
Hastings, Warren 131
Haweis, Mrs. H. R. 117, 338n4
Hawkes, Terrence 340n16
Hawkins, John 293
Hawthorne, Nathaniel 313
Hayley, William 277
Hazlitt, William 31
Heath, Shirley B. 335n20
Heinemann, William 34, 64, 72
Hemans, Patricia 270
Heminge & Condell 298
Henry, Julie 335n22, 344n6
Henty, George 203
Herodotus 270
heroes 186, 215, 217, 260, 266, 271, 275, 276, 280, 281, 282, 290, 315, 341n14
Hertel, John A. 165
Hiawatha 38
Highroads of History 230, 268–69, 342n31
Highroads of Literature 4, 9, 230, 251–58, 268, 341n13, n15, n18, n19
Hilliard, Nicholas 44
Hirsch, E. D. 333n6
history 4, 88–89, 96, 100, 104, 105, 111, 117, 126, 127, 130, 133, 134, 156, 157, 158, 174, 179, 186, 187, 197, 200–02, 206, 209–10, 211, 215, 248, 250, 251, 255, 259, 262–72, 275, 276, 285, 294–95, 299, 302, 305, 310, 311
History of Childhood 333n3
History of Children's Book Illustration 336n32

A History of Children's Reading and Literature 336n31, n36, 339n11, 343n9, n26
The History of Shylock 9
The History of Street Literature 334n6
Hoby, Thomas 150
Hodder & Stoughton 63, 65–66, 70
Hodgkins, Thomas 10, 17, 81, 336n30
Hodson & Son 6, 10, 335n13
Hoffman, Alice S. 4, 20, 108, 156, 215–25, 283, 318, 340n21, n22
Hogarth, William 19
Holinshed, Raphael 271
Holmes, Oliver Wendell 313
home libraries 2, 5, 273, 275–93
home study courses 14, 165–68
Home Treasury of Old Story Books 2, 14, 333n1
Homer 280, 282, 308, 315, 317
Horne, Alan 336n22, 337n13
Horton, Priscilla 253
Houfe, Simon 336n32, n7, 339n2
Houlbrooke, Ralph 334n3
Houston, T. A. 268
Howard, Frank 133, 134–40
Howard, Jerome 14
Howells, William Dean 275
Hoyer, M. A. 165
Huckleberry Finn 12
Hudson, Henry Norman 307
Hudson, R(obert) 4, 156, 197–99, 340n14
humor stories 280, 285, 298
Humphrey, Heman 2, 333n2
Humphrey, Ozias 167
Hunt, Peter 335n17, 340n4
Hunt, W. Holman 18
Huxley, T. H. 316

Idylls of the King 55
Iliad see Homer
Illustrated Children's Books 336n32
Illustrated History of England Series 262, 336n24, n25 Illustrated Story of England Series 231, 262
In Days of Old Series 296, 301
Indian Civil Service 14, 31
Ingoldsby Legends 34
Irving, Henry 169, 175, 283
Irving, Washington 34, 286, 313
Italy 90, 115, 117, 124, 135, 150, 152, 165, 173, 182, 204, 257
Ivanhoe 282, 313

Jack, T. C. & E. C. 40, 65, 155, 181–82, 184, 197, 281, 294, 301
Jackson, A. E. 46–55, 337n12
Jackson, Mary V. 334n6
Jackson, Russell 339n18
James, Henry 245
Jameson, Anna 129
Jane Eyre 261
The Jew of Malta 312

The Jew of Venice 2, 9, 252, 255
Jewett, Sarah Orne 313
Joan of Arc 75, 201, 269
Johnson, Jane 335n20
Johnson, Samuel 132, 302
Jonson, Ben 146, 166, 254, 298, 303, 309
Journeys through Bookland 5, 273, 285–89, 343n13
Julius Caesar 25, 57, 72, 78, 81, 85, 88, 89, 91, 100, 133, 135, 142–44, 149, 184, 202, 205, 206, 215, 248, 257, 278, 284, 289, 293, 306, 309, 312, 313, 318, 321, 322, 323
The Junior Classics 5, 273, 282–84, 343n11, n12
Juvenile Drama 9–10, 334n13, n14

Kauffmann, Angelica 28–29, 246
Kean, Edmund 76
Keats, John 316
Kemble, John 254
Kemble family 136
Kenilworth 295, 298, 305
Kennedy, Randy 344n8
Kermode, Frank 342n33
King, Dorothy 236, 341n3, n4
King Henry IV 73–74, 89, 90, 126, 134, 135, 197–98, 202, 210, 250, 262, 263, 265, 270, 284, 298–99, 309, 318
King Henry V 32, 74–75, 79, 91, 131, 135, 202, 211, 215, 219, 220, 248, 257, 263, 265–66, 268–69, 270, 293, 318
King Henry VI 75–76, 79, 88, 89, 134, 202, 210, 262, 265, 269, 270
King Henry VIII 32, 57, 78, 79, 104, 131, 135, 136, 205, 213, 269, 270, 284, 293
King John 76, 77, 135, 184, 187, 202, 212–13, 214, 215, 219, 257, 259, 262, 265, 270, 278, 284, 318, 319
King Lear 10, 17, 29, 33, 36, 42–44, 52–53, 55, 60, 66, 86, 87, 92, 93, 94, 96–97, 104, 116, 117, 127, 156, 165, 177, 178, 184, 188, 190–91, 193, 206, 208, 209, 210, 215, 219, 225, 227, 231, 233–34, 241–42, 243, 246, 249, 250, 25q, 262, 298, 300, 305, 318, 321, 322, 323
King Leir & His Three Daughters 9, 334n11, n12
King of the Golden River 123
King Richard II 32, 78, 91–92, 104, 135, 202–03, 210–11, 215, 219, 220, 257, 265, 270
King Richard III 10, 76, 78, 79, 92, 136, 184, 187, 202, 204–05, 211–12, 262, 263, 264, 268, 270, 178, 289, 320, 322, 323
kings (British): Alfred 268, 278; Arthur 122, 131, 133, 141, 172, 235, 247, 251, 255, 280, 301, 317, 322, 341n14; Edward I 268; Edward III 100, 111, 243; Edward VII 170; George V 187; Richard I (Lionheart) 212–13, 265; *see also* Shakespeare history plays
King's Treasuries of Literature Series 201, 205
Kingsley, Charles 315
Kingston, W. H. G. 114

Kipling, Rudyard 65
Kirk, M(aria) L. 89–91
Kirk, Thomas 30
Klimt, Gustav 190
Kline, Daniel T. 333n1
Knighton, Henry 271

The Lady of the Fountain 235
La Fontaine 108
Lamb, Charles 10, 11–12, 17, 31, 93, 238–39, 242–43, 278, 279, 286, 307, 313, 316, 335n19
Lamb, Mary 10, 25, 42, 82, 83, 92, 93, 105–07, 136, 138, 189, 233, 238–39, 249, 243–44, 278, 279, 307, 309, 313
Lamb's *Tales from Shakespeare* 3, 4, 10, 11–12, 14, 56–57, 71, 72–73, 81, 82–84, 86–87, 88, 111, 14, 149, 155, 156, 170, 173, 181, 199–200, 201, 202, 215, 228, 230, 231, 234, 238, 241–42, 243–44, 245, 255, 258, 270, 273, 276, 278, 281, 282, 286, 291, 298, 312, 313, 314, 315, 318, 320, 322
Lamb's *Tales from Shakespeare* (complete; illustrator/editor): Boydell Gallery 26–31, 336n2; Copping, Harold/F.J. Furnivall 71, 81–88, 157, 163, 222, 238, 239, 337n3, n4; Gilbert, Sir John 31–33, 336n6; Godwin, Frank 63–64, 337n16; Jackson, A. E. 46–55, 337n12; Kirk, M(aria) L./Winston Stokes 89–91, 337n6; Mulready, William/first ed. 17–18, 31, 81, 85, 257; Price, Norman M. 39–46, 337n11; Rackham, Arthur 34–39, 64–65, 336n8, 337n9; Rhead, Louis 55–62, 337n15
Lamb's *Tales from Shakespeare* (selected, editor/illustrator): Dulac, W.H. Robinson, Hugh Thomson, etc. 64–70, 337n17; Lang, Mrs. Andrew/Bacon, Dixon, etc. 92–99, 133, 338n7; Robarts, Edith 105–08, 338n12; Stead, W. T./Edith Ewen 71–72, 99–104, 338n11
Lance, William Coolidge 334n5
Lancelot 122
Landseer, Edwin 258
Lane, Allen 100
Lang, Andrew 40
Lang, Mrs. Andrew 71, 92–99, 133, 238, 338n7
Lang, Jeanie 4, 45, 155, 181–88, 199, 278, 281, 298, 340n10, n11
Langland, William 302
Langridge 124
Lanier, Sidney 10
The Last of the Mohicans 313
Laurie, William 20
Lawrence, Thomas 254
Layamon's *Brut* 250, 251
Lee, Sidney 172, 173, 174, 177, 248, 284
legends 114, 117, 145, 157, 235, 253, 262, 266, 273, 275, 276, 279, 280, 282, 285, 301, 302, 311, 315, 322
Leighton, Frederick 19
Leney, William S. 226

Lewis, C. S. 12
libraries for children 313–20, 343n26, n27, n28, n29
Lilly's *Latin Grammar* 298
Lincoln, Abraham 319
Linscott, Robert Newton 277–79, 342n3
Linton, James D. 257
Lippincott, J. B. 72
Literary Landmarks 274, 310–13, 343n25
Literary Reading Books 230, 258–60, 341n20
A Little Pretty Pocket-Book 8, 334n6, n7
Little Women 119
Living Purpose Series 251
Locke, John 7
Lodge, Thomas 118, 298
Long, William J. 5, 274, 308–10, 343n24
Longfellow, Henry Wadsworth 114, 142, 157, 274, 276, 284, 313
Longmans 20
The Lord of the Gleaming Globe 344n1
Lounsbury, T. R. 307
Love's Labour's Lost 25, 72, 73, 81, 134, 253, 298, 305
Lowell, James Russell 261, 313
Lucas, E. V. 315
Lyly, John 116, 338n3

Mabie, Hamilton Wright 9, 273, 279–82, 334n12, 342n8
Mabinogion 235
Macaulay, Thomas B. 286, 310
Macbeth 17, 26, 36, 45–46, 48–50, 55–56, 57, 58–60, 64, 83–84, 86, 90, 93, 94, 97, 104, 107, 109, 116, 117, 118, 127, 128–30, 135, 140, 165, 167, 174, 179–80, 184, 186–87, 188, 193, 206, 219, 225, 227, 238, 241, 247, 248, 249, 258, 259, 268, 278, 289, 307, 309, 312, 318, 321, 322, 323
Macfarlane, J. 241–42
MacKaye, Percy 274, 293–94, 307, 343n17
Mackintosh, Charles Rennie 181, 185
Macleod, Mary 4, 155, 160, 172–81, 184, 225, 227, 298, 340n8
Maclise, Daniel 3, 19, 39, 253–54
Macmillan 241, 315
Macmillan's Pocket Classics 242–44
Malone, E. 167
Malory, Thomas 110–11, 247, 250, 308
The Man Without a Country 280
Mancoff, Debra 338n1
Margetson, W. H. 251
marginalia 93–94, 95, 160–63, 252
Marlowe, Christopher 303, 312
Marryat, Frederich 114
Marsden, Jean 336n1
Marshall, H(enrietta) E. 5, 65, 250, 274, 294–98, 304, 343n18
Marshall, Horace 247, 269
Marshall, Logan 273–74
Martin, John 19

Martineau, Jane 336n34, n35, 339n18
Marvin, F. S. 315
Master Skylark 14
Mathews, Arthur 19
Matthews, David 337n4
Matthews, W. 95
Maud, Constance & Mary 4, 156, 225–29, 340n24
Maxey, K. 288
McCracken, Elizabeth 278, 342n4
Meade, L. T. 165
Measure for Measure 17, 26, 30, 44–45, 50, 57, 65, 86, 133, 134, 138, 174, 215, 245, 249
Mechanics Institute 157
medievalism 52, 79, 111, 181, 202, 208, 209, 210–11, 214, 338n1; *see also* chivalry; Middle Ages
Meigs, Cornelia 335n17, 336n26, 343n27
The Merchant of Venice 9, 10, 17, 28, 32, 33, 37, 50, 57–58, 68–69, 84, 90, 93, 94, 96, 100, 104, 107, 108, 109, 114–15, 116, 118, 124–26, 132, 135, 138, 150, 153–54, 156, 165, 167, 169, 170–71, 174, 182, 184, 188, 190, 197, 199, 206–07, 219, 220, 225, 231, 233, 234, 235, 236, 238, 241, 246, 252, 255, 257, 261, 277, 283, 284, 292, 293, 297, 298, 305, 307, 310, 312, 318, 320, 322, 323
Meres, Francis 298, 303
Merry Wives of Windsor 10, 25, 72, 73, 81, 88, 89, 90, 134, 137, 293
Mershon 341n9
Merton, Ambrose 333n1
Meyer, Susan E. 336n32
Michael, A. C. 255
Michaelangelo 29
Middle Ages 1, 4, 5, 21, 79, 97, 117–18, 160, 167, 178, 181, 204, 205, 210, 212–15, 250, 251, 255, 260, 263, 265–68, 271, 273, 276, 285, 290, 294–95, 302, 304, 317; *see also* medievalism
A Midsummer Night's Dream 1, 2, 10, 17, 19, 26, 27, 32, 34, 36–37, 40, 47, 48, 57, 58, 63, 64, 65, 68, 73, 82, 84, 87, 89, 92–93, 94–95, 104, 105–06, 107, 109, 116, 118–19, 127, 140, 142, 144–46, 150, 151, 156, 160, 165, 166–67, 169, 172, 174–75, 176, 177, 182, 183, 188, 189–90, 193, 1197, 206, 209, 216–18, 220, 222, 225, 231, 234, 235–36, 238, 239, 241, 246, 248, 249, 253, 260, 275, 278, 281, 283, 289, 291, 298, 301, 305, 310, 311–112, 318, 321, 322, 323
Mifflin, Houghton 276, 277, 304, 312, 319
Millais, Sir John Everett 3, 19, 36, 48, 254, 276
Miller, Naomi J. 344n2
Miller, Olive Beaupré 273, 282–84, 289–93, 343n14, n15, n16
Miller, William 228, 246
Milton, John 24, 105, 250, 263, 304, 339n17
The Mind and Art of Shakespeare 312
Minstrel Tales 341n21

miracle/mystery plays 291–92, 293, 295, 318
The Mirror for Magistrates 272
The Misfortunes of Arthur 302
Mr. William Shakespeare's Plays 32, 344n3
moral purpose/value 5, 11–13, 16, 21, 50, 50, 104, 106, 111–12, 115, 116–18, 119–20, 121–23, 126, 127–28, 129, 130–31, 135, 137–39, 143, 144, 145, 146–49, 151, 152, 153, 166, 171–72, 173–74, 177, 178–81, 183, 185, 186–87, 189, 190, 191–92, 193, 194, 198, 200, 204, 207, 210, 215, 218, 222, 223–28, 236, 238–41, 244, 248, 249, 250–51, 255, 257, 260, 265–66, 269, 278, 281, 283–84, 287–88, 292–93, 298–99, 300–01, 303, 305–06, 307, 308–10, 312–13, 317–18, 319, 322
Moreau, Gustave 19
Morris, Harrison S. 71, 72–81, 337n1
Morris, William 19, 124, 166, 223
Morris dancers 291
Moses, Montrose J. 12, 274, 314–16, 335n21, 343n28
Mother Goose's Melodies 8–9
Much Ado About Nothing 28, 33, 44, 58, 60, 64, 84, 133, 134, 138, 167, 174, 177, 197, 198, 235, 248, 243, 246, 249, 289, 299, 301, 322
Muir, Percy 334n6
Mulready, William 17–18, 31, 81, 85, 257
My Book House 5, 273, 289–93, 343n16
My Book of History 290
myths *see* legends

national/racial/patriotic identity 11, 20, 21–22, 35, 42, 48, 58, 65, 71, 75, 85, 100, 104, 110, 124, 135, 128, 130–31, 133, 142, 147, 149, 156, 170, 179, 184, 193, 201–05, 208, 209–13, 215, 219, 220, 222, 227, 244, 245, 248, 250–51, 257, 260–61, 263, 266, 269–71, 274, 275, 279, 281, 282, 285, 293–94, 295, 302, 305, 307, 310, 342n22
nature stories 95, 253, 274, 275, 276, 282, 285; *see also* Shakespeare, William, songs
Neilson, Julia 169
Neilson, William Allen 278
Nelson, Thomas 20, 71, 92, 133, 230, 251, 252, 254, 299, 316
Nelson Readers 4, 20, 251–58
Nesbit, E(dith) 4, 14, 47, 85, 87, 155, 156–65, 189, 198, 273, 282, 339n1, n3, n4, 340n5, n6
Nesbit, E(dith) *The Children's Shakespeare* (illustrator/edition): Brundage, Bowley, Grey/first ed.156–57, 339n1; Brundage, etc./Altemus 169, 340n5; Brundage, etc./Graham 169, 340n6; Copping, Bacon, Dixon, etc. *Children's Stories from Shakespeare* 157–65, 339n3; Brundage/Max Bihn, *Twenty Beautiful Stories* 165–68, 339n4; Brundage, etc.*The Winter's Tale and Other Stories* 165
Neubauer, John 342n7
Neuburg, Victor E. 334n6
The New Child: British Art 7, 334n4

Newbery, John 8, 33, 334n6
Newbolt, Henry 20, 261, 333n4, 335n23, 336n37, 338n7
Newbolt Report see *The Teaching of English*
Nielsen, Kay 200
Nister 315
Northcote, James 30, 202
Northern heritage (Saxons, Vikings) 42, 48, 66, 86, 90, 115, 124, 152, 180, 186, 203, 213, 215, 225, 242, 277
Norton, Charles Eliot 273, 342n1
novels 14, 114, 115, 121, 129, 155, 200, 203, 261, 266, 270, 280, 281, 282, 295, 300, 304, 308, 316, 318
Nymphidia 189

Oakden, E. C. 342n21
The Odyssey see Homer
Of the Decorative Illustration of Books 225
Olcott, Frances J. 275, 314, 316–20, 343n29
Old Story Books of England 333n1
Olivier, Lawrence 211
On the Art of Reading 200, 340n17
Opie, Iona & Peter 334n9
Opie, John 76
Opie Library Series 339n4
Orbis Pictus 7
Orientalism 41, 54, 55, 60–61, 64, 68, 70, 90, 116, 167, 207, 219, 221, 236–37, 247
Othello 10, 17, 30–31, 32, 41, 52, 54, 57–58, 60–61, 64, 70, 84, 90, 134, 165, 167, 174, 177, 238, 240–41, 246, 284
Ottoman Wonder Tales 219
Our Inheritance 250–51, 341n11
Our Island Story 250, 294
Outlines of English and American Literature 274, 308–10, 343n24
Oxford 173, 238, 241

The Pageant of British History 298
The Pageant of English Literature 274, 298–99, 343n19
Paget, Henry Marriott 96
paintings, historical 3, 4, 18–19, 28–33, 36, 42, 43, 44, 50, 66, 70, 72, 74–80, 136, 145, 158–62, 169, 170, 178, 180, 186, 197–98, 199, 230, 234, 252, 253, 254, 255, 257, 259, 264, 268, 283, 295, 298, 299, 338n5; *see also* Pre-Raphaelites
Palladis Tamia 303
Pape, Walter 336n34, n3, n4, n5
parent-child relations 28, 29, 30, 42–44, 52, 55, 64, 74, 96, 103, 108, 112, 114, 118, 125–26, 127–28, 135, 136, 152, 163, 171, 176, 178, 180, 190, 191, 192, 194, 199, 207, 208, 210, 218, 222, 227–28, 245, 246, 249, 250, 251, 257, 278, 287, 300, 303
The Parents' Institute 342n6
Paris, Matthew 271
Parker, James 29

Parris, Leslie 341n17
Parrott, Edward 274, 298–99, 302, 343n19
Parry, Judge E. A. 315
Pater, Walter 210
Paton, Joseph Noel 3, 19, 39
Patten, William 273, 282–84, 343n11, n12
Paul, Evelyn 262
Pearson, Meg 333n5, n4
pedagogy 4, 9, 20, 22–24, 61, 81, 90, 100, 130–31, 140, 188, 202, 235, 238–41, 245, 247–50, 252, 254, 255, 257, 258, 259, 260, 264, 269–70, 273–75, 276, 277, 278, 285–89, 310–13, 323, 341n9
Penguin Books 100
The Penny Histories 334n6
Penny Poets Series 100
Penny Shakespeare 14, 101
Pepys, Samuel 7, 8
Percy, Bishop Thomas 9, 81, 334n11
Pericles 17, 50, 53, 61, 83, 84–85, 116, 118, 121–23, 127, 139, 140, 156, 165, 167, 169, 174, 184, 219, 238, 247
Perrault, Charles 108
Peter Pan 34, 117
Peter Parley Tales 2, 340n20
Peter Rabbit 117
Petherick, Rosa C. 251
Pettie, John 268
Phoebe's Shakespeare 110, 150–54, 180, 184, 339n19
Pickering, Samuel F. 333n2
A Picturesque Tale of Progress 290
Pilgrim's Progress 13, 55, 116, 247, 276, 282, 313, 317
Pinocchio 219
Plantagenet 209, 211
Plautus 119
Plumb, J. H. 334n4
Plutarch 248, 315, 317
Poe, Edgar Allan 65
poems 16, 23, 100, 104, 117, 132, 151, 157, 204, 247, 269–70, 273, 275, 276, 281, 282, 283–84, 285, 303, 308, 312; *see also* Shakespeare, William, songs
Pollack, Linda 333n3
Pope, Alexander 250
Popular Literature 334n6
pop-up theatre 332–23, 344n5
Potter, Beatrix 116, 165
Potter, Harry 12, 46, 179
Poynter, Edwin 79, 257–58
Pre-Raphaelite 36, 42, 50, 52, 99, 158, 160, 208, 254, 341n17
Price, Norman M. 39–46, 55, 181, 278, 281, 315, 337n11
Prichard, Mari 86–87, 334n6, n9, 335n20, 337n5
Priestly, J. B. 5, 333n7
Prince Albert 128
Puffin Books 100

Pullman, Philip 12
Putnam 315
Pyle, Howard 141

queens (British): Alexandra 186; Anne 304; Elizabeth I 107, 136, 205, 209, 215, 264, 292, 295, 298, 305; Elizabeth II 322; Victoria 29, 128, 242, 270
Quiller-Couch, Sir Arthur 3, 4, 20–221, 65, 156, 199–205, 215, 264, 284, 315, 318, 340n15, n16, n17

Rackham, Arthur 3, 18, 19, 34–39, 63, 64–65, 219, 234, 250, 283, 336n8, 337n9, n10
Raleigh, Sir Walter 252, 255, 270
Ralph Roister Doister 295, 302
Raphael House Library of Gift Books 157
Raspe, Rudolph Erick 276
Raymond, Robert S. 110, 141–50, 313, 339n16
recommended book lists 278, 179, 298, 305, 309, 312–12, 315, 318, 319
religion 42, 50, 51, 64, 75, 92, 96, 100, 104, 107, 111–13, 115, 124–26, 128, 138, 153–54, 170, 171, 179, 180–81, 184, 188, 199, 204, 205, 207, 208, 209, 210, 212, 213, 222, 223, 227, 239, 240, 243, 244, 247, 251, 259, 261, 265, 266, 268, 271, 280, 285, 290, 292, 303, 308, 310, 317, 340n20
Religious Tract Society (RST) 100, 133, 312, 339n11
Reliques of Ancient English Poetry 9
The Return to Camelot 338n1, 342n7
reviews 20, 181, 238, 259, 266
Reward/prize books 4, 20, 40, 71, 81, 87, 92, 99, 105, 157, 159, 198, 205–06, 229, 231, 251, 255, 258, 274, 315, 339n11
Reynolds, Joshua 7, 29, 30
Rhead, Louis 55–62, 337n15
Rhys, Ernest 34, 108, 201, 337n8
Richardson, Abbey Sage 4, 110, 115–30, 313
Richmond, Hugh M. 337n2, 339n13
Richmond, Velma Bourgeois 335n24, 25, 336n34, 337n14, 338n4, 340n20
Rigaud, Francis 247, 259
Rip Van Winkle 34, 193
Riverside Classics 312
Riverside Literature Series 311
Riverside School Library 278, 312
Robarts, Edith 72, 105–08, 235, 338n12
Robert of Sicily 114
Robin Goodfellow 146, 183, 217, 283
Robin Hood 33, 35, 45, 55, 65, 84, 86, 89, 96, 106–07, 118, 126, 141, 149, 235, 236, 241, 254, 291, 301, 322, 341n4, n14
Robinson, Charles 108
Robinson, T. H. 105
Robinson, W. Heath 3, 19, 65, 69
Robinson Crusoe 2, 13, 46, 276, 280, 282, 313, 317
Roe, E. T. 165–66, 339n4

Roland 294, 341n14
Rolfe, William 5, 292, 307
romances 8, 14, 15, 25, 40, 56, 83, 84–85, 92, 93, 101, 111, 114, 116, 117–18, 123, 126, 134, 174, 185, 235, 236, 252, 260, 299, 300–01, 305–06, 317, 319, 338n7, 339n11, 342n21
Romantic 11, 31, 84, 93, 235, 249, 269, 298, 313
Romeo and Juliet 10, 17, 30, 32, 36, 44, 50–51, 60, 64, 68, 86, 89–90, 92, 94, 97–98, 100, 107, 109, 116, 118, 150, 151–52, 156, 158, 159, 163, 165, 166, 167, 169, 174, 176, 197, 206, 207–08, 219, 225, 228, 231, 234, 246, 250, 289, 293, 298, 318, 321, 322
Romney, George 19, 246, 277
Roosevelt, Theodore 281
Roscoe, William 17
Rosenthal, Joel T. 333n3
Ross, Estelle 262, 342n24
Rossetti, Dante Gabriel 36, 52, 241
Round Table *see* King Arthur
Routledge 42, 334n11
Rowling, J. K. 46, 179
Royal School Series 20, 251
Royal Treasury of Story and Song 251
Rubáiyyat of Omar Khayyam 65
Rubens, Peter Paul 7, 31
Ruskin, John 123, 255

Sabatelli, Giuseppe 41
Sadler, John E. 333n2
Saint George 104, 135, 291, 294
Saint Louis 293
Sandford and Merton 104
Sant, James 253
Santa Claus 169
Sargent, John Singer 19
Saure, Heinrich 140, 339n15
Sawyer, Robert 340n16
Schelling, Felix E. 307
Schiavonetti, Luigi 29
school stories 261, 275
schoolbooks: history 4–5, 200, 230, 248, 264–72; literature 230, 247–61; readers 4, 251–61, 311
Schoole of Vertue 157
schools (Elizabethan) 71, 85, 17, 157, 291, 292, 298, 302–03
Schoonover, Frank E. 55, 58
Scott, Grant F. 336n4
Scott, Sir Walter 12, 22, 100, 157, 250, 258, 280, 284, 295, 302, 308, 313, 317
Scribner's 278, 315
Scudder, Horace 2, 313
Sea Venture 151
Seager, Francis 157
Sesame Readers 9, 230, 250, 260–61
The Seven Champions of Christendom 13
The Seven Sages of Rome 114
Seymour, Mary S. 4, 110, 133–40, 225, 338n10, 339n12

Shakespeare, William: biography 5, 26, 71, 84, 85, 93–94, 117, 141–42, 147, 157, 220, 222, 238, 248, 249, 253, 255, 274, 279, 282, 291–92, 295, 297, 298–99, 299–301, 305, 310, 322; chronology 82, 84, 158, 248, 274, 297, 300, 303, 310; difficult for children 16, 23, 25, 117, 156, 182, 235, 253, 254, 274, 284, 286–87, 289; eminence 1, 13, 16, 22, 57, 84, 104, 117, 140, 157, 166, 170, 182, 202, 205, 220, 222, 254, 257, 260, 263, 264, 271, 272, 274–75, 276–77, 282–83, 284, 291, 295, 297, 298, 306, 309–10, 316, 320; performance 6, 9, 23–24, 29, 31, 40–41, 47, 57, 50, 53, 72, 76, 78, 79, 82–84, 92, 93, 97, 144–45, 132, 163, 215, 217, 245, 253, 254, 257, 277, 282, 291–92, 306, 318–19, 322; portraits 72, 93, 132, 167, 169, 170, 249, 252–53, 288, 297, 308, 142; quotations 94, 96, 97, 102, 111–12, 134, 135, 136, 138, 149, 141–49, 153, 166, 169, 174, 183, 186, 188, 190, 197, 199, 202, 206, 211, 212, 213, 215, 218, 238, 239, 240, 241–42, 249–50, 255, 257, 259, 260, 261, 262, 263–64, 271, 282, 283–84, 293–94, 323; songs 9, 48, 57, 58, 73, 94, 102, 111, 112, 123, 126, 149, 151, 153, 174, 206, 236, 241, 253, 254, 273, 282, 283, 291, 298; sonnets 250, 306, 307; sources 85, 93, 96, 117–18, 173, 189, 248, 250, 251, 252, 255, 259, 271, 297; theatre 23, 26, 29, 82, 85, 88, 93, 112, 117, 119, 131–32, 153, 158, 163, 248, 252, 295, 297, 298, 302, 303, 307, 309

Shakespeare and Appropriation 340n16
Shakespeare Association 22
Shakespeare Day 22
Shakespeare in Art 336n34, 339n18
Shakespeare Society 81, 238, 336n3
Shakespeare the Boy 5, 292
Shakespeare's Globe 322
Shakespeare's Heroines 129
Shake-speares Sweetheart 14
Sheed & Ward 20
Shelley, Percy Bysshe 81
Shepard, Leslie 334n6
Shephard, E. H. 96
Sheridan, Richard B 318
Shore, Emily 339n17
A Short History of America's Literature 274, 304, 307, 343n23
A Short History of England's Literature 274, 304–07, 343n23
Siddons, Sarah 78, 136, 226
Sidney, Philip 251–52
Siegfried 317, 341n14
Siegmund, Georg 228
Sim, Adelaide C. Gordon, *Phoebe's Shakespeare* 110, 150–54, 180, 339n19
Simon, Jean Pierre 28, 29, 30
Simpkin, Marshall 20
Simple Susan 280

Skeat, Walter W. 82, 157
Skelton, J(oseph) R. 295, 296, 304
Skinner, E. F. 97, 98
Sleeping Beauty and Other Fairy Tales 200
Sleigh, André 157
Smiles, Samuel 261, 300
Smirke, Robert 28, 246
Smith, Benjamin 277
Smith, David Murray 4, 110–15, 338n2
Society for Propagation of Christian Knowledge (SPCK) 133, 339n11
Sommerville, C. John 333n6
Sondheim, Stephen 181
A Song of the English 65
Sophocles 312
Southey, Robert 265
Spark, Muriel 270, 342n33
Sparkes, W. E. 338n7
Speaight, George 9, 10, 334n13, n14
Spenser, Edmund 24, 71, 116, 255, 281, 295, 315, 338n3
Spufford, Margaret 334n6
Spurgeon, Caroline 3, 20
Standard Catalog of High School Libraries 181, 320, 340n9
Staunton, Howard 32
Stead, W. T. 3, 71–72, 99–105, 181, 312
Steedman, Amy 338n5
Steele, Richard 8, 302
Steps to Literature 230, 258, 260, 342n22
Sterling, Sara Hawkins 14
Sterne, Laurence 8
Stevenson, R. L. 200, 284
Stewart, James 334n4
Stidolph, Ada Baynes, *The Children's Shakespeare* (actors' photographs) 155, 169–72, 340n7
Stokes, Winston, *All Shakespeare's Tales* (paintings) 71, 88–92, 337n6
Stories for the Children Series 105, 338n12
Stories from British History 231, 266–68, 342n30
Stories from English History 262–63, 342n26
Stories from History Series 197
Stories of Great Writers 274, 296, 301–04, 343n22
Stories Old & New Series 230, 234, 236, 341n3
The Story of a Bad Boy 275
storytelling 15, 22, 30, 32, 39, 46, 48, 51–52, 84, 86, 94, 96, 101, 130, 132, 134, 139, 155, 163, 171, 173, 188, 191, 200, 220, 245, 253, 266, 271, 274, 275, 294–95, 299, 316, 317, 318, 321
Stothard, Thomas 30–31, 246
Stowe, Harriet Beecher 313
Stratton, Helen 55
Stubbs, G. T. 335n17
Sturt, M(ary) 341n21
Styles, Morag 335n20
Summerly, Felix 2, 17

Swift, Jonathan 250, 276, 280, 315; *see also Gulliver's Travels*
Sylvester, Charles 273, 285–89, 343n13
Syms-Wood, A. 230, 238–41, 341n5

Tales and Talks from History 105
Tales for the Children Series 197
Tales from Many Lands Series 72, 108, 216, 219
Tales of a Grandfather 258
Tales of a Wayside Inn 114
Tales of Chivalry and Romance 110–15
Tales of the Homeland 260
The Taming of the Shrew 17, 29–30, 35, 40, 41–42, 44, 51–52, 61, 63, 70, 82, 86, 135, 136–37, 140, 150, 152, 156, 160, 161, 165, 167, 168, 169, 174, 182, 192, 219, 246, 248, 299, 318, 321
Tappan, Eva March 5, 273, 274, 275–79, 282, 304–07, 338n1, 342n2
Tarrant, Margaret W. 46
Tate, Nahum 29
The Tatler 8
Taylor, Dorothy Loring 289, 343n14
Taylor, John 308
The Teaching of English (Newbolt Report) 3, 4, 12, 13, 20–24, 99, 205, 284, 333n4, 335n23
The Tempest 1, 10, 17, 19, 26, 27, 28, 33, 40, 47, 57, 58, 65, 66–68, 83, 84, 86, 87, 94, 100, 101–02, 104, 109, 111–14, 116, 118, 123–24, 135, 138, 140, 150–51, 156, 163, 165, 167, 169, 174, 176, 182–83, 188, 193, 197, 207–09, 219, 220, 222, 225, 228, 231, 233, 241, 243, 246, 249, 253, 255, 258, 276, 277, 278, 281, 282, 83, 286–89, 291, 300, 306, 307, 309, 310, 318, 329, 323
Temple Shakespeare 21, 319
Temple Shakespeare for Children 318
Tenniel, John 34
Tennyson, Alfred 55, 71, 85, 131, 142, 157, 241, 250, 255, 261, 270, 274, 284, 295, 313, 316
Terry, Ellen 23, 169
Thackeray, William M. 206
Theaker, Harry 46
Thew, Robert 28
Thomas, Isaiah 8–9, 334n7
Thomas, Keith 333n3
Thoms, William 333n1
Thomson, Clara L. 230, 231, 247–51, 265–66, 269–71, 341n10, n11, 342n29, n32
Thomson, Hugh 19, 69
Thorndike, Ashley H. 284
Thwaite, Mary F. 14, 334n6, 335n19, n20
Ticker, Michael 321
Tillyard, E. M. W. 340n16
Tilney, F. C. 72, 108–09, 216, 219, 283, 338n13
Timon 10, 50, 60, 140, 174, 215, 247
Titian 124, 152, 160
Titus Andronicus 25, 72, 88, 89, 91, 133, 134, 139

Told Through the Ages Series 156, 205, 231, 262, 276
Told to the Children Series 4, 45, 65, 155, 181–82, 184, 197, 281, 294
Tolkien, J. R. R. 39, 223
Tolstoy, Leo 101
Tom Brown's Schooldays 261
Tommy Thumb's Pretty Song Book 9
Top Ten Shakespeare Stories 321, 344n1
Townsend, John Rowe 335n17
Towry, M. H. 315
Travels of Baron Munchausen 276, 281, 282
Treasure Island 55, 117
Trimmer, Sarah 11, 340n18
Trimpe, Pamela W. 339n18
Tristram Shandy 8
Troilus & Cressida 81, 85, 89, 133, 135, 140, 293
Truchet, Abel 257
True Stories from History 105
Tuck, Raphael 81, 85, 87, 157, 165, 198
Tudor 205, 209, 211, 212, 270
Tudor Shakespeare 284
Turner, J. M. W. 19, 112
Twelfth Night 17, 35, 45, 50, 61, 63–64, 65, 69, 83, 104, 139, 150, 156, 160, 162, 165, 169, 174, 178, 181, 225, 231, 233, 278, 299, 318, 320, 322, 323
Twenty Stories and Biographies 264–65
Two Gentlemen of Verona 28–29, 44, 50, 60, 64, 86, 133, 150, 152, 167, 174, 177, 181, 188, 197, 215, 246
Two Noble Kinsmen 118
Tyler, Wat 203
Typical Tales of Fancy, History & Romance from Shakespeare's Plays 110, 141–50, 313

Ulysses (Odysseus) 11, 12, 133, 280, 315, 317
Uncle Tom's Cabin 12
The University Society 281, 343n8, n10

Valentine and Orson 13
Valpy Shakespeare 245–46
Van Dyke, Anthony 7, 44
Vanity Fair 261
Variorum Edition 307
Velásques, Diego 7
Vergil, Polydore 204
Veronese, Paolo 152
Vicar of Wakefield 313
Victorian Fairy Painting 336n35, 339n18
Viguers, Ruth Hill 343n27
Villette 261
Vredenburg, Eric 157, 165, 339n3

Wagner, Richard 34, 318
Wannamaker, Sam 322
Ward, Lock 46, 72, 105
Warton, Thomas 9
Warwick Pageant 295

Watt, Ian 12
Watts, George Frederick 68, 282
Watts-Dunton, Theodore 298
Waverley Book Co. 279
Wawn, Andrew 340n12
Webster, Daniel 319
Wells Gardner, Darton 155, 172
Welsh, Charles 280
West, Benjamin 246
West, William 9–10, 335n13
Westall, Richard 29, 227, 246, 247
Westminster Historical Reading Books 231, 264–65, 342n28
Whalley, Joyce Irene 336n32
When Knights Were Bold 338n1
Whistler, James Abbott McNeill 47
White, Richard Grant 307, 313
Whittier, John Greenleaf 313
Whittington, Dick 117
Wigfull, W. Edward 94
Wiggin, Kate Douglas 313
Wijngard, Juan 322–23, 344n5
Willey, Basil 340n16
William Shakespeare and the Globe 322, 344n4
Williams, Marcia 322, 344n2, n3
Willmot, Robert Ari 334n11
Wilson, Clara Powers 188–89
Wilson, J. Dover 3, 21
Wilson, Lawrence 338n5
Winston, John C. Co. 63
The Wind in the Willows 82, 117, 137
Winnie the Pooh 117
The Winter's Tale 1, 8, 10, 28, 35, 50, 51, 53, 58, 84–85, 89, 109, 116, 117, 118, 119, 120–21, 136, 140, 156, 158, 163, 165, 167, 169, 174, 177, 178, 182, 183–84, 188, 191–92, 197, 198, 206, 218, 231, 233, 235, 236–37, 238, 239–41, 246, 249, 260, 284, 291, 293, 299, 306, 307, 310, 318, 321, 322
witches 17, 26, 33, 36, 45–46, 48, 60, 86, 90, 109, 117, 118, 129–30, 140, 167, 179, 180, 186–87, 193, 195, 197, 219, 227, 279, 287
Witham, Rose Adelaide 304
The Wizard of Oz 12
Wonderful Adventures of Old Brer Rabbit 100
Wood, Sally 338n10
Wordsworth, William 11, 131, 243, 270, 316
Working Men's Colleges 14, 15, 82, 157
World War I 20, 34, 56, 60, 65, 100, 104, 108, 219, 263, 274, 279, 281, 293–94, 295, 301, 307
World War II 13, 19, 20, 63, 109, 211, 273, 281, 340n2
Worthington, Katherine 282
Wright, Joseph 28, 50
Wycliffe, John 81

Yeames, W. F. 76, 77, 259, 264
Yonge, Charlotte 231, 264–65, 180, 342n28
Young Albert, The Roscius 9, 334n10
Young Folks' Book of Ideals 280
Young Folks' Library 273
Young Folks' Treasury 273, 279–82
Young People's Home Library 273–74
Yvain 122

Zefferelli, Franco 97
Ziegler, Georgiana 9, 334n10
Zoffany, Johann 19

www.ingramcontent.com/pod-product-compliance
Ingram Content Group UK Ltd.
Pitfield, Milton Keynes, MK11 3LW, UK
UKHW041921140426
5217IPUK00014B/265